Sams **Teach Yourself**

jQuery and JavaScript

in **24**
Hours

SAMS 800 East 96th Street, Indianapolis, Indiana, 46240 USA

D0516774

Sams Teach Yourself jQuery and JavaScript in 24 Hours

ISBN-13: 978-0-672-33734-5

ISBN-10: 0-672-33734-7

Library of Congress Control Number: 2013954604

Printed in the United States of America

First Printing December 2013

Trademarks

All terms mentioned in this book that are known to be trademarks or service marks have been appropriately capitalized. Sams Publishing cannot attest to the accuracy of this information. Use of a term in this book should not be regarded as affecting the validity of any trademark or service mark.

Warning and Disclaimer

Every effort has been made to make this book as complete and as accurate as possible, but no warranty or fitness is implied. The information provided is on an "as is" basis. The author and the publisher shall have neither liability nor responsibility to any person or entity with respect to any loss or damages arising from the information contained in this book.

Special Sales

For information about buying this title in bulk quantities, or for special sales opportunities (which may include electronic versions; custom cover designs; and content particular to your business, training goals, marketing focus, or branding interests), please contact our corporate sales department at corpsales@pearsoned.com or (800) 382-3419.

For government sales inquiries, please contact governmentsales@pearsoned.com.

For questions about sales outside the U.S., please contact international@pearsoned.com.

Acquisitions Editor
Mark Taber

Managing Editor
Sandra Schroeder

Senior Project Editor
Tonya Simpson

Copy Editor
Barbara Hacha

Indexer
Erika Millen

Proofreader
Anne Goebel

Technical Editor
Russell Kloepfer

Publishing Coordinator
Vanessa Evans

Book Designer
Gary Adair

Cover Designer
Mark Shirar

Compositor
Jake McFarland

For D!

—A & F

Contents at a Glance

Part V: jQuery UI

Part VI: jQuery Mobile

Table of Contents

About the Author

Brad Dayley is a senior software engineer with more than 20 years of experience developing enterprise applications. He has used HTML/CSS, JavaScript, and jQuery extensively to develop a wide array of web pages, ranging from enterprise application interfaces to sophisticated, rich Internet applications, to smart interfaces for mobile web services. He is the author of *Python Phrasebook* and *jQuery and JavaScript Phrasebook*.

Acknowledgments

I'd like to take this opportunity to thank all those who made this title possible. First, thanks to my wonderful wife and boys for giving me the inspiration and support I need. I'd never make it far without you.

Thanks to Mark Taber for getting this title rolling in the right direction, Russell Kloepfer, for keeping me honest with his technical review, Barbara Hacha, for turning the technical ramblings of my brain into a fine text, and Tonya Simpson, for managing everything on the production end and making sure the book is the finest quality.

We Want to Hear from You!

As the reader of this book, *you* are our most important critic and commentator. We value your opinion and want to know what we're doing right, what we could do better, what areas you'd like to see us publish in, and any other words of wisdom you're willing to pass our way.

We welcome your comments. You can email or write to let us know what you did or didn't like about this book—as well as what we can do to make our books better.

Please note that we cannot help you with technical problems related to the topic of this book.

When you write, please be sure to include this book's title and author as well as your name and email address. We will carefully review your comments and share them with the author and editors who worked on the book.

Email: feedback@samspublishing.com

Mail: Sams Publishing
         ATTN: Reader Feedback
         800 East 96th Street
         Indianapolis, IN 46240 USA

Reader Services

Visit our website and register this book at informit.com/register for convenient access to any updates, downloads, or errata that might be available for this book.

Introduction

With billions of people using the Internet today, there is a rapidly growing trend to replace traditional websites, where pages link to other pages with a single page, with applications that have richly interactive elements. The main reason for this is that users have become less patient with clicking, waiting, and then having to navigate back and forth between web pages. Instead, they want websites to behave more like the applications they are used to on their computers and mobile devices.

In fact, in just the next 24 hours, millions of new web pages will be added to the Internet. The majority of these pages will be written in HTML, with CSS to style elements and with JavaScript to provide interaction between the user and back-end services.

As you complete the 24 one-hour lessons in this book, you will gain a practical understanding of how to incorporate JavaScript with the powerful jQuery library to provide rich user interactions in your web pages. You will gain the valuable skills of adding dynamic code that allows web pages to instantly react to mouse clicks and finger swipes, interact with back-end services to store and retrieve data from the web server, and create robust Internet applications.

Each hour in the book provides fundamentals that are necessary to create professional web applications. The book includes some basics on using HTML and CSS to get you started, even if you've never used them before. You are provided with code examples that you can implement and expand as your understanding increases. In fact, in just the first lesson in the book, you create a dynamic web page using jQuery and JavaScript.

So pull up a chair, sit back, and enjoy the ride of programming rich Internet applications with jQuery and JavaScript.

Beyond jQuery and JavaScript

This book covers more than jQuery and JavaScript because you need to know more than the language structure to create truly useful web applications. The goal of this book is to give you the fundamental skills needed to create fully functional and interactive web applications in just 24 short, easy lessons. This book covers the following key skills and technologies:

▶ HTML is the most current recommendation for web page creation. Every example in this book is validated HTML5, the most recent recommended version.

▶ CSS is the standard method for formatting web elements. You not only learn how to write CSS and CSS3, but also how to dynamically modify it on the fly using jQuery and JavaScript.

▶ JavaScript is the best method to provide interactions in web pages without the need to load a new page from the server. This is the standard language on which most decent web applications are built.

▶ jQuery, jQueryUI, and jQueryMobile are some of the most popular and robust libraries for JavaScript. jQuery provides very quick access to web page elements and a robust set of features for web application interaction. jQuery provides additional UI and mobile libraries that provide rich UI components for traditional web applications as well as mobile web applications.

▶ AJAX is the standard method that web applications use to interact with web servers and other services. The book includes several examples of using AJAX to interact with web servers, Google, Facebook, and other popular web services.

Code Examples

Most of the examples in the book provide the following elements:

▶ **HTML code**—Code necessary to provide the web page framework in the browser.

▶ **CSS code**—Code necessary to style the web page elements correctly.

▶ **JavaScript code**—This includes both the jQuery and JavaScript code that provide interactions among the user, web page elements, and web services.

▶ **Figures**—Most of the examples include one or more figures that illustrate the behavior of the code in the browser.

The examples in the book are basic to make it easier for you to learn and implement. Many of them can be expanded and used in your own web pages. In fact, some of the exercises at the end of each hour have you expand on the examples.

All the examples in the book have been tested for compatibility with the latest version of the major web browsers, including Google's Chrome, Microsoft's Internet Explorer, and Mozilla's Firefox.

Special Elements

As you complete each lesson, margin notes help you immediately apply what you just learned to your own web pages.

Whenever a new term is used, it is clearly explained. No flipping back and forth to a glossary!

TIP

Tips and tricks to save you precious time are set aside in Tips so that you can spot them quickly.

NOTE

Notes highlight interesting information you should be sure not to miss.

CAUTION

When there's something you need to watch out for, you'll be warned about it in a Caution.

Q&A, Quizzes, and Exercises

Every hour ends with a short question-and-answer session that addresses the kind of "dumb questions" everyone wants to ask. A brief but complete quiz lets you test yourself to be sure you understand everything presented in the hour. Finally, one or two optional exercises give you a chance to practice your new skills before you move on.

HOUR 1
Intro to Dynamic Web Programming

What You'll Learn in This Hour:

▶ Getting ready for creating dynamic web pages
▶ Creating a jQuery- and a JavaScript-friendly development environment
▶ Adding JavaScript and jQuery to web pages
▶ Constructing web pages to support jQuery and JavaScript
▶ Creating your first dynamic web pages with jQuery and JavaScript

JavaScript and its amped up counterpart jQuery have completely changed the game when it comes to creating rich interactive web pages and web-based applications. JavaScript has long been a critical component for creating dynamic web pages. Now, with the advancements in the jQuery, jQuery UI, and jQuery Mobile libraries, web development has changed forever.

This hour quickly takes you through the world of jQuery and JavaScript development. The best place to start is to ensure that you understand the dynamic web development playground that you will be playing in. To be effective in JavaScript and jQuery, you need a fairly decent understanding of web server and web browser interaction, as well as HTML and CSS.

This hour includes several sections that briefly give a high-level overview of web server and browser interactions and the technologies that are involved. The rest of this hour is dedicated to setting up and configuring a jQuery and JavaScript friendly development environment. You will end with writing your very first web pages that include JavaScript and jQuery code.

Understanding the Web Server/Browser Paradigm

JavaScript and jQuery interact with every major component involved in communication between the web server and the browser. To help you understand that interaction better, this section provides a high-level overview of the concepts and technologies involved in web server/browser communication. This is not intended to be comprehensive by any means; it's a high-level overview that enables you to put things into the correct context as they are discussed later in the book.

Looking at Web Server to Browser Communication Terms

The World Wide Web's basic concept should be very familiar to you: An address is typed into or clicked in a web browser, and information is loaded in a form ready to be used. The browser sends a request, the server sends a response, and the browser displays it to the user.

Although the concept is simple, several steps must take place. The following sections define the components involved, their interactions with each other, and how JavaScript and jQuery are involved.

Web Server

The web server is the most critical component of the web. Without it, no data would be available at all. The web server responds to requests from browsers with data that the browsers then display. A lot of things happen on the web server, though. For example, the web server and its components check the format and validity of requests. They may also check for security to verify that the request is from an allowed user. Then, to build the response, the server may interact with several components and even other remote servers to obtain the data necessary.

Browser

The next most important component is the browser. The browser sends requests to the web server and then displays the results for the user. The browser also has a lot of things happening under the hood. The browser has to parse the response from the server and then determine how to represent that to the user.

Although several browsers are available, the three most popular are Firefox, Internet Explorer, and Chrome. For the most part, each browser behaves the same when displaying web pages; however, occasionally some differences exist, and you will need to carefully test your JavaScript and jQuery scripts in each of the browsers that you want to support.

JavaScript and jQuery can be very involved in the interactions that occur between the browser receiving the response and the final output rendered for the user. These scripts can change the format, content, look, and behavior of the data returned from the server. The following sections describe important pieces provided by the browser.

DOM

The browser renders a web page by creating a Document Object Model, or DOM. The DOM is a tree structure with the HTML document as the root object. The root can have several children, and those children can have several children. For example, a web page that contains a list would have a root object, with a child list object that contained several child list element objects. The following shows an example of a simple DOM tree for a web page containing a single heading and a list of three cities:

```
document
  + html
    + body
      + h1
        + text = "City List"
      + ul
        + li
          + text = "New York, US"
        + li
          + text = "Paris, FR"
        + li
          + text = "London, EN"
```

The browser knows how to display each node in the DOM and renders the web page by reading each node and drawing the appropriate pixels in the browser window. As you learn later, JavaScript and jQuery enable you to interact directly with the DOM, reading each of the objects, changing those objects, and even removing and adding objects.

Browser Events

The browser tracks several events that are critical to jQuery and JavaScript programs—for example, when a page is loaded, when you navigate away from a page, when the keyboard is pressed, mouse movements, and clicks. These events are available to JavaScript, allowing you to execute functionality based on which events occur and where they occur.

Browser Window

The browser also provides limited access to the browser window itself. This allows you to use JavaScript to determine the display size of the browser window and other important information that you can use to determine what your scripts will do.

URL

The browser is able to access files on the web server using a Uniform Resource Locator, or URL. A URL is a fully unique address to access data on the web server, which links the URL to a specific file or resource. The web server knows how to parse the URL to determine which file/resources to use to build the response for the browser. In some instances, you might need to use JavaScript to parse and build URLs, especially when dynamically linking to other web pages.

HTML/HTML5

Hypertext Markup Language, or HTML, provides the basic building blocks of a web page. HTML defines a set of elements representing content that is placed on the web page. Each element is enclosed in a pair of tags denoted by the following syntax:

```
<tag>content</tag>
```

For example:

```
<p>This is an HTML paragraph.</p>.
```

The web browser knows how to render the content of each of the tags in the appropriate manner. For example, the tag `<p>` is used to denote a paragraph. The actual text that is displayed on the screen is the text between the `<p>` start tag and the `</p>` end tag.

The format, look, and feel of a web page is determined by placement and type of tags that are included in the HTML file. The browser reads the tags and then renders the content to the screen as defined.

HTML5 is the next generation of the HTML language that incorporates more media elements, such as audio and video. It also provides a rich selection of vector graphic tags that allow you to draw sharp, crisp images directly onto the web page using JavaScript.

Listing 1.1 shows an example of the HTML used to build a simple web page with a list of cities. The HTML is rendered by the browser into the output shown in Figure 1.1.

LISTING 1.1 A Simple HTML Document That Illustrates the HTML Code Necessary to Render a List in a Browser

```
01 <!DOCTYPE html>
02 <html>
03   <head>
04     <title>Cities</title>
05     <meta http-equiv="content-type" content="text/html; charset=utf-8" />
06   </head>
07   <body>
08     <ul>
09       <li>New York, US</li>
10       <li>Paris, FR</li>
11       <li>Rome, IT</li>
12       <li>London, EN</li>
13     </ul>
14   </body>
15 </html>
```

- New York, US
- Paris, FR
- Rome, IT
- London, EN

FIGURE 1.1
List of cities rendered in a browser using the code from Listing 1.1.

CSS

One of the challenges with web pages is getting them to look sharp and professional. The generic look and feel that browsers provide by default is functional; however, it is a far cry from the sleek and sexy eye-candy that users of today's Internet have come to expect.

Cascading Style Sheets, or CSS, provide a way to easily define how the browser renders HTML elements. CSS can be used to define the layout as well as the look and feel of individual elements on a web page. To illustrate this, I've added some CSS code to our example from Listing 1.1. Listing 1.2 uses CSS to modify several attributes in lines 07 to 13. These attributes alter the text alignment, font style, and change the list bullet from a dot to an airplane image. Notice how the CSS style changes how the list is rendered in Figure 1.2.

LISTING 1.2   HTML with Some CSS Code in `<STYLE>` Element to Alter the Appearance of the List

```
01 <!DOCTYPE html>
02 <html>
03   <head>
04     <meta http-equiv="content-type" content="text/html; charset=utf-8" />
05     <style>
06     li {
07        text-align: center;
08        font-family: "Times New Roman", Times, serif;
09        font-size: 30px;
10        font-style: italic;
11        font-weight: bold;
12        list-style-type: none;
13        list-style-image: url('images/air.png');
14     }
15     </style>
16   </head>
17   <body>
18     <ul>
19        <li>New York, US</li>
20        <li>Paris, FR</li>
21        <li>Rome, IT</li>
22        <li>London, EN</li>
```

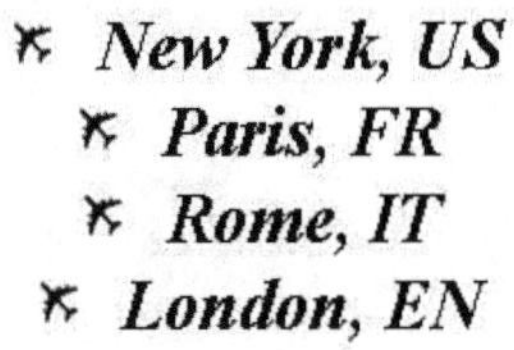

```
23    </ul>
24    </body>
25  </html>
```

✈ *New York, US*
  ✈ *Paris, FR*
   ✈ *Rome, IT*
   ✈ *London, EN*

FIGURE 1.2
The CSS code dramatically changes the look of the list in the browser.

HTTP/HTTPS Protocols

Hypertext Transfer Protocol (HTTP) defines communication between the browser and the web server. It defines what types of requests can be made, as well as the format of those requests and the HTTP response.

Hypertext Transfer Protocol with Secure Sockets Layer (HTTPS) adds an additional security layer, SSL/TLS, to ensure secure connections. When a web browser connects to a web server via HTTPS, a certificate is provided to the browser. The user is then able to determine whether to accept the certificate. Without the certificate, the web server will not respond to the user's requests, thus ensuring that the request is coming from a secured source.

The following sections discuss a little bit about HTTP headers and the two most common types of HTTP requests, GET and PUT.

HTTP Headers

HTTP headers allow the browser to define the behavior and format of requests made to the server and the response back to the web browser. HTTP headers are sent as part of an HTTP request and response. You can send HTTP requests to web servers from JavaScript, so you need to know at least a little bit about the headers required.

The web server reads the request headers and uses them to determine how to build a response for the browser. As part of the response, the web server includes response headers that tell the browser how to process the data in the response. The browser reads the headers first and uses the header values when handling the response and rendering the page.

Following are a few of the more common ones:

▶ ACCEPT—Defines content types that are acceptable in the response.

▶ AUTHORIZATION—Specifies authentication credentials used to authenticate the requesting user.

▶ COOKIE—Cookie value that was previously set in the browser by a server request. Cookies are key/value pairs that are stored on the client. They can be set via server requests or JavaScript code and are sent back to the server as part of HTTP requests from the browser.

▶ SET-COOKIE—Cookie value from the server that the browser should store if cookies are enabled.

▶ CONTENT-TYPE—Type of content contained in the response from the web server. For example, this field may be "text/plain" for text or "image/png" for a .png graphic.

▶ CONTENT-LENGTH—Amount of data that is included in the body of the request or response.

Many more headers are used in HTTP requests and responses, but the preceding list should give you a good idea of how they are used.

GET Request

The most common type of HTTP request is the GET request. The GET request is generally used to retrieve information from the web server—for example, to load a web page or retrieve images to display on a web page. The file to retrieve is specified in the URL that is typed in the browser, for example:

```
http://www.dayleycreations.com/tutorials.html
```

A GET request is composed entirely of headers with no body data. However, data can be passed to the server in a GET request using a query string. A query string is sent to the web server as part of the URL. The query string is formatted by specifying a ? character after the URL and then including a series of one or more key/value pairs separated by & characters using the following syntax:

```
URL?key=value&key=value&key=value...
```

For example, the following URL includes a query string that specifies a parameter `gallery` with a value of `01` that are sent to the server:

```
http://www.dayleycreations.com/user.html?gallery.html?gallery=01
```

POST Request

A POST request is different from a GET request in that there is no query string. Instead, any data that needs to be sent to the web server is encoded into the body of the request. POST requests are generally used for requests that change the state of data on the web server. For example, a web form that adds a new user would send the information that was typed into the form to the server as part of the body of a POST.

Web Server and Client-Side Scripting

Originally, web pages were static, meaning that the file that was rendered by the browser was the exact file that was stored on the server, as shown in Figure 1.3. The problem is that when you try to build a modern website with user interactions, rich elements, and large data, the number of web pages needed to support the different static web pages is increased dramatically.

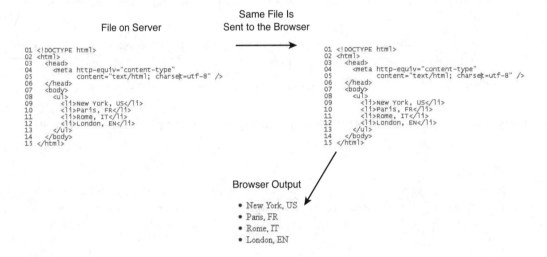

FIGURE 1.3
With static pages, the same page that is located on the web server is sent to the browser and rendered directly.

Rather than creating a web server full of static HTML files, it is better to use scripts that use data from the web server and dynamically build the HTML that is rendered in the browser.

Those scripts can either run on the server or in the client browser. The following sections discuss each of those methods. Most modern websites use a combination of server- and client-side scripting.

Server-Side Scripting

Server-side scripting is the process of formatting server data into an HTML response before it is sent back to the browser. The main advantages of server-side scripting are that data processing is done completely on the server side and the raw data is never transferred across the Internet; also, problems and data fix-ups can be done locally within the server processing. The disadvantage is that it requires more processing on the server side, which can reduce the scalability of some applications. Listing 1.3 shows a simple server-side PHP script that dynamically adds the list of cities to an HTML document before sending it to the browser.

Figure 1.4 shows an example of a simple PHP server-side script. Notice that the file located on the server is different from the one sent to the browser, but the same one sent to the browser is what is rendered.

LISTING 1.3   A PHP Script That Is Run at the Server Populates the City List Items

```
01 <!DOCTYPE html>
02 <html>
03   <head>
04     <meta http-equiv="content-type" content="text/html; charset=utf-8" />
05   </head>
06   <body>
07     <ul>
08       <?php
09         $cities = array("New York, US", "Paris, FR", "Rome, IT", "London, EN");
10         foreach ($cities as $city) {
11           echo "<li>$city</li>";
12         }
13       ?>
14     </ul>
15   </body>
16 </html>
```

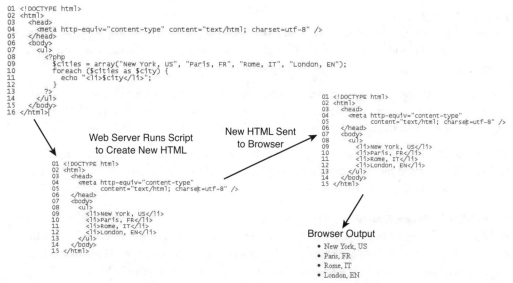

FIGURE 1.4
The PHP script is executed on the web server, and so the HTML document sent to the browser is different from what is actually contained on the server.

Client-Side Scripting

Client-side scripting is the process of sending code along with the web page. That code gets executed either during the loading of the web page or after the web page has been loaded.

There are a couple of great advantages of client-side scripting. One is that data processing is done on the client side, which makes it easier to scale applications with large numbers of users. Another is that browser events can often be handled locally without the need to send requests to the server. This enables you to make interfaces respond much more quickly to user interaction.

JavaScript and jQuery are by far the most common form of client-side scripting. Throughout this book, you learn why that is the case.

What Is JavaScript?

JavaScript is a programming language much like any other. What separates JavaScript the most from other programming languages is that the browser has a built-in interpreter that can parse and execute the language. That means that you can write complex applications that have direct access to the browser and the DOM.

Access to the DOM means that you can add, modify, or remove elements from a web page without reloading it. Access to the browser gives you access to events such as mouse movements and clicks. This is what gives JavaScript the capability to provide functionality such as dynamic lists and drag and drop.

What Is jQuery?

jQuery is a library that is built on JavaScript. The underlying code is JavaScript; however, jQuery simplifies a lot of the JavaScript code into simple-to-use functionality. The two main advantages to using jQuery are selectors and built-in functions.

Selectors provide quick access to specific elements on the web page, such as a list or table. They also provide access to groups of elements, such as all paragraphs or all paragraphs of a certain class. This allows you to quickly and easily access specific DOM elements.

jQuery also provides a rich set of built in functionality that makes it easy to do a lot more with a lot less code. For example, tasks such as hiding an element on the screen or animating the resize of an element take just one line of code.

Client-Side Scripting Example

Listing 1.4 shows an example of a simple JavaScript client-side script. Figure 1.5 diagrams the flow of data between the web server and the browser. Notice that this time the file located on the server is the same one sent to the browser, but the JavaScript changes the HTML that is loaded in the browser.

LISTING 1.4 A Simple JavaScript Client-Side Script That Is Run in the Browser to Populate the City List Items

```
01 <!DOCTYPE html>
02 <html>
03    <head>
04       <meta http-equiv="content-type" content="text/html; charset=utf-8" />
05         <script>
06           function loadCities(){
07                 var cities = ["New York, US", "Paris, FR", "Rome, IT", "London,
                   ➥EN"];
08                 var ulElement = document.getElementById("cityList");
09                 for (var city in cities){
10                     var listItem = ulElement.appendChild(document.
                       ➥createElement("li"));
11                     listItem.appendChild(document.createTextNode(cities[city]));
12                 }
13           }
14       </script>
15    </head>
16    <body onload="loadCities()">
17       <ul id="cityList">
18       </ul>
19    </body>
20 </html>
```

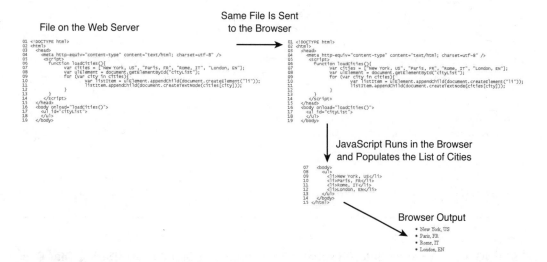

FIGURE 1.5
The JavaScript is executed in the browser, and so the HTML document rendered by the browser is different from the one that was originally sent.

AJAX

Asynchronous JavaScript and XML, or AJAX, is the process of using JavaScript to continue to communicate with the web server after the web page has been loaded. AJAX reduces the need to reload the web page or load other web pages as the user interacts. This reduces the amount of data that needs to be sent with the initial web server response and also allows web pages to be more interactive.

For a simple example of AJAX, I've constructed two scripts—Listing 1.5 and Listing 1.6. Listing 1.5 is an HTML document with JavaScript that runs on the client after the page is loaded. The JavaScript makes an AJAX request back to the server to retrieve the list of cities via a server-side PHP script, shown in Listing 1.6. The list of cities returned is then used to populate the HTML list element with items.

LISTING 1.5   A Simple JavaScript Client-Side Script Executes an AJAX Request to the Server to Retrieve a List of Cities to Use When Building the HTML List Element

```
01 <!DOCTYPE html>
02 <html>
03   <head>
04     <meta http-equiv="content-type" content="text/html; charset=utf-8" />
05     <script>
06       var xmlhttp = xmlhttp=new XMLHttpRequest();
07       function loadCities(){
08         xmlhttp.open("GET","php/hour01_06.php",false);
09         xmlhttp.send();
10         var cities = JSON.parse( xmlhttp.responseText );
11         var ulElement = document.getElementById("cityList");
12         for (var city in cities){
13           var listItem = ulElement.appendChild(document.createElement("li"));
14           listItem.appendChild(document.createTextNode(cities[city]));
15         }
16       }
17     </script>
18   </head>
19   <body onload="loadCities()">
20     <ul id="cityList">
21     </ul>
22   </body>
23 </html>
```

LISTING 1.6   A Server-Side PHP Script That Returns a Simple JSON String That Can Be Parsed and Used by the JavaScript in Listing 1.5

```
1 <?php
2   echo '["New York, US", "Paris, FR", "Rome, IT", "London, EN"]';
3 ?>
```

Figure 1.6 illustrates the flow of communication that happens during the AJAX request/response. Notice that a second request is made to the server to retrieve the list of cities.

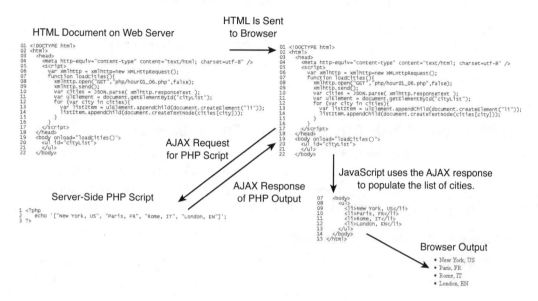

FIGURE 1.6
Using an AJAX request, JavaScript can send an additional request to the server to retrieve additional information that can be used to populate the web page.

Preparing to Write jQuery and JavaScript

With the brief introduction to dynamic web programming out of the way, it is time to cut to the chase and get your development environment ready to write jQuery and JavaScript.

The development environment can make all the difference when you are writing jQuery and JavaScript projects. The development environment should have these following characteristics:

- ▶ **Easy to Use IDE**—The IDE provides text editors that allow you to modify your code in the simplest manner possible. Choose an IDE that you feel comfortable with and that is extensible to support HTML, CSS, JavaScript, and jQuery.

- ▶ **Development Web Server**—You should never develop directly on a live web server (although most of us have done it at one point or another). A web server is required to test out scripts and interactions.

▶ **Development Web Browser(s)**—Again, you should initially develop to the browser that you are most comfortable with or will be the most commonly used. You will need to enable debugging tools on the browser to help you find and fix issues with your scripts.

▶ **Well-Structured Project**—Structure your project, directories, and filenames for growth. It is a difficult process to restructure a web project with a large number of files and directories. Too many files or confusing filenames can make a project cumbersome and difficult to manage.

Setting Up a Web Development Environment

Setting up a web development environment requires three steps. First, install an IDE that will provide the tools to create and edit code. Second, add and enable JavaScript debugging tools in your web browser(s). Third, set up a development web server that you can test your scripts from. The following sections take you through each of those tasks.

Installing a Web Development IDE

The IDE is the most important aspect when developing with JavaScript. An IDE integrates the various tasks required to write web applications into a single interface. In reality, you could use any text editor to write HTML, CSS, JavaScript, and jQuery code. However, you will find it much more productive and easy to use a good IDE.

Several IDEs are available. Some are open source; others cost a lot. Pick the one that best fits your needs. You should have an IDE with code completion and error checking, because those two features save the most time.

Possible IDEs include Dreamweaver, Visual Studio, and several others. However, Eclipse features numerous plug-ins that provide extensibility. For jQuery and JavaScript, consider using Aptana Studio because it is simple to set up and get going with, and it is supported on Mac, Windows, and Linux.

Installing Aptana Studio

For the purposes of this book, you step through the process of installing and configuring Aptana, although all the editing and debugging concepts apply equally to whatever IDE you are working with.

NOTE

You will need to have a Java JRE or JDK installed to be able to install Aptana Studio.

You can download Aptana Studio from the following location:
www.aptana.com/products/studio3/download

You should select Standalone Version and specify which operating system that you are installing it on, as shown in Figure 1.7. After the install is downloaded, execute it and follow the prompts; they are very straightforward.

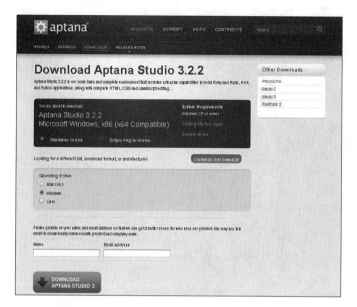

FIGURE 1.7
Aptana Studio download page.

After Aptana Studio is installed, launch it. When you launch it for the first time, you need to specify a location for your workspace. The workspace is where your projects and files will be stored, so pick a location that you can easily manage.

Configuring Aptana Studio
Now that Aptana Studio is installed, there are just a few more steps to configure it. Do the following:

1. Select Commands, Bundle Development, Install Bundle from the main menu. Then select jQuery from the bundles list and click the OK button.

2. Select Windows, Preferences from the main menu to load the Preferences dialog shown in Figure 1.8. From the Preferences dialog select Aptana Studio, Themes, also shown in Figure 1.8, and then select a theme from the drop-down list. The theme will set window, menu, selection, and code element colors and fonts. Choose a theme that works well for you. You can also customize the theme for this page.

NOTE

You can also import and export themes from this themes preferences dialog. On the book website is a file named AptanaTheme.tmTheme, which is the theme used in writing this book. You can import that theme here.

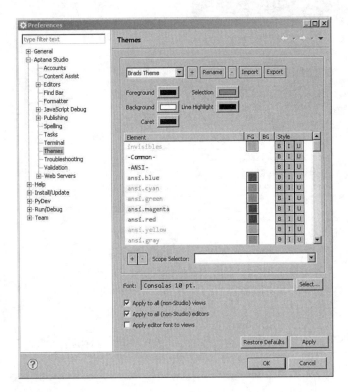

FIGURE 1.8
Aptana Studio Preferences dialog.

3. Select and drag the Outline tab in the bottom left and merge it next to the App Explorer tab. This gives you a better view of the outline in your scripts and allows you to close the snippets and sample tabs in the bottom that you do not need. The final result should look something like Figure 1.9.

4. Play around with the preferences and menus to familiarize yourself with the interface.

Aptana Studio is now set up and ready for you to begin creating projects.

Outline Tab

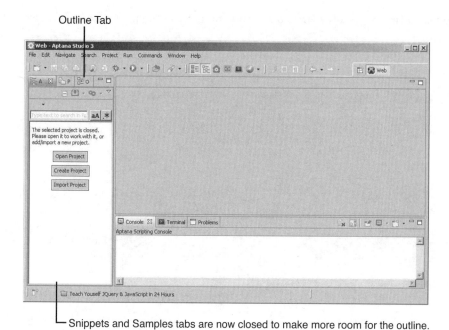

Snippets and Samples tabs are now closed to make more room for the outline.

FIGURE 1.9
Aptana Studio with Outline tab moved.

Configuring Browser Development Tools

After you have Aptana Studio set up, you are ready to configure your browsers to debug JavaScript. In this section, you follow the steps needed to enable JavaScript debugging on each of the three main browsers. It doesn't really matter which browser you choose; however, Firefox is used in the next section and throughout the book.

Firefox seems to have the most consistent experience and has been the most reliable. Firefox also seems to have the most consistent cross-platform support.

Installing Firebug on Firefox

Use the following steps to enable JavaScript debugging on Firefox:

1. Open Firefox.

2. Select Tools, Add-Ons from the main menu.

3. Type **Firebug** into the search box in the top right to search for Firebug, and then click the Install button to install it.

4. Type **FireQuery** into the search box in the top right to search for FireQuery, and then click the Install button to install it. FireQuery extends Firebug to also support jQuery.

5. When you reload Firefox, click the Firebug button to display the Firebug Console, as shown in Figure 1.10.

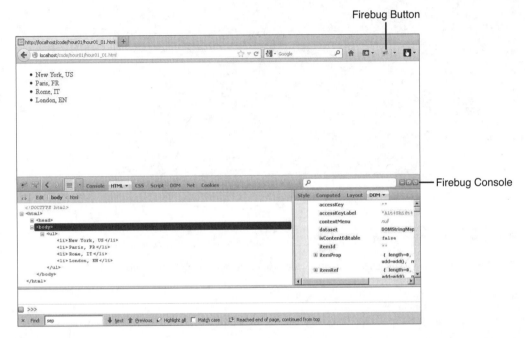

FIGURE 1.10
Firefox with Firebug enabled.

Enabling Developer Tools in Internet Explorer

Use the following steps to enable JavaScript debugging on Internet Explorer:

1. Open Internet Explorer.

2. Click the Settings button and select Developer Tools from the drop-down menu, or press the F12 key.

3. The Developer Console is displayed as shown in Figure 1.11.

Enabling the JavaScript Console in Chrome

Use the following steps to enable JavaScript debugging in Chrome:

1. Open Chrome.

2. Click the Settings button and select Tools, Developer Tools from the drop-down menu. You can also press Ctrl+Shift+j on PCs or CMD-Shift-j on Macs.

3. The JavaScript Console is displayed as shown in Figure 1.12.

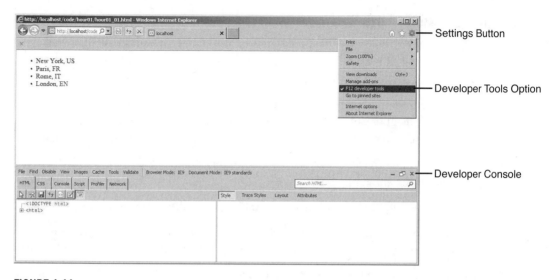

FIGURE 1.11
Internet Explorer with the Developer Console loaded.

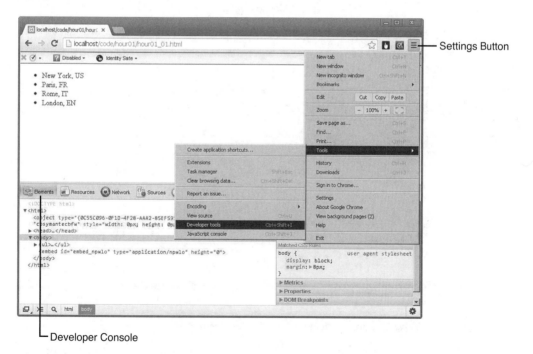

FIGURE 1.12
Chrome with the Developer Console loaded.

Installing a Simple Development Web Server

After you have your browser ready, the final step is to install and configure a simple development server. If possible, it is usually best to have a basic web server installed on your development machine.

You can choose from several options, but the two most common are Apache or IIS. The best option for a development server is using a prebuilt Apache stack that includes MySQL and PHP support. This book uses the XAMPP stack because it is available for Mac, Windows, and Linux.

The XAAMP stack can be downloaded from the following location: www.apachefriends.org/en/xampp.html

Use the following steps to install and configure XAMPP as your development server:

1. Download the XAMPP installer and install XAMPP. The installation is straightforward. Remember the location where you choose to install it. You will be using that location later.

2. Load the XAMPP Control Panel shown in Figure 1.13.

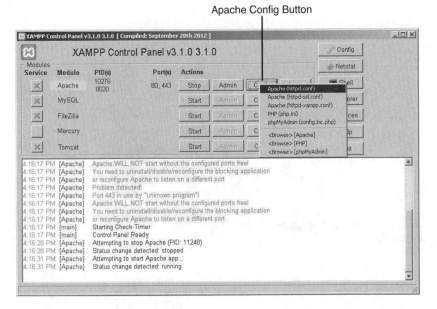

FIGURE 1.13
Selecting the Apache config file http.conf from the XAMPP Control Panel.

3. From the XAMPP Control Panel, click the Apache Config button and select the httpd.conf file to load the Apache configuration file in the editor.

4. Add the following directive to the httpd.conf file to enable a code directory for you to access directly when the server is running:

```
<Directory "C:/xampp/htdocs/code">
    # Allows Browser Access to Your jQuery and JavaScript code Directory
    Options Indexes FollowSymLinks Includes ExecCGI
    AllowOverride All
    Allow from All
</Directory>
```

CAUTION

The Allow from All option will allow anyone access to the files in that folder while the web server is running. It is perfect for debugging. If you would like stricter security, check out Apache's security guide at http://httpd.apache.org/docs/2.2/configuring.html.

NOTE

In step 4, the directory is a Windows path for the default settings of XAMPP. If you installed XAMPP to a different location or on Linux and Mac systems, you will need to make adjustments to the path specified in the Directory directive.

5. Save the file.

6. Create a directory named code in the /xamp/htdocs directory or wherever your Apache root directory is set to. This is the directory that you will be adding your code to.

7. Stop and then Start the Apache service using the XAMPP Control Panel.

8. Go to the following location in your web browser; an empty directory link similar to the one in Figure 1.14 should be displayed in the browser:

```
http://localhost/code
```

Your web server is now ready to be used for web development.

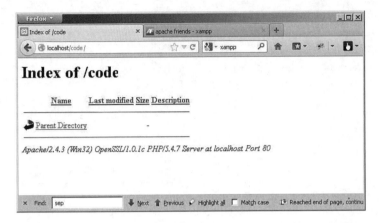

FIGURE 1.14
Verifying that the web browser has access to the newly created code directory.

Creating a Web Development Project

After you have installed your IDE and web server, you are ready to begin creating projects. In this section, you learn some concepts and go through the process of creating a project in Aptana Studio.

Directory Structure

When you first begin a web project, you typically start off small with a few images and only a couple of files. However, as time goes by and more files are added to the project, poorly organized projects can quickly become a mess.

To avoid that problem, plan your directory structure ahead of time. The best directory structure will depend on what your needs are, how many images you will be incorporating, what file types, and so on.

To give you a quick example, consider a basic directory structure similar to the following:

- ▶ **root**—Contains index.html, sitemaps, webcrawler items, and the like

- ▶ **root/html**—Contains only the HTML files

- ▶ **root/js**—Contains JavaScript files

- ▶ **root/php**—Contains any server-side PHP scripts

- ▶ **root/images**—Contains all graphics

- **root/images/visual**—Contains graphic elements, such as buttons, to build web pages

- **root/images/photos**—Contains any photos displayed on the website

The purpose of the preceding list is to give you an idea of one way to structure your files so that they remain organized. The best way is totally up to you. You may want more subdirectories; just don't add so many that the URL to reach files in them becomes a mess.

File Naming

Another area you need to pay attention to when creating a web project are filenames. Here are a few things to consider:

- **Not too long**—Filenames often become part of URLs and are parsed by JavaScript. Making filenames too long becomes cumbersome in code and in the browser.

- **Make them mean something**—When you create a script or HTML page, you will have to use that name when building web pages, and you will also need to find it in the editor. If the name doesn't reflect the purpose of the file, it can make development difficult.

TRY IT YOURSELF ▼

Creating a Project

In this section, you learn the process of creating a project in Aptana Studio. A project in Aptana Studio—and most IDEs, for that matter—is a way to organize, control, build, and often deploy websites and applications that require several files.

This section does not spend a lot of time discussing projects, but as you go along, you will get the idea of how a basic web project works.

Use the following steps to create a project in Aptana Studio:

1. Select File, New, Web Project to launch the Project Template dialog.
2. Select Default Project and click Next.
3. Type in a project name. Keep it short, but make it mean something. For example, TYjQueryCode is the project name for this book.
4. Unselect the Use Default Location option.
5. Add the location of the directory that you added to the httpd.conf file previously. In this case, it was c:\xampp\htdocs\code.
6. Click the Finish button and the project should show up in the workspace tab, as shown in Figure 1.15.

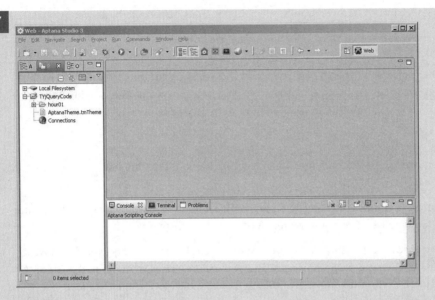

FIGURE 1.15
Creating a new project in Aptana Studio.

7. Right-click the project name and select New, Folder; then name the folder hour01 to store code for this hour.

8. Your first project has now been created.

▼ TRY IT YOURSELF

Creating a Dynamic Web Page with jQuery and JavaScript

Now that you have a project created, you are ready to create your dynamic web pages. In this section, you follow the steps to create a fairly basic dynamic web page. When you are finished, you will have a dynamic web page based on HTML, stylized with CSS with interaction through jQuery and JavaScript.

Adding HTML

The first step is to create a simple web page that has an HTML element that you can stylize and manipulate. Use the following steps in Aptana to create the HTML document that you will use as your base:

1. Right-click the hour01 folder that you created earlier.

2. Select New, File from the pop-up menu.

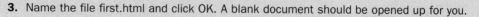

3. Name the file first.html and click OK. A blank document should be opened up for you.

4. Type in the following HTML code. Don't worry if you are not too familiar with HTML; you'll learn enough to use it a bit later in the book.

```
<!DOCTYPE html>
<html>
  <head>
    <meta http-equiv="content-type" content="text/html; charset=utf-8" />
  </head>
  <body>
    <span>Click Me</span>
  </body>
</html>
```

5. Save the file.

6. Open the following URL in your web browser and you should see the text "Click Me" appear:

```
http://localhost/code/hour01/first.html
```

That's it. All the basic HTML elements are now in place. In the next section, you stylize the `<span>` element so that Click Me looks more like a button.

Adding CSS

The simple text rendered by the browser is pretty plain, but that problem can quickly be solved by adding a CSS style. In this section, you use CSS to make the text appear more like a button.

Use the following steps to add the CSS style to the `<span>` element. For reference, the style changes you make in these steps are shown in the final script in Listing 1.7:

1. Add the following code inside the `<head>` tags of the web page to include a CSS `<style>` element for all `<span>` elements:

```
<style>
  span{
  }
</style>
```

2. Add the following property setting to the span style to change the background of the text to a dark blue color:

```
background-color: #0066AA;
```

3. Add the following property settings to the span style to change the font color to white and the font to bold:

```
color: #FFFFFF;
font-weight: bold;
```

4. Add the following property settings to the span style to add a border around the span text:

```
border-color: #C0C0C0;
border:2px solid;
border-radius:5px;
padding: 3px;
```

5. Add the following property settings to the span style to set an absolute position for the span element:

```
position:absolute;
top:150px;
left:100px;
```

6. Save the file.

7. Open the following URL in your web browser, and you should see the stylized text Click Me appear as shown in Figure 1.16:

```
http://localhost/code/hour01/first.html
```

FIGURE 1.16
`<span>` element stylized to look like a button.

Writing a Dynamic Script

Now that the HTML is stylized the way you want it, you can begin adding dynamic interactions. In this section, you add a link to a hosted jQuery library so that you will be able to use jQuery, and then you link the browser mouse event `mouseover` to a JavaScript function that moves the text.

Follow these steps to add the jQuery and JavaScript interactions to your web page:

1. Change the `<span>` element to include an ID so that you can reference it, and also add a handler for the `mouseover` event, as shown in line 30 of Listing 1.7:

```
<span id="elusiveText" onmouseover="moveIt()">Click Me</span>
```

2. Add the following line of code to the `<head>` tag, as shown in line 6 of Listing 1.7. This loads the jQuery library from a hosted source:

```
<script src="http://code.jquery.com/jquery- latest.min.js"></script>
```

3. Add the following JavaScript function to the `<head>` as shown in lines 6–13 of Listing 1.7. This function creates an array of coordinate values from 10 to 350, then randomly sets the top and left CSS properties of the span element each time the mouse is moved over it:

```
function moveIt(){
    var coords = new Array(10,50,100,130,175,225,260,300,320,350);
    var x = coords[Math.floor((Math.random()*10))];
    var y = coords[Math.floor((Math.random()*10))];
    $("#elusiveText").css({"top": y + "px", "left": x + "px"})
}
```

4. Save the file.

5. Open the following URL in your web browser, and you should see the stylized text Click Me appear, as shown in Figure 1.16:

```
http://localhost/code/hour01/first.html
```

6. Now try to click the Click Me button. The button should move each time the mouse is over it, making it impossible to click it.

7. Find someone who annoys you, and ask them to click the button.

LISTING 1.7   A Simple Interactive jQuery and JavaScript Web Page

```
01  <!DOCTYPE html>
02  <html>
03    <head>
04      <meta http-equiv="content-type" content="text/html; charset=utf-8" />
05      <script src="http://code.jquery.com/jquery-latest.min.js"></script>
06      <script>
07        function moveIt(){
08          var coords = new Array(10,50,100,130,175,225,260,300,320,350);
09          var x = coords[Math.floor((Math.random()*10))];
10          var y = coords[Math.floor((Math.random()*10))];
11          $("#elusiveText").css({"top": y + "px", "left": x + "px"})
12        }
13      </script>
14      <style>
15        span{
16          background-color: #0066AA;
17          color: #FFFFFF;
18          font-weight: bold;
```

```
19          border-color: #C0C0C0;
20          border:2px solid;
21          border-radius:5px;
22          padding: 3px;
23          position:absolute;
24          top:150px;
25          left:100px;
26      }
27     </style>
28    </head>
29    <body>
30      <span id="elusiveText" onmouseover="moveIt()">Click Me</span>
31    </body>
32 </html>
```

Summary

In this hour, you learned the basics of web server and browser communications. You learned differences between GET and POST requests, as well as the purposes of server-side and client-side scripts. You also learned about the DOM and how the browser uses it to render the web page that is displayed to the user.

You have set up a good web development environment and created your first project. As part of creating your first project, you created a dynamic web page that incorporates HTML, CSS, jQuery, and JavaScript.

Q&A

Q. Which is better—a client-side or a server-side script?

A. It really depends on what you are trying to accomplish. Some people say that one way or the other is the only way to go. In reality, it is often a combination of the two that provides the best option. A good rule to follow is that if the interaction with the data is heavier based on user interaction such as mouse clicks, use a client-side script. If validation or error handling of the data requires interaction with the server, use a server-side script.

Q. Why don't all browsers handle JavaScript the same way?

A. To render HTML and interact with JavaScript, the browsers use an engine that parses the data from the server, builds objects, and then feeds them into a graphical rendering engine that writes them on the screen. Because each browser uses a different engine, each interprets the scripts slightly differently, especially with fringe elements that have not yet become standardized. If you want to support all browsers, you need to test your web pages in each of them to verify that they work correctly.

Workshop

The workshop consists of a set of questions and answers designed to solidify your understanding of the material covered in this hour. Try answering the questions before looking at the answers.

Quiz

1. Would you send a GET or a POST request to a web server to open a web page?

2. What type of script has access to browser mouse events: server-side, client-side, or both?

3. True or False: JavaScript consoles are enabled by default on all browsers.

4. What type of script is the best to use when defining the appearance of DOM elements?

Quiz Answers

1. GET

2. Client-side

3. False. You must manually enable JavaScript debugging on all browsers.

4. CSS scripts are the simplest to use when defining the appearance of DOM elements.

Exercises

1. Modify your first.html file to change the background color of your button randomly each time it is moved. Add the following two lines to randomly select a color:

```
var colors = new Array("#0066AA", "#0000FF", "#FF0000", "#00FF00");
var color = colors[Math.floor((Math.random()*4))];
```

Then modify the CSS change in your JavaScript to include background-color, as shown next:

```
$("#elusiveText").css({"top": y + "px", "left": x + "px", "background-color":
➥color})
```

2. Add an additional `<span>` element to your first.html file with the same behavior as the first. To do this, add the following two lines in the appropriate locations. You should be able to figure out where they go:

```
$("#elusiveText2").css({"top": x + "px", "left": y + "px"})
<span id="elusiveText2" onmouseover="moveIt()">Click Me</span>
```

Debugging jQuery and JavaScript Web Pages

What You'll Learn in This Hour:

▶ Where to find information that is outputted from jQuery and JavaScript scripts

▶ How to debug problems with HTML elements

▶ Ways to more easily find and fix problems with CSS layout

▶ Methods to view and edit the DOM live in the web browser

▶ How to quickly find and fix problems in your JavaScript

▶ What information is available to analyze network traffic between the browser and the web server

A major challenge when writing JavaScript and jQuery applications is finding and fixing problems in your scripts. Simple syntax problems or invalid values can cause a lot of frustration and wasted time. For that reason, some excellent tools have been created to help you quickly and easily find problems in your scripts. In this hour, you learn some of the basics of debugging JavaScript via Firebug in Mozilla. Although the developer consoles in other browsers are a bit different, most of the principles are the same. Also, don't be alarmed if you don't recognize the code element in the examples. They'll be covered in upcoming hours, but you should be able to debug before you jump into coding heavily.

Viewing the JavaScript Console

One of the first debugging tools that you will want to become familiar with is the JavaScript console. The console is your interface to output from JavaScript scripts. Errors and log messages will be displayed as they occur in the JavaScript console.

For example, when an error in the script results in the browser not being able to parse it, the error will be displayed in the console. In addition to errors, by using the `console.log` statement, you can also add your own debug statements to be displayed in the JavaScript console.

NOTE

In addition to `console.log`, you can use `console.error()`, `console.assert()`, and a variety of other statements to log information to the JavaScript console. For more information about how to use the Firebug console log, see

https://getfirebug.com/wiki/index.php/Console_API

Understanding the JavaScript Console

The JavaScript console is a fairly basic and yet powerful tool. The console has two parts: the controls and the list of log entries. Figure 2.1 shows the Firebug JavaScript console.

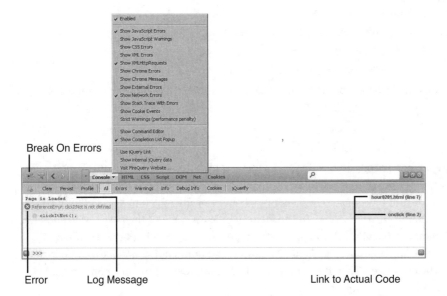

FIGURE 2.1
The JavaScript console in Firebug displays log messages and errors.

Notice the menu displayed when you click the down arrow in the Console tab. From that menu you can enable the console, as well as select which types of errors and log messages to include in the message list.

The console also provides a toolbar with several options. The options in the console toolbar are toggled by clicking them. The following list describes each of the options in the control bar:

▶ **Break On Errors**—When this is enabled, JavaScript will stop executing if an error is encountered in the script. This is very useful if you want to catch errors and see what the values of things are when they occur.

▶ **Clear**—Clears the messages in the message list.

▶ **Persist**—Retains the messages even if the page is reloaded. If this option is not set, the message list is emptied when the page is reloaded.

▶ **Profile**—Starts and stops the profiler to track time inside code.

▶ **All**—Displays all messages. For the most part, you should leave all messages on unless there are too many and you want to focus on a specific message.

▶ **Error**—Display only error messages.

▶ **Warnings**—Display only warning messages.

▶ **Debug Info**—Display only debug messages.

▶ **Cookies**—Display only cookie-related messages.

▶ **jQuerify**—Modifies the script that loads the jQuery library to include the latest jQuery code. This is part of the FireQuery plug-in.

Notice that in the messages portion in Figure 2.1, there are two types of messages. One is a log statement, and the second is an error. Both show the line number to the right. If you click the line number, you go directly to the code.

Notice in the error message, the top portion of text refers to the error that occurred and the bottom shows the actual JavaScript line. This is useful when debugging because you can often see the problem by looking at the error and the single line of code.

 TRY IT YOURSELF ▼

Using the JavaScript Console to Find Errors

The simplest way to understand using the console is to debug an actual script. Consider the HTML code in Listing 2.1, which contains several errors. Use the following steps to add the listing to your project in Aptana:

1. Right-click the project and select New, Folder from the menu.

2. Name the folder hour02 and click Finish.

3. Right-click the new folder and select New, File from the menu.

4. Name the file hour0201.html.

5. Type in the contents of Listing 2.1, or if you have the file from the website, cut and paste the contents into the new file.

6. Save the file.

LISTING 2.1   A Very Simple HTML Document with JavaScript Errors

```
01 <!DOCTYPE html>
02 <html>
03   <head>
04     <meta http-equiv="content-type" content="text/html; charset=utf-8" />
05     <script>
06       fnction loadedFunction(){
07         console.log("Page is Loaded");
08       }
09       function clickIt(){
10         console.log("User Clicked");
11       }
12     </script>
13   </head>
14   <body onload="loadedFunction()">
15     <span onclick="clickItNot()">Click Me</span>
16   </body>
17 </html>
```

The code in Listing 2.1 is supposed to display the message Page Is Loaded in the console after the page has been loaded in the browser. Another message, User Clicked, is displayed each time the user clicks the Click Me text in the browser. The problem is that the script has several bugs.

With the file now in place, use the following steps to debug the errors using the JavaScript console:

1. Open Firefox and click the Firebug icon.

2. Click the Console tab in Firebug to bring up the JavaScript console shown in Figure 2.2.

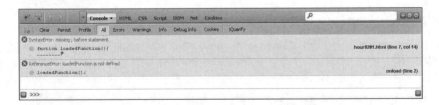

FIGURE 2.2
The JavaScript console showing two errors that occurred during the page load.

3. Open the following URL in Firefox to load the newly created web page:

   http://localhost/code/hour02/hour0201.html

4. Notice the errors displayed in the console, as shown in Figure 2.2. The first error shows that missing ";" in the definition for loadedFunction(). The second error shows that

`loadedFunction` is not defined. Taking these two errors together indicates that a problem exists with the definition for `loadedFunction()`. Looking at the failed definition statement, you can see that `function` is misspelled as `fnction`.

5. In Aptana, change the word `fnction` in line 6 to `function`.

6. Go back to Firefox and refresh the web page. Now in the console you should see Page Is Loaded, the text that is logged in the `loadedFunction()` function, but no errors.

7. Click the Click Me text. An error is added to the console, as shown in Figure 2.3. The error states that `clickItNot` is not defined. When you look at the HTML file and search for `clickItNot`, you can see on line 16 that an `onclick` event is linked to `clickItNot()`, but that the JavaScript function is named `clickIt()`.

FIGURE 2.3
The JavaScript console showing one successful log message and one error.

8. In Aptana, change `clickItNot` in line 15 to `clickIt` and save the file.

9. Reload the web pages.

10. Click the Click Me Text again. Figure 2.4 shows that both log statements are now displayed correctly and there are no errors. The page has been successfully debugged.

FIGURE 2.4
The JavaScript console showing two successful log messages and no errors.

Debugging HTML Elements

Debugging HTML elements can be a big challenge at times. Simple syntax errors can lead to major problems for the browser when it's trying to render an HTML document. In addition, HTML elements have property values that are not rendered to the screen but that will affect the behavior of the web page.

The HTML Inspector and the DOM editor help you find and fix problems in your HTML code. The following sections take you through some simple examples of using those tools.

Inspecting HTML Elements

The HTML Inspector enables you to view each of the HTML elements that have been parsed by the browser. This gives you a view of the HTML from the browser's perspective, which in the case of syntax errors is usually different from the one that was intended, making it more obvious where syntax errors are.

Figure 2.5 shows an example of the Firebug HTML Inspector. With the HTML Inspector, some very useful features are available to you as described next:

▶ **DOM Tree**—This is a simple view into the DOM tree. You can click the + icons to expand parts of the tree and click − icons to collapse parts of the tree.

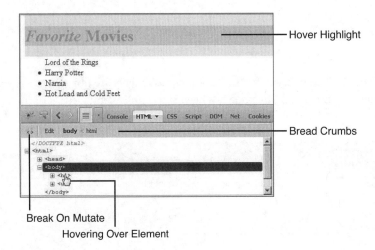

FIGURE 2.5
The HTML Inspector page in Firebug.

▶ **Break on Mutate**—When this option is enabled, the browser will break into the JavaScript debugger whenever the DOM element is changed dynamically. This helps you catch problems as they are occurring.

▶ **Edit**—When this option is enabled, the tree view changes to a text editor view that allows you to directly edit the HTML code in the browser. The browser changes what is rendered based on the changes you make here. Although this won't change the code in your project, it is much easier to use this feature to try things out until problems are fixed. Then you can copy the code from the editor and paste it into the actual file in your project.

▶ **Hover**—When you hover over the HTML code in the DOM tree, the element is highlighted in the browser. The hover feature of the HTML Inspector is one of my favorites because it gives a very visual way to see the relationship between the node in the DOM tree and the rendered web page. Notice in Figure 2.5 that as the `<h1>` element hovered, the heading is highlighted in the web page.

NOTE

When an element is hovered over in the DOM tree, the element is highlighted on the web page. The hover highlight is color coded, with light blue being the contents, purple being the padding, and yellow being the margin for the HTML element.

▶ **Bread Crumbs**—The bread crumbs show the hierarchy of nodes from the root `<html>` node down to the one that is currently selected in the tree or edit view. This makes it easy to navigate around, especially in the edit view.

TRY IT YOURSELF ▼

Debugging HTML Using the HTML Inspector

To illustrate how to use the HTML Inspector, consider the code in Listing 2.2. A basic HTML document with a list of movies and the word "Favorite" in the heading is supposed to be in italic. However, look at the rendered version in Figure 2.6. There are obviously some problems: Everything is in italic and there is no bullet point on the first list item. These problems are caused by just two characters in all the text.

LISTING 2.2   A Very Simple HTML Document with Some HTML Syntax Errors Illustrated in Figure 2.6

```
01 <!DOCTYPE html>
02 <html>
03    <head>
04       <meta http-equiv="content-type" content="text/html; charset=utf-8" />
```

```
05    </head>
06    <body>
07      <h1><i>Favorite<i> Movies</h1>
08      <ul>
09        <ll>Lord of the Rings</li>
10        <li>Harry Potter</li>
11        <li>Narnia</li>
12        <li>Hot Lead and Cold Feet</li>
13      </ul>
14    </body>
15  </html>
```

Favorite Movies

Lord of the Rings
- *Harry Potter*
- *Narnia*
- *Hot Lead and Cold Feet*

FIGURE 2.6
This web page has two problems: Only the word "Favorite" should be in italic, and there is no bullet point on the first list item.

Follow along with these steps to find and fix the HTML syntax problems using the HTML Inspector:

1. Add the code in Listing 2.2 to a new file hour0202.html in the hour02 folder of your project and save the document. You should be familiar with this process by now.

2. Open Firefox and click the Firebug icon to enable Firebug.

3. Open the following URL in Firefox; the web page should look like Figure 2.6.

   `http://localhost/code/hour02/hour0202.html`

4. Click the HTML tab in Firebug and expand the `<html>`, then `<body>`, and then `<i>` tags, as shown in Figure 2.7. Notice that the only element under the `<i>` tag is a second `<i>` tag. That isn't right, so go back to Aptana and look at the `<i>` tags on line 7 in the HTML. Notice that the / is missing from the closing `<i>` tag.

5. Change the second `<i>` tag to a closing tag `</i>` and save the document.

6. Refresh the document in the browser. Notice that the word "Favorite" is now in italic, as it should be, but the bullet point is still missing, as shown in Figure 2.8.

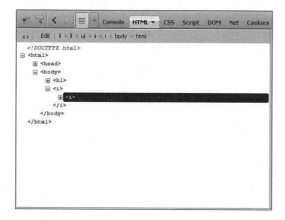

FIGURE 2.7
This HTML Inspector shows a second `<i>` in the DOM.

FIGURE 2.8
This web page now has only one problem—no bullet point on the first list item.

7. Go back to the HTML Inspector and expand the `<html>`, then `<body>`, then `<ul>`, then `<ll>`, as shown in Figure 2.9. Instead of a set of four `<li>` elements under the `<ul>` element, there is an `<ll>` element with the `<li>` elements underneath. We haven't covered the HTML tags yet, but if you are familiar with HTML lists, you will recognize that `ll` is not a valid HTML tag. It should be `<li>`.

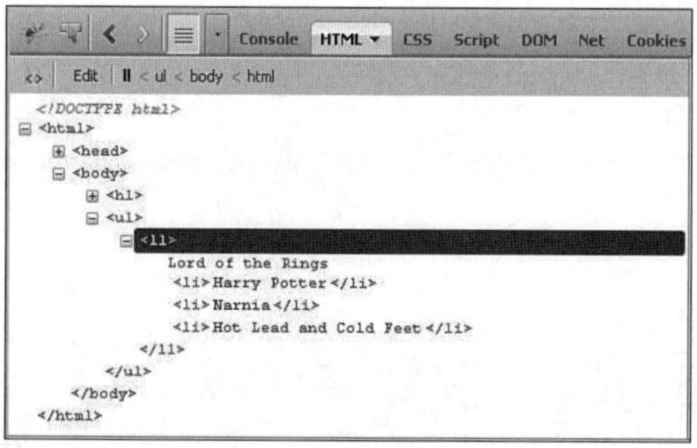

FIGURE 2.9
Viewing the DOM reveals that the browser sees an `<ll>` tag under the `<ul>` tag, not a set of `<li>` tags.

8. Go back to Aptana and change the `<11>` tag in line 9 to `<li>` and save the page.

9. Reload the web page in the browser. It is now displayed properly, as shown in Figure 2.10.

Favorite **Movies**

- Lord of the Rings
- Harry Potter
- Narnia
- Hot Lead and Cold Feet

FIGURE 2.10
The properly formatted web page.

Viewing and Editing the DOM

Another important tool when debugging HTML is the DOM inspector. The DOM inspector is extremely powerful. It allows you to view the attributes, properties, functions, children, parents, and everything else about each HTML element in the DOM. The information is displayed in tree form so that you can expand and collapse groups.

The DOM inspector can be found in two places: either by clicking the DOM tab in Firebug or, when you are inspecting HTML, you can click the DOM tab in the HTML Inspector.

Figure 2.11 shows the main DOM inspector. From the main DOM inspector, you have access to a variety of information about the browser environment. For example, in Figure 2.11, the screen attribute of the window object is expanded, revealing the values of the available and actual dimensions of the browser window.

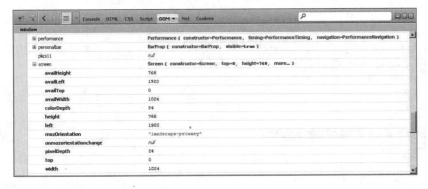

FIGURE 2.11
The main DOM inspector tab in Firebug.

Typically, it's preferable to use the DOM inspector from the HTML Inspector, as shown in Figure 2.12. When you use the DOM tab in the HTML Inspector, you see only the DOM for that HTML element, which reduces the amount of information that is displayed. It also makes it easy to quickly change attribute values of the HTML element directly in the browser, which makes debugging and developing much easier.

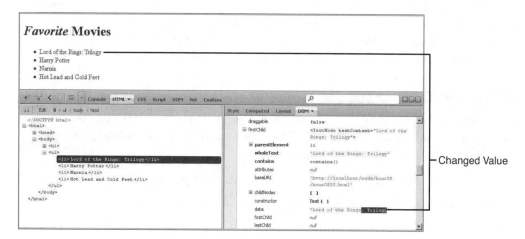

FIGURE 2.12
Editing HTML elements inside the DOM inspector.

TRY IT YOURSELF ▼

Editing HTML Element Values in the DOM Inspector

As an example, you can play with the previous example of code using the following steps:

1. Open the fixed code in file hour0202.html in Firefox and open Firebug.

2. Click the HTML tab in Firebug.

3. Expand the <html>, <body>, and <ul> nodes.

4. Select the first <li> node.

5. Click the DOM tab to the right, as shown in Figure 2.12.

6. Scroll down and find the firstChild node in the DOM inspector and expand that node. It should be a <TextNode> element.

7. Double-click the value to the right of the data attribute and change the text as shown in Figure 2.12. Notice that the HTML element rendered in the web page also changes. It is as easy as that to manipulate any editable attribute of your HTML nodes.

Debugging CSS

As part of debugging your dynamic web pages, you also need to be aware of how to debug CSS issues because a lot of the dynamics of web pages deal with modifying CSS layout in the JavaScript.

If your JavaScript or jQuery scripts modify the CSS layout of DOM elements, looking at the code in the web browser will not do you any good. You need to be able to see what CSS the browser has applied to the element. To do this, you need to use a combination of the CSS inspector as well as the layout inspector and style inspector inside the HTML Inspector.

Using the CSS Inspector

The CSS inspector, shown in Figure 2.13, provides access to all the CSS scripts loaded in the web page. There are two drop-down menus at the top of the CSS inspector. The menu on the left allows you to toggle between the following options:

▶ **Source Edit**—Displays the CSS that originally loaded with the web page.

▶ **Live Edit**—Displays the CSS that is currently applied to the HTML elements.

Disable

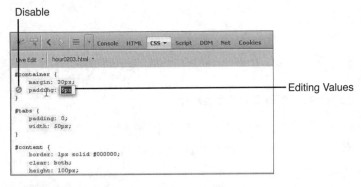

Editing Values

FIGURE 2.13
Editing CSS properties inside the CSS inspector.

The menu on the left provides a list of all the files containing CSS that have been loaded. This enables you to select which CSS document you would like to view and edit.

From the CSS inspector, you also have the capability to edit the CSS. Figure 2.13 shows the editing in process. Notice the disable icon. When you click this icon, that CSS property will be disabled, and the icon will go from red to gray. You can also directly edit the value of the CSS property, as shown in Figure 2.13.

Using the Style Inspector

In addition to editing the entire CSS file, you can view and edit the CSS properties for specific elements from the HTML Inspector. Figure 2.14 shows the Style tab in the HTML Inspector. From the Style inspector, you can view and modify the property values for a specific element.

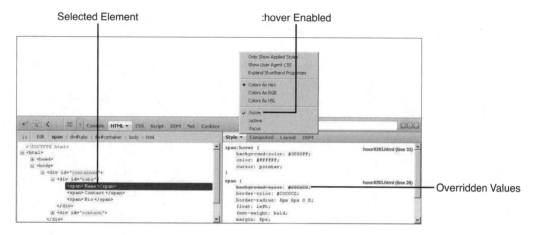

FIGURE 2.14
Editing CSS properties inside the Style inspector inside the HTML Inspector.

Figure 2.14 also illustrates some important features of the Style inspector. Notice that :hover is selected in the menu. That shows the CSS style that is applied to that element when it is hovered over by the mouse. Also notice that the span:hover selector overrides the background-color setting in the span selector. The entire CSS hierarchy is displayed in the style window so you can see which property values are coming from what CSS selector and which values have been overridden.

Using the Layout Inspector

Another extremely powerful tool when debugging CSS is the Layout inspector in the HTML Inspector. The Layout inspector, shown in Figure 2.15, provides an easy-to-use visual interface to the CSS layout of the selected HTML element.

From the Layout inspector you can use, view, and modify the following features:

▶ **Margin**—The margin is the outermost box shown in Layout inspector. There is a value on each of the four sides of the margin. You can double-click those values and change the CSS property directly in the Layout inspector.

▶ **Border**—The border is the next box. It also has four values you can change to adjust the CSS border properties of the HTML element.

▶ **Padding**—The padding is the next box. It also has four values you can change to adjust the CSS padding properties of the HTML element.

▶ **Content**—The content is the innermost box in the Layout inspector. It has two values, the length and width, that you change to set the CSS length and width properties of the HTML element.

▶ **Rulers**—The rulers are displayed in the web page to give you a specific size scale to work from.

▶ **Guidelines**—When you select the margin, border, padding, or content box in the Layout inspector, guidelines appear in the web page. The guidelines run horizontally and vertically to show the specific location of the edges of that CSS property. This can be extremely useful when trying to line up elements in your layouts.

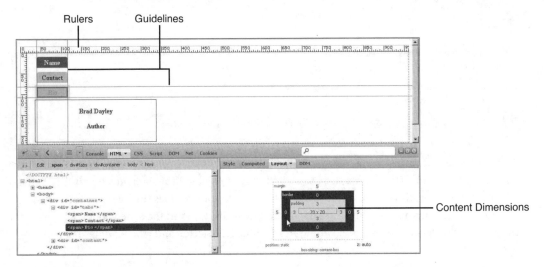

FIGURE 2.15
Viewing the CSS layout properties inside the Layout inspector inside the HTML Inspector.

▼ TRY IT YOURSELF

Editing the CSS Layout

To help you understand debugging and editing the CSS layout using Firebug, consider the code in Listing 2.3. The code is designed to display a simple tabbed box to display info. Some problems exist with the CSS properties that cause it to be displayed poorly, as shown in Figure 2.16. Notice that the tabs are stacked and there is space between them.

LISTING 2.3   A Very Simple HTML Document with Some HTML Syntax Errors Illustrated in Figure 2.16

```
01 <!DOCTYPE html>
02 <html>
03   <head>
04     <meta http-equiv="content-type" content="text/html; charset=utf-8" />
05     <style>
06       #container{
07         margin: 30px;
08         padding:5px;
09       }
10       #tabs{
11         padding: 0px;
12         width:50px;
13       }
14       #content{
15         border: 1px solid #000000;
16         height: 100px;
17         width: 300px;
18         clear: both;
19       }
20       span{
21         margin: 5px;
22         width: 70px;
23         background-color: #C0C0C0;
24         font-weight: bold;
25         border-color: #C0C0C0;
26         border:1px solid, #000000;
27         border-radius: 5px 5px 0px 0px;
28         padding: 3px;
29         float: left;
30         text-align: center;
31       }
32       span:hover{
33         background-color: #3030FF;
34         color: #FFFFFF;
35         cursor: pointer;
36       }
37       p{
38         font-weight: bold;
39         text-align: center;
40       }
41     </style>
42   </head>
43   <body>
44     <div id="container">
```

```
45        <div id="tabs">
46          <span>Name</span>
47          <span>Contact</span>
48          <span>Bio</span>
49        </div>
50        <div id="content">
51          <p>Brad Dayley</p>
52          <p>Author</p>
53        </div>
54      </div>
55    </body>
56 </html>
```

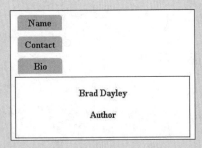

FIGURE 2.16
The poor CSS layout of the tabs makes the web page ugly.

Use the following steps to correct the CSS layout:

1. Add the code in Listing 2.3 to a new file hour0203.html in the hour02 folder of your project and save the document

2. Open Firefox and click the Firebug icon to enable Firebug.

3. Open the following URL in Firefox:

   `http://localhost/code/hour02/hour0203.html`

4. Click the HTML tab in Firebug and expand the `<html>`, then `<body>`, `<div id="container">`, and then `<div id="tabs">` elements, as shown in Figure 2.17.

5. Select the `<div id="container">` element and expand it.

6. Select the `<div id="tabs">` child.

7. Select Layout and click the margin box. Look at the guidelines for the margin of the element that is supposed to contain the tabs. It is barely wider than one of the tabs, so it could not possibly support all three side by side.

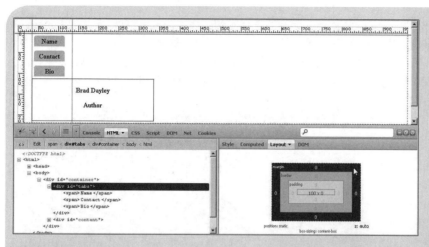

FIGURE 2.17
The Layout guidelines show that there is not enough room for three tabs side by side.

8. To fix this problem, click the Style tab and change the width property to 300px, as shown in Figure 2.18. Notice that the tabs now are all side by side, but there is still too much space between them.

NOTE

You can also modify the margin, border, height, width, and padding values directly in the Layout View.

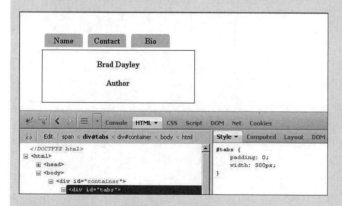

FIGURE 2.18
Changing the `<div>` width allows the tabs to be side by side, but they are still too far apart.

9. Right-click the Name tab in the web page and select Inspect Element with Firebug from the list. That element is automatically selected in the HTML Inspector.

10. Click the Layout tab and hover over the margin box, as shown in Figure 2.19. Notice that there is a margin of 5px around the `<span>` element. That is why they are not close to each other.

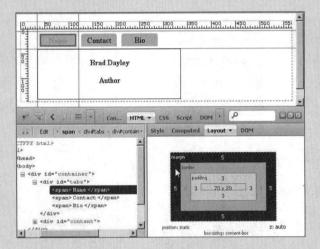

FIGURE 2.19
The Layout guidelines reveal that there is a margin around the `<span>` element keeping the tabs apart.

11. Go to the Style tab and disable the margin property for the `<span>` element, as shown in Figure 2.20. The tabs are now right together and sitting directly on top of the display box.

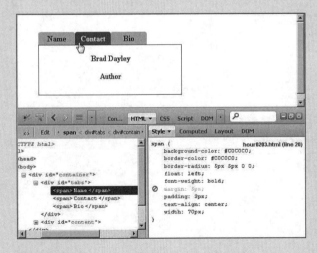

FIGURE 2.20
Disabling the margin allows the tabs to sit close to each other and the display box.

Debugging jQuery and JavaScript

You already have learned to look for errors in JavaScript and other scripts in the JavaScript console. What if your script isn't causing any browser errors, but it just isn't working the way you want it to? Firebug has a very nice integrated debugger to help you out.

Navigating the JavaScript Debugger

The JavaScript debugger allows you to view the JavaScript scripts that are loaded into the browser with the web page. In addition to viewing the scripts, you can set breakpoints, watch variable values, and view the call stack, just as you would with any other debugger.

Figure 2.21 shows the components of the JavaScript debugger available in Firebug. From the JavaScript debugger, you have access to the following features:

▶ **JavaScript View**—This shows you the actual JavaScript code.

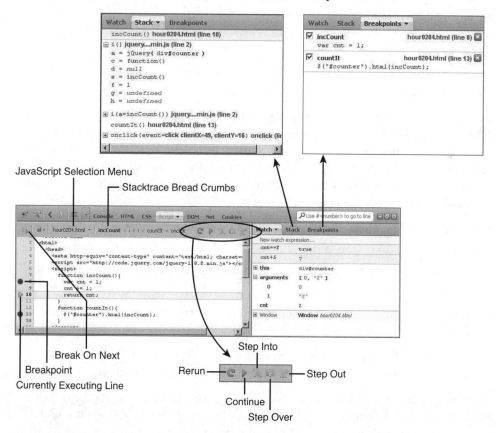

FIGURE 2.21
The Firebug debugger provides code, watch, stack, and breakpoint views.

▶ **JavaScript Selection Menu**—This menu shows a list of the JavaScript scripts loaded with the web page. You can click this menu to select which JavaScript file to load in the view.

▶ **Break on Next**—When this option is selected, the browser will break into the debugger and stop executing the JavaScript on the first line of the next script that is run.

▶ **Watch**—The Watch tab shown in Figure 2.21 gives you a list of functions, variables, properties, and so on that are available at the current execution of the code. This is an extremely valuable window. From here you can see what the values of variables and objects are as the code is executing. In addition, you can add your own expressions to the watch list by typing them in at the top of the watch list. A great feature of the Watch tab is that you can double-click variable values and change the value that is used in execution. This is a great way to test what-if scenarios.

▶ **Stack**—The Stack tab provides a history of the function calls that led up to the currently executing line of code. One of the most valuable aspects of the Stack tab is that you can see the parameter values passed into each function by expanding the function name. You can also click the function name, and that file will be loaded in the JavaScript view and that line of code highlighted.

▶ **Stack Bread Crumbs**—Similar to the Stack tab, these show the stack history and you can click them to load that JavaScript file and function into the JavaScript view.

▶ **Breakpoints**—Breakpoints allow you to specify where to stop when executing JavaScript. When you set a breakpoint, the browser stops executing and breaks into the debugger before it executes that line of code. You set breakpoints by clicking to the left of the line of code in the JavaScript view. They are denoted by a red dot. To remove the breakpoint, click it. The breakpoints tab shows you a list of breakpoints that have been set. You can disable the breakpoint by unchecking the box next to it.

▶ **Currently Executing Line**—The currently executing line of code is denoted by a yellow arrow.

▶ **Rerun**—When you click this icon, the currently executing script is restarted with the same inputs as before.

▶ **Continue**—This allows the script to continue executing normally until hitting another breakpoint if one is encountered.

▶ **Step Into**—When you click this icon, code advances one line. If the line of code is executing another function, you are taken to the first line of code in that function.

▶ **Step Over**—When you click this icon, code advances one line. If the line of code is executing another function, that function is executed and you are taken to the next line of code in the current function. If a breakpoint is encountered when stepping over a function, the browser will stop executing at that location in the script.

▶ **Step Out**—When you click this icon, the current function finishes executing and you are taken to the next line of code in the calling function.

Using the JavaScript Debugger

The following example will help you become more familiar with the JavaScript debugger. Consider the code in Listing 2.4. This is a basic web page that contains a button and a count string. The HTML contains two `<div>` elements. The first, `<div id="clicker" onclick="countIt()">`, is used for a simple button. When you click the button, the JavaScript function `countIt( )` is called. The second, `<div id="counter">`, is used to display a number.

The JavaScript is supposed to increase the number by 1 each time the button is clicked. A problem exists with the JavaScript code, though; the number will not increase past 2.

LISTING 2.4   **A Very Simple HTML Document with JavaScript Errors Illustrated**

```
01  <!DOCTYPE html>
02  <html>
03    <head>
04      <meta http-equiv="content-type" content="text/html; charset=utf-8" />
05      <script src="http://code.jquery.com/jquery-latest.min.js"></script>
06      <script>
07        function incCount(){
08          var cnt = 1;
09          cnt += 1;
10          return cnt;
11        }
12        function countIt(){
13          $("#counter").html(incCount);
14        }
15      </script>
16      <style>
17        #clicker{
18          background-color: #0066AA;
19          color: #FFFFFF;
20          font-weight: bold;
21          border:2px solid, #C0C0C0;
22          width: 65px;
23        }
24      </style>
25    </head>
26    <body>
27      <div id="clicker" onclick="countIt()">Click Me</div>
```

```
28      <div id="counter">1</div>
29    </body>
30  </html>
```

Walk through the following steps to set a breakpoint in the JavaScript Debugger and debug the problem:

1. Add the code in Listing 2.4 to a new file hour0204.html in the hour02 folder of your project and save the document.

2. Open Firefox and click the Firebug icon to enable Firebug.

3. Open the following URL in Firefox. Notice the single button and the count value of 1.

   ```
   http://localhost/code/hour02/hour0203.html
   ```

4. Click the Script tab in Firebug, and then select hour0204.html from the script selection menu. You should see the code from Listing 2.4 in the Script area of the debugger. Notice that the function that sets the value that is placed in the counter div is in lines 7–11.

5. Set a breakpoint on line 8 by clicking to the left of the line number. A red dot should appear, as shown in Figure 2.22. Also make sure the Watch tab is open in the debugger.

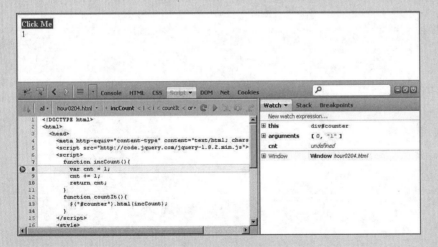

FIGURE 2.22
The JavaScript debugger in Firebug is stopped on line 8 because of a breakpoint. The Watch menu shows the value of the cnt variable as undefined.

6. Now click the button on the web page. You should see a yellow arrow appear and line 8 in the debugger highlighted. The script has stopped executing on that line. This function will determine what value will be placed in the counter. Notice that the value of the cnt variable in the Watch tab is undefined.

7. Click the Step Over icon. You should see the value of `cnt` go to 1.

8. Click the Step Over icon again. Now the value of `cnt` is 2, as expected, changed by the `cnt += 1;` line.

9. Click the Step Out icon three times to step out of this function and the jQuery functions in between. Notice that the value on the webpage has gone to 2.

10. Click the Continue button to allow the script to complete. So far, so good.

11. Click the button again in the web page. The debugger should activate again and be stopped in the same location as step 6. Notice that the value of `cnt` is undefined again.

12. Click the Step Over icon; `cnt` changes to 1. Click Step Over again and `cnt` changes to 2. As the button is clicked, `cnt` is reset to undefined, set to 1, and then incremented to 2.

13. To fix the problem, switch lines 7 and 8 in the original file in Aptana so that the definition of `cnt` happens before the definition of `incCount()`. This defines the variable `cnt` and sets the value only once when the script is loaded before the function is defined.

14. Save the file, then refresh the web page in Firefox. This time the script stops executing as the page is loading. Figure 2.23 shows the JavaScript debugger stopped on line 8 of hour0204.html. This occurred because the definition of the function is on line 8 instead of the definition of `cnt`.

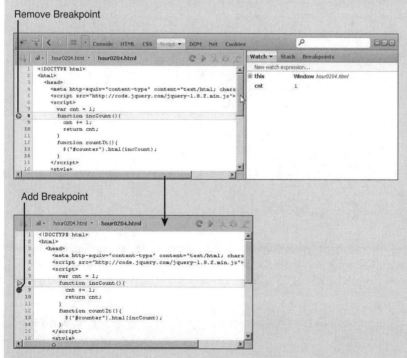

FIGURE 2.23
Changing the breakpoint from the function definition to the first line in the function.

15. Click the breakpoint on line 8 to remove it and add a breakpoint to line 9, as shown in Figure 2.23.

16. Click the Continue button to resume execution of the JavaScript and finish loading the web page.

17. Click the button in the web page, and the JavaScript should break again—this time on line 9. This time you will not see the `cnt` variable in the Watch window unless you expand the Window element, as shown in Figure 2.24.

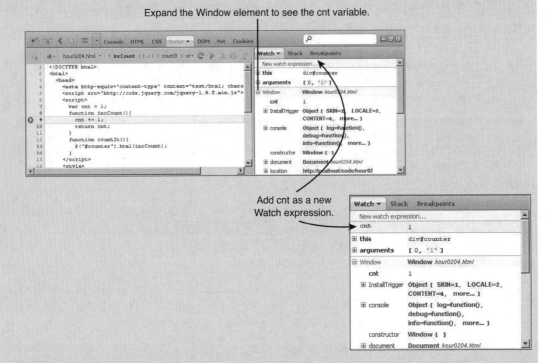

FIGURE 2.24
Adding a new Watch expression for `cnt` so you don't have to expand the Window element each time.

18. Rather than having to expand the Window element each time you want to debug, click New Watch Expression at the top of the Watch list shown in Figure 2.24, type **cnt**, and press Enter. This adds a new watch expression right at the top for the `cnt` variable, as shown in Figure 2.24.

19. Click the Step Over icon and `cnt` will go to 2. Then click the Continue button to resume execution.

20. Click the button in the web page again, and this time the `cnt` variable will show as 2. When you click the Step Over button, the `cnt` variable will go to 3.

21. The program appears to be working, so click the breakpoint on line 9 to remove the breakpoint, and then click the Continue button to resume execution.

22. Now every time you click the button, the number is incremented. You've just debugged the JavaScript.

This was a very basic example, but it was made simple so that it would be easy to follow the steps and get used to how the debugger works. You will likely come back to the debugger several times when doing exercises in the book. Keep in mind the basic steps. Set a breakpoint and watch the variables as you step through the code.

So How Do You Debug jQuery?

A question that comes up frequently, even with people that are experienced with debugging JavaScript, is how to debug jQuery. The answer is simple. jQuery and the numerous plug-ins and versions are just additional JavaScripts. To debug jQuery, download a non-minified version of the jQuery library from the Web and save it in your project. You learn how to do that later in this book.

The reason you download a non-minified version is that the minified is unreadable. Everything is crunched together in one line and doesn't show up well in the debugger. The non-minified version is formatted in a readable form.

NOTE

Even if you cannot get a non-minified version of a JavaScript file, you can always open the file in Aptana and select File, Format from the main menu. Aptana will automatically format the file to a pretty, readable form. Most IDEs will have that type of feature.

With the jQuery or any other JavaScript library formatted, you can debug it like any other JavaScript file.

Analyzing the Network Traffic

A very valuable tool available in Firebug that is often used in debugging JavaScript is the network traffic analyzer. The network traffic analyzer, shown in Figure 2.25, is available by clicking the Net tab in Firebug. The traffic analyzer displays information about each request from the browser to the web server. This allows you to get a better understanding about what data is being transferred and if requests are happening at all and in the right order.

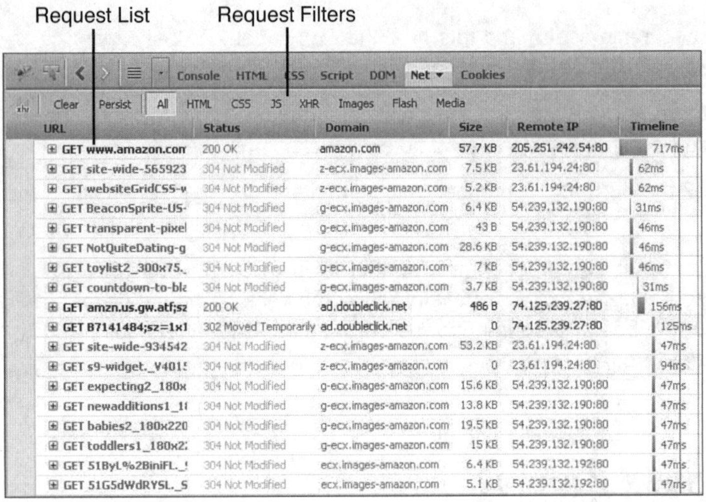

Request List   Request Filters

FIGURE 2.25
Network traffic required to load amazon.com.

Figure 2.25 shows the traffic involved in loading the amazon.com web page. There are numerous requests, each one represented by a single line in the traffic list. For each request, the following is shown in the traffic:

▶ **URL**—The URL of the request can be very useful. You can right-click the URL and copy it, or even open it in another tab or window. This allows you to debug a single request and not the full web page load.

▶ **Status**—I use the status to determine whether the request was successful and whether it is still running. For example, the web page may not look right because an image request failed to load, which is very easy to diagnose from the Net tab in Firebug.

▶ **Domain**—The domain is interesting, especially if you are dealing with cross-domain scripts.

▶ **Size**—The size may also be useful in that it allows you to quickly find requests that require a lot of disk space and network bandwidth.

▶ **Remote IP**—The IP address the request is going to.

▶ **Timeline**—Shows the time in milliseconds the request took. This is very useful in diagnosing slow-responding web pages and other problems related to speed.

With some complex web pages, you may have too much traffic to try to debug all the requests. The filter options in the Net tab allow you to view only certain types of requests, such as HTML,

CSS, or JS. The XHR filter stands for XMLHttpRequest, which is the communication used in AJAX. Selecting the XHR filter will show only AJAX communication.

When you expand a request, as shown in Figure 2.26, you get a lot of additional information about the request. What tabs are available in the expanded request depend on the request type and the response type, but here are some of the most useful items:

▸ **Headers**—Displays the HTML request and response headers that were sent. This is very useful if you are accessing a service via AJAX that requires specific headers to be sent.

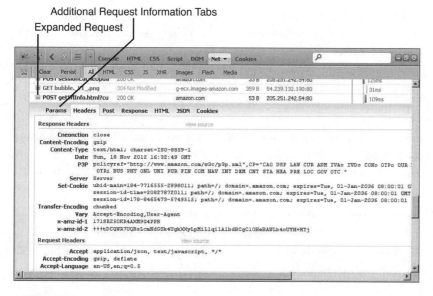

FIGURE 2.26
Expanding the request provides additional tabs with more information about the request and server response.

▸ **Response**—This will vary, depending on what the response is. For example, if you are downloading a JavaScript file from the web server, this displays the raw JavaScript.

▸ **Post**—This is available in POST requests and shows you the values of the parameters sent in the POST request to the server.

▸ **Cache**—This shows the cache information, such as the size in the cache, the last time the cache was used, and when it will expire. Many of the perceived issues in debugging JavaScript are due to data that has been cached by the browser, so it doesn't try to retrieve a fresh copy.

NOTE

If you click the down arrow on the Net tab in Firebug, there is an option to disable browser cache. This option can be very useful when you are updating files on the web server to debug and fix issues. When this option is checked, the browser will always retrieve the latest from the web server.

▶ **HTML**—Shows a rendered version of the HTML document that was included in the response.

▶ **Cookies**—Displays the cookies and values involved in the request.

▶ **JSON**—Displays the JSON code in an expandable tree form that is easy to navigate. This is useful if you are receiving JSON as the response to an AJAX request. You can view the data that was retrieved from the server.

Summary

In this hour, you learned a myriad of ways to debug problems in your dynamic web pages. You learned how to output messages from your scripts to the JavaScript console. You learned how to use the HTML Inspector to see the HTML elements that the browser has built while loading the web page.

You also followed several examples of debugging problems in HTML, CSS, and JavaScript. The methods you learned throughout this hour will be very helpful to you as you finish this book and in future projects because they will save a lot of time and frustration with simple syntax problems that always seem to creep up.

Q&A

Q. Is there a way to debug server-side scripts?

A. Yes, there is. It is really beyond the scope of this book; however, most good languages have a method of remotely debugging problems. If you are trying to debug PHP server-side scripts, look into the capabilities of ZEND at www.zend.com/en/community/pdt. If you are working with Python server-side scripts, check into using PyDev at pydev.org.

Q. Is there a way to debug cookies?

A. As far as debugging cookies, all you need to really know is whether cookies are enabled, which cookies are set in the browser, what the cookie values are, and when they expire. All of that information can be found in the Cookies tab in Firebug. There are similar features with both Chrome and Internet Explorer in their developer consoles.

Workshop

The workshop consists of a set of questions and answers designed to solidify your understanding of the material covered in this hour. Try to answer the questions before looking at the answers.

Quiz

1. Where do you go in Firebug to find what the background-color CSS property value is for a specific `<div>` tag?

2. Where would you go in Firebug to see the available size of the browser window?

3. How do you get your JavaScript to stop executing on a specific line of code?

4. When JavaScript execution is halted, how do you find the values of a variable?

Quiz Answers

1. The Style tab of the HTML Inspector with that `<div>` tag selected.

2. The DOM tab and expand the Screen node.

3. Set a breakpoint in the Script debugger tab.

4. Look in the Watch tab of the Script debugger.

Exercises

1. Modify the hour0204.html code to output the value of `cnt` to the JavaScript console by adding the following code at line 10.

   ```
   console.log("cnt=%d",cnt);
   ```

2. Use the Net traffic as you browse the traffic from some different pages. Expand some of the requests and look at the data represented in some of the tabs. This can help you understand the ebb and flow of browser to web server traffic a bit better.

HOUR 3
Understanding Dynamic Web Page Anatomy

What You'll Learn in This Hour:

▶ How to build a basic dynamic web page

▶ Where to add CSS and JavaScript in web pages

▶ What the difference is between block and inline elements

▶ How to add images to web pages

▶ How to build web forms

▶ How to add links to specific spots in a web page

▶ How to build tables into your web pages

▶ What HTML5 SVG graphics can do

▶ Ways to use HTML5 to prep for dynamic audio and video

Throughout the rest of this book, you will use a lot of HTML, CSS, jQuery, and JavaScript. For that purpose, this hour is designed to accomplish two tasks. The first is to familiarize you, in case you are not already familiar, with some important basics of HTML so that you will be able to easily understand the examples moving forward.

The second is to help you understand how to design your HTML to make it easier to add dynamics to your web pages later using jQuery and JavaScript. Understanding how to design your HTML elements will make it easier later to add some cool effects and dynamically update data stored in lists or tables.

The following sections discuss the basics of HTML and how they relate to jQuery and JavaScript.

Using HTML/HTML5 Elements to Build a Dynamic Web Page

You have already seen some examples of HTML code in Hour 1, "Intro to Dynamic Web Programming," and Hour 2, "Debugging jQuery and JavaScript Web Pages." Now it's time to delve a bit deeper in understanding the syntax and which HTML elements and attributes are important to dynamic web pages.

To properly build dynamic web pages, you need to understand the HTML syntax, some fundamental HTML elements, and how to organize and structure those elements. The following sections cover those topics.

Understanding HTML Structure

HTML documents are composed of three main parts: the `<!DOCTYPE>` tag, the head, and the body. Each of these parts plays a specific role in helping the browser to render the HTML document into a web page.

The `<!DOCTYPE>` tag must be the first statement in the HTML file and tells the browser how to read the rest of the file. Although this tag is not strictly required, it is a good idea to include it in your HTML documents. There are several forms of the `<!DOCTYPE>` element; a few of them are listed next:

▶ **HTML5**—Version used for HTML5 documents

```
<!DOCTYPE html>
```

▶ **HTML 4.01 Strict**—Enforces strict compliance with the HTML 4.01 standard and will remove deprecated elements such as `<font>`.

```
<!DOCTYPE HTML PUBLIC "-//W3C//DTD HTML 4.01//EN"
➥"http://www.w3.org/TR/html4/strict.dtd">
```

▶ **HTML 4.01 Transitional**—Relaxed compliance with the HTML 4.01 standard and will allow deprecated elements such as `<font>`.

```
<!DOCTYPE HTML PUBLIC "-//W3C//DTD HTML 4.01 Transitional//EN"
➥"http://www.w3.org/TR/html4/loose.dtd">
```

The `head` and `body` components are contained in the HTML tag. The purpose of the `head` element is to contain elements that are used in parsing the HTML document but are not rendered inside the browser window, such as scripts and metadata. The purpose of the `body` tag is to contain elements that will be rendered to the browser window and viewed by the user.

The following code shows an example of the basic HTML document structure with one head element and one body element:

```
<!DOCTYPE html>
<html>
  <head>
    <meta charset="UTF-8" />
  </head>
  <body>
    <h1>New Page</h1>
```

```
  </body>
</html>
```

Syntax is everything when working with HTML elements. If the browser cannot parse the document correctly, the page will not be rendered correctly to the user.

TIP

Most web development IDEs and editors have built-in error checking as well as code completing for HTML syntax. These are shown in a variety of ways, from highlighted or underlined code, to warning icons inline with the code, to a list of potential problems in a different pane. Pay attention to what the IDE is trying to tell you about possible problems.

An HTML element is composed of the following three main components:

- ▶ **Tag**—The tag is enclosed in `<>` characters and tells the browser what type of HTML element to parse and render. For example, the tag for a paragraph element is `<p>`, the tag for an unordered list is `<ul>`, and the tag for a list item is `<li>`.

- ▶ **Content**—The content portion of the HTML element can be another HTML element, simple text, or nothing. To define what is contained inside an HTML element, a closing tag is added at the end of the content. The following example illustrates that perfectly. Notice that there are several `<li>` elements—each with an opening tag `<li>`, some content, and then a closing tag `</li>`. The content of the `<li>` tags are the text in between. There is also an opening and closing `<ul>` and `</ul>` tag. The content of the `<ul>` element is all of the `<li>` elements in between.

  ```
  <ul>
    <li>New York, US</li>
    <li>Paris, FR</li>
    <li>Rome, IT</li>
    <li>London, EN</li>
  </ul>
  ```

- ▶ **Attribute**—Attributes provide a way of attaching additional information about the element that can be used by the browser. This information can be used to define how the element is rendered by the browser or provide a way to identify or classify the element. The following shows an example of adding an `align` attribute to a paragraph element to tell the browser to center the text when rendering it. Notice that the attribute value is assigned using an equal sign and that the value is enclosed in double quotes.

  ```
  <p align="center">This is some centered text.</p>
  ```

If an element does not have an end tag, you can include the / at the end of the first tag and completely leave out the end tag. For example, both of the following are acceptable to the browser:

```
<p align="center"></p>
<p align="center" />
```

Implementing HTML Head Elements

The HTML `<head>` element is designed as a container for nonvisual elements of the web page. The tags in the `<head>` element are parsed by the browsers into the DOM, but they are not rendered to the browser window.

The following sections describe some of the more important `<head>` elements and how they relate to using jQuery and JavaScript.

`<title>`

The `<title>` element is supposed to be required in all HTML documents. The browser will still render the page without it, but there are many reasons to include the title element in your web pages, including that the `<title>` element does the following:

▶ Defines the title that is displayed in the browser toolbar/tab.

▶ Provides the title that the web page is listed as when it is added to favorites.

▶ Determines what is displayed as the title when the web page is displayed by search engines.

The following code shows an example of adding a title to the web page:

```
<!DOCTYPE html>
<html>
  <head>
    <title>A Really Cool Web Page</title>
```

The value of the `<title>` element can easily be changed using jQuery and Java. For example, the code in Listing 3.1 uses JavaScript to change the title of the web page after it is loaded.

LISTING 3.1 JavaScript Code Changing the `<title>` Value After the Page Has Loaded

```
01 <!DOCTYPE html>
02 <html>
03   <head>
04     <title>A Really Cool Web Page</title>
05     <meta charset="UTF-8" />
06     <script>
07       function appendTitle(newTitle){
08         document.title += newTitle;
09       }
10     </script>
11   </head>
12   <body onload="appendTitle('... Loaded')">
13   </body>
14 </html>
```

Notice in Figure 3.1 that the Title in the tab has changed to read A Really Cool Web Page... Loaded.

FIGURE 3.1
The JavaScript function has changed the title of the web page that is displayed in the browser tab.

`<meta>`

The `<meta>` tag has many uses. Browsers use the `<meta>` tags to determine things such as what character sets to use when rendering the web page. Search engine crawlers use the `<meta>` tags to determine the purpose of the content of the web page for better optimized searches. The best way to introduce it is to show you some examples of syntax.

The meta tag required to set the character set in HTML5 web pages is

```
<meta charset="UTF-8">
```

The `<meta>` tag required to set the character set in HTML4 web pages is

```
<meta http-equiv="content-type" content="text/html; charset=UTF-8">
```

The `<meta>` tag to define keywords for search engines is as follows, where the value of content are the keywords you want the search engine to use when finding the web page:

```
<meta name="keywords" content="HTML, CSS, jQuery, JavaScript">
```

The `<meta>` tag to tell the browser to refresh the web page every 60 seconds is

```
<meta http-equiv="refresh" content="300">
```

`<style>`

The `<style>` tag allows you to add CSS code directly inside the HTML document. Everything included inside the `<style>` tag is treated like a CSS document and is used by the browser to render the web page.

As an example of the syntax, the Listing 3.2 HTML file includes CSS to turn the background of `<h1>` elements black and the foreground white, as shown in Figure 3.2.

LISTING 3.2 Adding CSS to an HTML Document Using the `<style>` Tag

```
01 <html>
02   <head>
03     <meta charset="UTF-8">
04     <style type="text/css">
05       h1 {
06         background-color:black;
07         color:white;
08       }
09     </style>
10   </head>
11   <body>
12     <h1>CSS Reversed Text</h1>
13   </body>
14 </html>
```

CSS Reversed Text

FIGURE 3.2
This `<h1>` element has had its style reversed by a CSS style script in the HTML document.

`<script>`

The `<script>` tag enables you to add JavaScript code directly inside the HTML document or link to a separate external JavaScript file. If you include inline JavaScript code, everything included inside the `<script>` tag is treated like a JavaScript document and loaded into the browser when the HTML document is parsed. If you include a link to an external file, that file is downloaded from the web server and loaded by the browser.

CAUTION

When using the `<script>` tag, scripts are loaded in the order they are parsed. That means that any subsequent scripts that have the same variable values will overwrite the ones already loaded. When adding multiple scripts to a web page, you should be careful to not override variable and function names that you do not intend to.

For example, the HTML document in Listing 3.3 includes two `<script>` elements: one to load the external jQuery library and the second with a simple JavaScript and jQuery function to turn the background of `<h1>` elements black and the foreground white, as shown in Figure 3.3.

LISTING 3.3　Adding JavaScript and jQuery to an HTML Document Using the `<script>` **Tag**

```
01  <!DOCTYPE html>
02  <html>
03    <head>
04      <meta charset="UTF-8">
05      <script src="http://code.jquery.com/jquery-latest.min.js"></script>
06      <script>
07        function reverseText(){
08          $("h1").css("background-color", "black");
09          $("h1").css("color", "white");
10        }
11      </script>
12    </head>
13    <body onload="reverseText()">
14      <h1>JavaScript Reversed Text</h1>
15    </body>
16  </html>
```

JavaScript Reversed Text

FIGURE 3.3
This `<h1>` element that has had its style reversed by a JavaScript function using jQuery directly in the HTML document.

`<noscript>`

Although it doesn't happen very often any more, occasionally people disable JavaScript on their web browsers. If JavaScript is disabled, any JavaScript, and consequently jQuery scripts, will not be executed. This can provide a very bad experience for users.

The `<noscript>` tag allows you to provide elements that will be rendered before items in the `<body>` element. This allows you to display warning messages or alternative forms of the page in the event that JavaScript is disabled.

The `<noscript>` tag supports the same child element types that the `<body>` tag supports. For example, the following code loads the JavaScript file if JavaScript is enabled, but if not, it adds a `<h3>` heading to the top of the web page that warns users that the web page will not function properly:

```
<head>
  <script src="DynamicPage.js"></script>
  <noscript>
    <h3>This web page uses JavaScript but it is disabled in your browser.
        The web page may not function properly.</h3>
  </noscript>
</head>
```

`<link>`

The `<link>` tag allows you to link separate resources to the current document. For the most part, it is used for CSS files. That means that when the browser loads the HTML document, linked CSS files are downloaded from the web server and loaded as well. For example, the following head block will load two different CSS documents:

```
<head>
  <link rel="stylesheet" type="text/css" href="styleA.css">
  <link rel="stylesheet" type="text/css" href="styleB.css">
</head>
```

In addition to CSS files, you can link things like icons, help documents, licenses, and searches to the web page. For example, the following code links an icon that is displayed in the browser tab when the web page is loaded:

```
<link rel="icon" type="image/png" href="http://example.com/myicon.png">
```

Adding HTML Body Elements

Most of the HTML elements that are added to the body block are rendered by the browser and displayed on the screen to the user. Each of the HTML body element tags provides different options that will help you show information on the web page in a meaningful and elegant way.

In the following sections, you'll see some specific attributes that are useful to apply to HTML elements when programming in jQuery and JavaScript. You also learn the syntax of some of the more common elements that you will see throughout the rest of the book so that the examples will be easier to follow.

Using Important Body Element Attributes

Each of the different body elements will have some attributes that are specific to the element only. However, some attributes are important and common for all elements. Those tags are the following:

- ▶ id—This is a string identifier that must be unique among all elements on the web page. This is used by CSS, JavaScript, and jQuery to identify, access, and modify a specific element on the web page.

- ▶ class—The class attribute allows you to specify a grouping of multiple elements. This option is used heavily with CSS stylizing to set styles such as background-color for several HTML elements at once. It is also useful in jQuery to select multiple elements based on their class value.

- ▶ style—The style attribute allows you to place CSS definitions directly in the HTML code inside of the HTML object. The values in the style override all other CSS directives.

The following code illustrates the syntax to add id, class, and style attributes to HTML elements. Notice that the classes "heading" and "content" are used multiple times, but the id attribute is different for every element. Also notice that for the first heading, an additional style attribute was added to force the first heading to always be bold.

```
<div id="Div1">
  <p id="Div1Heading" class="heading" style="font-weight:bold">Heading Text</p>
  <p id ="Div1Content" class ="content">Some Content</p>
</div>
<div id="Div2">
  <p id="Div2Heading" class="heading">Another Heading Text</p>
  <p id ="Div2Content" class ="content">Some More Content</p>
</div>
```

Understanding Block Versus Inline Elements

Remember that the web page is rendered to the display screen by the browser parsing each element in the HTML document and rendering it along with any children. The difference between block and inline elements is how much room the browser gives the element.

Block elements are given the full width available to render the item in the browser. That means that any elements before will be displayed above, and elements that come after will be displayed below. <div> and <p> are examples of block elements.

Inline elements are given only enough width to display the element on the page. That means that multiple inline elements are displayed side by side in the browser as long as there is enough room. <span>, <a>, and <img> are some examples of inline elements.

The following code and the rendered version shown in Figure 3.4 illustrate the difference between block and inline tags. Notice that the `<p>` tags take up the full width of the browser screen, and the `<span>` tags take only enough space to display the text and margin.

```
<p>Paragraph A</p>
<p>Paragraph B</p>
<p>Paragraph C</p>
<span>Span A</span>
<span>Span B</span>
<span>Span CA</span>
```

FIGURE 3.4
The block element `<p>` takes up the entire width, but the inline element `<span>` uses only the width that it needs.

Although elements are block or inline by default, you can always change them by setting the `display` CSS style. For example, setting a `<span>` display to block as follows will make it behave like a `<div>` element.

```
<span style="{display:block;}">Span Text</span>
```

The following is a list of values that you can set the display style to:

▶ `block`—Renders the element as a block element.

▶ `inline`—Renders the element as an inline element.

▶ `none`—Will not render the element to the screen even though it is parsed and exists in the DOM.

You can also force items to be rendered below other items by separating them by using one of the following line break tags:

▶ `<br>`—Adds a line break that causes the content after to be rendered below the current content, even if they are inline.

▶ `<hr>`—Similar to `<br>` but also causes the browser to render a horizontal line under the current content.

These tags do not require a closing tag. For example, the following code creates a set of three `<span>` elements that are separated by first the `<br>` tag and then the `<hr>` tag. The rendered results are shown in Figure 3.5. Notice that `<br>` inserted a line break and `<hr>` inserted a line break and rendered a line between the content:

```
<span>Text on</span>
<span> Line 1</span><br>
<span>Text on Line 2</span><hr>
<span>New section on Line 3</span>
```

```
Text on Line 1
Text on Line 2
───────────────────────────────
New section on Line 3
```

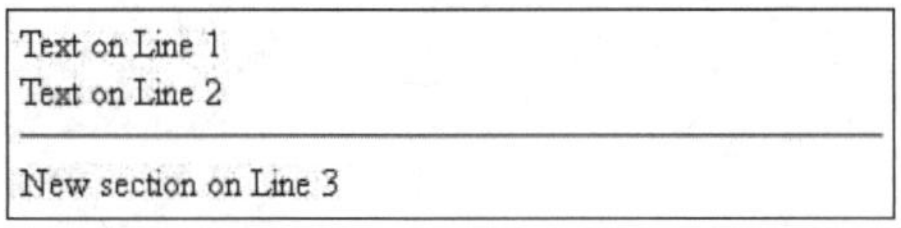

FIGURE 3.5
Using `<br>` adds a line break and `<hr>` adds a line break and renders a line between the content.

Creating Container Elements

Container elements are used for a variety of purposes, such as grouping and formatting sets of elements or text. This allows you to apply formatting and dimensions to the container and have it affect all the items within. Although just about any HTML element could be used as a container, three main ones are `<p>`, `<div>`, and `<span>`.

Container elements by themselves do not alter the appearance of the text or data within them. For example, the text inside all the following will render the same in the browser:

```
Some Text
<p>Some Text <p>
<div>Some Text </div>
<span>Some Text</span>
```

TRY IT YOURSELF ▼

Using Container Elements to Group and Style

Container elements are typically used to group elements for layout and style settings. The following exercise creates the code in Listing 3.4. The code is designed to introduce you to grouping and styling elements.

1. Start by creating a folder in your Aptana project called hour03.

2. Create a new HTML document in the hour03 folder called hour0304.html (to match the filename on the book's website).

3. Add the appropriate `<html>`, `<head>`, and `<body>` tags.

4. Add the following <div> element with the id attribute set to "heading" as shown in lines 19–23. This will be the container for your heading items.

```
19      <div class="heading">
20        <p>Heading A</p>
21        <p>Heading B</p>
22        <p>Heading C</p>
23      </div>
```

5. Add the following second <div> element with the id attribute set to "content" as shown in lines 24–28. This is the container for your content items.

```
24      <div class="content">
25        <p>Paragraph A</p>
26        <p>Paragraph B</p>
27        <p>Paragraph C</p>
28      </div>
```

6. Save the file and load the following URL in the web browser to view the unformatted code, as shown in Figure 3.6:

```
http://localhost/code/hour03/hour0304.html
```

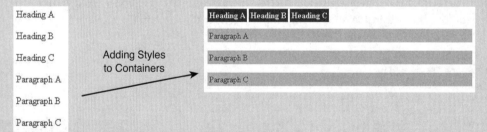

FIGURE 3.6
Using <div> container elements makes it easy to change the look and behavior of <p> elements in different areas of the web page.

7. Go back to Aptana and add a <style> tag to the header of the file.

8. Inside the <style> tag, add the following code that formats the content elements with a gray background and a bit of padding around the edges:

```
05      .content p{
06        background-color:#C0C0C0;
07        padding: 3px;
08      }
```

9. Add the following additional rule to style the header elements. This rule changes the `<p>` elements in the heading container to be inline, with bold white text and a black background.

```
09          .heading p{
10             display: inline;
11             background-color:black;
12             color: white;
13             font-weight:bold;
14             padding:3px;
15          }
```

10. Save the document and then reload it in the web browser. Notice in Figure 3.6 that the elements in the "heading" class `<div>` element are rendered as inline with a black background and white text as defined in lines 11 and 12, and the elements in the "content" class `<div>` element are rendered with a gray background and remain block style.

LISTING 3.4 Adding CSS to an HTML Document Using the `<style>` Tag

```
01 <html>
02   <head>
03     <meta charset="UTF-8">
04     <style type="text/css">
05       .content p{
06         background-color:#C0C0C0;
07         padding: 3px;
08       }
09       .heading p{
10         display: inline;
11         background-color:black;
12         color: white;
13         font-weight:bold;
14         padding:3px;
15       }
16     </style>
17   </head>
18   <body>
19     <div class="heading">
20       <p>Heading A</p>
21       <p>Heading B</p>
22       <p>Heading C</p>
23     </div>
24     <div class="content">
25       <p>Paragraph A</p>
26       <p>Paragraph B</p>
27       <p>Paragraph C</p>
28     </div>
29   </body>
30 </html>
```

You will be using the container elements heavily in JavaScript and jQuery development to group, format, and control various aspects of the dynamic web page.

Adding Link Elements

Web pages often contain a series of links to additional pages. Links are easy to add to a web page using the anchor tag `<a>`. The `<a>` tag has three purposes:

▶ **Link to External Web Page**—Displays a link on the web page. When the user clicks the link, the browser requests the web page in the link from the server. The following is an example of adding a link to an external web page:

```
<a href="http://www.dayleycreations.com/">Dayley Creations</a>
```

▶ **Link to Location on Current Web Page**—Displays a link on the web page. When the user clicks the link, the browser changes the scroll down to the location so that the anchor linked to is visible.

```
<a href="#local link">Link to Some Text Below</a>
```

▶ **Web Page Anchor**—Adds a link inside the web page that can be directly linked to either by the current page or by another web page. To define an anchor, you need to use the `id` attribute. For example, to add the anchor for the above link, use the following:

```
<a id="local_link">Page Anchor</a>
```

Web page anchors can be useful when using JavaScript to build the link elements. For example, you can dynamically change the `url` attribute of the link to control where the link takes the user.

Using Image Elements

One of the greatest aspects of web pages is the capability to display images along with other graphics and text. Images are displayed using the `<img>` tag.

The actual image file on the web server to display in the `<img>` tag is determined by the `src` attribute. The size of the image on the screen is determined by the `height` and `width` attributes.

The following code shows some examples of displaying an image with different sizes and whitespace, as shown in Figure 3.7. Notice that when only the `height` or `width` is specified, the image is scaled to keep the aspect ratio, but when both are specified, the image is stretched to fit the specific height and width settings:

```
<img src="/code/hour03/images/hour0301.jpg" height="200px"/>
<img src="/code/hour03/images/hour0301.jpg" width="200px"/>
<img src="/code/hour03/images/hour0301.jpg" height="200px" width="200px"/>
```

FIGURE 3.7
Using `<img>` to add images to a web page and specify height and width.

You will also be dealing with images frequently when creating dynamic web pages using jQuery and JavaScript because they allow you to quickly resize, move, hide, and add them to the web page. This allows your images to interact with mouse actions and other input from users.

Applying List Elements

List elements allow you to group a set of items together and have the browser automatically format them with bullets or numbers. Ordered lists are created using the `<ol>` tag, and bulleted lists are created using the unordered list tag `<ul>`. Items within the list are contained in the `<li>` tag. For example, the following code renders to Figure 3.8:

```
<ul>
  <li>Yellowstone</li>
  <li>Yosemite</li>
  <li>Glacier</li>
  <li>Arches</li>
  <li>Zion</li>
</ul>
```

- Yellowstone
- Yosemite
- Glacier
- Arches
- Zion

FIGURE 3.8
Adding a list to a web page using the `<ul>` and `<li>` tags.

Creating Table Elements

Table elements are some of the more complex HTML elements. They are used to organize other elements on the screen in a series of rows and columns. They can be used for a variety of purposes, from laying out entire web pages to a simple table of data. This section covers the basics that you need to know for this book.

Tables are constructed using a series of tags that define the table, headers, body, and cells. The following lists the various tags that can be used when constructing a table:

- ▶ `<table>`—Acts as the container element for all other table elements and defines the overall table.

- ▶ `<thead>`—This element is not required, but it can be useful in that it allows you to group and define the header elements in a table, or refer to the parent of header elements directly from jQuery or JavaScript via the `id` attribute.

- ▶ `<tbody>`—This is also not required, but it is useful to define the overall body of the table or refer to the parent of body elements directly from jQuery or JavaScript via the `id` attribute.

- ▶ `<th>`—Defines a single header cell in a table.

- ▶ `<td>`—Defines a cell in a table.

- ▶ `<tr>`—Defines a single row in a table. This acts as a container for either `<th>` and/or `<td>` elements or cell elements.

- ▶ `<caption>`—Provides a container for caption content. The caption content can be either text or other HTML elements.

- ▶ `<colgroup>`—Enables you to place one or more columns in a table into a group that can be formatted together. This is also useful if you want to access a specific set of columns from jQuery or JavaScript via the `id` attribute.

- ▶ `<col>`—Specifies the column properties for a single column within a `<colgroup>` element.

- ▶ `<tfoot>`—This element is not required, but it can be useful in that it allows you to group and define the footer elements in a table or refer to the parent of footer elements directly from jQuery or JavaScript via the `id` attribute.

In HTML4, several attributes can be set on the table elements. Many of those have been deprecated in HTML5 because they were used for formatting size, alignment, and color, which should really be done with CSS styles. The following is a list of the more important attributes that you will still need to use on table elements:

- ▶ `border`—Specifies whether the table cells should have borders.

- ▶ `colspan`—Specifies the number of columns a cell should span. This allows an individual `<td>` or `<th>` element to occupy more than one column in the table.

▶ rowspan—Specifies the number of rows a cell should span. This allows an individual `<td>` or `<th>` element to occupy more than one row in the table.

▶ headers—Added to `<td>` or `<th>` elements. Allows you to specify the id value of one or more `<th>` elements. This creates an association to the header element that can be accessed from jQuery and JavaScript.

TRY IT YOURSELF ▼

Creating HTML Tables

The easiest way to explain tables is to show you an example of creating a basic table. Use the following steps to create the table code in Listing 3.5:

1. Create a new HTML document in the hour03 folder called hour0305.html (to match the file-name on the book's website).

2. Add the appropriate `<html>`, `<head>`, and `<body>` tags.

3. Add the following `<table>` element with the `border` attribute set to 1:

```
06      <table border=1></table>
```

4. Add the following `<caption>` element inside the `<table>` element to give the table a caption:

```
07      <caption>Favorite U.S. National Parks</caption>
```

5. Create the table headers by adding the following `<thead>` element to the `<table>` element. Notice that the third `<th>` sets the `colspan` to 2 so that it will cover the last two columns, as shown in Figure 3.9.

```
08      <thead>
09        <th>Park</th>
10        <th>Location</th>
11        <th colspan=2>Established</th>
12      </thead>
```

Favorite U.S. National Parks			
Park	Location	Established	
Yellowstone	Montana, Wyoming, Idaho	March 1, 1872	
Yosemite	California	March 1, 1872	
Zion	Utah	November 19, 1919	

FIGURE 3.9
An HTML table example showing headers in rows and columns and a caption.

6. Add the `<tr>` elements shown in lines 13 through 18 of Listing 3.5. Notice in the example that follows that each of these `<tr>` elements contains four cells. The first cell is a row header because it uses the `<th>` tag. The next two cells are simple text in `<td>` elements, but in the fourth cell, the `<td>` element contains an `<img>` element (the .jpg files can be found on the book's website).

```
13        <tr>
14          <th>Yellowstone</th>
15          <td>Montana, Wyoming, Idaho</td>
16          <td>March 1, 1872</td>
17          <td><img src="images/hour0302.jpg" width="100" />
18        </tr>
```

7. Save the document and open the following URL in the web browser to view the rendered results shown in Figure 3.9:

```
http://localhost/code/hour03/hour0305.html
```

LISTING 3.5 HTML Generating a Table with Headers, Rows, and Columns

```
01 <html>
02    <head>
03      <meta charset="UTF-8">
04    </head>
05    <body>
06      <table border=1>
07        <caption>Favorite U.S. National Parks</caption>
08        <thead>
09          <th>Park</th>
10          <th>Location</th>
11          <th colspan=2>Established</th>
12        </thead>
13        <tr>
14          <th>Yellowstone</th>
15          <td>Montana, Wyoming, Idaho</td>
16          <td>March 1, 1872</td>
17          <td><img src="images/hour0302.jpg" width="100" />
18        </tr>
19        <tr>
20          <th>Yosemite</th>
21          <td>California</td>
22          <td>March 1, 1872</td>
23          <td><img src="images/hour0303.jpg" width="100" />
24        </tr>
25        <tr>
26          <th>Zion</th>
27          <td>Utah</td>
```

```
28            <td>November 19, 1919</td>
29            <td><img src="images/hour0304.jpg" width="100" /></td>
30          </tr>
31      </table>
32    </body>
33 </html>
```

Implementing Form Elements

Another extremely useful set of tags in HTML are the form tags. These tags provide the building blocks to render user input forms that enable you to gain input from the user. Browsers know how to render the form elements to display things like text boxes, buttons, and lists.

Following is a list of the more common form tags you will use in jQuery and JavaScript to create dynamic form elements:

▶ <form>—This is the root element of the form. All other elements are contained inside.

▶ <fieldset>—Acts as a container allowing you to group several form elements together. In HTML5, you can set the disabled attribute of the fieldset to disable it from user input. You can also use jQuery and JavaScript to access the children of the fieldset and modify them from code.

▶ <legend>—Tells the browser to add a caption to the fieldset.

▶ <label>—Allows you to tie a label element to an <input> element in the form by setting the for attribute to the id attribute value of the <input> element. This adds the advantage that the mouse events for the input element are also triggered for the <label>.

▶ <input>—The input tag is really a wrapper for several types of input components. The input that is rendered by the browser will depend on the value of the type attribute. The following is a list of type elements that can be specified in the input tag: button, checkbox, color, date, datetime, email, file, hidden, image, month, number, password, radio, range, reset, search, submit, tel, text, time, url, and week.

▶ <textarea>—Different from the other inputs, this provides a resizable area where the user can type in multiple lines of text. The cols and rows attributes define the initial size.

▶ <select>—Acts a container for a drop-down list of items.

▶ <option>—Used inside the <select> element to define a single item in the list. The value attribute of the selected item is also the value of the <select> element.

▶ <button>—Defines a clickable button element. The type attribute of button tells the browser whether to use the button to submit the form, reset the values, or act as a simple input button.

The form elements have a different set of attributes that provide access to and modify the look and behavior of the element. The following are some of the more important ones:

▶ name—This option specifies a name that can be used when submitting the form.

▶ value—This option specifies the value of the form element. For elements such as text `<input>`, what you specify for value will be added as text in the rendered text box. The value attribute is also accessible via JavaScript, so you can get the value of any form element directly from JavaScript.

▶ disabled—When this attribute is added, the element will be displayed; however, it will appear disabled so the user cannot interact with the form element. When you enable and disable elements from JavaScript or jQuery, this value is modified dynamically. The disabled attribute is a Boolean, so you do not need to include a value. The following shows an example of how to include the disabled attribute:

```
<input type="text" disabled />
```

▼ TRY IT YOURSELF

Adding Forms to Web Pages

In this example, you add a form with different elements to a web page. The finished example, shown in Listing 3.6, renders the web form shown in Figure 3.10 with several types of form elements. Using the basics you learn in the following example, you will be able to create just about any custom form you need.

1. Create a new HTML document in the hour03 folder called hour0306.html (to match the filename on the book's website).

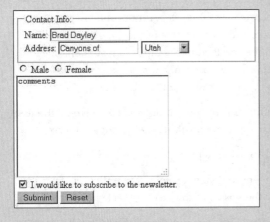

FIGURE 3.10
An HTML form example showing the various form elements created by Listing 3.6.

2. Add the appropriate `<html>`, `<head>`, and `<body>` tags.

3. Add a `<form>` element.

4. Inside the `<form>` element add the following `<fieldset>` to request contact info. The `<fieldset>` includes a `<legend>` element that provides a caption, two basic text `<input>` tags for name and address, and then a `<select>` element with three `<option>` children to provide a drop-down list of states. Figure 3.10 shows the rendered `<fieldset>` with a box around it and the elements.

```
07          <fieldset>
08              <legend>Contact Info:</legend>
09              Name: <input type="text" name="name"><br>
10              Address: <input type="text" name="name">
11              <select name="state">
12                <option value="UT">Utah</option>
13                <option value="CA">California</option>
14                <option value="NY">New York</option>
15              </select>
16          </fieldset>
```

5. Next add the radio buttons to select gender. Add the following `<label>` and `<input>` fields to the form. The `type` attribute of the `<input>` elements is set to `radio`. Also, notice that the `<label>` elements include a `for` attribute that links them to the `radio` `<input>` elements. Because the `<label>` is linked to the `<input>`, when you click the label it toggles the radio button.

```
17          <input id="maleRB" type="radio" name="gender" value="male">
18          <label for="maleRB">Male</label>
19          <input id="femaleRB" type="radio" name="gender" value="female">
20          <label for="femaleRB">Female</label><br>
```

6. Add a comments element by adding the following `<textarea>` element. Notice that the `rows` and `cols` attributes define the size, and we include the word "`comments`" initially in the text area rather than adding a label outside. The `<br>` tag at the end causes the following form elements to be on a new line.

```
21          <textarea rows="10" cols="30">comments</textarea><br>
```

7. Provide a check box to enable a subscription to a newsletter by adding the following `<input>` and `<label>`. The type of the `<input>` element is set to `checkbox` so the browser knows to render it as a check box. Also, the `<label>` element uses the `for` attribute so that the user can click the check box or the label to toggle it on or off.

```
22          <input id='newsCB' type="checkbox" name="news" value="news">
23            <label for="newsCB">
24              I would like to subscribe to the newsletter.
25            </label><br>
```

8. Add the following code to include two button elements: a `submit` button and a `reset` button. When the `submit` button is pressed, the browser submits the form. When the reset button is pressed, the values in the form are reset.

```
26        <button type="submit" name="SubmitButton" value="Submit">Submit</
button>
27        <button type="reset" name="ResetButton" value="Reset">Reset</button>
```

9. Save the document and open the following URL in the web browser to view the rendered results shown in Figure 3.10:

```
http://localhost/code/hour03/hour0306.html
```

LISTING 3.6   HTML Generating a Form with Text Inputs and Selects

```
01 <html>
02   <head>
03     <meta charset="UTF-8">
04   </head>
05   <body>
06     <form>
07       <fieldset>
08         <legend>Contact Info:</legend>
09         Name: <input type="text" name="name"><br>
10         Address: <input type="text" name="name">
11         <select name="state">
12           <option value="UT">Utah</option>
13           <option value="CA">California</option>
14           <option value="NY">New York</option>
15         </select>
16       </fieldset>
17       <input id="maleRB" type="radio" name="gender" value="male">
18       <label for="maleRB">Male</label>
19       <input id="femaleRB" type="radio" name="gender" value="female">
20       <label for="femaleRB">Female</label><br>
21       <textarea rows="10" cols="30">comments</textarea><br>
22       <input id='newsCB' type="checkbox" name="news" value="news">
23         <label for="newsCB">
24           I would like to subscribe to the newsletter.
25         </label></br>
26       <button type="submit" name="SubmitButton" value="Submit">Submit</button>
27       <button type="reset" name="ResetButton" value="Reset">Reset</button>
28     </form>
29   </body>
30 </html>
```

Adding Some Advanced HTML5 Elements

HTML5 adds several more advanced elements that you can use to enhance dynamic web pages. A few of the graphic and media elements are covered in the following sections because a direct relationship exists between those and JavaScript/jQuery programming.

Using HTML5 Graphical Elements

The two main HTML5 graphical elements are `<svg>` and `<canvas>`. These two elements can be added and manipulated via jQuery and JavaScript. This allows you to dynamically change complex graphics in your web pages by drawing directly to the browser window from your scripts.

That means you can dynamically add graphical elements in the browser without needing to load files from the server.

Creating SVG Graphics in HTML5

The `<svg>` element allows you to add scalable vector graphics to your web pages. Scalable vector graphics are composed of a series of lines, arcs, and fills that make up paths. When rendered by the browser, these paths can produce simple to complex graphics. The advantage to using vector graphics is that they retain their crisp edges even when scaled inside the browser. They look sharper onscreen and when printed.

Adding SVG graphics can get extremely complex, so the next section gives you an idea of the HTML elements involved so that you can understand attributes and style properties. From JavaScript and jQuery, you will be able to access the properties for various reasons, such as creating and animating graphics in your web page.

Adding Basic Geometric Shapes

First, you'll create some basic geometric shapes. The following code from Listing 3.7 creates a simple ellipse and a polygon, shown in Figure 3.11. In the `<ellipse>` element, you specify the center of the ellipse as `cx` and `cy` coordinates; then you specify the radius in both the horizontal and vertical directions using the `rx` and `ry` attributes. Notice that you also specify a `stroke` color and width, as well as the `fill` color. The `<polygon>` element is a bit different—the points attribute is set to a series of `x,y` coordinates separated by spaces.

```
08    <svg xmlns="http://www.w3.org/2000/svg" version="1.1" height="200">
09      <ellipse cx="100" cy="100" rx="80" ry="50"
10              stroke="black" stroke-width="2" fill="red" />
11      <polygon points="100,10 40,180 110,120 160,180"
12        style="fill:gold; stroke:black; stroke-width:5; fill-rule:evenodd;" />
13    </svg>
```

FIGURE 3.11
Using SVG graphics makes it easy to add basic geometric shapes to a web page.

Adding Paths

Another example is using paths to draw some more complex shapes. A path is simply a collection of lines that are all connected. The lines may be straight, parabolic arcs, or Bezier curves. To create a path, add a `<path>` element to the `<svg>` element and define the d attribute. The d attribute contains a series of commands that tells the browser how to render the path on the screen. The following is a list of the more common commands:

▶ M x,y—Specifies to move to coordinates x,y. Capital M specifies absolute coordinates; lowercase m will specify relative coordinates.

▶ h n—Specifies to draw a horizontal line n pixels. This value can be positive or negative. Negative means left. Capital H is absolute and lowercase h is relative.

▶ v n—Specifies to draw vertical line n pixels. This value can be positive or negative. Negative means up. Capital V is absolute and lowercase v is relative.

▶ l x,y—Draws a line from the current coordinates to the coordinate x,y. You can specify additional sets of coordinates separated by a space to add additional line segments. Capital L is absolute and lowercase l is relative.

▶ c x1 y1 y2 y2 x y—Draws a Bezier curve from the current coordinates to x,y using x1,y1 as a control point of the curve for the start and x2,y2 as control points for the curve. Figure 3.12 illustrates how the control points work. Capital C is absolute and lowercase c is relative.

▶ a rx ry x-axis-rotation large-arc-flag sweep-flag x y—Draws an arc from the current coordinates to x,y. The size and orientation of the ellipse are defined by two radii rx, ry as well as the x-axis-rotation value, which specifies the angle of the x axis of the arc. The large-arc-flag and sweep-flag are set to 0 or 1 and define which part of the parabolic curve is rendered to the screen. Capital A is absolute and lowercase a is relative.

▶ z—Close the path, which means that the last coordinate will be connected to the beginning of the path.

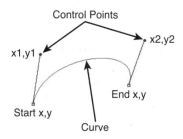

FIGURE 3.12
The control points define the shape of the curve.

The following code in Listing 3.7 illustrates utilizing a couple of paths to create a disconnected pie graph, as shown in Figure 3.13. Notice that the `<path>` data begins with an M command to move to a specific absolute coordinate. Then an h50 command draws a line to the right 50 pixels; next, an a command draws an arc with a 50-pixel radius in both directions up 50 pixels and to the right 50 pixels. Finally, the z command closes the arc and you have the first piece of pie. The next `<path>` element draws the main portion of the pie in the same way.

```
14      <svg xmlns="http://www.w3.org/2000/svg" version="1.1" height="200">
15          <path d="M100,90 h-50 a50,50 0 1,0 50,-50 z"
16              fill="none" stroke="blue" stroke-width="1" />
17          <path d="M90,80 v-50 a50,50 0 0,0 -50,50 z"
18              fill="green" stroke="none" stroke-width="2" />
19      </svg>
```

FIGURE 3.13
Using vector paths to create a pie chart.

In addition to using paths to create graphical elements, you can also use paths to create some cool textual effects. For example, the following code adds a path with no fill as an SVG definition in a `<defs>` container. The path draws a full circle using two arc segments. The id attribute is set to path1. Next, an SVG `<text>` element is created that defines some text.

Notice that inside the `<text>` element is a `<textPath>` element that references the `path1` definition. The result is that the text is drawn on the path, as shown in Figure 3.14. I also added a path element to the `<svg>` tag that draws the hands using a couple of line segments.

```
20    <svg xmlns="http://www.w3.org/2000/svg" version="1.1" height="350">
21      <defs>
22        <path id="path1" d="M 77,210 a 1,1 0 1,1 200,0 a 1,1 0 1,1 -200,1"/>
23      </defs>
24      <text x="10" y="10" style="fill:blue;font-size:31px;">
25        <textPath xlink:href="#path1">
26          Teach Yourself jQuery and JavaScript in 24 Hours
27        </textPath>
28      </text>
29      <path d="M 175,130 v90 h60" stroke="black" stroke-width="5" fill="none"/>
30    </svg>
```

FIGURE 3.14
Using vector paths, you can link text to the path to create some cool visual effects.

The SVG examples can be found in the code/hour03/hour0307.html file on the website. Using these techniques, you can create a vast amount of graphical shapes.

LISTING 3.7   JavaScript and HTML Code That Uses `<svg>` Elements to Create a Pie Graph and a Text Border Around a Clock

```
01  <!DOCTYPE html>
02  <html>
03    <head>
04      <title>Hour 3-7</title>
05      <meta charset="UTF-8" />
06    </head>
07    <body>
08      <svg xmlns="http://www.w3.org/2000/svg" version="1.1" height="200">
09        <ellipse cx="100" cy="100" rx="80" ry="50"
```

```
10                    stroke="black" stroke-width="2" fill="red" />
11        <polygon points="100,10 40,180 110,120 160,180"
12           style="fill:gold; stroke:black; stroke-width:5; fill-rule:evenodd;" />
13      </svg>
14      <svg xmlns="http://www.w3.org/2000/svg" version="1.1" height="200">
15        <path d="M100,90 h-50 a50,50 0 1,0 50,-50 z"
16              fill="none" stroke="blue" stroke-width="1" />
17        <path d="M90,80 v-50 a50,50 0 0,0 -50,50 z"
18              fill="green" stroke="none" stroke-width="2" />
19      </svg>
20      <svg xmlns="http://www.w3.org/2000/svg" version="1.1" height="350">
21        <defs>
22          <path id="path1" d="M 77,210 a 1,1 0 1,1 200,0 a 1,1 0 1,1 -200,1"/>
23        </defs>
24        <text x="10" y="10" style="fill:blue;font-size:31px;">
25          <textPath xlink:href="#path1">
26            Teach Yourself jQuery and JavaScript in 24 Hours
27          </textPath>
28        </text>
29        <path d="M 175,130 v90 h60" stroke="black" stroke-width="5" fill="none"/>
30      </svg>
31    </body>
32 </html>
```

This section only scratched the surface of SVG. If you would like to learn more about SVG graphics in HTML5, you can check out the docs here: www.w3.org/TR/SVG/Overview.html.

Adding a Canvas for Dynamic Design

The <canvas> element also allows you to dynamically add and manipulate image-type graphics to your web pages. The canvas allows you to paint color, lines, text, and images onto an area of the browser screen from JavaScript.

The difference between <svg> elements and <canvas> elements is that rather than being a path, the graphics are stored as a pixel by pixel map where each pixel is a different color and opaqueness.

Most of the work done with <canvas> element will be done in jQuery and JavaScript scripts. In HTML, all you need to do is add the canvas element with an id that you can access from your scripts. To get an idea of the relationship between <canvas> elements and JavaScript, consider the code in Listing 3.8.

The canvas element only defines a container that can be drawn on. All the work is done in the <script> element. Inside the script, the first two lines get the myCanvas element and get a 2d context object. The context object is the graphical object that provides methods to draw on the canvas. Lines 13 and 14 set the line width and color that will be rendered by a stroke() call.

```
11        var c=document.getElementById("myCanvas");
12        var ctx=c.getContext("2d");
13        ctx.lineWidth="1";
14        ctx.strokeStyle="blue";
```

The rest of the JavaScript draws three sides of a cube onto the canvas. For each side, the beginPath() call starts a new path. Then you use createLinearGradient() and addColorStop() to create a gradient fill and set the context fill style.

```
17        var grd=ctx.createLinearGradient(100,50,100,5);
18        grd.addColorStop(0,"blue");
19        grd.addColorStop(1,"white");
20        ctx.fillStyle=grd;
```

Next, to build the cube side, begin with a moveTo() call to move to a specific coordinate in the canvas and then a series of lineTo() to add the lines. At this point, there is still nothing written to the canvas. To write the pixels to the canvas, you can use the stroke() call and/or fill() calls to draw lines and fill colors on the canvas. The results are shown in Figure 3.15.

FIGURE 3.15
Using JavaScript to draw pixels on a canvas.

LISTING 3.8   **JavaScript and HTML Code That Draws a Cube onto a** <canvas>
Element

```
01 <html>
02   <head>
03     <title>Hour 3-8</title>
04     <meta charset="UTF-8" />
05   </head>
06   <body>
07     <canvas id="myCanvas" width="300" height="300">
08       Sorry Your Browser Doesn't Support HTML5 Canvas
09     </canvas>
10     <script>
11       var c=document.getElementById("myCanvas");
12       var ctx=c.getContext("2d");
```

```
13          ctx.lineWidth="1";
14          ctx.strokeStyle="blue";
15          //top
16          ctx.beginPath();
17          var grd=ctx.createLinearGradient(100,50,100,5);
18          grd.addColorStop(0,"blue");
19          grd.addColorStop(1,"white");
20          ctx.fillStyle=grd;
21          grd.addColorStop(0,"blue");
22          ctx.moveTo(1,25);
23          ctx.lineTo(100,5);
24          ctx.lineTo(200,25);
25          ctx.lineTo(100,50);
26          ctx.fill();
27          ctx.stroke();
28          //left
29          ctx.beginPath();
30          var grd=ctx.createLinearGradient(0,125,0,25);
31          grd.addColorStop(0,"blue");
32          grd.addColorStop(1,"white");
33          ctx.fillStyle=grd;
34          ctx.moveTo(1,25);
35          ctx.lineTo(100,50);
36          ctx.lineTo(100,165);
37          ctx.lineTo(1,125);
38          ctx.lineTo(1,25);
39          ctx.fill();
40          ctx.stroke();
41          //right
42          ctx.beginPath();
43          var grd=ctx.createLinearGradient(100,50,200,25);
44          grd.addColorStop(0,"blue");
45          grd.addColorStop(1,"white");
46          ctx.fillStyle=grd;
47          ctx.moveTo(100,50);
48          ctx.lineTo(200,25);
49          ctx.lineTo(200,125);
50          ctx.lineTo(100,165);
51          ctx.fill();
52          ctx.stroke();
53      </script>
54   </body>
55 </html>
```

This section only scratched the surface of <canvas> elements. If you would like to learn more about canvas graphics in HTML5, you'll find some good docs and examples here: www.w3schools.com/tags/ref_canvas.asp

Adding Media Elements

Some additional HTML5 elements that you should be aware of are the `<video>` and `<audio>` tags. These tags allow you to add media elements to web pages in the form of audio and video. Using jQuery and JavaScript, you can reference these elements and manipulate them dynamically. This allows you to change the size, notify the user when the media has loaded, or just control the playback:

The following code shows an example of the `<video>` and `<audio>` tags, and Figures 3.16 and 3.17 show the rendered components:

```
<video width="320" height="240" controls>
  <source src="images/movie.mp4" type="video/mp4">
  <source src="images/movie.ogg" type="video/ogg">
  Sorry, your browser does not support the video tag.
</video>
<audio controls>
  <source src="song.mp3" type="audio/mp3">
  Sorry, your browser does not support the audio element.
</audio>
```

FIGURE 3.16
Rendered `<video>` element allows you to play back a movie.

FIGURE 3.17
Rendered `<audio>` element allows you to play back songs or other audio.

Summary

This hour, you learned the basics of HTML web page development. You also learned how some of the elements can be dynamically accessed via jQuery and JavaScript so that you can better design interactions into your web pages. In addition, you learned the basics necessary to design your HTML elements to support implementing CSS layouts and styling.

Several Try It Yourself walkthroughs took you step by step through adding styled containers, tables, and web forms. In subsequent hours, you use the basics learned in this hour to implement dynamic jQuery and JavaScript.

Q&A

Q. Why is there HTML5 and HTML4 and not just HTML? Which one should I use?

A. It takes web browsers some time to adopt the standards in the newer versions of HTML. Many of the HTML5 features will not work in older browsers, causing errors on the HTML pages and a very poor user experience. Because of that, HTML4 is kept as a different standard until HTML5 is fully supported on all web browsers. Which one you select to use depends on who will be viewing your web pages. If the web pages are for everyone on the Internet, you need to continue to support HTML4 until the browsers fully support HTML5. If the web pages are only for users internal to your company, and you can require a certain level of web browser, you can choose a web browser and version that fully supports HTML5 and run with the new features.

Q. Why even bother creating HTML documents with elements when you can dynamically create them from JavaScript?

A. The best paradigm to use for dynamic web pages is to build the bare bones in HTML, style them in CSS, and then add interactions with JavaScript. The reason you should use HTML documents with the full bare bones is that it is much easier to understand and adjust the structure of the web pages via HTML rather than in JavaScript. Also, if you are localizing your web pages, it is often easier to localize an HTML document in contrast to dynamic JavaScript strings.

Workshop

The workshop consists of a set of questions and answers designed to solidify your understanding of the material covered in this hour. Try to answer the questions before looking at the answers.

Quiz

1. What HTML element attribute is used to change things such as the background color and size of elements?

   2. What is the `<noscript>` element used for?

   3. What is the difference between the `<canvas>` and `<svg>` elements?

   4. True or False: You cannot have an HTML page link to a location on the same page.

   5. What is the difference between a block and inline HTML elements?

Quiz Answers

   1. `style`.

   2. The `<noscript>` allows you to display a message on the HTML page if JavaScript is not active in the user's web browser.

   3. The `<canvas>` element displays images as pixel-based graphics and supports images such as JPEG and PNG; `<svg>` supports vector-based graphics as a series of paths that remain crisp when scaled.

   4. False. You can use the `<a href"#` syntax to link to a local anchor on the web page.

   5. Block elements take up the full width of the screen so elements after them flow below, whereas multiple inline elements can be displayed on the same line because they take up only the amount of room necessary for the content within them.

Exercises

   1. Extend the example in Listing 3.5 to include some additional National Parks.

   2. Use the example in Listing 3.8 as a base and change the cube to a sphere by making all the top points in the path go to the same point (100,15). You will need to remove the portion that draws the top of the cube, change the moves, and remove some of the `lineTo()` functions.

Adding CSS/CSS3 Styles to Allow Dynamic Design and Layout

What You'll Learn in This Hour:

▶ Adding CSS to HTML documents

▶ How to use CSS selectors to apply styles to specific HTML elements

▶ How to apply color, images, and backgrounds to HTML elements

▶ Creating cool borders around HTML elements

▶ Using CSS to define the look and layout of web pages

▶ Designing CSS to be used by your jQuery and JavaScript code

One of the most important aspects of dynamic web pages is their capability to dynamically adjust the design and layout of elements as users interact with the page. This hour focuses on adding CSS styles to your HTML documents. CSS provides a way to very easily apply style changes to HTML elements on the web page.

It is important to add an initially good design that can be easily altered in your jQuery and JavaScript code. With a good design, simple style changes through jQuery and JavaScript can dramatically alter the appearance and behavior of the HTML components, providing a rich user experience.

The following sections cover CSS syntax and using CSS to modify the look of HTML elements and the layout of the web page.

Adding CSS Styles to the Web Page

You can add CSS styles to web pages in a number of ways. You can add them as a separate file, in the HTML <head> element, in the HTML <body> element, inline inside of a specific HTML element, or even dynamically from jQuery and JavaScript.

You can apply as many styles in as many different ways as you would like. However, you need to keep in mind that the styles are applied in order, with the latest style overriding the values of previous styles. Styles are loaded in the following order:

1. `<link>` or `<style>` elements from the header. The lower elements override the ones above them.

2. `<style>` elements in the web page body. The lower elements override the ones above them.

CAUTION

If you define different CSS definitions for the same element(s) in two different CSS files or `<style>` sections, the ones that are loaded last will overwrite the previous ones. This is very useful; however, it can be a pain if it is not intended. For example, if you have a selector that changes several properties for `<p>` elements and then a subsequent selector that directly references the ID of a specific `<p>` element, you would likely want to place the general definition before the specific so that you retain the specific property values.

---

3. Styles applied to HTML elements directly via the style attribute of the element.

4. Styles applied dynamically via jQuery or JavaScript. These are dynamically applied when the JavaScript is executed.

The following sections discuss how to add styles using each of the different options and when to use them.

Loading CSS Styles from a File

Typically, the best method of loading CSS styles is from a separate file, which means you create a file with a .css extension and then add it to your website. This provides several advantages:

▶ You can link several HTML documents to the same CSS file.

▶ Your HTML files remain much cleaner because there is not a lot of extra CSS code encumbering them.

▶ It is easy to re-skin your website by changing out the CSS file for another.

To load CSS styles from a separate file, you need to add the .css file to your website and then add a `<link>` element to the HTML `<head>` element. When the web page is loaded, the browser parses the `<link>` element, requests the .css file from the web server, and applies the styles when rendering the HTML elements.

The following is an example of the syntax used in the `<link>` element. Notice that the rel attribute is set to `stylesheet`, the `type` to `text/css`, and the `href` points to the location of the .css file on the web server.

```
<link rel="stylesheet" type="text/css" href="css/test.css">
```

Adding CSS Styles to the Header

You can also add CSS styles directly to a web page in the `<head>` element using the `<style>` tag. All the text inside the `<style>` tab will be treated as CSS, read into the browser, and applied to the elements as they are rendered.

Applying CSS styles in the header does have some advantages, including the following:

▶ It is easy to apply them to the header to test out the web page without needing to manage an additional .css file.

▶ You can override global styles loaded from a .css file with some that apply specifically to that page.

The following is an example of a `<head>` element that includes a `<style>` element with CSS. Notice that the `type` attribute is set to `text/css`; this is not required, but it is good practice for a time when other style types are supported by browsers.

```
<html>
  <head>
    <meta charset="UTF-8">
    <style type="text/css">
      p{
        background-color:#C0C0C0;
        padding: 3px;
      }
      span{
        font-weight:bold;
      }
    </style>
  </head>
...
```

Using CSS Styles in the HTML Body

You can also use the `<script>` tag to add CSS style settings directly inside the HTML `<body>` element. This is not a good practice, because it can make the web page styles very difficult to change and fix. You should limit your use of this method to times when you want to quickly add a style for testing purposes. After testing, you should always move them to the `<head>` or a separate file.

Defining CSS Styles in HTML Elements

HTML elements provide a `style` attribute that allows you to directly set the CSS style inside the HTML statement. This provides advantages, but one huge disadvantage.

The advantage is that you can override the CSS styles that are applied globally to the website or web page. This makes it possible to customize the look and feel of a specific element without the need to include a special rule in another location.

The disadvantage is that if you do this very much, it makes it really difficult to update the style of your website when you decide on a different web design or branding.

The following line of code shows an example of adding a CSS `style` directly inside of a `<span>` element:

```
<span style="background-color:blue; color:white font-weight:bold">Styled Text
➥</span>
```

Adding CSS Styles to HTML Elements

You have already seen some brief examples of CSS being applied in previous examples in this book. Now it is time to introduce you to the syntax and properties that you can apply to HTML elements via CSS. This section is by no means comprehensive; however, it will give you an understanding of what can be done to HTML elements via CSS.

As you read through and try out the examples, keep in mind that you will have access to the CSS properties via jQuery and JavaScript and can therefore set them dynamically as the user interacts with the web page.

Understanding the Basic CSS Syntax

CSS is composed of a set of one or more rules that define values of properties that the web browser uses when rendering the HTML element. Each rule is started by a selector that defines which HTML element(s) to apply the style change to. Then inside the {} brackets are specific property settings. The property values are set using the `property:value` syntax. Each property setting is separated by a semicolon.

The following listing shows an example of a simple CSS rule that sets the font style, background color, and width of a `<p>` element:

```
p {
  font-style:italic;
  background-color:#DDDDDD;
  width:250px;
}
```

You should use a separate line for each of the elements to make the file more readable and clean. You can combine multiple elements on the same line as long as they are enclosed in the {} brackets. For example:

```
p { font-style:italic, background-color:#DDDDDD, width:250px, }
```

NOTE

Several of the CSS properties support multiple settings for a single property. This helps keep your CSS files a bit more concise and yet maintains the readability. For example, the following single CSS property setting sets the font to `bold`, `italic`, 12 pixels, and `Times New Roman`. The multiple settings are separated by spaces. There are two typefaces specified, `Times New Roman` and `serif`, so if the browser can't find the first, it will use the second. Notice that because `Times New Roman` includes spaces, it must be encapsulated in double or single quotes. Also notice that the two typefaces are separated by a comma indicating they are still part of the same setting value.

```
font:italic bold 12px "Times New Roman",serif;
```

Figure 4.1 shows the basic CSS to apply background and color changes to a `<p>` element and a `<span>` element. Notice that there are two rules—one for each element type. The property values listed in each rule are applied only to the element specified by the selector.

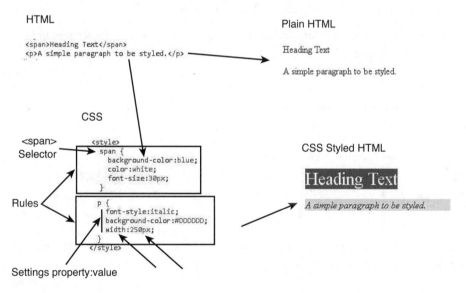

FIGURE 4.1
CSS rules are composed of a selector, followed by a list of property values to be applied to HTML elements.

NOTE

Some of the CSS properties are supported only in specific types of browsers. CSS has a naming convention that allows for the browser engine to be prepended onto the property name to identify the browser that the property setting is intended for. This provides a couple of benefits: one is that you can specify different CSS property values for different browsers; the second is that it allows you to set the CSS property only for browsers that support the functionality. The prefixes are `-ms-` for

Internet Explorer, `-moz-` for Firefox, `-webkit-` for Safari and Chrome, and `o-` for Opera. The following shows an example of using the prefixes to set the rotate property value:

```
-ms-transform:rotate(5deg);          /* IE 9 */
-moz-transform:rotate(5deg);         /* Firefox */
-webkit-transform:rotate(5deg);      /* Safari and Chrome */
-o-transform:rotate(5deg);           /* Opera */
```

Using CSS Selectors to Style HTML Elements

One of the most important pieces of styling HTML elements is the CSS selector. The CSS selector is used to define which HTML elements the CSS rule applies to. CSS selectors can seem a bit daunting at first; however, when you understand the basic concepts in some examples, the syntax falls into place.

The following series of examples will help you understand selectors:

To apply a CSS rule to all `<div>` elements, use the following (HTML elements are referred to by tag name):

```
div {...
```

To apply a CSS rule to a specific HTML element with the `id` attribute equal to `myDiv`, use the following (in CSS, the `id` attribute is designated using #):

```
#myDiv {...
```

To apply a CSS rule to a group of HTML elements all with the `class` attribute equal to `container`, use the following (in CSS, the `id` attribute is designated using .):

```
.container {...
```

To apply a CSS rule to `<span>` elements when the mouse is hovering over them, use the following (in CSS, states are designated by `:state`):

```
span:hover {...
```

To apply a CSS rule to `<a>` elements that have the target attribute set to `_blank`, use the following (in CSS, attributes are designated by [] brackets):

```
a[target=_blank]
```

You can also chain multiple selectors together using commas. For example, to apply a CSS rule to all `<div>`, `<span>`, `<p>`, and elements with `class="menu"`, you could use the following:

```
div, span, p, .menu {...
```

Also keep in mind that CSS stands for Cascading Style Sheets. You may have different selectors that apply to several groups of objects that overlap. For example, consider the following selectors. The first applies to all `<div>` elements, the second applies only to "menu" class elements—some of which are `<div>` elements—and the final applies only to "menu" class elements that are currently under the mouse cursor. Property settings in the `.menu` and `.menu:hover` rules will override settings made in the div rule:

```
div {...
.menu {...
.menu:hover{...
```

Table 4.1 provides a list of several types of selectors; it shows an example and describes how the selector works. You can do much more with selectors than what is shown in the preceding examples and in Table 4.1, but these should give you an idea of how we are using selectors in the rest of the exercises in this book.

TABLE 4.1 List of Some of the More Commonly Used CSS Selectors

Selector	Example	Description
.class	.menu	Selects all elements with class="menu"
#id	#myClass	Selects the element with id="myClass"
*	*	Selects all elements
element	p	Selects all `<p>` elements
element,element	div, .menu	Selects all `<div>` elements and all elements with class="menu"
element element	div span	Selects all `<span>` elements inside `<div>` elements
element> element	div>span	Selects all `<span>` elements where the parent is a `<div>` element
element+ element	div+table	Selects all `<table>` elements that are placed immediately after `<div>` elements
element1~ element2	h1~ul	Selects every `<ul>` element that is preceded by a `<h1>` element
[attribute]	[target]	Selects all elements with a target attribute
[attribute=value]	[value= 1]	Selects all elements with value="1"
[attribute~= value]	[src~= css]	Selects all elements with a src attribute containing "css"
[attribute^= value]	a[src^="https"]	Selects the `<a>` elements with a src attribute value that begins with "https"

Selector	Example	Description
[attribute$= value]	a[src$=".png"]	Selects the `<a>` elements with a `src` attribute value ending with ".png"
[attribute*= value]	img[src*="bkground"]	Selects every `<img>` element with a `src` attribute value containing "bkground"
:link	a:link	Selects all unvisited links
:visited	a:visited	Selects all visited links
:active	a:active	Selects the active link
:hover	a:hover	Selects links that the mouse is over
:focus	input:focus	Selects the currently focused input element
:empty	div:empty	Selects every `<div>` element that has no children
:enabled	input:enabled	Selects the enabled `<input>` elements
:disabled	input:disabled	Selects the disabled `<input>` elements
:checked	input:checked	Selects the checked `<input>` elements

Using CSS Design Properties

Most of the CSS properties are aimed at altering the appearance of the HTML items. Unfortunately, the out-of-the-box HTML elements look pretty bland. However, by adding color, borders, backgrounds, images, and other design properties, you can dramatically change the appearance of your HTML elements with only a little bit of CSS code.

The following sections cover the CSS properties that alter the look of HTML components.

CSS Colors

One of the most frequently used settings applied via CSS is the color property. Most elements have a color property that defines the color the browser uses to render them—for example, a table border, a list bullet, or text characters in a paragraph.

You can use several methods for setting the exact color to support the different backgrounds and situations of people who are defining the color. The color value can be specified via one of the following methods:

▶ **Name**—The CSS color name, such a red, blue, green, or yellow. There are 147 predefined color names, such as aqua, crimson, silver. You can find a list of color names at www.w3.org/TR/css3-color/#svg-color.

- ▶ **Hex**—You can specify a hex number that represents the amount of red, green, and blue to include in the color. The syntax is #RRGGBB. A value of 00 represents none of that color, and a value of FF represents all of that color. For example, red is #FF0000, green is #00FF00, and blue-green is #00FFFF.

- ▶ **RGB**—Similar to Hex, except that you can specify values between 0 and 255. For example, blue-green is rgb(0, 255, 255).

- ▶ **RGBA**—Same as RGB; however, you can also specify an alpha parameter that controls the opaqueness, with 0.0 being fully transparent and 1.0 being opaque. For example: rgba(0, 255, 255, 0.5) is blue-green that is 50% opaque.

- ▶ **HSL**—Enables you to specify the color based on the Hue/Saturation/Lightness color scheme. For example, a color with a hue of 100, saturation of 45%, and a lightness of 75% would be hsl(100, 45%, 75%).

- ▶ **HSLA**—Same as HSL, except you can also specify an alpha parameter that controls the opaqueness, with 0.0 being fully transparent and 1.0 being opaque. For example, an 80% transparent color would be hsla(100, 45%, 75%, .20).

For example, the following CSS rules all define the text color of a <p> element as blue and are completely interchangeable:

```
p {color:blue;}
p {color:#0000FF;}
p {color:rgb(0,0,255);}
p {color:rgba(0,0,255,1.0);}
p {color:hsl(240,100%,50%);}
p {color:hsl(240,100%,50%,1.0);}
```

TRY IT YOURSELF ▼

Applying Text Styles via CSS

CSS provides several properties that enable you to define the look of text in HTML elements. The following are some of the more common text properties you might be dealing with:

- ▶ color—Allows you to set the color and transparency of the text.

- ▶ font—Allows you to set the various properties of the font used to render the text. The properties that you can set are font-style, font-variant, font-weight, font-size, and font-family. The font property allows these to be set on a single line or as a series of separate properties. For example, the following lines are equivalent and produce the output shown in Figure 4.2:

```
#roman{font: italic bold 30px "Times New Roman", serif}
#roman{
```

```
font-family:"Times New Roman", serif;
font-style:italic;
font-weight:bold;
font-size: 30px;
}
```

Some Times New Roman Text

FIGURE 4.2
Changing the font style, weight, size, and face.

NOTE

Font families are applied in the order specified in the font-family property. The first font found is used. It is a good idea to always provide one of the common fonts, such as serif, as a backup in case the font you specify doesn't exist on the browser's system.

▶ text-align—Allows you to set the text alignment to right, left, or centered. For example, the following CSS settings render the output shown in Figure 4.3:

```
#align-left{text-align:left}
#align-center{text-align:center}
#align-right{text-align:right}
```

Left Text

Centered Text

Right Text

FIGURE 4.3
Changing the alignment repositions the text in the browser.

▶ letter-spacing—Allows you to specify an amount of spacing between the letters in the words. This value can be either positive or negative and can be specified as px/pt/cm. Figure 4.4 shows an example of using the following CSS setting to tighten the letter spacing by 1 pixel:

```
#tight{letter-spacing:-1px}
```

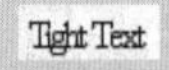

Tight Text

FIGURE 4.4
Changing the letter-spacing to 1px tightens the text.

► `word-spacing`—Enables you to specify an amount of spacing between the letters in the words. This value can be either positive or negative and can be specified as `px/pt/cm`.

► `line-height`—Enables you to control the amount of space between lines. You can specify the value as a number that is multiplied by the height of the text, a size amount using a number with an `em/px/pt/cm` suffix, or a % for percentage of the height of the line. Figure 4.5 shows an example of using the following CSS setting to tighten the line spacing to only 50% the normal height:

```
#half-height{line-height:50%}
```

Close Text Line 1
Close Text Line 2

FIGURE 4.5
Changing the line-height to 50% tightens the lines of text.

► `text-decoration`—Enables you to add a line below, above, or through the text using the `overline`, `underline`, or `line-through` values. You can also specify `blink` as the value to have the text blink in the browser. The following lines of CSS cause the element to render an underline and strikethrough, as shown in Figure 4.6:

```
#underline{text-decoration:underline;}
#strike-through{text-decoration:line-through;}
```

Underlined Text

Strike-Through Text

FIGURE 4.6
Changing the text to underline or strikethrough.

► `text-indent`—Enables you to specify an amount to indent the first line of the text either by a specific value, such as 20px, or as a percentage of the width of the element, such as 20%.

► `text-transform`—Enables you to change the capitalization of the text using capitalize to capitalize the first character in each word, uppercase to make the text all caps, or lowercase to remove all capital letters.

► `text-overflow`—Allows you to define what happens when the text is wider than the size allowed by the element. The options are `clip` to just cut the text off, `ellipsis` to add a ... representing the clipped text, or a string that will be added to replace the clipped text. For example, the following line of CSS will clip text if it is too long and append the string `" (more) "` at the end:

```
#overflow{text-overflow:" (more)";}
```

Use the following steps to create an HTML document and add CSS styles to text elements. The full versions of the files you are creating are in Listing 4.1-html and Listing 4.1-css:

1. From Aptana create a folder named Hour04.

2. Add a subfolder to Hour04 called css.

3. Right-click the Hour04 folder and create a new HTML document named hour0401.html; then add the following basic HTML elements:

```
01 <!DOCTYPE html>
02 <html>
03   <head>
04     <title>Hour 4 - Example 1</title>
05     <meta charset="UTF-8">
...
07   </head>
08   <body>
...
23   </body>
24 </html>
```

4. Now add the following `<p>` elements that you will format using CSS. Notice that each has a different `id` property that you can use in the CSS selector to isolate just that element.

```
09       <p id="plain">Plain Text</p>
10       <p id="blue">Blue Text</p>
11       <p id="tight">Tight Text</p>
12       <p id="half-height">Close Text Line 1<br>
13                           Close Text Line 2</p>
14       <p id="align-center">Centered Text</p>
15       <p id="align-right">Right Text</p>
16       <p id="indent">Indented Text</p>
17       <p id="underline">Underlined Text</p>
18       <p id="strike-through">Strike Through Text</p>
19       <p id="first-cap">capitalize the first letter</p>
20       <p id="uppercase">change to upper case</p>
21       <p id="blackadder">Some BlackAdder Text</p>
22       <p id="roman">Some Times New Roman Text</p>
```

5. Right-click the new css folder and add a new CSS file named hour0401.css.

6. Add the following CSS rules to the new file to define different property settings for the different textual elements created in step 4:

```
01 #blue{color:blue;}
02 #tight{letter-spacing:-1px}
```

```
03 #half-height{line-height:50%}
04 #align-center{text-align:center}
05 #align-right{text-align:right}
06 #indent{text-indent:50px;}
07 #underline{text-decoration:underline;}
08 #strike-through{text-decoration:line-through;}
09 #first-cap{text-transform:capitalize;}
10 #uppercase{text-transform:uppercase;}
```

7. Add the following `<link>` element to the header of hour0401.html to link to the new CSS document:

```
06      <link rel="stylesheet" type="text/css" href="css/hour0401.css">
```

8. Save both files and open the following location in a browser. You should see output similar to Figure 4.7 with the various looks of each of the paragraphs altered.

```
http://localhost/code/hour04/hour0401.html
```

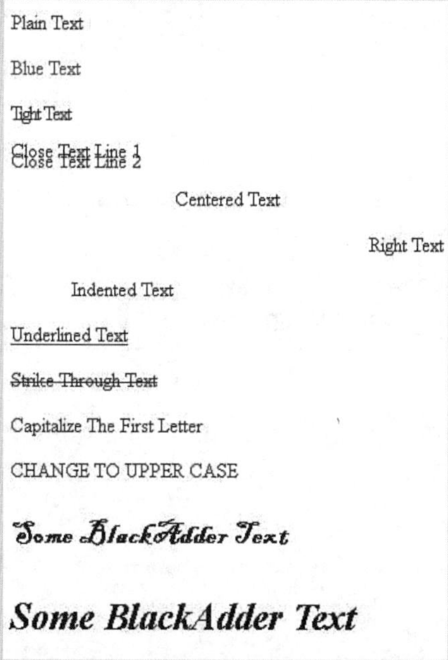

FIGURE 4.7
Applying CSS styles to paragraph elements enables you to completely change their look and behavior.

▼
LISTING 4.1-html   HTML Code with Several Paragraph Elements to Be Stylized

```
01 <!DOCTYPE html>
02 <html>
03   <head>
04     <title>Hour 4 - Example 1</title>
05     <meta charset="UTF-8">
06     <link rel="stylesheet" type="text/css" href="css/hour0401.css">
07   </head>
08   <body>
09     <p id="plain">Plain Text</p>
10     <p id="blue">Blue Text</p>
11     <p id="tight">Tight Text</p>
12     <p id="half-height">Close Text Line 1<br>
13                         Close Text Line 2</p>
14     <p id="align-center">Centered Text</p>
15     <p id="align-right">Right Text</p>
16     <p id="indent">Indented Text</p>
17     <p id="underline">Underlined Text</p>
18     <p id="strike-through">Strike Through Text</p>
19     <p id="first-cap">capitalize the first letter</p>
20     <p id="uppercase">change to upper case</p>
21     <p id="blackadder">Some BlackAdder Text</p>
22     <p id="roman">Some Times New Roman Text</p>
23   </body>
24 </html>
```

LISTING 4.1-css   CSS Code That Stylizes the Various Textual Elements by Adjusting the Color, Alignments, Adding Lines, and Adjusting the Spacing

```
01 #blue{color:blue;}
02 #tight{letter-spacing:-1px}
03 #half-height{line-height:50%}
04 #align-center{text-align:center}
05 #align-right{text-align:right}
06 #indent{text-indent:50px;}
07 #underline{text-decoration:underline;}
08 #strike-through{text-decoration:line-through;}
09 #first-cap{text-transform:capitalize;}
10 #uppercase{text-transform:uppercase;}
11 #roman{font: italic bold 30px "Times New Roman", serif}
12 #blackadder{
13   font-family:"blackadder itc";
14   font-size: 25px;
15   font-weight:bold;
16 }
```

Adding Backgrounds via CSS

Altering the background properties of elements is an excellent way to completely change the look and feel. You should be aware of several background properties, such as the following:

▶ background-attachment—Can be set to scroll or fixed, which will scroll the background with the rest of the page or leave it as fixed.

▶ background-color—Enables you to define the color of the background using the normal color commands; for example:

```
#top-left {background-color:rgb(255,255,0);}
```

▶ background-size—Enables you to specify the size of the background of the element. The values can be a width/height set in pixels or percentages, cover which will scale the background to fill the area of the element, or contain which will scale the image so that the entire image fits in the element. Keep in mind that with cover, some parts of the image may not be displayed in the element if the dimension ratios are different. Some examples that follow set the size to 200 pixels wide by 100 pixels high, 20% the width of the element by 200% the height, and contained fully within the size of the element.

```
#top-left {background-size:200px 100px;}
#top-left {background-position:20% 100%;}
#top-left {background-position:contain;}
```

▶ background-position—This sets the location the background is placed in the element, such as top left, bottom center, and so on. You can also specify a position coordinate of width and height in pixels or percentages for the top-left corner of the background image. For example, the following code places the background image in the middle, 10% to the right 50% down, and 100px to the right 20px down:

```
#top-left {background-position:center center;}
#top-left {background-position:10% 50%;}
#top-left {background-position:100px 20px;}
```

▶ background-image (url)—Enables you to specify the url to an image that will be applied as a background. For example:

```
#rocs{background-image:url("images/rocks.png");}
```

▶ background-image (gradient)—In CSS3, you can also specify a gradient that will fill the background with transitions to different colors. When specifying the gradient, you can set the position, size, and colors. Each of the browsers has its own specific property name.

Following is an example of CSS that defines a horizontal linear gradient. Figure 4.8 shows how the gradient is applied. Notice that the position is set to top. It starts with the color blue at the top, goes to white at 70%, and then to green at 100%, or the bottom:

```
background-image: -moz-linear-gradient(top, blue 0%, white 70%, green 100%);
```

FIGURE 4.8
Creating a linear background image gradient.

▶ The following line of CSS defines the radial gradient shown in Figure 4.9. The center of the radiant is set to 50% from the left and 50% from the top; `circle` ensures that it isn't skewed into an ellipse, and `contain` scales it down to the right size. The color starts at white at the center, moves to blue at 75% and then back to transparent white on the outside, using the `rgba()` color setting.

```
background-image: -moz-radial-gradient(50% 50%, circle contain,white,blue
➥75%,rgba(255,255,255,0));
```

FIGURE 4.9
Creating a radial background image gradient.

▶ `background-repeat`—You can use this option to repeat the background image multiple times. The values are `repeat` to repeat in all directions, `repeat-y` to repeat in the vertical direction, and `repeat-x` to repeat in the horizontal direction. You can also specify `no-repeat` to display the image only once. Repeating images are used for borders and as a design element for bars and buttons. Figure 4.10 shows the results for the different `background-repeat` values in the following code:

```
body{
    background-size:50px 50px;
    margin:5px;
    background-image: -moz-radial-gradient(20px 20px, circle
    ➥contain,white,blue 75%,white);
    background-repeat:repeat;
}
```

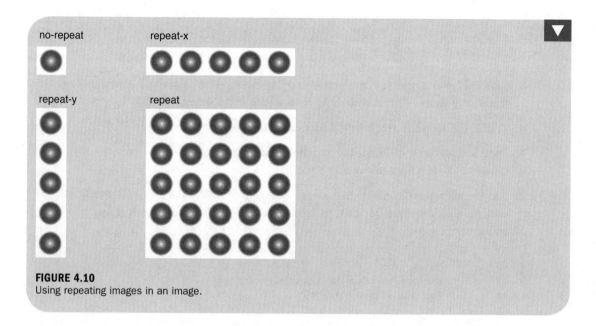

FIGURE 4.10
Using repeating images in an image.

Use the following steps to create an HTML document and add CSS styles to text elements. These are the basics with a few `<div>` and `<span>` elements. The full versions of the files you will be creating are in Listing 4.2:

1. Create a new HTML document named hour0402.html in the hour04 folder in Aptana.

2. Add the following basic HTML elements:

```
01 <!DOCTYPE html>
02 <html>
03   <head>
04     <title>Hour 4 - Example 1</title>
05     <meta charset="UTF-8">
06     <style>
...
30     </style>
31   </head>
32   <body>
33     <div id="heading">jQuery Rocks</div>
34     <div id="content">
35       <div id="menu">
36         <span>Home</span>
37         <span>Info</span>
38         <span>Examples</span>
39       </div>
40       <p>Page Content</p>
```

```
41       </div>
42     </body>
43 </html>
```

3. Save the file and open it in your browser using the `localhost` address. Notice that the text is very plain. All that is about to change with just a little bit of CSS.

4. Create a folder under the hour04 folder called images.

5. Copy a 200-pixel wide image file into that folder. You can use the file /code/hour04/images/rocks.png from the website if you like.

6. Add the following CSS rule to the `<style>` element in the header of the HTML file. This adds the image you just copied into the images folder to the web page. It repeats the image vertically.

```
07        body {
08           margin:0px;
09           background-image:url("images/rocks.png");
10           background-repeat:repeat-y;
11        }
```

7. Then add the following rule to style the text for the `heading` element and add a horizontal linear gradient as the background:

```
12        #heading {
13           background-image: -moz-linear-gradient(left, #0055ff 0%, #AACCFF
             ➥100%);
14           height:200px;
15           font:150px bold;
16           text-align: center;
17           color:rgba(255,255,255,.4);
18        }
```

8. The vertical repeating image we added to the body is 200 pixels wide, so change the left margin for the content container to 200px using the following rule so that the content will be to the right of the image:

```
19        #content {
20           margin-left:200px;
21        }
```

9. Style the menu by changing the background color to #555555 and adding a vertically linear gradient to the `<span>` elements that make up the options.

```
22        #menu{
23           padding:3px;
24           background-color:#555555;
```

```
25          }
26          span {
27             padding:3px;
28             background-image: -moz-linear-gradient(top, #0022ff 0%, #AACCFF
               ➥85%, #0022ff 100%);
29             font:20px bold;
30             color:white;
31          }
```

10. Save the file and refresh the web page in your browser, as shown in Figure 4.11. Notice the difference that adding some background elements can have to some otherwise very plain HTML.

Before Adding CSS Background Styles   After Adding CSS Background Styles

FIGURE 4.11
Adding CSS background styles greatly improves the appearance of elements.

LISTING 4.2   HTML and CSS Code That Add Different Types of Background Styles to Elements

```
01 <!DOCTYPE html>
02 <html>
03   <head>
04     <title>Hour 4 - Example 1</title>
05     <meta charset="UTF-8">
06     <style>
07       body {
08          margin:0px;
09          background-image:url("images/rocks.png");
```

```
10          background-repeat:repeat-y;
11        }
12        #heading {
13          background-image: -moz-linear-gradient(left, #0055ff 0%, #AACCFF 100%);
14          height:200px;
15          font:150px bold;
16          text-align:center;
17          color:rgba(255,255,255,.4);
18        }
19        #content {
20          margin-left:200px;
21        }
22        #menu{
23          padding:3px;
24          background-color:#555555;
25        }
26        span {
27          padding:3px;
28          background-image: -moz-linear-gradient(top, #0022ff 0%, #AACCFF 85%,
            ➥#0022ff 100%);
29          font:20px bold;
30          color:white;
31        }
32      </style>
33    </head>
34    <body>
35      <div id="heading">jQuery Rocks</div>
36      <div id="content">
37        <div id="menu">
38          <span>Home</span>
39          <span>Info</span>
40          <span>Examples</span>
41        </div>
42        <p>Page Content</p>
43      </div>
44    </body>
45  </html>
```

▼ TRY IT YOURSELF

Adding Borders to HTML Elements

Another CSS attribute that can be modified to completely change the look and feel of an HTML component is the border attribute. All the container elements, such as `<div>`, `<span>`, and `<p>`, enable you to define a border style through CSS.

Table 4.2 describes some of the CSS properties that can be modified in CSS to define various styles of borders.

TABLE 4.2   CSS Properties That Define Border Styles

Property	Description

`border`	Enables you to define the `border-width`, `border-style`, and `border-color` properties in a single CSS property using the following syntax:
	
	`border: border-width border style border-color;`
	`border: 1px solid blue;`

`border-width`	Specifies the weight of the line used to build the border. Values are `thin`, `medium`, `thick`, or a size such as `1px`.
`border-color`	Specifies the color of the border based on the normal CSS color methods.
`border-style`	Defines the type of line that is drawn on the HTML page. You can use `none`, `dotted`, `dashed`, `solid`, `double`, `groove`, `ridge`, `inset`, `outset`, and `inherit`.
`border-radius`	Defines the radius of the corners of the border. The value can be a size, such as 5px, or a percentage, such as 10%.
`box-shadow`	Adds a box shadow to the HTML element by setting the following properties: ▶ `h-shadow`—Position of the horizontal shadow. ▶ `v-shadow`—Position of the vertical shadow. ▶ `blur`—Distance to blur. ▶ `spread`—Size of the shadow. ▶ `color`—Color of the shadow. ▶ `inset`—If this is set, the shadow is displayed inside the border; otherwise, it is displayed outside the border. Example: `box-shadow:5px 5px 3px 2px red inset;`

You can specify different values of the `border-width`, `border-color`, and `border-style` attributes on a single property setting using the following syntax:

```
property: top right bottom left;
border-width: 1px 2px 1px 2px;
border-color: red blue red blue;
```

You can also set individual border component properties using the location properties, such as `border-top` or `border-top-width`. For example, the following CSS will style only the top and left components of the border:

```
border-top: 1px solid black;
border-left-color: blue;
border-left-style: solid;
border-left-width: 2px;
```

The following steps take you through the process of adding several types of borders to HTML `<div>` elements by creating the code in Listing 4.3-html and Listing 4.3-css:

1. Create a new HTML document named hour0403.html in the hour04 folder in Aptana.

2. Add the code shown in Listing 4.3-html. The code links to an external style sheet named css/hour0403.css and then defines a series of `<div>` elements.

3. Create a new CSS document named hour0403.css in the hour04/css folder in Aptana.

4. Add the following line to the new CSS file to set basic spacing and size for the `<div>` elements:

```
01 div { width:200px; margin:5px; padding:2px; text-align:center}
```

5. Add the lines of code 2–8 from Listing 4.3-css to define several border styles that apply to the different `<div>` elements.

6. Add the following CSS rules to create rounded borders on two of the `<div>` elements:

```
09 #round { border: 1px solid; border-radius:5px;}
10 #veryround { border: 1px solid; border-radius:50%;}
```

7. Add lines 11–20 from Listing 4.3-css. These lines of code create shadows on the `<div>` element. The first is an outset shadow and the second included the inset value that defines it as an inner shadow.

8. Add the following lines of code that create a mixed border. This is included to show you that you have a great deal of control on each side of the border. The top is `solid`, with a radius on the right side; the left is `dotted`, and the bottom is a `ridge` with a radius on the right side.

```
21 #mixed {
22    border-top: 1px solid;
23    border-top-left-radius: 5px;
24    border-left: 1px dotted;
25    border-bottom: 5px ridge;
26    border-bottom-right-radius: 10px;
27 }
```

9. Add the following code that uses only the border with a large radius and a background color to create a good-looking button:

```
28 #button {
29    width:150px;
30    background-color: #2233FF;
31    color: white;
32    border:5px outset blue;
33    border-radius:50%;
34 }
```

10. Save the files and open the HTML file in a web browser. You should see results similar to what is shown in Figure 4.12. Notice the different styles of borders applied with only a few CSS styling statements.

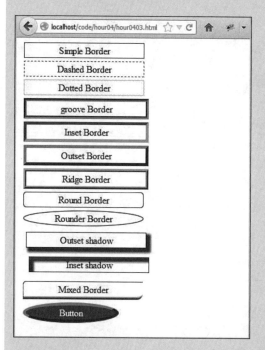

FIGURE 4.12
Adding CSS border elements can apply a variety of borders to HTML elements.

LISTING 4.3-html   **HTML That Creates a Series of `<div>` Elements That Are Styled by Listing 4.3-css**

```
01 <html>
02    <head>
03       <meta charset="UTF-8">
04       <link rel="stylesheet" type="text/css" href="css/hour0403.css">
```

```
05   </head>
06   <body>
07     <div id="simple">Simple Border</div>
08     <div id="dashed">Dashed Border</div>
09     <div id="dotted">Dotted Border</div>
10     <div id="groove">Groove Border</div>
11     <div id="inset">Inset Border</div>
12     <div id="outset">Outset Border</div>
13     <div id="ridge">Ridge Border</div>
14     <div id="round">Round Border</div>
15     <div id="veryround">Rounder Border</div>
16     <div id="shadow">Outset shadow</div>
17     <div id="ishadow">Inset shadow</div>
18     <div id="mixed">Mixed Border</div>
19     <div id="button">Button</div>
20   </body>
21 </html>
```

LISTING 4.3-css   **CSS Rules That Define Several Border Styles**

```
01 div { width:200px; margin:5px; padding:2px; text-align:center}
02 #simple { border:1px solid black; }
03 #dashed { border:1px dashed black; }
04 #dotted { border:1px dotted gray; }
05 #groove { border:5px groove blue; }
06 #inset { border:5px inset red; }
07 #outset { border:5px outset blue; }
08 #ridge { border:5px ridge black; }
09 #round { border: 1px solid; border-radius:5px;}
10 #veryround { border: 1px solid; border-radius:50%;}
11 #shadow {
12   margin:10px;
13   border:1px solid black;
14   box-shadow: 5px 5px 3px 2px blue;
15 }
16 #ishadow {
17   margin:15px;
18   border:1px solid black;
19   box-shadow: 5px 5px 3px 2px blue inset;
20 }
21 #mixed {
22   border-top: 1px solid;
23   border-top-left-radius:5px;
24   border-left: 1px dotted;
25   border-bottom: 5px ridge;
```

```
26    border-bottom-right-radius: 10px;
27 }
28 #button {
29    width:150px;
30    background-color: #2233FF;
31    color: white;
32    border:5px outset blue;
33    border-radius:50%;
34 }
```

Cursor

An important part of browser interaction with users is the mouse cursor. You can let the user know the purpose or behavior of an HTML element just by changing the way the cursor looks when the mouse is over it.

The `cursor` CSS property enables you to define what cursor should be used when the mouse is over a specific element. The following shows an example of setting the `cursor` to a pointer:

```
div { cursor:pointer; }
```

You can choose from several `cursor` values. Figure 4.13 shows an example of some of the cursor values that are available via the `cursor` CSS property.

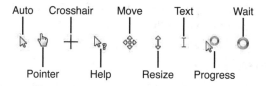

FIGURE 4.13
Examples of some of the cursor types available via the `cursor` CSS property.

Opacity

The `opacity` CSS property enables you to set the transparency of an HTML element as well as all elements contained within. The `opacity` is specified as a decimal value between 0 and 1, where 0 is transparent and 1 is opaque.

Changing the `opacity` is a great way to let users know that an HTML element is inactive. For example, the following CSS and HTML define two button definitions. The definition for `button2` includes an opacity of .4 to make it partially transparent. The results are shown in Figure 4.14.

FIGURE 4.14
Two <span> elements styled as buttons, with one having an opacity set to .4.

CSS rules:

```
#button, #button2 {
  margin: 5px; padding:3px;
  text-align: center;
  background-color: #2233FF;
  color: white;
  border:5px outset blue;
  border-radius:50%;
}
#button2 { opacity:.4; }
```

HTML elements:

```
<span id="button">Active</span>
<span id="button2">Inactive</span>
```

Visibility

Another useful CSS property is visibility. You can set visibility to hidden, and the HTML element and all elements contained will not be rendered to the browser. Then setting it to visible again will display it in the browser window. This capability is very useful in jQuery and JavaScript to enable you to show and hide page elements dynamically.

Applying CSS Layout Properties

One of the biggest challenges with creating HTML web pages is that HTML does not lend itself to creating attractive-looking layouts very easily. That is why many of the CSS properties are aimed at altering the size, position, and relation to other HTML elements.

Using the CSS Layout properties, you will be able to position items correctly on your web page, and with JavaScript and jQuery you can alter those positions efficiently to provide more of an application experience for your users, rather than a simple point-and-click web page. The following sections cover the CSS properties that alter the layout of HTML components.

Understanding the Box Model

HTML elements are rendered to the browser window using the box model. In the box model, the content of the HTML element is made up of the following four parts shown in Figure 14.15:

▶ **Content**—The HTML component content itself

▶ **Padding**—Space between the component and the border

▶ **Border**—Border surrounding the HTML element

▶ **Margin**—Space between the HTML element and other elements around it

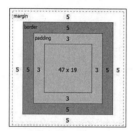

FIGURE 4.15
CSS Box Model includes four parts: content, padding, border, and margin.

The amount of space that each of these takes in the web browser can be set using CSS.

Setting the Content Size

The content is set by specifying a size value of the height and width CSS properties. The size value can be specified as px, cm, auto, %, and so on. You can also specify a maximum and minimum height and width using max-height, max-width, min-height, and min-width properties.

The following shows an example of setting the height and width properties of <p> element:

```
p {height:100px; width: 50px;}
```

Adding Padding Around HTML Content

Padding is an important part of element layout, especially if you are using borders. Padding keeps the content inside the HTML element from touching the border.

Padding can be added to all sides of the HTML element by specifying a padding value, such as

```
padding:3px;
```

You can also specify the padding for each side of the element, for example:

```
padding:1px 2px 1px 2px;
```

Adding Margins Around HTML Elements

Margins work similar to padding, except they are outside the border of the element and keep other HTML elements from touching the border. A margin can be added to all sides of the HTML element by specifying a `margin` value, such as

```
margin:3px;
```

You can also specify the `margin` for each side of the element, for example:

```
margin:1px 2px 1px 2px;
```

The `margin` property also supports the value of `auto`. Using `auto` splits the `margin` values equally, based on the size constraints that are placed in the HTML element.

Modifying HTML Element Flow

Unless you specify otherwise, HTML elements flow to the top-left corner of the browser window.

As you learned in the previous hour, some HTML elements are block elements and some are inline elements. The block elements take up the full width, and so items after them flow down to the next line. Inline elements take up only the amount necessary for the content.

Using the `display` CSS property, you can set elements to be `block` or `inline`. Another value of the `display` attribute worthy of mention is `inline-block`. `inline-block` allows the element to be displayed inline; however, unlike inline elements, you can still set the block properties, such as `height` and `width` as well as `margin`. For example:

```
span {
  height: 200px; width:200px;
  display:inline-block;
}
```

Another way to modify the HTML element flow is to use the `float` property. The `float` property allows an element to float either to the `left` or `right` of the containing element. Other elements that are not floating will be displayed next to the floating element on the side away from the edge of the containing element.

When using the `float` attribute, you need to use the `clear` property to define which sides of the floating element other elements are not allowed to flow around. To illustrate this, consider the following CSS and HTML code. Notice that in Figure 4.16, the paragraph element that does not include the `clear:both` attribute is rendered next to the image that is floating to the left.

CSS rules:

```
#image1 {float:left;}
#image2 {float:right;}
#cleared {clear:both;}
```

HTML elements:

```
<img id="image1" src="images/hour0302.jpg" width="100" />
<img id="image2" src="images/hour0303.jpg" width="100" />
<p id="uncleared">Uncleared Line of Text</p>
<p id="cleared">Cleared Line of Text</p>
```

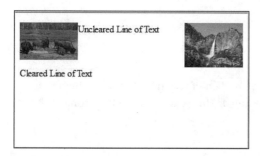

FIGURE 4.16
Floating an element to the left or right modifies the flow. However, you need to `clear` property that you do not want to flow next to them.

Positioning HTML Elements from CSS

The `position` property enables you to define how an element is positioned by the browser. By default, elements are static and simply flow with the other elements in the document. However, by changing the value of the `position` property, you can change that behavior.

The following list describes each of the different nonstatic position values:

▶ `fixed`—Positions the element relative to the browser window.

▶ `absolute`—Positions the element relative to the first nonstatic container element. At least one of the element's containers must already be defined in a nonstatic position.

▶ `relative`—Positions the element relative to the normal position it would have been in.

After you change the position property to a nonstatic value, you can use the `top`, `left`, `bottom`, and `right` properties to set the positioning. For example, to set the top-left corner of an element to 50 pixels from the top and 100 pixels from the top-left edge of the browser window, you would use the following CSS code:

```
position:fixed;
top:50px;
left:100px;
```

z-index

When you begin positioning HTML elements using nonstatic positioning, you may find a situation where one element overlaps another. The z-index property allows you to specify which element should be in front. Elements with a higher z-index number are in front of elements with lower z-index values. The following CSS <div> elements would be in front of <p> paragraph elements.

```
div { z-index:2; }
p { z-index:2; }
```

Overflow

The overflow CSS property is provided to solve the problem of trying to display an item that is too large for the area in the web page you have designed. The overflow property can be set to the following:

- ▶ visible—Default behavior.

- ▶ hidden—Will hide the element if the content is too big.

- ▶ scroll—Adds scrollbars on the bottom and right. If the content exceeds the size constraint, the scrollbars become active so you can view the full contents of the container without affecting the flow of the rest of the page.

- ▶ auto—Will add the scrollbars, if necessary, to keep the element to the size constraints you place on it.

Figure 4.17 shows an example of a list that gets constrained inside of a <ul> element that has the following CSS rule with the overflow property:

```
ul{
  border:1px solid;
  height:150px; width:300px;
  overflow:auto;
}
li{ width:800px; }
```

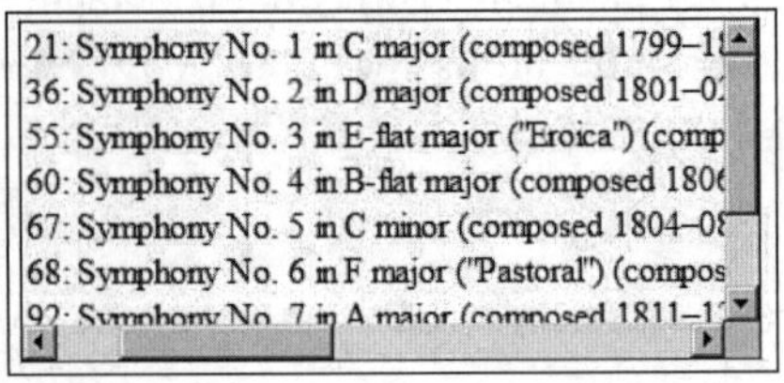

FIGURE 4.17
Adding the overflow property to a <ul> element results in the list being constrained within scrollbars.

Using CSS to Lay Out Web Page Components

In this example, you put into practice several of the layout properties. In the example, you create two `<div>` elements and place them in fixed positions in the web page using the following steps. The full HTML and CSS code can be found in Listing 4.4-html and Listing 4.4-css.

1. Create a new HTML document named hour0404.html in the hour04 folder in Aptana.

2. Add the code shown in Listing 4.4-html. The code links to an external style sheet named css/hour0404.css and then defines two `<div>` elements: one that contains a set of images and the second that contains `<p>` elements to display song info.

3. Copy the image files listed in Listing 4.4-html from the book's website under code/hour04/ images to the hour04/images folder in your Aptana project.

4. Create a new CSS document named hour0404.css in the hour04/css folder in Aptana.

5. Add the following lines to the new CSS file to set basic spacing and size for the `<img>` elements. The `margin` property gives them space around each other and in the div element. The `float` property allows them to float to the left of their container.

```
01 img{
02    width:48;height:48px;
03    margin:5px;
04    float:left;
05 }
```

6. Add the following lines of code to define the look and feel of both `<div>` elements. The `position` is set to `fixed`, but no positioning is specified yet. We also add `padding` to give the items inside the `<div>` room away from the border.

```
06 #buttons, #songInfo{
07    position:fixed;
08    background-color: black;
09    padding:5px;
10    display:inline-block;
11    border:8px ridge blue;
12    border-radius:5px;
13 }
```

7. Add the following CSS rules to position each of the `<div>` elements individually. Remember that they keep all the values from the previous step. Notice that you set the elements' position by specifying the `top` and `left` positions in the browser window. Also notice that you give the buttons a higher `z-index` number to ensure that it will always be on top of the `songInfo`.

```
14 #songInfo{
15    top:70px;
```

```
16    left:100px;
17    height:150px;width:300px;
18    z-index:1;
19 }
20 #buttons{
21    top:200px;
22    left:140px;
23    z-index:2;
24 }
```

8. Add lines 25–44, which define the formatting for the text elements in the `songInfo` container. Following is the rule for one of the rules. Notice that you set the `position` to `relative` so that you can position them relative to where they would normally flow inside of the `<div>` container. Then when you set the `top` and `left` values, they are relative to the `<p>` items' normal position. By specifying a negative number, you can move the item up toward the top.

```
32 #artist{
33    color:cyan;
34    font-size:20px;
35    position:relative;
36    left:30px;
37    top:-50px;
```

9. Save the files and open the HTML file in a web browser. You should see results similar to what is shown in Figure 4.18. Notice that the CSS layout styles have positioned the elements in specific positions in the browser.

FIGURE 4.18
Adding CSS layout properties allows you to position elements at specific locations in the browser.

LISTING 4.4-html   HTML That Creates a Pair of `<div>` Elements That Are Styled by Listing 4.4-css to Be Song Info and a Set of Playback Controls

```
01 <html>
02   <head>
03     <meta charset="UTF-8">
04     <link rel="stylesheet" type="text/css" href="css/hour0404.css">
05   </head>
06   <body>
07     <div id="buttons">
08       <img src="images/skipBack.png" />
09       <img src="images/seekBack.png" />
10       <img src="images/play.png" />
11       <img src="images/stop.png" />
12       <img src="images/seekForward.png" />
13       <img src="images/skipForward.png" />
14     </div>
15     <div id="songInfo">
16       <p id="title">Canon in D major</p>
17       <p id="artist">Johann Pachelbel</p>
18       <p id="album">London Symphony Performances</p>
19     </div>
20     <h1>Song Controls</h1>
21   </body>
22 </html>
```

LISTING 4.4-css   CSS Code Used to Apply a Page Layout That Places Elements in Fixed Positions

```
01 img{
02   width:48;height:48px;
03   margin:5px;
04   float:left;
05 }
06 #buttons, #songInfo{
07   position:fixed;
08   background-color: black;
09   padding:5px;
10   display:inline-block;
11   border:8px ridge blue;
12   border-radius:5px;
13 }
14 #songInfo{
15   top:70px;
16   left:100px;
17   height:150px;width:300px;
```

```
18    z-index:1;
19 }
20 #buttons{
21    top:200px;
22    left:140px;
23    z-index:2;
24 }
25 #title{
26    color:lime;
27    font-weight:bold;
28    font-size:30px;
29    position:relative;
30    top:-20px;
31 }
32 #artist{
33    color:cyan;
34    font-size:20px;
35    position:relative;
36    left:30px;
37    top:-50px;
38 }
39 #album{
40    color:yellow;
41    position:relative;
42    left:60px;
43    top:-70px;
44 }
```

Preparing CSS Styles for Dynamic Design

One of the coolest features of jQuery and JavaScript is the capability to adjust CSS styles dynamically. A little bit later in the book you learn how to do just that to create some cool effects. In this section, you are introduced to the concept of preparing for dynamic styles while CSS is still fresh in your mind.

As you define your CSS styling rules, keep in mind that there are a few methods to applying styles dynamically. That way you can design the CSS in such a way that the dynamic code will be much simpler to implement. The following sections describe some of the methods that you will learn later.

Preparing to Add Classes to HTML Elements Dynamically

The simplest way to dynamically adjust the style of an HTML element is to change which CSS rules are associated with the element. The easiest way to change CSS rules is to use `class` selectors for the different rules that you want to use. That way, from jQuery and JavaScript, you can add a `class` to apply a style or remove a `class` to remove the style.

This provides two main advantages. First, dynamic code is much simpler because it is easy to add and remove classes. The second is that it is easy to make adjustments to the CSS styles that will be applied, because they will be done inside a .css file or a `<style>` tag.

Using dynamic class rules requires that the rules for the class selectors be completely defined somewhere in the CSS code loaded with the web page. It also requires some thinking about how to implement each CSS rule.

For example, think about adding dynamic interaction with a `<span>` element that is styled to be used as a button. You want the button to be able to have four different states of up, down, inactive, and state changing. You can create a different CSS rule with a selector for the class of those button states. When the button is up, the `class` attribute assigned to the `<span>` would be up; when the user clicks the button, you could change the `class` to state changing, and then when the mouse is released, change the `class` to down.

Preparing to Directly Adjust CSS Properties

You can also directly access and modify specific CSS properties of an element or a set of elements via jQuery and JavaScript. This provides the advantage of being able to create static CSS definitions in .css files or `<style>` tags and then dynamically change a subset of the property values.

A great example of using JavaScript with CSS property values is moving items around the web page. For instance, suppose you were to define an HTML image element for a scrolling banner that was supposed to scroll horizontally across the screen. You would define the static CSS style that styles the banner as a fixed position in the browser window. Then, because the CSS already defines all the necessary properties to render the banner fixed, all you need to do from jQuery and JavaScript is to adjust the CSS position properties to scroll the banner.

Summary

This hour discussed using CSS to quickly and easily alter the look and feel of your web pages. Understanding these concepts is critical to implementing JavaScript and jQuery to create dynamic web pages and rich Internet applications.

You learned how the CSS rules are structured and how to define selectors that will apply a CSS rule to a specific set of HTML elements. You were introduced to some of the common design and layout styles of CSS.

You learned how to style text, apply color and background images, and create cool borders around HTML elements. You also learned how to understand and control the flow of the HTML elements on the page as well as applying fixed positioning.

Q&A

Q. **Is it better to use a fixed size and position for HTML elements, or should I try to use more of the HTML flow based on the content size?**

A. That is a tough question. For most web pages, consider using more of a flow with relative positioning within elements as much as possible. The reason for that is because of the wide range of displays that may be looking at the web pages. If you need to support mobile displays up to 36-inch monitors, the flow allows for the content to more easily match the browser size. However, if you are designing a dynamic web page as more of a web application, use more fixed sizes that support an average size monitor and then implement a mobile version using the jQuery Mobile techniques you learn later in this book.

Q. **Why bother with CSS—can't I just apply the CSS styles directly from jQuery and JavaScript?**

A. Sure, everything that you can do with CSS can be applied from JavaScript. However, it is more difficult to maintain the changes, especially when more than one person is involved in the design. Often, some of the best web page designers won't know any jQuery or JavaScript. Also, think about how easy it is to keep multiple versions of a CSS file and tweak them to apply different skins to the web page.

Workshop

The workshop consists of a set of questions and answers designed to solidify your understanding of the material covered in this hour. Try to answer the questions before looking at the answers.

Quiz

1. What selector would you use to apply a CSS rule to all `<div>` elements?

2. What CSS property allows an element to float past other elements either to the right or to the left?

3. How would you apply a border with rounded corners around a `<div>` element?

4. True or False: You cannot specify exact coordinates in the browser to position an HTML element.

5. What selector would you use to apply a CSS rule only to an HTML element with the `class` attribute set to "myClass" and the `id` set to "mainContainer"?

Quiz Answers

1. `div {...`

2. `float:right` or `float:left`

3. `border:1px solid;border-radius:5px;`

4. False. You can set the `display:fixed` property and then set the top, left, bottom, or right pixel offset to place the HTML element, regardless of where other elements are on the page.

5. `#mainContainer {...`

Exercises

1. Modify the code that you applied in Listing 4.2 to include the following CSS rule that will apply to the span you defined as buttons. The rule should change the style of the HTML element and consequently the look of the menu item when the mouse hovers over it:

```
span:hover {
  width:150px;
  background-color: #2233FF;
  color: white;
  border:5px outset blue;
  border-radius:50%;
}
```

2. Modify the code in Listing 4.4-html and Listing 4.4-css to wrap the heading in its own border and position it above the other `<div>` elements. You will need to change the position of the existing `<div>` elements to do so.

Jumping into jQuery and JavaScript Syntax

What You'll Learn in This Hour:

▶ Ways to add jQuery and JavaScript to your web pages

▶ Creating and manipulating arrays of objects

▶ Adding code logic to JavaScript

▶ Implementing JavaScript functions for cleaner code

Throughout the book, you'll see several examples of using jQuery and JavaScript to perform various dynamic tasks. jQuery doesn't replace JavaScript, it enhances it by providing an abstract layer to perform certain common tasks, such as finding elements or values, changing attributes and properties of elements, and interacting with browser events.

In this hour, you learn the basic structure and syntax of JavaScript and how to use jQuery to ease some of the development tasks. The purpose of this hour is to help you become familiar with the JavaScript language syntax, which is also the jQuery language syntax.

Adding jQuery and JavaScript to a Web Page

Browsers come with JavaScript support already built in to them. That means all you need to do is add your own JavaScript code to the web page to implement dynamic web pages. jQuery, on the other hand, is an additional library, and you will need to add the jQuery library to your web page before adding jQuery scripts.

Loading the jQuery Library

Because the jQuery library is a JavaScript script, you use the `<script>` tag to load the jQuery into your web page. jQuery can either be downloaded to your code directory and then hosted on your web server, or you can use the hosted versions that are available at jQuery.com. The following statement shows an example of each; the only difference is where jQuery is being loaded from:

```
<script src="http://code.jquery.com/jquery-latest.min.js"></script>
<script src="includes/js/jquery-latest.min.js"></script>
```

CAUTION

Remember that you need to place the `<script>` element to load the jQuery library before any script elements that are using it. Otherwise, those libraries will not be able to link up to the jQuery code.

The jQuery library downloads and hosted links can be found at the following location: http://jquery.com/download/

Implementing Your Own jQuery and JavaScript

jQuery code is implemented as part of JavaScript scripts. To add jQuery and JavaScript to your web pages, first add a `<script>` tag that loads the jQuery library, and then add your own `<script>` tags with your custom code.

The JavaScript code can be added inside the `<script>` element, or the `src` attribute of the `<script>` element can point to the location of a separate JavaScript document. Either way, the JavaScript will be loaded in the same manner.

The following is an example of a pair of `<script>` statements that load jQuery and then use it. The `document.write()` function just writes text directly to the browser to be rendered:

```
<script src="http://code.jquery.com/jquery-latest.min.js"></script>
<script>
  function writeIt(){
    document.write("jQuery Version " + $().jquery + " loaded.");
  }
</script>
```

NOTE

The `<script>` tags do not need to be added to the `<head>` section of the HTML document; they can also be added in the body. It's useful to add simple scripts directly inline with the HTML elements that are consuming them.

Accessing HTML Event Handlers

So after you add your JavaScript to the web page, how do you get it to execute? The answer is that you tie it to the browser events. Each time a page or element is loaded, the user moves or clicks the mouse or types a character, an HTML event is triggered.

Each supported event is an attribute of the object that is receiving the event. If you set the attribute value to a JavaScript function, the browser will execute your function when the event is triggered.

For example, the following will execute the writeIt() function when the body of the HTML page is loaded:

```
<body onload="writeIt()">
```

TRY IT YOURSELF ▼

Implementing JavaScript and jQuery

Those are the basic steps. Now it is time to try it yourself. Use the following steps to add jQuery to your project and use it dynamically in a web page:

1. In Aptana, create a source folder named hour05.

2. In the same folder as the hour05 folder, add an additional directory called js.

3. Go to jQuery.com/download and download the latest jQuery library to that folder and name the file jquery.min.js. The file may come up as clear text in the browser. If so, just press Ctrl+s (Command-s on Macs) and save the file that way.

4. Now create a source file named hour0501.html in the hour05 folder.

5. Add the usual basic elements (html, head, body).

6. Inside the <head> element, add the following line to load the library you just downloaded:

```
06    <script src="../js/jquery.min.js"></script>
```

7. Now you can add your own <script> tag with the following code to print out the jQuery version to the browser windows:

```
07    <script>
08      function writeIt(){
09        document.write("jQuery Version " + $().jquery + " loaded.");
10      }
11    </script>
```

8. To have your script execute when the document is loaded, tie the writeIt() function to the <body> onload event using the following line:

```
13    <body onload="writeIt()">
```

9. Save the file, shown in Listing 5.1, and view it in a web browser. The output should be similar to Figure 5.1.

FIGURE 5.1
The function `writeIt()` is executed when the body loads and writes the jQuery version to the browser.

LISTING 5.1 Very Basic Example of Loading Using jQuery in a Web Page to Print Out Its Own Version

```
01 <!DOCTYPE html>
02 <html>
03   <head>
04     <title>Hour 5-1</title>
05     <meta charset="utf-8" />
06     <script src="../js/jquery.min.js"></script>
07     <script>
08       function writeIt(){
09         document.write("jQuery Version " + $().jquery + " loaded.");
10       }
11     </script>
12   </head>
13   <body onload="writeIt()">
14   </body>
15 </html>
```

Accessing the DOM

One of the most important aspects of JavaScript, and especially jQuery, is the capability to access and manipulate the DOM. Accessing the DOM is how you make the web page dynamic by changing styles, size, position, and values of elements.

In the following sections, you learn about accessing the DOM through traditional methods via JavaScript and the much improved methods using jQuery selectors. These sections are a brief introduction. You will get plenty of practice as the hours roll on.

Using Traditional JavaScript to Access the DOM

Traditionally, JavaScript uses the global document object to access elements in the web page. The simplest method of accessing an element is to directly refer to it by id. For example, if you have a paragraph with the id="question" you can access it via the following JavaScript getElementById() function:

```
var q = document.getElementById("question");
...
<p id="question">Which method do you prefer?</p>
```

Another helpful JavaScript function that you can use to access the DOM elements is getElementsByTagName(). This returns a JavaScript array of DOM elements that match the tag name. For example, to get a list of all the <p> elements, use the following function call:

```
var paragraphs = document.getElementsByTagName("p");
```

Using jQuery Selectors to Access HTML Elements

Accessing HTML elements is one of jQuery's biggest strengths. jQuery uses selectors that are very similar to CSS selectors to access one or more elements in the DOM, hence, the name jQuery. jQuery returns back either a single element or an array of jQuerified objects. jQuerified means that additional jQuery functionality has been added to the DOM object, allowing for much easier manipulation.

The syntax for using jQuery selectors is $(*selector*).*action*(), where *selector* is replaced by a valid selector and *action* is replaced by a jQuerified action attached to the DOM element(s).

For example, the following command finds all paragraph elements in the HTML document and sets the CSS font-weight property to bold:

```
$("p").css('font-weight', 'bold');
```

TRY IT YOURSELF ▼

Using jQuery and JavaScript to Access DOM Elements

Now to solidify the concepts, you'll run through a quick example of accessing and modifying DOM elements using both jQuery and JavaScript. Use the following steps to build the HTML document shown in Listing 5.2:

1. Create a source file named hour0502.html in the hour05 folder.

2. Add the usual basic elements (html, head, body).

3. Inside the `<head>` element, add the following line to load the library you just downloaded.

```
06      <script src="../js/jquery.min.js"></script>
```

4. Add the following `<script>` element that accesses the DOM using both the JavaScript and jQuery methods. Notice that with jQuery two actions are chained together. The first sets the CSS `font-weight` property and the second changes text contained in element. With JavaScript, you use the `getElementById()` method, and then you set the `innerHTML` property directly in the DOM to change the text displayed in the browser.

```
07      <script>
08        function writeIt(){
09          $("#heading").css('font-weight', 'bold').html("jQuery");
10          var q = document.getElementById("question");
11          q.innerHTML = "I Prefer jQuery!";
12        }
13      </script>
```

5. To have your script execute when the document is loaded, tie the `writeIt()` function to the `<body>` onload event using the following line:

```
15      <body onload="writeIt()">
```

6. Add the following `<p>` elements to the `<body>` to provide containers for the JavaScript code to access:

```
16      <p id="heading">jQuery or JavaScript</p>
17      <p id="question">Which method do you prefer?</p>
```

7. Save the file and view it in a web browser. The output should be similar to Figure 5.2.

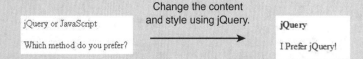

FIGURE 5.2
The function `writeIt()` is executed when the body loads and changes the content and appearance of the text.

LISTING 5.2   **Very Basic Example of Using JavaScript and jQuery to Access DOM Elements**

```
01 <!DOCTYPE html>
02 <html>
03   <head>
04     <title>Hour 5-2</title>
```

```
05      <meta charset="utf-8" />
06      <script src="../js/jquery.min.js"></script>
07      <script>
08        function writeIt(){
09          $("#heading").css('font-weight', 'bold').html("jQuery");
10          var q = document.getElementById("question");
11          q.innerHTML = "I Prefer jQuery!";
12        }
13      </script>
14    </head>
15    <body onload="writeIt()">
16      <p id="heading">jQuery or JavaScript</p>
17      <p id="question">Which method do you prefer?</p>
18    </body>
19  </html>
```

Understanding JavaScript Syntax

Like any other computer language, JavaScript is based on a rigid syntax where specific words mean different things to the browser as it interprets the script. This section is designed to walk you through the basics of creating variables, working with data types, and using looping and functions in JavaScript to manipulate your web pages.

Creating Variables

The first place to begin with in JavaScript is variables. Variables are a means to name data so that you can use that name to temporarily store and access data from your JavaScript files. Variables can point to simple data types, such as numbers or strings, or they can point to more complex data types, such as objects.

To define a variable in JavaScript, you must use the `var` keyword and then give the variable a name; for example:

```
var myData;
```

You can also assign a value to the variable in the same line. For example, the following line of code creates a variable `myString` and assigns it the value of `"Some Text"`:

```
var myString = "Some Text";
```

This works as well as

```
var myString;
myString = "Some Text";
```

After you have declared the variable, you can use the name to assign the variable a value and access the value of the variable. For example, the following code stores a string into the `myString` variable and then uses it when assigning the value to the `newString` variable:

```
var myString = "Some Text";
var newString = myString + "Some More Text";
```

Your variable names should describe the data that is stored in them so that it is easy to use them later in your program. The only rule for creating variable names is that they must begin with a letter, $, or _, and they cannot contain spaces. Also remember that variable names are case sensitive, so using `myString` is different from `MyString`.

Understanding JavaScript Data Types

JavaScript uses data types to determine how to handle data that is assigned to a variable. The variable type will determine what operations you can perform on the variable, such as looping or executing. The following list describes the most common types of variables that we will be working with through the book:

▶ **String**—Stores character data as a string. The character data is specified by either single or double quotes. All the data contained in the quotes will be assigned to the string variable. For example:

```
var myString = 'Some Text';
var anotherString = "Some Other Text";
```

▶ **Number**—Stores the data as a numerical value. Numbers are useful in counting, calculations, and comparisons. Some examples are

```
var myInteger = 1;
var cost = 1.33;
```

▶ **Boolean**—Stores a single bit that is either true or false. Booleans are often used for flags. For example, you might set a variable to false at the beginning of some code and then check it on completion to see whether the code execution hit a certain spot. The following shows an example of defining a true and a false variable:

```
var yes = true;
var no = false;
```

▶ **Array**—An indexed array is a series of separate distinct data items all stored under a single variable name. Items in the array can be accessed by their zero-based index using the `[index]`. The following is an example of creating a simple array and then accessing the first element, which is at index 0:

```
var arr = ["one", "two", "three"]
var first = arr[0];
```

▶ **Associative Array/Objects**—JavaScript does support the concept of an associative array, meaning accessing the items in the array by a name instead of an index value. However, a better method is to use an object literal. When you use an object literal, you can access items in the object using `object.property` syntax. The following example shows how to create and access an object literal:

```
var obj = {"name":"Brad", "occupation":"Hacker", "age", "Unknown"};
var name = obj.name;
```

▶ **Null**—At times you do not have a value to store in a variable, either because it hasn't been created or you are no longer using it. At this time you can set a variable to `null`. That way you can check the value of the variable in your code and use it only if it is not `null`.

```
var newVar = null;
```

NOTE

JavaScript is a typeless language, meaning you do not need to tell the browser what data type the variable is; the interpreter will automatically figure out the correct data type for the variable.

Using Operators

JavaScript operators provide the capability to alter the value of a variable. You are already familiar with the = operator because you used it several times in the book already. JavaScript provides several operators that can be grouped into two types—arithmetic and assignment.

Arithmetic Operators

Arithmetic operators are used to perform operations between variable and direct values. Table 5.1 shows a list of the arithmetic operations along with the results that get applied.

TABLE 5.1 Table Showing JavaScript's Arithmetic Operators as Well as Results Based on y=4 to Begin With

Operator	Description	Example	Resulting x	Resulting y
+	Addition	x=y+5	9"49"	444
		x=y+"5"	"Four44"	
		x="Four"+y+"4"		
-	Subtraction	x=y-2	2	4
++	Increment	x=y++	4	5
		x=++y	5	5

Operator	Description	Example	Resulting x	Resulting y
`--`	Decrement	`x=y--`	4	3
		`x=--y`	3	3
`*`	Multiplication	`x=y*4`	16	4
`/`	Division	`x=10/y`	2.5	4
`%`	Modulous (remainder of Division)	`x=y%3`	1	4

TIP

The + operator can also be used to add strings or strings and numbers together. This allows you to quickly concatenate strings and add numerical data to output strings. Table 5.1 shows that when adding a numerical value and a string value, the numerical value is converted to a string, and then the two strings are concatenated.

Assignment Operators

Assignment operators are used to assign a value to a variable. You are probably used to the = operator, but there are several forms that allow you to manipulate the data as you assign the value. Table 5.2 shows a list of the assignment operations along with the results that get applied.

TABLE 5.2 JavaScript's Assignment Operators as Well as Results Based on x=10 to Begin With

Operator	Example	Equivalent Arithmetic Operators	Resulting x
`=`	`x=5`	`x=5`	5
`+=`	`x+=5`	`x=x+5`	15
`-=`	`x-=5`	`x=x-5`	5
`*=`	`x*=5`	`x=x*5`	25
`/=`	`x/=5`	`x=x/5`	2
`%=`	`x%=5`	`x=x%5`	0

Applying Comparison and Conditional Operators

Conditionals are a way to apply logic to your applications so that certain code will be executed only under the correct conditions. This is done by applying comparison logic to variable values. The following sections describe the comparisons available in JavaScript and how to apply them in conditional statements.

Comparison Operators

A comparison operator evaluates two pieces of data and returns true if the evaluation is correct or false if the evaluation is not correct. Comparison operators compare the value on the left of the operator against the value on the right.

The simplest way to help you understand comparisons is to provide a list with some examples. Table 5.3 shows a list of the comparison operators along with some examples.

TABLE 5.3 JavaScript's Comparison Operators as Well as Results Based on x=10 to Begin With

Operator	Example	Example	Result
==	Is equal to (value only)	x==8	false
		x==10	true
===	Both value and type are equal	x===10	true
		x==="10"	false
!=	Is not equal	x!=5	true
!==	Both value and type are not equal	x!=="10"	true
		x!==10	false
>	Is greater than	x>5	true
>=	Is greater than or equal to	x>=10	true
<	Is less than	x<5	false
<=	Is less than or equal to	x<=10	true

You can chain multiple comparisons together using logical operators. Table 5.4 shows a list of the logical operators and how to use them to chain comparisons together.

TABLE 5.4   JavaScript's Comparison Operators as Well as Results Based on x=10 and y=5 to Begin With

Operator	Description	Example	Result
&&	and	(x==10 && y==5)	true
		(x==10 && y>x)	false
||	or	(x>=10 || y>x)	true
		(x<10 && y>x)	false
!	not	!(x==y)	true
		!(x>y)	false
	mix	(x>=10 && y<x || x==y)	true
		((x<y || x>=10) && y>=5)	true
		(!(x==y) && y>=10)	false

If

An `if` statement enables you to separate code execution based on the evaluation of a comparison. The syntax is shown in the following lines of code where the conditional operators are in `()` parentheses and the code to execute if the conditional evaluates to true is in `{}` brackets:

```
if(x==5){
  do_something();
}
```

In addition to executing code only within the `if` statement block, you can specify an `else` block that will get executed only if the condition is false. For example:

```
if(x==5){
  do_something();
} else {
  do_something_else();
}
```

You can also chain `if` statements together. To do this, add a conditional statement along with an `else` statement. For example:

```
if(x<5){
  do_something();
} else if(x<10) {
  do_something_else();
} else {
  do_nothing();
}
```

switch

Another type of conditional logic is the `switch` statement. The `switch` statement allows you to evaluate an expression once and then, based on the value, execute one of many sections of code.

The syntax for the `switch` statement is the following:

```
switch(expression){
  case value:
    code to execute
    break;
  case value2:
    code to execute
    break;
  default:
    code to execute if not value or value2.
}
```

This is what is happening. The `switch` statement will evaluate the expression entirely and get a value. The value may be a string, a number, a Boolean, or even an object. The `switch` value is then compared to each value specified by the `case` statement. If the value matches, the code in the `case` statement is executed. If no values match, the `default` code is executed.

NOTE

Typically, each `case` statement will include a break command at the end to signal a break out of the `switch` statement. If no break is found, code execution will continue with the next `case` statement.

TRY IT YOURSELF ▼

Applying `if` Conditional Logic in JavaScript

To help you solidify using JavaScript conditional logic, use the following steps to build conditional logic into the JavaScript for a dynamic web page. The final version of the HTML document is shown in Listing 5.3:

1. Create a source file named hour0503.html in the hour05 folder.

2. Create a folder under hour05 named images.

3. Copy the day.png and night.png images from the website under code/hour05/images, or substitute your own into the images folder.

4. Add the usual basic elements (html, head, body).

5. Add the following `<script>` element that gets the hour value using the
`Date().getHours()` JavaScript code. The code uses `if` statements to determine the
time of day and does two things: It writes a greeting onto the screen and sets the value of
the `timeOfDay` variable.

```
06    <script>
07      function writeIt(){
08        var hour = new Date().getHours();
09        var timeOfDay;
10        if(hour>=7 && hour<12){
11          document.write("Good Morning!");
12          timeOfDay="morning";
13        } else if(hour>=12 && hour<18) {
14          document.write("Good Day!");
15          timeOfDay="day";
16        } else {
17          document.write("Good Night!");
18          timeOfDay="night";
19        }
32      }
33    </script>
```

6. Now add the following `switch` statement that uses the value of `timeOfDay` to determine
which image to display in the web page:

```
20        switch(timeOfDay){
21          case "morning":
22          case "day":
23            document.write("<img src='images/day.png' />")
24            break;
25          case "night":
26            document.write("<img src='images/night.png' />")
27            break;
28          default:
29            document.write("<img src='images/day.png' />")
30            break;
31        }
```

7. Save the file and view it in a web browser. The output should be similar to Figure 5.3,
depending on what time of day it is.

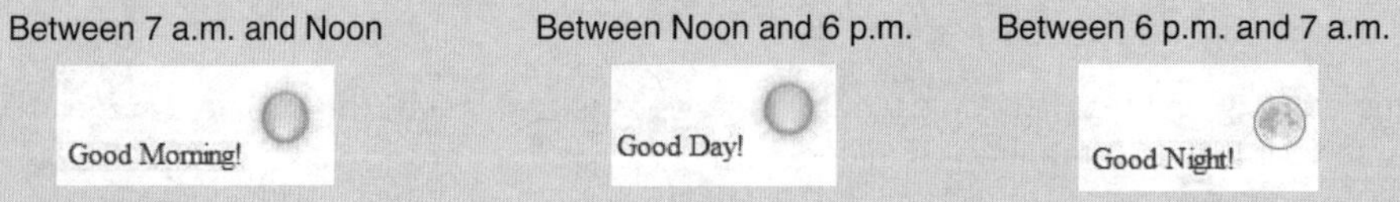

Between 7 a.m. and Noon   Between Noon and 6 p.m.   Between 6 p.m. and 7 a.m.

Good Morning!   Good Day!   Good Night!

FIGURE 5.3
The function `writeIt()` is executed when the body loads and changes the greeting and image displayed on
the web page.

LISTING 5.3   Simple Example of Using Conditional Logic Inside JavaScript

```
01 <!DOCTYPE html>
02 <html>
03   <head>
04     <title>Hour 5-3</title>
05     <meta charset="utf-8" />
06     <script>
07       function writeIt(){
08         var hour = new Date().getHours();
09         var timeOfDay;
10         if(hour>=7 && hour<12){
11           document.write("Good Morning!");
12           timeOfDay="morning";
13         } else if(hour>=12 && hour<18) {
14           document.write("Good Day!");
15           timeOfDay="day";
16         } else {
17           document.write("Good Night!");
18           timeOfDay="night";
19         }
20         switch(timeOfDay){
21           case "morning":
22           case "day":
23             document.write("<img src='images/day.png' />")
24             break;
25           case "night":
26             document.write("<img src='images/night.png' />")
27             break;
28           default:
29             document.write("<img src='images/day.png' />")
30             break;
31         }
32       }
33     </script>
34   </head>
35   <body onload="writeIt()">
36   </body>
37 </html>
```

Implementing Looping

Looping is a means to execute the same segment of code multiple times. This is extremely use-ful when you need to perform the same tasks on a set of DOM objects, or if you are dynamically creating a list of items.

JavaScript provides functionality to perform `for` and `while` loops. The following sections describe how to implement loops in your JavaScript.

`while` **Loops**

The most basic type of looping in JavaScript is the `while` loop. A `while` loop tests an expression and continues to execute the code contained in its {} brackets until the expression evaluates to false.

For example, the following `while` loop executes until the value of `i` is equal to 5:

```
var i = 1;
while (i<5){
  document.write("Iteration " + i + "<br>");
  i++;
}
```

The resulting output to the browser is as follows:

```
Iteration 1
Iteration 2
Iteration 3
Iteration 4
```

`do/while` **Loops**

Another type of `while` loop is the `do/while` loop. This is useful if you always want to execute the code in the loop at least once and the expression cannot be tested until the code has executed at least once.

For example, the following `do/while` loop executes until the value of day is equal to Wednesday:

```
var days = ["Monday", "Tuesday", "Wednesday", "Thursday", "Friday"];
var i=0;
do{
  var day=days[i++];
  document.write("It's " + day + "<br>");
} while (day != "Wednesday");
```

The resulting output to the browser is

```
It's Monday
It's Tuesday
It's Wednesday
```

`for` **Loops**

The JavaScript `for` loop allows you to execute code a specific number of times by using a `for` statement that combines three statements into one using the following syntax:

```
for (statement 1; statement 2; statement 3;){
  code to be executed;
}
```

The `for` statement uses those three statements as follows when executing the loop:

- ▶ **statement 1**—Executed before the loop begins and not again. This is used to initialize variables that will be used in the loop as conditionals.

- ▶ **statement 2**—Expression that is evaluated before each iteration of the loop. If the expression evaluates to true, the loop is executed; otherwise, the `for` loop execution ends.

- ▶ **statement 3**—Executed each iteration after the code in the loop has executed. This is typically used to increment a counter that is used in statement 2.

To illustrate a `for` loop, check out the following example. The example not only illustrates a basic `for` loop, it also illustrates the capability to nest one loop inside another:

```
for (var x=1; x<=3; x++){
  for (var y=1; y<=3; y++){
    document.write(x + " X " + y + " = " + (x*y) + "<br>");
  }
}
```

The resulting output to the web browser is as follows:

```
1 X 1 = 1
1 X 2 = 2
1 X 3 = 3
2 X 1 = 2
2 X 2 = 4
2 X 3 = 6
3 X 1 = 3
3 X 2 = 6
3 X 3 = 9
```

`for/in` **Loops**

Another type of `for` loop is the `for/in` loop. The `for/in` loop executes on any data type that can be iterated on. For the most part, you will use the `for/in` loop on arrays and objects. The following example illustrates the syntax and behavior of the `for/in` loop in a simple array:

```
var days = ["Monday", "Tuesday", "Wednesday", "Thursday", "Friday"];
for (var idx in days){
```

```
    document.write("It's " + days[idx] + "<br>");
}
```

Notice that the variable `idx` is adjusted each iteration through the loop from the beginning array index to the last. The resulting output is

```
It's Monday
It's Tuesday
It's Wednesday
It's Thursday
It's Friday
```

Interrupting Loops

When working with loops, at times you need to interrupt the execution of code inside the code itself without waiting for the next iteration. There are two ways to do this using the `break` and `continue` keywords.

The `break` keyword stops execution of the `for` or `while` loop completely. The `continue` keyword, on the other hand, stops execution of the code inside the loop and continues on with the next iteration. Consider the following examples:

Using a `break` if the `day` is `Wednesday`:

```
var days = ["Monday", "Tuesday", "Wednesday", "Thursday", "Friday"];
for (var idx in days){
  if (days[idx] == "Wednesday")
    break;
  document.write("It's " + days[idx] + "<br>");
}
```

When the value is `Wednesday`, loop execution stops completely:

```
It's Monday
It's Tuesday
```

Using a `continue` if the `day` is `Wednesday`:

```
var days = ["Monday", "Tuesday", "Wednesday", "Thursday", "Friday"];
for (var idx in days){
  if (days[idx] == "Wednesday")
    continue;
  document.write("It's " + days[idx] + "<br>");
}
```

Notice that the `write` is not executed for `Wednesday` because of the `continue`; however, the loop execution did complete:

```
It's Monday
```

```
It's Tuesday
It's Thursday
It's Friday
```

Creating Functions

One of the most important parts of JavaScript is making code that is reusable by other code. To do this, you combine your code into functions that perform specific tasks. A function is a series of code statements combined in a single block and given a name. The code in the block can then be executed by referencing that name.

Defining Functions

Functions are defined using the keyword `function` followed by a function name that describes the use of the function, list of zero or more arguments in `()` parentheses, and a block of one or more code statements in `{}` brackets. For example, the following is a function definition that writes "Hello World" to the browser.

```
function myFunction(){
  document.write("Hello World");
}
```

To execute the code in `myFunction()`, all you need to do is add the following line to the main JavaScript or inside another function:

```
myFunction();
```

Passing Variables to Functions

Frequently, you will need to pass specific values to functions that they will use when executing their code. Values are passed in comma-delimited form to the function. The function definition will need a list of variable names in the `()` parentheses that match the number being passed in. For example, the following function accepts two arguments, a `name` and `city`, and uses them to build the output string:

```
function greeting(name, city){
  document.write("Hello " + name);
  document.write(". How is the weather in " + city);
}
```

To call the `greeting()` function, we need to pass in a `name` value and a `city` value. The value can be a direct value or a previously defined variable. To illustrate this, the following code will execute the `greeting()` function with a `name` variable and a direct string for the `city`:

```
var name = "Brad";
greeting(name, "Florence");
```

Returning Values from Functions

Often, functions will need to return a value to the calling code. Adding a `return` keyword followed by a variable or value will return that value from the function. For example, the following code calls a function to format a string, assigns the value returned from the function to a variable, and then writes the value to the browser:

```
function formatGreeting(name, city){
  var retStr = "";
  retStr += "Hello <b>" + name + "</b><br>";
  retStr += "Welcome to " + city + "!";
 return retStr;
}
var greeting = formatGreeting("Brad", "Rome");
document.write(greeting);
```

You can include more than one `return` statement in the function. When the function encounters a `return` statement, code execution of the function is stopped immediately. If the `return` statement contains a value to return, that value is returned. The following example shows a function that tests the input and returns immediately if it is zero:

```
function myFunc(value){
  if (value == 0)
    return;
  code_to_execute_if_value_nonzero;
}
```

▼ TRY IT YOURSELF

Creating JavaScript Functions

To help solidify functions, use the following steps to integrate some functions into a JavaScript application. The following steps take you through the process of creating a function, calling it to execute code, and then handling the results returned:

1. Create a source file named hour0504.html in the hour05 folder.

2. Add the usual basic elements (html, head, body).

3. Add a `<script>` tag to the `<head>` element to house the JavaScript.

4. Insert the following object literal definition at the beginning of the script. The object will have planet names for attributes, and each planet name is a reference to an array of moons.

```
07        var moonData = {"Earth":["Luna"],
08                        "Jupiter":["Io", "Europa"],
09                        "Saturn":["Titan", "Rhea"],
```

```
10                              "Mars":["Phobos"]};
```

5. Add the following function that will be called by the `onload` event. In this function you use a nested `for/in` loop to iterate through the `moonData` object attributes. The outer loop gets the planet `name` and the inner loop loops through the index of the `moon` array.

```
11          function writeIt(){
12            for (planet in moonData){
13              var moons = moonData[planet];
14              for (moonIdx in moons){
15                var moon = moons[moonIdx];
16                var listItem = makeListItem(planet, moon);
17                document.write(listItem);
18              }
19            }
20          }
```

6. Notice that on line 16 of the `writeIt()` function is a call to `makeListItem()`. That function needs to return a value that can be used in line 17 to write to the document. Add the following code to create the function. The function takes two arguments: a `name` and a `value`, then generates an HTML string to create a `<li>` element and returns the string.

```
21          function makeListItem(name, value){
22            var itemStr = "<li>" + name + ": " + value + "</li>";
23            return itemStr;
24          }
```

7. Save the file, shown in Listing 5.4, and open it in a web browser. You should see the results shown in Figure 5.4. You have just created two JavaScript functions: one that takes no arguments and does not return a value and the other that takes two arguments and returns a formatted HTML string containing the argument strings.

- Earth: Luna
- Jupiter: Io
- Jupiter: Europa
- Saturn: Titan
- Saturn: Rhea
- Mars: Phobos

FIGURE 5.4
The function `writeIt()` is executed, which iterates through the `moonData` object and makes calls to the `makeListItem()` function to format the planet and moon names as an HTML `<li>` element.

LISTING 5.4   Simple Example of Using Conditional Logic Inside JavaScript

```
01 <!DOCTYPE html>
02 <html>
```

```
03    <head>
04      <title>Hour 5-4</title>
05      <meta charset="utf-8" />
06      <script>
07        var moonData = {"Earth":["Luna"],
08                        "Jupiter":["Io", "Europa"],
09                        "Saturn":["Titan", "Rhea"],
10                        "Mars":["Phobos"]};
11        function writeIt(){
12          for (planet in moonData){
13            var moons = moonData[planet];
14            for (moonIdx in moons){
15              var moon = moons[moonIdx];
16              var listItem = makeListItem(planet, moon);
17              document.write(listItem);
18            }
19          }
20        }
21        function makeListItem(name, value){
22          var itemStr = "<li>" + name + ": " + value + "</li>";
23          return itemStr;
24        }
25      </script>
26    </head>
27    <body onload="writeIt()">
28    </body>
29  </html>
```

Understanding Variable Scope

After you start adding conditions, functions, and loops to your JavaScript applications, you need to understand variable scoping. Variable scope is simply this: "what is the value of a specific variable name at the current line of code being executed."

JavaScript enables you to define both a global and a local version of the variable. The global version is defined in the main JavaScript, and local versions are defined inside functions. When you define a local version in a function, a new variable is created in memory. Within that function, you will be referencing the local version. Outside that function, you will be referencing the global version.

To understand variable scoping a bit better, consider the following code:

```
01 <script>
02   var myVar = 1;
03   function writeIt(){
```

```
04      var myVar = 2;
05      document.write(myVar);
06      writeMore();
07    }
08    function writeMore(){
09      document.write(myVar);
10    }
11  </script>
```

The global variable `myVar` is defined on line 2. Then on line 4, a local version is defined within the `writeIt()` function. So, line 5 will write 2 to the document. Then in line 6, `writeMore()` is called. Because there is no local version of `myVar` defined in `writeMore()`, the value of the global `myVar` is written in line 9.

Adding Error Handling

An important part of JavaScript coding is adding error handling for instances where there may be problems. By default, if a code exception occurs because of a problem in your JavaScript, the script fails and does not finish loading. This is not usually the desired behavior.

Try/Catch **Blocks**

To prevent your code from totally bombing out, use `try`/`catch` blocks that can handle problems inside your code. If JavaScript encounters an error when executing code in a `try`/`catch` block, it will jump down and execute the `catch` portion instead of stopping the entire script. If no error occurs, all of the `try` will be executed and none of the `catch`.

For example, the following `try`/`catch` block will execute any code that replaces `your_code_here`. If an error occurs executing that code, the error message followed by the string `": happened when loading the script"` will be written to the document:

```
try {
    your_code_here
} catch (err) {
  document.write(err.message + ": happened when loading the script");
}
```

Throw Your Own Errors

You can also throw your own errors using a `throw` statement. The following code illustrates how to add throws to a function to `throw` an error, even if a script error does not occur:

```
01 <script>
02    function sqrRoot(x) {
03      try {
04        if(x=="")    throw "Can't Square Root Nothing";
05        if(isNaN(x)) throw "Can't Square Root Strings";
```

```
06        if(x<0)        throw "Sorry No Imagination";
07        return "sqrt("+x+") = " + Math.sqrt(x);
08      } catch(err){
09        return err;
10      }
11    }
12    function writeIt(){
13      document.write(sqrRoot("four") + "<br>");
14      document.write(sqrRoot("") + "<br>");
15      document.write(sqrRoot("4") + "<br>");
16      document.write(sqrRoot("-4") + "<br>");
17    }
18 </script>
```

The function sqrRoot() accepts a single argument x. It then tests x to verify that it is a positive number and returns a string with the square root of x. If x is not a positive number, the appropriate error is thrown and returned to writeIt().

Using finally

Another valuable tool in exception handling is the finally keyword. A finally keyword can be added to the end of a try/catch block. After the try/catch blocks are executed, the finally block is always executed. It doesn't matter if an error occurs and is caught or if the try block is fully executed.

Following is an example of using a finally block inside a web page:

```
function testTryCatch(value){
  try {
    if (value < 0){
      throw "too small";
    } else if (value > 10){
      throw "too big";
    }
    your_code_here
  } catch (err) {
    document.write("The number was " + err.message");
  } finally {
    document.write("This is always written.");
  }
}
```

Summary

In this hour, you learned the basics of adding jQuery and JavaScript to web pages. The basic data types that are used in JavaScript and, consequently, jQuery, were described. You learned some of the basic syntax of applying conditional logic to JavaScript applications. You also learned how to compartmentalize your JavaScript applications into functions that can be reused in other locations. Finally, you learned some ways to handle JavaScript errors in your script before the browser receives an exception.

Q&A

Q. When should you use a regular expression in string operations?

A. That depends on your understanding of regular expressions. Those who use regular expressions frequently and understand the syntax well would almost always rather use a regular expression because they are so versatile. If you are not very familiar with regular expressions, it takes time to figure out the syntax, and so you will want to use them only when you need to. The bottom line is that if you need to manipulate strings frequently, it is absolutely worth it to learn regular expressions.

Q. Can I load more than one version of jQuery at a time?

A. Sure, but there really isn't a valid reason to do that. The one that gets loaded last will overwrite the functionality of the previous one. Any functions from the first one that were not overwritten may be completely unpredictable because of the mismatch in libraries. The best bet is to develop and test against a specific version and update to a newer version only when there is added functionality that you want to add to your web page.

Workshop

The workshop consists of a set of questions and answers designed to solidify your understanding of the material covered in this hour. Try to answer the questions before looking at the answers.

Quiz

1. What is the difference between `==` and `===` in JavaScript?

2. What is the difference between the `break` and `continue` keywords?

3. When should you use a `finally` block?

4. What is the resulting value when you add a string "1" to a number 1, ("1"+1)?

Quiz Answers

1. `==` compares only the relative value; `===` compares the value and the type.

2. `break` will stop executing the loop entirely, whereas `continue` will only stop executing the current iteration and then move on to the next.

3. When you have code that needs to be executed even if a problem occurs in the `try` block.

4. The string "11" because the number is converted to a string and then concatenated.

Exercises

1. Open hour0504.html and modify it to create a table instead of a list. You will need to add code to the `writeIt()` function that writes the `<table>` open tag before iterating through the planets and then the closing tag after iterating through the planets. Then modify the `makeListItem()` function to return a string in the form of

   `<tr><td>planent</td><td>moon</td></tr>`

2. Modify hour0503.html to include some additional times with different messages and images. For example, between 8 and 9 you could add the message "go to work" with a car icon, between 5 and 6 you could add the message "time to go home" with a home icon. You will need to add some additional cases to the `switch` statement and set the `timeOfDay` value accordingly.

HOUR 6
Understanding and Using JavaScript Objects

What You'll Learn in This Hour:

▶ How to access JavaScript objects
▶ Creating and manipulating strings
▶ Sorting JavaScript arrays
▶ Searching arrays and strings
▶ How to create your own custom objects

Much of the code in JavaScript revolves around objects. Objects are a convenient and easy way to group functionality and data together for a variety of purposes. Objects allow you to more easily write code that is clear and easy to implement.

There are four main types of objects that you will be working with in jQuery and JavaScript: DOM, built-in, user-defined, and jQuery. The following sections define object syntax, take you through the most common built-in objects, and show you how to create your own custom objects. DOM objects and jQuery objects are covered in upcoming hours.

Using Object Syntax

To use objects in JavaScript effectively, you need to have an understanding of their structure and syntax. An object is really a container to group multiple values and, in some instances, functions together. The values of an object are called properties, and functions are called methods. Object syntax is very straightforward—you use the object name, then a dot, then the property or method name.

Creating a New Object Instance

To use a JavaScript object, you must first create an instance of the object. Object instances are created using the new keyword with the object constructor name. For example, to create a Number object you use the following line of code:

```
var x = new Number("5");
```

Accessing Object Properties

Almost all JavaScript objects have values that are accessible via a standard dot naming syntax. For example, consider an object with the variable name `user` that contains a property `firstName`. The following statement accesses the value of the `firstName` property of the `user` object:

```
user.FirstName
```

Accessing Object Methods

Many JavaScript objects also have methods. An object method is a function that is attached to the object as a name. The function can be called by using the dot syntax to reference the method name. For example, if the object named `user` had a method called `getFullName()`, that function can be called by the following statement:

```
user.getFullName()
```

Assigning New Values and Methods to Objects

One of the coolest things about objects in JavaScript is that you can assign new property and method values to them at any point using the dot syntax. It doesn't matter if it is a built-in object or one of your own custom objects. That value can then be accessed later using the same dot syntax.

The following is an example of adding a method and property to the main document object that we have been using for several examples. Notice that we define a simple function that writes the `document.me` property to the browser. Then we assign a value to `document.me` and the function `writeMe()` without the `()` as `document.writeMe`. At that point we can call `document.writeMe` and access the property `document.me`:

```
<script>
  function writeMe(){
    document.write(document.me);
  }
  document.me = "Brad Dayley";
  document.writeMe = writeMe;
  document.writeMe();
</script>
```

CAUTION

If you assign a new value to an object, the existing properties or methods with the same name will be overwritten. When assigning values to objects, be careful that you do not accidentally overwrite an existing property or method.

Understanding Built-In Objects

JavaScript has several built-in objects that provide a specific set of functionality. Using these built-in objects will save time because they provide already coded and tested methods to handle data. The following sections don't include all the JavaScript objects, but cover the ones that you need for this book.

Number

The `Number` object provides functionality that is useful when dealing with numbers. Creating a `number` object is different from just assigning a number to a variable. When you create a `Number` object, you also get a set of methods that can be used with it.

The `Number` object provides the methods listed in Table 6.1. Follow the output results for each of these methods in Table 6.1 based on the following object creation:

```
var x = new Number("5.55555555");
```

I chose to pass the number `5.555555555` in as a string instead of a number to illustrate that `Number()` can accept a string, number, or variable representing a string or a number. The string must be a number string or the value of the `Number` objects will be `NaN` (not a number).

TABLE 6.1 Using the Built-in Number Object Methods

Method	Description	Output
`x.toExponential()`	Exponential form of number	`5.55555555e+0`
`x.toFixed(2)`	Reduce to fixed decimal places	`05.56`
`x.toPrecision(5)`	Reduce to specific length	`5.5556`
`x.toString()`	String form of number	`"5.55555555"`
`x.valueOf()`	Actual numerical value	`5.55555555`

It is a good idea to test values before creating the `Number` object. To test a value and determine whether it is a number, use the `isNaN()` function. `isNaN()` returns `false` if the value is a number or a string that can be a number.

NOTE

You can use a hexadecimal string when checking for numbers. This is very useful if you are working with hex color values, such as `#e0ffff`. The string format to use in JavaScript is `"0xe0ffff"`.

String

The `String` object is by far the most commonly used in JavaScript. JavaScript automatically creates a `String` object anytime you define a variable that has a string data type. For example:

```
var myStr = "Teach Yourself jQuery & JavaScript in 24 Hours";
```

When you create a string, several special characters can't be directly added to the string. For these characters, JavaScript provides a set of escape codes described in Table 6.2.

TABLE 6.2 Escape Codes Used in JavaScript Strings

Escape	Description	Example	Output String
\'	Single quote mark	"couldn\'t be"	couldn't be
\"	Double quote mark	"I \"think\" I \"am\""	I "think" I "am"
\\	Backslash	"one\\two\\three"	one\two\three
\n	New line	"I am\nI said"	I am I said
\r	Carriage return	"to be\ror not"	to be or not
\t	Tab	"one\ttwo\tthree"	one two three
\b	Backspace	"correction\b\b\bion"	correction
\f	Form feed	"Title A\fTitle B"	Title A then Title B on a new page (mostly for printing)

To get the length of the string, you can use the `length` property of the string object, for example:

```
var numOfChars = myStr.length;
```

The `String` object has several functions that allow you to access and manipulate the string in various ways. The methods for string manipulation are described in Table 6.3.

TABLE 6.3 `String` Object Methods Used to Manipulate JavaScript Strings

Method	Description
charAt(index)	Returns the character at the specified index.
charCodeAt(index)	Returns the unicode value of the character at the specified index.

Method	Description
`concat(str1, str2, ...)`	Joins two or more strings and returns a copy of the joined strings.
`fromCharCode()`	Converts unicode values to actual characters.
`indexOf(subString)`	Returns the position of the first occurrence of a specified `subString` value. Returns −1 if the substring is not found.
`lastIndexOf(subString)`	Returns the position of the last occurrence of a specified `subString` value. Returns −1 if the substring is not found.
`match(regex)`	Searches the string and returns all matches to the regular expression.
`replace(subString/regex, replacementString)`	Searches the string for a match of the `subString` or regular expression, and replaces the matched substring with a new substring.
`search(regex)`	Searches the string based on the regular expression and returns the position of the first match.
`slice(start, end)`	Returns a new string that has the portion of the string between the `start` and `end` positions removed.
`split(sep, limit)`	Splits a string into an array of substrings based on a separator character or regular expression. The optional `limit` argument defines the maximum number of splits to make, starting from the beginning.
`substr()`	Extracts the characters from a string, beginning at a specified start position, and through the specified number of characters.
`substring(from, to)`	Returns a substring of characters between the `from` and `to` index.
`toLowerCase()`	Converts the string to lowercase.
`toUpperCase()`	Converts a string to uppercase.
`valueOf()`	Returns the primitive string value.

To get you started on using the functionality provided in the `String` object, the following sections describe some of the common tasks that can be done using `String` object methods.

Combining Strings

Multiple strings can be combined either by using a + operation or by using the `concat()` function on the first string. For example, in the following code, `sentence1` and `sentence2` will be the same:

```
var word1 = "Today ";
var word2 = "is ";
var word3 = "tomorrows\' ";
var word4 = "yesterday.";
var sentence1 = word1 + word2 + word3 + word4;
var sentence2 = word1.concat(word2, word3, word4);
```

Searching a String for a Substring

To tell if a string is a substring of another, you can use the `indexOf()` method. For example, the following code writes the string to the browser only if it contains the word "think":

```
var myStr = "I think, therefore I am.";
if (myStr.indexOf("think") != -1){
  document.write(myStr);
}
```

Replacing a Word in a String

Another common `String` object task is replacing one substring with another. To replace a word/ phrase in a string, use the `replace()` method. The following code replaces the text `"<username>"` with the value of the variable username:

```
var username = "Brad";
var output = "<username> please enter your password: ";
output = output.replace("<username>", username);
```

Splitting Strings into an Array

A common task with strings is to split them into arrays using a separator character. For example, the following code splits a time string into an array of its basic parts using the `split()` method on the `":"` separator:

```
var t = "12:10:36";
var tArr = t.split(":");
var hour = tArr[0];
var minute = tArr[1];
var second = tArr[2];
```

▼ TRY IT YOURSELF

Manipulating Strings in JavaScript

In this section, you follow step by step the process of manipulating some strings to produce a mini-madlib. It is just a basic example, but it should help solidify `String` objects a bit for you. The full code is in Listing 6.1, and the results are displayed in Figure 6.1.

1. In Aptana, create a source folder named hour06.

FIGURE 6.1
Outputted madlib text.

2. Create a source file named hour0601.html in the hour06 folder.

3. Add the usual basic elements (html, head, body).

4. Inside the `<head>` element, add a `<script>` element with a function named `writeIt()` and link it to the `onload` event of the `<body>` element, as shown next:

```
06 <script>
07    function writeIt(){
...
19   }
20 </script>
21   </head>
22   <body onload="writeIt()">
```

5. Add the following three string definitions that will house each line of the madlib text:

```
08    var line1 = "In a [place] a long time ago, ";
09    var line2 = "there lived an [animal] that liked to ";
10    var line3 = "[action] people.";
```

6. Add the following three string definitions be used to populate items in the madlib:

```
11    var place = "golf course";
12    var animal = "gopher";
13    var action = "drive";
```

7. Add the following line to combine the lines of text as a single string:

```
14    var madlib = line1.concat(line2, line3);
```

8. Fill in the blanks in the madlib string by replacing them with the appropriate variable value. The following lines use the `replace()` method to replace the value of the variable with the correct location in the string:

```
15      madlib = madlib.replace("[place]", place);
16      madlib = madlib.replace("[animal]", animal);
17      madlib = madlib.replace("[action]", action);
```

9. Add the following command to write the fully processed madlib string to the browser:

```
18      document.write(madlib);
```

10. Open the page in the browser, and the string should be formatted as shown in Figure 6.1.

LISTING 6.1   **Example of Combining Multiple Lines of Text into a Single String and Using** `replace()` **to Fill in Specifically Formatted Sections of the String with Variable Values**

```
01 <!DOCTYPE html>
02 <html>
03   <head>
04     <title>Hour 5-1</title>
05     <meta charset="utf-8" />
06 <script>
07   function writeIt(){
08     var line1 = "In a [place] a long time ago, ";
09     var line2 = "there lived an [animal] that liked to ";
10     var line3 = "[action] people.";
11     var place = "golf course";
12     var animal = "gopher";
13     var action = "drive";
14     var madlib = line1.concat(line2, line3);
15     madlib = madlib.replace("[place]", place);
16     madlib = madlib.replace("[animal]", animal);
17     madlib = madlib.replace("[action]", action);
18     document.write(madlib);
19   }
20 </script>
21   </head>
22   <body onload="writeIt()">
23   </body>
24 </html>
```

Array

The `Array` object provides a means of storing and handling a set of other objects. Arrays can store numbers, strings, or other JavaScript objects. You can use a couple of methods to create JavaScript `Arrays`; for example, the following statements create three identical versions of the same array:

```
var arr = ["one", "two", "three"];
var arr2 = new Array();
arr2[0] = "one";
arr2[1] = "two";
arr3[2] = "three";
var arr3 = new Array();
arr3.push("one");
arr3.push("two");
arr3.push("three");
```

To get the number of elements in the array, you can use the `length` property of the `Array` object. For example:

```
var numOfItems = arr.length;
```

Arrays are a zero-based index, meaning that the first item is at index 0, and so on. You can access the array backward by subtracting using the `length` attribute. For example, in the following code, the value of variable first will be Monday and the value of variable last will be Friday:

```
var week = ["Monday", "Tuesday", "Wednesday", "Thursday", "Friday"];
var first = week[0];
var last = week[week.length-1];
```

The `Array` object has several built-in functions that allow you to access and manipulate the array in various ways. Table 6.4 describes the method attached to the `Array` object that enables you to manipulate the array contents.

TABLE 6.4 Array Object Methods Used to Manipulate JavaScript Arrays

Method	Description
`concat(arr1, arr2, ...)`	Returns a joined copy of the array and the arrays passed as arguments.
`indexOf(value)`	Returns the first index of the `value` in the array or −1 if the item is not found.
`join(separator)`	Joins all elements of an array separated by the `separator` into a single string. If no separator is specified, a comma is used.
`lastIndexOf(value)`	Returns the last index of the `value` in the array or −1 if the `value` is not found.
`pop()`	Removes the last element from the array and returns that element.
`push(item1, item2, ...)`	Adds one or more new elements to the end of an array, and returns the new length.
`reverse()`	Reverses the order of all elements in the array.
`shift()`	Removes the first element of an array and returns that element.

Method	Description
slice(start, end)	Returns the elements between the start and end index.
sort(sortFunction)	Sorts the elements of the array. The sortFunction is optional.
splice(index, count, item1, item2...)	At the index specified, count number items are removed, and then any optional items passed in as arguments are inserted at index.
toString()	Returns the string form of the array.
unshift()	Adds new elements to the beginning of an array and returns the new length.
valueOf()	Returns the primitive value of an Array object.

To get you started on using the functionality provided in the Array object, the following sections describe some of the common tasks that can be done using Array object methods.

Combining Arrays

You can combine arrays the same way that you combine String objects, using + statements or using the concat() method. In the following code, arr3 ends up being the same as arr4:

```
var arr1 = [1,2,3];
var arr2 = ["three", "four", "five"]
var arr3 = arr1 + arr2;
var arr4 = arr1.concat(arr2);
```

TIP

You can combine an array of numbers and an array of strings. Each item in the array will keep its own object type. However, as you use the items in the array, you need to keep track of arrays that have more than one data type so that you do not run into problems.

Iterating Through Arrays

You can iterate through an array using a for or a for/in loop. The following code illustrates iterating through each item in the array using each method:

```
var week = ["Monday", "Tuesday", "Wednesday", "Thursday", "Friday"];
for (var i=0; i<week.length; i++){
  document.write("<li>" + week[i] + "</li>");
}
for (dayIndex in week){
  document.write("<li>" + week[dayIndex] + "</li>");
}
```

Converting an Array into a String

A useful feature of `Array` objects is the capability to combine the elements of a string to make a string object separated by a specific separator using the `join()` method. For example, the following code results in the time components being joined together into the format 12:10:36:

```
var timeArr = [12,10,36];
var timeStr = timeArr.join(":");
```

Checking to See Whether an Array Contains an Item

Often, you will need to check to see whether an array contains a certain item. You can do this by using the `indexOf()` method. If the item is not found in the list, a –1 will be returned. The following function writes a message to the browser if an item is in the week array:

```
function message(day){
  var week = ["Monday", "Tuesday", "Wednesday", "Thursday", "Friday"];
  if (week.indexOf(day) != -1){
    document.write("Happy " + day);
  }
}
```

Adding Items to and Removing Items from Arrays

You can use several methods to add items or remove them from `Array` objects using the various built-in methods. Table 6.5 gives you some ideas on the various methods used in this book.

TABLE 6.5 `Array` **Object Methods Used to Add or Remove Elements from Arrays**

Statement	Value of `x`	Value of `arr`
`var arr = [1,2,3,4,5];var x = 0;`	0	1,2,3,4,5
`x = arr.unshift("zero");`	6 (length)	zero,1,2,3,4,5
`x = arr.push(6,7,8);`	9 (length)	zero,1,2,3,4,5,6,7,8
`x = arr.shift();`	zero	1,2,3,4,5,6,7,8
`x = arr.pop()`	8	1,2,3,4,5,6,7
`x = arr.splice(3,3,"four","five","six")`	4,5,6	1,2,3,four,five,six,7
`x = arr.splice(3,1)`	four	1,2,3,five,six,7
`x = arr.splice(3)`	five,six,7	1,2,3

▼ TRY IT YOURSELF

Creating and Manipulating Arrays

In this exercise, you learn the creation and manipulation of arrays using various methods attached to the `Array` object. Use the following steps to build the file in Listing 6.2:

1. Create a source file named hour0602.html in the hour06 folder.

2. Add the usual basic elements (html, head, body).

3. Inside the `<head>` element, add a `<script>` element with a function named `writeIt()` and link it to the `onload` event of the `<body>` element, as shown next:

```
06 <script>
...
11    function writeIt(){
...
29    }
30 </script>
31    </head>
32    <body onload="writeIt()">
```

4. Add the following JavaScript function that accepts a message and an array argument as `msg` and `arr`. The array is converted to a string using the `join()` method. The method also writes the message and joined array string to the browser with some HTML formatting.

```
07    function writeArray(msg, arr){
08      var arrString = arr.join(" | ");
09      document.write("<b>"+ msg + ": </b>" + arrString + "<br><br>");
10    }
```

5. Add the following lines of code to the `writeIt()` function to create a couple of arrays and call the `writeArray()` function to write them to the browser. The `weekDays` array is created by the declaration; the `weekEnd` array is generated by creating a blank array and then pushing items into it.

```
12      var weekDays = ["Monday", "Tuesday", "Wednesday", "Thursday",
        ➡"Friday"];
13      writeArray("Week Days", weekDays);
14      var weekEnd = new Array();
15      weekEnd.push("Saturday");
16      weekEnd.push("Sunday");
17      writeArray("Weekend", weekEnd);
```

6. Use the following lines to create a new array with the full week array by combining the weekEnd. In line 18, the `concat([])` is a way of creating a copy of `weekDays`. We want Sunday at the first and Saturday at the end, so we use `unshift()` to push Sunday on to the front of the array and `push()` to append Saturday to the end.

```
18      var week = weekDays.concat([]);
19      week.unshift(weekEnd[1]);
```

```
20      week.push(weekEnd[0]);
21      writeArray("Week", week);
```

7. Create a `midWeek` array using the `slice()` function, as follows:

```
22      var midWeek = week.slice(2,5);
23      writeArray("Mid Week", midWeek);
```

8. Use the following code to create a sorted version of the full week and then iterate through each item in the `sortedWeek` array and write them out to the browser:

```
24      var sortedWeek = week.sort();
25      document.write("<b>Sorted Days :</b> <br>");
26      for (dayIndex in sortedWeek){
27        document.write(sortedWeek[dayIndex] + "<br>");
28      }
```

9. Open the page in the browser, and the output of the arrays that you created should be displayed, as shown in Figure 6.2.

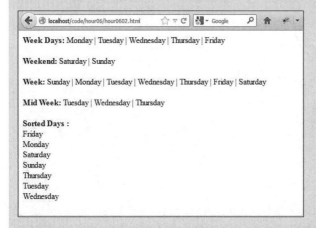

FIGURE 6.2
Output of Listing 6.2.

LISTING 6.2 Example of Creating and Manipulating `Array` Objects in JavaScript

```
01 <!DOCTYPE html>
02 <html>
03   <head>
04     <title>Hour 6-2</title>
05     <meta charset="utf-8" />
06 <script>
```

```
07    function writeArray(msg, arr){
08      var arrString = arr.join(" | ");
09      document.write("<b>"+ msg + ": </b>" + arrString + "<br><br>");
10    }
11    function writeIt(){
12      var weekDays = ["Monday", "Tuesday", "Wednesday", "Thursday", "Friday"];
13      writeArray("Week Days", weekDays);
14      var weekEnd = new Array();
15      weekEnd.push("Saturday");
16      weekEnd.push("Sunday");
17      writeArray("Weekend", weekEnd);
18      var week = weekDays.concat([]);
19      week.unshift(weekEnd[1]);
20      week.push(weekEnd[0]);
21      writeArray("Week", week);
22      var midWeek = week.slice(2,5);
23      writeArray("Mid Week", midWeek);
24      var sortedWeek = week.sort();
25      document.write("<b>Sorted Days :</b> <br>");
26      for (dayIndex in sortedWeek){
27        document.write(sortedWeek[dayIndex] + "<br>");
28      }
29    }
30  </script>
31    </head>
32    <body onload="writeIt()">
33    </body>
34  </html>
```

Date

The Date object provides access to the current time on the browser's system. This can be useful in a lot of ways, such as displaying time on the page, comparing time with the server via AJAX, timing certain events, and the like.

To get the current time on the system, use the following syntax:

```
var cDate = new Date();
document.write(cDate);
```

The string version of the date will be similar to the following:

```
Mon Dec 10 2012 17:30:27 GMT-0700 (Mountain Standard Time)
```

You can create a `Date` object using a string or a set of values based on the following syntax:

```
Date(year, month, day, hours, minutes, seconds, milliseconds)
```

For example, the following will create the same `Date` object:

```
var d1 = Date("2012, 12, 12, 12, 12, 12, 00");
var d2 = Date("December 12, 2012 12:12:12");
```

JavaScript enables you to compare dates using the normal logical comparisons (<, >, ==, and so on). For example, you could use the following code to compare the current time on the browser with what has been sent from the server as a timestamp: `"December 12, 2012 12:12:12"`.

```
var currentTime = new Date();
var serverTime = new Date("December 12, 2012 12:12:12");
if (currentTime>serverTime){
    alert("Mayans Wrong?");
}
```

Math

The `Math` object is really an interface to a mathematical library that provides a ton of time-saving functionality. The math library is much too large to go over in this book, but Table 6.6 introduces you to some of the more useful functions.

TABLE 6.6 Using the `Math` Object in JavaScript

Property/Method	Description	Output
Math.PI	Returns PI	3.14...
Math.E	Returns Euler's number	2.718...
Math.LN10	Returns the natural logarithm	2.302...
Math.floor(5/2)	Round down always	2
Math.ceil(5/2)	Round up always	3
Math.round(5/2)	Round up >= .5	3
Math.abs(1-10)	Absolute value	9
Math.exp(5)	Returns e^x	148.4131...
math.pow(2,16)	Returns x^y	65536
math.sqrt(16)	Returns square root	4
Math.floor ((Math.random()*100)+1)	Random number	0<?<100
Math.min(2,8,7,3,1)	Minimum of set	1
Math.max(2,8,7,3,1)	Maximum of set	8

Property/Method	Description	Output
`Math.sin(1)`	Returns sine	`0.84147...`
`Math.cos(1)`	Returns cosine	`0.54030...`

RegExp

When dynamically processing user input or even data coming back from the web server, an important tool is regular expressions. Regular expressions allow you to quickly match patterns in text and then act on those patterns.

JavaScript enables you to create a `RegExp` object that can be used to match patterns in strings using the following syntax:

```
var re = new RegExp(pattern,modifiers);
```

Or, more simply:

```
var re =/pattern/modifiers;
```

The pattern is a standard regular expression pattern, and the modifiers define the scope to apply the expression. Following is a list of the available modifiers in JavaScript:

▶ i—Perform matching that is not case sensitive.

▶ g—Perform a global match on all instances rather than just the first.

▶ m—Perform multiline match rather than stopping on the first `LF`/`CR` character.

The following shows an example of using a regular expression with a string `replace()` function to do a search for "yourself" that is not case sensitive and replace it with `"Your Friends"`.

```
var myStr = "Teach Yourself jQuery & JavaScript in 24 Hours";
var re = /yourself/i;
var newStr = myStr.replace(re, "Your Friends");
```

The value of `newStr`:

```
Teach Your Friends jQuery & JavaScript in 24 Hours
```

If you are not familiar with regular expressions, consider doing some research into it. There are some good books on the topic and several resources on the Web.

Creating Custom-Defined Objects

As you have seen so far, using the built-in JavaScript objects has several advantages. As you begin to write code that uses more and more data, you will find that you want to build your own custom objects with specific properties and methods. The following sections take you through the process of building custom JavaScript objects.

Defining JavaScript Objects

JavaScript objects can be defined using a couple of different ways. The simplest is the on-the-fly method, meaning that you create a generic object and then add properties to it as you need it.

For example, to create a user object and assign a first and last name, you use the following code:

```
var user = new Object();
user.first="Brad";
user.last="Dayley";
```

You could also accomplish the same effect through a direct assignment using the following syntax where the object is enclosed in { } brackets and the properties are defined using property:value syntax, as shown next:

```
var user = {'first':'Brad','last':'Dayley'};
```

These first two options work very well for simple objects that you do not need to reuse later. A better method is to enclose the object inside its own function block. This has the advantage of enabling you to keep all the code pertaining to the object local to the object itself. For example:

```
function User(first, last){
  this.first = first;
  this.last = last;
}
var user = new User("Brad", "Dayley");
```

The end result of these methods is essentially the same. You have an object with properties that that can be referenced using dot syntax, as shown next:

```
document.write(user.first + " " + user.last);
```

Adding Methods to JavaScript Objects

If there is code specific to a custom object, you want to attach that code as methods to the object itself. There are a couple of ways to do this depending on how the object was created.

The first way is to define a static function and then assign it as a property of the object. Following is an example of assigning a static function when defining objects on-the-fly:

```
var user = new Object();
user.first="Brad";
user.last="Dayley";
user.getFullName = makeFullName;
var user2 = {'first':'Brad', 'last':'Dayley',
             'getFullName':makeFullName};
function makeFullName(){
  return this.first + " " + this.last;
}
document.write(user.getFullName());
```

The function `makeFullName()` combines and returns the first and last properties of the object as a string. Notice that the function accesses the properties using the `this` keyword. `this` refers to the current instance of the object. Also notice that the assignment of the `makeFullName()` to `getFullName` omits the `()` parentheses; this sets `user.getFullName` equal to the function itself instead of the value it returns.

If you created the object using the better enclosed method, the function can be defined inside the object using the following syntax. Notice that `getFullName` is set to a newly defined function that returns the value in the same way that the static function `makeFullName()` did.

```
function User(first, last){
  this.first = first;
  this.last = last;
  this.getFullName = function(){
      return this.first + " " + this.last;
    };
}
```

Using a Prototyping Object Pattern

An even more advanced method of creating objects is using a prototyping pattern. The prototyping pattern is implemented by defining the functions inside the prototype attribute of the object instead of the object itself. The reason prototyping is better is that the functions defined in the prototype are created only once when the JavaScript is loaded, instead of each time a new object is created.

The following example shows the code necessary to implement the prototyping pattern. Notice that you define the object `UserP` and then you set `UserP.prototype` to include the `getFullName()` function. You can include as many functions in the `prototype` as you like. Each time a new object is created, those functions will be available.

```
function UserP(first, last){
  this.first = first;
  this.last = last;
}
```

```
UserP.prototype = {
  getFullName: function(){
      return this.first + " " + this.last;
    }
};
```

Creating and Using Custom Objects

In this section, you use the prototyping pattern to create and use an array of custom JavaScript objects. Use the following steps to build the file in Listing 6.3:

1. Create a source file named hour0603.html in the hour06 folder.

2. Add the usual basic elements (html, head, body).

3. Inside the `<head>` element, add a `<script>` element with a function named `writeIt()` and link it to the `onload` event of the `<body>` element, as shown next:

```
06 <script>
07    function writeIt(){
...
38    }
39 </script>
40    </head>
41    <body onload="writeIt()">
```

4. Add the following function below `writeIt()`. This function will be used to create custom `Character` objects. The function accepts a `first` and `last` name, the `land` where the character is from, and the `race`.

```
25    function Character(first, last, land, race){
26       this.first = first;
27       this.last = last;
28       this.race = race;
29       this.land = land;
30    }
```

5. Add the following prototype definition that provides two functions, `getFullName()` and `getDetails()`:

```
31    Character.prototype = {
32       getFullName: function(){
33          return this.first + " " + this.last;
34       },
35       getDetails: function(){
36          return "is a " + this.race + " of the " + this.land;
37       }
38    }
```

6. Inside the `writeIt()` function, add the following lines of code that create the characters array and populate it with character objects. The objects are created using the `new` keyword.

```
08      var characters = new Array();
09      characters.push(new Character("Gandolf", "the White", "Middle Earth",
        ➥"Wizard"));
10      characters.push(new Character("Bilbo", "Baggins", "Shire", "Hobbit"));
11      characters.push(new Character("Frodo", "Baggins", "Shire", "Hobbit"));
12      characters.push(new Character("Aragorn", "son of Arathorn", "Dunedain",
        ➥"Man"));
```

7. Add the following code to create the `Legolas` object. Notice that we pass in only the `first` name. Lines 14 and 15 assign the additional `land` and `race` values. This provides an example of another method to assign values to objects.

```
13      legolas = new Character("Legolas", "", "", "");
14      legolas.land = "Woodland Realm";
15      legolas.race = "Elf";
16      characters.push(legolas);
```

8. Add the following `for` loop that iterates through each element of the characters array and writes information about the character to the browser. Line 19 assigns a new property value of `number` to the `Character` object. Notice that after it is assigned, we are able to access `character.number` to write it out as part of the string.

```
17      for (var i=0; i<characters.length; i++){
18          var character = characters[i];
19          character.number = i+1;
20          document.write(character.number + ". " +
21                          character.getFullName() + " " +
22                          character.getDetails() + "<br>");
23      }
```

9. Open the page in the browser, and the output of the objects that you created should be displayed, as shown in Figure 6.3.

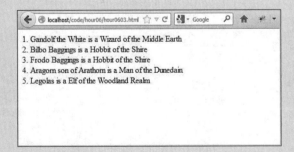

FIGURE 6.3
Output of Listing 6.3.

LISTING 6.3 Example of Creating and Manipulating `Array` Objects in JavaScript ▼

```
01 <!DOCTYPE html>
02 <html>
03   <head>
04     <title>Hour 6-3</title>
05     <meta charset="utf-8" />
06 <script>
07   function writeIt(){
08     var characters = new Array();
09     characters.push(new Character("Gandolf", "the White", "Middle Earth",
       ➥"Wizard"));
10     characters.push(new Character("Bilbo", "Baggins", "Shire", "Hobbit"));
11     characters.push(new Character("Frodo", "Baggins", "Shire", "Hobbit"));
12     characters.push(new Character("Aragorn", "son of Arathorn", "Dunedain",
       ➥"Man"));
13     legolas = new Character("Legolas", "", "", "");
14     legolas.land = "Woodland Realm";
15     legolas.race = "Elf";
16     characters.push(legolas);
17     for (var i=0; i<characters.length; i++){
18       var character = characters[i];
19       character.number = i+1;
20       document.write(character.number + ". " +
21                      character.getFullName() + " " +
22                      character.getDetails() + "<br>");
23     }
24   }
25   function Character(first, last, land, race){
26     this.first = first;
27     this.last = last;
28     this.race = race;
29     this.land = land;
30   }
31   Character.prototype = {
32     getFullName: function(){
33         return this.first + " " + this.last;
34     },
35     getDetails: function(){
36         return "is a " + this.race + " of the " + this.land;
37     }
38   };
39 </script>
40   </head>
41   <body onload="writeIt()">
42   </body>
43 </html>
```

Summary

In this hour, we discussed how JavaScript objects provide a way to create much cleaner and more efficient code. You learned how objects support attaching properties and methods to a single variable name.

You also were introduced to several built-in objects such as `Array` and `String`. The built-in objects provide properties and methods that provide quick functionality with little code—for example, using the `Date` object to get the system time, compare times, and create time-based output to the browser.

Finally, you got a chance to create and manipulate your own JavaScript objects with properties and methods. Creating custom objects will help you organize your scripts to be more efficient.

Q&A

Q. What is the difference between built-in, custom, DOM objects and jQuery objects?

A. Only how they are defined. Built-in objects are automatically defined and available as part of the language sometimes; as with arrays or strings, they are automatically instantiated during an assignment statement. DOM objects are also built in to the JavaScript language. You can create an instance of them in JavaScript, but they are also created based on the tags in the HTML file. jQuery objects are defined and created inside the jQuery library. At the low level, they are all just JavaScript objects. Each has properties and methods that can be used to simplify JavaScript tasks.

Q. The new keyword creates a new instance of an object, but how do I get rid of an instance of an object to free up memory and such?

A. JavaScript automatically cleans up memory for you when a variable goes out of scope. To clean up an instance of a JavaScript object, make it go out of scope. For example, if it is part of an array, you can use the `pop()` function to remove it, or, if you want all of an array of objects to be freed up, set the array variable to `null`.

Workshop

The workshop consists of a set of questions and answers designed to solidify your understanding of the material covered in this hour. Try to answer the questions before looking at the answers.

Quiz

1. What is the `new` keyword for?
2. How do you find the length of a JavaScript array?

3. True or False: The following statement creates a copy of the `Array` object named `myArr`:

```
var newArr = myArr.concat([])
```

4. True or False: You cannot assign new properties to an existing JavaScript object.

Quiz Answers

1. The `new` keyword is used to create a new instance of an object.

2. The length of JavaScript `String` and `Array` objects can be found using the `length` property. For example:

```
myArr.length
```

3. True.

4. False.

Exercises

1. Extend the code in Listing 6.1 to include a much more complete madlib. Add several attributes that should be included in the final string.

2. Use the code in Listing 6.2 as an outline to create and display arrays that contain the summer months, winter months, autumn months, and spring months. Then combine the arrays into a single array containing all the months of the year.

3. Extend Listing 6.3 to add all the members of the "Fellowship of the Rings." A listing can be found by doing an Internet search. Also include additional attributes such as weapon, age, or height.

Accessing DOM Elements Using JavaScript and jQuery Objects

What You'll Learn in This Hour:

▶ The difference between jQuery and JavaScript DOM objects

▶ How to tell if an object is jQuery or DOM

▶ How to get a jQuery object from a DOM object

▶ How to get a DOM object from a jQuery object

▶ How to use jQuery selectors to quickly find DOM elements

The most important part of dynamic web development is the capability to access the DOM elements quickly and efficiently. JavaScript inherently provides functionality to access the DOM elements. It can be useful at times; however, this is the area where jQuery really stands out and you understand the need for jQuery on top of JavaScript.

In the following sections, you learn about the basic structure of jQuery and JavaScript DOM objects, how to determine whether an object is jQuery or DOM, and how to switch between them. The rest of the hour discusses methods you can use to find and access the DOM elements using jQuery and JavaScript.

Understanding DOM Objects Versus jQuery Objects

You need to understand the difference between DOM objects and jQuery objects and how to manipulate and use both to be effective when creating dynamic web pages. In this section, you learn about these types of objects and how to navigate between them.

Introducing JavaScript DOM Objects

DOM objects are the objects that the web browser is using to render elements on the web page. Consequently, DOM objects have a great deal of functions and attributes. The advantage with working with DOM objects is that you have direct access to everything you need to manipulate the HTML element.

The disadvantage of DOM objects is that most of the attached functions and attributes are things that the browser needs and are not necessarily useful when you're working with JavaScript. That means that the DOM object has a lot of properties and methods that encumber your debugging environment, such as Firebug or other JavaScript consoles.

Table 7.1 provides a list of some of the important attributes and methods of DOM objects that you should be aware of. The list is not comprehensive; it is intended to give you an idea of things that you can access from a DOM object.

TABLE 7.1 Some of the More Commonly Used Attributes/Methods Attached to DOM Objects

Attribute/Method	Description
parentNode	Because DOM objects are part of a tree, they always have a link to their direct parent.
childNodes	As with parent nodes, if the DOM object has children, this attribute allows you to access them as an array.
click()	This enables you to execute and/or change the event handler that gets called when the HTML element is clicked.
innerHTML	Access to the content text that is placed between the elements' starting and ending tags. For example, the following line of code changes the inner HTML of an object. Notice that you are able to include DOM tags in with the HTML text. These will be rendered with the page: `obj.innerHTML = "This is <span>SOME</span> text";`
outerHTML	Access to the full text, including tags of the HTML element.
value	Some elements such as options and inputs contain a `value` attribute.
id	Direct access to the `id` attribute of the HTML element.
class	Direct access to the `class` attribute of the HTML element.
style	Direct access to the CSS `style` of the element. For example, to set the color you could use `obj.style.color="red";`
getAttribute(attribute)	Gets the `attribute` value in the DOM object. For example, to get the `name` attribute of an object, use `obj.getAttribute("name")`
setAttribute(attribute, value)	Sets the `value` of `attribute` in the DOM object. For example, to set the `href` attribute of an object, you could use `obj.setAttribute("href", "http://dayleycreations.com");`

Attribute/Method	Description
appendChild(object)	Appends a child DOM element to the object. For example, to add a new `<option>` element to a `<select>` object, you could use
	`var o = new Option("New", 1, false, false);` `selectObj.appendObject(o);`

Introducing jQuery Objects

jQuery objects are basically wrapper objects around a set of DOM elements. The jQuery objects are still JavaScript objects and provide access to the DOM elements—however, in a much different, much easier, and often much more effective way.

The most important thing to remember is that a jQuery object may represent a single DOM object or it may represent a set of many DOM objects. So if you apply an operation on the jQuery object, it may apply to many DOM objects.

The biggest advantage to jQuery objects is how easy it is to search HTML elements in a web page. Another advantage is that the jQuery library wraps methods and attributes specifically to make it easier for JavaScript and jQuery developers to manipulate and work with different groups of objects. Calling a method on a jQuery object can apply to one or many DOM elements without the need to iterate through a list.

Table 7.2 provides a list of some of the important methods of jQuery objects that you should be aware of. The list is not comprehensive; it is intended to give you an idea of things that you can access from a jQuery object.

TABLE 7.2 Some of the More Commonly Used Methods Attached to jQuery Objects

Method	Description
html([newHTML])	Gets the inner HTML text of the object or sets it to the optional newHTML.
val([newValue])	Gets the value of the object or sets it to the optional newValue argument if one is passed. For example, to set the value of an element, use
	`$("#myInput").val("test");`
attr(attribute, [value])	Enables you to get the value of an attribute or set it to the optional value argument if one is passed. For example, to set the value of the href attribute, use
	`$("#mainLink").attr("href", "www.dayleycreations.com");`

Method	Description
addClass(class)	Enables you to add a class attribute value that can result in new CSS rules being applied to the object.
css(property, [value])	Enables you to get or set a CSS property value for the jQuery object. For example, to set the background-color for all <div> elements, use $("div").css("backgorund-color", "yellow");
click([function])	Enables you to get the onclick hander for the jQuery object or set a function definition for a new onclick handler.
height([value])	Gets or sets the height of the DOM elements. If the value is specified, the object's height is set; otherwise, the value of the object's height is returned.
width([value])	Gets or sets the width of the DOM elements.
hide()	Enables you to hide the DOM objects represented by the jQuery object.
show()	Enables you to unhide the DOM objects represented by the jQuery object.

Determining Whether an Object Is DOM or jQuery

Occasionally, you find yourself in a situation where you have an object and you are not sure whether it is a jQuery object, a DOM object, or some other JavaScript object. There is a simple way to tell the difference.

To tell whether an object is a jQuery object, use the following if syntax to check to see whether the object has the jquery attribute:

```
if( obj.jquery ) {
  . . .
```

To tell whether an object is a DOM object, use the following if syntax to check to see whether the object has the nodeType attribute:

```
if( obj.nodeType ) {
  . . .
```

Changing an Object from DOM to jQuery and Back

What do you do if you have a jQuery object but you want to use code intended for DOM objects, or vice versa? The answer is to convert the object to the other type.

The `.get()` method returns the JavaScript version of the jQuery element set in the form of an array of DOM objects. Use the following code to call the `get()` function that returns the DOM object of the HTML element represented by the jQuery object:

```
var domObj = jqueryObj.get();
```

Conversely, the `$()` or `jquery()` method creates a new jQuery object from JavaScript. Use the following code to execute the `$()` function to wrap the DOM object as a jQuery object:

```
var jqueryObj = $(domObj);
```

Accessing DOM Objects from JavaScript

To be able to manipulate HTML elements from JavaScript, you first need to gain access to the DOM object. You can use a few different methods to do that.

Finding DOM Objects by ID

The simplest is to find an HTML element using the value of the `id` attribute using the `getElementById(id)` function. `getElementById(id)` searches the DOM for an object with a matching `id` attribute.

For example, the following code searches for the HTML element with `id="container"`:

```
var containerObj = document.getElementById("container");
```

Finding DOM Objects by Class Name

You can also search for HTML elements by their `class` attribute using the `getElementsByClassName(class)`. This function returns a list of DOM objects with matching `class` attributes. You can then iterate over that list using a JavaScript loop and apply changes to each DOM element.

For example, the following retrieves a list of HTML elements with `class="myClass"` and then iterates through them:

```
var objs = document.getElementsByClassName("myClass");
for (var i=0; i<objs.length; i++){
  var htmlElement = objs[i];
  ...
}
```

Finding DOM Objects by Tag Name

Another way to search for HTML elements is by their HTML tag, using the `getElementsByTagName(tag)`. This function returns a list of DOM objects with matching

HTML tag. You can then iterate over that list using a JavaScript loop and apply changes to each DOM element.

For example, the following code retrieves a list of the `<div>` HTML elements and then iterates through them:

```
var objs = document.getElementsByClassName("div");
for (var i=0; i<objs.length; i++){
  var htmlElement = objs[i];
  ...
}
```

▼ TRY IT YOURSELF

Using JavaScript to Access DOM Objects

In this example, you use JavaScript to find different elements and read values and write values to them. This is a basic example designed to give you a chance to use JavaScript to access DOM objects. The full scripts used in the example are shown in Listing 7.1.

1. In Aptana, create a source folder named hour07. Inside the hour07 folder, create a js and css folder.

2. Create a source file named hour0701.html in the hour07 folder.

3. Add the usual basic elements (html, head, body).

4. Inside the `<head>` element, add the following `<script>` and `<link>` elements, shown in Listing 7.1-html, which will be used to load the JavaScript and CSS rules that will be defined later:
```
06    <script type="text/javascript" src="js/hour0701.js"></script>
07    <link rel="stylesheet" type="text/css" href="css/hour0701.css">
```

5. Add the following `<input>` elements to define a text box and a button. Notice that on the button you need to add the `onclick` handler, which allows you to run your dynamic script when the button is clicked. The text input has the `id="textIn"`.
```
10    <input id="textIn" type="text"/>
11    <input type="button" onclick="textChange()" value="Update" /><br>
```

6. Add the following `<span>` and `<p>` elements. For now they are empty; the dynamic code will update them.
```
12    <span class="heading"></span>
13    <p id="p1"></p>
14    <span class="heading"></span>
15    <p id="p2"></p>
```

7. Create a file called hour07/js/hour0701.js.

8. Create a function called `textChange()`, as shown in Listing 7.1-js. This function will be called when the button is clicked.

9. Add the following variable definition to the `textChange()` function to find the text input by the id `"textIn"`:

```
02    var inElement = document.getElementById("textIn");
```

10. Add the following variable definition to get all the `<p>` elements by tag name:

```
03    var outElements = document.getElementsByTagName("p");
```

11. Add the following variable definition to get all the elements with the `class="heading"`.

```
04    var headingElements = document.getElementsByClassName("heading");
```

12. Add the `for` loop shown in Listing 7.1-js that iterates through the `outElements` that were found in the document. For each element, you set the `innerHTML` text to the `inElement.value`, which is what is typed into the text box.

13. Create a file called hour07/css/hour0701.css and add the code shown in Listing 7.1-css. This stylizes the `out` elements a bit.

14. Save the three files and open the hour0701.html file in a web browser to check out the web page shown in Figure 7.1. Try typing in some text and clicking the Update button.

FIGURE 7.1
A simple JavaScript web page that allows the user to enter text and update components.

LISTING 7.1-html   HTML File That Loads JavaScript and Attaches an Event Handler to a Button Element to Update the Page

```
01 <!DOCTYPE html>
02 <html>
03   <head>
04     <title>Hour 7-1</title>
05     <meta charset="utf-8" />
06     <script type="text/javascript" src="js/hour0701.js"></script>
07     <link rel="stylesheet" type="text/css" href="css/hour0701.css">
08   </head>
09   <body>
10     <input id="textIn" type="text"/>
11     <input type="button" onclick="textChange()" value="Update" /><br>
12     <span class="heading"></span>
13     <p id="p1"></p>
14     <span class="heading"></span>
15     <p id="p2"></p>
16   </body>
17 </html>
```

LISTING 7.1-js   JavaScript File Contains a Function Showing Examples of Accessing Variables by id, tag, and class Attributes

```
01 function textChange(){
02   var inElement = document.getElementById("textIn");
03   var outElements = document.getElementsByTagName("p");
04   var headingElements = document.getElementsByClassName("heading");
05   for(var i=0; i<outElements.length; i++){
06     var outItem = outElements[i];
07     headingElements[i].innerHTML = "Updating " + (i+1) + " to " +
      ➡inElement.value;
08     outItem.innerHTML = inElement.value;
09   }
10 }
```

LISTING 7.1-css   CSS That Styles <p> Elements

```
1 p{
2   font-weight:bold;
3   font-size:50px;
4   margin:5px;
5 }
```

Using jQuery Selectors

Unlike JavaScript, jQuery enables you to find HTML elements in countless ways using selectors. Yes, just like CSS selectors. In fact, most of the jQuery selectors were taken from CSS, providing a more seamless transition between the two.

As you will find in upcoming sections, jQuery selectors make it very easy to select just about any group of HTML elements. Keep in mind, though, that jQuery selectors return jQuery objects, not DOM objects.

jQuery selector syntax is very straightforward. After the jQuery library is loaded, use `$(selector)`. For example:

`$("#myElement")`

CAUTION

Several meta characters are used in jQuery selector syntax. If you want to use any of the meta characters, such as `!"#$%&'()*+,./:;<=>?@[\]^`{|}~` ), as a part of a class/ID/name, you will need to escape the character with `\\` two backslashes. For example, if you have an element with `id="my.element"`, you would use the selector `$("#my\\.element")`.

As with CSS selectors, the best way to introduce you to jQuery selectors is to show you some examples. The following sections take you through some examples of different types of jQuery selectors. These sections only scratch the surface. You can go to the following location to review the selector documentation when you get a chance:

`http://api.jquery.com/category/selectors/`

Applying Basic Selectors

The most commonly used selectors are the basic ones. The basic selectors focus on the `id` attribute, `class` attribute, and `tag` name of HTML elements. Table 7.3 list some examples to show you how to define some of the basic selectors.

TABLE 7.3 Examples of Using Basic jQuery Selectors

Selector Syntax/Example	Description
`$("*")`	Selects all HTML elements.
`$(".class")` `$(".container")`	Selects elements based on the `class` attribute. Example: Selects all HTML elements with `class="container"`. The `.` character prefix denotes a class name.

Selector Syntax/Example	Description
$("#id") $("#menu")	Selects an element based on the id attribute. Example: Selects the HTML elements with id="menu". The # character prefix denotes an id value.
$("element") $("div")	Selects elements based on tag type. Example: Selects all the <div> elements.
$("element,element...") $("div, span, p")	Selects multiple types of elements based on tag. Example: Selects all <div>, <span>, and <p> elements. You can also specify multiple elements separated by a comma.
$("element.class") $("ul.bigLists")	Selects elements of a specific tag and class. Example: Selects all <ul> elements that have class="bigList" by combining the element name and class. Note that there is no space between the element and the class name.

Applying Attribute Selectors

Another way to use jQuery selectors is to select HTML elements by their attribute values. It can be a default attribute or one that you have added to the HTML elements. Attribute values are denoted in the selector syntax by being enclosed in [] brackets. Table 7.4 shows some of the ways that attribute selectors can be applied.

TABLE 7.4 Examples of Using Attribute jQuery Selectors

Selector Syntax/Example	Description
$([attribute=value]") $("input[value=0]")	Selects elements where attribute attr=value. Example: Selects all <input> elements that have a value attribute equal to 0.
$([attr*=value]) $("p[class*=Content")	Attribute attr contains value. Example: Selects all HTML elements with "Content" in the class name. For example, all of the following <p> elements would be selected: <p class="leftContent">...</p> <p class="cenerContent">...</p> <p class="rightContent">...</p>

Selector Syntax/Example	Description
`$("[attr^=value]")` `$("img[src^='icons\\/']")`	Attribute `attr` begins with value. Example: Selects all `<img>` elements whose `src` attribute starts with `"icons/"`. Notice that because the expression was not simple text, quotes were required around the value. Also notice that the / character had to be escaped with `\\`.

`$("[attr!=value]")`
`$("input[value!=`
`'default text']")`
	Attribute `attr` does not equal value.
	
	Example: Selects all the `<input>` elements where the value does not equal `"default text"` or that do not have a value attribute.

`$("[attr]")` `$("p[id]")`	Selects elements that have attribute `attr`. Example: Selects all `<p>` elements that have an `id` attribute.

`$("[attr][attr2$=value]")`
`$("p[id][class$=Menu]")`
	Selects elements that have attribute `attr` and have attribute `attr2` equal to `value`.
	
	Example: Selects all `<p>` elements that have an `id` attribute and have a `class` attribute that ends with `"Menu"`. For example, only the top two of the following HTML elements would be selected:
	`<p id="topMenu" class=" topMenu ">...</p>`
	`<p id="topMenu" class="leftMenu">...</p>`
	`<p id="contentMenu" class="contentMenuItem">...</p>`
	`<p class="contentMenu">...</p>`

Applying Content Selectors

Another set of useful jQuery selectors are the content filter selectors. These selectors allow you to select HTML elements based on the content inside the HTML element. Table 7.5 shows examples of using content selectors.

TABLE 7.5   Examples of Using Content jQuery Selectors

Selector Syntax/Example	Description
`$(":contains(value)")` `$("div:contains('Open Source')")`	Selects elements that have the text in value in their contents. Example: Selects all `<div>` elements that contain the text `"Open Source"`.

Selector Syntax/Example	Description

`$(":has(element)")`
 `$("div:has(span) ")`
	Selects elements that contain a specific child element.
	
	 Example: Selects all `<div>` elements that contain a `<span>` element. For example, only the first of the following elements would be selected:
	 `<div><span>Span Text</span></div>`
	 `<div>No Span Text</div>`

`$(":empty")` `$("div:empty")`	Selects elements that have no content. Example: Selects all `<div>` elements that have no content.
`$(":parent")` `$("div:parent")`	Inverse of `:empty`, selects elements that have at least some content. Example: Selects all `<div>` elements that have at least some content.

Applying Hierarchy Selectors

An important set of jQuery selectors are the hierarchy selectors. These selectors allow you to select HTML elements based on the DOM hierarchy. This enables you to write dynamic code that is more content aware by only selecting elements based on parents, children, or other elements around them in the DOM tree. Table 7.6 shows some examples of hierarchy selectors.

TABLE 7.6   Examples of Using Hierarchy jQuery Selectors

Selector Syntax/Example	Description
`$(" ancestor element")` `$("div span")`	Selects elements of a type that have an ancestor of type ancestor and match `element`. Example: Selects all `<span>` elements that have an ancestor that is a `<div>`. The `<div>` element does not need to be the immediate ancestor. For example, the following `<span>` element would still be selected: `<div><p>Some <span>Span Text</span></p></div>`
`$("parent > child")` `$("div.menu > span ")`	Selects elements with a specific parent type. Example: Selects all `<span>` elements that have an immediate parent element that is a `<div>` with `class="menu"`.

Selector Syntax/Example	Description
`$("prev + next")` `$("label + input.textItem")`	Selects elements immediately followed by a specific type of element. Example: Selects all `<label>` elements that are immediately followed by an `<input>` element that has `class="textItem"`.

`$("prev ~ siblings")`
`$("#menu ~ div")`
	Selects elements that are after the `prev`, have the same parent, and match the siblings selector.
	
	Example: Selects all `<div>` elements that are siblings of the element that has `id="menu"` and that come after the "#menu" item in the DOM tree. Note that `<div>` elements that come before will not be selected. For example, only the last two elements will be selected:
	
	`<div>...</div>`
	`<ul id="menu> ... </ul>`
	`<span> ... <span>`
	`<div> ... </div>`
	`<div> ... </div>`

NOTE

It is always best to be as specific as possible when designing your jQuery selectors. For example, if you want to select all the span elements with `class="menu"` and these elements are only under the `<div>` element with `id="menuDiv"`, then `$("div#menuDiv .menu")` would be much more efficient than `$(".menu")` because it would limit the search to the `<div>` element before checking from the menu `class` attribute.

Applying Form Selectors

An extremely useful set of selectors when working with dynamic HTML forms are the form jQuery selectors. These selectors enable you to select elements in the form based on the state of the form element. Table 7.7 shows some examples of form selectors.

TABLE 7.7 Examples of Using Form jQuery Selectors

Selector Syntax/Example	Description
`$(":checked")` `$("input:checked")`	Selects elements with checked attribute true. Example: Selects all `<input>` elements that are currently in a checked state.

Selector Syntax/Example	Description
`$(":selected")` `$("option:selected")`	Selects elements with the `selected` attribute true. Example: Selects all `<option>` elements that are currently selected.
`$(":focus")` `$(":focus")`	Selects elements that are in focus in the form. Example: Selects all HTML elements that are currently in focus.
`$(":enabled")` `$("input:enabled")`	Selects enabled elements. Example: Selects all the `<input>` elements that are in the enabled state.
`$("disabled")` `$("input:disabled")`	Selects disabled elements. Example: Selects all the `<input>` elements that are in the disabled state.

Applying Visibility Selectors

If you are using visibility to control the flow and interactions of your web page components, using the visibility jQuery selectors makes it simple to select the HTML elements that are hidden or visible. Table 7.8 shows some examples of visibility selectors.

TABLE 7.8 Examples of Using Visibility jQuery Selectors

Selector Syntax/Example	Description
`$(":visible")` `$("div:visible")`	Selects visible elements. Example: Selects all `<div>` elements that currently have at least some height and width, meaning they consume space in the browser. This will even include elements that are hidden by `visibility:hidden` or `opacity:0` because they still take up space.
`$(":hidden")` `$("div:hidden ")`	Selects hidden elements. Example: Selects all `<div>` elements that currently have the CSS property of `visibility:hidden` or `opacity:0`.

Applying Filtered Selectors

Often you will need to refine your jQuery selectors down to a more specific subset. One way to accomplish that is to use filtered selectors. Filtered selectors append a filter on the end of the selector statement that limits the results returned by the selector. Table 7.9 shows some examples of adding filters to selectors.

TABLE 7.9 Examples of Using Filtered jQuery Selectors

Selector Syntax/Example	Description
`$(":even")` `$("tr:even")`	Filters out all the odd indexed elements. Example: Selects all `<tr>` elements and then filters the results down to only the even-numbered items; for example, second, fourth, sixth, and so on.
`$(":odd")` `$("li:odd")`	Filters out all the even indexed elements. Example: Selects all `<li>` elements and then filters the results down to only the odd-numbered items; for example, first, third, fifth, and so on.
`$(":first")` `$("div:first")`	Filters out everything but the first element. Example: Selects only the first `<div>` element encountered.
`$(":last")` `$("div:last")`	Filters out all but the last element. Example: Selects only the last `<div>` element encountered.
`$(":header")` `$(":header")`	Selects elements that are header types, such as `<h1>`, `<h2>`, `<h3>`, and so on. Example: Selects all header elements.
`$(":eq(index)")` `$("div:eq(5)")`	Selects the element at a specific zero-based index. Example: Selects the sixth `<div>` element encountered. The reason that the sixth element and not the fifth is selected is that the index is zero based, so 0 would be the first.
`$(":gt(index)")` `$("li:gt(1)")`	Greater than, filters the list to only include elements after a specific zero-based index. Example: Selects every `<li>` element after the second one encountered. Again, this index is zero based.
`$(":lt(index)")` `$("li:lt(2)")`	Less than, filters the list to only include elements before a specific zero-based index. Example: Selects only the first and second `<li>` elements encountered. Again, this index is zero based.
`$(":animated")` `$(":animated")`	Selects elements that are currently being animated. Example: Selects all elements that are currently being animated.

▼ TRY IT YOURSELF

Using jQuery to Access DOM Objects

In this example, you use jQuery to find different elements and read values and write values to them. This is another basic example designed to help solidify the concepts of how jQuery selectors enable you to find and access DOM elements. You see some more advanced examples later in this hour. The full scripts used in the example are shown in Listing 7.2.

1. In the hour07 folder, create the source files named hour0702.html, js/hour0702.js, and css/hour0702.css.

2. Open hour0702.html and add the usual basic elements (html, head, body).

3. Inside the `<head>` element, add the following `<script>` and `<link>` elements, shown in Listing 7.2-html, that will be used to load the jQuery, JavaScript, and CSS:

```
06      <script src="../js/jquery.min.js"></script>
07      <script type="text/javascript" src="js/hour0702.js"></script>
08      <link rel="stylesheet" type="text/css" href="css/hour0702.css">
```

4. Now add the following `<span>` elements that will be styled as buttons. Each `<span>` element contains a different `onclick` handler that will allow you to run your dynamic script when it is clicked.

```
11      <span onclick="setEven()">Even</span>
12      <span onclick="setOdd()">Odd</span>
13      <span onclick="setFirst4()">First 4</span>
```

5. Add the `<p>` and `<ul>` elements shown in lines 14–24 of Listing 7.2-html to add a list of planets to the page.

6. Open the file hour0702.css and add the contents of Listing 7.2-css that style the `<span>` elements as buttons and the `<p>` element as a list header.

7. Open the hour0702.js files so that you can add the event handlers for the `<span>` elements.

8. Add a JavaScript function named `setEven()` to act as an event handler.

9. Add the following line that uses jQuery to select all `<li>` and `<span>` elements and clears the CSS `font-weight` value:

```
02   $("li, span").css("font-weight","");
```

10. Add the following lines that define a variable named $evenItems to the results of the selector that selects all `<li>` elements and then filters the list to only those with an even index. Line 3 uses the $evenItems variable to set the CSS `font-weight` property of those items to bold.

```
03   var $evenItems = $("li:even");
04   $evenItems.css("font-weight","bold");
```

11. Add the following line that uses jQuery to select all `<span>` elements that contain "Even" in their contents and sets the CSS `font-weight` property to `bold`.

```
05    $("span:contains(Even)").css("font-weight","bold");
```

12. Add the following line that uses jQuery to select the elements with `class="label"` to select the `<p>` element. The `.html("Even")` part of the statement changes the `innerHTML` property of the selection to "Even", thus changing the heading.

```
06    $(".label").html("Even");
```

13. Add the other two event handlers, `setOdd()` and `setFirst4()`, shown in Listing 7.2-js, which basically do the same thing, but for a different set of list items.

14. Save the three files and open the hour0702.html file in a web browser to check out the web page shown in Figure 7.2. Try clicking the different buttons and watch the button, heading, and list items change.

FIGURE 7.2
A simple JavaScript web page that uses jQuery to dynamically change page elements based on user interaction.

LISTING 7.2-html **HTML File That Loads jQuery and JavaScript and Attaches Event Handler Elements to Provide User Interaction**

```
01 <!DOCTYPE html>
02 <html>
03    <head>
04      <title>Hour 7-2</title>
05      <meta charset="utf-8" />
06      <script src="../js/jquery.min.js"></script>
07      <script type="text/javascript" src="js/hour0702.js"></script>
08      <link rel="stylesheet" type="text/css" href="css/hour0702.css">
```

```
09    </head>
10    <body>
11      <span onclick="setEven()">Even</span>
12      <span onclick="setOdd()">Odd</span>
13      <span onclick="setFirst4()">First 4</span>
14      <p class="label">Planets</p>
15      <ul>
16        <li>Mercury</li>
17        <li>Venus</li>
18        <li>Earth</li>
19        <li>Mars</li>
20        <li>Jupiter</li>
21        <li>Saturn</li>
22        <li>Uranus</li>
23        <li>Neptune</li>
24      </ul>
25    </body>
26  </html>
```

LISTING 7.2-js JavaScript File Containing Event Handler Functions That Use jQuery in Various Ways to Select and Alter Page Elements

```
01 function setEven(){
02    $("li, span").css("font-weight","");
03    var $evenItems = $("li:even");
04    $evenItems.css("font-weight","bold");
05    $("span:contains(Even)").css("font-weight","bold");
06    $(".label").html("Even");
07 }
08 function setOdd(){
09    $("li, span").css("font-weight","");
10    var $oddItems = $("li:odd");
11    $oddItems.css("font-weight","bold");
12    $("span:contains(Odd)").css("font-weight","bold");
13    $(".label").html("Odd");
14 }
15 function setFirst4(){
16    $("li, span").css("font-weight","");
17    var $first4 = $("li:lt(4)");
18    $first4.css("font-weight","bold");
19    $("span:contains('First 4')").css("font-weight","bold");
20    $(".label").html("First 4");
21 }
```

LISTING 7.2-css **CSS That Styles `<span>` Elements and Elements with class="label"**

```
01 span{
02    padding:2px;
03    border:3px ridge blue;
04    color:white;
05    background:blue;
06    cursor:pointer;
07 }
08 .label{
09    font-size:25px;
10    margin:10px;
11 }
```

Summary

In this hour, you learned about using jQuery and JavaScript objects to find and access DOM elements. This is the most critical piece of dynamic programming, because you must be able to provide efficient access to the DOM elements to be able to manipulate them dynamically. You learned the basic syntax and structure of JavaScript DOM objects as well as a few of the methods and attributes attached to those objects.

Q&A

Q. **When should I use the** `getObjectById()` **rather than** `$("#id")`**?**

A. It's likely that you will rarely use `getObjectById()`. The only times you might use it is when you don't want to take the time to link the jQuery library to your HTML docs. jQuery is so much more extensible.

Workshop

The workshop consists of a set of questions and answers designed to solidify your understanding of the material covered in this hour. Try to answer the questions before looking at the answers.

Quiz

1. How to would you convert a DOM object named `myDiv` into a jQuery object?

2. True or False: A jQuery selector returns a list of DOM objects.

3. How can you tell if an object is a jQuery object?

4. What jQuery selector would you use if you wanted all elements with `class="heading"`?

5. What jQuery selector would you use to get all `<p>` elements that are children of `<div>` elements?

6. How can you get a JavaScript array of the DOM elements represented in a jQuery object?

Quiz Answers

1. Use `$(myDiv)` to create a new jQuery object with the DOM element as the only item in the set.

2. False. A jQuery selector returns a jQuery object that contains a set of DOM elements.

3. Test to see whether it has the `jquery` property set.

4. `$(".heading")`

5. `$(div p)`

6. Use the `get()` method on the jQuery object.

Exercise

1. Add an additional button to the example in hour0702.html that will select only the first and last planets in the list. You will need to add the HTML and JavaScript code necessary to do so.

Navigating and Manipulating jQuery Objects and DOM Elements with jQuery

---

What You'll Learn in This Hour:

▶ Chaining jQuery operations together for efficiency

▶ Ways to filter the DOM elements in a jQuery object

▶ Methods to use jQuery objects to traverse the DOM

▶ Iterating through each element in the jQuery object set

jQuery selectors return a jQuery object that represents zero or more elements that match the selector definition. Simple selectors are great for a lot of different things. However, as your web pages become more complex, you will find that the selectors do not do everything that you need.

jQuery objects provide additional functionality and enhance the selector results by allowing you to easily refine the list of DOM elements represented, navigate the DOM tree to find other elements, and manipulate the values of the HTML elements. The following sections cover how to chain jQuery operations together to efficiently find, filter, and navigate around the DOM elements in the web page.

Chaining jQuery Object Operations

One of the great things about jQuery objects is that you can chain multiple jQuery operations together into a single statement. Each consecutive statement will operate on the results of the previous operation in the chain. This can help reduce and simplify your selectors and reduce the amount of class and ID definitions required in your CSS.

Think of the results of the chained jQuery operations as a stack of jQuery objects, with each object representing a set of DOM elements. Each operation in the chain will place a jQuery object onto the stack, but the current operation will be applied only to the top jQuery.

To help illustrate this, consider the following statements. The code first finds the `<div>` element with `id="content"` and then finds the first `<p>` element inside and changes the `font-weight` to `bold`. Then it finds the `<span>` elements inside the `<p>` and sets the `color` to `red`:

```
var $contentDiv = $("div#content");
var $firstP = $contentDiv.children("p:first");
$firstP.css("font-weight","bold");
var $spans = $firstP.children("span");
$spans.css("color","red");
```

The code above took five lines to accomplish all the tasks it does. The following single line of chained jQuery operations does the same things but with only a single line:

```
$("div#content").children("p:first").css("font-weight","bold").children("span").
➥css("color","red");
```

Because each of the operations return a jQuery object, you can chain as many jQuery operations together as you would like. Even though the `.css()` operation is designed to alter the DOM objects and not find them, it still returns the same jQuery object so you can perform other operations on the results.

Filtering the jQuery Object Results

jQuery objects provide a good set of methods that allow you to alter the DOM objects represented in the query. Reducing the results is helpful when you are trying to pinpoint a specific set of elements within a jQuery selector result. Table 8.1 provides some examples of chaining jQuery selectors.

TABLE 8.1 jQuery Object Methods with Examples That Filter the DOM Elements Represented

Method/Example	Description
`.eq(index)` `$("div").eq(1);`	Selects the element at the zero-based index in the set. Example: Returns the second `<div>` element.

`.filter(selector or element or function(index) or index or object)`
 	
`$("option").filter(`
`  function (index) {`
`    return (this.value>5);`
`});`
	Reduces the set to match the filter. The filter can be a selector, a specific DOM element, a jQuery object, or a function that tests each element and returns true if it should be included.
	
	Example: Executes the function on each item in the current set and includes only those items where the `value` > 5. The `this` keyword refers to the current DOM object during each loop through the set.

`.first()` `$("li").first()`	Selects the first element in the set. Example: Reduces to just the first `<li>` element.

Method/Example	Description
`.last()` `$("p").last()`	Selects the last element in the set. Example: Reduces to just the last `<p>` element.
`.has(selector or element)` `$("div").has("p")`	Reduces the set to those elements that have descendant elements that match the selector or contain the specified DOM element. Example: Reduces to only `<div>` elements that have `<p>` children elements.
`.not(selector or elements or function(index) or object)` `$(".menu").not("span")`	Reduces the set to match the filter. The filter can be a selector, one or more specific DOM elements, a jQuery object, or a function that tests each element and returns true if it should be included. Example: Selects elements where `class="menu"` but are not `<span>` elements.
`.slice(start, [end])` `$("tr").slice(2,5)`	Remove elements before index start and after index end. The indexes are zero based. Example: Selects the `<tr>` elements with index 2, 3, and 4.

TIP

The jQuery selectors that are the same as the CSS selectors are able to use the native DOM method `querySelectorAll()`, which has some advanced optimizations on DOM objects. Other jQuery selectors cannot take advantage of that optimization, so it is better to use a CSS-based selector first and then add the filter as a chained selector. For example, rather than using `$("div:animated")`, you should use `$("div").filter(":animated")`. http://api.jquery.com/category/selectors/jquery-selector-extensions/

Traversing the DOM Using jQuery Objects

Another important set of methods attached to the jQuery object are the DOM traversing methods. DOM traversal enables you to select elements based on their relationship to other elements.

The DOM is sometimes referred to as the DOM tree because it is organized in a tree structure, with the document as the root and nodes that can have parents, siblings, and children. To visualize this better, check out the following HTML code:

```
<body>
  <div>
    <p>Paragraph 1</p>
    <p>Paragraph 2</p>
```

```
    <ul>
        <li>Item 1</li>
         <li>Item 2</li>
        </ul>
  </div>
</body>
```

The `<p>` element and `<ul>` element are siblings to each other, and they are all children of the `<div>` element. The `<div>` element is the parent of the `<p>` and `<ul>` elements, and the `<ul>` element is the parent of the `<li>` elements, and so forth.

jQuery DOM traversing methods enable you to move from one layer in the DOM to another to select elements—for example, if you want to access all `<p>` elements that are children of `<div>` elements, or if you want to find a `<label>` element that is a sibling of an `<input>` element.

jQuery objects provide an incredible set of methods that allow you to traverse the DOM in almost innumerable ways by allowing you to use the current selection of DOM elements in the jQuery object to select other sets of DOM elements in the tree. Table 8.2 lists the methods that you can use to traverse the DOM.

TABLE 8.2 jQuery Object Methods with Examples That Allow You to Traverse the DOM to Select Elements

Method/Example	Description
`.children([selector])` `$("div").children("p")`	Returns a jQuery object representing the children of the elements represented by the current object. You can specify an optional selector that limits the results to include only children that match the selector.
	Example: Selects the `<p>` elements that are direct `children` of all `<div>` elements.

`.closest(selector, [context]` or
`object or element)`
`$("p.menu").closest("div")`
	Returns a jQuery object representing the first element that matches the argument that is passed in. The argument can be a selector, a selector with context of where to begin searching, a jQuery object, or a DOM object. The search begins at the current set of elements and then searches ancestors.

	Example: Selects the closest `<div>` ancestor for `<p>` elements that have `class="menu"`.
`.contents()` `$("div").contents()`	Returns a jQuery object representing the immediate children of the current set of elements.
	Example: Selects all the immediate child elements in `<div>` elements.

Method/Example	Description

`.find(selector or object or element)`
 	
`$("table").find("span")`
	Returns a jQuery object representing descendants of the current set that match the argument supplied. The argument can be a selector, a jQuery object to match elements against, and an element tag name.
	
	Example: Selects all `<span>` elements contained somewhere in `<table>` elements.

`.next([selector])`
 	
`$("p#title").next("p")`
	Returns a jQuery object representing the next sibling of each element in the current set. If the optional selector is provided, the next sibling is added only if it matches the selector.
	
	Example: Finds the `<p>` element with `id="title"` and selects the very next `<p>` element that is a sibling.

`.nextAll([selector])`
 	
`$("p:first").nextAll()`
	Returns a jQuery object representing all the following sibling objects of each element in the current set. Also accepts an optional selector.
	
	Example: Selects the first `<p>` element that it finds and then selects all the `<p>` siblings to that element.

`.nextUntil([selector] or [element] [,filter])`
 	
`$("p:first").nextUntil("ul")`
	Returns a jQuery object representing all the sibling objects after each element in the current set, up until an object matching the element or selector argument is encountered. The first argument can be a DOM object or a selector. The second optional argument is a filter selector to limit the items returned in the results.
	
	Example: Selects the first `<p>` element that it finds and then selects all the siblings until it finds a `<ul>` element.

`.offsetParent()`
 	
`$("#notify").offsetParent()`
	Returns a jQuery object representing the closest ancestor element that has a CSS position attribute of relative, absolute, or fixed. This allows you to get the element used for positioning.
	
	Example: Finds the element with `id="notify"` and then selects the ancestor that is used to position that element.

`.parent([selector])`
 	
`$("div#menu").parent()`
	Returns a jQuery object representing the immediate parent objects of each of the elements represented in the current set. An optional selector argument allows you to limit the results to those parents matching the selector.
	
	Example: Selects the `<div>` element with `id="menu"` and then finds its immediate parent.

Method/Example	Description
`.parents([selector])` `$("#data").parents("div")`	Returns a jQuery object representing the ancestors of each of the elements represented in the current set. An optional selector argument allows you to limit the results to those parents matching the selector. Example: Finds the element with `id="data"` and then returns a set with all `<div>` ancestors.
`.parentsUntil([selector] or [element] [, filter])`	Returns a jQuery object representing the ancestors of each of the elements represented in the current set, up until an object matching the element or selector argument is encountered. The first argument can be an element tag name or a selector. The second optional argument is a filter selector to limit the items returned in the results.
`.prev()` `$("p#footer").prev("p")`	Returns a jQuery object representing the previous sibling of each element in the current set. If the optional selector is provided, the previous sibling is added only if it matches the selector. Example: Finds the `<p>` element with `id="footer"` and selects the previous `<p>` element that is a sibling.
`.prevAll()` `$("div#footer").prevAll("div")`	Returns a jQuery object representing all the previous sibling objects of each element in the current set. Also accepts an optional selector. Example: Selects the `<div>` element with `id="footer"` and then selects all the `<div>` siblings prior to that element.
`.prevUntil([selector] or [element] [,filter])`	Returns a jQuery object representing all the sibling objects that come before each element in the current set, up until an object matching the element or selector argument is encountered. The first argument can be a DOM object or a selector. The second optional argument is a filter selector to limit the items returned in the results.
`.siblings([selector])` `$(".menu").siblings("span")`	Returns a jQuery object representing all the sibling objects for each element in the current set. An optional selector argument allows you to limit the results to those siblings matching the selector. Example: Selects all `<span>` elements that are siblings to elements with `class="menu"`.

Looking at Some Additional jQuery Object Methods

When filtering the jQuery object or using it to traverse the DOM, there are some additional methods that you should be aware of. Table 8.3 lists a set of methods that you can use in conjunction with filtering and traversing elements, to iterate through the DOM elements in the jQuery object, add additional elements to the set, end filtering, and test items. You will find that you'll use these methods more and more frequently as your jQuery code becomes more natural to you.

NOTE

When using functions with jQuery methods that iterate through the DOM elements, you can use the `this` keyword to access the current DOM object that is being iterated on. This is a DOM object and not a jQuery object. If you need to use the jQuery form of the DOM object, then use `$(this)` instead. Keep in mind, though, that it takes work in the browser's rendering engine to build the jQuery form of the DOM object, so create the jQuery form only if you want the functionality that is provided.

TABLE 8.3   A Few Additional Methods and Examples That Allow You to Work with jQuery Objects

Method/Example	Description
`.add(selector, [context] or elements or html or object)` `$("div.left").add("div.right")`	Returns a new jQuery with additional elements. The arguments to `.add()` can be another jQuery sector with optional context to start from, another set of elements, an HTML fragment, or a jQuery object. Example: Selects all `<div>` elements with `class="left"` and then adds all `<div>` elements with `class="right"`.
`.andSelf()` `$("#title").nextAll().andSelf()`	Adds the previous set of elements on the stack to the current set so that you can apply operations on both. Selects the element with `id="title"`, gets all the siblings after it, and finally returns an object that includes all the siblings and the element itself.

`.each(function(index, Element))`
`$("span").each(function(i){`
`  $(this).css('width','300px');`
`})`
	Iterates through the current set of elements and executes the specified function by passing in the index and DOM object. `.each()` returns the same jQuery object that it operated on.
	
	Example: Sets the `width` of all `<span>` elements to 300 pixels.

Method/Example	Description

`.end()`
 	
`$("p").first().css("font-width", "bold").end().eq(1)`
	Ends the current filtering operations in chained jQuery statements and returns to the jQuery object in the stack from the previous state.
	
	Example: Selects all `<p>` elements, then selects the first one and sets the font to bold. Then the `end()` method returns to the jQuery object with all `<p>` elements, and you are able to select the second one in that set.

`.is(selector or index or object or element)`
 	
`$(".menu").each(function(i){`
`  $v = $(this);`
`  if($v.is("span")){`
`     $v.css('color','red');`
`  }`
`})`
	Check the current set of objects against a selector, function, jQuery object, or DOM object. If the elements match, true is returned; otherwise, false is returned.
	
	Example: Selects all elements with `class="menu"`, then iterates through the elements, and if it is a `<span>` element, it changes the `color` CSS property to `red`.

`.map(function(index, element))`
 	
`$(":selected").map(function(i) {`
`     return $(this).val();`
`  }).get();`
	Iterates through the current set of elements and executes a function on each item. The `.map()` function returns a jQuery object that represents a set of the results from each time the map function was executed.
	
	Example: Gets all the selected elements, then uses `map` to iterate through them and returns a JavaScript array of the value of each of the selected elements using `.get()`.

Using `.each()`

The `.each(function)` method is one of the most important jQuery object methods because it allows you to traverse all elements in the jQuery set and perform actions on each of them individually. This is different from just applying the same action to all items in the query.

The `.each()` method allows you to specify a function that will be run for each element in the jQuery object set. The function will be passed an index number as the first argument. Inside the function, the `this` variable will point to the current DOM element.

The following snippet of code illustrates using `.each()`. It iterates through all paragraph elements and sets the content, including the index number of the element:

```
$("p").each(function (idx){
    $(this).html("This is paragraph " + idx);
  });
```

Notice that idx is passed in as an index number, 0 for the first <p> element, 1 for the second, and so on. Also note that this was converted to a jQuery object using $(this) so that the .html() method could be called.

Using .map()

The .map(function) method also iterates through each element in the jQuery object set. Although very similar to .each(), there is one big difference, which is that .each() will return the same jQuery object, but .map() will return a new jQuery object with the values returned by each iteration.

The following snippet of code illustrates using .map(). It will iterate through all <li> elements and return a comma-separated string of the elements' text:

```
var liValues = $("li").map(function (idx){
    return $(this).html();
}).get().join(",");
```

Notice that for each iteration, the function returns the HTML content in the <li> element. You call .get() to return a JavaScript array version of the new jQuery object returned by .map() and then call .join(",") on that array to build the comma-separated string.

TRY IT YOURSELF ▼

Using the jQuery .map() and .each() Methods to Navigate, Access, and Manipulate the DOM Elements

In this example, you learn the process of using a jQuery selector to find all paragraph elements. You then use the .map() function to read the content and use it to create a new <span> box. You also use .each() to iterate through the <p> elements and restyle them. The full sample files can be found in Listing 8.1. Use the following steps to implement the example:

1. In Aptana, create a source folder named hour08. Inside the hour08 folder, create a js and css folder.

2. In the hour08 folder, create the source files named hour0801.html, js/hour0801.js, and css/hour0801.css.

3. Open hour0801.html and add the usual basic elements (html, head, body).

4. Inside the <head> element, add the following <script> and <link> elements, shown in Listing 8.1-html, that will be used to load the jQuery, JavaScript, and CSS:

```
06      <script src="../js/jquery.min.js"></script>
07      <script type="text/javascript" src="js/hour0801.js"></script>
08      <link rel="stylesheet" type="text/css" href="css/hour0801.css">
```

5. Add the code shown in lines 11–19 of Listing 8.1-html to the css/hour0801.css file. This code defines two input buttons, a bunch of `<p>` elements, and a `<div>` that will be used to place content.

6. Add the styling code from Listing 8.1-css to the hour0801.css file. The styling code will style the `<span>` elements so that they will display as inline-block so that you can set their size.

7. Open the js/hour0801.js file and add the following lines that will create a `.ready()` function that will be executed when the page is loaded:

```
01  $(document).ready(function () {
    . . .
21  });
```

8. Add the following code that will add a `click` event handler to the first button. The function uses a simple `.each()` function to iterate through the `<p>` elements; it gets the string, splits it into a color and size, and then sets the `font-size` and `color` CSS properties.

```
02      $("input:eq(0)").click(function () {
03          $("p").each(function(){
04              var parts = $(this).html().split(" ");
05              $(this).css({"font-size":parts[1]+"px", color:parts[0]});
06          });
07      });
```

9. Add the following code that will add a `click` event handler to the second button. The function uses a simple `.map()` function to iterate through the `<p>` elements; it gets the string and splits it into a color and size. This time, however, the function returns a JavaScript object with a `color` and `size` attribute. The `.get()` at the end converts the results of the `.map()` to a JavaScript array named `items`.

```
08      $("input:eq(1)").click(function () {
09          var items = $("p").map(function(){
10              var parts = $(this).html().split(" ");
11              return {color:parts[0], size:parts[1]};
12          }).get();
```

10. Add the following `for` loop that iterates through items and creates a new `<span>` element with the color and size based on the values read from the `<p>` elements:

```
13          for (var idx in items){
14              var item = items[idx];
15              var span = $("<span>" + item.color + "</span>");
16              var size = item.size*5;
17              span.css({"background-color":item.color,  "font-size":
                  ➥item.size+"px", width:size, height:size});
18              $("div").append(span);
19          }
```

11. Save the three files and open the HTML document in a web browser. When you click the
`.each()` button, the text of the `<p>` elements should change, as shown in Figure 8.1.
When you click the `.map()` button, new boxes should be displayed in the `<div>`.

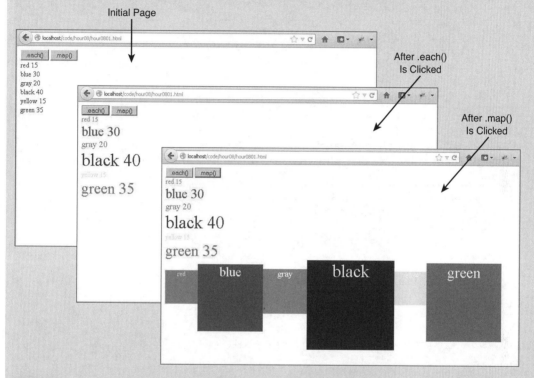

Initial Page

After .each() Is Clicked

After .map() Is Clicked

FIGURE 8.1
A simple JavaScript web page that uses `.map()` and `.each()` to read the text in `<p>` elements and make
dynamic changes to the web page for each of those elements.

LISTING 8.1-html   HTML File That Loads jQuery and JavaScript

```
01 <!DOCTYPE html>
02 <html>
03   <head>
04     <title>Hour 8-1</title>
05     <meta charset="utf-8" />
06     <script type="text/javascript" src="../js/jquery.min.js"></script>
07     <script type="text/javascript" src="js/hour0801.js"></script>
08     <link rel="stylesheet" type="text/css" href="css/hour0801.css">
09   </head>
10   <body>
```

```
11      <input type="button" value=".each()">
12      <input type="button" value=".map()">
13      <p>red 15</p>
14      <p>blue 30</p>
15      <p>gray 20</p>
16      <p>black 40</p>
17      <p>yellow 15</p>
18      <p>green 35</p>
19      <div></div>
20    </body>
21  </html>
```

LISTING 8.1-js   jQuery and JavaScript Code Gets the `<p>` Elements and Iterates Through Them Using `.map()` and `.each()` to Apply Different Changes for Each Element

```
01 $(document).ready(function (){
02   $("input:eq(0)").click(function (){
03     $("p").each(function(){
04       var parts = $(this).html().split(" ");
05       $(this).css({"font-size":parts[1]+"px", color:parts[0]});
06     });
07   });
08   $("input:eq(1)").click(function (){
09     var items = $("p").map(function(){
10         var parts = $(this).html().split(" ");
11         return {color:parts[0], size:parts[1]};
12       }).get();
13     for (var idx in items){
14       var item = items[idx];
15       var span = $("<span>" + item.color + "</span>");
16       var size = item.size*5;
17       span.css({"background-color":item.color,  "font-size": item.size+"px",
18               width:size, height:size});
19       $("div").append(span);
20     }
21   });
22 });
```

LISTING 8.1-css   CSS Code That Styles the `<span>` and `<p>` Elements

```
1 p{margin:0; padding:0;}
2 span{
3   display:inline-block;
```

```
4    color: white;
5    text-align:center;
6  }
```

Using jQuery Objects to Traverse the DOM

In this example, you use jQuery objects to dynamically access DOM elements relative to their position from each other. The purpose of this example is to illustrate how easy it is use jQuery objects to navigate and find other related DOM elements. The result will be a simple web page that allows users to input ratings and provides a graphical indicator of their value. The full scripts used in the example are shown in Listing 8.2.

1. In the hour08 folder, create the source files named hour0802.html, js/hour0802.js, and css/hour0802.css.

2. Open hour0802.html and add the usual basic elements (html, head, body).

3. Inside the `<head>` element, add the following `<script>` and `<link>` elements, shown in Listing 8.2-html, that will be used to load the jQuery, JavaScript, and CSS:

```
06    <script src="../js/jquery.min.js"></script>
07    <script type="text/javascript" src="js/hour0802.js"></script>
08    <link rel="stylesheet" type="text/css" href="css/hour0802.css">
```

4. Add the code shown in lines 11–25 of Listing 8.2-html. This code defines a set of `<div>` elements containing a label, a text input, and a set of 5 `<span>` elements. The `onkeyup="update()"` attribute of the `<input>` elements provides the dynamic interaction when the user types into the text box.

5. Add the styling code from Listing 8.2-css to the hour0802.css file. The styling code styles the `<span>` elements with a certain `height` and `width` and adds the `margin` and `padding` necessary.

6. Open the hour0802.js file in Aptana and create a JavaScript function named `update()` to be called by the `onkeyup` event handler.

7. Add the following line to set the `background-color` of all `<span>` elements to `lightgrey`:

```
2    $("span").css("background-color","lightgrey");
```

8. Add the following jQuery code to select all `<div>` elements, and then use `.each()` to iterate on each of them and apply a function:

```
3    $("div").each(function(i){
```

```
      . . .
 8    })
```

9. Inside the function, add the following line that gets the first `<input>` child of the `<div>` element:

```
 4      var $input = $(this).children("input:first");
```

10. Add the following lines that get the value of the `<input>` element and create a jQuery selector string to filter on only the first *n* number of `<span>` elements, where n is the value of `<input>`:

```
 5      var $value = $input.val();
 6      var filter = "span:lt(" + $value + ")";
```

11. Add the following line that uses the `$input` jQuery object to search for siblings based on the `filter` defined in step 10. The `css()` method changes the background color to blue. Notice the simplicity of the function. You can add as many `<div>` sections as you want. As long as they follow the same structure `<div><input><span>...</div>`, the jQuery code will work on all of them.

```
 7      $input.siblings(filter).css("background-color","blue");
```

12. Save the files and open hour0802.html in a web browser. Notice that as you type in the text boxes, the `<span>` elements are changed to blue to match the value of the input, as shown in Figure 8.2.

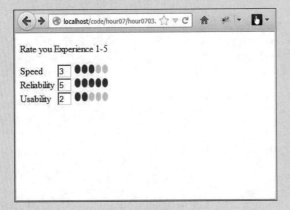

FIGURE 8.2
A simple JavaScript web page that allows users to input a rating and dynamically changes based on the value typed in.

LISTING 8.2-html   HTML File That Loads jQuery and JavaScript and Attaches Event
Handler Elements to Provide User Interaction

```
01  <!DOCTYPE html>
02  <html>
03    <head>
04      <title>Hour 8-2</title>
05      <meta charset="utf-8" />
06      <script type="text/javascript" src="../js/jquery.min.js"></script>
07      <script type="text/javascript" src="js/hour0802.js"></script>
08      <link rel="stylesheet" type="text/css" href="css/hour0802.css">
09    </head>
10    <body>
11      <p>Rate you Experience 1-5</p>
12      <div>
13        <label>Speed</label>
14        <input type="text" onkeyup="update()"></input>
15        <span></span><span></span><span></span><span></span><span></span>
16      </div>
17      <div><label>Reliability</label>
18        <input type="text" onkeyup="update()"></input>
19        <span></span><span></span><span></span><span></span><span></span>
20      </div>
21      <div>
22        <label>Usability</label>
23        <input type="text" onkeyup="update()"></input>
24        <span></span><span></span><span></span><span></span><span></span>
25      </div>
26    </body>
27  </html>
```

LISTING 8.2-js   JavaScript Code That Handles the Key Up Event and Uses jQuery to
Manipulate the Color of the <span> Elements Based on the Input Value

```
1 function update(){
2   $("span").css("background-color","lightgrey");
3   $("div").each(function(i){
4     var $input = $(this).children("input:first");
5     var $value = $input.val();
6     var filter = "span:lt(" + $value + ")";
7     $input.siblings(filter).css("background-color","blue");
8   })
9 }
```

LISTING 8.2-css   **CSS Code That Styles the** `<span>`, `<input>`, **and** `<label>`
Elements

```
01 span{
02    display:inline-block;
03    height:15px;
04    width:10px;
05    background-color:lightgrey;
06    margin:1px;
07    border-radius:50%;
08 }
09 input {
10    width:20px;
11 }
12 label {
13    display:inline-block;
14    width:60px;
15 }
```

Summary

In this hour, you learned about using jQuery and JavaScript objects to find and navigate through the DOM elements. This adds a critical piece in implementing dynamic code because often you will want to act, not on the elements that you search for, but for elements related to them.

You learned how to chain jQuery requests together to apply multiple operations to the same set of DOM elements. This reduces the number of statements required in your scripts.

You also learn how to iterate through the DOM element set associated with the jQuery objects returned by the selector. This allows you to apply a different set of operations to each individual element in a set without the need to look each one up individually.

Q&A

Q. What is the difference between `$("div:eq(n)")` **and** `$("div").eq(n)`?

A. The biggest difference is that `.eq()` enables you to specify a negative number and count backward from the end. For example, `.eq(-1)` is the last element in the list. `:eq()` does not allow negative indexes.

Q. How many jQuery options should be chained together?

A. Good question. It depends on the circumstances. It is really a question of performance versus readability/reusability. Keep in mind that there is a bit of code behind each jQuery lookup, so the more you can use the same jQuery stack, the better off you are. At some point, what is really in the current stack can become confusing; however, at that point you should save yourself future headaches and move on. A better approach is to break the operations into separate groups that can be reused and then define variable names for those.

Workshop

The workshop consists of a set of questions and answers designed to solidify your understanding of the material covered in this hour. Try to answer the questions before looking at the answers.

Quiz

1. What jQuery method would you use to filter out elements that have a `<p>` element as a child?

2. What jQuery method would you use to get all sibling `<p>` elements before an element with `id="middleEarth"`?

3. What is the difference between `.map()` and `.each()`?

Quiz Answers

1. `.has("p");`

2. `$("#middleEarth").prevAll("p");`

3. `.map()` is used to iterate through the set of elements and return a new object containing the results of the specified function of each iteration. `.each()` will just iterate through the elements applying the function specified.

Exercise

1. Extend the HTML code in hour0801.html to include more `<div>` sections like the others. Notice that the same functionality is automatically applied to each.

Applying Events for Richly Interactive Web Pages

What You'll Learn in This Hour:

▶ Ways that events can be triggered by the user and browser

▶ What properties are accessible on event objects

▶ How to add handlers that are able to dynamically respond to events

▶ Ways to pass extra data to event handlers

▶ Methods to manually trigger events

▶ Ways to create your own custom events

▶ How to implement and fire off callback functions in your code

One of the major goals of jQuery and JavaScript is to provide developers with the capability to create incredibly sophisticated and richly active web pages. At the heart of interactive web pages are events. An event is basically any time anything happens in the browser environment, from a page loading, to a mouse movement or click, to keyboard input, to resizing the window.

Understanding events, the objects that represent them, and how to apply them in your web pages will enable to you to create some spectacular user interaction. In this hour, you learn the concepts required to understand events and how to utilize them in building rich, interactive web pages. You will be using the concepts in this hour throughout the rest of the book.

Understanding Events

You have already been using events in several of the examples used so far in this book. However, to get the most out of them, you need to understand what is happening in the entire process from the physical interaction to the jQuery and JavaScript interactions that will modify screen elements and data. The following sections describe the event process, as well the components involved, and how to implement events in web pages.

Understanding the Event Process

The event-handling concept is pretty easy to catch at a high level; you click a button on the web page and things happen. This section delves a little bit deeper so you can understand what is going on. The following list describes the important things that happen when a user interacts with the web page or browser window.

1. **A physical event happens**—A physical event occurs; for example, a user clicks or moves the mouse or presses a key.

2. **Events are triggered in the browser**—The user interaction results in events being triggered by the web browser—often, multiple events at the same time. For example, when a user types a key on the keyboard, three events are triggered: the `keypressed`, `keydown`, and `keyup` events.

3. **The browser creates an object for the event**—The web browser creates a separate object for each event that is triggered. The objects contain information about the event that can be used by handlers.

4. **User event handlers are called**—User-defined event handlers are called. You have the capability to create handlers in JavaScript that will interact with the event objects and/or page elements to provide interactivity with HTML elements. There are three phases that the event handlers can be acting in. The following describes the three phases shown in Figure 9.1:

   ▶ **Capturing**—The capturing phase is on the way down to the target HTML element from the document directly through each of the parent elements. By default, behavior for event handlers for the capturing phase is disabled.

   ▶ **Targeting**—The target phase occurs when the event is in the HTML element where it was initially triggered.

   ▶ **Bubbling**—The bubbling phase is on the way up through each of the parents of the target HTML element all the way back to the document. By default, the bubbling phase is enabled for events.

5. **Browser handlers are called**—In addition to user event handlers, the browser has default handlers that do different things based on the event that was triggered. For example, when the user clicks a link, the browser has an event handler that gets called and navigates to the `href` location specified in the link.

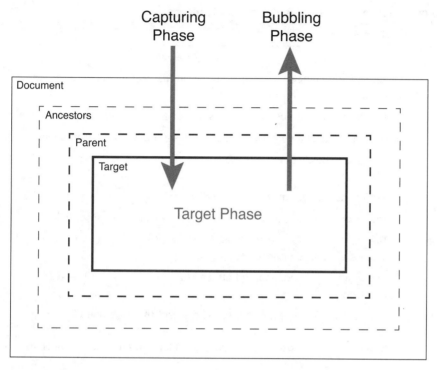

FIGURE 9.1
Events are handled first in the capturing phase from the document down to the target, then in the target phase, and finally, the bubbling phase from the target up through the document.

Looking at Event Objects

Event objects get created by the browser when it detects that an event has occurred. If the event handler was defined by jQuery, the event object is converted to a jQuery event object that has a few more attributes and methods. Therefore, you need to be aware of which event object type you are working with.

The event object provides you with additional information about the event, such as what type the event was—for instance, a `click` or `keypress`—which key(s) were pressed, the position of the mouse, what HTML element the event occurred on, and so on. Table 9.1 describes the most commonly used event attributes that you will be working with.

TABLE 9.1   JavaScript and jQuery Event Object Attributes

Property	Description
altKey	True if the Alt key was pressed during the event; otherwise, false.
button	Returns the number of the mouse button that was pressed: 0 for left, 1 for middle, and 2 for right.
cancelable	True if the default action for the event can be stopped; otherwise, false.
charCode	Ordinal value of the character that is pressed if it is a keyboard event.
clientX	Horizontal coordinate of the mouse pointer relative to the current window.
clientY	Vertical coordinate of the mouse pointer relative to the current window.
ctrlKey	True if the Ctrl key was pressed during the event; otherwise, false.
currentTarget	The DOM object for the HTML element that the event handler currently being executed is attached to.
data	User data that is defined and attached to the event when the event is triggered.
delegateTarget	This is the DOM object of the HTML element that was used in the jQuery .delegate() or .on() method to attach the event handler. (.on() and .delegate() are discussed later in this hour.) Available only on jQuery event objects.
eventPhase	The current phase that the event handler is operating in, where 1 is at the target, 2 is bubbling, and 3 is capturing.
metaKey	True if a "meta" key was pressed during the event; otherwise false. For example, true if Ctrl, Alt, Cmd or other meta key is pressed.
relatedTarget	Identifies a secondary target relative to the UI event. For example, when using the mouseover and mouseexit events, it indicates the target being exited or entered.
results	Last value returned by an event handler that was triggered by this event. Available only on jQuery event objects.
screenX	Horizontal coordinate based on the actual display coordinate system.
screenY	Vertical coordinate based on the actual display coordinate system.
shiftKey	True if the Shift key was pressed during the event; otherwise, false.
target	The DOM object for the HTML element where the event originated.
type	Text describing the event, such as click or keydown.
timeStamp	Time in milliseconds since January 1, 1970 and when the event was triggered.
which	Actual numerical value.

Events also provide a few methods that allow you some control into the behavior of the event—for example, stopping propagation and default web behavior. Table 9.2 describes the important methods on event methods.

TABLE 9.2   JavaScript and jQuery Event Object Methods

Method	Description
isDefaultPrevented()	True if the default action has been disabled; otherwise, false.
isImmediatePropagationStopped()	True if immediate propagation has been disabled; otherwise, false.
isPropagationStopped()	Returns true if propagation has been stopped; otherwise, false.
preventDefault()	If an event can be cancelled, this method will disable the default action that would be applied by the browser. For example, you could disable a link from navigating away from the web page.
stopImmediatePropagation()	Stops the event from propagating to any other event handlers that are attached to the current target, as well as from propagating through the DOM tree.
stopPropagation()	Stops the event from propagating to other HTML elements in the DOM tree. Other events on the current target will still complete.

Reviewing Event Types

An event type is a keyword that is used by JavaScript and jQuery to identify the physical event that took place. These keywords are used to attach handlers to specify types of events. Also, as you will see later, the keywords are used in the names of methods that can be used to attach event handlers or trigger events manually.

JavaScript provides several event types that correspond to the different events that occur during dynamic page interaction. jQuery event handling supports all the JavaScript and also adds a few of its own events. Table 9.3 lists the different event types supported by JavaScript and jQuery.

TABLE 9.3   JavaScript and jQuery Event Types

Event Type	Description
abort	Triggered when an image load is stopped before completing.
blur	Triggered when a form element loses focus.
change	Triggered when the content, selection, or check state of a form element changes. Applies to `<input>`, `<select>`, and `<textarea>` elements.
click	Triggered when the user clicks an HTML element.
dblclick	Triggered when the user double-clicks an HTML element.
error	Triggered when an image does not load correctly.
focus	Triggered when a form element gets the focus.
focusin	Triggered when a form element or any descendant element inside of it gets the focus. Different from the focus event type in that it supports bubbling up to parents. This is a jQuery-only event.
focusout	Triggered when a form element or any element inside of it loses the focus. Different from blur in that it supports bubbling up to parents. This is a jQuery-only event.
keydown	Triggered when a user begins pressing a key.
keypress	Triggered when a user presses a key.
keyup	Triggered when a user releases a key.
load	Triggered when a document, frameset, or DOM element is loaded.
mousedown	Triggered when a user presses a mouse button. The target element is the one the mouse is over when the button is pressed.
mousemove	Triggered when the mouse cursor is moving over an element.
mouseover	Triggered when the mouse cursor moves onto an element or any of its descendants.
mouseout	Triggered when the mouse cursor moves out of an element or any of its descendants.
mouseup	Triggered when a user releases a mouse button. The target element is the one that the mouse is over when the button is released.
mouseenter	Triggered when the mouse cursor enters an element. Different from `mouseover` in that it is triggered only by the element and not its descendants. This is a jQuery-only event.
mouseleave	Triggered when the mouse cursor leaves an element. Different from `mouseout` in that it is triggered only by the element and not its descendants. This is a jQuery-only event.
reset	Triggered when a form is reset.

Event Type	Description
resize	Triggered when the document view is resized by resizing the browser window or frame.
scroll	Triggered when a document view is scrolled.
select	Triggered when a user selects text in an `<input>` or `<textarea>`.
submit	Triggered when a form is submitted.
unload	Triggered when a page is unloaded from the `<body>` or `<frameset>` element.

Using the Page Load Events for Initialization

When the HTML document loads, the JavaScript code specified in the `<script>` tags will be loaded and executed. Typically, the JavaScript and jQuery logic will be inside functions that will be executed later. However, there will be some code that does initialization work, such as attaching event handlers to page elements or even adding additional elements to existing ones.

The problem is that the HTML element objects may not have been built by the browser at the point when the JavaScript code is loaded. An exception will be thrown if you try to reference the HTML object before it is created, so you need to wait until the page has fully loaded.

That is where the load event comes in extremely handy. Placing your initialization code inside an event handler that gets triggered when the page is loaded allows you to be sure all HTML objects have been created and the DOM is fully ready.

Using the JavaScript `onload` Event

To add initialization code that runs when pages are loaded in JavaScript, create a function in JavaScript that performs the initialization. For example, consider the following JavaScript code that shows a simple skeleton initialization function:

```
function onloadHandler(){
  (initialization code here...)
}
```

Now you have two options to cause the `onloadHandler()` to trigger when the page is fully loaded. The first is to attach your initialization code to the `onload` attribute of the `<body>` element in the HTML. For example:

```
<body onload="onloadHandler()">
```

The second method is to assign it directly to the `window` object in your JavaScript code. For example:

```
window.onload = onloadHandler;
```

Adding Initialization Code in jQuery

In jQuery, initialization code can be triggered and executed at two different times: when the DOM is ready and when the document and its resources have fully loaded. Which of these options you use will depend on what needs to happen in your initialization code.

Using the `.ready()` jQuery method will trigger the initialization code to run when the DOM is fully ready. All of the DOM objects will have been created and the page will be displayed to users. All page resources, such as images, may not have fully downloaded at this point, however. This is the option that enables you to add interactions and functionality as soon as possible. The following shows an example of using `.ready()` to attach a simple initialization function:

```
$(document).ready(function(){
   (initialization code here...)
}
```

Using the `.load()` jQuery method will trigger the initialization code to run after all page resources have loaded and are rendered to the user. On occasion you might use this option if you need resource information, such as image dimensions, when you are applying the initialization code. The following shows an example of using `load()` to attach a simple initialization function:

```
$(document).load(function(){
   (initialization code here...)
}
```

CAUTION
_____

The `.ready()` and `.load()` methods are not compatible with using the `onload="..."` attribute in the `<body>` tag. If you are using jQuery, use `.ready()` or `.load()`; if not, use the `onload` attribute.
_____

Adding and Removing Event Handlers to DOM Elements

To provide interaction to events that occur in a web page, an event handler must be added for each specific event type you want to interact with. An event handler is just a JavaScript function that adds, removes, or alters DOM elements, or whatever else is necessary to complete the interaction. For example, the following code is an example of an event handler that changes the text displayed in the `<p>` elements to `"clicked"`:

```
function clickHandler(){
  $("p").html("clicked");
}
```

Several methods enable you to add event handlers to DOM elements. The following section describes each of these methods along with their advantages and disadvantages.

Assigning Event Handlers in HTML

The most basic methods of adding an event handler to a DOM element is directly in the HTML code. The advantage of this method is that it is simple and easy to see what event handler gets assigned to a particular DOM object.

Event handlers are added to DOM objects in HTML by setting the value of the handler attribute in the tag statement. For each event that the element supports, there is an attribute that starts with "on" followed by the name of the event. For example, the `click` event attribute is `onclick` and the `load` event attribute is `onload`. To see a list of the events, see Table 9.1.

The following example shows just how easy it is to add a `click` event handler to DOM element in the HTML code:

```
<div onclick="clickHandler()">Click Here</div>
```

This would call the following function when the `<div>` element is clicked:

```
function clickHandler(){
  $("div").html("clicked");
}
```

You can also include the DOM event object as a parameter to the event handler using the `event` keyword. This allows you to access the event information in event handler; for example:

```
<div onclick="clickHandler(event)">Click Here</div>
```

This would call the following function when the `<div>` element is clicked and change the text to display the x coordinate of the mouse cursor by reading `e.screenX`:

```
function clickHandler(e){
  $("div").html("clicked at X postion: " + e.screenX);
}
```

You can also define that specific arguments are passed to an event, allowing you to distinguish specific functionality. The parameters can be numbers or strings surrounded by single quotes or even the `id` value of DOM objects, in which case the DOM element will be passed. For example, the following code adds event handlers that pass the event object, as well as the DOM object for the `<h1>` element with `id="heading"` along with a number and string:

```
<h1 id="heading"></h1>
<div onclick="clickHandler(event,heading,1,"Yes")">Click Here</div>
<div onclick="clickHandler(event,heading,2,"No")">Or Here</div>
```

When clicked, the elements would call the following function and use the DOM objects' `innerHTML` property to change the text to display the number, message, and x coordinate of the mouse cursor:

```
function clickHandler(e,obj,num,msg){
  obj.innerHTML = "DIV " + num + " says " + msg +" at X postion: " + e.screenX;
}
```

There are a couple of major disadvantages to this method, though. The first is that the DOM element has to be defined in the HTML and never removed and read dynamically. The second is that if you want the same event handler assigned to several DOM elements, you have to add code to the tag to every one of them in the HTML.

Typically, you use the HTML method of assigning event handlers only for basic examples with very little JavaScript.

Adding Event Handlers in JavaScript

You can also add and remove event handlers dynamically to DOM objects inside of JavaScript code. This method provides the advantage that you can dynamically add event handlers at any point in time, not just when the page is loaded. Thus, it enables you to add event listeners to elements created after the page load.

To add an event handler in JavaScript, simply call `addEventListener()` on the DOM object. The `addEventListener()` function takes three parameters: the first is the event `type` (event types are defined in Table 9.1), the second is the function to call, and the third is a Boolean that specifies true if the handler should be called during the capturing phase and the bubbling phase, or false if the handler should be called only during the bubbling phase.

The trick with using `addEventListener()` is how to pass custom data into the handler call. One method is to wrap the actual function handler inside of a simple wrapper function that passes the arguments to the event handler. The following code illustrates this:

```
function clickHandler(e,objId,num,msg){
  var obj = document.getElementById(objId);
  obj.innerHTML = "DIV " + num + " says " + msg +" at X postion: " + e.screenX;
}
...
document.getElementById("div1").addEventListener('click',
  function(e){
```

```
    clickHandler (e, "heading", 1, "yes");
},false);
```

So here is what is going on in the addEventListener() calls in the preceding code. The event type 'click' is specified, and then a new anonymous function with no name is defined that accepts the event object as the only parameter represented by e. Inside the wrapper function, the actual event handler is called with the custom parameters, including the e variable to pass the event object along. In the example, false is used to indicate that the handler should be called only during the bubbling phase.

You can also remove event handlers from the event using the removeEventListener() function on the DOM object. You will need to specify the event type and the name of the event handler to remove. For example, the following code adds an event handler and then removes it:

```
var obj = document.getElementById("div1");
obj.addEventListener('click', clickHandler);
obj.removeEventListener('click', clickHandler);
```

TIP

You can also set the access event handler on the DOM object itself using the handler attribute. The handler attribute will be "on" plus the event type. For example, for the click event, the attribute is obj.onclick. You can call the event handler using obj.onclick() or assign it directly using obj.onclick= function handler(){ ...};

TRY IT YOURSELF ▼

Adding Event Handlers to DOM Objects via JavaScript

In this example, you attach event handlers to DOM objects dynamically using the JavaScript method. Use the following steps to create the files shown in Listing 9.1:

1. In Aptana, create the hour09, hour09/js, and hour09/css folders.

2. Create the hour09/hour0901.html, hour09/js/hou0901.js, and hou09/cs/hour0901.css files.

3. Add the code shown in Listing 9.1-html to the HTML file. You should recognize almost everything in this file. Notice the onload event handler for the <body> tag is set to onloadHandler().

4. Add the CSS from Listing 9.1-css to the CSS file. You should also recognize the CSS statements by now.

5. Open the hour0901.js file and the following function that will be used to handle click events. Notice that it takes several arguments. The first argument is the DOM event object,

which is used to get the x position via e.screenX. It also accepts an object ID that is used to get the object that should be written to. The rest of the arguments are used to write out the message the innerHTML of the object specified by objId.

```
01 function clickHandler(e,objId,num,msg){
02    var obj = document.getElementById(objId);
03    obj.innerHTML = "DIV " + num + " says " + msg +" at X postion: " +
    ➥e.screenX;
04 }
```

6. Create the following wrapper functions that will be used to pass arguments to the actual event handler. The wrapper functions only accept the event object as argument e. Then they call the clickHandler() function with the appropriate values. In this example, the event handler is then removed from the target object by calling removeEventListener(). It is not typical to remove event handlers; this is just to provide an example.

```
05 function yesWrapper(e){
06    clickHandler(e, "heading", 1, "yes");
07    e.target.removeEventListener('click', yesWrapper);
08 }
09 function noWrapper(e){
10    clickHandler(e, "heading", 1, "no");
11    e.target.removeEventListener('click', noWrapper);
12 }
```

7. Add the following onloadHandler() function that calls addEventListener() to add a click event handler to each of the <div> elements:

```
13 function onloadHandler(){
14    document.getElementById("div1").addEventListener('click', yesWrapper,
    ➥false);
15    document.getElementById("div2").addEventListener('click', noWrapper,
    ➥false);
16 }
```

8. Save all three files and then open the HTML document in a web browser and play around with the Say Yes and Say No buttons shown in Figure 9.2. Notice that the buttons work only once because the event handler was removed. If we had not removed the event handler, the buttons would continue to handle the event and change the <h1> element text.

LISTING 9.1-html **HTML File That Loads jQuery and JavaScript, Attaches Event Handler Elements to Provide User Interaction, and Then Defines the** <div> **and** <h1> **Elements Used in the Example**

```
01 <!DOCTYPE html>
02 <html>
03    <head>
04       <title>Hour 9-1</title>
```

```
05      <meta charset="utf-8" />
06      <script type="text/javascript" src="../js/jquery.min.js"></script>
07      <script type="text/javascript" src="js/hour0901.js"></script>
08      <link rel="stylesheet" type="text/css" href="css/hour0901.css">
09    </head>
10    <body onload="onloadHandler()">
11      <div id="div1")">Say Yes</div>
12      <div id="div2")">Say No</div>
13      <h1 id="heading"></h1>
14    </body>
15  </html>
```

FIGURE 9.2
A simple JavaScript web page that dynamically adds event handlers to `<div>` elements and responds to
mouse clicks.

LISTING 9.1-js JavaScript Code That Defines an Event Handler and Dynamically
Attaches It to the `<div>` Elements

```
01 function clickHandler(e,objId,num,msg){
02   var obj = document.getElementById(objId);
03   obj.innerHTML = "DIV " + num + " says " + msg +" at X postion: " + e.screenX;
04 }
05 function yesWrapper(e){
06   clickHandler(e, "heading", 1, "yes");
07   e.target.removeEventListener('click', yesWrapper);
08 }
09 function noWrapper(e){
10   clickHandler(e, "heading", 2, "no");
11   e.target.removeEventListener('click', noWrapper);
12 }
13 function onloadHandler(){
14   document.getElementById("div1").addEventListener('click', yesWrapper, false);
15   document.getElementById("div2").addEventListener('click', noWrapper, false);
16 }
```

LISTING 9.1-css   CSS Code That Styles the `<div>` Elements

```
1 div{
2   border-radius:5px;
3   margin:3px;
4   padding:5px;
5   background-color:lightgrey;
6   font-weight:bold;
7   display:inline-block;
8   cursor:pointer;
9 }
```

Applying Event Handlers in jQuery

The best method of attaching event handlers to DOM elements is using jQuery. Using jQuery objects makes it simple to select different sets of objects and apply the same event handler to all of them at the same time.

In the past, jQuery has had a couple of different ways to add and remove event handlers, including `bind()`/`unbind()` and `delegate()`/`undelegate()`. The `bind()` method mimicked the behavior of `addEventListener()`, and `delegate()` made it possible to add an event to a jQuery object and then, as additional child elements were added to the event handler, would automatically be delegated to those as well.

As of jQuery 1.7, these methods have all been replaced by a simple pair, `on()` and `off()`. Event handlers are attached to jQuery objects using the `on()` method. The `on()` method can be called in one of the two following formats:

```
on(events [, selector] [, data], handler(eventObject))
on(events-map [, selector][, data])
```

The following list describes the purpose of each of the arguments that can be added to the `on()` method when adding event handlers to jQuery objects:

- `events`—One or more space-separated event types and optional namespaces denoted by dot syntax; for example, `"click"`, `"mouseenter mouseleave"`, or `"keydown.myPlugin"`. The list of event types can be found in Table 9.1.

- `events-map`—A mapping object in which the string keys specify one or more space-separated event types, and then the values specify handler functions that will be called when the event is triggered; for example, `{'click':myhandler}` or `{'click':function myHandler(e){return true;}}`.

▶ `selector`—Optional. Selector string that specifies which descendants should also call the event handler when the event is triggered. This replaces the functionality of the `delegate()` method. If you add the event handler to a set of parent objects that will always exist in the page, any of their descendants that match the selector will also call the handler when the event is triggered, even if they get added after the event is attached.

▶ `data`—Optional. This can be a number, a string, or an object that will get passed to the handler as the data part of the `event` as `event.data` when an event is triggered.

▶ `handler(eventObject)`—If you are not using an `events-map`, you will need to specify the handler function that will be executed when the event is triggered.

To remove an event handler from elements using jQuery, call the `off()` method on the jQuery object. The syntax for the off method is one of the following:

```
off(events [, selector] [, handler(eventObject)])
off(events-map [, selector])
```

If no handler is specified, the `off()` function removes all event handlers for the events specified. The following example shows a basic example of adding an event handler to all `<div>` elements using `on()` and then removing it using `off()`:

```
$("div").on("click",clickHandler);
$("div").off("click",clickHandler);
```

NOTE

The `on()` and `off()` methods work for all jQuery event types, including your own custom events. jQuery also provides some simple helper functions that are discussed later in the hour to make it easier to attach handlers for certain events.

TIP

Often you will want an event handler to run only once, the first time the event occurs. jQuery provides the very helpful `one()` method that will add an event, then automatically remove it after it triggers for the first time. The `one()` method uses the same syntax as the `on()` method.

TRY IT YOURSELF ▼

Adding Event Handlers Using jQuery

In this example, you attach event handlers to DOM objects dynamically using the jQuery method. Use the following steps to create the files shown in Listing 9.2:

1. In Aptana, create the hour09/hour0902.html, hour09/js/hou0902.js, and hou09/cs/hour0902.css files.

2. Add the code shown in Listing 9.2-html to the HTML file. You should recognize almost everything in this file.

3. Add the CSS from Listing 9.2-css to the CSS file.

4. Open the hour0902.js file and the following function that will be used to handle click events. The event takes only the event object as argument e. It relies on the data portion of the event object to provide the `objId` of the element that text should be added to. It also uses the `e.target.id`, `e.screenX`, and `e.data.answer` values as part of the message written to the `<h1>` element.

```
01 function clickHandler(e){
02    $("#"+e.data.objId).html(e.target.id + " says " + e.data.answer +
03                              " at X postion: " + e.screenX);
04 }
```

5. Create the following `ready()` function that will automatically be called when the document has been loaded and is ready:

```
05 $(document).ready(function(){
...
12 });
```

6. Add the following jQuery code that finds the `#div1` element and then uses `on()` to add an event handler. In this example, an `events-map` object is passed specifying `clickHandler()` for the click event type. In addition, an object is passed in that will add the heading and answer attributes to the event object data. This is where the values came from that we used in step 4.

```
06    $("#div1").on({"click":clickHandler},
07                {"objId":"heading", "answer":"yes"});
```

7. Add the following jQuery code that gets the `document` object and then adds the event handler to the `#div2` element. The difference between this method and the one in step 6 is that we use a selector. By using a selector, you can delete and re-add the `#div2` element, and it will still call the event handler. Also notice that, rather than an `event-map`, you use the events method and add the handler as the final argument.

```
08    $(document).on("click",
09                "#div2",
10                {"objId":"heading", "answer":"no"},
11                clickHandler);
```

8. Save all three files and then open the HTML document in a web browser and play around with the Say Yes and Say No buttons shown in Figure 9.3.

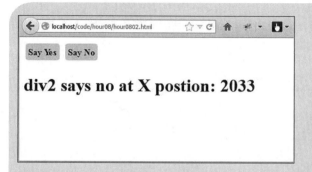

FIGURE 9.3
A simple JavaScript web page that uses jQuery to dynamically add event handlers to `<div>` elements and responds to mouse clicks.

LISTING 9.2-html   HTML File That Loads jQuery and JavaScript, Attaches Event Handler Elements to Provide User Interaction, and Then Defines the `<div>` and `<h1>` Elements Used in the Example

```
01 <!DOCTYPE html>
02 <html>
03   <head>
04     <title>Hour 9-2</title>
05     <meta charset="utf-8" />
06     <script type="text/javascript" src="../js/jquery.min.js"></script>
07     <script type="text/javascript" src="js/hour0902.js"></script>
08     <link rel="stylesheet" type="text/css" href="css/hour0902.css">
09   </head>
10   <body>
11     <div id="div1">Say Yes</div>
12     <div id="div2">Say No</div>
13     <h1 id="heading"></h1>
14   </body>
15 </html>
```

LISTING 9.2-js   jQuery and JavaScript Code That Defines an Event Handler and Dynamically Attaches It to the `<div>` Elements

```
01 function clickHandler(e){
02   $("#"+e.data.objId).html(e.target.id + " says " + e.data.answer +
03                          " at X postion: " + e.screenX);
04 }
05 $(document).ready(function(){
06   $("#div1").on({"click":clickHandler},
07               {"objId":"heading", "answer":"yes"});
```

```
08    $(document).on("click",
09              "#div2",
10              {"objId":"heading", "answer":"no"},
11              clickHandler);
12 });
```

LISTING 9.2-css   CSS Code That Styles the `<div>` Elements

```
1 div{
2    border-radius:5px;
3    margin:3px;
4    padding:5px;
5    background-color:lightgrey;
6    font-weight:bold;
7    display:inline-block;
8    cursor:pointer;
9 }
```

Using jQuery Event Helper Function to Assign Event Handlers

In addition to using the `addEventListener()` method to add event handlers, jQuery also provides helper functions that enable you to set the event handler. These helper functions are named after the event, so it helps your code look a bit cleaner.

The helper functions use the following syntax similar to `addEventListener()` but without the need to specify the event type:

```
.<event type>( [eventData], handler(eventObject))
```

The `eventData` argument is optional and, as with `addEventListener()`, will set the `data` value for the event object. The handler argument is required and specifies the function to call. Replace `<event type>` with the event name listed in Table 9.3. For example, the following two jQuery statements are equivalent ways to assign a handler to the click event:

```
obj.click( dataObj, function myHandler(e){...});
obj.addEventListener("click", dataObj, function myHandler(e){...});
```

In addition to the helper functions based on the event type name, jQuery also provides one additional helper function that is useful for mouse hovering events. The `hover()` helper function allows you to set the handlers for the `mouseenter` and `mouseleave` events at the same time. For example:

```
obj.hover(function enterHandler(e){...}, function leaveHandler(e){...});
```

is equivalent to

```
obj.addEventListener("mouseenter", function enterHandler(e){...});
obj.addEventListener("mouseenter", function leaveHandler(e){...});
```

You can also set the same handler for both the `mouseenter` and `mouseleave` by specifying only one handler. For example:

```
obj.hover(function hoverHandler(e){...});
```

Triggering Events Manually

JavaScript and jQuery allow you to trigger events manually. This provides advantages such as simulating user interactions, tying page element interactions together, or interactions with your own custom events.

The following sections describe how to trigger events in both JavaScript and jQuery.

Triggering Events in JavaScript

The simplest way to trigger an event in JavaScript is to use the event method attached to the DOM object if there is one. Simple events such as `click`, `select`, `blur`, and `focus` have corresponding methods attached to DOM objects that support them. For example, you can trigger the `click` event on most DOM objects using the following syntax:

```
obj.click();
```

The more advanced method of triggering events in JavaScript is to create an event object and then use the `document.dispatchEvent()` call to trigger the event mechanism. This method provides much more control over event information and is the only way to trigger many of the events. The `dispatchEvent()` method involves a three-step process.

The first step is to create an event object using the `document.createEvent()` method. The `createEvent()` method requires that you specify the event `type` for the object that is being created. Table 9.4 lists some of the common event types accepted by `createEvent()`. For example, to create a mouse `click` event object, you would use the following statement:

```
var clickEvent = document.createEvent("MouseEvents");
```

The next step is to initialize the event object with values by calling the events' initialization function. Table 9.4 lists the corresponding initialization function for the event types along with the parameters supported.

For example, to initialize the `click` event object, you would use the following statement. The type is specified as `"click"` and `bubbling` and `cancelable` attributes are both true. Here, window is used as the view element. The coordinates don't really matter, so they remain at 0, and the additional keyboard keys don't matter, so those are set to false. The button argument is set to 0 for the left-click, and no related target is specified:

```
clickEvent.initMouseEvent("click", true, true, window, 0, 0, 0, 0, 0, 0,
                          false, false, false, false, 0, null);
```

For the most part, the parameters to the initialization functions should be self-explanatory. However, you will likely need to check on some of the specific arguments. You can find the definitions for the event objects and methods at

www.w3.org/TR/DOM-Level-2-Events/events.html

The final step is to call dispatchEvent() on the HTML object that you want to trigger the event for. For example, the following code looks up an object and then triggers the click event:

```
var obj = document.getElementById("someId");
obj.dispatchEvent(clickEvent);
```

TABLE 9.4 Common Event Types Supported by createEvent()

Event Type	Initialization Method
CustomEvent	event.initCustomEvent(type, canBubble, cancelable, detail)
HTMLEvents	event.initEvent(type, bubbles, cancelable)
KeyboardEvent	event.initKeyboardEvent(type, bubbles, cancelable, viewArg, ctrlKeyArg, altKeyArg, shiftKeyArg, metaKeyArg, keyCodeArg, charCodeArg)
MouseEvents	event.initMouseEvent(type, canBubble, cancelable, view, detail, screenX, screenY, clientX, clientY, ctrlKey, altKey, shiftKey, metaKey, button, relatedTarget)
MutationEvents	event.initMutationEvent(type, canBubble, cancelable, relatedNode, prevValue, newValue, attributeName, attributeChange)
UIEvents	event.initUIEvent(type, canBubble, cancelable, view, detail)

CAUTION

Prior to IE9, IE used a different set of methods to create and trigger an event. Instead of `createEvent()`, you need to use `createEventObject()` and instead of `dispatchEvent()`, you would need to use `fireEvent()`. If you need to trigger events and support earlier IE browsers, then you should review the documentation at MSDN on using `fireEvent()`.

 TRY IT YOURSELF ▼

Triggering Events Manually in JavaScript

In this example, you step through the process of using an event handler from a `<span>` element to trigger a `click` event on a completely different element. The result will be that you can click the span element to select or deselect a check box. Use the following steps to create the files shown in Listing 9.3:

1. In Aptana, create the hour09/hour0903.html, hour09/js/hou0803.js, and hour09/cs/hour0903.css files.

2. Add the code shown in Listing 9.3-html to the HTML file. This is just a basic HTML file that loads additional JavaScript and CSS files. There are two check boxes and two `<span>` elements added to the web page.

3. Add the CSS from Listing 9.3-css to the CSS file. This code stylizes the `<span>` element to look like a button.

4. Open the hour0903.js file and the following `onloadHandler()` initialization function that attaches an event listener to both of the `<span>` elements:

```
01 function onloadHandler(){
02    var employee = document.getElementById("Employee");
03    employee.addEventListener('click', simpleClick, false);
04    var registered = document.getElementById("Registered");
05    registered.addEventListener('click', eventClick, false);
06 }
```

5. Create the `simpleClick()` handler function added to the first button. The code uses the `target.id` from the event to find the corresponding check box element. Then the `click()` function is called on the check box object, which triggers the `click` event just as if the mouse had clicked it.

```
07 function simpleClick(e){
08    var cb = document.getElementById("check"+e.target.id);
09    cb.click();
10 }
```

6. Add the following `eventClick()` handler function to the second button. This code first creates a "MouseEvents" object and then initializes it to a "click" type with the

appropriate parameters. This code also uses the `target.id` from the event to find the corresponding check box element, then calls `dispatchEvent()` on the check box element's object, triggering a mouse `click` event.

```
11 function eventClick(e){
12     var event = document.createEvent("MouseEvents");
13     event.initMouseEvent("click", true, true, window,
14                          0, 0, 0, 0, 0, false, false,
15                          false, false, 0, null);
16     var cb = document.getElementById("check"+e.target.id);
17     cb.dispatchEvent(event);
18 }
```

7. Save all three files and then open the HTML document in a web browser, as shown in Figure 9.4. Play around with the check boxes and buttons. Notice that the buttons provide the same interaction with the check box as directly clicking the check box.

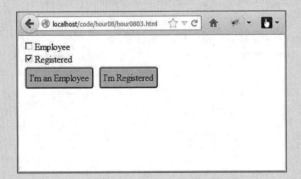

FIGURE 9.4
A simple web page that triggers the `click` event for check boxes from `<span>` elements.

LISTING 9.3-html **HTML File That Loads CSS and JavaScript and Defines the Check Boxes and `<span>` Elements**

```
01 <!DOCTYPE html>
02 <html>
03   <head>
04     <title>Hour 9-3</title>
05     <meta charset="utf-8" />
06     <script type="text/javascript" src="js/hour0903.js"></script>
07     <link rel="stylesheet" type="text/css" href="css/hour0903.css">
08   </head>
09   <body onload="onloadHandler()">
10     <input id="checkEmployee" type="checkbox" /><label>Employee</label><br>
```

```
11      <input id="checkRegistered" type="checkbox" /><label>Registered</label><br>
12      <span id="Employee">I'm an Employee</span>
13      <span id="Registered">I'm Registered</span>
14   </body>
15 </html>
```

LISTING 9.3-js JavaScript Code Manually Triggers the Click Event for the Check Box Elements from the `<span>` Elements

```
01 function onloadHandler(){
02   var employee = document.getElementById("Employee");
03   employee.addEventListener('click', simpleClick, false);
04   var registered = document.getElementById("Registered");
05   registered.addEventListener('click', eventClick, false);
06 }
07 function simpleClick(e){
08   var cb = document.getElementById("check"+e.target.id);
09   cb.click();
10 }
11 function eventClick(e){
12     var event = document.createEvent("MouseEvents");
13     event.initMouseEvent("click", true, true, window,
14                          0, 0, 0, 0, 0, false, false,
15                          false, false, 0, null);
16     var cb = document.getElementById("check"+e.target.id);
17     cb.dispatchEvent(event);
18 }
```

LISTING 9.3-css CSS Code That Styles the `<span>` Elements

```
1 span{
2   border-radius:5px;
3   margin:3px;
4   padding:5px;
5   background-color:#C0C0C0;
6   border:3px ridge;
7   display:inline-block;
8   cursor:pointer;
9 }
```

Using jQuery to Trigger Events Manually

Now that you've had a chance to trigger events from JavaScript, you are ready to find out just how much easier jQuery will make your life if you are able to use it. jQuery also supports two methods to trigger events manually.

As with JavaScript, jQuery objects also have methods that correspond to many of the event types that you can call directly. For example, most elements have `click()` and `dblclick()` methods. Form elements add additional methods such as `blur()`, `focus()`, `keypress()`, `keydown()`, and `keyup()` that can be called to trigger specific events. For example, the following statement will trigger the `click` event for all `<span>` elements:

```
$("span").click();
```

jQuery also provides a way to trigger events while specifying the values of the event object using the `trigger()` method. There are two different syntaxes for the `trigger()` method, as listed next:

```
trigger(eventType [, extraParameters])
trigger( eventObject)
```

Following is an example of using the first method to trigger the `click` event for all elements with `class="checkbox"`:

```
$(".checkbox").trigger("click");
```

The following is an example of using the second method on all input items with `class="bigText"`. This method actually passes in a simple event object for the `keypress` event, then sets the `charCode` attribute of the event object to 13 or the return key.

```
$("input.bigText").trigger({'type':'keypress', 'charCode':13});
```

Notice that this is much simpler than the JavaScript method because `trigger()` accepts a simple object with the appropriate attribute names to set whatever values in the event object you might want to pass in. Occasionally, you might end up having to use the JavaScript method, but you should use jQuery as often as possible.

▼ TRY IT YOURSELF

Triggering Events Manually in jQuery

In this example, you step through the process of using an event handler from a `<span>` element to trigger a `keypress` event on a text `<input>` element. The result will be that the click on the `<span>` will pass through the same event handler as a keystroke in the `<input>` element. Use the following steps to create the files shown in Listing 9.4:

1. In Aptana, create the hour09/hour0904.html, hour09/js/hou0904.js, and hou09/cs/hour0904.css files.

2. Add the code shown in Listing 9.4-html to the HTML file. This is a basic HTML file that loads additional jQuery, JavaScript, and CSS files. There is a `<p>` element, an `<input>` element, and a series of `<span>` elements that will act as buttons.

3. Add the CSS from Listing 9.4-css to the CSS file. This code stylizes the `<span>` element to look like a button and the `<p>` element to provide nice formatting.

4. Open the hour0904.js file and add the following `ready()` initialization function that attaches a `keypress` event handler to the `<input>` element as well as a `click` handler to all the `<span>` elements:

```
09 $(document).ready(function(){
10   $("input").keypress(function (e){inputHandler(e)});
11   $("span").click(function (e){spanHandler(e)});
12 });
```

5. Create the `inputHandler()` handler function that gets the `charCode` from the event object and appends the string form to the `<p>` element. At this point as you type in the text `<input>`, it will be displayed in the `<p>` element as well.

```
01 function inputHandler(e){
02   var chr = String.fromCharCode(e.charCode);
03   $("p").append(chr);
04 }
```

6. Add the following `spanHandler()` handler function that gets the `innerHTML` of the `<span>` element and converts the first character to a code. Line 7 then triggers a keypress event on the `<input>` element passing in the character code for the button as the `charCode` value. This allows the user to click a button and apply the currency symbol using the event handler for the text `<inputs>`.

```
05 function spanHandler(e){
06   var chrCode = e.target.innerHTML.charCodeAt(0);
07   $("input").trigger({'type':'keypress', 'charCode':chrCode});
08 }
```

7. Save all three files and then open the HTML document in a web browser, as shown in Figure 9.5. Type some text into the input and also click the `<span>` elements and notice that the result is the same.

LISTING 9.4-html   **HTML File That Loads CSS and JavaScript and Defines the `<p>`, Text `<input>`, and `<span>` Elements**

```
01 <!DOCTYPE html>
02 <html>
03   <head>
```

```
04        <title>Hour 9-4</title>
05        <meta charset="utf-8" />
06        <script type="text/javascript" src="../js/jquery.min.js"></script>
07        <script type="text/javascript" src="js/hour0904.js"></script>
08        <link rel="stylesheet" type="text/css" href="css/hour0904.css">
09     </head>
10     <body>
11        <p>Price: </p>
12        <input type="text" />
13        <span>&#x24;</span>
14        <span>&#xa3;</span>
15        <span>&#xa5;</span>
16        <span>&#x20ac;</span>
17     </body>
18  </html>
```

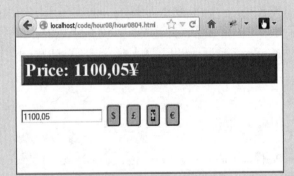

FIGURE 9.5
A simple web page that triggers the `keypress` event for the `<input>` element from the `<span>` elements'
event handler.

LISTING 9.4-js JavaScript Code That Triggers the `keypress` Event for the
`<input>` Element from the `<span>` Elements' Event Handler

```
01 function inputHandler(e){
02    var chr = String.fromCharCode(e.charCode);
03    $("p").append(chr);
04 }
05 function spanHandler(e){
06    var chrCode = e.target.innerHTML.charCodeAt(0);
07    $("input").trigger({'type':'keypress', 'charCode':chrCode});
08 }
09 $(document).ready(function(){
10    $("input").keypress(function (e){inputHandler(e)});
11    $("span").click(function (e){spanHandler(e)});
12 }),
```

▼ **LISTING 9.4-css**   CSS Code That Styles the `<span>` and `<p>` Elements

```
01 span{
02    border-radius:5px;
03    margin:3px;padding:5px;
04    background-color:#C0C0C0;
05    border:3px ridge;
06    display:inline-block;
07    cursor:pointer;
08 }
09 p{
10    border:4px outset blue;
11    padding:3px;
12    color:white;background-color:blue;
13    font-size:30px;font-weight:bold;
14 }
```

Creating Custom Events

An extremely powerful aspect of the JavaScript and jQuery event-handling mechanism is the capability to add custom events. This solves the problem that the built-in events are all tied to DOM elements and specific behaviors supported by the browser. What if you want an event for every time the number of items in an array is greater than 100?

Custom events enable you to extend the events that can be added to elements. Custom events do not directly correspond to the physical interaction with the user, but rather to events that happen in your code based on the interactions that the user is performing.

The advantage of creating custom events is that you can use the already in-place event-handling system that allows you to add/remove events, bubble them up, and trigger them.

The following sections describe the different methods you can use in JavaScript and jQuery to add your own custom events.

Adding Custom Events Using JavaScript

Adding a custom event in JavaScript is similar to triggering an event in that you create a custom event object and then initialize it. The following code shows an example of creating a basic custom event:

```
var myEvent = document.createEvent("CustomEvent");
myEvent .initCustomEvent(
  "worldEnds",
  true,
```

```
   false,
   {
       'fire': false,
       'ice': false,
       'time': new Date()
   }
);
```

The first parameter defines the `type` name, the second sets the `bubbles` property to true, the third sets `cancelable` to false, and the fourth defines the `details` of the event. The values of `fire`, `ice`, and `time` will be available via the `details` attribute of the event object.

After the event has been created, you can trigger the event by calling the `dispatchEvent()` method on a DOM object. For example:

```
var obj = document.getElementById("#notify");
obj.dispatchEvent(myEvent);
```

Event handlers for the event can be added to DOM elements in the normal way using the `addEventListener()` method. For example:

```
document.addEventListener("worldEnds ", endOfWorldHandler, false);
```

Adding Custom Events Using jQuery

Adding custom events in jQuery is a very simple process. It is a simple matter of calling `$.event.trigger()` and passing in the new event object. You must specify a type attribute for the event object, but after that, you can define whatever default values for the event object that you would like. For example, the following code will define a new event:

```
var custEvent = $.Event("worldEnds", {
  fire: false,
  ice: false,
  time: new Date()
});
```

The next line of code will trigger the event in the event system:

```
$.event.trigger(custEvent);
```

After the event has been added to the system, you can attach event handlers for it. For example:

```
$(document).on("worldEnds", endOfWorldHandler);
```

Implementing Callbacks

Although they are not really events, callbacks have some similarities. A callback is a function that can be registered in jQuery and then fired off at specific times from your code. When a callback list is fired, each of the functions are executed in order.

An example where callbacks are useful is if you want users to have the option to specify that they want a notification when a background process, such as downloading data via AJAX, completes. If a user selects the option to enable the notification, a callback can be added. Then, anytime a download completes, the callback function will execute and display a notification to the user.

Understanding the Callback Mechanism

The callback mechanism is used by calling $.Callbacks(flags) to create a callbacks object. The purpose of the flags attribute is to provide the capability to specify the behavior that should occur when different callback functions are executed. The possible values for flags are as follows:

- ▶ once—Functions added are fired only once.

- ▶ memory—As new functions are added, they are fired right away with the same values as the last time callbacks were fired.

- ▶ unique—Allows the callback functions to be added only once.

- ▶ stopOnFalse—Stops firing other callback functions if one of the functions fired returns a false.

The callbacks object supports adding functions using the add(functionName) method and removing functions using the remove(functionName) method. To fire the callback list, call the fire() method. You can also disable the list using the disable() method.

The simplest way to understand implementing callbacks is to look at some examples. The following code defines a list of callbacks that must have unique function names and that also stop if one of the functions returns false:

```
function functionA(){return true;}
function functionB(){return true;}
function functionC(){return true;}
var callbacks = $Callbacks("unique stopOnFalse");
callbacks.add(functionA);
callbacks.add(functionB);
callbacks.fire()
callbacks.remove(functionB);
callbacks.add(functionC);
```

```
callbacks.fire();
callbacks.disable();
callbacks.fire();
```

The first time that `callbacks` is fired, `functionA` and `functionB` are executed. The second time, `functionA` and `functionC` are executed because `functionB` was removed. The third time, no functions are executed because the list has been disabled.

Using Deferred Objects

jQuery provides an intriguing option to implement callbacks in a different way, the deferred object. A deferred object is an object that contains a set of functions that can be run at a later time. The actual arguments passed to the function are not added until the deferred object is resolved and the functions are executed.

This allows you to apply a set of functions to a single object that can be applied at any time.

The following code illustrates creating a simple deferred object with multiple functions and then executing those functions:

```
var resultString = "";
function function1(n1, n2, p3) { resultString += "Problem: "; }
function function2(n1, n2) { resultString += n1 + " + "; }
function function3(n1, n2) { resultString += n2 + " = "; }
var deferredObj = $.Deferred();
deferredObj.done( [function1, function2], function3).done(function(n1, n2) {
    resultString += n1 + n2;
    $("div").append(resultString);
  });
deferredObj.resolve(5,6);
```

So this is what is happening in the preceding code. The three defined functions all add to the `resultString` variable. A new deferred object named `deferredObj` is created. The `.done(functions [, functions])` method is called to add the functions to the deferred object. All three ways were used to add functions. The first argument is a list of functions to execute, the second is a single function, and the third is an anonymous function.

The functions are not executed until `.resolve(args)` is called. Notice that the arguments of `.resolve()` match those required by the functions. Each function is executed in order. The result is that the following string is appended to the `<div>` element:

```
Problem: 5 + 6 = 11
```

Summary

This hour focused on the different ways to implement event handling in web pages. Event handling is at the heart of interactive web pages. JavaScript and jQuery differ in how you create and add events to DOM elements. You learned the methods used to add event handlers in both.

You also learned how to access the event object and pass your own custom objects into event handlers, and you learned how to create and trigger your own custom events.

Q&A

Q. When is it better to use JavaScript to create and trigger custom functions rather than jQuery?

A. Never. Okay, not necessarily. jQuery has a lot more cross-browser support right now for events. Also, it is much easier to create the objects necessary. For those reasons, you should almost always use jQuery. If jQuery isn't an option for your environment because of backward compatibility or the like, then use JavaScript.

Q. Can't you do everything with custom events that you can do with callbacks?

A. Not very easily. Remember that you can create as many callback lists as you want with different flags and only fire off the functions tied to a specific list. Trying to manage all of that in event handlers would get out of hand pretty quickly

Workshop

The workshop consists of a set of questions and answers designed to solidify your understanding of the material covered in this hour. Try to answer the questions before looking at the answers.

Quiz

1. What HTML attribute of the `<body>` tag can be used to call JavaScript code when the page has finished loading?

2. True or False: An event will trigger the handler function only for the target element in which it occurs.

3. When would you use the `.ready()` method rather than the `.load()` method?

4. True or False: Mouse events can be triggered only by mouse movement or mouse clicks.

Quiz Answers

1. `onload`.

2. False. Most events will bubble up through ancestor objects all the way through the document object.

3. `.ready()` is used when you need only the DOM to be loaded. `.load()` is used if you also require other resources, such as images, to be finished loading as well.

4. False. Mouse events can be manually triggered in both jQuery and JavaScript.

Exercises

1. Extend the example in Listing 9.4 to add additional buttons for other nonstandard characters. You will need to get the Unicode character codes from the web.

2. Extend the example in Listing 9.4 to include a third button that will trigger the events for both check boxes.

Dynamically Accessing and Manipulating Web Pages

What You'll Learn in This Hour:

▶ Tracking the mouse position and other information

▶ Manipulating the size and other attributes of page elements

▶ How to show and hide elements dynamically

▶ Layering page elements

▶ Dynamically creating DOM elements and adding them to web pages

▶ Adding and removing classes in jQuery

▶ Modifying the layout of the web page

This hour is a big one. So far you have been given most of the tools that you will need to implement highly dynamic and interactive web pages. In this hour, you take the next step and learn how to use those tools and some new ones to access information about web page elements. Then you use that information to manipulate and arrange them.

After you are able to access and modify the properties and values of the different page elements, you will be able to change basic web pages into true web applications. The following sections will take you on that ride, so hang on.

Accessing Browser and Page Element Values

One of the core fundamentals of both jQuery and JavaScript are access to the DOM objects that represent the elements on the web page. This section guides you through accessing property values, position, size, and other attributes of the elements, as well as showing you how to modify many of them.

Getting Mouse Position

Mouse movement is one of the most common web interactions that you will be dealing with. Often, you will need to make adjustments to elements on the page based on the position of the mouse.

The mouse position is accessible from the event object when a mouse event is triggered. Keep in mind that there are three mouse coordinates specified by the event. Table 10.1 describes each of these.

TABLE 10.1 Event Object Attributes That Specify the Mouse Position

Attribute	Description
screenX	Specifies the x coordinate based on the mouse position relative to the left edge of the screen, regardless of the position of the browser window.
screenY	Specifies the y coordinate based on the mouse position relative to the top of the screen, regardless of the position of the browser window.
pageX	Specifies the x coordinate based on the mouse position relative to the left edge of the web page, regardless of the horizontal scrolling position.
pageY	Specifies the y coordinate based on the mouse position relative to the top of the web page, regardless of the vertical scrolling position.
clientX	Specifies the x coordinate based on the mouse position relative to the left edge browser window view area.
clientY	Specifies the y coordinate based on the mouse position relative to the top edge browser window view area.

The following code shows an example of getting the mouse coordinates from an event object named e and applying them to a string variable:

```
var screenPosition = e.screenX + ", " + e.screenY;
var pagePosition = e.pageX + ", " + e.pageY;
var browserPosition = e.clientX + ", " + e.clientY;
```

Getting and Setting Values

Several HTML elements, especially input elements, have values that are associated with them. It is a simple matter in both jQuery and JavaScript to access the values of elements.

In JavaScript, the value can be accessed directly by accessing the value attribute of the object; for example:

```
domObject.value = 5;
var value = domObject.value;
```

jQuery, on the other hand, provides the .val() method to retrieve and set the value. For example, the following code will set and then get the value of a jQuery object representing the HTML <input> element with id="textInput":

```
$("#textInput").val(5);
var value = $("#textInput ").val();
```

Getting and Setting Attributes and Properties in jQuery

DOM objects provide direct access to the DOM object attributes and the DOM element properties of the HTML elements they represent. This is not reasonable in jQuery, because jQuery objects often represent multiple elements with varying attributes. For that reason, jQuery provides the .attr() and .prop() methods to get and set the attributes and properties of these elements.

The .attr(attribute, [value]) method allows you to specify an attribute name only to get the current value, as well as an optional value to set the current value. For example, the following code gets the src value for a specific image element with id="bannerImg":

```
var state = $("#bannerImg").attr("src");
```

Then the following statement sets the src attribute value for all <img> elements:

```
$("img").attr("src","images/default.jpg");
```

The .prop(property, [value]) method allows you to specify the property to get the current value and an optional value to set the current value. For example, the following code gets the checked state for a specific element with id="firstCheckbox":

```
var state = $("#firstCheckbox").prop("checked");
```

And the following statement will set the checked value of all <input> elements to true:

```
$("input").prop("checked", true);
```

NOTE

The only difference between a property and attribute as far as jQuery goes is that attributes are values that define the HTML structure and properties are values that affect the dynamic state of the object. For example, in an <input> element, "type" is an attribute because it defines the structure, whereas "checked" is a property because it affects only the state.

Getting and Setting CSS Properties

Another important aspect of dynamic web programming is the dynamic manipulation of CSS.

JavaScript enables you to access the CSS properties via the style attribute of the DOM object. For example, you can get the color and background-color CSS properties of an element from a DOM object using the following code. Notice that you need to use style["background-color"] syntax because style.background-color is not valid in JavaScript:

```
var domObj = document.getElementById("banner");
var color = domObj.style.color;
var color = domObj.style.["background-color"];
```

Another example is that you can set `position`, `top`, and `left` CSS properties for an element using the following code:

```
domObj.style.position = "absolute";
domObj.style.top = "100px";
domObj.style.left = "100px";
```

jQuery also makes it extremely easy to get and set CSS values using the `.css(property, [value])` method. For example, the following code retrieves the `cursor` CSS property value of an element:

```
$("#buttonA").css("cursor");
```

Then the following sets the `border-radius` value:

```
$("#buttonA").css("border-radius", "10px 15px");
```

The `.css()` method also allows you to pass a map object with properties and values. This enables you to set several settings at once. For example, the following code uses `.css()` to set the `margin`, `padding`, `float`, and `font-weight` attributes at the same time:

```
$("span").css({margin:0, padding:2, float:"left", "font-weight":"bold"});
```

Notice that the property names can either be enclosed in quotes or not. You need to use quotes if the property name contains a – or other character that is not valid in a JavaScript object name. The values can be numbers or strings. The numerical values represent distance, which can be expressed in px, cm, or %; the default is px, so if you want to specify pixels, you only need to enter the number. If you want to specify cm, %, or some other value type, you need to use a string—for example, `"100%"`.

Getting and Setting Element Size

Another important aspect when dynamically working with HTML elements is the capability to get the element's size. jQuery makes this very simple. Table 10.2 shows the methods provided in the jQuery object that enable you to get the height and width of an element.

TABLE 10.2   jQuery Object Methods to Get and Set the Element Size

Attribute	Description
height([value])	If a value is specified, the height of all HTML elements in the set is changed; otherwise, the current height of the first HTML element is returned.

Attribute	Description
width([value])	If a value is specified, the width of all HTML elements in the set is changed; otherwise, the current width of the first HTML element is returned.
innerHeight()	Returns the current height, including padding, of the first element in the set.
innerWidth	Returns the current width, including padding, of the first element in the set.
outerHeight([includeMargin])	Returns the current height, including padding, border, and margin, if specified, of the first element in the set.
outerWidth([includeMargin])	Returns the current width, including padding, border, and margin, if specified, of the first element in the set.

CAUTION

The height and width methods return only the size of the first element in the jQuery objects' set. For single object sets, that is not a problem. Just keep in mind that other objects in the set may have different sizes.

Getting and Setting Element Position

In addition to the size of HTML elements, you often need to get their position. When you're working with HTML elements, there are two types of positions. The first is the position relative to the full document. The second is the position relative to the HTML element that acts as an offset parent. Which element is the offset parent depends on the position settings in CSS.

jQuery provides the .position([position]) method to get the position relative to the offset parent. The .offset([position]) method provides the position relative to the document. Both of these methods can be called with no argument. They return a simple object with a left and right attribute that represent the number of pixels from the left and top of the document when using .position() or offset parent when using .offset(). They can also be called with a simple position attribute, which is an object that has left and right attributes. When called with a position parameter, they will set the position of the element.

For example, the following code will get the number of pixels from the top and the left of the document and the offset parent to an element with id="myElement". Notice that to get the statements on one line, you reference the top and left attributes directly after the call:

```
var pixelsFromPageTop = $("#myElement").offset().top;
var pixelsFromPageLeft = $("#myElement").offset().left;
```

```
var pixelsFromParentTop = $("#myElement").position().top;
var pixelsFromParentLeft = $("#myElement").position().left;
```

To set the distance of that element exactly 10 pixels down and 10 pixels to the right of the top-left corner of the document, use the following statement that defines a simple object with `left` and `top` values and passes it to the `.offset()` method:

```
$("#myElement").offset({"top":10,"left":10);
```

Accessing the Class

The simplest way to get the classes associated with an HTML element is to look at the `className` attribute of the DOM object. The `className` attribute is a string containing the names of the class(es) attached to the element. Keep in mind that an element may have more than one class name attached to it. In those cases, the names will be separated by a space.

The following example shows how to get the `className` attribute of an element with `id="mainList"` from jQuery:

```
var class = $("#mainList").get().className;
```

Getting Browser and Screen Size and Color Information

An important part of dynamically manipulating web pages is the capability to access information about the screen and browser. This section focuses on the size and color capability.

Getting the screen or browser window size allows you to adjust the size of HTML elements based on the available area on the screen or browser window.

You can access the screen size using the `Screen` object in JavaScript. The `Screen` object provides the `width` and `height` attributes that are the screen resolution dimensions. For example, the following code stores the screen `width` and `height` in variable:

```
var sWidth = screen.width;
var sHeight = screen.height;
```

To get the supported colors by the screen and thus the web browser, use the `colorDepth` attribute of the `Screen` object. This returns a value of the number of bits supported—for example, 8, 16, 24. Following is an example of getting the color depth supported by the screen:

```
var colorBits = screen.colorDepth;
```

Even if the screen is large, the browser window may not be taking up the full screen amount. Although the browser window provides scrollbars for web pages that exceed the size of the window, it often looks better to resize elements on the page or adjust the layout as the browser size changes.

The browser dimensions can be accessed from the `innerWidth`, `outerWidth`, `innerHeight`, and `outerHeight` attributes of the window object available in JavaScript. The `innerHeight` and `innerWidth` values refer to the actual area available for the web page. The `outerWidth` and `outerHeight` refer to the total area, including the browser menu, borders, and bars. The following is an example of getting the web page display area dimensions:

```
var pageWidth = window.innerWidth;
var pageHeight = window.innerHeight;
```

TRY IT YOURSELF ▼

Getting Screen, Browser, Mouse, and Element Info Using jQuery and JavaScript

Now it's time to put everything together. In this example, you build a basic web page with some different HTML elements. One of the elements will be a `<div>` that displays screen, browser, mouse, and element information and is updated with each movement of the mouse. The code is shown in Listing 10.1. It may look like a lot of code at first, but it really is pretty basic and will help you see how to get information from jQuery and JavaScript about the current state of things.

Use the following steps to implement the example:

1. In Aptana, create the hour10, hour10/js, hour10/css, and hour10/images folders.

2. Create the hour10/hour1001.html, hour10/js/hour1001.js, and hour10/css/ hour1001.css files.

3. Add the code shown in Listing 10.1-html to the HTML file. You should recognize the HTML components. There are two main sections: The first part defines several types of elements for you to interact with, and the second part, the really long `<div>`, provides a place to display information about the mouse, screen, browser, and elements.

4. Add the CSS from Listing 10.1-css to the CSS file. You should also recognize the CSS statements by now. Some of the lines in the CSS are combined to make it fit better in the book.

5. Open the hour1001.js file and the following `ready()` function that adds event handlers for the `mousemove`, `mouseover`, `change`, `keypress`, and `resize` events. You will create these event handlers in later steps. The `mousemove` event handler is attached to the document to catch the mouse movements at the document level. The resize handler is attached to the window so that you can display info when the browser is resized.

```
01 $(document).ready(function(){
02    $(document).mousemove(mousePosition);
03    $("*").mouseover(elementInfo);
04    $("*").change(elementInfo);
05    $("*").keypress(elementInfo);
```

```
06    $(window).resize(windowResize);
07 });
```

6. Add the following handler that will be called on mouse movement. Notice that propagation is stopped so that you try to display the information only once. The `Screen` object is used to get and display the screen dimensions and color bits. The event object `e` is used to get and display the various mouse position coordinates.

```
08 function mousePosition(e){
09    e.stopPropagation();
10    $("#screenSize").html(screen.width + "x" + screen.height);
11    $("#colors").html(screen.colorDepth+"bit");
12    $("#browserSize").html(window.innerWidth + "x" + window.innerHeight);
13    $("#mousePosition").html("X:" + e.screenX + "  Y:" + e.screenY);
14    $("#pagePosition").html("X:" + e.pageX + "  Y:" + e.pageY);
15    $("#scrollPosition").html("X:" + e.clientX + "  Y:" + e.clientY);
16 }
```

7. Create the following functions that will display all the element information. Propagation is stopped. The contents of the `.infoContainer` `<span>` elements are removed by line 19. Using the event object, the `domObj` variable is assigned the `target` DOM object that the event occurred on, and `jObj` is set to the jQuery version of the `target` object:

```
17 function elementInfo(e){
18    e.stopPropagation();
19    $(".infoContainer span").html("");
20    var domObj = e.target;
21    var jObj = $(domObj);
...
33 }
```

8. Add the following statements that use the DOM and jQuery objects to display the `id`, `tag`, and `class` attributes:

```
22    $("#elementId").html(domObj.id);
23    $("#elementType").html(jObj.prop('tagName'));
24    $("#elementClass").html(domObj.className);
```

9. Add the following statements that display the element's size and position:

```
25    $("#elementSize").html(jObj.width() + "x" + jObj.height());
26    $("#elementPosition").html(jObj.offset().top + ", " + jObj.offset().
➥left);
```

10. Add the following miscellaneous statements. Line 27 uses the `.css()` method to get the CSS color attribute, line 28 uses `.val()` to get the value of the element if there is one, line 30 gets the checked state of the element if available, and line 32 gets the `src` attribute of `<img>` elements.

```
27    $("#elementColor").html(jObj.css("color"));
28    $("#elementValue").html(jObj.val());
29    try{
30      $("#elementChecked").html(jObj.prop('checked').toString());
31    } catch (e) {}
32    $("#elementSource").html(jObj.attr('src'));
```

11. Add the following handler that sets the browser window size each time you resize the browser:

```
34 function windowResize(e){
35    $("#browserSize").html(window.innerWidth + "x" + window.innerHeight);
36 }
```

12. Save all three files and then open the HTML document in a web browser. Play around with the HTML elements and see the information change, as shown in Figure 10.1. Mouse coordinates, screen, and browser size, as well as element info, are displayed as available. Don't forget to try resizing the browser and scrolling.

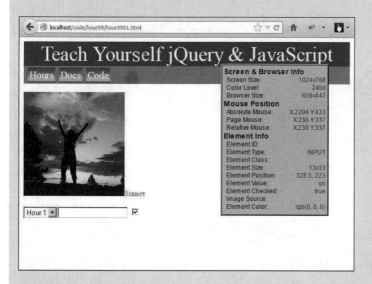

FIGURE 10.1
A web page that displays the screen, browser, mouse, and element info as you play around with the web page.

LISTING 10.1-html   **HTML File That Provides Several Elements to Play with, as Well as an Independent `<div>` That Displays Info**

```
01 <!DOCTYPE html>
02 <html>
```

```
03    <head>
04      <title>Hour 10-1</title>
05      <meta charset="utf-8" />
06      <script type="text/javascript" src="../js/jquery.min.js"></script>
07      <script type="text/javascript" src="js/hour1001.js"></script>
08      <link rel="stylesheet" type="text/css" href="css/hour1001.css">
09    </head>
10    <body>
11      <div>
12        <div id="banner" class="header">Teach Yourself jQuery & JavaScript</div>
13        <div id="menu" class="menu">
14          <span class="menuItem">Hours</span>
15          <span class="menuItem">Docs</span>
16          <span class="menuItem">Code</span>
17        </div>
18        <div id="content">
19          <p class="imageArea"><img id="sunset" src="images/sunset.jpg"
          ➥width="200px"/>Sunset</p>
20          <select>
21            <option value=1>Hour 1</option>
22            <option value=2>Hour 2</option>
23            <option value=3>Hour 3</option>
24            <input type=text />
25          </select>
26          <input type="checkbox" />
27        </div>
28      </div>
29
30      <div class=infoContainer>
31        <p>Screen & Browser Info</p>
32        <div>Screen Size: <span id="screenSize"></span></div>
33        <div>Color Level: <span id="colors"></span></div>
34        <div>Browser Size: <span id="browserSize"></span></div>
35        <p>Mouse Position</p>
36        <div>Absolute Mouse: <span id="mousePosition"></span></div>
37        <div>Page Mouse: <span id="pagePosition"></span></div>
38        <div>Relative Mouse: <span id="scrollPosition"></span></div>
39        <p>Element Info</p>
40        <div>Element ID: <span id="elementId"></span></div>
41        <div>Element Type: <span id="elementType"></span></div>
42        <div>Element Class: <span id="elementClass"></span></div>
43        <div>Element Size: <span id="elementSize"></span></div>
44        <div>Element Position: <span id="elementPosition"></span></div>
45        <div>Element Value: <span id="elementValue"></span></div>
46        <div>Element Checked: <span id="elementChecked"></span></div>
47        <div>Image Source: <span id="elementSource"></span></div>
```

```
48        <div>Element Color: <span id="elementColor"></span></div>
49      </div>
50    </body>
51 </html>
```

LISTING 10.1-js   jQuery and JavaScript Code That Retrieves and Displays
Information About the Screen, Browser, Mouse, and HTML Elements

```
01 $(document).ready(function(){
02   $(document).mousemove(mousePosition);
03   $("*").mouseover(elementInfo);
04   $("*").change(elementInfo);
05   $("*").keypress(elementInfo);
06   $(window).resize(windowResize);
07 });
08 function mousePosition(e){
09   e.stopPropagation();
10   $("#screenSize").html(screen.width + "x" + screen.height);
11   $("#colors").html(screen.colorDepth+"bit");
12   $("#browserSize").html(window.innerWidth + "x" + window.innerHeight);
13   $("#mousePosition").html("X:" + e.screenX + "  Y:" + e.screenY);
14   $("#pagePosition").html("X:" + e.pageX + "  Y:" + e.pageY);
15   $("#scrollPosition").html("X:" + e.clientX + "  Y:" + e.clientY);
16 }
17 function elementInfo(e){
18   e.stopPropagation();
19   $(".infoContainer span").html("");
20   var domObj = e.target;
21   var jObj = $(domObj);
22   $("#elementId").html(domObj.id);
23   $("#elementType").html(jObj.prop('tagName'));
24   $("#elementClass").html(domObj.className);
25   $("#elementSize").html(jObj.width() + "x" + jObj.height());
26   $("#elementPosition").html(jObj.offset().top + ", " + jObj.offset().left);
27   $("#elementColor").html(jObj.css("color"));
28   $("#elementValue").html(jObj.val());
29   try{
30     $("#elementChecked").html(jObj.prop('checked').toString());
31   } catch (e) {}
32   $("#elementSource").html(jObj.attr('src'));
33 }
34 function windowResize(e){
35   $("#browserSize").html(window.innerWidth + "x" + window.innerHeight);
36 }
```

LISTING 10.1-css   CSS Code That Styles the `<div>` and Other Elements

```
01  .infoContainer{
02    border:3px ridge;
03    padding:3px;
04    position:fixed; display:inline-block;
05    top:50px; right:50px;
06    background-color:#C0C0C0;
07    width:200px; height:280px;
08    font:12px arial;
09  }
10  .infoContainer div{ margin-left:5px; }
11  .infoContainer div span{
12    color:blue;
13    float:right; }
14  .infoContainer p{
15    margin:0px; padding:0px;
16    font-size:14px; font-weight:bold;
17  }
18  #banner{
19    height:100;
20    color:white; background-color:blue;
21    font-size:40px; text-align:center;
22  }
23  #menu{ background-color:gray; padding:5px; }
24  .menuItem{
25    padding:3px; margin-left:3px;
26    background-image: -moz-linear-gradient(top, #0022ff 0%, #AACCFF 85%, #0022ff
       ➡100%);
27    font:20px bold;
28    color:white;
29  }
30  .imageArea{color:red;}
```

Dynamically Manipulating Page Elements

In the previous section, you not only learned how to access the components, but also how to change values, attributes, properties, and CSS settings. This section extends those concepts by discussing some additional ways to dynamically manipulate the web page by adding and removing elements, changing classes, and toggling visibility.

Adding Page Elements Dynamically

Often, you will not know all the elements that belong on a web page until a user logs in, or you receive addition information from a web service, or some other interaction. In those cases, you must be able to add elements on-the-fly in your jQuery and JavaScript code.

Adding Page Elements in JavaScript

There are several ways to add HTML elements dynamically. The most basic is to set the `innerHTML` attribute of a container object to an HTML string. For example, the following code sets the contents of an existing object to a new `<p>` element:

```
domObj.innerHTML = "<p>Paragraph 1 goes here</p>";
domObj.innerHTML += "<p>Paragraph 2 goes here</p>";
```

The problem with this method is that it lends itself to really ugly string statements that will likely become a major headache later. So JavaScript provides a way to create the DOM objects and then append them to the parent object.

The `document.createElement(tag)` method allows you to create an element object, and the `document.createTextNode(text)` allows you to create the text node that is part of the element. Then the `appendChild(object)` method can be called on the DOM objects to append the newly created elements and nodes.

To illustrate this, check out the following code that adds a couple of paragraphs to an existing object named `domObj`:

```
var newP = createElement("p");
var newT = createTextNode("Paragraph 1 goes here");
newP.appendChild(newT);
domObj.appendChild(newP);
```

It takes a bit more code, but the flow is much safer. Plus, the upside of creating objects is that you have an actual DOM object that you can add additional values to the element. For example, the following code allows you to add an `<img>` element and set the `src` and `height` attributes before appending it to the existing object:

```
var newImg = createElement("img");
newImg.src = "images/sunset.jpg";
newImg.height = 200;
domObj.appendChild(newImg);
```

Adding Page Elements in jQuery

Now you can look at how to add new elements in jQuery. You can apply the same `innerHTML` shortcut in jQuery as in JavaScript by using the `.html()` method, which will get or set the `innerHTML` string. For example:

```
$("#myDiv").html("<p>Paragraph 1 goes here</p>");
```

This method, however, has the same limitations and should be used sparingly. The better method is to create a new jQuery object and append it. The following code takes you through that process. The first step is to create the object by passing the tag name or HTML string to the jQuery object $. For example, the following statement creates a new jQuery object with one <p> element in the set:

```
var newP = $("<p></p>");
```

You can then add text to the paragraph using the following:

```
newP.html("Paragraph 1 goes here");
```

Then you can append an element to one or more existing elements using .append(jQueryObject). For example, the following code adds the paragraph to all <div> elements:

```
$("div").append(newP);
```

To illustrate this, the following code creates a new jQuery object with an <img> element in the set and adds it to all <li> elements:

```
var newImg = $("<img></img>");
newImg.attr("src", "images/sunset.jpg");
newImg.height(30);
$("li").append(newImg);
```

jQuery also provides the .appendTo(target) method, which allows you to append an object to another object. This works the same way as .append() but in reverse. The method is called from the child object and not the new parent. For example, the newImg object from the example above could be appended by the following statement instead:

```
newImg.appendTo("li");
```

Removing Page Elements

Page elements can be removed in a couple of ways. The most basic way is to get the parent object and then set domObj.innerHTML = "" for DOM objects or call jObj.html("") for jQuery objects. This erases all content inside the parent element and thus removes any child elements.

Try to design your html components so that you can remove elements using the .html("") method because it keeps the cleanup code so simple. Another advantage is that adding new elements to the container is easier because you don't have to deal with existing elements.

In JavaScript, you can also call the `.removeElement(child)` on the parent element. For example, the following code gets an element with `id="container"` and then removes a child with `id="paragraphA"`:

```
var parent=document.getElementById("container");
var child=document.getElementById("paragraphA");
child.parentNode.removeChild(child);
```

jQuery provides two methods to remove elements. The first is `.empty()`, which is equivalent to `.html("")`. With `.empty()`, all child elements and text will be removed. The second method is `.remove([selector])`, which removes elements based only on the original query and an optional `selector`.

If no selector is specified, the elements from the original query are removed. For example, to remove all `<div>` elements, use the following statement:

```
$("div").remove()
```

If a selector is specified, child elements from the original query that match the selector will be removed. For example, to remove the `<p>` elements inside `<div>` elements, use the following:

```
$("div").remove("p");
```

jQuery provides one additional method that is useful when removing elements: the `.detach([selector])` method. The detach method works the same way as the `.remove([selector])` method, with one important difference. The actual element DOM data is not deleted, even though the elements are removed from the parents. You still have the elements in the existing jQuery object and can insert them back into the DOM at another location.

For example, the following code detaches all paragraphs from one element and appends them to another:

```
var ps = $("#div1").detach("p");
ps.appendTo("#div2");
```

Replacing Elements in jQuery

As you have seen in the previous sections, you can easily add and remove elements via jQuery. You also need to be aware of the capability to replace existing sets of elements with other sets of elements. This is required in jQuery because after you remove the elements, you will no longer be able to perform the same queries because the elements will be gone.

You can use three methods to replace elements in jQuery. The simplest is to use `.html()`. The `.html()` method in jQuery is extremely useful for replacing the contents of an existing element with completely different content. The `.html()` method accepts a string or an object and replaces the content of the set of elements in the jQuery with the object or string. For example, the following statement replaces the contents of all `<div>` elements with a new paragraph:

```
$("div").html($("<p>New Paragraph</p>"));
```

Another method of replacing a set of elements in the document with new content is the `.replaceAll(target)` method. This method replaces the set of elements that match the `target` selector with those of the current set. For example, to replace all `<div>` elements in a `parentB` with `<span>` elements from `parentA`, you could use the following:

```
$("#parentA span").replaceAll("#parentB div");
```

The final method is to use `.replaceWith(newContent)`, which does the opposite of `.replaceAll()`. The `.replaceWith()` function replaces the elements in the current set with the content specified. For example, to replace all `<div>` elements with a single new blank `<div>`, you could use the following:

```
$("div").replaceWith($("<div></div>"));
```

Inserting Elements in jQuery

Another important feature of jQuery is the capability to easily insert elements into existing content. You have already seen how to append items to the end; however, what if you want to put content into the middle? That is where the `.before()` and `.after()` methods come in handy.

The `.after(content [,content])` method allows you to specify an element that should be inserted after each element in the current jQuery object's set. For example, to insert a new paragraph after the third `<p>` element in the document, you would use the following:

```
$("p:eq(2)").after($("<p>New Fourth Paragraph</p>"));
```

The `.before(content [,content])` method allows you to specify an element that should be inserted before each element in the current jQuery object's set. For example, to insert a new paragraph before the third `<p>` element in the document, you would use the following:

```
$("p:eq(2)").before($("<p>New Third Paragraph</p>"));
```

NOTE

Both the `.after()` and `.before()` methods allow you to pass in multiple objects to insert, separated by a comma. This enables you to prepare sets of objects and then insert them all together in the correct spot.

Changing Classes

A very important part of rich interactive web pages is good CSS design. JavaScript and jQuery can enhance the CSS design by dynamically adding and removing classes from elements.

jQuery makes it extremely simple to add, remove, and toggle classes on and off. If you design your CSS code well, it is very simple to apply some nice effects very easily.

Classes are added using the `.addClass(className)` method. For example, to add a class named active to all `<span>` elements, you could use the following statement:

```
$("span").addClass("active");
```

Classes are removed using the `.removeClass([className])` method. For example, to remove the active class from the `<span>` elements, you would call

```
$("span").removeClass("active");
```

You can also use remove with no `className`, which removes all classes from the elements. For example, the following statement removes all classes from `<p>` elements:

```
$("p").removeClass();
```

You can also toggle classes on and off using the `.toggleClass(className [, switch)` method. In addition to the `className`, you can specify a `true` or `false` for the optional `switch` parameter indicating to turn the class on or off.

For example, to turn the active class and the inactive class off for all `<span>` elements, the code would be the following:

```
$("span").toggleClass("active", true);
$("span").toggleClass("inactive", false);
```

Toggling Visibility

A simple way of changing the look and feel of web pages is to toggle the visibility of elements. You can do this from JavaScript by setting the `style.display` property to `"none"` or to `""`; however, jQuery provides much more elegant and extensible solutions.

To display an element using jQuery, simply call the `.show()` method on that object. Then to hide the element, use the `.hide()` method. It's as simple as that. For example, to hide an object named jObj, use the following statement:

```
jObj.hide();
```

To display it again, use

```
jObj.show();
```

One problem with .hide() is that once it is applied, the element will no longer take up any page space. This may be the way that you want it, or in some instances you may only want the element to be invisible, but still take up space. To make an element invisible, set the opacity CSS property to 0. For example:

```
jObj.css("opacity", "0");
```

To make the element visible again, set the opacity back to 1:

```
jObj.css("opacity", "1");
```

TIP
_____

Setting the opacity lower but not to 0 can be a great way to show that elements are not currently active while still showing them. For example, you can set menu and button elements that are not yet implemented and active to .5 opacity so that they still show up but are obviously not clickable.
_____

▼ TRY IT YOURSELF

Dynamically Manipulating Web Page Elements

Now it's time to put everything together again. In this example, you start with a basic web page and then dynamically add, modify, and remove elements based on user interactions, as shown in Figure 10.2. The purpose of this example is to get you going on adding content dynamically, as well as accessing properties of existing elements and manipulating the content, visibility, and classes.

The code is shown in Listing 10.2. After you grasp this example, it should open up your mind to more elaborate and rich implementations. Use the following steps to implement the example:

1. In Aptana, create the hour10/hour1002.html, hour10/js/hour1002.js, and hour10/css/hour1002.css files.

2. Add the code shown in Listing 10.2-html to the HTML file. You should recognize the HTML components. There is a set of <span> elements that will be buttons, a content <div> where you will dynamically place new elements, and a free-floating menu that provides buttons with links to jQuery docs.

3. Add the CSS from Listing 10.2-css to the CSS file. There is quite a bit of CSS code to style the different elements. However, all of it should be familiar to you by now.

4. Open the hour1002.js file and add the following ready() function. Line 2 hides the docMenu div, which will be shown only when the user clicks on the Docs button. The rest of the lines add click handlers for the buttons.

```
01 $(document).ready(function(){
02    $("docMenu").hide();
```

```
03    $("#hours").click(setHourNav);
04    $("#docs").click(setDocNav);
05    $("#fade").click(fade);
06  });
```

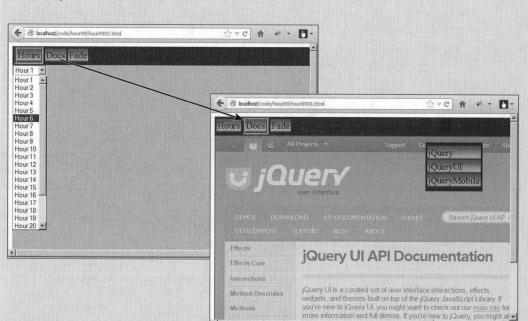

FIGURE 10.2
A web page that dynamically builds the elements displayed in the left pane and then changes the content based on user selections.

5. Add the code shown in lines 7 through 22. This is two functions. The `setHourNav()` function is called when the user clicks the Hours button. This function goes through the process of creating a new `<select>` element and adding 24 `<option>` elements to it. On line 16, a `change` event handler is added to the `<select>` element to catch when the hour changes. The second function sets the content paragraph element to match the hour selected.

```
24    $("#content").append(select).append("<br><p></p>");
```

6. Add the following function that will be called when a user clicks the Docs button. This function shows the doc menu, removes the active class from all `<span>` elements, and then adds it to the Docs button to show it is active.

```
27  function setDocNav(){
28    $("docMenu").show();
29    $("span").removeClass("active");
```

```
30    $("#docs").addClass("active");
31 }
```

7. Add the following handler for when the user clicks one of the options in the doc menu. This function creates a new `<iframe>` element that points to the selected doc and then replaces the contents of the #content `<div>` with that new element.

```
32 function setDoc(doc){
33    var frame = $("<iframe></iframe>");
34    frame.attr("src", doc);
35    $("#content").html(frame);
36 }
```

8. Add the following handler for when the user clicks the Fade button. This checks the current opacity CSS property and increases it or decreases it to cause the content to fade in and out.

```
37 function fade(){
38    var opacity = $("#content").css("opacity");
39    if (opacity < 1){ $("#content").css("opacity", 1);}
40    else { $("#content").css("opacity", .5); }
41 }
```

9. Save all three files and then open the HTML document in a web browser. Play around with the Hours and Docs buttons to see the elements dynamically displayed. Try the Fade button to fade the content in and out.

LISTING 10.2-html   HTML File Basic Web Page Used in the Example

```
01 <!DOCTYPE html>
02 <html>
03   <head>
04     <title>Hour 10-2</title>
05     <meta charset="utf-8" />
06     <script type="text/javascript" src="../js/jquery.min.js"></script>
07     <script type="text/javascript" src="js/hour1002.js"></script>
08     <link rel="stylesheet" type="text/css" href="css/hour1002.css">
09   </head>
10   <body>
11     <div id="container">
12       <div id="menu" class="menu">
13         <span id="hours" class="menuItem">Hours</span>
14         <span id="docs" class="menuItem">Docs</span>
15         <span id="fade" class="menuItem">Fade</span>
16       </div>
17       <div id="content"></div>
18     </div>
```

```
19      <div id="docMenu">
20        <span onclick="setDoc('http://api.jquery.com/')">jQuery</span>
21        <span onclick="setDoc('http://api.jqueryui.com/')">jQueryUI</span>
22        <span onclick="setDoc('http://jquerymobile.com/
          ➥demos/1.2.0/')">jQueryMobile</span>
23      </div>
24    </body>
25  </html>
```

LISTING 10.2-js   jQuery and JavaScript Code That Dynamically Builds the Left
Navigation Items Based on the Button Clicked in the Top Menu

```
01 $(document).ready(function(){
02   $("#docMenu").hide();
03   $("#hours").click(setHourNav);
04   $("#docs").click(setDocNav);
05   $("#fade").click(fade);
06 });
07 function setHour(e){
08   var hour = $("#hourSelect").val();
09   $("#content p").html("Hour "+ hour);
10 }
11 function setHourNav(){
12   $("#docMenu").hide();
13   $("span").removeClass("active");
14   $("#hours").addClass("active");
15   var select = $('<select id="hourSelect"></select>');
16   select.change(setHour);
17   for(var x=1; x<25; x++){
18     var option = $("<option></option>");
19     option.val(x);
20     option.html("Hour "+x);
21     select.append(option);
22   }
23   $("#content").html("");
24   $("#content").append(select).append("<br><p></p>");
25   setHour();
26 }
27 function setDocNav(){
28   $("#docMenu").show();
29   $("span").removeClass("active");
30   $("#docs").addClass("active");
31 }
32 function setDoc(doc){
33   var frame = $("<iframe></iframe>");
34   frame.attr("src", doc);
```

```
35   $("#content").html(frame);
36 }
37 function fade(){
38   var opacity = $("#content").css("opacity");
39   if (opacity < 1){ $("#content").css("opacity", 1);}
40   else { $("#content").css("opacity", .5); }
41 }
```

LISTING 10.2-css CSS Code That Styles the Banner, Buttons, and Other Elements

```
01 #banner{
02   height:100px;
03   color:white; background-color:blue;
04   font-size:40px; text-align:center;
05 }
06 #menu, #docMenu{
07   background-color:black;
08   padding:6px 4px 9px 4px;
09 }
10 .menuItem, #docMenu span{
11   padding:2px;
12   background-image: -moz-linear-gradient(top, #2244ff 0%, #AACCFF 85%, #0022ff
      ➥100%);
13   font:20px bold;
14   cursor:pointer;
15 }
16 .active{
17   border:5px groove;
18 }
19 #docMenu span{
20   display:block;
21   margin-top:1px;
22 }
23 #content, iframe{
24   display:inline-block;
25   width:700px; height:500px;
26 }
27 #container{ width:800px; background-color:#C0C0C0}
28 #docMenu{
29   position:fixed; right:60px; top:60px;
30 }
```

Dynamically Rearranging Elements on the Web Page

One of the coolest interactions that you can make with web pages is to rearrange elements based on user interaction. For instance, you can make elements bigger or smaller, or change the position. These were already covered as part of getting and setting element attributes in the first section of this hour. This section builds further on those concepts by discussing a final way to position page elements using the `z-index`; then you step through an example that shows the different methods of rearranging the elements.

Adjusting the `z-index`

The `z-index` is a CSS property that specifies the position of an HTML element with respect to other elements, not vertically or horizontally but projected out toward the user, as if it were papers stacked on top of one another on the screen. The element with the highest `z-index` is displayed on top of other elements when the page is rendered by the browser.

To get and set the `z-index` in jQuery, use the `.css()` method. For example, to get the `z-index` for an item, use the following:

```
var zIndex = $("#item").css("z-index");
```

To set the `z-index` for an item to read 10, use the following statement:

```
$("#item").css("z-index", "10");
```

▼ TRY IT YOURSELF

Dynamically Rearranging Page Elements

In this example, you learn the process of using jQuery and JavaScript to move, resize, and rearrange images. You use images because they are one of the most commonly rearranged elements. You can apply these same principles to any HTML element. The code for the example is shown in Listing 10.3. Use the following steps to implement the example:

1. In Aptana, create the hour10/hour1003.html, hour10/js/hour1003.js, and hour10/css/hour1003.css files.

2. Add the code shown in Listing 10.3-html to the HTML file. You should recognize the HTML components. The HTML code contains several `<span>` elements that will be styled as buttons and three images that will be rearranged as the user clicks the buttons.

3. Add the CSS from Listing 10.3-css to the CSS file. This code styles the buttons and puts a frame around the images.

4. Open the hour1003.js file and the following global definitions, which will be used later to keep track of the starting coordinates when tiling and stacking images, as well as the current image with the top z-index and max image index:

```
01 var startX = startY = 60;
02 var topIndex, maxIndex;
```

5. Add the following ready() function. Lines 3 and 4 set the current top index and the max index to the number of files minus 1 to make it zero-based. Then lines 6–12 add click handlers for each of the buttons.

```
03 $(document).ready(function(){
04    topIndex = $(".photo").length-1;
05    maxIndex = topIndex;
06    $("#right").click(function(e){move(e, "right");});
07    $("#left").click(function(e){move(e, "left");});
08    $("#bigger").click(function(e){resize(e, "bigger");});
09    $("#smaller").click(function(e){resize(e, "smaller");});
10    $("#stack").click(stack);
11    $("#tile").click(tile);
12    $("#flip").click(flip);
13    stack();
14 });
```

6. Add the following resize handler that accepts a direction and uses the value to either enlarge or shrink the image by adjusting the width using the width() method. Notice that the topIndex variable is used to determine which image to adjust:

```
15 function resize(e, direction){
16    var img = $("img:eq(" + topIndex + ")");
17    if (direction == "bigger"){ img.width(img.width()+20); }
18    else { img.width(img.width()-20); }
19 }
```

7. Add the following move handler that adjusts the offset() of the image to the left or right based on the direction argument. Also startX and startY are adjusted to the new position.

```
20 function move(e, direction){
21    var img = $("img:eq(" + topIndex + ")");
22    var pos = img.offset();
23    if (direction == "right"){ pos.left += 10;}
24    else {pos.left -= 10;}
25    img.offset(pos);
26    startX = pos.left;
27    startY = pos.top;
28 }
```

8. Add the following `stack()` function that iterates through all the `.photo` elements and stacks them by adjusting the `top` and `left` offset values each iteration:

```
29 function stack(){
30    var x = startX,  y = startY;
31    $(".photo").each(function(indx){
32       $(this).offset({ top:y, left:x });
33       x += 20;
34       y += 20;
35    });
36 }
```

9. Add the following `tile()` function that also iterates through all the `.photo` elements and places them next to each other, rotating to the next line if the current set has surpassed 400 pixels. Notice that I use several variables through each iteration to keep track of the max height and current x and y coordinates.

```
37 function tile(){
38    var x = startX, y = currTop = startY;
39    var maxH = 0;
40    $(".photo").each(function(indx){
41       maxH = Math.max(maxH, $(this).outerHeight());
42       $(this).offset({ top:y, left:x });
43       x += $(this).outerWidth();
44       if (x > 400){
45          y = currTop + maxH;
46          x = startX;
47          maxH = 0;
48       }
49    });
50 }
```

10. Add the `flip()` function that will adjust the `z-index` so that when images overlap each other, you can change which is on top:

```
51 function flip(){
52    if (topIndex >= $(".photo").length-1){ topIndex=0; }
53    else { topIndex++; }
54    var lastObj = null;
55    $(".photo").each(function(indx){
56       if (indx>topIndex){ z = indx-topIndex; }
57       else { var z = indx + maxIndex - topIndex; }
58       $(this).css("z-index", z);
59       lastObj = $(this);
60    });
61    lastObj.css("z-Index", 0);
62 }
```

11. Save all three files and then open the HTML document in a web browser, as shown in Figure 10.3. Play around with the buttons and notice how the interactions of the images matches the rearrangements made by the click handler functions.

FIGURE 10.3
Using the `width()`, `offset()`, and `css("z-index")` methods on image objects, you can easily rearrange them on the web page.

LISTING 10.3-html   HTML File Basic Web Page Used in the Example That Defines Several `<span>` Elements Used for Buttons and `<img>` Elements

```
01 <!DOCTYPE html>
02 <html>
03   <head>
04     <title>Hour 10-3</title>
05     <meta charset="utf-8" />
06     <script type="text/javascript" src="../js/jquery.min.js"></script>
07     <script type="text/javascript" src="js/hour1003.js"></script>
08     <link rel="stylesheet" type="text/css" href="css/hour1003.css">
09   </head>
10   <body>
11     <div id="container">
12       <span id="left">Left</span>
13       <span id="right">Right</span>
14       <span id="bigger">Bigger</span>
15       <span id="smaller">Smaller</span>
16       <span id="stack">Stack</span>
17       <span id="flip">Flip</span>
18       <span id="tile">Tile</span>
```

```
19        <div id="photos">
20            <img class="photo" src="images/sunset.jpg" />
21            <img class="photo" src="images/boy.jpg" />
22            <img class="photo" src="images/flower.jpg" />
23        </div>
24    </div>
25    </body>
26 </html>
```

LISTING 10.3-js jQuery and JavaScript Code That Dynamically Moves, Resizes, and Adjusts the z-index of Several <img> Elements

```
01 var startX = startY = 60;
02 var topIndex, maxIndex;
03 $(document).ready(function(){
04    topIndex = $(".photo").length-1;
05    maxIndex = topIndex;
06    $("#right").click(function(e){move(e, "right");});
07    $("#left").click(function(e){move(e, "left");});
08    $("#bigger").click(function(e){resize(e, "bigger");});
09    $("#smaller").click(function(e){resize(e, "smaller");});
10    $("#stack").click(stack);
11    $("#tile").click(tile);
12    $("#flip").click(flip);
13    stack();
14 });
15 function resize(e, direction){
16    var img = $("img:eq(" + topIndex + ")");
17    if (direction == "bigger"){ img.width(img.width()+20); }
18    else { img.width(img.width()-20); }
19 }
20 function move(e, direction){
21    var img = $("img:eq(" + topIndex + ")");
22    var pos = img.offset();
23    if (direction == "right"){ pos.left += 10;}
24    else {pos.left -= 10;}
25    img.offset(pos);
26    startX = pos.left;
27    startY = pos.top;
28 }
29 function stack(){
30    var x = startX,  y = startY;
31    $(".photo").each(function(indx){
32        $(this).offset({ top:y, left:x });
33        x += 20;
```

```
34      y += 20;
35    });
36  }
37  function tile(){
38    var x = startX, y = currTop = startY;
39    var maxH = 0;
40    $(".photo").each(function(indx){
41      maxH = Math.max(maxH, $(this).outerHeight());
42      $(this).offset({ top:y, left:x });
43      x += $(this).outerWidth();
44      if (x > 400){
45        y = currTop + maxH;
46        x = startX;
47        maxH = 0;
48      }
49    });
50  }
51  function flip(){
52    if (topIndex >= $(".photo").length-1){ topIndex=0; }
53    else { topIndex++; }
54    var lastObj = null;
55    $(".photo").each(function(indx){
56      if (indx>topIndex){ z = indx-topIndex; }
57      else { var z = indx + maxIndex - topIndex; }
58      $(this).css("z-index", z);
59      lastObj = $(this);
60    });
61    lastObj.css("z-Index", 0);
62  }
```

LISTING 10.3-css   CSS Code That Styles the Buttons and Images

```
01  .photo{
02    border:6px groove;
03    width:200px;
04    position:absolute; top:40px; left:20px;
05  }
06  span{
07    padding:5px;
08    background-color:blue; color:white;
09    border-radius:10px 15px; border:5px ridge blue;
10    cursor:pointer;
11  }
12  #container{ padding:5px; }
```

Summary

This hour has covered a lot of ground. You already had the tools to understand the JavaScript code, CSS styling, and the various objects involved in jQuery and JavaScript. In this hour, you learned how to access the attributes, properties, methods, and other parts of those objects and them modify them to apply interactivity and dynamics to web pages.

You also learned how to create HTML objects dynamically and add them to web pages, and how to remove and modify existing elements based on user interaction.

Q&A

Q. You showed how to add and remove classes in jQuery; is there a way to do the same in JavaScript?

A. Yes, but you probably shouldn't use it. The `className` attribute of the DOM object contains a space-separated list of classes. You can add a class by appending the new class name to that attribute—for example `obj.className += " " + newClass;`. Removing the `className` is more difficult. You need to either use a `regex` statement or split the string, remove the class, and then rebuild it. These methods are a lot more risky than jQuery because you can end up mangling the string and then none of the classes will work.

Q. Is there a way to rotate an image element?

A. Yes, in some browsers. You can use the `transform` CSS property for Firefox and Chrome and the `filter` property for Internet Explorer. The following code illustrates rotating an image 90 degrees using jQuery in Firefox, IE, and Chrome:

```
$("img").css({
    "-webkit-transform": "rotate(90deg)",
    "-moz-transform": "rotate(90deg)",
    "filter": "progid:DXImageTransform.Microsoft.BasicImage(rotation=1)"
});
```

Workshop

The workshop consists of a set of questions and answers designed to solidify your understanding of the material covered in this hour. Try to answer the questions before looking at the answers.

Quiz

1. How do you make an element disappear and yet keep taking up space in the web browser?

2. What CSS property allows you to specify which HTML element is displayed on top when two elements overlap?

3. What is the difference between `screenX`, `pageX`, and `clientX` properties of a mouse event?

4. What jQuery would you use to remove all `<p>` elements from an element with `id="container"`?

5. True or False: An HTML element can have only one class assigned to it at a time.

Quiz Answers

1. By setting the `opacity` CSS property to 0.

2. `z-index`

3. `screenX` is relative to the left edge of the `screen`, `pageX` is relative to the left edge of the document, and `clientX` is relative to the left edge of the browser window.

4. `$("#container p").remove();`

5. False. Elements can have many classes assigned to them.

Exercises

1. Open the code in Listing 10.1 and add a link with a `target` and `href` value. Then modify the JavaScript to also display those values in the info portion of the web page so that you can hover over the link and see them.

2. Open the code in Listing 10.3 and add four new buttons. Add two buttons to move the image up and down. Then add two buttons that change the opacity of the image up .1 or down .1. You will need to make certain that the opacity stops at 0 and 1.

Accessing Data Outside the Web Page

What You'll Learn in This Hour:

▶ Adding timers to web pages
▶ Getting and setting cookies
▶ Creating pop-ups

Dynamic web pages often require you to access and, in some cases, even manipulate things beyond the HTML elements. JavaScript provides a rich set of objects and functions that allow you to access information about the screen, browser window, history, and more.

The first part of this hour describes the `screen`, `window`, `location`, and `history` objects that provide JavaScript with an interface to access information beyond the web page. The second part covers utilizing those objects to implement cookies, pop-up windows, and timers.

Understanding the Screen Object

You have already seen the screen object in use in previous hours. You have used the screen object to get the color depth as well as the height and width of the screen. Getting the screen dimensions has become more important with the shift toward mobile devices and tablets.

A wide range of screen sizes is available; therefore, you must be able to design your web pages and dynamic interactions to take the screen size into account.

Table 11.1 describes the full set of properties available on the screen object.

TABLE 11.1 Screen Object Properties

Property	Description
availHeight	Height of the physical screen minus the Windows taskbar.
availWidth	Width of the physical screen minus the Windows taskbar.
colorDepth	Number of bits in the color palette available to display images.
height	Full height of the physical screen.

Property	Description
pixelDepth	Color resolution of the screen in bits per pixel.
width	Full width of the physical screen.

Using the Window Object

The window object is by far the most robust of the external object set. The window object provides access to the browser window, allowing you to get information such as the dimensions and position of the browser window.

Using the window object, you can also create and control new browser windows when you want to display additional web content but do not want to navigate away from the current page.

The following sections describe some of the methods and properties attached to the window object.

Accessing the Window Object Properties

The window object provides you with important information about browser windows. You can access the size and position of the current window or even its parent window. For example, the following code gets the pixels down and left from the top left of the screen to the top left of the browser:

```
var fromTop = window.self.screenY;
var fromLeft = window.self.screenX;
```

Table 11.2 shows a list of some of the more important window object properties and what they are used for.

TABLE 11.2 Window Object Properties

Property	Description
closed	True if window has been closed; false if it is still open.
innerHeight	Settable. Inner height of a window's content area.
innerWidth	Settable. Inner width of a window's content area.
name	Settable. Name of a window.
opener	Window object for the parent window that created this one.
outerHeight	Settable. Outer height of a window, including additional bars.

Property	Description
outerWidth	Settable. Outer width of a window, including additional bars.
pageXOffset	Number of pixels the current page has been scrolled down.
pageYOffset	Number of pixels the current page has been scrolled up.
parent	Parent window object of the current window.
screenX	X coordinate of the window relative to the screen.
screenY	Y coordinate of the window relative to the screen.
self	Current window object.
top	Topmost browser window object.

Using the Window Object Methods

The window object also provides a set of methods that allow you to create and manage additional child windows from your JavaScript code.

For example, the following code opens a new browser window and loads the URL specified:

```
var tempWindow = window.open("http://jquery.com");
```

Later, from the JavaScript code in your original web page, you can close the new window using the following statement:

```
tempWindow.close();
```

Table 11.3 shows a list of some of the more important window object properties and what they are used for.

TABLE 11.3 Window Object Methods

Method	Description
alert()	Launches a dialog box with a message and an OK button.
blur()	Removes focus from the current window.
clearInterval()	Clears a timer set with setInterval().
clearTimeout()	Clears a timer set with setTimeout().
close()	Closes the current window.
confirm()	Launches a dialog box with a message and an OK and Cancel button.
createPopup()	Launches a dialog box.

Method	Description
focus()	Sets focus to the current window.
moveBy()	Moves a window relative to its current position.
moveTo()	Moves a window to the specified position.
open()	Opens a new browser window.
print()	Prints the content of the current window.
prompt()	Displays a dialog box that prompts the visitor for input.
resizeBy()	Resizes the window by the specified pixels.
resizeTo()	Resizes the window to the specified width and height.
scrollBy()	Scrolls the content by the specified number of pixels.
scrollTo()	Scrolls the content to the specified coordinates.
setInterval()	Calls a function or evaluates expression at *n* ms intervals.
setTimeout()	Calls a function or evaluates expression after *n* ms.

Using the Browser Location Object

The browser location object gives you access to the current location in the browser. This allows you to access all the URL information as well as reload the current page or load a new one in the current window.

For example, the following statement gets the following URL from the current page and then loads a new page at a different URL:

```
var oldURL = location.href;
location.assign("http://jquery.com");
```

Also, if the URL was linked to a specific anchor on the web page, you can get that portion of the URL using location.hash. You can use the anchor points that have existed in static web pages as a way to provide backward compatibility with other web pages that link to specific locations. You read the anchor hash and then adjust the dynamic content to match what was located at that portion of the original web page.

```
var anchor = location.hash;
```

Table 11.4 shows a list of the location object properties and methods.

TABLE 11.4 Location Object Properties and Methods

Property	Description
hash	Anchor portion of a URL if specified.
host	Hostname and port of a URL.
hostname	Hostname of a URL.
href	Entire URL.
pathname	Path portion of a URL.
port	Port number of the server.
protocol	Protocol of a URL (http/https/and so on).
search	Query portion of a URL (?k=v&k2=v2...).
assign(url)	Loads a new document.
reload()	Reloads the current document.
replace(url)	Replaces the current document with a new one.

Using the Browser History Object

The history object provides access to the browser navigation history, allowing you to move forward and backward dynamically without the user needing to click the browser Forward and Back buttons.

Navigating Forward in the Browser History

To move forward, you can use `history.forward()` to move to the next URL in the history, or you can use `history.go(n)`, where n is a positive number that represents the number of steps to move forward. For example, the following statement moves three URLs forward:

```
history.go(3);
```

Navigating Backward in the Browser History

To move backward, you can use `history.back()` to move to the previous URL in the history, or you can use `history.go(n)`, where n is a negative number that represents the number of steps to move backward. For example, the following statement moves two URLs back:

```
history.go(-2);
```

Controlling External Links

An important part of dynamic web programming also involves controlling the linkage outside of the web page. The following sections describe some of the ways that you can control the behavior of external links by preventing them from happening or forcing them to open new browser windows.

Stopping External Links on a Web Page

A useful task that you can perform with a simple jQuery script is stopping external links from happening. This allows you to lock linking away from the web page using one of the `<a>` elements within it.

To lock down external links from a web page, you need to first add a click event handler to the `<a>` tags that link externally and then call `preventDefault()` on the click event object. For example, the following code finds `<a>` tags where the `href` begins with `http://` and then adds a click handler function that prevents the default browser action:

```
$('a[href^="http://"').click(function (e){
    any of your own handler code . . .
    e.preventDefault();
  });
```

Forcing Links to Open in New Browser Windows

Another useful task that you can perform with a simple jQuery script is forcing external links to open in new windows. This allows the current window to remain available.

To force external links to open in a new window, set the `target` attribute to `"_blank"` for `<a>` tags that link externally. For example, the following code finds `<a>` tags where the `href` begins with `http://` and then sets the `target` attribute to `"_blank"`, forcing the links to open in a new browser window when clicked:

```
$('a[href^="http://"').attr("target", "_blank");
```

▼ TRY IT YOURSELF

Getting and Setting Cookies

Cookies that allow you to store bits of information statically in the client's browser are an important part of the web paradigm. Often, cookies are read by server-side scripts; however, it can also be helpful if you can get and set cookies from JavaScript without the need for additional server communication.

You can get and set cookies by reading or writing to the `document.cookie` attribute. The `document.cookie` is in a string format that includes the `name`, `value`, `expiration`, and `path` in the following format:

```
name=value;expiration;path
```

The simplest way to help you understand how to implement cookies is to show you by example. The following example takes you through the process of creating simple JavaScript to get and set cookies from a web page. The code for the example is shown in Listing 11.1. Use the following steps to implement the example:

1. In Aptana, create the hour11/hour1101.html, hour11/js/hou1001.js, and hour11/css/hour1101.css files.

2. Add the code shown in Listing 11.1-html to the HTML file. You should recognize the HTML components. The HTML code contains several `<span>` elements that are styled as buttons, text inputs to input cookie names and values, and then a list of cookies.

3. Add the CSS from Listing 11.1-css to the CSS file. This code styles the buttons.

4. Open the hour1101.js file and add the following `ready()` function that adds click handlers for the get, set, and delete cookie buttons. Notice that the handlers get the cookie names from the name `<input>` field.

```
01 $(document).ready(function(){
02   $("#set").click(function(e){setCookie($("#cookieName").val(),
03                               $("#cookieValue").val(), 1);});
04   $("#get").click(function(e){getCookie($("#cookieName").val());});
05   $("#delete").click(function(e){setCookie($("#cookieName").val(), "",
     ➥-1);});
06   displayCookies();
07 });
```

5. Add the following `setCookie()` handler function that gets the date and uses it to create an expires time string. The code then sets `document.cookie` using the `name`, `value`, `expires`, and a root path as the string value:

```
08 function setCookie(name, value, days) {
09   var date = new Date();
10   date.setTime(date.getTime()+(days*24*60*60*1000));
11   var expires = "; expires="+date.toGMTString();
12   document.cookie = name + "=" + value + expires + "; path=/";
13   displayCookies();
14 }
```

6. The following `getCookie()` handler gets the `document.cookie` string, splits it by `;` and then iterates through the cookie array until it finds a cookie where the name matches the one passed in. The function then sets the value `<input>` field to the value of the cookie.

```
15 function getCookie(name) {
16   var cookieStr = $("#cookieName").val() + "=";
17   var cArr = document.cookie.split(';');
18   for(var i=0;i < cArr.length;i++) {
19     var cookie = cArr[i];
20     while (cookie.charAt(0)==' '){
21       cookie = cookie.substring(1, cookie.length);
22     }
23     if (cookie.indexOf(cookieStr) == 0){
24       $("#cookieValue").val(cookie.substring(cookieStr.length,
          ➥cookie.length));
25       break;
26     }
27   }
28 }
```

7. Add the following `displayCookies()` function that renders the list of currently set cookies:

```
29 function displayCookies(){
30   $("#cookieList").html("");
31   var cArr = document.cookie.split(';');
32   for(var i=0;i < cArr.length;i++) {
33     var cookie = cArr[i];
34     $("#cookieList").append($("<li></li>").html(cookie));
35   }
36 }
```

8. Save all three files and then open the HTML document in a web browser, as shown in Figure 11.1. Play around with setting, getting, and deleting cookies. Also navigate away from the page and then back, and the cookies should still be set.

FIGURE 11.1
Getting, setting, and deleting cookies using JavaScript.

LISTING 11.1-html   HTML File Basic Web Page Used in the Example That Defines Several `<span>` Elements Used for Buttons and `<input>` Elements to Input Cookie Names and Values

```
01  <!DOCTYPE html>
02  <html>
03    <head>
04      <title>Hour 11-1</title>
05      <meta charset="utf-8" />
06      <script type="text/javascript" src="../js/jquery.min.js"></script>
07      <script type="text/javascript" src="js/hour1101.js"></script>
08      <link rel="stylesheet" type="text/css" href="css/hour1101.css">  </head>
09    <body>
10      <div>
11        <span id="set">Set Cookie</span>
12        <span id="get">Get Cookie</span>
13        <span id="delete">Delete Cookie</span>
14      </div>
15      <div>
16        <label>Cookie Name: </label><input id="cookieName" type="text" />
17      </div>
18      <div>
19        <label>Cookie Value: </label><input id="cookieValue" type="text" />
20      </div>
21      <div id="cookieList"></div>
22    </body>
23  </html>
```

LISTING 11.1-js   jQuery and JavaScript Code That Gets, Sets, and Deletes Cookies

```
01  $(document).ready(function(){
02    $("#set").click(function(e){setCookie($("#cookieName").val(),
03                                   $("#cookieValue").val(), 1);});
04    $("#get").click(function(e){getCookie($("#cookieName").val());});
05    $("#delete").click(function(e){setCookie($("#cookieName").val(), "", -1);});
06    displayCookies();
07  });
08  function setCookie(name, value, days) {
09    var date = new Date();
10    date.setTime(date.getTime()+(days*24*60*60*1000));
11    var expires = "; expires="+date.toGMTString();
12    document.cookie = name + "=" + value + expires + "; path=/";
13    displayCookies();
14  }
15  function getCookie(name) {
16    var cookieStr = $("#cookieName").val() + "=";
```

```
17    var cArr = document.cookie.split(';');
18    for(var i=0;i < cArr.length;i++) {
19      var cookie = cArr[i];
20      while (cookie.charAt(0)==' '){
21        cookie = cookie.substring(1, cookie.length);
22      }
23      if (cookie.indexOf(cookieStr) == 0){
24        $("#cookieValue").val(cookie.substring(cookieStr.length, cookie.length));
25        break;
26      }
27    }
28  }
29  function displayCookies(){
30    $("#cookieList").html("");
31    var cArr = document.cookie.split(';');
32    for(var i=0;i < cArr.length;i++) {
33      var cookie = cArr[i];
34      $("#cookieList").append($("<li></li>").html(cookie));
35    }
36  }
```

LISTING 11.1-css   CSS Code That Styles the Buttons and Images

```
1 span{
2   padding:5px;
3   background-color:blue; color:white;
4   border-radius:10px 20px; border:5px ridge blue;
5   cursor:pointer;
6 }
7 div{ padding:10px; }
```

Adding Pop-up Boxes

The window provides several methods that allow you to launch pop-up windows that you can interact with for alerts, prompts, and notifications. The pop-up windows are displayed, and the user needs to interact with the pop-up before continuing to access the web page.

NOTE

It is often much better to create a fixed position `<div>` element with an overlay rather than using these pop-up boxes because you have much more control over them. You learn how to do just that a little later in the book.

Notifying the User

The most common type of pop-up is an alert pop-up designed to notify the user that something has happened. The user will see the message; however, the only option given is to close the pop-up message.

To create a simple alert message, use the `window.alert()` method as shown next and displayed in Figure 11.2:

```
window.alert("It's 12/12/12 12:12:12!!!");
```

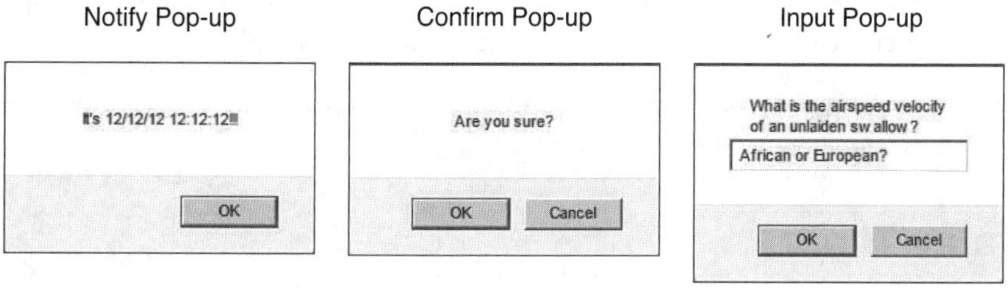

Notify Pop-up   Confirm Pop-up   Input Pop-up

FIGURE 11.2
JavaScript pop-up boxes.

Asking the User to Confirm

The next most common type of pop-up is a confirmation pop-up designed to notify the user that something is about to happen. The user will see the message and then be given the option to click OK to allow the action to occur or click Cancel to reject the action.

To create a confirmation dialog box that allows the user to respond with yes or no, use the `window.confirm()` method, as shown next and displayed in Figure 11.2:

```
var response = window.confirm("Are you sure?");
if (response == true) { do something; }
else { don't do something; }
```

Prompting the User for Input

Another type of pop-up is the prompt. The prompt displays a text box that allows the user to type a text string into the pop-up box. That string is returned to the JavaScript code and can be used in various ways.

To create a prompt dialog that allows the user to input a single text string as input, use the `window.prompt()` method, as shown next and displayed in Figure 11.2:

```
var response = window.prompt("What is the airspeed velocity of an unlaiden
➡swallow?");
if (response == "African or European?"){ pass }
else { no pass }
```

Setting Timers

Another useful feature of JavaScript is the capability to set timers that execute a function or evaluate an expression after a certain amount of time or on a specific interval.

Using timers allows you to delay the execution of code so that it does not need to happen at the exact moment an event is triggered or the page is loaded.

Adding a Delay Timer

To delay the execution of code for a certain amount of time, use the `setTimeout(code, ms)` method, where `code` is either a statement or a function that will execute when the time expires. `ms` is the number of milliseconds. For example, to execute a function named `myTimer()` in 10 seconds, you would use the following:

```
var timerId = setTimeout(myTimer, 10000);
```

At any point before the time runs out and the code is executed, you can clear the timer by calling `clearTimeout(id)` method using the ID returned from `setTimeout()`. For example:

```
clearTimeout(timerId);
```

Adding a Reccurring Timer

You can also start a timer that will trigger on a regular interval using the `setInterval(code, ms)` method. This method also accepts a `code` statement or a function name and milliseconds as arguments. For example, the following code creates a timer that triggers every minute and calls a function `checkStatus()`:

```
var timerId = setInterval(checkStatus, 60000);
```

You can also turn off an interval timer using the `clearInterval()` method, as shown next:

```
clearInterval(timerId);
```

Creating Simple Timers and Dialogs

In this example, you create a simple web page that displays a clock and updates it on a per-second basis. The web page also pops up a notification message every few seconds until you tell it to stop. This exercise should solidify timers and alerts in your mind. The code for the example is shown in Listing 11.2. Use the following steps to implement the example:

1. In Aptana, create the hour11/hour1102.html, hour11/js/hou1002.js, and hour11/css/hour1102.css files.

2. Add the code shown in Listing 11.2-html and Listing 11.2-css to the HTML and CSS files. Just basic stuff.

3. Open the hour1102.js file and add the following `ready()` function that adds a timeout and interval timer to the web page:

```
01 $(document).ready(function(){
02   setTimeout(continueNotify, 3000);
03   setInterval(displayTime, 1000);
04 });
```

4. Add the following `continueNotify()` function that will execute after 3 seconds. The function prompts users to answer whether they want to continue to receive notifications; if they do, the timeout is reset so the function will run again in another 3 seconds:

```
05 function continueNotify(){
06   var result = confirm("Do you wish to continue\nto receive
     ➥notifications?");
07   if (result==true) { setTimeout(continueNotify, 3000); }
08 }
```

5. Add the following `displayTime()` function that will run every second when the interval timer is triggered. This function updates the `#clock` element with the current time string. The `padNumber()` function is used to add a leading zero for numbers less than 10.

```
13 function displayTime(){
14   var date = new Date();
15   $("#clock").html(padNumber(date.getHours()) +":"+
16                    padNumber(date.getMinutes()) +":"+
17                    padNumber(date.getSeconds()));
18 }
```

6. Save all three files and then open the HTML document in a web browser, as shown in Figure 11.3. The time should automatically begin to update. When the prompt appears, try canceling it first and then accepting it the second time. You shouldn't see it again.

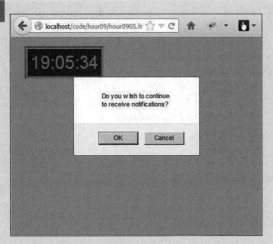

FIGURE 11.3
Simple timer and dialog app.

LISTING 11.2-html   HTML File Basic Web Used to Display a Time Element

```
01 <!DOCTYPE html>
02 <html>
03   <head>
04     <title>Hour 11-2</title>
05     <meta charset="utf-8" />
06     <script type="text/javascript" src="../js/jquery.min.js"></script>
07     <script type="text/javascript" src="js/hour1102.js"></script>
08     <link rel="stylesheet" type="text/css" href="css/hour1102.css">
09   </head>
10   <body>
11     <div><span id="clock"></span></div>
12   </body>
13 </html>
```

LISTING 11.2-js   jQuery and JavaScript Code That Implements a Timeout and
Interval Timer

```
01 $(document).ready(function(){
02   setTimeout(continueNotify, 3000);
03   setInterval(displayTime, 1000);
04 });
05 function continueNotify(){
06   var result = confirm("Do you wish to continue\nto receive notifications?");
```

```
07    if (result==true) { setTimeout(continueNotify, 3000); }
08 }
09 function padNumber(num){
10    if (num<10){ return "0"+num; }
11    return num;
12 }
13 function displayTime(){
14    var date = new Date();
15    $("#clock").html(padNumber(date.getHours()) +":"+
16                 padNumber(date.getMinutes()) +":"+
17                 padNumber(date.getSeconds())));
18 }
```

LISTING 11.2-css   **CSS Code That Styles the Clock**

```
1 div {padding:15px;}
2 span{
3    background-color:black;
4    color:#00FF00;
5    font:30px arial;
6    padding:5px;
7    border:5px groove;
8 }
```

Summary

This hour has focused on using JavaScript objects to access data outside the web page. You learned that there are screen, window, browser, location, and history objects that provide a myriad of details about the physical screen, browser, and client history, as well as access to cookies.

You saw how to open and close browser windows. Using JavaScript, you also learned how to create basic pop-ups that allow you to interact with the user.

Q&A

Q. Is there a way to find out what operating system and browser is being used?

A. Yes. The navigator object will show you the browser in the `window.navigator.appCodeName` attribute. You can also get the operating system using `window.navigator.platform`.

Workshop

The workshop consists of a set of questions and answers designed to solidify your understanding of the material covered in this hour. Try to answer the questions before looking at the answers.

Quiz

1. What are the three types of pop-up boxes supported by JavaScript?

2. How do you use JavaScript to find the full URL that was used to load the web page?

3. True or False: You can navigate backward through the browser history but not forward.

Quiz Answers

1. Alert, confirmation, and prompt.

2. Access the `location.href` attribute.

3. False. You can navigate forward using `history.forward()` or `history.go(n)`.

Exercises

1. Open the code in Listing 11.1 and modify the `ready()` function to get a cookie named `buttonColor`. If the `buttonColor` cookie is set, change the color of the buttons using the following jQuery line:

   ```
   $("span").css("color", getCookie("buttonColor"));
   ```

2. Open the code in Listing 11.2 and modify the prompt to ask the user for a number of seconds before the next notification. If the user enters 0, terminate the notification. Otherwise, use the value in the `setTimeout()` call. Remember that you need to multiply the number of seconds by 1000 to get milliseconds.

HOUR 12

Enhancing User Interaction Through Animation and Other Special Effects

---

What You'll Learn in This Hour:

▶ Understanding animation fundamentals
▶ Creating sliding elements
▶ Creating image galleries using simple resize and transparency animations
▶ Implementing expandable and collapsible elements
▶ How to delay animations for better effects
▶ How to animate element movement for dynamic web apps

One of the most important features of jQuery is the capability to add animations to changes you are making to elements. This provides the user with the feel of a slick, well-developed application rather than a clunky, traditional web page.

This is especially true if you are moving, resizing, or dynamically adding elements to the web page. It is very frustrating as a user to all of a sudden have a bunch of new things appear or disappear. Using transitions, it gives users a chance to see where things are leaving or coming from and adjust their mindset to accept the changes.

This hour focuses on helping you understand the fundamentals of animation. Then you will get a chance to apply those new skills in a series of practical examples.

Understanding jQuery Animation

jQuery animation is the process of modifying a property of an HTML element from one value to another in an incremental fashion visible to the user. This section describes that process and how to implement animations on CSS attributes.

Animating CSS Settings

Most animation in jQuery is done via the `.animate()` method. The `.animate()` jQuery method allows you to implement animations on one or more CSS properties. Keep in mind that the `.animate()` method acts on all elements in the jQuery object set at the same time. Often you will want to act on only a single element so you will need to filter the set down to one.

The `.animate()` method accepts a CSS property object mapping as the first argument. You can specify more than one property in the object to animate multiple properties at the same time. For example, the following code animates the `height` and `width` properties for `<img>` elements:

```
$("img").animate({height:100, width:100});
```

> **NOTE**
>
> The `.animate()` method can animate only properties that have a numerical value. For example, you will not be able to animate border styles, but you can animate border size.

There are a couple of different ways to call the animate method. The following shows the syntax of both:

```
.animate(properties [, duration] [, easing] [, complete])
.animate(properties, options)
```

The first method allows you to specify the `duration`, `easing`, and `complete` functions as optional arguments. The second method allows you to specify the options as a single option map object. For example, the following calls `.animate()` with a `duration` and `easing` object map:

```
$("img").animate({height:100, width:100}, {duration:1000, easing:"linear"});
```

> **TIP**
>
> You cannot animate color changes using the color names; however, you can animate color changes using the hex values, such as `#ff0000`.

Table 12.1 describes the different options available for the `.animate()` method. These options are also available on some of the other animation methods that are discussed later in this hour.

TABLE 12.1 Animation Options

Option	Description
complete	Defines a function that will be called when the animation has completed.
duration	A string or number specifying how long the animation will run. The optional string values are `"slow"` or `"fast"`. A number specifies the number of milliseconds the animation will run. If no duration is specified, the default is 400 ms.

Option	Description
`easing`	A string indicating which easing function to use for the transition. Currently, the values are `"swing"` (default) or `"linear"`, which provides a more constant speed to the animation. Additional easing functions are available in the jQueryUI library that is discussed later.
`queue`	Can be true, meaning the animation will be queued up behind any others for the object; false, meaning that the animation will start immediately; or a string specifying the name of a specific queue.
`step`	Specifies a function that will be executed each step in the animation until the animation completes.
`specialEasing`	You can also map the easing directly in the properties map, allowing you to do different easing for different elements. For example: `$("img").animate({height:[100, "swing"], width:[100,"linear"]}, 1000);`

Understanding Animation Queues

Animations happen asynchronously with code executing, meaning that the code continues to execute while the animation is happening. What happens if you specify another animation for an object before the first one completes? The answer is that jQuery queues the animations and then executes them in order, one after another, until all are competed. That is, unless you specify `queue:false` in the animation options.

You must understand the animation queue because if you allow user interactions to queue too many animations by moving the mouse or clicking, the animations will be sluggish and behind the users' actions.

CAUTION

You must pay attention to where you trigger your animations from. Remember that events will bubble up. If you execute the same animation from all levels during the bubble up phase, you could have some seriously undesired results. To prevent this, you can use the `stopPropagation()` and `stopImmediatePropagation()` methods.

Stopping Animation

jQuery enables you to stop the current animations currently executing on elements contained in the jQuery object set. The `.stop([clearQueue] [, jumpToEnd])` method allows you to stop animations in a few ways.

Calling `.stop()` with no parameters pauses the animations that are in the queue. The next animation that starts will begin executing, then animations in the queue again. For example, the following code pauses all animations:

```
$("*").stop();
```

Calling `.stop(true)`, with the `clearQueue` option set to `true`, stops animations at the current point and removes all animations from the queue. For example, the following stops all animations on images and removes the animations from the queue:

```
$("img").stop(true);
```

Calling `.stop(true, true)`, with the `jumpToEnd` option set to `true`, causes the currently executing animation to jump to the end value immediately, clear the queue, and then stop all animations. For example, the following stops all animations on images but finishes the adjustment made by the current animation and then removes the animations from the queue:

```
$("img").stop(true, true);
```

The `.stop()` method returns the jQuery object, so you can chain additional methods onto the end. For example, the following code stops all animations on images and then starts a new one to set the `opacity` to `.5`:

```
$("img").stop(true, true).animate({opacity:.5}, 1000);
```

Delaying Animation

A great option when implementing animations is adding a delay before the animation is added to the queue. This can be used to provide animations in a more advanced way because you delay the execution of the animation queue, allowing the user a better visual experience.

The `.delay(duration, [, queueName])` method enables you to specify the delay `duration` in milliseconds, as well as an optional `queueName` that specifies what queue to apply the delay to. For example, the following code adds a size animation to images; then after the size is complete, there will be a delay of 2 seconds and the `opacity` will animate up to 1:

```
$("img").animate({width:500}, 1000).delay(2000).animate({opacity:1} 1000);
```

NOTE
_____

The `.delay()` method is great for delaying between queued jQuery effects; however, it is not a replacement for the JavaScript `setTimeout()` function, which may be more appropriate for certain use cases—especially those cases that you require to have the capability to cancel the delay.
_____

Applying `.promise()` to Animations

The `.promise([type], [, target])` method allows you to apply functionality after all actions bound to the jQuery object's set are completed. It does this by returning a new object that will observe the actions and not execute any attached methods until the actions have completed.

The `.promise()` returns an object similar to a deferred object. It has a `.done()` method that enables you to pass in a function that will be run after the `.promise()` functionality has been executed.

For example, the following code waits for animations to complete, then changes the text to "complete":

```
$("span").animate({opacity:0}, 30000).promise().done(function(){
    $("p").html("complete");
});
```

The `.promise()` method accepts two optional arguments. The first is `type`, which specifies the type of action. The default type is `fx`, which applies to animations; so for animations, you do not need to specify the type. The second parameter is `target`, which specifies an optional target jQuery object to return rather than a newly created one.

Animating Show and Hide

You have already seen the `.show()` and `.hide()` methods in action in Hour 9, "Applying Events for Richly Interactive Web Pages." It is common practice to animate this functionality, so jQuery has nicely provided animation options for these methods to make your life easier.

Animating `hide()`

The `.hide( [duration] [, easing] [, callback])` method provides the optional `duration`, `easing`, and `callback` options allowing you to animate the hide effect, making less of a jump when the element disappears.

For example, the following code applies an animation of 1 second with `linear` easing and executes a simple callback function when hiding an element:

```
$("#box").hide(1000, "linear", function() { $("#label").html("Hidden!") });
```

Animating `show()`

The `.show( [duration] [, easing] [, callback])` method provides the optional `duration`, `easing`, and `callback` options allowing you to animate the show effect, making a more easy transition as an element appears.

For example, the following code applies an animation of 1 second with `linear` easing and executes a simple callback function when showing an element:

```
$("#box").show(1000, "linear", function() { $("#label").html("Shown!") });
```

Animating `toggle()`

The `.toggle( [duration] [, easing] [, callback])` method provides the optional `duration`, `easing`, and `callback` options allowing you to animate the toggle between the show or hide effect when toggling between them.

For example, the following code applies an animation of 1 second with `linear` easing and executes a simple callback function when toggling an element between hidden or shown:

```
$("#switch").toggle(1000, "linear", function() { $("#label").html("Switch
➥Toggled!") });
```

▼ TRY IT YOURSELF

Using Show and Hide Animations to Create an Expand/Collapse Element

In this example, you create a simple web element that provides a title bar with a collapse and expand button on the left, allowing you to expand and collapse an image. The purpose of the exercise is to provide you with a chance to use the show and hide animations. The code for the example is in Listing 12.1.

Use the followings steps to create the dynamic web page:

1. In Aptana, create the hour12, hour12/js, hour12/css, and hour12/images folders, and then add the hour12/hour1201.html, hour12/js/hour1201.js, and hou12/css/hour1201.css files. You also need to copy the images from the website at code/hour12/images to the hour12/images folder in Aptana.

2. Add the code shown in Listing 12.1-html and Listing 12.1-css to the HTML and CSS files. It's just basic stuff—a `<div>` with `<span>` used for a handle, an `<img>`, and a footer `<div>`.

3. Open the hour1201.js file and add the following `ready()` function that adds a click handler to the #handle element:

```
01 $(document).ready(function(){
02   $("#handle").click(toggleImage);
03 });
```

4. Add the following handler to toggle the visibility of the image. The `if` statement checks the text in #handle and then either calls `show()` to display the image or `hide()` to hide it. Notice that on `show()`, there is a complete function that displays the footer, letting the user know that the image is ready. On hide, the footer is hidden:

```
04 function toggleImage(){
05    if ($("#handle").html() == '+'){
06       $("#photo").show(1000, function(){$("#footer").show();});
07       $("#handle").html('-');
08    } else {
09       $("#footer").hide();
10       $("#photo").hide(1000);
11       $("#handle").html('+');
12    }
13 }
```

5. Save all three files and then open the HTML document in a web browser, as shown in Figure 12.1. You should be able to expand the image and collapse it and see the footer displayed at the appropriate time.

Expanded   Collapsing   Collapsed

Collapse button

FIGURE 12.1
Simple expand/collapsible image element.

LISTING 12.1-html **HTML File Basic Web Used to Display the Collapsible Image Element**

```
01 <!DOCTYPE html>
02 <html>
03   <head>
04     <title>Hour 12-1</title>
05     <meta charset="utf-8" />
06     <script type="text/javascript" src="../js/jquery.min.js"></script>
07     <script type="text/javascript" src="js/hour1201.js"></script>
```

```
08          <link rel="stylesheet" type="text/css" href="css/hour1201.css">
09        </head>
10        <body>
11          <div>
12            <div id="title"><span id="handle">-</span>Image</div>
13            <img id="photo" src="images/img7.jpg" width="200px"/>
14            <div id="footer">Image Ready</div>
15          </div>
16        </body>
17      </html>
```

LISTING 12.1-js jQuery and JavaScript Code That Implements the Collapsible Image

```
01 $(document).ready(function(){
02   $("#handle").click(toggleImage);
03 });
04 function toggleImage(){
05   if ($("#handle").html() == '+'){
06     $("#photo").show(1000, function(){$("#footer").show();});
07     $("#handle").html('-');
08   } else {
09     $("#footer").hide();
10     $("#photo").hide(1000);
11     $("#handle").html('+');
12   }
13 }
```

LISTING 12.1-css CSS Code That Styles the Collapsible Image Element

```
01 div{ width:200px; text-align:center; }
02 #title, #handle, #footer{
03   background-color:blue; color:white;
04   font-weight:bold;
05 }
06 #handle{
07   display:inline-block; width:15px; float:left;
08   background-color:black; cursor:pointer;
09 }
10 #footer{
11   font-size:10px; background-color:black;
12   margin-top:-5px
13 }
```

Animating Visibility

jQuery also provides animation capability in fade methods attached to the jQuery objects. In the end, the fade methods are equivalent to using `.animate()` on the `opacity` property.

The following sections describe applying animation to the various fading methods.

fadeIn()

The `.fadeIn( [duration] [, easing] [, callback])` method provides the optional duration, easing, and `callback` options allowing you to animate fading the `opacity` of an element from its current value to 1.

For example, the following code applies an animation of 1 second with `swing` easing to all image elements:

```
$("img").fadeIn(1000, "swing");
```

fadeOut()

The `.fadeOut( [duration] [, easing] [, callback])` method provides the optional duration, easing, and `callback` options allowing you to animate fading the `opacity` of an element from its current value to 0.

For example, the following code applies an animation of 1 second with `swing` easing to all image elements and then, when completed, fades them back in again:

```
$("img").fadeOut(1000, "swing", function() { $(this).fadeIn(1000);});
```

fadeToggle()

The `.fadeToggle( [duration] [, easing] [, callback])` method provides the optional duration, easing, and `callback` options allowing you to animate fading the `opacity` of an element from its current value to 0 or 1, depending on its current value.

For example, the following code applies an animation of 3 seconds with `swing` easing to all image elements. Images that are currently visible are faded out, and images that are currently transparent are faded in:

```
$("img").fadeToggle(3000, "swing");
```

fadeTo()

The `.fadeTo( duration, opacity [, easing] [, callback])` method provides the `duration` and `opacity` options that specify a specific opacity to end at and how long to animate the transition. It also provides optional `easing` and `callback` arguments.

For example, the following code applies an animation of 2 seconds for all images to transition from the current opacity to .5:

```
$("img").fadeTo(2000, .5);
```

▼ TRY IT YOURSELF

Using Fade Animation to Implement an Image Selection Effect

In this example, you apply a fade animation to an image set, allowing you to alter the transparency as the mouse hovers over an image. The purpose of the exercise is to provide you with a chance to use some of the fading techniques discussed in this section. The code for the example is in Listing 12.2.

Use the followings steps to create the image selection page:

1. In Aptana, create the hour12/hour1202.html, hour12/js/hour1202.js, and hour12/css/hour1202.css files.

2. Add the code shown in Listing 12.2-html and Listing 12.2-css to the HTML and CSS files—just a basic `<div>` with five `<img>` elements.

3. Open the hour1202.js file and add the following `ready()` function that adds a `mouseover` and `mouseout` handler to all the `<img>` elements. The `mouseover` handler fades the image to an `opacity` of 1, which makes it fully opaque; the mouse out fades it back to .3 so that it will be transparent when the mouse is not over it.

```
1 $(document).ready(function(){
2     $("img").mouseover(function(){$(this).fadeTo(1000, 1);});
3     $("img").mouseout(function(){$(this).fadeTo(1000, .3);});
4 });
```

4. Save all three files and then open the HTML document in a web browser, as shown in Figure 12.2. You should be able to move the mouse over the images and see the transparency change.

LISTING 12.2-html   HTML File Basic Web Used to Display the Images

```
01 <!DOCTYPE html>
02 <html>
03   <head>
04     <title>Hour 12-2</title>
```

```
05        <meta charset="utf-8" />
06        <script type="text/javascript" src="../js/jquery.min.js"></script>
07        <script type="text/javascript" src="js/hour1202.js"></script>
08        <link rel="stylesheet" type="text/css" href="css/hour1202.css">
09    </head>
10    <body>
11      <div>
12        <div id="photos">
13        <img src="images/img1.jpg"/>
14        <img src="images/img2.jpg"/>
15        <img src="images/img3.jpg"/>
16        <img src="images/img4.jpg"/>
17        <img src="images/img5.jpg"/>
18      </div>
19    </body>
20 </html>
```

FIGURE 12.2
A simple image selection that adjusts transparency as the mouse moves over an image.

LISTING 12.2-js   jQuery and JavaScript Code That Implements Image Selection
Fades

```
1 $(document).ready(function(){
2    $("img").mouseover(function(){$(this).fadeTo(1000, 1);});
3    $("img").mouseout(function(){$(this).fadeTo(1000, .3);});
4 });
```

LISTING 12.2-css   CSS Code That Styles the Collapsible Image Element

```
1 div{padding:0px;}
2 img{
3    float:left;
4    opacity:.3;
5    width:100px;
6 }
```

Sliding Elements

A common animation is the sliding effect. A sliding effect transitions an element from taking no space to taking space from a starting edge to the finish edge. Using sliding animations gives the user a richer experience because menus, images, and other elements can be "tucked" away until the user moves the mouse over them or clicks them.

You can use a couple of different ways to create a sliding element. One way is to use the built-in jQuery slide methods. The second is to animate the height and width properties. The following sections describe each of these methods.

Animating `slideUp()`, `slideDown()`, and `slideToggle()`

The `.fadeTo( duration, opacity [, easing] [, callback])`, `.fadeTo( duration, opacity [, easing] [, callback])`, and `.fadeTo( duration, opacity [, easing] [, callback])` methods provide the `duration`, `easing`, and `callback` arguments allowing you to animate sliding effects in the vertical direction.

For example, the following code applies an animation of 1 second to slide an element down, and then applies a delay of 3 seconds and slides the element back up:

```
$("#menu").slideDown(1000).delay(3000).slideUp(1000);
```

You can also animate the `.slideToggle()` method in a similar fashion. For example, the following code animates visibility of a `<div>` element using a slide animation:

```
$("div").slideToggle(1000);
```

Sliding Using Width and Height

I also like to use the width and height properties to create a sliding element. You can create a vertical slide animation by animating the height and create a horizontal slide animation by animating the width.

There are a couple of tricks. You need to provide both a width and a height value for the element if you want to have the full slide effect and not just a resize effect. Also, if you want the element to maintain space on the page, you cannot animate the value all the way down to 0. However, you can animate down to .1 and the other dimension will retain its space.

The following example shows an animation that animates sliding down by changing the height to 100 and then back up by changing the height to .1:

```
$("img").animate({height:100}, 1000);
$("img").animate({height:.1}, 1000);
```

Using Sliding Animation to Implement a Dynamic Menu

In this example, you create a simple web element that provides a title bar with a sliding effect that reveals an image menu. As you hover over each item in the menu, an image slides down and then slides back up as you leave the menu. The purpose of the exercise is to provide you with a chance to use some of the sliding techniques discussed in this section. The code for the example is in Listing 12.3.

Use the followings steps to create the dynamic web page:

1. In Aptana, create the hour12/hour1203.html, hour12/js/hour1203.js, and hour12/css/hour1203.css files.

2. Add the code shown in Listing 12.3-html and Listing 12.3-css to the HTML and CSS files—just basic stuff: a `<div>` with a `<p>` for a title bar, and an inner `<div>` containing the `<span>` used for menus and `<img>` elements.

3. Open the hour1203.js file and a basic `ready()` function. Inside the `ready()` function, add the following line that will hide the inner `<div>`:

```
02    $("div div").hide();
```

4. Add the following statements to add `mouseover` and `mouseout` handlers to the `<span>` elements. On `mouseover`, you get the index of the `<span>` and then use it to find the corresponding `<img>` element and animate setting the `height` to 100, thus sliding down the image. On `mouseout` you do the opposite, setting the `height` to .1 to slide it up:

```
03    $("span").mouseover(function(){
04      var i = $(this).index("span");
05      $("img").eq(i).animate({height:100}, 1000);
06    });
07    $("span").mouseout(function(){
08      var i = $(this).index("span");
09      $("img").eq(i).animate({height:.1}, 1000);
10    });
```

5. Add the following statements to add `mouseenter` and `mouseleave` handlers to the `#container` element. On `mouseenter`, you first stop propagation so that you apply the slide toggle only once during bubbling. Then you stop all animation on the `#images` element and use `slideToggle()` to animate sliding the entire menu. The same occurs on `mouseleave`. The result is that when the mouse is over the `#container` element, it slides down and slides back up when the mouse leaves:

```
11    $("#container").mouseenter(function(e){
12      e.stopPropagation();
13      $("#images").stop(true).slideToggle(1000);
14    });
```

```
15    $("#container").mouseleave(function(e){
16        e.stopPropagation();
17        $("#images").stop(true).slideToggle(1000);
18        });
```

6. Save all three files and then open the HTML document in a web browser, as shown in Figure 12.3. You should be able to expand the menu, and as you hover over each menu item, the image should slide down and back up when you leave.

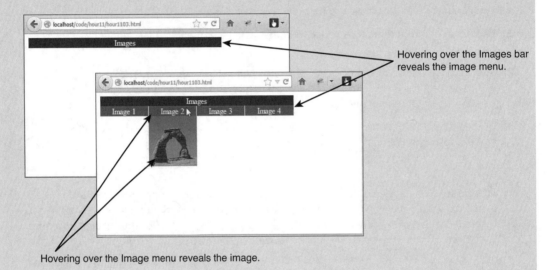

Hovering over the Images bar reveals the image menu.

Hovering over the Image menu reveals the image.

FIGURE 12.3
Simple sliding menu element.

LISTING 12.3-html   HTML File Basic Web Used to Display the Sliding Menu Element

```
01  <!DOCTYPE html>
02  <html>
03    <head>
04      <title>Hour 12-3</title>
05      <meta charset="utf-8" />
06      <script type="text/javascript" src="../js/jquery.min.js"></script>
07      <script type="text/javascript" src="js/hour1203.js"></script>
08      <link rel="stylesheet" type="text/css" href="css/hour1203.css">
09    </head>
10    <body>
11      <div id="container">
12        <p>Images</p>
```

```
13        <div id="images">
14          <span>Image 1</span><span>Image 2</span><span>Image 3</span><span>
          ➥ Image 4</span><br>
15          <img src="images/img1.jpg" />
16          <img src="images/img2.jpg" />
17          <img src="images/img3.jpg" />
18          <img src="images/img4.jpg" />
19        </div>
20      </div>
21    </body>
22 </html>
```

LISTING 12.3-js jQuery and JavaScript Code That Implements the Sliding Image Menu

```
01 $(document).ready(function(){
02    $("div div").hide();
03    $("span").mouseover(function(){
04      var i = $(this).index("span");
05      $("img").eq(i).animate({height:100}, 1000);
06      });
07    $("span").mouseout(function(){
08      var i = $(this).index("span");
09      $("img").eq(i).animate({height:.1}, 1000);
10      });
11    $("#container").mouseenter(function(e){
12        e.stopPropagation();
13        $("#images").stop(true).slideToggle(1000);
14      });
15    $("#container").mouseleave(function(e){
16        e.stopPropagation();
17        $("#images").stop(true).slideToggle(1000);
18        });
19 });
```

LISTING 12.3-css CSS Code That Styles the Sliding Menu

```
01 img{
02    display:inline-block; width:100px; height:.1px;
03    margin:0px; padding:0px; float:left;
04 }
05 p, span {
06    display:inline-block; width:400px;
07    background-color:black; color:white;
```

```
08    margin:0px; padding:0px; text-align:center;
09 }
10 span {
11    width:100px; margin:-1px;
12    border:1px solid; background-color:blue; float:left;
13 }
```

Creating Resize Animations

Similar to using the height and width to create a sliding effect, you can also use them to create a resize animation. The difference between a slide and a resize is that the aspect ratio of the image is maintained on a resize, giving the overall appearance that the element is growing or shrinking rather than being unfolded or untucked.

The trick to creating a resize animation is that you either need to specify both height and width in the `.animate()` statement, or one of them has to be auto in the CSS settings, and you animate only the one that has a value.

For example, the following code shows a resize animation of an image up to 500 pixels over 1 second, and then slowly over 5 seconds back down to 400 pixels:

```
$("img").animate({height:500, width:500}, 1000).animate({height:500, width:500}, 5000);
```

▼ TRY IT YOURSELF

Using a Resize Animation to Create a Simple Image Gallery View

In this example, you create a simple image gallery view that resizes an image and applies opacity changes in the same animation. The purpose of the exercise is to provide you with a chance to use some of the resizing techniques discussed in this section. The code for the example is in Listing 12.4.

Use the followings steps to create the dynamic web page:

1. In Aptana, create the hour12/hour1204.html, hour12/js/hour1204.js, and hour12/css/hour1204.css files.

2. Add the code shown in Listing 12.4-html and Listing 12.4-css to the HTML and CSS files—just a basic `<div>` with `<img>` elements. In the CSS file, the `<img>` elements are styled to a width of 100px, but no height is set. That way we can animate the size without using the height property.

3. Now open the hour1204.js file and a basic `ready()` function that adds `mouseover` and `mouseout` handlers to the `<img>` elements. On `mouseover`, you get the animation by increasing the `width` and `opacity`, and do the opposite on `mouseout`.

```
1 $(document).ready(function(){
2   $("img").mouseover(function(){
3       $(this).animate({width:"200px", opacity:1}, 1000);
4   });
5   $("img").mouseout(function(){
6       $(this).animate({width:"100px", opacity:.3}, 1000);
7   });
8 });
```

4. Save all three files and then open the HTML document in a web browser, as shown in Figure 12.4. You should be able to hover over the images and see the resize animation.

FIGURE 12.4
Simple sliding menu element.

LISTING 12.4-html   HTML File Basic Web Used to Display the Images

```
01 <!DOCTYPE html>
02 <html>
03   <head>
04     <title>Hour 12-4</title>
05     <meta charset="utf-8" />
06     <script type="text/javascript" src="../js/jquery.min.js"></script>
07     <script type="text/javascript" src="js/hour1204.js"></script>
08     <link rel="stylesheet" type="text/css" href="css/hour1204.css">
09   </head>
10   <body>
11     <div>
12       <div id="photos">
```

```
13          <img src="images/img1.jpg"/>
14          <img src="images/img2.jpg"/>
15          <img src="images/img3.jpg"/>
16          <img src="images/img4.jpg"/>
17          <img src="images/img5.jpg"/>
18      </div>
19    </body>
20 </html>
```

LISTING 12.4-js   jQuery and JavaScript Code That Implements the Resize Effect

```
1 $(document).ready(function(){
2   $("img").mouseover(function(){
3       $(this).animate({width:"200px", opacity:1}, 1000);
4     });
5   $("img").mouseout(function(){
6       $(this).animate({width:"100px", opacity:.3}, 1000);
7     });
8 });
```

LISTING 12.4-css   CSS Code That Styles the Images

```
1 div{padding:0px;}
2 img{
3   opacity:.3;
4   width:100px;
5   float:left;
6 }
```

Implementing Moving Elements

Another dynamic that is good to animate is repositioning of elements—specifically, moving an element from one location to another. Users hate it when they do something and page elements are all of a sudden in a different location. Animating the move enables them to see where things go and make the necessary adjustments in their thinking.

The following sections describe methods of animating the repositioning of elements. You also get a chance to implement some code that should solidify the concepts for you.

Animating Element Position Changes on Static Elements

You cannot directly alter the position of static page elements, because they simply flow with the items around them. However, you can animate the margin and padding properties. For example, the following code animates a move of all <p> elements to the right by animating the margin-left property:

```
$("p").animate({"margin-left":30}, 1000);
```

Animating Element Position Changes on Nonstatic Elements

Most of the move animation you do will be on nonstatic elements, and usually it will be on fixed elements, simply because it is much easier and safer to move those without needing to worry about other element positions.

Either way, it doesn't matter if it is a fixed, absolute, or relative positioned element—you will still be animating the same two values, top and left. To animate movement vertically, you use top, and to animate horizontally, you will use left. For example, the following statements animate moving an element to the right 10 pixels and then down 10 pixels:

```
var position = $("#element").offset();
$("#element").animate({top:position.top+10}, 1000);
$("#element").animate({top:position.left+10}, 1000);
```

You can also animate in a diagonal direction by animating both top and left at the same time. For example, the following code animates movement down 10 pixels and to the right 100 pixels in the same animation:

```
var position = $("#element").offset();
$("#element").animate({top:position.top+10, top:position.left+100}, 1000);
```

TRY IT YOURSELF ▼

Creating a Simple Paper Airplane App with jQuery Animation

In this example, you create a simple web app that provides controls to fly a paper airplane around a set of cones. The purpose of the exercise is to provide you with a chance to use some of the move animation techniques to move the airplane around the page. The code for the example is in Listing 12.5.

Use the followings steps to create the dynamic web page:

1. In Aptana, create the hour12/hour1205.html, hour12/js/hou1205.js, and hour12/css/hour1205.css files.

2. Add the code shown in Listing 12.5-html and Listing 12.5-css to the HTML and CSS files. The HTML code displays a set of images for the controls. You can use a couple of `<span>` elements as spacers for the controls. The rest of the images are the plane and the cones. Each cone has its own ID so that it can be positioned in CSS.

3. Open the hour1205.js file and the following global variables and basic `ready()` function. The variables store the `height` and `width` of the browser pane so that you can use that to know when to stop the animation. It is also used in line 4 to position the plane image in the middle of the web page:

```
01 var rightEdge = window.innerWidth;
02 var bottomEdge = window.innerHeight;
03 $(document).ready(function(){
04    $("#plane").offset({top:bottomEdge/2, left:rightEdge/2});
...
22 });
```

4. Add the following handlers for the control buttons. Notice that each handler first changes the image `src` for the plane, stops the current animation, and then animates the left or top properties to move the plane. The `#stop` handler stops all animation and clears the animation queue:

```
05    $("#up").click(function(){
06        $("#plane").attr("src","images/planeUp.png");
07        $("#plane").stop(true).animate({top:0}, 5000);
08    });
09    $("#left").click(function(){
10        $("#plane").attr("src","images/planeLeft.png");
11        $("#plane").stop(true).animate({left:0}, 5000);
12    });
13    $("#right").click(function(){
14        $("#plane").attr("src","images/planeRight.png");
15        $("#plane").stop(true).animate({left:rightEdge}, 5000);
16    });
17    $("#down").click(function(){
18        $("#plane").attr("src","images/planeDown.png");
19        $("#plane").stop(true).animate({top:bottomEdge}, 5000);
20    });
21    $("#stop").click(function(){ $("#plane").stop(true) });
```

5. Save all three files and then open the HTML document in a web browser, as shown in Figure 12.5. You should be able to fly the plane around using the control buttons. It's a very basic example, but a good way to help you understand movement animation.

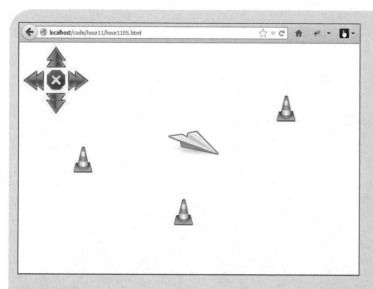

FIGURE 12.5
A simple web app that allows the user to fly a paper plane around the screen.

LISTING 12.5-html HTML File Basic Web Used to Display the Controls, Cones, and Plane

```
01 <!DOCTYPE html>
02 <html>
03   <head>
04     <title>Hour 12-5</title>
05     <meta charset="utf-8" />
06     <script type="text/javascript" src="../js/jquery.min.js"></script>
07     <script type="text/javascript" src="js/hour1205.js"></script>
08     <link rel="stylesheet" type="text/css" href="css/hour1205.css">
09   </head>
10   <body>
11     <div>
12       <span></span>
13       <img id="up" src="images/up.png" /></br>
14       <img id="left" src="images/left.png" />
15       <img id="stop" src="images/stop.png" />
16       <img id="right" src="images/right.png" /><br>
17       <span></span>
18       <img id="down" src="images/down.png" />
19       <img id="plane" src="images/planeRight.png" />
20       <img id="cone1" src="images/cone.png" />
21       <img id="cone2" src="images/cone.png" />
```

```
22        <img id="cone3" src="images/cone.png" />
23     </div>
24    </body>
25 </html>
```

LISTING 12.5-js jQuery and JavaScript Code That Implements the Plane
Movement Animation Using Click Handlers

```
01 var rightEdge = window.innerWidth;
02 var bottomEdge = window.innerHeight;
03 $(document).ready(function(){
04    $("#plane").offset({top:bottomEdge/2, left:rightEdge/2});
05    $("#up").click(function(){
06        $("#plane").attr("src","images/planeUp.png");
07        $("#plane").stop(true).animate({top:0}, 5000);
08    });
09    $("#left").click(function(){
10        $("#plane").attr("src","images/planeLeft.png");
11        $("#plane").stop(true).animate({left:0}, 5000);
12    });
13    $("#right").click(function(){
14        $("#plane").attr("src","images/planeRight.png");
15        $("#plane").stop(true).animate({left:rightEdge}, 5000);
16    });
17    $("#down").click(function(){
18        $("#plane").attr("src","images/planeDown.png");
19        $("#plane").stop(true).animate({top:bottomEdge}, 5000);
20    });
21    $("#stop").click(function(){ $("#plane").stop() });
22 });
```

LISTING 12.5-css CSS Code That Styles the Controls, Cones, and Plane

```
1 img{ width:40px;}
2 span{ width:40px; display:inline-block; }
3 #plane{ position:fixed; width:100px;}
4 #cone1{ position:fixed; top:100px; left: 500px; width:50px;}
5 #cone2{ position:fixed; top:200px; left: 100px; width:50px;}
6 #cone3{ position:fixed; top:300px; left: 300px; width:50px;}
```

Summary

In this chapter, you learned the basics of web animations and how to apply them to changes you make to elements. Most animations can be done using the `.animate()` method that is available on jQuery objects. You learned about the animation queue, how to stop animations and clear the queue, as well as delay the animations.

jQuery also provides several helper functions, such as `fadeIn()`/`fadeOut()` and `show()`/`hide()`, that simplify some of the more common animation tasks. You got a chance to create some practical page elements as well as a simple app to waste time flying paper airplanes.

Q&A

Q. Is there a way to globally disable all animations?

A. Yes. You can set `jQuery.fx.off` to set all animations to the final state and disable animations. This is a useful feature if you want to disable animations for testing or if you want to allow users to disable the animations on slower devices. Setting the value to false enables animations again.

Q. Is there a way to control the number of steps required to compete the animation?

A. Sort of. You can set the `jQuery.fx.interval` value to the number of milliseconds between steps. This controls the frames per second at which the animations run. You should be careful with this setting, though; lowering the number will make the transitions smoother but will also take up more system resources.

Workshop

The workshop consists of a set of questions and answers designed to solidify your understanding of the material covered in this hour. Try to answer the questions before looking at the answers.

Quiz

1. Is it possible to control when an animation occurs?
2. How do you animate color changes?
3. True or False: Animating the width property only will always keep the image aspect ratio.
4. True or False: You cannot animate movement in static elements.
5. Is there a way to execute a function after all animations have completed?

Quiz Answers

1. Yes, partially. Using the `.delay()` method or `setTimeout()`, you can delay an animation for a period of time.

2. You must use the hex color values, such as #ffffff.

3. False. If height is auto, then that is correct; however, if height is a specific value, the aspect ratio will be ignored.

4. False. You can animate margins and padding to provide some movement animations.

5. Yes, using the `.promise()` method.

Exercises

1. Open up the code in Listing 12.1. Add a second `<span>` to the `#title` `<div>` to place the "Image" text in. Then hide and expand that `<span>` as well as the image.

2. Open the code in Listing 12.4. Modify the code by adding a click handler for the images. In the click handler, stop all animation without completing the current animation. Then turn off the `mouseover` and `mouseout` event handler using `$(this).off("mouseover");` and so on.

3. Open the code for Listing 12.5. Modify the code to add four new buttons for diagonal movement. You will need to find your own images. You will also need to add handlers for those buttons that apply the movement animation by setting the top and left properties in the same animation.

HOUR 13
Interacting with Web Forms

What You'll Learn in This Hour:

- ▶ How to get and set form element values
- ▶ Dynamically building form elements
- ▶ How to use form element animations to help users navigate the form
- ▶ How to automatically focus elements for users
- ▶ Creating a basic e-commerce web form
- ▶ Simple methods of validating web forms

Web forms are an integral part of dynamic web programming. You may think of forms only in terms of credit card payments, online registration, and the like; however, anytime you need actual data input from the user, you will be using web forms to collect the data input.

Web forms can be a positive or negative experience for users. Think about it for a second. They know they need to input data. If it seems difficult to input the data because the form is clunky or difficult to understand, they hate it and have a bad experience. If the form elegantly guides them through fast and efficiently, then they say, "Wow! That was easy."

So how do you give the user a good experience?

1. Use dynamic programming to access the data they are entering to provide a dynamic workflow that fits what they are doing.

2. Provide visual effects, such as highlights or expanding elements, that help guide them through the page.

3. Provide inline validation to let them know as soon as possible if they begin to go astray.

The following sections go through each of the concepts. By the time you are finished, you will be able to implement some fantastic web forms.

Accessing Form Elements

The most important part of interacting with web forms is being able to access the data that they represent. Accessing the form data allows you to get and set the values, change selections, and serialize the data to be used in other ways.

There are numerous types of form elements. Unfortunately, there is not a single standard method for getting and setting the value the element represents. The following sections describe ways to access the data in each of the types of form elements.

Getting and Setting Form Element Values

Getting the value a form element represents depends on the form element type. For example, a text element represents the text inside, whereas a select element represents the value(s) of the selected element(s).

In the following sections, the form elements are broken into groups based on the methods to get the form values. For example, all the textual elements are accessed in the same way, regardless of type.

Accessing Form Element Attributes

The different elements have many of the same attributes as well as a few unique to the element type. There are several attributes you need to access when implementing dynamic code:

- id—Used to query for and identify the form element.
- name—Used in multiple fashions. For radio inputs, this attribute is used to group the elements together so that only one can be selected at a time. For serialization and submission of the form, the name attribute is used as the name given to the element's value.
- type—Used to identify the type of <input> element.
- value—Stores a value that is associated with the element. For text elements, the value is displayed in the text box; for buttons, it is the string in the button; for <option> elements, it is the value associated with the option.
- checked—Used to access the selection state of a radio or check box <input> element.

These attributes can be accessed directly in JavaScript by attribute name. For example, to get and set the value attribute, you could use the following:

```
domObj.value = "New Text";
var newValue = domObj.value;
```

In jQuery, there are three ways to get the properties and attributes of the form objects: the `.attr()`, `.prop()`, and `.val()` methods. The `.attr()` method is used to access attributes of the DOM object that correspond to the HTML attributes, such as id, name, and type, whereas the `.prop()` method is used to access properties of the DOM object that are more JavaScript specific, such as `selectedIndex` of `<select>` elements.

CAUTION

The `.attr()`, `.prop()`, and `.val()` methods get the values of only the first element in the matched jQuery set. If you are working with multiple elements in the set, you might need to use a `.map()` or `.each()` method to get values from all elements.

jQuery provides the `.val()` method to access values represented by the form element. In jQuery, the value can be accessed using the `.val()` method of the jQuery object. For example, the following statements set the value of all `<input>` elements with `type="text"` element and get the value of the first:

```
$("input:text").val("New Text");
var newValue = $("input:text").val();
```

Accessing Text Input Elements

The most common type of form elements are the textual inputs. These elements include the `<textarea>` element as well as `<input>` elements with the following type attribute values: color, date, datetime, datetime-local, email, month, number, password, range, search, tel, text, time, url, and week.

Although all of these are a bit different in usage, they all render the same basic text box and are accessed in the same basic way. Each has a value attribute that can be set in HTML that will be displayed in the text box as the image is rendered. For example, the following code shows a basic example of rendering a text form element with an initial value as shown in Figure 13.1:

```
<input type="text" value="Initial Text"/>
```

FIGURE 13.1
A simple text input with an initial value.

That value can be accessed directly from JavaScript by accessing the value attribute. For example, the following sets the value of a text input element and then gets the value:

```
textDomObj.value = "New Text";
var newValue = textDomObj.value;
```

In jQuery, the value can be accessed using the `.val()` method of the jQuery object. For example, the following statements set the value of all `<input>` elements with `type="text"` element and then get the value of the first:

```
$("input:text").val("New Text");
var newValue = $("input:text").val();
```

Accessing Check Box Inputs

Check box input elements have a Boolean value based on whether the element is checked. The value is accessed by getting the value of the `checked` attribute. If the element is checked, then checked has a value such as `true` or `"checked"`; otherwise, it does not—for example, undefined or false.

You can get and set the state of a check box element from JavaScript in the following manner:

```
domObj.checked = true;
domObj.checked = false;
var state = domObj.checked;
```

With jQuery determining if an item is checked, it is a bit different. Remember, in jQuery you may be dealing with multiple check boxes at once, so the safest way to see if the jQuery object represents an object that is checked is the `.is()` method. For example:

```
jObj.is(":checked");
```

To set the state of a jQuery object representing check boxes to checked, you set the `checked` attribute as follows:

```
jObj.attr("checked", true);
```

To set the state of a jQuery object representing check boxes to unchecked is a bit different. You need to remove the `checked` attribute using `removeAttr()`. For example:

```
jObj.removeAttr("checked");
```

Accessing Radio Inputs

Individual radio inputs work the same way as check boxes. You can access the checked state the same way.

However, radio inputs are almost always used in groups. The value of a radio input group represents is not Boolean. Instead, it is the `value` attribute of the currently selected element.

When submitting the form or serializing the form data, the value of the radio input group is automatically populated. To get the value of a radio input group in code, you need to first access all the elements in the group, find out which one is selected, and then get the `value` attribute from that object. The following code will get the value of a radio input group that is grouped by name="myGroup" in jQuery:

```
var groupValue = $("input[name=myGroup]").filter(":checked").val();
```

The code first finds the `<input>` elements with name="myGroup", then filters them down to the ones that are checked, and finally returns the value.

Accessing Select Inputs

Select inputs are really container inputs for a series of `<option>` elements. The value of the select element is the value(s) of the currently selected option(s). Again, the submission and serialization in jQuery and JavaScript automatically handle this for you. However, to do it manually requires a bit of code.

NOTE

If you do not specify a value attribute for an `<option>` element, the value returned will be the value of the innerHTML. For example, the value of the following option is "one":
`<option>one</option>`

There are a couple of different values that you may want when accessing a `<select>` element. One is the full value represented by the element. To get that value is very simple in jQuery using the `.val()` method. For example, consider the following code:

HTML:

```
<select id="mySelect">
  <option value="one">One</option>
  <option value="two">Two</option>
  <option value="three">Three</option>
</select>
```

jQuery:

```
$("#mySelect").val();
```

The value returned by the jQuery statement if the first option is selected is

```
"one"
```

For multiple selects, the `.val()` method returns an array of the values instead of a single value. For example, on a multiple select, the value returned by the jQuery statement if the first option is selected is

```
["one"]
```

On a multiple select, the value returned by the jQuery statement if the first three options are selected is

```
["one", "two", "three"]
```

You can also use the `.val()` method to set the selected elements. For example, the following statement selects the second element from the select listed above:

```
$("#mySelect").val("two");
```

The following statement selects the second and third options in a multiple select element:

```
$("#mySelect").val(["two", "three"]);
```

Accessing Button Inputs

For the most part, you will not need to access button data, with the possible exception of the `value` attribute, which defines the text displayed on the button. The adding/removing event handlers and CSS properties are all the same as for other HTML elements.

Accessing File Inputs

The file input is an interestingly different type of form element. It provides both a button and text box. The button links into the OS's file browser and the text box displays the path to the file that needs to be uploaded to the web server.

The `value` attribute of the file input will be the name of the file, so you can access it directly from JavaScript or by using the `.val()` method in jQuery.

In Firefox and Chrome, the DOM object also provides a `files` attribute that is an array of File objects representing the files selected by this element. You can access files selected by the user from JavaScript using the following code.

HTML:

```
<input id=fileSelect type="file" />
JavaScript:
var fileSelector = document.getElementById("fileSelect");
var fileList = fileSelector.files;
for (var i in fileList){
  var fileObj = fileList[i];
  var fileName = fileObj.name;
  var filePath = fileObj.mozFullPath;
  var fileSize = fileObj.size;
  var fileType = fileObj.type;
}
```

CAUTION

You must be careful when playing around with the file input because that seems to be a sore spot for malicious behavior. Internet Explorer will fail a submit event on a page if it detects that the file objects have been tampered with. Also, many browsers have security settings that prevent some to all of the file information from being available to scripts.

Each file object contains several attributes that are useful in dynamic programming. Some of the most commonly used are listed in Table 13.1.

TABLE 13.1   Properties of the DOM File Object

Attribute	Description
name	Filename excluding the path.
path	This is a bit different for each browser. Mozilla provides this attribute as `mozFullPath`, `webkitRelativePath`.
size	Size of the file in bytes.
type	File type specified by the HTTP standard. For example: `image/jpeg`.

Accessing Hidden Inputs

A great HTML element to use if you need to supply additional information to the browser from a form is the hidden input. The hidden input will not be displayed with the form; however, it can contain a name and value pair that is submitted, or even just values that you want to store in the form and have accessible during dynamic operations.

The parts that will be sent with the form are the name and value attributes. However, you can attach additional values to a hidden form object, or any HTML DOM object from jQuery using the `.data(key [,value])` method. This method works like `.attr()` and `.prop()` in that you pass it a key if you want to get the value, and a key and value if you want to set the value. For example, the following code defines a simple hidden element and then uses jQuery to assign the submission value as well as an extended attribute:

HTML:

```
<input id="invisibleMan" name="InvisibleMan" type="hidden" />
```

jQuery:

```
$("#invisibleMan").val("alive");
$("#invisibleMan").data("hairColor", "clear");
var state $("#invisibleMan").val();
var state $("#invisibleMan").data("hairColor");
```

Serializing Form Data

Many of the input elements in a form can be easily serialized into strings or arrays. Serializing the form data makes it easier to deal with when storing it, sending it to a server, or dynamically making adjustments based on a form event.

For a form to be serialized, it needs two things: a `name` attribute and a `value` attribute that can be assigned to the name. Table 13.2 describes the different value sources for types of attributes:

TABLE 13.2 Properties of the DOM File Object

Input Type	Value Source
`textarea, color, date, datetime, datetime-local, email, month, number, password, range, search, tel, text, time, url, week`	Text value displayed inside the input's text box.
`checkbox`	The value is "on" if no `value` attribute is specified; otherwise, it is the value of the `value` attribute.
`radio`	The value of the selected radio input for the group.
`select`	Value of the selected option for single selects. For multiple selects, it is an array of the values of the selected options.

Converting a Form into a Query String

One of the most common serialization tasks is converting the form data into a serialized array. jQuery makes this a snap with the `.serialize()` method. The `.serialize()` method will access the form and convert the name/value pairs into a URL-encoded string ready to be transmitted across the web.

For example, check out the following code that creates a form and then serializes it based on the values set in Figure 13.2.

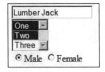

FIGURE 13.2
Simple form with `text`, `select`, and `radio` inputs.

HTML:

```
<form id="simpleForm">
  <input name="title" type="text" /><br>
  <select name="mySelection" multiple size=3 id="mySelect">
    <option value="one">One</option>
    <option value="two">Two</option>
    <option value="three">Three</option>
  </select><br>
  <input type="radio" name="gender" value="male">Male</input>
  <input type="radio" name="gender" value="female">Female</input><br>
</form>
```

jQuery:

```
var qString = $("#simpleForm").serialize();
```

Value of qString:

```
title=Lumber+Jack&mySelection=one&mySelection=two&gender=male
```

Converting a Form into a JavaScript Object

Another very useful serialization technique is to convert the form data into a JavaScript object that can then be accessed. The jQuery .serializeArray() method will do just that. All name/value pairs are converted to an array that can be accessed via your code.

For example, consider the following jQuery statement running on the same form shown in Figure 13.2:

```
var formArr = $("#simpleForm").serializeArray();
```

The resulting value of formArr would be the following:

```
{0: {"name":"title", "value":"Lumber Jack"},
 1: {"name":"mySelection", "value":"one"},
 2: {"name":"mySelection", "value":"two"},
 3: {"name":"gender", "value":"male"}};
```

TRY IT YOURSELF ▼

Accessing and Manipulating Form Element Data

Now that you have had a chance to review the methods of accessing and interacting with form data, it is time to jump in and do it yourself. In this exercise, you create a couple of forms to get data from and the other to set the data in. The result will be that as you update one form, the other is updated as well.

The purpose of the exercise is to provide you with a chance to get and set form element values in a variety of ways. The code for the example is in Listing 13.1.

Use the followings steps to create the dynamic web page:

1. In Aptana, create the hour13, hour13/js, hour13/css, and hour13/images folders, and then add the hour13/hour1301.html, hour13/js/hour1301.js, and hour13/css/hour1301.css files. You will also need to copy the images from the book's website at code/hour13/images to the hour13/images folder in Aptana.

2. Add the code shown in Listing 13.1-html and Listing 13.1-css to the HTML and CSS files. There is a lot of HTML code, but it is all just defining form elements. Notice that there are two forms: formA and formB.

3. Open the hour1301.js file and a basic `.ready()` function that you will add lines of code to that implement event handlers to update formB from formA data.

4. Add the following line that attaches a `keyup` handler to the text input so that when it is changed in formA, the value also changes in formB. The values are retrieved and set by `.val()` method:

```
02   $("#formA input:text").keyup(function(){$("#formB
   ➥input:text").val($(this).val());});
```

5. Add the following lines that attach a `keyup` handler to the text and `<textarea>` inputs so that when it is changed in formA, the value also changes in formB. The values are retrieved and set by `.val()` method:

```
02   $("#formA input:text").keyup(function(){$("#formB
   ➥input:text").val($(this).val());});
03   $("#formA textarea").keyup(function(){$("#formB
   ➥textarea").val($(this).val());});
```

6. Add the following lines that attach a change handler to the radio input group. Notice that to get the same radio input element in the other form, you need to get the input element with the same value using `$("#formB input[value=" + $(this).val() + "]");`. The value is set using `.prop()`.

```
04   $("#formA input:radio").change(function(){
05      var radioB = $("#formB input[value=" + $(this).val() + "]");
06      radioB.prop("checked", $(this).is(":checked"));
07   });
```

7. Add the following lines that attach a click handler to the check box in formA and uses the `.prop()` method to check the same check box in formB when clicked.

```
08   $("#formA input:checkbox").click(function(){
09      $("#formB input:checkbox").prop("checked", $(this).prop("checked"));
10   });
```

8. Add the following line that attaches a click handler to the select in `formA` so that when the selection changes, the `.val()` can be called to get the value from `formA` and set `formB`.

```
11    $("#formA select").change(function(){$("#formB
      ►select").val($(this).val());});
```

9. Add the following lines that attach a `click` handler to the image input so that when it is clicked, the `src` attribute of the image input in `formB` will be changed to match:

```
15    $("#formA input:image").click(function(e){
16        $("#formB input:image").attr("src", $(this).attr("src"));
17        e.preventDefault();
18    });
```

10. Add the following click handler for the Reset button. The handler calls the `.reset()` function on `formB` by getting the `formB` DOM element using `$("#formB").get(0)`. It then removes the `check` attribute from all checked elements and resets the `src` attribute of the image element.

```
19    $("#resetB").click(function(){
20        $("#formB").get(0).reset();
21        $("#formB input:checked").removeAttr("checked");
22        $("#formB input:image").attr("src", "");
23    });
```

11. Add the following click handler for the serialize button. The handler first calls `.serialize()` on form and writes the string out to the serialized paragraph element. Then it retrieves a serialized array by calling `.serializeArray()`. The `jQuery.each()` method is used to iterate through the array and append a new paragraph with name and value pair to the `serializedA` paragraph.

```
24    $("#serializeB").click(function(e){
25        $("#serialized").html($("#formA").serialize());
26        $("#serializedA").empty();
27        var arr = $("#formA").serializeArray();
28        jQuery.each(arr, function(i, prop){
29            $("#serializedA").append($("<p>" + prop.name + " = " + prop.value +
             ►"</p>"));
30        });
31    });
```

12. Save all three files and then open the HTML document in a web browser, as shown in Figure 13.3. You should be able to change the elements in the left form and see them also change in the right. When you click the Serialize button, the two `<div>` elements at the bottom should be populated with the serialized data from `formA`.

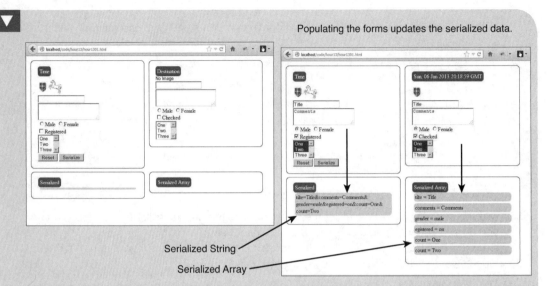

FIGURE 13.3
Form-to-form manipulation illustrating how to read and write data to forms as well as serialize the form values.

LISTING 13.1-html HTML Document That Implements the Form Elements Used in the Example

```
01  <!DOCTYPE html>
02  <html>
03    <head>
04      <title>Hour 13-1</title>
05      <meta charset="utf-8" />
06      <script type="text/javascript" src="../js/jquery.min.js"></script>
07      <script type="text/javascript" src="js/hour1301.js"></script>
08      <link rel="stylesheet" type="text/css" href="css/hour1301.css">
09    </head>
10    <body>
11        <div><form id="formA">
12          <label>Time</label><br>
13          <input type="image" src="images/shield.png" />
14          <input type="image" src="images/horse.png" /><br>
15          <input name="title" type="text" /><br>
16          <textarea name="comments"></textarea><br>
17          <input type="radio" name="gender" value="male">Male</input>
18          <input type="radio" name="gender" value="female">Female</input><br>
19          <input type="checkbox" name="registered">Registered</input><br>
20          <select size=3 multiple name="count">
```

```
21          <option>One</option><option>Two</option><option>Three</option>
22        </select><br>
23        <input id="resetB" type="button" value="Reset"></input>
24        <input id="serializeB" type="button" value="Serialize"></input>
25      </form></div>
26      <div><form id="formB">
27        <label>Destination</label><br>
28        <input type="image" alt="No Image"></input><br>
29        <input type="text" /><br>
30        <textarea></textarea><br>
31        <input type="radio" name="gender" value="male">Male</input>
32        <input type="radio" name="gender" value="female">Female</input><br>
33        <input type="checkbox">Checked</input><br>
34        <select size=3 multiple>
35          <option>One</option><option>Two</option><option>Three</option>
36        </select>
37      </form></div>
38      <div><label>Serialized</label><p id="serialized"></p></div>
39      <div><label>Serialized Array</label><span id="serializedA"></span></div>
40    </body>
41  </html>
```

LISTING 13.1-js jQuery and JavaScript Code That Implements a Series of Event Handlers That Read Data from an Element in One Form as It Changes and Updates the Second

```
01  $(document).ready(function(){
02    $("#formA input:text").keyup(function(){$("#formB input:text").val($(this).
    ➥val());});
03    $("#formA textarea").keyup(function(){$("#formB textarea").val($(this).
    ➥val());});
04    $("#formA input:radio").change(function(){
05      var radioB = $("#formB input[value=" + $(this).val() + "]");
06      radioB.prop("checked", $(this).is(":checked"));
07    });
08    $("#formA input:checkbox").click(function(){
09      $("#formB input:checkbox").prop("checked", $(this).prop("checked"));
10    });
11    $("#formA select").change(function(){$("#formB select").val($(this).val());});
12    $("#formA label").click(function(){
13      $("#formB label").html(new Date().toUTCString());
14    });
15    $("#formA input:image").click(function(e){
16      $("#formB input:image").attr("src", $(this).attr("src"));
17      e.preventDefault();
18    });
```

```
19    $("#resetB").click(function(){
20        $("#formB").get(0).reset();
21        $("#formB input:checked").removeAttr("checked");
22        $("#formB input:image").attr("src", "");
23    });
24    $("#serializeB").click(function(e){
25        $("#serialized").html($("#formA").serialize());
26        $("#serializedA").empty();
27        var arr = $("#formA").serializeArray();
28        jQuery.each(arr, function(i, prop){
29            $("#serializedA").append($("<p>" + prop.name + " = " + prop.value +
            ➥"</p>"));
30        });
31    });
32 });
```

LISTING 13.1-css   CSS Code That Styles the Form Elements

```
1 input[type=image] {height:40px; margin-top:15px;}
2 div{
3   vertical-align:top; width:300px; height:auto;
4   display:inline-block; padding:20px; margin:5px;
5   border-radius:10px; border:1px solid;
6 }
7 label{ background-color:blue; color:white; border-radius:8px; padding:5px; }
8 p { margin:5px; padding:3px; background-color:lightgrey; border-radius:8px; }
```

Intelligent Form Flow Control

Another important aspect of dynamic form control is dynamically helping the user navigate through the web form. This is especially true when working with more complex web forms. The way that you help users navigate through the web form is by automatically changing the focus for them, hiding elements that become irrelevant, showing new elements when needed, and disabling elements that cannot be changed.

Using these methods provides the web form with an interactive and rich feel. This will make the web form a lot easier for the user to go through. The following sections discuss the basic concepts of web form control.

Automatically Focusing and Blurring Form Elements

A great flow control feature for web forms is to automatically focus elements when you know the user is ready to enter them. For example, if the user selects a year and the next element is a month selection, it makes sense to make the month active for the user automatically.

To set the focus of an element in jQuery, call the `.focus()` method on that object. For example, the following code sets the focus for an object with `id="nextInput"`:

```
$("#nextInput").focus();
```

You can also blur an element that you want to navigate the user away from by calling the `.blur()` method:

```
$("#nextInput").blur();
```

Intelligently Hiding and Showing Elements

Another great trick when providing flow control for a web form is to dynamically hide and show elements. In effect, less is more, meaning that you shouldn't necessarily show users more than the elements they will need to fill out.

For example, if the form has elements for both men's sizes and women's sizes, don't show both. Wait for the user to select the gender and then display the appropriate size elements.

Form elements can be shown and hidden in jQuery using the `.show()` and `.hide()` methods. Alternatively, if you only want to make the element invisible but still take up space, you can set the opacity CSS attribute to 0 or 1.

Disabling Elements

Disabling web elements will still display them, but the user will not be able to interact with them. Typically, it makes sense to disable a form element instead of disable it only if you still want the user to be able to see the values of the elements.

To disable a form element, you need to set the `disabled` attribute. In JavaScript, you can do this directly on the DOM object. In jQuery, you use the `.attr()` method. For example:

```
$("#deadElement").attr("disabled", "disabled");
```

To reenable a disabled element, you remove the `disabled` attribute. For example:

```
$("#deadElement").removeAttr("disabled");
```

Controlling Submit and Reset

Another important aspect of form flow control dynamically is intercepting the submit and reset event and performing actions based on various conditions. For example, you might want to validate form values before you allow the form to be submitted.

You control the form submission functions by attaching a `submit` event handler to the form. Inside the event handler, you have access to information about the event as well as the form data that will be submitted. You can perform whatever tasks you need and then either allow the form to be submitted or reset or prevent the default browser action.

The following code illustrates an example of stopping the form submission by calling `.preventDefault()` on the event:

```
$("form").submit(function(e){
    alert("Sorry. Not yet Implemented.");
    e.preventDefault();
 });
```

jQuery does not provide an event handler for the form `reset` event for some reason. To get past this in jQuery, change the input `type` from `reset` to `button` for the Reset button. Then add a `click` handler to the button event where it will call `.reset()` on the DOM element of the form. The following code does just that based on a user prompt:

```
$("#resetB").click(function(e){
    if(confirm("Are you sure?")){ $("form").get(0).reset(); }
 });
```

▼ TRY IT YOURSELF

Adding Dynamic Flow Control to Forms

Now that you have had a chance to review the concepts of form flow control, you are ready to try some yourself. In this exercise, you add some basic flow control to an e-commerce web form for accepting payments.

The purpose of the exercise is to provide you with experience hiding, showing, disabling, and autofocusing web elements as the user interacts with the form. The code for the example is in Listing 13.2.

Use the followings steps to create the dynamic web page:

1. In Aptana, create the hour13/hour1302.html, hour13/js/hour1302.js, and hour13/css/hour1302.css files.

2. Add the code shown in Listing 13.2-html and Listing 13.2-css to the HTML and CSS files. There is a lot of HTML and CSS code, but you should be able to follow it by now. The code defines and styles a basic payment form.

3. Open the hour1302.js file and create the `.ready()` function shown in lines 35–47 of Listing 13.2-html. You should recognize the first few lines as just adding click handlers, which is discussed later. Lines 40–46 are shown below and implement the flow control for submitting and resetting the form. The `submit` handler displays a message that the form submission is not implemented and prevents the default submit. The `click` handler for the reset button prompts the user with a message before calling `.reset()` to reset the form.

```
40    $("form").submit(function(e){
41        alert("Sorry. Not yet Implemented.");
42        e.preventDefault();
43    });
44    $("#resetB").click(function(e){
45        if(confirm("Are you sure?")){ $("form").get(0).reset(); }
46    });
```

4. Add the `updateAddr()` function that will update the billing address to match that of the shipping and disable the billing elements if the check box is selected. If the check box is not selected, line 22 will remove the `disabled` attribute so that the user can choose a different billing address.

```
13 function updateAddr(){
14    var cb = $("#cbSame");
15    if (cb.attr("checked")){
16        $("#nameB").val($("#name").val());
17        $("#addrB").val($("#addr").val());
18        $("#cityB").val($("#city").val());
19        $("#stateB").val($("#state").val());
20        $("#zipB").val($("#zip").val());
21        $("#addrB, #cityB, #stateB, #zipB").attr("disabled", "disabled");
22    } else{ $("#addrB, #cityB, #stateB, #zipB").removeAttr("disabled"); }
23 }
```

5. Add the following function to update the payments section when the user selects a credit card or PayPal. Notice that when users select a credit card, the PayPal information is hidden and the credit card information is shown; the reverse occurs if PayPal is selected. Also notice that the focus is changed in both instances to the first text element in the area where the user will begin entering payment information. That way, the user doesn't need to tab to or click the next element:

```
24 function updatePaymentType(){
25    if(this.id == "ppal"){
26        $("#ccInfo").hide();
27        $("#ppInfo").show();
28        $("#ppEmail").focus();
29    } else {
30        $("#ppInfo").hide();
```

```
31      $("#ccInfo").show();
32      $("#cardNum").focus();
33    }
34  }
```

6. Save all three files and then open the HTML document in a web browser, as shown in Figure 13.4. Populate the shipping information and then see it populate the billing information when the same check box is selected. Also try selecting different payment types and watch the elements hide and the autofocus work.

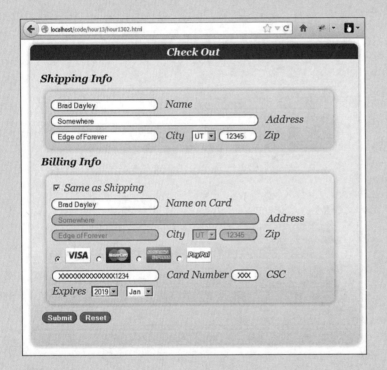

FIGURE 13.4
Basic e-commerce web form with intelligent flow control as the user enters data.

LISTING 13.2-html **HTML Document That Implements the Payment Form Used in the Example**

```
01 <!DOCTYPE html>
02 <html>
03   <head>
04     <title>Hour 13-2</title>
05     <meta charset="utf-8" />
```

```
06    <script type="text/javascript" src="../js/jquery.min.js"></script>
07    <script type="text/javascript" src="js/hour1302.js"></script>
08    <link rel="stylesheet" type="text/css" href="css/hour1302.css">
09  </head>
10  <body>
11    <div id="box">
12      <p>Check Out</p>
13      <form>
14        <span>Shipping Info</span><br>
15          <div id="billInfo">
16          <input type="text" id="name"/><label>Name</label><br>
17          <input type="text" id="addr" /><label>Address</label><br>
18          <input type="text" id="city" /><label>City</label>
19          <select class="state" id="state"></select>
20          <input type="text"  id="zip"/><label>Zip</label><br>
21        </div>
22        <span>Billing Info</span><br>
23        <div id="billInfo">
24          <input type="checkbox" id="cbSame"/>
25            <label for="cbSame">Same as Shipping</label><br>
26          <input type="text"  id="nameB"/><label>Name on Card</label><br>
27          <input type="text"  id="addrB"/><label>Address</label><br>
28          <input type="text"  id="cityB"/><label>City</label>
29          <select class="state"  id="stateB"></select>
30          <input type="text"  id="zipB"/><label>Zip</label><br>
31          <input type="radio" name="ptype" id="visa" />
32            <label for="visa"><img src="images/visa.png" /></label>
33          <input type="radio" name="ptype" id="mc" />
34            <label for="mc"><img src="images/mc.png" /></label>
35          <input type="radio" name="ptype" id="amex" />
36            <label for="amex"><img src="images/amex.png" /></label>
37          <input type="radio" name="ptype" id="ppal" />
38            <label for="ppal"><img src="images/ppal.png" /></label><br>
39          <div id="ccInfo">
40            <input type="text"  id="cardNum"/><label>Card Number</label>
41            <input type="text"  id="csc"/><label>CSC</label><br>
42            <label>Expires</label><select id="expiresY"></select>
43            <select id="expiresM"></select><br>
44          </div>
45          <div id="ppInfo">
46            <input type="text"  id="ppEmail"/><label>PayPal Email</label><br>
47            <input type="text"  id="ppPW"/><label>PayPal Password</label><br>
48          </div>
49        </div>
50        <input type="submit" value="Submit" id="submitB" />
51        <input type="button" value="Reset" id="resetB" />
```

```
52          </form>
53        </div>
54      </body>
55  </html>
```

LISTING 13.2-js   jQuery Code That Provides the Intelligent Flow Control for the Payment Form

```
01 var months = ["Jan", "Feb", "Mar", "Apr", "May", "Jun", "Jul",
02              "Aug", "Sep", "Oct", "Nov", "Dec" ];
03 var sArr = ["AK","AL","AR","AS","AZ","CA","CO","CT","DC","DE","FL",
04   "GA","GU","HI","IA","ID","IL","IN","KS","KY","LA","MA","MD","ME","MH","MI",
     ➥"MN",
05   "MO","MS","MT","NC","ND","NE","NH","NJ","NM","NV","NY","OH","OK","OR","PA",
     ➥"PR", ͯ
06   "PW","RI","SC","SD","TN","TX","UT","VA","VI","VT","WA","WI","WV","WY"];
07
08 function buildSelects(){
09   for(var i in sArr){$("#state, #stateB").append($('<option>'+sArr[i]+
     ➥'</option>"'));}
10   for(var i in months){ $("#expiresM").append($('<option>'+months[i]+
     ➥'</option>"')); }
11   for(var y=2013; y<2020;y++){ $("#expiresY").append($('<option>'+y+
     ➥'</option>"')); }
12 }
13 function updateAddr(){
14   var cb = $("#cbSame");
15   if (cb.attr("checked")){
16     $("#nameB").val($("#name").val());
17     $("#addrB").val($("#addr").val());
18     $("#cityB").val($("#city").val());
19     $("#stateB").val($("#state").val());
20     $("#zipB").val($("#zip").val());
21     $("#addrB, #cityB, #stateB, #zipB").attr("disabled", "disabled");
22   } else{ $("#addrB, #cityB, #stateB, #zipB").removeAttr("disabled"); }
23 }
24 function updatePaymentType(){
25   if(this.id == "ppal"){
26     $("#ccInfo").hide();
27     $("#ppInfo").show();
28     $("#ppEmail").focus();
29   } else {
30     $("#ppInfo").hide();
31     $("#ccInfo").show();
32     $("#cardNum").focus();
33   }
```

```
34 }
35 $(document).ready(function(){
36   $("#ppInfo").hide();
37   buildSelects();
38   $("#cbSame").click(updateAddr);
39   $("input:radio").click(updatePaymentType);
40   $("form").submit(function(e){
41     alert("Sorry. Not yet Implemented.");
42     e.preventDefault();
43   });
44   $("#resetB").click(function(e){
45     if(confirm("Are you sure?")){ $("form").get(0).reset(); }
46   });
47 });
```

LISTING 13.2-css   CSS Code That Styles the Payment Form Elements

```
01 input[type=text] {
02    width:200px; margin-right:15px; padding-left:10px;
03    border-radius: 10px; border:2px groove blue;}
04 select {margin-left:10px}
05 img {margin-top:10px; }
06 #addr, #addrB { width:400px; }
07 #zip, #zipB { width:60px ; }
08 #csc { width:40px; }
09 #box, #billInfo, #shipInfo{
10    font:italic 20px/30px Georgia, serif;
11    width:650px; height:auto; padding-bottom:20px; margin:10px;
12    background: -moz-linear-gradient(bottom, #DDDDDD, #F0F0F0 175px);
13    border-radius: 10px; box-shadow: 0px 0px 8px rgba(0, 0, 0, 0.3); }
14 #billInfo, #shipInfo { width:550px; padding:10px;}
15 #submitB, #resetB{
16    background-color:#3377FF; color:white; font-weight:bold;
17    border:2px groove blue; border-radius:15px; }
18 p{ color:white; background-color:blue; font-weight:bold; margin:0px;
19    text-align:center; border-radius: 10px 10px 0px 0px ; }
20 span{display:inline-block; margin-left:-15px -15px; color:black;
   ➥font-weight:bold;}
21 form{ padding:20px; color:blue}
```

Dynamically Controlling Form Element Appearance and Behavior

In addition to the intelligent flow control, it is also helpful to provide visual indicators to the users about what is happening as they interact with the form. These indicators may adjust font or element sizes, change classes, add/change borders, and so on.

Many of the changes can be made by simple CSS settings based on element states such as :hover or :checked. However, with the capability to add animations to these changes, you can give your forms more of a rich application look and feel.

▼ TRY IT YOURSELF

Adding Animated Elements to Improve User Experience

You already have all the tools necessary to add whatever graphical interactions to your web forms that you want. The purpose of this section is to give you an idea of some of the things that you can do. The example is a very basic registration form, but includes select, styled radios and check boxes and some other form effects. The code is designed to give you a chance to see several techniques in the same example with the smallest amount of code. Feel free to expand on any of these as you play around with the example.

The code for the example is in Listing 13.3. Use the followings steps to create the dynamic web page:

1. In Aptana, create the hour13/hour1303.html, hour13/js/hour1303.js, and hour13/css/hour1303.css files.

2. Add the code shown in Listing 13.3-html and Listing 13.3-css to the HTML and CSS files. There HTML is a pretty basic form. The CSS is fairly big and has a few intermediate selectors that are based on attribute values, but you should be able to follow it. The CSS styles the radio inputs to look like buttons by hiding the radio and showing only a styled label. A similar technique is used for the check box displaying an image instead of a check box.

3. Open the hour1303.js file and create a basic .ready() function to implement the handlers in the following steps.

4. Add the following lines of code that hide the form and then slowly show it as the user clicks the header and hides it when the form is submitted:

```
16    $("form").hide();
17    $("p").click(function(){$("form").toggle(1000); return false;}); ;
18    $("input:submit").mousedown(function(){$("form").toggle(1000); return
      ➥false;});
```

5. Add the following lines that will animate resizing the `<textarea>` element when it is in and out of focus:

```
19    $("textarea").focus(function(){ $(this).animate({width:350, height:100},
      ➥1000);});
20    $("textarea").blur(function(){ $(this).animate({width:200, height:50},
      ➥1000);});
```

6. Add the following handler for when the radio inputs change. The handler animates the opacity down to .1, then when that is complete, it changes the class to a darker color and animates the opacity back up. This gives the appearance of clicking the button. With the CSS style, this makes the radio input group act like a button bar:

```
08 function changeRadio(){
09    $(this).animate({opacity:.1}, 400, function(){
10       $("input:radio").next("label").removeClass("rb_checked");
11       $(this).addClass("rb_checked");
12       $(this).animate({opacity:1}, 800);
13    });
14 }
```

7. Add the following handler for when the check boxes are clicked. The handler animates changing the size of the image, border, and opacity, giving the element a visual indicator of whether the character has a horse or armor:

```
01 function changeCheckbox(){
02    var checkbox = $("#"+$(this).attr("for"));
03    if(checkbox.prop("checked")){
04       $(this).children("img").animate({opacity:.25, height:20,
         ➥"border-size":1}, 500);}
05    else {
06       $(this).children("img").animate({opacity:1, height:40,
         ➥"border-size":.5}, 500); }
07 }
```

8. Add the following lines that attach a handler to the text inputs so that as the user types, the labels are replaced with the text content:

```
24    $("input:text").keyup(function(){
25       $(this).next("label").html($(this).val());});
```

9. Add the code in lines 26–31 that animate the Submit button size as it is in focus or hovered over by the user.

10. Add the following lines that attach a mouseover handler option element that animates a font size increase as the mouse hovers over them, giving users a better idea of what they will select:

```
32    $("option").mouseover(function(){
33       $(this).stop(true).animate({"font-size":20}, 400); return false;});
34    $("option").mouseout(function(){
35       $(this).stop(true).animate({"font-size":15}, 400); return false;});
```

11. Save all three files and then open the HTML document in a web browser, as shown in Figure 13.5. You should be able to interact with the web form and see the visual elements that you have implemented.

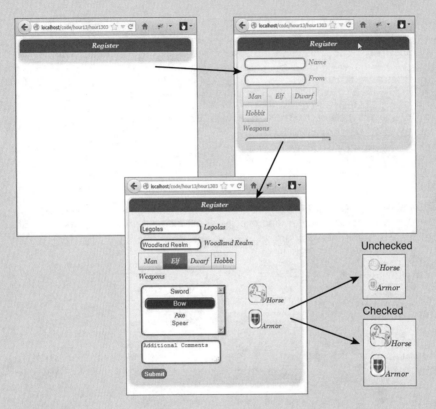

FIGURE 13.5
A simple registration form that provides some dynamic visual effects to make the form more interactive and user friendly.

LISTING 13.3-html   HTML Document That Implements the Registration Form Used in the Example

```
01  <!DOCTYPE html>
02  <html>
03    <head>
04      <title>Hour 13-3</title>
05      <meta charset="utf-8" />
06      <script type="text/javascript" src="../js/jquery.min.js"></script>
07      <script type="text/javascript" src="js/hour1303.js"></script>
```

```
08      <link rel="stylesheet" type="text/css" href="css/hour1303.css">
09    </head>
10    <body>
11      <div>
12        <p>Register</p>
13        <form>
14          <input type="text" /><label>Name</label><br>
15          <input type="text" /><label>From</label><br>
16      <input type="radio" name="race" id="man" /><label class="rb" for="man">Man
        ➥</label>
17      <input type="radio" name="race" id="elf" /><label class="rb" for="elf">Elf
        ➥</label>
18      <input type="radio" name="race" id="dwarf" /><label class="rb"
        ➥for="dwarf">Dwarf</label>
19      <input type="radio" name="race" id="hobbit" /><label class="rb"
        ➥for="hobbit">Hobbit</label><br>
20          <label>Weapons</label><br>
21          <select size=4 multiple>
22            <option>Sword</option><option>Bow</option><option>Axe
            ➥</option><option>Spear</option>
23          </select>
24          <input type="checkbox" id="horse" />
25            <label class="cb" for="horse"><img src="images/horse.png" />
            ➥<span>Horse</span></label>
26          <input type="checkbox" id="shield" />
27            <label class="cb" for="shield"><img src="images/shield.png" />
            ➥<span>Armor</span></label><br>
28          <textarea>Additional Comments</textarea><br>
29          <input type="submit" value="Submit" id="submit" />
30        </form>
31      </div>
32    </body>
33 </html>
```

LISTING 13.3-js   jQuery Code Implements the Animated Visual Elements

```
01 function changeCheckbox(){
02   var checkbox = $("#"+$(this).attr("for"));
03   if(checkbox.prop("checked")){
04     $(this).children("img").animate({opacity:.25, height:20, "border-size":1},
       ➥500);}
05   else {
06     $(this).children("img").animate({opacity:1, height:40, "border-size":.5},
       ➥500); }
07 }
08 function changeRadio(){
09   $(this).animate({opacity:.1}, 400, function(){
```

```
10      $("input:radio").next("label").removeClass("rb_checked");
11      $(this).addClass("rb_checked");
12      $(this).animate({opacity:1}, 800);
13    });
14  }
15  $(document).ready(function(){
16    $("form").hide();
17    $("p").click(function(){$("form").toggle(1000); return false;});
18    $("input:submit").mousedown(function(){$("form").toggle(1000); return
    ↪false;});
19    $("textarea").focus(function(){ $(this).animate({width:350, height:100},
    ↪1000);});
20    $("textarea").blur(function(){ $(this).animate({width:200, height:50},
    ↪1000);});
21    $(".rb").click(changeRadio);
22    $("input:checkbox").prop("checked",false);
23    $(".cb").click(changeCheckbox);
24    $("input:text").keyup(function(){
25        $(this).next("label").html($(this).val());});
26    $("#submit").mouseover(function(){
27      $(this).animate({"background-color":"#0000FF", "width":"140px"},
      ↪400,"linear");});
28    $("#submit").mouseout(function(){
29      $(this).animate({"background-color":"#3377FF", "width":"60px"}, 400,
      ↪"linear");});
30    $("#submit").focus(function(){
31      $(this).animate({"background-color":"#0000FF","border-width":"5px"},
      ↪400,"linear");});
32    $("option").mouseover(function(){
33      $(this).stop(true).animate({"font-size":20}, 400); return false;});
34    $("option").mouseout(function(){
35      $(this).stop(true).animate({"font-size":15}, 400); return false;});
36  });
```

LISTING 13.3-css   CSS Code That Styles the Form Elements and Provide Classes for Dynamic Adjustments

```
01  br{clear:both;}
02  select, textarea, input, option:checked{
03    border-radius: 10px; margin:5px; border:4px groove blue; float:left }
04  select:focus, textarea:focus, input:focus {
05    border-radius: 10px; margin:5px; border:6px groove #3377FF; }
06  select{width:200px; text-align:center;}
07  img{}
08  input[type="radio"], input[type="checkbox"] {display:none;}
09  .rb {
```

```
10    background: -moz-linear-gradient(bottom, #CCCCCC, #EEEEEE 10px);
11    width: 50px; padding: 3px; margin-right:-1px; display: inline-block;
12    text-align:center; float:left; border: 1px solid gray; }
13 .rb_checked {
14    background: -moz-linear-gradient(bottom, #0000FF, #7272FF 15px);
15    color:white;
16 }
17 .cb { padding: 3px; margin-right:-1px; float:right; width:100px; }
18 .cb img{ border:.5px dotted; border-radius:10px; opacity:.2; height:20px; }
19 #submit{
20    background-color:#3377FF; color:white; font-weight:bold;
21    border:2px groove blue; border-radius:15px; }
22 div{
23    width:400px; height:auto; padding-bottom:20px;
24    background: -moz-linear-gradient(bottom, #DDDDDD, #F0F0F0 175px);
25    border-radius: 10px; box-shadow: 0px 0px 8px rgba(0, 0, 0, 0.3);
26    font:italic 15px/30px Georgia, serif;}
27 p{
28    color:white; background-color:blue; font-weight:bold; margin:0px;
29    text-align:center; border-radius: 10px 10px 0px 0px ; }
30 form{ padding:20px; }
```

Validating a Form

One of the most important parts of web forms is validating the information that is being entered. There are many different types and levels of validation depending on the data being entered.

Some elements, for example, are totally optional and require no validation. Others, such as a comment, may be required but the contents do not really matter. Others, such as an email address or data, may be required and must adhere to specific formatting requirements, perhaps even value ranges.

Often, this is done by a server-side script. The problem with that method is that all the data must be sent to the server and then the error is formulated and returned back to the user.

A much better option is to validate the form data in your jQuery code before it is submitted to the server. The following sections describe the different methods for validating form data.

Manually Validating a Web Form

The most basic way of validating forms is by accessing their values and checking the actual contents against the requirements. This can be done when the user is entering data by adding, for example, a `blur`, `change`, or `keypress` event handler, and then inside the event handler checking the value of the data. The following code implements validation in a `keypress` handler, validating that the value of the form element is numeric, and if it isn't, adding warning text to a label:

```
$("input:text").keypress(function (){
    if(!$.isNumeric($(this).val())) {
        $("#validLabel").html("Not a Number"));
    }
});
```

You can also implement the validation when the user submits the form by adding the validation to a `submit` handler. For example, the following code adds a validation function to a submit handler so that if the element does not begin with the text `"vfx"`, an `alert` is displayed and the form is not submitted:

```
$("form").submit(function (){
    if (!$("#vfxField").val().match("^vfx")){
        alert("Invalid vfx element");
        e.preventDefault();
    }
});
```

Getting the jQuery Validation Plug-in

Using the techniques in the previous section, you can validate pretty much any type of form element. The problem is that it takes a lot of code and time to add validation. Rather than reinventing the wheel, you can use the jQuery validation plug-in that takes care of most of the validation needs.

As a plug-in, the validator is implemented by loading the .js file after the jQuery .js file has been loaded. For example:

```
<script type="text/javascript" src="../js/jquery.min.js"></script>
<script type="text/javascript" src="js/jquery.validate.min.js"></script>
```

The plug-in can be downloaded from http://jqueryvalidation.org/.

The documentation for the validation plug-in can be found at http://docs.jquery.com/Plugins/Validation/.

Applying Simple jQuery Validation Using HTML

The validator can be implemented in HTML using the `class` and `title` attributes. The validator uses a set of rules, such as `required` or `email`, to validate the form element. Setting the `class` attribute to one or more of these rules applies the validation when `.validate()` is called on the form. Table 13.3 lists several of the validation rules.

For example, to validate that a text element has text and is in email format, you use the following code:

HTML:

```
<form id="myForm">
  <input type="text" class="required email" />
</form>
```

jQuery:

```
$(document).ready(function(){
    $("#myForm").validate();
  };
```

The `.ready()` function adds the validation to the form, and as the user types in the element, a message displays that the element is required if it is empty and that a valid email address is required if it does not contain a valid email address, as shown in Figure 13.6.

FIGURE 13.6
Validation messages of an email element.

You can also add your own text messages instead of the defaults provided by the validation library. This is done by setting the `title` attribute to the message string you want to display. For example, the following input statement adds the title element that will be displayed if the element is invalid:

```
<input type="text" class="required email"
  title="This Element requires a valid Email Address such as name@here.com"/>
```

Applying Complex Validation

A better way to add validation using the validation library is inside the jQuery validate method. The validate method accepts an object that defines how a form is validated. This section covers using the values of rules and messages. The validation object supports several attributes; you can review the online jQuery documentation to see the rest.

Adding Validation Rules

The rules method allows you to define the different rules, listed in Table 13.3, that apply to a form element by referencing the `name` attribute. For example, the following code adds the `required` and `email` rules to an element with `name="emailField"` using the validator object:

HTML:

```
<form id="myForm">
  <input type="text" name="emailField" />
</form
```

jQuery:

```
$(document).ready(function(){
    $("#myForm").validate({
        emailField: {
           required:true,
           email:true
        }
      );
  };
```

TABLE 13.3   Validation Rules and Usage

Rule	Value Source/Usage
`accept`	Element requires a certain file extension. `accept:"jpg|png|gif"`
`creditcard`	Element requires a valid credit card number. `creditcard:true`
`date`	Element requires a valid date. `date:true`
`dateISO`	Element requires a valid International Standards Organization (ISO) date. `dateISO:true`
`digits`	Element requires digits only. `digits:true`
`email`	Element requires a valid email. `email:true`
`equalTo`	Requires the element to have the same value as another. `equalTo:"#passwordVerify"`
`min`	Element value requires a given minimum. `min:10`

Rule	Value Source/Usage
`minlength`	Element value string length must be more than. `minlength:8`
`max`	Element value requires a given maximum. `max:100`
`maxlength`	Element value string length must be less than. `maxlength:12`
`number`	Element requires a decimal number. `number:true`
`rangelength`	Element value string length must fall in a specific range. `rangelength:[3,9]`
`remote`	Will execute an HTTP AJAX request that calls a server-side script that must return back a valid JSON response as true or false. The parameter name and value will be passed to the server-side script as the query string in GET request. `remote:"validation.php"`
`required`	Element requires a value. `required:true`
`range`	Element requires a given value range. `range:[1,5]`
`url`	Element requires a valid URL. `url:true`

TIP

The `validate()` method accepts a debug option that will disable form submission, allowing you to implement and test the form validation without submitting data to the server. To implement the form validation debug mode, use the following:

```
$(form).validate({
  debug:true,
  other options . . .
});
```

Adding Validation Messages

The messages attribute of the validation object allows you to specify custom messages that will be applied to the individual rules for the element. The messages attribute is also based on the name attribute of the element. The following code illustrates adding messages to the validation:

```
$(document).ready(function(){
  $("#simpleForm").validate(
    {rules: {
      emailField: {
        required:true,
        email:true,
        accept:"jpg|cvs"
        }
      },
      messages: {
        emailField: {
          required:"Must add Email",
          email:"Email format = me@here.com"
        }
      }
    }
  );
};
```

The .validate() method returns a Validator object, which provides several methods that are valuable for checking form validation. Table 13.4 lists the methods available from the Validator object. The following code illustrates using the validator object to check the validity of the form by calling the .form() method:

```
$(document).ready(function(){
  var validator = $("#simpleForm").validate( ...);
  if(!validator.form()){ alert("Form is not valid"));
});
```

TABLE 13.4 Validator Object Methods

Rule	Value Source/Usage
element(element)	Returns true if the element is valid; otherwise, false.
form()	Returns true if the form elements are all valid; otherwise, false.
numberOfInvalids()	Returns the number of form elements failing validation.
resetForm()	Resets the values in the form.
showErrors(errors)	Shows the specified error messages.

When errors are detected in a form element, a label is added to the form to display the error message. The plug-in adds a class named `error` to both the element and the new label for the message. This makes it very easy to style the message as well as the element.

To style the element, you can add a CSS rule for the element type and add the `.error`. For example, to style input elements that have errors to display the text in red, you use the following CSS rule:

```
input.error { color:red; }
```

You can use the same method to style the error message displayed using the `label.error` selector. For example, the following sets the font color of the error messages to red:

```
label.error { color:red; }
```

Placing Validation Messages

The validation plug-in places the error messages directly after the element that was validated. That is often not the desired location. For example, you may want the validation to come before some elements or in a totally different location.

NOTE

The jQuery Validation tool provides a simple method for localizing web form validation. If you include the messages_##.js file found in the localization folder, the validation error messages will be localized. The two-digit number (##) in messages_##.js stands for the two-character ISO country code.

A good example of this is radio input groups. If you validate the group, the message appears after the first radio input element, as shown in Figure 13.7. That is not the desired location. Instead, you want the error message to come after the full set of radio inputs and their labels.

Without Using errorPlacement

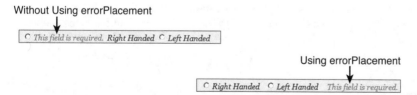

Using errorPlacement

FIGURE 13.7
Using the `errorPlacement` option in the `.validate()` method allows you to define the placement of the error messages.

That is where the `errorPlacement` attribute of the Validation object comes in handy. The `errorPlacement` attribute value is a function that gets called to add an error element to the web form. The `errorPlacement` function will be passed two parameters. The first parameter is the jQuery object that represents the new error message, and the second is a jQuery object that represents the element that failed validation. Using these parameters, you can define your own function that places the elements wherever you want them.

To illustrate this, look at the following code. The `errorPlacement` is set to a function that receives the `error` and `element` arguments. The `element` is tested to see if it is a radio. If the `element` is a radio input, the `error` is inserted after the label that follows the last radio input in the form, as shown in Figure 13.7. If the `element` is not a radio input, the `error` is inserted immediately after the `element`.

```
$("#simpleForm").validate({
  rules: {
    gender: {required:true}
    errorPlacement: function(error, element){
      if (element.is(":radio")){
        error.insertAfter($("input:radio:last").next("label"))}
      else {error.insertAfter(element)}}
});
```

▼ TRY IT YOURSELF

Validating Web Forms Using jQuery

In this example, you use the jQuery validation plug-in to validate a basic web form. The purpose of the example is to help you understand how to implement the validation plug-in in your own scripts.

The code for the example is in Listing 13.4. Use the followings steps to create the web form with validation:

1. In Aptana, create the hour13/hour1304.html, hour13/js/hour1304.js, and hour13/css/hour1304.css files.

2. Add the validation plug-in. You can download the plug-in from the following location or copy the code/hour13/js/jquery.validation.min.js file from the book's website to hour13/js/jquery.validation.min.js in your project. The following line in Listing 13.4-html loads the validation plug-in:

   ```
   07    <script type="text/javascript" src="js/jquery.validate.min.js">
         ➥</script>
   ```

3. Add the code shown in Listing 13.4-html and Listing 13.4-css to the HTML and CSS files. The HTML is a basic form and shouldn't contain any surprises. The CSS does include some specific formatting for the validation code. Line 3 formats the `<input>` and `<select>` elements to have a red background and text to make them stand out. Line 4 formats the message to be in red text.

   ```
   03 input.error, select.error{ background-color:#FFDDDD; color:darkred}
   04 label.error{color:red;}
   ```

4. Open the hour1304.js file and create a basic `.ready()` function to implement the handlers in the following steps. Also add a `.validate()` call on the form as shown next. Include a `rules`, `messages`, and `errorPlacement` section. Notice that the `validationObj` object variable is defined in line 2 so that we can use it later.

```
02    var validationObj = $("#simpleForm").validate({
03      rules: {
. . .
11      messages: {
. . .
16      errorPlacement: function(error, element){
. . .
22    });
```

5. Add the following validation rules for the form elements. The elements are all referenced by the element's `name` attribute. The `password1` element has three rules: `required`, `rangelength`, and `equalTo`. The `equalTo` is set to the `id` attribute of the `password2` element. The `weapon` element uses a `rangelength` of `[2,2]`, which forces the user to pick exactly two weapons.

```
04      name: { required:true, minlength:5 },
05      email: { required:true, email:true },
06      password1: { required:true, rangelength:[6,12], equalTo:"#password2" },
07      battle: { required:true, date:true },
08      weapon: { required:true, rangelength:[2,2]},
09      hands: {required:true},
10      armor: {required:true, minlength:2 }},
```

6. Add the following custom messages to be more specific for the `password`, `weapon`, and `armor` elements:

```
12        password1: { equalTo:"Passwords Do Not Match"},
13        weapon: { rangelength:"Select 2 Weapons"},
14        armor: { minlength:"2 Pieces of Armor Required"},
```

7. Finish off the `errorPlacement` function. There is a radio group for `hands` and a button group for `armor`. You want the error message to be displayed after the `<label>` of the last element in the group, so you modify the `.insertAfter()` method to query for the last `checkbox` or `radio` and then get the very next `label`:

```
16      errorPlacement: function(error, element){
17        if (element.is(":radio")){
18          error.insertAfter($("input:radio:last").next("label"))}
19        else if (element.is(":checkbox")){
20          error.insertAfter($("input:checkbox:last").next("label"))}
21        else {error.insertAfter(element)}}
```

8. Add the following lines. Line 23 validates the form, which will display the requirements after the page has loaded. Lines 24 and 25 are a submit handler. The handler checks to see whether the form is valid by calling `.form()`. If the form is invalid, an alert message is displayed and the submit is prevented by `.preventDefault()`:

```
23    validationObj.form();
24    $("form").submit(function(e){
25        if(!validationObj.form()){ alert("Form Errors"); e.preventDefault(); }
➥});
```

9. Save all three files and then open the HTML document in a web browser, as shown in Figure 13.8. You should immediately see validation errors. Watch the errors change and disappear as you fill out the form. Also try to submit the form with and without errors to see the alert message.

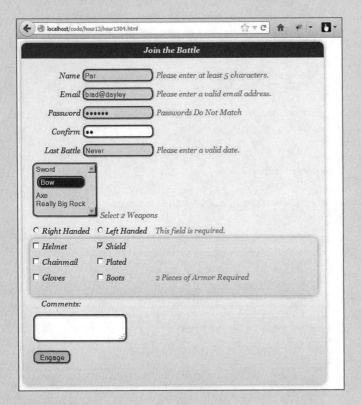

FIGURE 13.8
Simple registration form with validation.

LISTING 13.4-html   HTML Document That Implements the Registration Form Used in the Example

```
01  <!DOCTYPE html>
02  <html>
03    <head>
04      <title>Hour 13-4</title>
05      <meta charset="utf-8" />
06      <script type="text/javascript" src="../js/jquery.min.js"></script>
07      <script type="text/javascript" src="js/jquery.validate.min.js"></script>
08      <script type="text/javascript" src="js/hour1304.js"></script>
09      <link rel="stylesheet" type="text/css" href="css/hour1304.css">
10    </head>
11    <body>
12      <div id="container"><p>Join the Battle</p>
13      <form action="test.html" method="get" name="test" id="simpleForm">
14        <label>Name</label><input name="name" type="text" /><br>
15        <label>Email</label><input name="email" type="text" /><br>
16        <label>Password</label><input name="password1" type="password" /><br>
17    <label>Confirm</label><input name="password2" id="password2"
    ➡type="password" /><br>
18        <label>Last Battle</label><input name="battle" type="text" /><br>
19        <select name="weapon" multiple size=4>
20          <option>Sword</option><option>Bow</option><option>Axe</option>
21          <option>Really Big Rock</option>
22        </select><br>
23        <input type="radio" name="hands" value="right" /><label>Right Handed
    ➡</label>
24        <input type="radio" name="hands" value="left" /><label>Left Handed
    ➡</label><br>
25        <div>
26          <input type="checkbox" name="armor" value="helmet" /><label>Helmet
    ➡</label>
27          <input type="checkbox" name="armor" value="shield" /><label>Shield
    ➡</label><br>
28          <input type="checkbox" name="armor" value="chainmail" />
    ➡<label>Chainmail</label>
29          <input type="checkbox" name="armor" value="plated" /><label>Plated
    ➡</label><br>
30          <input type="checkbox" name="armor" value="gloves" /><label>Gloves
    ➡</label>
31          <input type="checkbox" name="armor" value="boots" /><label>Boots</label>
32        </div>
33        <label>Comments:</label><br><textarea></textarea><br>
34        <input type="submit" value="Engage"/>
35      </form>
36      </div>
37    </body>
38  </html>
```

LISTING 13.4-js jQuery Code Implements the Validation of Form Elements

```
01 $(document).ready(function(){
02   var validationObj = $("#simpleForm").validate({
03     rules: {
04       name: { required:true, minlength:5 },
05       email: { required:true, email:true },
06       password1: { required:true, rangelength:[6,12], equalTo:"#password2" },
07       battle: { required:true, date:true },
08       weapon: { required:true, rangelength:[2,2]},
09       hands: {required:true},
10       armor: {required:true, minlength:2 }},
11     messages: {
12       password1: { equalTo:"Passwords Do Not Match"},
13       weapon: { rangelength:"Select 2 Weapons"},
14       armor: { minlength:"2 Pieces of Armor Required"},
15     },
16     errorPlacement: function(error, element){
17       if (element.is(":radio")){
18         error.insertAfter($("input:radio:last").next("label"))}
19       else if (element.is(":checkbox")){
20         error.insertAfter($("input:checkbox:last").next("label"))}
21       else {error.insertAfter(element)}}
22   });
23   validationObj.form();
24   $("form").submit(function(e){
25     if(!validationObj.form()){ alert("Form Errors"); e.preventDefault(); } });
26 });
```

LISTING 13.4-css CSS Code That Styles the Form Elements and Errors

```
01 label{display:inline-block;min-width:100px; text-align:right;}
02 input+label{text-align:left;}
03 input.error, select.error{ background-color:#FFDDDD; color:darkred}
04 label.error{color:red;}
05 br{clear:both;}
06 form{margin:15px;}
07 div{vertical-align:middle;
08   padding-bottom:20px;
09   background: -moz-linear-gradient(bottom, #FFDDDD, #FFF0F0 175px);
10   border-radius: 10px; box-shadow: 0px 0px 8px rgba(0, 0, 0, 0.3);
11   font:italic 15px/30px Georgia, serif;}
12 #container{width:600px; height:auto; }
13 p{
14   color:white; background-color:darkred; font-weight:bold; margin:0px;
15   text-align:center; border-radius: 10px 10px 0px 0px ; }
```

```
16 select, textarea, input, option:checked{
17   border-radius: 10px; margin:5px; border:4px groove blue; }
18 select:focus, textarea:focus, input:focus {
19   border-radius: 10px; margin:5px; border:6px groove #3377FF; }
```

Summary

In this hour, you learned how to access the data that form elements represent. Using that data, you can provide dynamic work flow by setting values automatically, autofocusing the next element, showing new necessary elements, or hiding unnecessary ones.

You also learn how to apply some great visual effects to your elements, allowing you to guide users better. Some of the effects can be created in CSS; however, jQuery provides much more variations and control.

Validation of web forms is one of the most critical pieces of dynamic programming. You can save a lot of user time by catching problems right at the browser in jQuery rather than after the form is submitted to the server.

Q&A

Q. Is there a way to create my own validation rules with the jQuery Validation plug-in?

A. Yes. You can call the `.addMethod(name, function(value, element, parameters) [,message])` method on the `Validator` object returned by `.validate()`. The name you specify will be the new rule, the function will be called, and the current value and element will be passed to it. The function should return true or false if the element value is valid. The option message parameter is the message that will be displayed.

Q. Isn't there a way to hide the ugly slide bar on a `<select>` element?

A. Not really. There are a bunch of workarounds, such as adding a `div` that masks it. One thing you can do is create a `<div>` element the exact size of the element. You could also use CSS clipping to try to hide it. None of them is a perfect solution, though.

Workshop

The workshop consists of a set of questions and answers designed to solidify your understanding of the material covered in this hour. Try to answer the questions before looking at the answers.

Quiz

1. How do you access the value of a `<select>` element from jQuery?

2. How do you disable a form element from jQuery?

3. List two methods to tell you if a check box input is checked from jQuery.

4. What does the following statement do?

   ```
   $("input:text").blur();
   ```

Quiz Answers

1. You call the `.val()` method on the jQuery object representing it.

2. Call `.attr("disabled","disabled")` on the jQuery object representing it.

3. `.prop("checked")` or `.is(":selected")` on the jQuery object.

4. It removes focus from all `<input>` elements of type `text`.

Exercises

1. Open the code in Listing 13.1 and modify the code so that `formB` also updates some of the elements in `formA`.

2. Open the code in Listing 13.2 and modify the code so that when the user selects a new year, the month element is autofocused.

3. Open the code in Listing 13.4 and add a new check box group for skills such as archery, strategy, hand to hand, or just make up your own. Add validation that the users must select between two and four skills.

HOUR 14
Creating Advanced Web Page Elements

What You'll Learn in This Hour:

▶ Creating an image gallery with slider controls
▶ Adding sorting to table elements
▶ Adding filtering to table elements
▶ How to create a multitype tree view
▶ How to implement custom dialogs
▶ Creating visual elements using basic HTML and jQuery
▶ How to use jQuery to create dynamic sparklines

In this hour, you have some fun creating some more advanced page elements. The purpose of this hour is to give you a chance to apply everything that you have learned so far in this book in some more advanced ways. The elements you build in this hour include an image gallery, interactive table, tree view, overlays, equalizer, and sparklines.

The following sections are written as examples that first explain some of the concepts used in the advanced elements; then you step through implementing them yourself. You will be able to apply the concepts learned in this chapter to implement a variety of types of advanced elements in your own web pages.

Adding an Image Gallery

One of the most visually interactive components of web pages are image galleries. An image is truly worth a thousand words. Images allow users to make decisions faster than any other type of visual element. The best way to apply images in allowing users to make decisions is to provide an interactive gallery.

An interactive gallery should enable users to quickly scan through several images and then easily select one to lead to the next step on the web page. Therefore, the necessary components are image thumbnails and controls. The thumbnails should be small versions of the original image that allow you to provide several options to select from at a time. Controls are whatever you apply to navigate through the thumbnails.

The most effective method of implementing an image gallery is to create a slider that contains the thumbnails with arrows that slide through the thumbnails until the user finds and clicks the desired image. Sliders are a good choice because they can be implemented in vertical or horizontal fashion to fit the design of the web page.

To implement the slider, you create a container <div> element that has a fixed size and hidden overflow, then a child <div> element that contains all the thumbnail images. The position of the child <div> can then be adjusted to reveal different sets of the images in the slider. The following section describes that process.

▼ TRY IT YOURSELF

Adding a Slider-Based Image Gallery

The purpose of the exercise is to give you some ideas about how to implement an image gallery with slider controls. The code for the example is in Listing 14.1.

Use the followings steps to create the dynamic web page:

1. In Aptana, create the hour14, hour14/js, hour14/css, and hour14/images folders, and then add the hour14/hour1401.html, hour14/js/hour1401.js, and hour14/css/hour1401.css files. You will also need to copy the images from the book's website at code/hour14/images to the hour14/images folder in Aptana.

2. Add the code shown in Listing 14.1-html and Listing 14.1-css to the HTML and CSS files. The HTML code lays out a set of <div> elements that will contain the image slider, control buttons, and the displayed image. The CSS code styles the images and the <div> elements. Specifically, notice the following lines. These lines define the slide selector area with a specific width with hidden overflow, a child <div> area that contains all the image elements, and the look of the images themselves.

```
06 #selector { max-width:640px; height:140px; overflow-x:hidden;
   ↪overflow-y:hidden; }
07 #imageSlide { position:relative; top:0px; left: 0px; height:100px; }
08 #imageSlide img {
09   height:100px; opacity:.6; vertical-align:top;  margin:10px;
10   border:3px ridge white; box-shadow: 5px 5px 5px #888888; }
```

3. Open the hour1401.js file and add a basic .ready() function that you will use to implement all the handlers to handle the interactions.

4. Add the following lines to add mouseenter and mouseleave event handlers to the #left and #right elements to provide a hover effect.

```
35   $("#left").mouseenter(function(){ slide(50); });
36   $("#left").mouseleave(function(){ $("#imageSlide").stop(true); return
     ➥false; });
37   $("#right").mouseenter(function(){ slide(-50); });
38   $("#right").mouseleave(function(){ $("#imageSlide").stop(true); return
     ➥false; });
```

5. Add the following lines that will add a hover animation effect for the thumbnails in the `#imageSlide` element. The hover effect animates increasing the `opacity` and `size` for images that are hovered over to give the user an indication that the item is clickable and which one is selected. A click handler is also added so that when the user clicks a thumbnail, it sets the main image.

```
39   $("#imageSlide img").mouseenter(function(){
40     $(this).stop(true).animate({height:120, opacity:1},500); return false;
       ➥});
41   $("#imageSlide img").mouseleave(function(){
42     $(this).stop(true).animate({height:100, opacity:.5},500); return false;
       ➥});
43   $("#imageSlide img").click(setPhoto);
```

6. Add the following line that calls the `click()` handler on the first thumbnail image to initially select a main image:

```
44   $("#imageSlide img:first").click();
```

7. Add the following `setPhoto()` click handler that animates changing the main image. Notice that the code fades the image out and then back in. Also, because the aspect ratios of the images are not all the same, the aspect ratio of the thumbnail is used to determine whether to set the `height` or `width` property for the image to fit properly.

```
23 function setPhoto(){
24   var newPhoto = $(this).attr("src");
25   var horizontal = (minHorizontalRatio > $(this).height()/$(this).width());
26   $("#photo img").stop(true).fadeTo(500, .1, "linear", function (){
27     $("#photo img").attr("src", newPhoto); });
28     if (horizontal) { $("#photo img").css({width:600,height:"auto"}) }
29     else { $("#photo img").css({width:"auto",height:400}) }
30   $("#photo img").fadeTo(500, 1);
31   return false;
32 }
```

8. Add the following `slide()` code that handles the sliding of the thumbnail images. Basically, this code determines where the new `left` position of the `#imageSlide` element should be. When the slide is all the way to the left, the `left` position is 0; when it is all the way to the right, the `left` position is set to a negative value clear off the web page so that only the right edge of the slide is visible.

```
12 function slide(value){
13   var oldLeft = sliderLeft;
14   sliderLeft = sliderLeft + value;
15   if (sliderLeft >= 0) { sliderLeft = 0; }
16   if (sliderLeft <= sliderMax) { sliderLeft = sliderMax; }
17   if(oldLeft != sliderLeft) {
18     $("#imageSlide").animate({left:sliderLeft}, 300, 'linear', function(){
19         slide(value); });
20   }
21   return false;
22 }
```

9. Add the initialization function `addImages()` shown in lines 3–11 and the `addImages()` call in line 34 of Listing 14.1-js. This code dynamically adds a set of image elements to the `#imageSlide` element.

10. Save all three files and then open the HTML document in a web browser, as shown in Figure 14.1. You should see the thumbnail slider and be able to navigate through it by hovering over the arrows. When you click a thumbnail image, the main image should change.

FIGURE 14.1
Image gallery with slider controls to select an image from thumbnails.

LISTING 14.1-html   HTML Document That Implements the Slider, Control, and Image Elements

```
01 <!DOCTYPE html>
02 <html>
03   <head>
04     <title>Hour 14-1</title>
05     <meta charset="utf-8" />
06     <script type="text/javascript" src="../js/jquery.min.js"></script>
07     <script type="text/javascript" src="js/hour1401.js"></script>
08     <link rel="stylesheet" type="text/css" href="css/hour1401.css">
09   </head>
10   <body>
11     <div id="viewer">
12       <div id="left"><img src="images/left.png" /></div>
13       <div id="selector">
14         <div id="imageSlide"></div>
15       </div>
16       <div id="right"><img src="images/right.png" /></div><br>
17       <div id="photo"><img src="" /></div>
18     </div>
19   </body>
20 </html>
```

LISTING 14.1-js   jQuery and JavaScript Code Implements the Mouse Event Handlers for the Image Slider Controls and Thumbnails

```
01 var sliderMax = sliderWidth = sliderLeft = 0;
02 var minHorizontalRatio = 400/600;
03 function addImages(){
04   var images = ["boy", "flower", "sunset", "bison", "canyon", "falls", "peak"];
05   for (i in images){
06     $("#imageSlide").append('<img src="images/'+ images[i] + '.jpg" />'); }
07   $("#imageSlide img").each(function(){ sliderWidth += $(this).width() + 26; });
08   sliderWidth += 40;
09   $("#imageSlide").width(sliderWidth);
10   sliderMax = $("#selector").width() - sliderWidth;
11 }
12 function slide(value){
13   var oldLeft = sliderLeft;
14   sliderLeft = sliderLeft + value;
15   if (sliderLeft >= 0) { sliderLeft = 0; }
16   if (sliderLeft <= sliderMax) { sliderLeft = sliderMax; }
17   if(oldLeft != sliderLeft) {
18     $("#imageSlide").animate({left:sliderLeft}, 300, 'linear', function(){
19         slide(value); });
```

```
20    }
21    return false;
22 }
23 function setPhoto(){
24    var newPhoto = $(this).attr("src");
25    var horizontal = (minHorizontalRatio > $(this).height()/$(this).width());
26    $("#photo img").stop(true).fadeTo(500, .1, "linear", function (){
27       $("#photo img").attr("src", newPhoto); });
28       if (horizontal) { $("#photo img").css({width:600,height:"auto"}) }
29       else { $("#photo img").css({width:"auto",height:400}) }
30    $("#photo img").fadeTo(500, 1);
31    return false;
32 }
33 $(document).ready(function(){
34    addImages();
35    $("#left").mouseenter(function(){ slide(50); });
36    $("#left").mouseleave(function(){ $("#imageSlide").stop(true); return false;
   ➥});
37    $("#right").mouseenter(function(){ slide(-50); });
38    $("#right").mouseleave(function(){ $("#imageSlide").stop(true); return false;
   ➥});
39    $("#imageSlide img").mouseenter(function(){
40       $(this).stop(true).animate({height:120, opacity:1},500); return false; });
41    $("#imageSlide img").mouseleave(function(){
42       $(this).stop(true).animate({height:100, opacity:.5},500); return false; });
43    $("#imageSlide img").click(setPhoto);
44    $("#imageSlide img:first").click();
45 });
```

LISTING 14.1-css CSS Code That Styles the Images and Controls

```
01 div { display:inline-block;}
02 #viewer { background-color:black; border:10px solid black; }
03 #right, #left {width:30px; height:100px; float:left; color:white; }
04 #right { float:right; }
05 #right img, #left img { margin-top:30px; width:32px; height:56px; }
06 #selector { max-width:640px; height:140px; overflow-x:hidden; overflow-y:hidden;
   ➥}
07 #imageSlide { position:relative; top:0px; left: 0px; height:100px; }
08 #imageSlide img {
09    height:100px; opacity:.6; vertical-align:top;  margin:10px;
10    border:3px ridge white; box-shadow: 5px 5px 5px #888888; }
11 #photo {
12    height:500px; width:700px;
13    display:table-cell; vertical-align:middle; text-align:center;
14 }
15 #photo img { border:5px ridge white; box-shadow: 10px 10px 5px #888888;}
```

Implementing Tables with Sorting and Filters

Tables are basic HTML. You should already be familiar with the concepts of adding tables with rows that include one or more `<th>` or `<td>` elements that provide column values. Tables are a great way to present data that can be organized into columns or rows.

For simple amounts of data, a basic static HTML table is adequate. But, what do you do if there is a lot of data in the table? Some web pages scroll on and on with tabular data. They are a pain to navigate, and in the end it's easier to use the web browser search capability to try to find what you are looking for.

One solution to this is to implement sorting and filtering in server-side scripts via AJAX request. Occasionally that is the best method when dealing with extremely large amounts of data stored in a database or extremely complex filtering algorithms. However, for most web pages, it is over-kill and requires a bunch of slow server requests that make the web page interaction disjointed.

A much better approach is to add filtering and sorting to those large tables directly in jQuery and JavaScript. That allows the user to filter the data down to a specific set and then order by columns very quickly. The page flow is much smoother, and no external server requests are required. The following section takes you through the process of implementing column sorting and filtering to a table.

TRY IT YOURSELF ▼

Creating an Interactive Table with Sorting and Filtering

The purpose of the exercise is to provide you with a chance to get and set form element values in a variety of ways. The code for the example is in Listing 14.2.

Use the following steps to create the dynamic web page:

1. In Aptana, create the hour14/hour1402.html, hour14/js/hour1402.js, and hour14/css/hour1402.css files.

2. Add the code shown in Listing 14.2-html and Listing 14.2-css to the HTML and CSS files. The HTML code defines the table and headers; the body will be added dynamically. The CSS code styles the table elements. Notice that the following lines of CSS define background images that will be used to indicate that the column is sortable, sorted ascending or sorted descending. The state of the column can then be changed by switching classes to `.ascending/.descending`. A search icon also is added as a background image to the `<input>` element to indicate its purpose:

```
14 input {  height:20px; width: 20px; border-radius:15px; padding: 0 7px 2px
   ➡25px;
15   background:url("../images/search.png") no-repeat scroll left bottom 0
   ➡#FFFFFF;
```

```
16    background-size:20px 20px;
17 }
18 input:focus { width:100px; }
19 span { background:url("../images/sort.png") no-repeat scroll left;
20    background-size:20px 20px;
21    padding: 0 7px 2px 25px;
22 }
23 .ascending{ background:url("../images/down.png") no-repeat scroll left;
24    background-size:20px 20px;
25 }
26 .descending{ background:url("../images/up.png") no-repeat scroll left;
27    background-size:20px 20px;
28 }
```

3. Open the hour1402.js file and the following `.ready()` function that will populate the table data, and add the sorting and filter handlers to the `<th>` elements. Notice that you use the jQuery `.data()` method to store the order and indicate whether the column data type is numeric. You also need to the add the `randInt()` and `buildData()` functions shown in lines 36–46 of Listing 14.2-js that will populate the table data:

```
47 $(document).ready(function(){
48    buildData();
49    $("th").each(function(i) {
50        var header = $(this);
51        header.data({numeric:header.hasClass("numeric"), order:-1});
52        header.children("span").click(function(){ sortColumn(header, i); });
53        var filter = $('<input type="text" />');
54        filter.keyup(function(){ filterColumn(filter, i); });
55        header.append(filter);
56    });
57 });
```

4. Add the following `keyup` event handler `filterColumn()` that will filter the column based on the text typed in the input for that column. The input and column arguments are passed to the handler in line 54. The `.each()` method is used to get the cell value of the specified column for each row. For numeric columns, if the value is less than the input value, the row is hidden. For string columns, the row is hidden if the string value of input is not found in the string value of the cell:

```
26 function filterColumn(input, column){
27    $("tbody tr").show().each(function(){
28        var header = $("th:eq("+ column +")");
29        var filterVal = input.val();
30        var rowVal = this.cells[column].innerHTML;
31        if(header.data("numeric") ){
```

```
32        if(parseFloat( filterVal ) > parseFloat( rowVal )) { $(this).hide();
    ➥}}
33      else {if(rowVal.indexOf(filterVal) < 0) { $(this).hide(); }}
34    });
35  }
```

5. Add the following compare() function that will accept two row elements, a and b, a column number, a numeric flag, and a sort order value. The code compares the column value of row a with row b and returns the correct sorting value based on whether the cell value is bigger, smaller, or equal.

```
04 function compare(a, b, column, numeric, order){
05    var aValue = a.cells[column].innerHTML;
06    var bValue = b.cells[column].innerHTML;
07    if (numeric) { aValue = parseFloat(aValue );
08                   bValue = parseFloat(bValue ); }
09    if (aValue < bValue) return order;
10    if (aValue > bValue) return -order;
11    return 0;
12  }
```

6. Add the following click handler sortColumn() that will sort the column when the user clicks the column heading. The handler uses the compare() function to sort the table rows and then appends them back to the table in the correct order. The handler also sets the correct classes for the header and cell elements for the column.

```
13 function sortColumn(header, column){
14    var rows = $("tbody tr");
15    rows.sort(function(a, b){
16        return compare(a, b, column, header.data("numeric"),
        ➥header.data("order"));
17      });
18    $(rows).each(function(){ $("tbody").append($(this)); });
19    header.data("order", -header.data("order"));
20    $("span").removeClass("ascending descending");
21    $("td").removeClass("sortColumn");
22    if(header.data("order") > 0) {
    ➥header.children("span").addClass("ascending"); }
23    else { header.children("span").addClass("descending"); }
24    $("tbody tr td:nth-child("+ (column + 1) +")").addClass("sortColumn");
25  }
```

7. Save all three files and then open the HTML document in a web browser, as shown in Figure 14.2. You should be able to change the sort order for the columns and use the text inputs to filter the rows displayed.

Sortable   Sorted Ascending   Filter Input

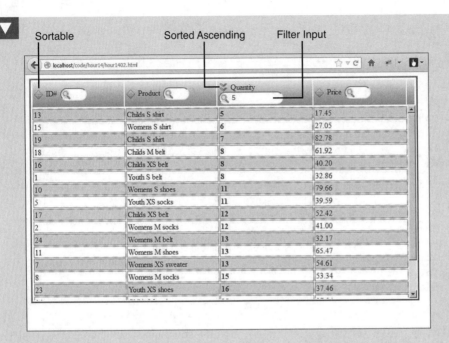

FIGURE 14.2
Dynamic table that allows you to sort and filter the elements displayed.

LISTING 14.2-html   HTML Document That Implements the Table Elements Used in the Example

```
01  <!DOCTYPE html>
02  <html>
03    <head>
04      <title>Hour 14-2</title>
05      <meta charset="utf-8" />
06      <script type="text/javascript" src="../js/jquery.min.js"></script>
07      <script type="text/javascript" src="js/hour1402.js"></script>
08      <link rel="stylesheet" type="text/css" href="css/hour1402.css">
09    </head>
10    <body>
11      <table>
12        <thead><tr>
13          <th class="numeric"><span>ID#</span></th>
14          <th ><span>Product</span></th>
15          <th class="numeric"><span>Quantity</span></th>
16          <th class="numeric"><span>Price</span></th>
17          <td class="spacer"></td>
18        </tr></thead>
```

```
19      <tbody></tbody>
20     </table>
21   </body>
22 </html>
```

LISTING 14.2-js   **jQuery and JavaScript Code Define the Interactions of the Table, Including Sorting and Filtering**

```
01 var tArr = ["Mens", "Womens", "Youth", "Childs"];
02 var sArr = ["XL", "M", "S", "XS"];
03 var kArr = ["pants", "shirt", "shoes", "socks", "sweater", "belt"];
04 function compare(a, b, column, numeric, order){
05   var aValue = a.cells[column].innerHTML;
06   var bValue = b.cells[column].innerHTML;
07   if (numeric) { aValue = parseFloat(aValue );
08                  bValue = parseFloat(bValue ); }
09   if (aValue < bValue) return order;
10   if (aValue > bValue) return -order;
11   return 0;
12 }
13 function sortColumn(header, column){
14   var rows = $("tbody tr");
15   rows.sort(function(a, b){
16       return compare(a, b, column, header.data("numeric"),
           ➥header.data("order"));
17     });
18   $(rows).each(function(){ $("tbody").append($(this)); });
19   header.data("order", -header.data("order"));
20   $("span").removeClass("ascending descending");
21   $("td").removeClass("sortColumn");
22   if(header.data("order") > 0) { header.children("span").addClass("ascending");
     ➥}
23   else { header.children("span").addClass("descending"); }
24   $("tbody tr td:nth-child("+ (column + 1) +")").addClass("sortColumn");
25 }
26 function filterColumn(input, column){
27   $("tbody tr").show().each(function(){
28     var header = $("th:eq("+ column +")");
29     var filterVal = input.val();
30     var rowVal = this.cells[column].innerHTML;
31     if(header.data("numeric") ){
32       if(parseFloat( filterVal ) > parseFloat( rowVal )) { $(this).hide(); }}
33     else {if(rowVal.indexOf(filterVal) < 0) { $(this).hide(); }}
34   });
35 }
36 function randInt(max) { return Math.floor((Math.random()*max)+1); }
```

```
37 function buildData(){
38   for(var x=1;x<26;x++){
39       var row =$("<tr></tr>");
40       row.append($("<td></td>").html(x));
41       row.append($("<td></td>").html(
42         tArr[randInt(3)]+" "+sArr[randInt(3)]+" "+kArr[randInt(5)]));
43       row.append($("<td></td>").html(randInt(20)));
44       row.append($("<td></td>").html(((Math.random()*80)+5).toFixed(2)));
45       $("tbody").append(row);}
46 }
47 $(document).ready(function(){
48   buildData();
49   $("th").each(function(i) {
50       var header = $(this);
51       header.data({numeric:header.hasClass("numeric"), order:-1});
52       header.children("span").click(function(){ sortColumn(header, i); });
53       var filter = $('<input type="text" />');
54       filter.keyup(function(){ filterColumn(filter, i); });
55       header.append(filter);
56     });
57 });
```

LISTING 14.2-css   CSS Code That Styles the Table Elements

```
01 table{ border:3px ridge blue; padding:0px;}
02 thead { display:block; width:820px; text-align:left; }
03 tbody { display:block;  max-height:400px; width:820px; overflow-y:scroll;}
04 th { background-image: -moz-linear-gradient(center top , #f1f1f1, #8F8F8F);
05    width:200px; height:30px; font:16px Arial Black; padding:3px;
06 }
07 .spacer {  background-image: -moz-linear-gradient(center top , #f1f1f1,
   ➥#8F8F8F);
08    width:15px; border:none;
09 }
10 td { width:200px; border: .5px dotted; }
11 .sortColumn { font-weight:bold; }
12 tr:nth-child(even){ background-color:#BBDDFF; }
13 img { height:26px; }
14 input {  height:20px; width: 20px; border-radius:15px; padding: 0 7px 2px 25px;
15    background:url("../images/search.png") no-repeat scroll left bottom 0 #FFFFFF;
16    background-size:20px 20px;
17 }
18 input:focus { width:100px; }
19 span { background:url("../images/sort.png") no-repeat scroll left;
20    background-size:20px 20px;
```

```
21   padding: 0 7px 2px 25px;
22 }
23 .ascending{ background:url("../images/down.png") no-repeat scroll left;
24   background-size:20px 20px;
25 }
26 .descending{ background:url("../images/up.png") no-repeat scroll left;
27   background-size:20px 20px;
28 }
```

Creating a Tree View

A tree view can be one of the most useful components when trying to present a large number of options to users. That is why tree views are used in so many places. Virtually all users will be familiar with them to at least a certain extent because it is the most common element used by OSes when displaying files and folders.

A tree view is simple to implement in jQuery and JavaScript. A very cool thing about tree views in your web pages is that they can contain any content that you want to display. The following section takes you through the process of implementing a tree view using jQuery and JavaScript.

Adding a Dynamic Tree View with Expanding and Collapsing Branches

The purpose of the exercise is to provide you with a chance to implement a tree view with items of different types. Each node in the tree is composed of a series of elements defined next:

```
<div class="tree">
  <span></span><label></label>
  <div class="content"></div>
  <div class="tree">one or more child elemnts</div>
</div>
```

The `<span>` element is used to display the collapsed or expanded image. The `<label>` element displays the text shown next to the expand/collapse button. The `<div class="content">` element can contain whatever content you would like to include. You can also add additional `<div class="tree">` elements that are child nodes.

The code for the example is in Listing 14.3. Use the followings steps to create the dynamic web page:

1. In Aptana, add the hour14/hour1403.html, hour14/js/hour1403.js, and hour14/css/hour1403.css files.

2. Add the code shown in Listing 14.3-html and Listing 14.3-css to the HTML and CSS files. The code in these files is fairly basic and should be familiar to you.

3. Open the hour1403.js file and add the following `.ready()` function. Add the code in lines 14–34. This code is used to populate the tree with random items, including images and form elements. This is to show you that the content of each node can be totally heterogeneous.

```
35 $(document).ready(function(){
36   var root = addLevels($("#treeContainer"), 4);
37   root.show();
38 });
```

4. Add the following `addItem()` function that is used to add a new node to the tree view. This function accepts jQuery objects `parentItem` and `item`. The `item` argument is a JavaScript object with a label and content value. These are used to build up the full node and append it to the parent:

```
06 function addItem(parentItem, item){
07   var newItem = $('<div class="tree"></div>').hide();
08   newItem.append($("<span></span>").click(toggleItem));
09   newItem.append($("<label></label>").html(item.label));
10   newItem.append($('<div class="content">
   ➥</div>').append(item.content).hide());
11   parentItem.append(newItem);
12   return newItem;
13 }
```

5. Add the following `click` handler `toggleItem()` that toggles the visibility of the child `<div>` elements when the user clicks the expand/collapse button:

```
01 function toggleItem(){
02   $(this).parent().children("div").toggle();
03   $(this).toggleClass("collapse");
04   return false;
05 }
```

6. Save all three files and then open the HTML document in a web browser, as shown in Figure 14.3. You should be able to expand and collapse levels of the tree view.

LISTING 14.3-html **HTML Document That Implements the Root Tree Element**

```
01 <!DOCTYPE html>
02 <html>
03   <head>
04     <title>Hour 14-3</title>
05     <meta charset="utf-8" />
06     <script type="text/javascript" src="../js/jquery.min.js"></script>
```

```
07        <script type="text/javascript" src="js/hour1403.js"></script>
08        <link rel="stylesheet" type="text/css" href="css/hour1403.css">
09      </head>
10      <body>
11        <div id="treeContainer"></div>
12      </body>
13    </html>
```

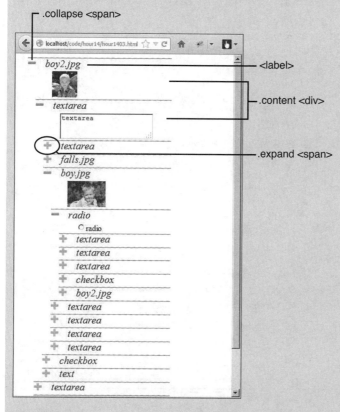

FIGURE 14.3
Collapsible tree view with multiple types of content.

LISTING 14.3-js jQuery and JavaScript Code Populates and Controls the Expansion
and Collapsing of the Tree

```
01  function toggleItem(){
02      $(this).parent().children("div").toggle();
03      $(this).toggleClass("collapse");
04      return false;
```

```
05 }
06 function addItem(parentItem, item){
07   var newItem = $('<div class="tree"></div>').hide();
08   newItem.append($("<span></span>").click(toggleItem));
09   newItem.append($("<label></label>").html(item.label));
10   newItem.append($('<div class="content"></div>').append(item.content).hide());
11   parentItem.append(newItem);
12   return newItem;
13 }
14 function randInt(max) { return Math.floor((Math.random()*max)); }
15 function getRandomItem(){
16   var itemTypes=["image", "input", "textarea"];
17   var images=["boy.jpg", "flower.jpg", "falls.jpg", "canyon.jpg", "sunset.jpg"];
18   var inputs=["text","checkbox", "radio"];
19   switch(itemTypes[randInt(3)]){
20     case "image":
21       var img = images[randInt(5)];
22       return {label:img, content:$('<img src="images/' + img + '" />')};
23     case "input":
24       var type = inputs[randInt(3)];
25       return {label:type, content:$('<input type="'+type+'">'+type+'</input>')};
26     case "textarea":
27       return {label:"textarea", content:$('<textarea>textarea</textarea>')};
28   }
29 }
30 function addLevels(parent, levels){
31   var element = addItem(parent, getRandomItem());
32   if( levels > 0 ){for(var x=0; x<5; x++){ addLevels( element, levels-1 ) }; }
33   return element;
34 }
35 $(document).ready(function(){
36   var root = addLevels($("#treeContainer"), 4);
37   root.show();
38 });
```

LISTING 14.3-css   CSS Code That Styles the Form Elements

```
01 #treeContainer { width:300px; }
02 .tree { margin-left: 16px; border-top:.5px dotted; }
03 .content { margin-left: 48px; }
04 .tree span {
05   display:inline-block; height:24px; width:24px; margin-right:10px;
06   border-radius:8px; vertical-align:middle;
07   background:url("../images/expand.png") no-repeat scroll left top 0;
08 }
```

```
09 .tree span.collapse {
10   background:url("../images/collapse.png") no-repeat scroll left top 0;
11 }
12 img { height:50px; }
13 .tree label { font:italic 20px/20px "Arial Black";}
```

Using Overlay Dialogs

You have already learned how to add several types of dialogs to your web pages using JavaScript. The problem is that the built-in dialogs are extremely limited in what you can do with them. You could open a new pop-up window to get more control, but pop-up windows have their own problems, the biggest of which is that users hate them and usually disable them in their browsers.

A much better option is to create your own dialog element using jQuery and JavaScript. Implementing a dialog requires two things: an overlay element that will mask off everything that is happening behind on the web pages and a dialog component that provides the dialog interaction.

The overlay needs to have a higher z-index than the main web page elements below. The overlay should also be somewhat transparent so that the user can see the web page in the background but is unable to click any of the web page elements under the overlay.

The dialog needs to have a higher z-index than the overlay so that it is visible when the overlay is displayed. The dialog also needs to have a means of closing, which makes the dialog and overlay elements hidden. You can include anything else in the dialog that you desire to provide user interaction.

The dialog and overlay need to be in a fixed position and initially hidden. When you want to display the dialog, unhide the overlay and dialog and then hide them when you are finished displaying the dialog. The following section takes you through that process.

TRY IT YOURSELF ▼

Adding Dynamic Dialogs Using Overlays in jQuery and JavaScript

The purpose of the exercise is to provide you with the capability to implement your own custom dialogs with an overlay that masks off the rest of the web page. The code for the example is in Listing 14.4.

Use the followings steps to create the dynamic web page:

1. In Aptana, create the hour14/hour1404.html, hour14/js/hour1404.js, and hour14/css/ hour1404.css files.

2. Add the code shown in Listing 14.4-html and Listing 14.4-css to the HTML and CSS files. The HTML code implements a basic web page with two exceptions. Notice the overlay and dialog <div> elements. Those elements are not part of the main web page and will be used to simulate a pop-up dialog with only jQuery and JavaScript.

3. Open the hour1404.js file and add the following `.ready()` function that hides the overlay and dialog <div> elements, and then add a click handler to display them and another to update the web page and hide the dialog.

```
12 $(document).ready(function(){
13    $("#overlay, #dialog").hide();
14    $("span").click(function(){ $("#overlay, #dialog").show(); });
15    $("#updateB").click(update);
16 });
```

4. Add the following `click` handler `update()` that updates the values of the web page based on information obtained in the dialog <div>. This illustrates the interaction between the dialog and the rest of the web page:

```
01 function update(){
02    $("#overlay, #dialog").hide();
03    $("#title p").html($("#titleT").val());
04    $("#content").html($("#contentT").val());
05    $("#leftNav span").remove();
06    $("input:checkbox").each(function(){
07       if($(this).prop("checked")){
08          $("#leftNav").append($("<span></span>").html($(this).val()));
09       }
10    });
11 }
```

5. Save all three files and then open the HTML document in a web browser, as shown in Figure 14.4. You should be able to open the dialog by clicking the Update button. Update the form and then see the web page close when the Update button in the dialog is clicked.

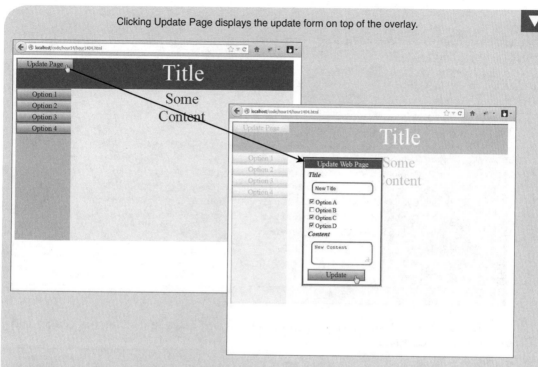

FIGURE 14.4
Form to page manipulation illustrating how to read data from forms and use it to update other elements on the web.

LISTING 14.4-html   HTML Document That Implements the Page, Overlay, and Dialog

```
01 <!DOCTYPE html>
02 <html>
03   <head>
04     <title>Hour 14-4</title>
05     <meta charset="utf-8" />
06     <script type="text/javascript" src="../js/jquery.min.js"></script>
07     <script type="text/javascript" src="js/hour1404.js"></script>
08     <link rel="stylesheet" type="text/css" href="css/hour1404.css">
09   </head>
10   <body>
11     <div><div id="title">
12       <span>Update Page</span><p>Title</p></div><br>
13     <div>
14       <div id="leftNav">
15         <span>Option 1</span>
16         <span>Option 2</span>
```

```
17          <span>Option 3</span>
18          <span>Option 4</span>
19       </div>
20       <div id="content">Some<br>Content</div>
21     </div></div>
22     <div id="overlay"></div>
23     <div id="dialog">
24       <p id="dialogTitle">Update Web Page</p>
25       <label>Title</label><br><input id="titleT" type="text" /><br>
26       <input type="checkbox"value="Option A">Option A</input><br>
27       <input type="checkbox"value="Option B">Option B</input><br>
28       <input type="checkbox"value="Option C">Option C</input><br>
29       <input type="checkbox"value="Option D">Option D</input><br>
30       <label>Content</label><br><textarea id="contentT"></textarea><br>
31       <span id="updateB">Update</span>
32     </div>
33   </body>
34 </html>
```

LISTING 14.4-js jQuery and JavaScript Code That Shows and Hides the Dialog and Updates the Web Page

```
01 function update(){
02   $("#overlay, #dialog").hide();
03   $("#title p").html($("#titleT").val());
04   $("#content").html($("#contentT").val());
05   $("#leftNav span").remove();
06   $("input:checkbox").each(function(){
07     if($(this).prop("checked")){
08       $("#leftNav").append($("<span></span>").html($(this).val()));
09     }
10   });
11 }
12 $(document).ready(function(){
13   $("#overlay, #dialog").hide();
14   $("span").click(function(){ $("#overlay, #dialog").show(); });
15   $("#updateB").click(update);
16 });
```

LISTING 14.4-css CSS Code That Styles the Page, Overlay, and Dialog Elements

```
01 div { margin:0px; display:inline-block; float:left; text-align:center; }
02 span { background-image: -moz-linear-gradient(center top , #f1f1f1, #8F8F8F);
```

```
03    color:black; border:3px ridge blue; font-size:20px; float:left;
    ↪cursor:pointer;
04    width:150px; text-align:center;
05 }
06 p { margin:0px; }
07 #title { background-color:blue; color:white; height:80px; width:750px;
    ↪font-size:60px; }
08 #leftNav{width:150px; height:400px; font-size:20px; background-color:#AACCFF; }
09 #content{ height:400px; width: 600px; font-size:40px;  background-color:#EEEEEE;
    ↪}
10 #overlay { position:fixed; top:10px; left:10px; height:480px; width:750px;
11    opacity:.8; background-color:white;
12 }
13 #dialog { border: 5px groove blue;  text-align:left; padding:10px;
14    position:fixed; top:100px; left:200px; background-color:white;
15 }
16 #dialogTitle { text-align:center; font:20px bold;
17    background-color:blue; color:white; margin:-10px -10px 5px -10px;
18 }
19 #contentT, #titleT { border-radius: 10px;  width:150px; padding:5px;
20    margin:10px; border:3px groove blue;
21 }
22 label { font:bold italic 18px "Arial Black" }
```

Implementing a Graphical Equalizer Display

The total purpose of this section is to help you see a method of using basic HTML elements along with dynamic jQuery and JavaScript interactions with data to provide a rich user experience with a visual indicator of what is happening with data. The data could be coming from a variety of sources, including JavaScript running on the web page or external services collected by AJAX requests.

A graphic equalizer element provides a great way to view several values at once and is something that many users are already familiar with. The following sections walk you through the process of implementing a graphical equalizer.

TRY IT YOURSELF ▼

Creating a Dynamic Graphic Equalizer with Simple jQuery and CSS

The purpose of the exercise is to illustrate how to implement graphical elements using the basic web elements with CSS styling and some background jQuery. In this exercise, you create a bunch of `<span>` elements, use CSS to style them into an element representing a graphical equalizer display, and then add jQuery to dynamically update the display to provide a rich UI element. The code for the example is in Listing 14.5.

Use the followings steps to create the dynamic web page:

1. In Aptana, create the hour14/hour1405.html, hour14/js/hour1405.js, and hour14/css/hour1405.css files.

2. Add the code shown in Listing 14.5-html and Listing 14.5-css to the HTML and CSS files. These files should be basic for you by now. The CSS provides class styles for the different colors used in the equalizer and then styles the look of the elements.

3. Open the hour1405.js file and add the following `.ready()` function that dynamically builds the equalizer by adding `<div>` and `<span>` elements:

```
20 $(document).ready(function(){
21    for(var i=0; i< 10; i++){
22      $("#equalizer").append($("<div></div>"));
23    }
24    $("#equalizer div").each(function (idx){
25      $(this).append($("<p></p>").html(idx));
26      for(var i=0; i< 2; i++){ $(this).append($('<span class="red">
         ➥</span>')); }
27      for(var i=0; i< 2; i++){ $(this).append($('<span class="orange">
         ➥</span>')); }
28      for(var i=0; i< 3; i++){ $(this).append($('<span class="yellow">
         ➥</span>')); }
29      for(var i=0; i< 8; i++){ $(this).append($('<span class="green">
         ➥</span>')); }
30      adjValues();
31    });
32 });
```

4. Add the following `updateEqualizer()` function that updates the opacity of the span elements so that only values below a certain level show as fully opaque. The data comes from a global array:

```
13 function updateEqualizer(){
14    $("span").css({opacity:.3});
15    $("#equalizer div").each(function(i){
16      $(this).children("span:gt("+ (15 - valueArr[i]) +")").css({opacity:1});
17      $(this).children("p:first").html(valueArr[i]);
18    });
19 }
```

5. Add the following functions that populate the global array every .5 seconds, via `setTimeout()`, with new data that is rendered in the equalizer by calling `updateEqualizer()`:

```
01 var valueArr = [10,8,3,12,12,15,15,3,4,5];
02 function randInt(max) { return Math.floor((Math.random()*max)-3); }
```

```
03 function adjValues(){
04    for (var i=0; i<valueArr.length; i++) {
05        var adj = valueArr[i] + Math.floor((Math.random()*7)-3);
06        adj = Math.max(3, adj);
07        adj = Math.min(15, adj);
08        valueArr[i] = adj;
09    }
10    updateEqualizer();
11    setTimeout(adjValues, 500);
12 }
```

6. Save all three files and then open the HTML document in a web browser, as shown in Figure 14.5. You should see the graphical equalizer element updating automatically.

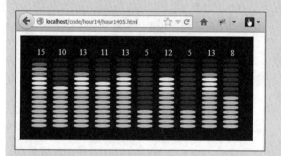

FIGURE 14.5
Graphical equalizer element.

LISTING 14.5-html   HTML Document That Implements a Web Page

```
01 <!DOCTYPE html>
02 <html>
03    <head>
04       <title>Hour 14-5</title>
05       <meta charset="utf-8" />
06       <script type="text/javascript" src="../js/jquery.min.js"></script>
07       <script type="text/javascript" src="js/hour1405.js"></script>
08       <link rel="stylesheet" type="text/css" href="css/hour1405.css">
09    </head>
10    <body>
11       <div id="equalizer"></div>
12    </body>
13 </html>
```

LISTING 14.5-js   **jQuery and JavaScript Code Dynamically Build and Populate the Graphical Equalizer**

```
01 var valueArr = [10,8,3,12,12,15,15,3,4,5];
02 function randInt(max) { return Math.floor((Math.random()*max)-3); }
03 function adjValues(){
04   for (var i=0; i<valueArr.length; i++) {
05       var adj = valueArr[i] + Math.floor((Math.random()*7)-3);
06       adj = Math.max(3, adj);
07       adj = Math.min(15, adj);
08       valueArr[i] = adj;
09   }
10   updateEqualizer();
11   setTimeout(adjValues, 500);
12 }
13 function updateEqualizer(){
14   $("span").css({opacity:.3});
15   $("#equalizer div").each(function(i){
16       $(this).children("span:gt("+ (15 - valueArr[i]) +")").css({opacity:1});
17       $(this).children("p:first").html(valueArr[i]);
18   });
19 }
20 $(document).ready(function(){
21   for(var i=0; i< 10; i++){
22       $("#equalizer").append($("<div></div>"));
23   }
24   $("#equalizer div").each(function (idx){
25       $(this).append($("<p></p>").html(idx));
26       for(var i=0; i< 2; i++){ $(this).append($('<span class="red"></span>')); }
27       for(var i=0; i< 2; i++){ $(this).append($('<span class="orange"></span>'));
➥}
28       for(var i=0; i< 3; i++){ $(this).append($('<span class="yellow"></span>'));
➥}
29       for(var i=0; i< 8; i++){ $(this).append($('<span class="green"></span>')); }
30       adjValues();
31   });
32 });
```

LISTING 14.5-css   **CSS Code That Styles Elements to Render the Graphical Equalizer**

```
01 #equalizer { background-color:black; color:white;
02   width:420px; height:160px; padding:20px;
03 }
04 div{ display:inline-block; width:40px;  padding:1px; }
05 p{ text-align:center; margin:0px;}
06 span{ display:block; width:30px; height:7px; margin:2px; border-radius: 40%; }
```

```
07  .green{ background-color:#00FF00; }
08  .yellow{ background-color:#FFFF00; }
09  .orange{ background-color:#FFAA00; }
10  .red{ background-color:#FF0000; }
```

Adding Sparkline Graphics

The purpose of this section is to help you see a method of using some of the new HTML5 elements along with dynamic jQuery and JavaScript interactions with data to provide a rich user experience with a visual indicator of trending data. The data could be coming from a variety of sources, including JavaScript running on the web page or external services collected by AJAX requests.

In this section, you implement a series of sparklines. A sparkline is a mini-graph that is updated frequently with the latest values from the web server. A sparkline element provides a great way for you to see how to use the new HTML elements to provide users with a great visual indicator of data trends. The following sections walk you through the process of implementing the sparkline.

TRY IT YOURSELF ▼

Creating Dynamic Sparklines with Simple jQuery, JavaScript, and CSS

The purpose of the exercise is to illustrate how to implement new HTML5 graphical elements to render useful visual components to your web page. In this exercise, you use `<canvas>` elements to implement sparklines and dynamically update them using jQuery and JavaScript. The code for the example is in Listing 14.6.

Use the followings steps to create the dynamic web page:

1. In Aptana, create the hour14/hour1406.html, hour14/js/hour1406.js, and hour14/css/hour1406.css files.

2. Add the code shown in Listing 14.6-html and Listing 14.6-css to the HTML and CSS files. The HTML and CSS are fairly basic. Notice that there are just `<div>`, `<span>`, `<label>`, and `<canvas>` elements.

3. Open the hour1406.js file and add the following `.ready()` function that populates the data used for the sparklines and starts off the `adjValues()` timer function. You also need to add the `adjValues()` and `getRandomArray()` functions shown in Listing 14.6-js. These functions populate and continuously update the values used for the sparklines. Notice that the data array is stored in the `<div>` element using the `.data()` method.

```
33 $(document).ready(function(){
34   $("div").each(function(){ $(this).data("valueArr", getRandomArray()); });
35   adjValues();
36 });
```

4. Add the following function `renderSpark()` that uses the set of values in the data array and draws a series of lines on the canvas to create the sparkline. Line 13 is a bit of a trick; setting the width of the canvas to its current value will erase the current data on the canvas, so the last sparkline is erased before drawing the new one:

```
12 function renderSpark(c, lineValues){
13   c.width = c.width;
14   var xAdj = c.width/lineValues.length;
15   var ctx = c.getContext("2d");
16   ctx.fillStyle = "#000000";
17   ctx.strokeStyle = "#00ff00";
18   ctx.lineWidth = 3;
19   var x = 1;
20   ctx.moveTo(x,(c.height));
21   for (var idx in lineValues){
22     var value = parseInt(lineValues[idx]);
23     ctx.lineTo(x+xAdj, (c.height - value));
24     x += xAdj;
25   }
26   ctx.stroke();
27 }
```

5. Save all three files and then open the HTML document in a web browser, as shown in Figure 14.6. You should see the sparklines automatically updating.

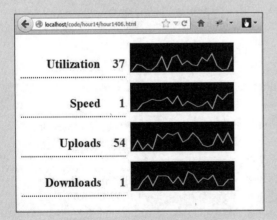

FIGURE 14.6
Web page with dynamic sparkline elements that update automatically.

LISTING 14.6-html   **HTML Document That Implements Page Elements**

```
01 <!DOCTYPE html>
02 <html>
03   <head>
04     <title>Hour 14-6</title>
05     <meta charset="utf-8" />
06     <script type="text/javascript" src="../js/jquery.min.js"></script>
07     <script type="text/javascript" src="js/hour1406.js"></script>
08     <link rel="stylesheet" type="text/css" href="css/hour1406.css">
09   </head>
10   <body>
11     <div><label>Utilization</label><span>1</span><canvas></canvas></div>
12     <div><label>Speed</label><span></span><canvas></canvas></div>
13     <div><label>Uploads</label><span></span><canvas></canvas></div>
14     <div><label>Downloads</label><span></span><canvas></canvas></div>
15   </body>
16 </html>
```

LISTING 14.6-js   **jQuery and JavaScript Code Dynamically Populates and Updates the Sparklines**

```
01 function randInt(max) { return Math.floor((Math.random()*max)+1); }
02 function adjValues(){
03   $("div").each(function(){
04     var lineValues = $(this).data("valueArr");
05     lineValues.shift();
06     lineValues.push(randInt(100));
07     $(this).children("span").html(lineValues[0]);
08     renderSpark($(this).children("canvas").get(0), lineValues);
09   });
10   setTimeout(adjValues, 1000);
11 }
12 function renderSpark(c, lineValues){
13   c.width = c.width;
14   var xAdj = c.width/lineValues.length;
15   var ctx = c.getContext("2d");
16   ctx.fillStyle = "#000000";
17   ctx.strokeStyle = "#00ff00";
18   ctx.lineWidth = 3;
19   var x = 1;
20   ctx.moveTo(x,(c.height));
21   for (var idx in lineValues){
22     var value = parseInt(lineValues[idx]);
23     ctx.lineTo(x+xAdj, (c.height - value));
```

```
24      x += xAdj;
25   }
26   ctx.stroke();
27 }
28 function getRandomArray(){
29   var arr = new Array();
30   for(var x=0; x<20; x++){ arr.push(randInt(100)); }
31   return arr;
32 }
33 $(document).ready(function(){
34   $("div").each(function(){ $(this).data("valueArr", getRandomArray()); });
35   adjValues();
36 });
```

LISTING 14.6-css   CSS Code That Styles the Page Elements and Sparkline

```
1 canvas{ height:50px; width: 200px; vertical-align:bottom;
2   border:3px solid black; background-color:black; margin:10px;
3 }
4 label, span { display:inline-block; text-align:right; width:160px;
5   font:bold 24px/50px "Arial Black"; border-bottom:2px dotted;
6 }
7 span{ width:50px; color:blue; }
```

Summary

In this hour, you got a chance to implement several more advanced web elements. You learned the basics of implementing image galleries, how to add sorting and filtering to a table, and how to dynamically create a tree view. You also got a chance to implement some graphical elements, such as sparklines and an equalizer display.

Q&A

Q. In your example, you populated the image slider using an array. Is that the best method?

A. Not necessarily. That was used for simplicity in the example. You can also use a static file located on the web server to get the list of files, or use an AJAX request to a server-side script that returns the list of images to display.

Q. Is it better to use a `<canvas>` or an `<svg>` element to draw chart type data such as the sparkline?

A. I used a `<canvas>` because it is simple to implement the changing lines. An `<svg>` chart would be too large to include in this book. The downside is that the canvas gets blurry if you zoom in on the web page. For the best charts, you should use `<svg>` so that the user can zoom in and it is still clean.

Workshop

The workshop consists of a set of questions and answers designed to solidify your understanding of the material covered in this hour. Try to answer the questions before looking at the answers.

Quiz

1. How do you use jQuery to move the slider in the image gallery?

2. Why do you use an overlay element along with the dialog when creating custom dialogs?

3. How do you make the dialog box appear on top of other elements?

Quiz Answers

1. The slider is really just a big `div`. To adjust the position, change the relative position using the `.css()` or `.animate()` methods.

2. The overlay keeps the user from clicking on the rest of the web page until the dialog is closed.

3. Set the `z-index` to a higher value.

Exercises

1. Modify the code in Listing 14.2 so that the filter for numerical columns will filter out items less than the value specified when the column is in ascending order and items greater than the value specified when the column is in descending order.

2. Modify the code in Listing 14.3 to add expand all and collapse all buttons. The buttons should expand or collapse all elements in the tree.

3. This exercise is for more advanced CSS and HTML users. In the code in Listing 14.1, modify the slider to be vertical. You will need to change positioning code to adjust the top instead of the left, move things around on the page, and do quite a number of CSS changes to get the slider to look right.

Accessing Server-Side Data via AJAX

What You'll Learn in This Hour:

▶ Using AJAX requests to load data into page elements

▶ Sending AJAX GET and POST requests

▶ How to serialize parameters for GET and POST requests

▶ How to handle JSON and XML data in the web server AJAX response

▶ Implementing AJAX event handlers to handle completion, success, and failure events

In this hour, you explore the world of asynchronous communication with the server using AJAX requests in jQuery and JavaScript. AJAX communications are one of the most vital parts of most websites. They allow jQuery and JavaScript to get additional data from the server and update the page instead of reloading or loading a new web page.

The following sections try to demystify AJAX a bit for you and they provide you with some practical examples. By the end of this hour, you will be able to implement AJAX in a variety of ways.

Making AJAX Easy

Despite its importance, AJAX tends to be a bit daunting at first. With all the communication terms, it might seem easy to get confused. That really shouldn't be the case. If you take a quick step back to look at the basics of AJAX from a high level, the details shouldn't seem daunting at all.

AJAX is a request from jQuery or JavaScript to the web server. The request may send data to the server, and the server will respond with a success or failure and possibly additional data. That is it—nothing more, nothing less. The following sections help clarify the request/response process.

Clarifying AJAX Versus Page Requests

The first step is to define the difference between AJAX and normal page linking request. You are already familiar with page links; when you click a link, a new web page appears. Often that is the case even if all the controls, tables, graphics, and so on are the same, but only some data has changed. In the case of form submission, none of the data changes, but the web page must still be reloaded from the server.

CAUTION

Don't confuse server-side dynamic creation of web pages with AJAX. Dynamic creation of web pages is still the old traditional method—it is just a bit easier to manage. Each request back to the server still requires a full new web page to be returned. The only advantage is that the web page is generated in memory instead of read from disk.

AJAX is completely different. An AJAX request does not request a new web page from the server. Instead, an AJAX request only sends and receives bits of data necessary. If the new data received from the web server requires the web page to be updated, then jQuery and JavaScript can update the page elements, as you have already seen.

The following is a list of a few of the benefits of AJAX requests:

▶ Less data requested from the web server.

▶ Allows the user to continue using the web page even while the request is being processed.

▶ Errors can be caught and handled on the client side before a request is ever made to the server.

Figure 15.1 illustrates the difference between the two methods of updating data in the browser.

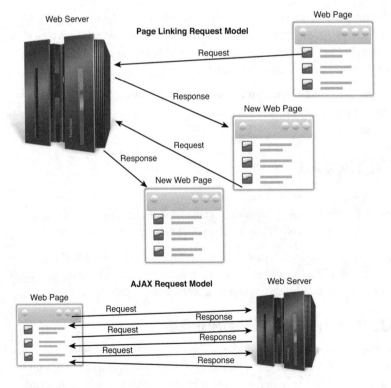

FIGURE 15.1
Comparison of AJAX requests versus traditional page linking.

Understanding Server-Side Services Such as ASP, PHP, MySQL

The next step is to understand how the AJAX requests are handled. Great detail is not necessarily important. What you need to understand is that for each AJAX request you send to a web server, a process will read the request, do some work, and then send back a response.

The back-end processes can be the web server returning a static HTML, text, XML, or JSON file. The back-end process often is an ASP, JSP, PHP, Python, or CGI script that is running on the server reading data from memory, files, databases, and other sources. The back-end process can also be a myriad of other frameworks that are integrated into the web server.

None of that really matters to the AJAX script running in the browser. All that matters is that the server sends back a status and data.

Understanding Asynchronous Communication

You need to be clear on asynchronous communication. When you request a web page from the web server, the communication is synchronous to your browser. That means the browser waits until the HTML document is downloaded from the server before it begins rendering it and retrieving the additional resources necessary.

TIP

You can do synchronous AJAX requests with both jQuery and JavaScript. The jQuery `.ajax()` method and the JavaScript `send()` function both have a Boolean field that allows this. You shouldn't use this, though, because you can cause the browser to lock up, which will create some very unhappy users. In fact, in jQuery 1.8 and later, that option is deprecated.

AJAX communication is different when you send an AJAX request. Control is returned immediately back to jQuery or JavaScript, which can do additional things. Only when the request has completed or timed out will events be triggered in the browser that allow you to handle the request data.

Understanding Cross-Domain Requests

Cross-domain requests occur when you send AJAX requests to separate servers from different domains. The browser prevents this, and correctly so because of a multitude of security reasons.

The only problem with blocking cross-domain requests is that you often want to get data from services external to the current website. You can get around this in a couple of ways.

The first method to overcome the cross-domain restriction is to have the web server act as a proxy to the other servers or services, meaning that instead of directly communicating via

JavaScript, you send the request to the server and have the server do it for you. The only downside is that it requires additional server-side scripting, and you pay an extra time penalty because data has to first be downloaded to the web server and then to the web browser.

Another option is to do what is called on-demand JavaScript, which is used by JSONP (JSON with Padding). This method takes advantage of the fact that you can download a script from another website as a resource using the following syntax:

```
<script type="text/javascript"
        src="http://new.domain.com/getData?jsonp=parseData">
</script>
```

The trick is that the address specified by the `src` attribute cannot return the JSON response directly. If the browser detects that the data in the script is JSON, as shown next, it throws a cross-domain error:

```
{ "title": "photoA", "rating": 7 };
```

Instead, the third-party service must support JSONP, in which case it pads the response with the function call specified by the request, as shown next. In that way, you will be able to access the data from JavaScript by calling the function.

```
parseData({ "title": "photoA", "rating": 7 });
```

Looking at GET Versus POST Requests

This section clarifies GET and POST requests. The two main types of requests that you send to the web server are GET and POST. There are only a few differences between the two, but they are important. A GET request passes parameters as part of the URL, whereas a POST request passes them as part of the request data.

To help you quickly see this, the following illustrates the basic URL and data involved to send a first and last name to the server in a GET and POST request:

GET request URL:

```
http://localhost/code/example1.html?first=Brad&last=Dayley
```

GET request data:

```
<empty>
```

POST request URL:

```
http://localhost/code/example1.html
```

POST request data:

```
first=Brad
last=Dayley
```

Which request type should you use? The basic rule is to use a GET for retrieving information from the server and a POST if you are changing data on the server.

Understanding Response Data Types—Binary Versus Text Versus XML Versus JSON

It's important to be clear on the response data types that may come back from the server. The data that comes back to an AJAX request will be either in some sort of binary or text format. Typically, binary is reserved for images, zip files, and the like. However, text may be raw text, HTML, XML, JSON, and so on.

What does that mean? This is where it can get a bit tricky. When the browser receives a response from the server, it attempts to determine the type of data received by the server and create the appropriate response object for you to use.

For XML and HTML data, a DOM object is created, whereas for JSON, a JavaScript object is created. For raw text or binary objects, an object is constructed that provides access to the raw text or binary data.

Implementing AJAX

Now that you have your head wrapped around the AJAX concepts, you are ready to begin implementing the basic details. To implement AJAX requests, you need to access the HTTP request object, format the data that needs to be sent to the server, send the request, and then handle the response.

Both JavaScript and jQuery have methods to send an AJAX request to the web server. You'll see both methods in the following sections. jQuery is able to do everything that JavaScript can do, but in a much easier and extensible manner.

The following sections discuss and provide some examples of implementing basic AJAX requests.

AJAX from JavaScript

To implement an AJAX request in JavaScript, you need access to a new window.XMLHttpRequest object. Table 15.1 describes the important methods and attributes of the XMLHttpRequest object:

TABLE 15.1 Important Methods and Attributes of the `XMLHttpRequest` Object

Method/Attribute	Description
`open()`	Allows you to construct a GET or POST request.
`send()`	Sends the request to the server.
`onreadystatechange`	Event handler that will be executed when the state of the `XMLHttpRequest` object changes.
`response`	Object created by the browser based on the data type.
`responseText`	Raw text returned in the response data from the server.
`setRequestHeader`	This allows you to set HTTP request headers necessary to implement the request.
`status`	Status response code from server; that is, 200 for success, 404 for not found, and so on.

To illustrate this, check out the following code that sends a GET AJAX request to the server to get the email address based on first and last name parameters:

```
var xmlhttp = new XMLHttpRequest();
xmlhttp.onreadystatechange=function() {
  if (xmlhttp.readyState==4 && xmlhttp.status==200)
    { document.getElementById("email").innerHTML=xmlhttp.responseText;}
  }
xmlhttp.open("GET","getUserEmail.php?userid=brad",true);
xmlhttp.send();
```

The following code illustrates how to send a basic POST AJAX request to the server to set the email address. Notice that for the POST request, the added `Content-length` and `Content-type` headers make sure that the data is treated correctly at the server. The `Content-length` is set to the length of the `params` string.

```
var xmlhttp = new XMLHttpRequest();
var params = "first=Brad&last=Dayley&email=brad@dayleycreations.com";
http.setRequestHeader("Content-type", "text/plain");
http.setRequestHeader("Content-length", params.length);
xmlhttp.onreadystatechange=function() {
  if (xmlhttp.readyState==4 && xmlhttp.status==200)
    { alert("Email Updated");
  }
xmlhttp.open("POST","setUserEmail.php",true);
xmlhttp.send(params);
```

NOTE

In Internet Explorer browsers earlier than IE7, you need to use the following line to create the `xmlhttp` object because the window object doesn't support the `XMLHttpRequest` attribute:

```
xmlhttp=new ActiveXObject("Microsoft.XMLHTTP");
```

AJAX from jQuery

This section looks at implementing AJAX requests from jQuery. jQuery provides very simple-to-use wrapper methods to implement AJAX requests, `.load()`, `.get()`, and `.post()`.

The helper functions are wrappers around the `.ajax()` interface, which is discussed later. These helper functions are the following:

▶ `.load(url [, data ] [, success(data, textStatus, jqXHR) ] )`—This method is used to load data directly into elements represented by the jQuery object.

▶ `.getScript (url [, data ] [, success(data, textStatus, jqXHR) ] ) )`—This method is used to load and then immediately execute a JavaScript/jQuery script.

▶ `.getJSON(url [, data ] [, success(data, textStatus, jqXHR) ] ) )`—This method is used to load data in JSON format using a JSONP request to servers on different domains.

▶ `.get(url [, data ] [, success(data, textStatus, jqXHR) ] [, dataType ]) )`—This method is used to send a generic GET request to the server.

▶ `.post(url [, data ] [, success(data, textStatus, jqXHR) ] [, dataType ]) )`—This method is used to send a generic POST request to the server.

Each of these methods enables you to specify the `url` of the request. The `.load()` method is used to load data directly into elements represented by jQuery object. The `.get()` and `.post()` methods are used to send GET and POST requests.

The `data` argument can be a string or basic JavaScript object. For example, in the following example, `obj`, `objString`, and `formString` are all valid data arguments:

```
var obj ={"first":"Brad", "last":"Dayley"};
var objString = $.param(obj);
var formString = $("form").serialize();
```

You can also specify the function that executes when the response from the server succeeds. For example, the following success handler sets the value of the `#email` element to the value response data:

```
$.get("getEmail.php?first=Brad&last=Dayley", null, function (data, status, xObj){
  $("#email").html(data);
}));
```

The .get() and .post() methods also enable you to specify a dataType parameter as a string, such as "xml", "json", "script", "html", and so on, that formats the expected format of the response data from the server. For example, to specify a response type of JSON, you would use the following:

```
$.get("getUser.php?first=Brad&last=Dayley", null, function (data, status, xObj){
  $("#email").html(data.email);
}), "json");
```

▼ TRY IT YOURSELF

Sending an AJAX Request from jQuery

In this exercise, you get a chance to implement some simple AJAX requests using the jQuery .load() method. The resulting web page contains a left navigation that uses AJAX requests to load lorem ipsum article data from the web server and populate the web page with the results. The purpose of the exercise is to give you a chance to see how the .load() method works.

The code for the example is in Listing 15.1. Use the followings steps to create the dynamic web page:

1. In Aptana, create the hour15, hour15/js, and hour15/css folders, and then add the hour15/hour1501.html, hour15/js/hour1501.js, and hour15/css/hour1501.css files. You also need to copy the images, data, and php folders from the book's website at code/hour15 to the hour15 folder in Aptana.

2. Add the code shown in Listing 15.1-html and Listing 15.1-css to the HTML and CSS files. The code in these files should be familiar to you, with the exception of an article attribute to the <span> element, as shown next. This is used in the jQuery to identify which article should be loaded when the span is clicked.

   ```
   <span class="navItem" article="article1">jQuery Under the Hood</span>
   ```

3. Now open the hour1501.js file and add the following .ready() that adds a click handler setArticle() to the left navigation items on the web page:

   ```
   4 $(document).ready(function(){
   5   $(".navItem").click(setArticle);
   6 });
   ```

4. Add the following click handler setArticle() that calls the jQuery AJAX method .load() and populates the #content <div> with new data loaded from the server. Notice that the article attribute in the span is read and a .html extension added so that the .load() method requests a different article for each link.

```
1 function setArticle(){
2   $("#content").load("data/"+$(this).attr("article")+".html");
3 }
```

5. Save all three files and then open the HTML document in a web browser, as shown in Figure 15.2. You should be able to click the left navigation items and load different articles.

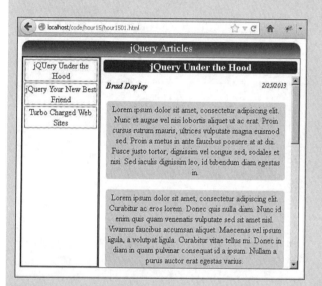

FIGURE 15.2
Article viewer that uses AJAX requests to populate the article content.

LISTING 15.1-html   HTML Document That Adds Menu and Content

```
01 <!DOCTYPE html>
02 <html>
03   <head>
04     <title>Hour 15-1</title>
05     <meta charset="utf-8" />
06     <script type="text/javascript" src="../js/jquery.min.js"></script>
07     <script type="text/javascript" src="js/hour1501.js"></script>
08     <link rel="stylesheet" type="text/css" href="css/hour1501.css">
09   </head>
10   <body>
11     <div><div id="banner">jQuery Articles</div>
12     <div>
13       <div id="leftNav">
```

```
14            <span class="navItem" article="article1">jQuery Under the Hood</span>
15            <span class="navItem" article="article2">jQuery Your New Best Friend
   ➡</span>
16            <span class="navItem" article="article3">Turbo Charged Web Sites</span>
17        </div>
18        <div id="content">
19          <span id="title"> </span>
20          <div id="article"></div>
21        </div>
22      </div>
23    </body>
24    </body>
25 </html>
```

LISTING 15.1-js **jQuery and JavaScript That Implements the AJAX** `.load()`
Requests

```
1 function setArticle(){
2   $("#content").load("data/"+$(this).attr("article")+".html");
3 }
4 $(document).ready(function(){
5   $(".navItem").click(setArticle);
6 });
```

LISTING 15.1-css **CSS Code That Styles the Page**

```
01 div { margin:0px; display:inline-block; float:left; text-align:center; }
02 p { margin:2px; }
03 #banner { border-radius: 15px 15px 0px 0px;
04   background-image: -moz-linear-gradient(center top , #0000FF, #88BBFF);
05   color:white; height:30px; width:550px; font-size:20px; }
06 #leftNav { width:150px; height:400px; border:3px groove #000088; }
07 .navItem { border:1px dotted; display:block; margin:3px; }
08 .navItem:hover { border:1px solid; background-color:#00FF00; cursor:pointer; }
09 #content {border:1px solid blue;}
10 #article { width: 372px; height:350px; padding:10px; overflow-y:scroll; }
11 #title { font-weight:bold; font-size:20px; display:block; margin:5px;
12   background-color:#0000AA; color:white; border-radius:5px; }
13 #by { text-align:right; font:bold italic 16px arial black; float:left;
14   margin-bottom:20px; }
15 #date { text-align:right; font:italic 12px arial black; float:right;}
16 #article p {margin-top:20px; background-color:#DDDDDD; border-radius:5px;
17   clear:both; padding:5px; }
```

Handling AJAX Responses

In addition to specifying the `success` handler, the wrapper methods also enable you to attach additional handlers using the following methods:

▶ `.done(data, textStatus, jqXHR)`—Called when a successful response is received from the server.

▶ `.fail(data, textStatus, jqXHR)`—Called when a failure response is received from the server or the request times out.

▶ `.always(data, textStatus, jqXHR)`—Always called when a response is received from the server.

For example, the following code adds an event handler that is called when the request fails:

```
$.get("getUser.php?first=Brad&last=Dayley", null, function (data, status, xObj){
  $("#email").html(data.email);
}), "json").fail(function(data, status, xObj){
  alert("Request Failed");
});
```

Handling Login Request Successes and Failures

In this exercise, you get a chance to implement the `.done()`, `.fail()`, and `.always()` AJAX event handlers on a basic jQuery `.get()` request. The resulting web page is a simple login that sends the username and password to a server-side PHP script that checks for `username="user"` and `password="password"`. If the correct username and password are entered, the request succeeds; otherwise, the request fails. The purpose of the exercise is to apply the AJAX handlers to a practical concept.

The code for the example is in Listing 15.2. Use the followings steps to create the dynamic web page:

1. In Aptana, create the hour15, hour15/js, and hour15/css folders, and then add the hour15/hour1502.html, hour15/js/hour1502.js, and hour15/css/hour1502.css files.

2. Add the code shown in Listing 15.2-html and Listing 15.2-css to the HTML and CSS files. The HTML and CSS code define a basic login dialog.

3. Open the hour1502.js file and add the following `.ready()` function that will add a click handler to the input button:

```
09 $(document).ready(function(){
10   $("#loginButton").click(login);
11 });
```

4. Add the following click handler `login()` that will be called when the user clicks the login button. The handler makes an AJAX `.get()` request to the hour15/php/login.php file that should already be in place. Notice that the data from the `#loginForm` is serialized using `.serialize()` to create the query string. Also notice that `.done()`, `.fail()`, and `.always()` are attached to the `.get()` request to handle the AJAX completion events.

```
04 function login(){
05    $.get("php/login.php",
06      $("#loginForm").serialize()).done(success).fail(failure).always(always);
07    return false;
08 }
```

5. Add the following three AJAX event handlers to handle completion, failure, and successful login attempts:

```
01 function failure(){ alert("Login Failed"); }
02 function success(){ alert("Login Succeeded"); }
03 function always(){ alert("Login Attempt Completed"); }
```

6. Save all three files and then open the HTML document in a web browser, as shown in Figure 15.3. You should see the completion alert pop up whenever you click the login button. You should also see the success alert when you use the correct credentials of `username="user"` and `password="password"`.

LISTING 15.2-html   **HTML Document That Creates the Login Dialog**

```
01 <!DOCTYPE html>
02 <html>
03   <head>
04     <title>Hour 15-2</title>
05     <meta charset="utf-8" />
06     <script type="text/javascript" src="../js/jquery.min.js"></script>
07     <script type="text/javascript" src="js/hour1502.js"></script>
08     <link rel="stylesheet" type="text/css" href="css/hour1502.css">
09   </head>
10   <body>
11     <div id="login">
12       <div id="title">Login</div>
13       <form id="loginForm">
14         <label>Username: </label><input type="text" name="user" /><br>
15         <label>Password: </label><input type="password" name="pw" /><br>
16         <input id="loginButton" type="button" value="Login" />
17       </form>
18     </div>
19   </body>
20   </body>
21 </html>
```

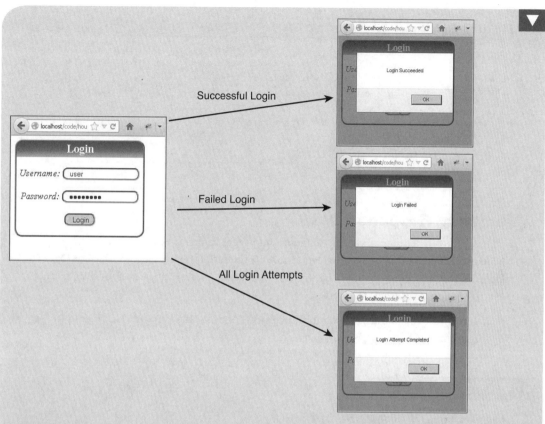

FIGURE 15.3
Simple login dialog.

LISTING 15.2-js jQuery and JavaScript That Sends the Login Request to the Server via an AJAX GET Request and Handles Success and Failure Conditions

```
01 function failure(){ alert("Login Failed"); }
02 function success(){ alert("Login Succeeded"); }
03 function always(){ alert("Login Attempt Completed"); }
04 function login(){
05   $.get("php/login.php",
06     $("#loginForm").serialize()).done(success).fail(failure).always(always);
07   return false;
08 }
09 $(document).ready(function(){
10   $("#loginButton").click(login);
11 });
```

LISTING 15.2-css   CSS Code That Styles the Page

```
01 #login { border-radius: 15px; text-align:center;
02   height:180px; width:250px; border: 3px ridge blue;
03 #title { border-radius: 10px 10px 0px 0px;
04   background-image: -moz-linear-gradient(center top , #0000FF, #88BBFF);
05   height:30px; color:white;  font:bold 22px arial black; }
06 input { border-radius:10px; border:3px groove blue; margin-top:20px;
07   padding-left:10px; }
08 label { font:italic 18px arial black; }
```

Handling Response Data

You have already learned about the different data types that can be generated by the response. The four main types that you will be working with are script, text, JSON, and XML/HTML. The script and text are handled simply by the `.load()` and `.getScript()` methods. JSON and XML/HTML can be a bit more complex.

The following sections walk you through the process of handling JSON and XML data in the response from the server.

▼ TRY IT YOURSELF

Handling JSON Response Data

JSON data is by far the easiest to work with in jQuery AJAX responses. This is because the response data is in object form, so you can access it via dot naming. For example, the following JSON response from the server:

```
{"first":"Brad", "last":"Dayley"}
```

can be accessed in the response data as the following:

```
var name  = data.first + " " + data.last;
```

Even if the response data object comes as a string, you can use the `.parseJSON()` to get a JavaScript object. For example:

```
var data = $.parseJSON('{"first":"Brad", "last":"Dayley"}');
var name  = data.first + " " + data.last;
```

In this exercise, you get a chance to handle JSON data coming back from an AJAX request. The resulting web page contains several images that have captions. The image caption and the image filename come from a JSON file located on the server at hour15/data/images.json. The purpose of the exercise is to familiarize you with using JSON data returned from an AJAX request to dynamically populate a page.

The code for the example is in Listing 15.3. Use the followings steps to create the dynamic web page:

1. In Aptana, create the hour15, hour15/js, and hour15/css folders, and then add the hour15/hour1503.html, hour15/js/hour1503.js, and hour15/css/hour1503.css files.

2. Add the code shown in Listing 15.3-html and Listing 15.3-css to the HTML and CSS files. These are very basic files because the image elements will be dynamically generated.

3. Open the hour1503.js file and add the following `.ready()` function that makes a `.get()` request to the server to get the hour15/data/images.json file and calls the `updateImages()` AJAX request complete event handler. The contents of the JSON file can be seen in Listing 15.3-json.

```
10 $(document).ready(function(){
11    $.get("data/images.json", updateImages);
12 });
```

4. Add the following AJAX request complete event handler `updateImages()`. Notice that the JSON response `data` has been converted to a JavaScript object array that you are able to iterate through and create the image elements and add them to the web page.

```
01 function updateImages(data){
02    for (i=0; i<data.length; i++){
03       var imageInfo =data[i];
04       var img = $('<img />').attr("src", "images/"+imageInfo.image);
05       var title = $("<p></p>").html(imageInfo.title);
06       var div = $("<div></div>").append(img, title);
07       $("#images").append(div);
08    }
09 }
```

5. Save all three files and then open the HTML document in a web browser, as shown in Figure 15.4. You should see the images loaded with the captions from the JSON file.

LISTING 15.3-html   **HTML Document That Loads the jQuery and JavaScript**

```
01 <!DOCTYPE html>
02 <html>
03    <head>
04       <title>Hour 15-3</title>
05       <meta charset="utf-8" />
06       <script type="text/javascript" src="../js/jquery.min.js"></script>
07       <script type="text/javascript" src="js/hour1503.js"></script>
08       <link rel="stylesheet" type="text/css" href="css/hour1503.css">
```

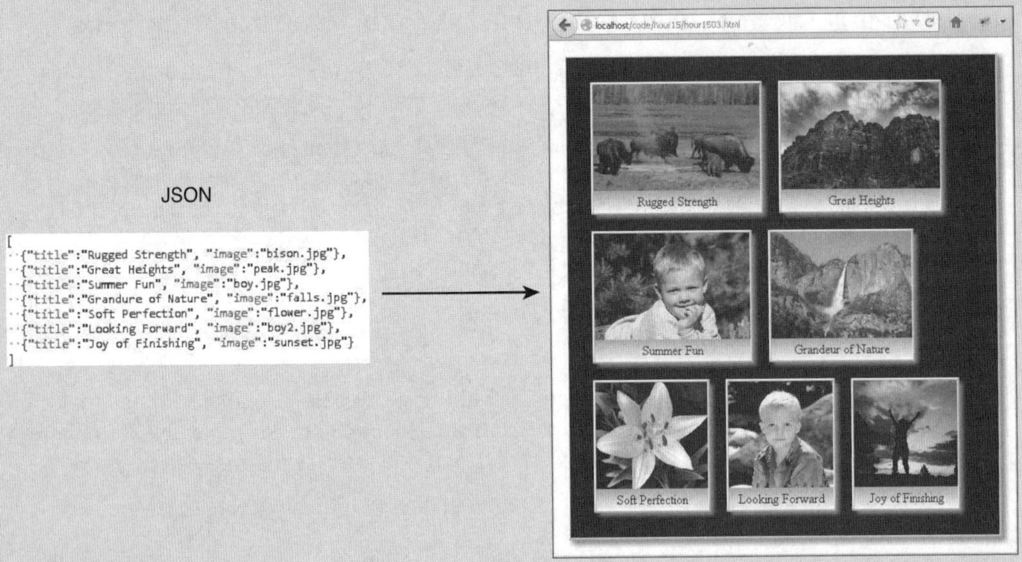

```
09    </head>
10    <body>
11      <div id="images"></div>
12    </body>
13 </html>
```

JSON

```
[
  {"title":"Rugged Strength", "image":"bison.jpg"},
  {"title":"Great Heights", "image":"peak.jpg"},
  {"title":"Summer Fun", "image":"boy.jpg"},
  {"title":"Grandure of Nature", "image":"falls.jpg"},
  {"title":"Soft Perfection", "image":"flower.jpg"},
  {"title":"Looking Forward", "image":"boy2.jpg"},
  {"title":"Joy of Finishing", "image":"sunset.jpg"}
]
```

FIGURE 15.4
Image gallery populated with JSON data.

LISTING 15.3-js   jQuery and JavaScript Code That Implements the AJAX Request and Handles the JSON Response

```
01 function updateImages(data){
02   for (i=0; i<data.length; i++){
03     var imageInfo =data[i];
04     var img = $('<img />').attr("src", "images/"+imageInfo.image);
05     var title = $("<p></p>").html(imageInfo.title);
06     var div = $("<div></div>").append(img, title);
07     $("#images").append(div);
08   }
09 }
10 $(document).ready(function(){
11   $.get("data/images.json", updateImages);
12 });
```

LISTING 15.3-json   JSON Data from the Book Website at code/hour15/data/imag-
es.json Containing Image Filenames and Captions

```
1  [
2     {"title":"Rugged Strength", "image":"bison.jpg"},
3     {"title":"Great Heights", "image":"peak.jpg"},
4     {"title":"Summer Fun", "image":"boy.jpg"},
5     {"title":"Grandeur of Nature", "image":"falls.jpg"},
6     {"title":"Soft Perfection", "image":"flower.jpg"},
7     {"title":"Looking Forward", "image":"boy2.jpg"},
8     {"title":"Joy of Finishing", "image":"sunset.jpg"}
9  ]
```

LISTING 15.3-css   CSS Code That Styles the Images

```
1  div {border:3px ridge white; box-shadow: 5px 5px 5px #888888;
2     display:inline-block; margin:10px; }
3  p { background-image: -moz-linear-gradient(center top , #B1B1B1, #FFFFFF);
4     margin:0px; padding:3px; text-align:center; }
5  img { height:130px; vertical-align:top;  }
6  #images { background-color:black; padding:20px; }
```

Handling XML/HTML Response Data

XML/HTML data is not as easy as JSON, but jQuery does make it fairly easy to work with.
XML data in the response is returned as a DOM object, which can be converted to jQuery and
searched/navigated using jQuery's extensive options. For example, the following XML response
from the server:

```
<person><first>Brad</first><last>Dayley</last></person>
```

can be accessed in the response data as the following:

```
var name  = $(data).find("first").text() + " " + $(data).find("last").text();
```

Similar to JSON, if the response data object comes as a string, you can use the .parseXML()
to get a DOM object. For example:

```
var data = $.parseXML("<person><first>Brad</first><last>Dayley</last></person>");
var name  = $(data).find("first").text() + " " + $(data).find("last").text();
```

In this exercise, you get a chance to handle XML data coming back from an AJAX request. The resulting web page contains a basic table with cell data derived from the XML data contained in the file hour15/data/parkdata.xml located on the server. The purpose of the exercise is to familiarize you with using XML data returned from an AJAX request to dynamically populate a page.

The code for the example is in Listing 15.4. Use the followings steps to create the dynamic web page:

1. In Aptana, create the hour15, hour15/js, and hour15/css folders, and then add the hour15/hour1504.html, hour15/js/hour1504.js, and hour15/css/hour1504.css files.

2. Add the code shown in Listing 15.4-html and Listing 15.4-css to the HTML and CSS files. These are very basic files because the table body will be dynamically generated.

3. Open the hour1504.js file and add the following `.ready()` function that will make a `.get()` request to the server to get the hour15/data/parkdata.xml file and call the `updateTable()` AJAX request complete event handler. The contents of the XML file can be seen in Listing 15.4-xml.

```
13 $(document).ready(function(){
14    $.get("data/parkdata.xml", updateTable);
15 });
```

4. Add the following AJAX request complete event handler `updateTable()`. Notice that the XML response data has been converted to a DOM element that is converted to a jQuery object using `$(data)`. The jQuery object can then be iterated using `.each()`, and each element can be searched using the `.children()` method to get the different values in the XML data.

```
01 function updateTable(data){
02    var parks = $(data).find("park");
03    parks.each(function(){
04       var tr = $("<tr></tr>");
05       tr.append($("<td></td>").html($(this).children("name").text()));
06       tr.append($("<td></td>").html($(this).children("location").text()));
07       tr.append($("<td></td>").html($(this).children("established").text()));
08       var img = $('<img />').attr("src", "images/"+$(this).children("image").
          ➥text());
09       tr.append($("<td></td>").append(img));
10       $("tbody").append(tr);
11    });
12 }
```

5. Save all three files and then open the HTML document in a web browser, as shown in Figure 15.5. You should see the table populated from the XML file.

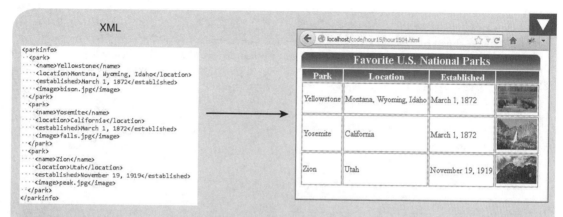

FIGURE 15.5
Table populated with XML data.

LISTING 15.4-html   HTML Document That Loads the jQuery and JavaScript

```
01 <!DOCTYPE html>
02 <html>
03   <head>
04     <title>Hour 15-4</title>
05     <meta charset="utf-8" />
06     <script type="text/javascript" src="../js/jquery.min.js"></script>
07     <script type="text/javascript" src="js/hour1504.js"></script>
08     <link rel="stylesheet" type="text/css" href="css/hour1504.css">
09   </head>
10   <body>
11     <table>
12       <caption>Favorite U.S. National Parks</caption>
13       <thead><th>Park</th><th>Location</th><th>Established</th><th> </th>
       ➥</thead>
14       <tbody></tbody>
15     </table>
16     <p></p>
17   </body>
18 </html>
```

LISTING 15.4-js   jQuery and JavaScript Code That Implements the AJAX Request
and Handles the XML Response

```
01 function updateTable(data){
02   var parks = $(data).find("park");
03   parks.each(function(){
```

```
▼   04      var tr = $("<tr></tr>");
    05      tr.append($("<td></td>").html($(this).children("name").text()));
    06      tr.append($("<td></td>").html($(this).children("location").text()));
    07      tr.append($("<td></td>").html($(this).children("established").text()));
    08      var img = $('<img />').attr("src", "images/"+$(this).children("image").
            ➥text());
    09      tr.append($("<td></td>").append(img));
    10      $("tbody").append(tr);
    11    });
    12  }
    13  $(document).ready(function(){
    14      $.get("data/parkdata.xml", updateTable);
    15  });
```

LISTING 15.4-xml   XML Data File with Raw Table Data

```
01  <parkinfo>
02    <park>
03      <name>Yellowstone</name>
04      <location>Montana, Wyoming, Idaho</location>
05      <established>March 1, 1872</established>
06      <image>bison.jpg</image>
07    </park>
08    <park>
09      <name>Yosemite</name>
10      <location>California</location>
11      <established>March 1, 1872</established>
12      <image>falls.jpg</image>
13    </park>
14    <park>
15      <name>Zion</name>
16      <location>Utah</location>
17      <established>November 19, 1919</established>
18      <image>peak.jpg</image>
19    </park>
20  </parkinfo>
```

LISTING 15.4-css   CSS Code That Styles the Table

```
1  img {width:80px;}
2  caption, th {
3    background-image: -moz-linear-gradient(center top , #0000FF, #88BBFF);
4    color:white; font:bold 18px arial black; }
5  caption { border-radius: 10px 10px 0px 0px; font-size:22px; height:30px; }
6  td { border:1px dotted; padding:2px; }
```

Updating Server Data from jQuery Using AJAX

In this exercise, you get a chance to implement a more complex AJAX web page with `.get()` and `.post()` requests, as well as some different AJAX event handlers. The resulting web page provides links to different vacation spots that you can rate. The data for the vacations is located in a JSON file that is accessed via a PHP script on the server. When you change the rating, the PHP script writes the change out to the JSON file, making it permanent. The purpose of the exercise is to solidify the jQuery AJAX concepts.

The code for the example is in Listing 15.5. Use the following steps to create the dynamic web page:

1. In Aptana, create the hour15, hour15/js, and hour15/css folders, and then add the hour15/hour1505.html, hour15/js/hour1505.js, and hour15/css/hour1505.css files.

2. Add the code shown in Listing 15.5-html and Listing 15.5-css to the HTML and CSS files. These files define the style and framework for the vacations page. There shouldn't be anything new in these files that you haven't already seen.

3. Open the hour1505.js file and add the following `.ready()` function that will make a `.get()` request to the server to get the list of vacations from the tripInfo.php script. Notice that a parameter list with `option:"getList"` is sent to tell the script what data is requested. Also, a `.done()` function is added so that when the data has been returned and the links are populated, the first link is automatically clicked to set the vacation content. Notice that the `sendRating()` event handler is added to the start elements to handle rating changes via the mouse:

```
29 $(document).ready(function(){
30    $.get("php/tripInfo.php", {option:"getList"}, setList).done(function(){
31       $("span:first").click(); return false; });
32    $(".star").click(sendRating);
33 });
```

4. Add the following click handler `setList()` for the left navigation buttons. For each of the buttons, the `getTrip()` event handler is added.

```
14 function setList(data){
15    var items = [];
16    $.each(data, function(key, val) {
17       var item = $("<span></span>").html(val);
18       item.click(function(){getTrip($(this).html())});
19       $("#leftNav").append(item);
20    });
21 }
```

5. Add the following `getTrip()` event handler that will send a `.get()` AJAX request to get a specific trip's info by specifying `option:"getTrip"` and `title:<trip title>`. The

`setTrip()` handler is called when the AJAX request is complete, so you need to add the code shown in Listing 15.5-js lines 1–9. This function takes the JSON data and populates the content elements.

```
10 function getTrip(title){
11    var params = [{name:"option", value:"getTrip"}, {name:"title",
       ➥value:title}]
12    $.get("php/tripInfo.php", params, setTrip);
13 }
```

6. Add the following `sendRating()` function that gets called when the user clicks a star. The index of the `.star` element is sent to the server via a `.post()` method with parameters `option:"setRating"`, `title:<trip title>`, and `value:<start index>`. The resulting POST request updates the JSON file on the server, permanently storing the new rating value.

```
22 function sendRating(){
23    var rating = $(".star").index($(this))+1;
24    var params = [{name:"option", value:"setRating"},
25                  {name:"title", value:$("#title").html()},
26                  {name:"rating", value:rating}]
27    $.post("php/tripInfo.php", params, setTrip);
28 }
```

7. Save all three files and then open the HTML document in a web browser, as shown in Figure 15.6. You should be able to link to the different vacations, see the images, and set the ratings.

LISTING 15.5-html   **HTML Document That Loads the jQuery and JavaScript**

```
01 <!DOCTYPE html>
02 <html>
03   <head>
04     <title>Hour 15-5</title>
05     <meta charset="utf-8" />
06     <script type="text/javascript" src="../js/jquery.min.js"></script>
07     <script type="text/javascript" src="js/hour1505.js"></script>
08     <link rel="stylesheet" type="text/css" href="css/hour1505.css">
09   </head>
10   <body>
11     <div><div id="banner">Vacations</div>
12     <div>
13       <div id="leftNav"></div>
14       <div id="content">
15         <p id="title">Title</p>
16         <img id="photo" src="images/falls.jpg" width="200px"/>
17         <p id="date">date</p>
```

```
18              <p id="info"><label>5</label> days of fun in <label>Location</label></p>
19              <img class="star" src="images/star.ico" />
20              <img class="star" src="images/star.ico" />
21              <img class="star" src="images/star.ico" />
22              <img class="star" src="images/star.ico" />
23              <img class="star" src="images/star.ico" />
24          </div>
25      </div>
26   </body>
27 </html>
```

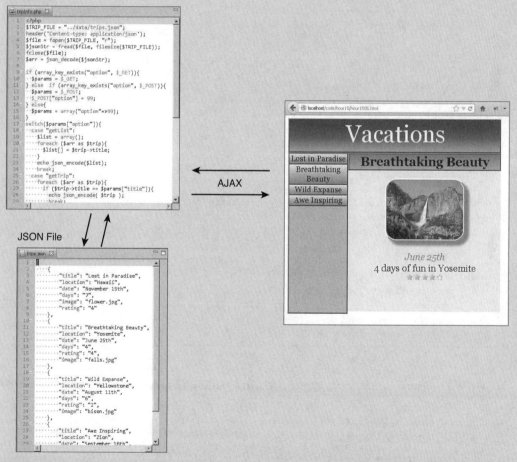

FIGURE 15.6
Simple vacation page with the capability to load data dynamically and update the rating via AJAX.

▼ **LISTING 15.5-js** jQuery and JavaScript Code That Implements the AJAX Request That Populates the Page and Updates the Server Data

```
01 function setTrip(data){
02   $("#title").html(data.title);
03   $("#photo").attr("src", "images/"+data.image);
04   $("#date").html(data.date);
05   $("label:first").html(data.days);
06   $("label:last").html(data.location);
07   $(".star:gt("+(parseInt(data.rating)-1)+")").attr("src", "images/empty.ico");
08   $(".star:lt("+(parseInt(data.rating))+")").attr("src", "images/star.ico");
09 }
10 function getTrip(title){
11   var params = [{name:"option", value:"getTrip"}, {name:"title", value:title}]
12   $.get("php/tripInfo.php", params, setTrip);
13 }
14 function setList(data){
15   var items = [];
16   $.each(data, function(key, val) {
17     var item = $("<span></span>").html(val);
18     item.click(function(){getTrip($(this).html())});
19     $("#leftNav").append(item);
20   });
21 }
22 function sendRating(){
23   var rating = $(".star").index($(this))+1;
24   var params = [{name:"option", value:"setRating"},
25                 {name:"title", value:$("#title").html()},
26                 {name:"rating", value:rating}]
27   $.post("php/tripInfo.php", params, setTrip);
28 }
29 $(document).ready(function(){
30   $.get("php/tripInfo.php", {option:"getList"}, setList).done(function(){
31     $("span:first").click(); return false; });
32   $(".star").click(sendRating);
33 });
```

LISTING 15.5-css CSS Code That Styles the Page Elements

```
01 * { font-family:Georgia; }
02 div { margin:0px; display:inline-block; float:left; text-align:center; }
03 span { background-image: -moz-linear-gradient(center top , #f1f1f1, #8F8F8F);
04   color:black; font-size:20px; float:left; cursor:pointer;
05   width:150px; text-align:center; border-bottom:3px ridge; }
06 p { margin:0px; }
07 #banner {
```

```
08   background-image: -moz-linear-gradient(center top , #0000FF, #88BBFF);
09   color:white; height:80px; width:550px; font-size:60px;
10   border:3px ridge blue; }
11 #title { font-weight:bold; font-size:32px; border:3px ridge;
12 background-image: -moz-linear-gradient(center top , #5588FF, #88BBFF);}
13 #leftNav {width:150px; height:400px; font-size:20px; background-color:#AACCFF;
14 border:3px ridge;}
15 #content { height:400px; width: 400px; background-color:#EEEEEE; }
16 #photo { margin:20px; border:5px ridge white; box-shadow: 10px 10px 5px #888888;
17   border-radius:30px;}
18 #date { color:red; font-style:italic; font-size:24px; }
19 #info, label { font-size:24px; }
```

Using Advanced jQuery AJAX

The concepts already covered in this hour should take care of most of your AJAX needs. However, they do not cover the full power of the jQuery AJAX interface. The following sections discuss some of the additional AJAX functionality built directly into jQuery.

Reviewing Global Setup

jQuery provides the `.ajaxSetup()` method that allows you to specify options that configure AJAX requests globally throughout the script. Table 15.3 lists some of the options that can be specified when calling `.ajaxSetup()`. For example, the following code sets the default global URL for requests:

```
$.ajaxSetup({url:"service.php", accepts:"json"})
```

Using Global Event Handlers

jQuery provides methods to create global event handlers that are called on events, such as initialization or completion for all AJAX requests. The global events are fired on each AJAX request. Table 15.2 lists the methods that you can use to register global event handlers.

An example of using global event handlers to set the class of a form is shown next:

```
$(document).ajaxStart(function(){
  $("form").addClass("processing");
});
$(document).ajaxComplete(function(){
  $("form").removeClass("processing");
});
```

NOTE

Global events are never fired for cross-domain script or JSONP requests, regardless of the value of the global property in `jQuery.ajaxSetup()`.

TABLE 15.2 jQuery Global AJAX Event Handler Registration Methods

Method	Description
`.ajaxComplete(function)`	Registers a handler to be called when AJAX requests are fully complete.
`.ajaxError(function)`	Registers a handler to be called when AJAX requests fail.
`.ajaxSend(function)`	Registers a function to be executed before an AJAX request is sent.
`.ajaxStart(function)`	Registers a handler to be called when the first AJAX request starts.
`.ajaxStop(function)`	Registers a handler to be called when all AJAX requests have completed.
`.ajaxSuccess(function)`	Registers a function to be executed whenever an AJAX request completes successfully.

Implementing Low-Level AJAX Requests

All AJAX request wrapper methods that you have been working with in this hour are handled underneath through the `.ajax(url [, settings])` interface. This interface is a bit more difficult to use, but it gives you much more flexibility and control of the AJAX request.

The `.ajax()` method is called the same way that `.get()` and `.post()` are; however, the settings argument allows you to set a variety of settings used when making the request.

Table 15.3 lists the more common settings that can be applied to the `.ajax()` method.

TABLE 15.3 Common Settings Available in the `.ajax()` Request Method

Method/Attribute	Description
`accepts`	Specifies the content type(s) the server can send back in the response; for example, application/json.
`async`	Boolean, default is true, meaning the request will be sent and then received asynchronously.
`beforeSend`	Specifies a function that should be run before sending the request.

Method/Attribute	Description
complete	Function to execute when the response is fully received.
contentType	Sets the content type to send with the request. The server uses the content type to determine how to parse the data.
crossDomain	Boolean. Enables you to send a cross-domain request, such as JSONP.
data	Specifies the data payload to send with the request.
error	Specifies a function to execute if the request fails.
headers	Object that contains the headers with values that should be sent to the server. For example: `{"Content-length": data.length}`
success	Function to execute if the response comes back with a 200 status, meaning the request was successful.
timeout	Specifies the milliseconds to wait before giving up on getting a response.
type	Set to GET or PUT to specify request type.
url	Specifies the URL on the web server to send the request.

A simple example of using the .ajax() interface is shown in the following code:

```
$.ajax({
  url:"setEmail",
  type:"get",
  accepts:"json",
  contentType: 'application/x-www-form-urlencoded; charset=UTF-8',
  data: {"first":"Brad", "last":"Dayley"}
}).fail(function(){ alert("request Failed"); });
```

The .ajax() method returns a jqXHR method that provides some additional functionality, especially when handling the response. Table 15.4 lists some of the methods and attributes attached to the jqXHR object.

TABLE 15.4 Common Methods and Attributes of the jqXHR Object Returned by .ajax()

Method/Attribute	Description
abort()	Aborts the request.
always(function)	Specifies a function to be called when the request completes.

Method/Attribute	Description
`done(function)`	Specifies a function to be called when the request completes successfully.
`fail(function)`	Specifies a function to be called when the request fails.
`getAllResponseHeaders()`	Returns the headers included in the response.
`getResponseHeader(name)`	Returns the value of a specific response header.
`setRequestHeader(name, value)`	Sets the value of an HTTP header that will be sent with the AJAX request.
`readyState`	Values: 1—Has not started loading yet 2—Is loading 3—Has loaded enough and the user can interact with it 4—Fully loaded
`status`	Contains the response status code returned from the server; for example, 200 status means the request was successful.
`statusText`	Contains the status string returned from the server.

Summary

AJAX is the basic communication framework between jQuery/JavaScript and the web server. Using AJAX allows you to get additional data from the web server and use it to dynamically update the web page instead of completely reloading it. This enables you to provide a much better experience for the user.

In this hour, you learned the ins and outs of AJAX. You were able to implement several examples that gave you experience with GET and POST requests, as well as handling different types of data, such as HTML, JSON, and XML.

Q&A

Q. Why is there a GET and a POST request and not just one request?

A. The answer is optimization. Although you could do everything with just POST requests, optimizations can be made at the web server as well as the browser by using GET requests that have the parameters directly in the URL. This is especially true with caching.

Q. Are there any other methods to send cross-domain requests besides JSONP?

A. Yes. Flash and Silverlight both have mechanisms that allow you to send cross-domain requests. HTML5 also introduces the `postMessage` interface designed to allow cross-domain requests.

Workshop

The workshop consists of a set of questions and answers designed to solidify your understanding of the material covered in this hour. Try to answer the questions before looking at the answers.

Quiz

1. Would you use a GET or a POST request to set a new password on a web server?

2. True or False: The `.done()` event handler function is called only if the AJAX request succeeds.

3. What data type is the response data converted to for XML data?

4. What data type is the response data converted to for JSON data?

5. Is it possible to specify the request headers sent with a GET request via jQuery?

Quiz Answers

1. POST.

2. True.

3. DOM object.

4. Basic JavaScript object.

5. Yes. You can use `.ajax()` with the headers parameter, or you can use `.ajaxSetup()` to set the headers parameter globally.

Exercises

1. Modify the example in Listing 15.3. Add an additional date value to each image in the JSON file. Then add the date value along with the image on the web page by including it in the image caption.

2. Modify the example in Listing 15.4. Add an additional column for rating. You will need to update the XML file, as well as the AJAX response handlers, to add the additional column to the rows. Also, you will need to fix up the CSS.

HOUR 16

Interacting with External Services, Facebook, Google, Twitter, and Flickr

What You'll Learn in This Hour:

▶ How to implement Facebook Like and Follow buttons
▶ Ways to implement Facebook comments in web pages
▶ Adding Google Maps to web pages
▶ Dynamically controlling the pan and zoom of Google Maps
▶ Creating Google Map markers in JavaScript
▶ Implementing a Custom Google search
▶ Displaying Twitter elements on your web page
▶ Allowing users to Tweet directly from your web page
▶ Adding Flickr photo streams to web pages

The sole purpose of this hour is to expand your ideas of what is possible through third-party interactions on your web pages. There are a lot of great services out there that you can incorporate directly into your web pages without needing to implement them yourself.

This hour covers a few of the most common external services that get incorporated into web pages: Facebook, Twitter, Google Maps, Google Search, and Flickr. Using these external services will save you a lot of time and provide your users with a better overall experience.

Using jQuery and JavaScript to Add Facebook Social Elements to Your Web Pages

The social aspect of the Internet has been one of the biggest shifts since its inception. No longer is there a simple one-on-one interaction between a user and an Internet website. With the advancements of Facebook, you now take your friends along for the ride by sharing your experiences with them.

The main pieces this section focuses on are using Facebook controls to provide users with the capability to "like" your website, post specific pieces of your website on their walls, and make comments that appear in timelines.

NOTE

There is a lot more to the Facebook SDK and the plug-ins than what is covered in this book. You might look at some additional possibilities: https://developers.facebook.com/docs/plugins/.

Adding the Facebook API Library to a Web Page

The first step in adding Facebook elements is to add the Facebook API to the web page. Facebook gives you the code snippet to add to your web pages to the API library. To see this, go to the following address, scroll down, and click the Get Code button to see the pop-up shown in Figure 16.1: https://developers.facebook.com/docs/reference/plugins/like/

FIGURE 16.1
Autogenerated code by Facebook.

TIP

If you have a Facebook developer account and an application ID, you can add the `appId` parameter to the library path, as shown next:

```
js.src = "//connect.facebook.net/en_US/all.js#xfbml=1&appId={YOUR_ID_HERE}";
```

If you add the `appId`, you can use Facebook Insights to get statistical information about the Like button clicks. You can register as a Facebook developer at the following location: https://developers.facebook.com/.

The code Facebook generates is shown next and is intended to be placed in your web page right after the `<body>` element:

```
<div id="fb-root"></div>
<script>(function(d, s, id) {
  var js, fjs = d.getElementsByTagName(s)[0];
  if (d.getElementById(id)) return;
  js = d.createElement(s); js.id = id;
  js.src = "//connect.facebook.net/en_US/all.js#xfbml=1";
  fjs.parentNode.insertBefore(js, fjs);
}(document, 'script', 'facebook-jssdk'));</script>
```

You may prefer to work with JavaScript and jQuery code directly, so the following code is converted script that can be added in an external JS file. The converted script, shown next, does the same thing that Facebook's script does. It adds the `#fb-root` element and then loads the SDK from Facebook into the web page:

```
function addFBsdk() {
  $("body").prepend('<div id="fb-root"></div>');
  if ($("#facebook-jssdk").length == 0){
    var fbSDK = document.createElement("script"); fbSDK.id = 'facebook-jssdk';
    fbSDK.src = "//connect.facebook.net/en_US/all.js#xfbml=1";
    $("head").get(0).appendChild(fbSDK);
  }
}
$(document).ready(function(){
   addFBsdk();
});
```

Adding a Like Button

After you have the Facebook SDK loading properly in your page, adding a Like button is a simple matter of adding a `<div>` element with `class="fb-like"`. The following code shows an example of adding a Facebook Like button:

```
<div class="fb-like" data-send="true" data-width="450" data-show-faces="true">
➥</div>
```

The simplest method to getting the `<div>` code for the Facebook Like button is go to the following URL and scroll down to the Get Like Button Code section. Fill out the form to style the Like button, and then click Get Code. You can ignore the code to load the SDK because you've already got it in the previous section.

https://developers.facebook.com/docs/reference/plugins/like/

Adding a Send Button

Adding a Send button for users to send your content to their friends is also very simple. All you need to do is add a `<div>` element with `class="fb-send"` and a `data-href` that specifies the URL to send. The following code shows an example of adding a Facebook Send button:

```
<div class="fb-send" data-href="http://dayleycreations.com"></div>
```

To get the code for the Facebook Send button, go to the following URL and scroll down to the Get Send Button Code section. Fill out the form to style the Send button and then click Get Code. You can ignore the code to load the SDK because you've already got it in the previous section. https://developers.facebook.com/docs/reference/plugins/send/

Adding a Comment Field

A Facebook comment field can be a very important part of your user's social experience. Users can see others comments, add their own, and even post comments directly to their own Facebook page (see Figure 16.2).

FIGURE 16.2
Facebook comments field.

Adding a Facebook comments field for users to comment on your content is also very simple. Add a `<div>` element with `class="fb-comments"` and a `data-href` that specifies the URL of the content. You can also set the height and number of comments to show using the `data-width` and `data-num-posts` attributes. The following code shows an example of adding a Facebook comments field:

```
<div class="fb-comments" data-href="http://dayleycreations.com"
     data-width="470" data-num-posts="2"></div>
```

To get the code for the Facebook comments field, go to the following URL and scroll down to the Get Send Button Code section. Fill out the form to style the Comments field and then click Get Code. You can ignore the code to load the SDK because you've already got it in the previous section. https://developers.facebook.com/docs/reference/plugins/comments/

Adding Facebook Elements to Your Web Pages

It's time to jump in and add some Facebook elements in a practical example. In this example, you add a Like button, several Send buttons, and a Comment field to a web page.

The code for the example is in Listing 16.1. Use the followings steps to create the dynamic web page:

1. In Aptana, create the hour16, hour16/js, and hour16/css folders, and then add the hour16/hour1601.html, hour16/js/hour1601.js, and hour16/css/hour1601.css files. You will also need to copy the images folder from the book's website at code/hour16 to the hour16 folder in Aptana.

2. Add the code shown in Listing 16.1-html and Listing 16.1-css to the HTML and CSS files.

3. Open the hour1601.js file and add the following `.ready()` that will call `addFBsdk()` to load the Facebook SDK. It also calls the functions to add the Like, Send, and Comment elements to the website and attaches a click handler function to the left `nav` items to switch the `src` attribute of the `#photo` element when clicked.

```
30 $(document).ready(function(){
31     addFBsdk();
32     addFBlike("http://www.dayleycreations.com", $("#like"));
33     addFBsend("http://www.dayleycreations.com", $(".navItem"));
34     addFBcomment("http://www.dayleycreations.com", $("#content"));
35     $(".navItem img").click(function(){
36         $("#photo").attr("src", $(this).attr("src"));
37     });
38 });
```

4. Add the following `addFBsdk()` function. This is the code you saw earlier that is converted to jQuery from what Facebook gives you.

```
01 function addFBsdk() {
02     $("body").prepend('<div id="fb-root"></div>');
03     if ($("#facebook-jssdk").length == 0){
04         var fbSDK = document.createElement("script"); fbSDK.id =
           ➥'facebook-jssdk';
05         fbSDK.src = "//connect.facebook.net/en_US/all.js#xfbml=1";
06         $("head").get(0).appendChild(fbSDK);
07     }
08 }
```

5. Add the creation function shown in lines 9–29 of Listing 16.1-js. These functions build the Facebook Like button, Send buttons, and Comments field dynamically. You can use the HTML code returned from Facebook, but this illustrates how to create the elements inside JavaScript and jQuery.

6. Save all three files and then open the HTML document in a web browser, as shown in Figure 16.3. You should see the Like, Send, and Comments fields added to the web page.

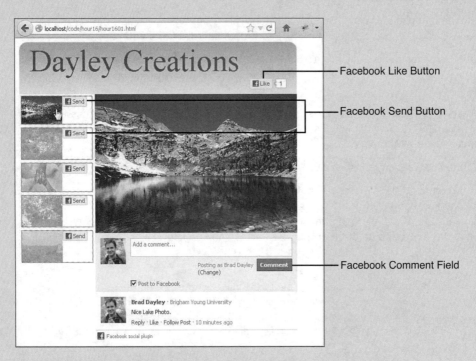

FIGURE 16.3
Article viewer that uses AJAX requests to populate the article content.

LISTING 16.1-html   HTML Document That Adds the Web Page

```
01   <html>
02     <head>
03     <title>Hour 16-1</title>
04     <meta charset="utf-8" />
05     <script type="text/javascript" src="../js/jquery.min.js"></script>
06     <script type="text/javascript" src="js/hour1601.js"></script>
07     <link rel="stylesheet" type="text/css" href="css/hour1601.css" />
08     </head>
09     <body>
10       <div>
11         <div id="banner">Dayley Creations
12           <div id="like"></div>
13         </div><br>
```

```
14        <div id="leftNav">
15           <div class="navItem"><img  src="images/lake.jpg" /></div>
16           <div class="navItem"><img  src="images/tiger.jpg" /></div>
17           <div class="navItem"><img  src="images/flower.jpg" /></div>
18           <div class="navItem"><img  src="images/pool.jpg" /></div>
19           <div class="navItem"><img  src="images/jungle.jpg" /></div>
20        </div>
21        <div id="content">
22           <div><img id="photo" src="images/lake.jpg" /''></div>
23           <div id="send"></div><br>
24        </div>
25     </div>
26   </body>
27 </html>
```

LISTING 16.1-js jQuery and JavaScript Loads the Facebook SDK and Adds the Social Elements

```
01 function addFBsdk() {
02   $("body").prepend('<div id="fb-root"></div>');
03   if ($("#facebook-jssdk").length == 0){
04     var fbSDK = document.createElement("script"); fbSDK.id = 'facebook-jssdk';
05     fbSDK.src = "//connect.facebook.net/en_US/all.js#xfbml=1";
06     $("head").get(0).appendChild(fbSDK);
07   }
08 }
09 function addFBlike(href, element){
10   var like = $('<div class="fb-like"></div>');
11   like.attr("data-href", href);
12   like.attr("data-width",400);
13   like.attr("data-layout","button_count");
14   like.attr("data-show-faces","true");
15   like.attr("data-font","arial");
16   element.append(like);
17 }
18 function addFBsend(href, element){
19   var like = $('<div class="fb-send"></div>');
20   like.attr("data-href", href + "/" +element.children("img").attr("src"));
21   element.append(like);
22 }
23 function addFBcomment(href, element){
24   var like = $('<div class="fb-comments"></div>');
25   like.attr("data-href", href);
26   like.attr("data-width", 400);
27   like.attr("data-num-posts", 2);
```

```
28    element.append(like);
29 }
30 $(document).ready(function(){
31    addFBsdk();
32    addFBlike("http://www.dayleycreations.com", $("#like"));
33    addFBsend("http://www.dayleycreations.com", $(".navItem"));
34    addFBcomment("http://www.dayleycreations.com", $("#content"));
35    $(".navItem img").click(function(){
36      $("#photo").attr("src", $(this).attr("src"));
37    });
38 });
```

LISTING 16.1-css CSS Code That Styles the Page

```
01 div { margin:0px; display:inline-block; float:left; text-align:center; }
02 p { margin:2px; }
03 #banner { border-radius: 15px 15px 0px 0px;
04    background-image: -moz-linear-gradient(center top , #88BBFF, #DDEEFF);
05    color:blue; height:100px; width:550px; font-size:60px; }
06 #leftNav { width:150px; }
07 .navItem { border:1px dotted; display:block; margin:3px; width:140px;}
08 .navItem img {width:80px; float:left; opacity:.5; }
09 .navItem img:hover { opacity:1; cursor:pointer; }
10 #like { float:right; margin-top:70px; margin-right:20px; }
11 #photo { width:400px; }
```

Adding Google Maps to Your Web Pages

An extremely important element of web pages can be a map that shows the location(s) of your business or resources. Google Maps makes it extremely easy to add maps that are interactive to your web pages.

To add Google Maps to your web pages, you will need to have an API access key. However, if you are following along with this book and using only the localhost webserver, a key is not required.

When implementing Google Maps on a nonlocal host domain, you need to go to the following location and follow the instructions to get the API key. The key is free as long as your usage remains low.
https://developers.google.com/maps/documentation/javascript/tutorial

After you get a key, you will be able to use that key to load the Google Maps API using a <script> block similar to the one shown next:

```
<script type="text/javascript"
src="https://maps.googleapis.com/maps/api/js?key={YOUR_API_KEY}&sensor={TRUE_OR_
➥FALSE}">
</script>
```

The sensor option specifies if your application uses a GPS or other type of sensor to determine the user's location.

After the Google Maps API is loaded, you can add a map to your web page by adding a google.maps.Map object to <div> element, as shown next:

HTML code:

```
<div id="mapCanvas"></div>
JavaScript/jQuery Code:
var mapOptions = {
  center: new google.maps.LatLng(-34.397, 150.644),
  zoom: 6,
  mapTypeId: google.maps.MapTypeId.SATELLITE
};
var map = new google.maps.Map($("#mapCanvas").get(0), mapOptions);
```

The Map() function accepts the HTML DOM element object that will contain the map as well as a mapOptions object. Table 16.1 describes the settings in the mapOptions object.

TABLE 16.1 Map Options Object Attributes

Attribute	Description
center	Specifies the google.maps.LatLng() object, which contains the latitude and longitude values for the center of the map.
zoom	Specifies the zoom level where 0 is no zoom.
mapTypeId	Specifies the type of map to display. The following are valid options:
	▶ ROADMAP—Displays the normal, default 2D tiles of Google Maps.
	▶ SATELLITE—Displays photographic tiles.
	▶ HYBRID—Displays a mix of photographic tiles and a tile layer for prominent features (roads, city names).
	▶ TERRAIN—Displays physical relief tiles for displaying elevation and water features (mountains, rivers, and so on).

After the Map object is created, it is added to the <div> element. You can then use the Map object in JavaScript to directly control the behavior of the map. The Map object also includes events that fire when actions occur based on user interaction.

Google `Map` events are attached to Map objects using the following syntax:

```
google.maps.event.addListener(mapObject, event, function);
```

Google `Map` coordinates are specified by a `google.maps.LatLng(x,y)` object, where x and y define the latitude and longitude. For example:

```
var mapPosition = google.maps.LatLng(50.555, 1.3);
```

As an example, the following code attaches a `center_changed` event handler that sets the `innerHTML` of an element #coordinates with the current map center coordinates:

```
var map = new google.maps.Map($("#mapCanvas").get(0),
  {center:new google.maps.LatLng(51,2),zoom:3,apTypeId:google.maps.MapTypeId.HYBRID
  ➥});
google.maps.event.addListener(map, "center_changed", function(){
  $("#coordinates").html(map.getCenter().toString());
});
```

Table 16.2 lists several of the methods, properties, and events that are attached to the `Map` object.

TABLE 16.2 `Map` Object Methods, Attributes, and Events

Method/Attribute/Event	Description
getCenter()	Returns a `google.maps.LatLng()` object of the center coordinates of the map.
getMapTypeId()	Returns the `mapTypeId` string.
getTilt()	Returns the map tilt angle.
getZoom()	Returns the map zoom value.
panBy(x, y)	Pans the map x to the right and y down.
panTo(latLng)	Pans the map to `google.maps.LatLng()`.
setCenter(latLng)	Sets the center coordinates as `google.maps.LatLng()`.
setMapTypeId(typString)	Sets the map type.
setTitle(value)	Sets the title to a specified level.
setZoom(value)	Adjusts the zoom to a specified level.
controls	Array of control objects attached to the `Map` object.
center_changes	Map event triggered when the center changes.
maptypeid_changed	Map event triggered when the `mapIdType` changes.
tilt_changed	Map event triggered when the tilt changes.
zoom_changed	Map event triggered when the zoom changes.

There is much more to the Google Maps API interface. You can find additional information at https://developers.google.com/maps/documentation/javascript/.

Adding Google Maps to a Web Page

You are now ready to add Google Maps to your websites. In this example, you add multiple Google Maps and then use the `Map` object to link them together by adjusting the zoom and pan for all map elements on the page. You will also get a chance to dynamically add your own markers.

The code for the example is in Listing 16.2. Use the followings steps to create the dynamic web page:

1. In Aptana, create the hour16, hour16/js, and hour16/css folders, and then add the hour16/hour1602.html, hour16/js/hour1602.js, and hour16/css/hour1602.css files.

2. Add the code shown in Listing 16.2-html and Listing 16.2-css to the HTML and CSS files. These are basic HTML and CSS, with the exception that the following line is added before you load the page JavaScript so that the Google Maps library is loaded first.

```
07      <script src="http://maps.googleapis.com/maps/api/js?sensor=false">
        ➡</script>
```

3. Open the hour1602.js file and add the `.ready()` shown in lines 34–39 of the Listing 16.2-js file. This function calls the `addMap()` init function that creates the maps on the page and then adds the event handlers to the zoom buttons and the add marker button.

4. Add the `addMaps()` function, shown next, to create the `Map` objects on the web page and add them to the `mapArr` array. The options for the map are coming from `mapProp` defined at the top in lines 3 and 4. Notice that each iteration through the loop increments the `zoom` value to make the maps progressively zoom in.

```
26 function addMaps(){
27   $(".map").each(function(){
28     var map = new google.maps.Map(this, mapProp)
29     google.maps.event.addListener(map, 'center_changed', pan);
30     mapArr.push(map);
31     mapProp.zoom += 3;
32   });
33 }
```

5. Add the `pan()` function shown next, which gets the current position of the map that is being changed using `getCenter()`. It then uses this position to adjust the center position of all maps.

```
05 function pan() {
06   var newPosition = this.getCenter();
07   if (newPosition !== position){
08     $("p").html(newPosition.toString());
09     position = newPosition;
10     for (var i=0; i<mapArr.length; i++){ mapArr[i].setCenter(position); }
11   }
12   return false;
13 }
```

6. Add the following zoom function that increments the current value of each of the maps using `getZoom()` and `setZoom()`:

```
14 function zoom(value){
15   for (var i=0; i<mapArr.length; i++){ mapArr[i].setZoom(map.getZoom()
     ➥+value); }
16   return false;
17 }
```

7. Add the following `placeMarker()` that creates a new `google.maps.Marker()` object on each of the maps based on the current center position.

```
18 function placeMarker(){
19   for (var i=0; i<mapArr.length; i++){
20     var markerInfo = { position: mapArr[i].getCenter(), map: mapArr[i],
21                        visible:true, title:$("#markText").val() };
22     var marker = new google.maps.Marker(markerInfo);
23   }
24   return false;
25 }
```

8. Save all three files and then open the HTML document in a web browser, as shown in Figure 16.4. You should see the maps appear. As you pan on one, it should pan on all of them. You also should be able to use the custom Zoom button to zoom in or out on all of them. Then type some text into the text box and click the marker button; a new marker should be added to the map.

LISTING 16.2-html   **HTML Document That Adds the Web Page**

```
01 <!DOCTYPE html>
02 <html>
03   <head>
04     <title>Hour 16-2</title>
05     <meta charset="utf-8" />
06     <script type="text/javascript" src="../js/jquery.min.js"></script>
07     <script src="http://maps.googleapis.com/maps/api/js?sensor=false"></script>
08     <script type="text/javascript" src="js/hour1602.js"></script>
```

```
09      <link rel="stylesheet" type="text/css" href="css/hour1602.css">
10    </head>
11    <body>
12      <div id="controls">
13        <img id="zoomin" src="images/in.png" />
14        <img id="zoomout" src="images/out.png" /><br>
15        <input id="markText" type="text" />
16        <img id="mark" src="images/marker.png" />
17        <p></p>
18      </div>
19      <div id="mainMap" class="map"></div>
20      <div id="smallMaps">
21        <div class="map"></div>
22        <div class="map"></div>
23        <div class="map"></div>
24        <div class="map"></div>
25      </div>
26    </body>
27 </html>
```

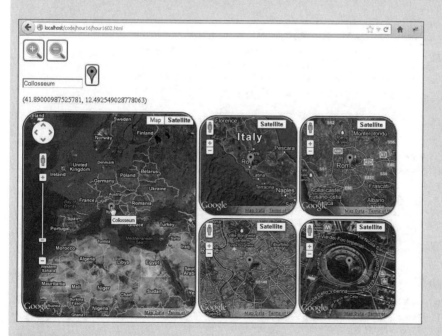

FIGURE 16.4
Custom implementation of Google Maps on a web page.

▼ **LISTING 16.2-js** jQuery and JavaScript That Creates the Google Maps Elements and Controls Them

```
01 var mapArr = new Array();
02 var position;
03 var mapProp = { center:new google.maps.LatLng(51.508742,-0.120850),
04               zoom:3, mapTypeId:google.maps.MapTypeId.HYBRID };
05 function pan() {
06   var newPosition = this.getCenter();
07   if (newPosition !== position){
08     $("p").html(newPosition.toString());
09     position = newPosition;
10     for (var i=0; i<mapArr.length; i++){ mapArr[i].setCenter(position); }
11   }
12   return false;
13 }
14 function zoom(value){
15   for (var i=0; i<mapArr.length; i++){ mapArr[i].setZoom(map.getZoom()+value); }
16   return false;
17 }
18 function placeMarker(){
19   for (var i=0; i<mapArr.length; i++){
20     var markerInfo = { position: mapArr[i].getCenter(), map: mapArr[i],
21                        visible:true, title:$("#markText").val() };
22     var marker = new google.maps.Marker(markerInfo);
23   }
24   return false;
25 }
26 function addMaps(){
27   $(".map").each(function(){
28     var map = new google.maps.Map(this, mapProp)
29     google.maps.event.addListener(map, 'center_changed', pan);
30     mapArr.push(map);
31     mapProp.zoom += 3;
32   });
33 }
34 $(document).ready(function(){
35   addMaps();
36   $("#zoomin").click(function(){ zoom(1);});
37   $("#zoomout").click(function(){ zoom(-1);});
38   $("#mark").click(placeMarker);
39 });
```

LISTING 16.2-css   **CSS Code That Styles the Page**   ▼

```
1 div { display:inline-block; }
2 img { height:40px; border:3px ridge; border-radius:7px; padding:2px; }
3 .map {width:220px; height:220px; border:4px groove blue; border-radius:40px; }
4 #mainMap { width:400px; height:460px; }
5 #smallMaps { width:460px; height:460px; }
6 #controls { width:900px; }
```

Adding a Custom Google Search

As websites become more and more complex, the need to provide users with a way to quickly find what they are looking for becomes more critical. A simple way to do this is to add a custom Google search engine to the web page.

The custom Google search engine leverages the Google search technology to search your local web page. Google provides some simple controls with a text input and Search button, and then it automatically overlays the search results on top of your web page.

To get started, you will need to do the following:

1. Create a Google account if you do not already have one. An account can be created at

   https://accounts.google.com/NewAccount

2. Go to the Google Custom Search page at the following address and click on a new search engine:

   http://www.google.com/cse/manage/all

3. In the Sites to Search field, specify the URL(s) of your website and then give your site a name and click Create.

4. After you have created the custom engine, you will get a code snippet back similar to the following. You can use this code snippet to add the search controls to your website. You can get the custom control at any time by clicking the Get Code link in the Google Custom Search page.

```
<script>
 (function() {
  var cx = '####;
  var gcse = document.createElement('script'); gcse.type = 'text/javascript';
  gcse.async = true;
  gcse.src = (document.location.protocol == 'https:' ? 'https:' : 'http:') +
        '//www.google.com/cse/cse.js?cx=' + cx;
```

```
    var s = document.getElementsByTagName('script')[0];
  ➥s.parentNode.insertBefore(gcse, s);
    })();
</script>
<gcse:search></gcse:search>
```

This code is then placed in the actual HTML page where you want the search to appear. The code is basic JavaScript that loads the custom search engine JavaScript into a `<script>` element on the web page. The `<gcse>` tag ends up being replaced with the necessary HTML to implement the Google Custom Search by the Google API JavaScript.

Because you might prefer to work with jQuery, I've broken down the JavaScript from Google into a basic jQuery function shown next. This gives you more control as to when and how the search elements are added to the page:

```
function addCustomSearchEngine(){
  var cx = "####";
  var src = 'http:///www.google.com/cse/cse.js?cx=' + cx;
  var search = $("<script></script>");
  search.attr("src", src).attr("async",true);
  $("head").prepend(search);
}
```

NOTE

There are other customized options for the Google custom search engine that you can configure at the Google Custom Search page. You might prefer to turn off the ads displayed in the search results by clicking the Business Settings link. You also might want to enable searching for the entire web with a preference to your website.

The basic search is usually good enough for most applications. There is a lot more that you can do with the Google custom search engine and controls. For more information, you can visit https://developers.google.com/custom-search/v1/overview.

▼ TRY IT YOURSELF

Adding Custom Google Search to a Web Page

You are now ready to add a Custom Google Search web page. In this example, you add a basic custom search to an existing website. You should have already gone through the steps earlier to set up the Custom Google Search engine and get a code snipped back with a `cx` number. You will need that number for this exercise.

The code for the example is in Listing 16.3. Use the followings steps to create the dynamic web page:

1. In Aptana, create the hour16, hour16/js, and hour16/css folders, and then add the hour16/hour1603.html, hour16/js/hour1603.js, and hour16/css/hour1603.css files.

2. Add the code shown in Listing 16.3-html and Listing 16.3-css to the HTML and CSS files.

3. Open the hour1603.js file and add the following `.ready()` that calls the `addCustomSearchEngine()` function to load the Google Custom Search Engine library. It then prepends the `<gcse>` element to the `#content` element on the pages.

```
08 $(document).ready(function() {
09   addCustomSearchEngine();
10   $("#content").prepend("<gcse:search></gcse:search>");
11 });
```

4. Add the following `addCustomSearchEngine()` that loads the Google Search Engine library into a `<script>` element that gets added to `<head>`. You will need to fill in the value of `cx` from the ID that you got from Google when you created your own custom search engine:

```
01 function addCustomSearchEngine(){
02   var cx = "####";
03   var src = 'http:///www.google.com/cse/cse.js?cx=' + cx;
04   var search = $("<script></script>");
05   search.attr("src", src).attr("async",true);
06   $("head").prepend(search);
07 }
```

5. Save all three files and then open the HTML document in a web browser, as shown in Figure 16.5. You should be able to search your website to find items using the new search control.

LISTING 16.3-html   HTML Document That Adds the Web Page

```
01 <!DOCTYPE html>
02 <html>
03   <head>
04     <title>Hour 16-3</title>
05     <meta charset="utf-8" />
06     <script type="text/javascript" src="../js/jquery.min.js"></script>
07     <script type="text/javascript" src="js/hour1603.js"></script>
08     <link rel="stylesheet" type="text/css" href="css/hour1603.css">
09   </head>
10   <body>
11     <div>
12       <div id="banner">jQuery in 24</div><br>
```

```
13          <div id="leftNav"><span class="navItem">Navigation</span></div>
14          <div id="content">
15          </div>
16      </div>
17  </body>
18 </html>
```

Google Custom Search results displayed on top of page

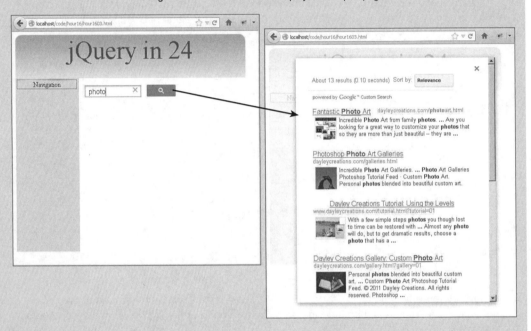

FIGURE 16.5
Article viewer that uses AJAX requests to populate the article content.

LISTING 16.3-js   **jQuery and JavaScript Implements the Google Custom Search Code**

```
01 function addCustomSearchEngine(){
02   var cx = "####";
03   var src = 'http:///www.google.com/cse/cse.js?cx=' + cx;
04   var search = $("<script></script>");
05   search.attr("src", src).attr("async",true);
06   $("head").prepend(search);
07 }
08 $(document).ready(function() {
09   addCustomSearchEngine();
10   $("#content").prepend("<gcse:search></gcse:search>");
11 });
```

LISTING 16.3-css   CSS Code That Styles the Page ▼

```
1 div { margin:0px; display:inline-block; float:left; text-align:center; }
2 #banner { border-radius: 15px 15px 0px 0px;
3   background-image: -moz-linear-gradient(center top , #88BBFF, #DDEEFF);
4   color:blue; height:100px; width:550px; font-size:60px; }
5 #leftNav { width:150px; background-color:#DDDDDD; height:400px; }
6 .navItem { border:1px dotted; display:block; margin:3px; width:140px;}
```

Adding Twitter Elements to Your Web Pages

An important part of web pages today is the social interaction available. Twitter is one of the most prolific social mechanisms because of the simplicity. It is almost expected today that if a users desires, they can tweet about experiences interacting directly with websites as they are using them.

Twitter provides some great controls that are extremely easy to implement with minimal understanding of JavaScript. Specifically, you can add Tweet and Follow buttons as well as timeline displays and tweet displays. This allows you to easily incorporate Twitter elements to keep your website up to date.

Adding the Twitter JavaScript API Library

To add Twitter controls to your web page, you need to load the Twitter JavaScript API library. Twitter provides the following code snippet that is added to the beginning of the `<body>` element of the web page:

```
<script>!function(d,s,id){
  var js,fjs=d.getElementsByTagName(s)[0];
  if(!d.getElementById(id)){
    js=d.createElement(s);
    js.id=id;
    js.src="//platform.twitter.com/widgets.js";
    fjs.parentNode.insertBefore(js,fjs);
  }
}(document,"script","twitter-wjs");</script>
```

You might want to use the following jQuery version:

```
function addTwitter(){
  if ( $("#twitter-wjs").length == 0 ) {
    var twitter = $("<script></script>");
    twitter.attr("id", "twitter-wjs");
    twitter.attr("src", "https://platform.twitter.com/widgets.js");
```

```
    $("head").append(twitter);
  }
}
```

You can learn more about the Twitter API as well as adding Twitter elements at the following location:

https://dev.twitter.com/

Adding a Tweet Button

To add a Tweet button to a web page, you need to add an `<a>` element with the `class="twitter-share-button"`. The Twitter JavaScript library adds the necessary interactions behind the scenes. When users click the Tweet button, it prompts them to log in if they haven't already, and then it displays a Tweet pop-up dialog that allows the user to send the tweet about your web page.

You can specify several additional attributes listed in Table 16.3.

TABLE 16.3 Attributes When Adding a Twitter Button

Attribute	Description
`data-url`	URL of the web page to share in the tweet.
`data-via`	Screen name of the user to attribute the tweet.
`data-text`	Default text for the tweet.
`data-related`	Related accounts that will be recommended when the user tweets; for example, `"bwdayley:jQuery in 24"`.
`data-count`	Count box position as `"none"`, `"horizontal"`, `"vertical"`.
`data-lang`	The language for the Tweet button.
`data-counturl`	URL to which your shared URL resolves.
`data-hashtags`	Comma-separated hashtags appended to tweet text.
`data-size`	The size of the rendered Tweet button.

The following shows an example of a basic Tweet button element:

```
<a href="https://twitter.com/share" class="twitter-share-button"
   data-url="https://dev.twitter.com" data-via="bwdayley"
   data-lang="en">Tweet</a>
```

Adding a Follow Button

To add a Follow button to a web page, you need to add an `<a>` element with the `class="twitter-follow-button"`. The Twitter JavaScript library adds the necessary interactions behind the scenes. When users click the Follow button, they are prompted to log in if they haven't already, and then it adds the user's Twitter account to the following list of the specified accounts in the `href`.

You can specify several additional attributes listed in Table 16.4.

TABLE 16.4   Attributes When Adding a Twitter Follow Button

Attribute	Description
`data-show-count`	Display the number of users currently following; `"true"` or `"false"`.
`data-show-screen-name`	Screen name of the user.
`data-width`	Width of the Follow button.
`data-align`	Alignment of the Follow button as `"left"` or `"right"`.
`data-lang`	The language for the Follow button.
`data-size`	The size of the rendered Follow button.

The following shows an example of a basic Follow button element:

```
<a href="https://twitter.com/bwdayley" class="twitter-follow-button"
   data-show-count="false" data-lang="en">Follow @bwdayley</a>
```

Adding Embedded Tweets

Another useful feature of the Twitter JavaScript API is the capability to embed a specific tweet in your website. This allows users visiting the website to retweet the embedded tweet for those following them.

To embed the tweet, you need to get a `<blockquote>` string directly from Twitter by clicking the Details link at the bottom of the tweet and then clicking the Embed This Tweet link, as shown in Figure 16.6.

FIGURE 16.6
Getting the embedded tweet code.

The following shows a code snippet of the embedded tweet:

```
<blockquote class="twitter-tweet">
  <p>New Update.
    <a href="http://t.co/n9Pfzfsc"
      title="http://dayleycreations.com">dayleycreations.com</a> via @
    <a href="https://twitter.com/bwdayley">bwdayley</a>
  </p>
  &mdash; Brad Dayley (@bwdayley)
  <a href="https://twitter.com/bwdayley/status/291618492191477761"
    data-datetime="2013-01-16T18:50:41+00:00">January 16, 2013</a>
</blockquote>
<script async src="//platform.twitter.com/widgets.js" charset="utf-8"></script>
```

If you have already embedded the Twitter API in the web page, you can ignore the `<script>` element. The `<blockquote>` code element is added to the web page wherever you would like the embedded tweet to be rendered.

Adding Embedded Timelines

Another useful feature of the Twitter JavaScript API is the capability to embed a timeline in your website. A timeline, shown in Figure 16.7, is an interactive control that lists tweets and allows users to reply, retweet, and add favorites. This is a great feature for websites that need a good social presence because the user never needs to leave the web page.

FIGURE 16.7
Twitter timeline embedded in a web page.

To embed the timeline, you need to get an `<a>` string directly from Twitter by creating a timeline widget at the following location. Click the Create New button and then click the user timeline tab to create the widget:

https://twitter.com/settings/widgets

In the bottom of the timeline widget window, you will see a text box with text similar to the following:

```
<a class="twitter-timeline"  href="https://twitter.com/bwdayley"
   data-widget-id="291668761717653506">Tweets by @bwdayley</a>
<script>!function(d,s,id){
  var js,fjs=d.getElementsByTagName(s)[0];
  if(!d.getElementById(id)){js=d.createElement(s);
    js.id=id;js.src="//platform.twitter.com/widgets.js";
    fjs.parentNode.insertBefore(js,fjs);
  }
}(document,"script","twitter-wjs");</script>
```

If you have already embedded the Twitter API in the web page, you can ignore the `<script>` element. The `<a>` code element is added to the web page wherever you would like the embedded tweet to be rendered.

▼ TRY IT YOURSELF

Adding Twitter Elements to a Web Page

In this example, you get a chance to implement a Tweet and a Follow button. You will also get a chance to display an existing tweet to the web page and add a timeline.

The code for the example is in Listing 16.4. Use the followings steps to create the dynamic web page:

1. In Aptana, create the hour16, hour16/js, and hour16/css folders, and then add the hour16/hour1604.html, hour16/js/hour1604.js, and hour16/css/hour1604.css files.

2. Add the code shown in Listing 16.4-html and Listing 16.4-css to the HTML and CSS files. You will end up replacing some of the code shown in the listing with your own tweet code.

3. Open the hour1604.html hour and modify the code in line 13 to include your own Twitter account.

4. Log in to Twitter and find a tweet that you would like to embed in the web page; then click Details and then Embed to get the `<blockquote>` code for the tweet. Replace the block code in lines 17–23 with your own block of code.

5. Go to the following location and create a new timeline widget. Get the `<a>` link code for the widget and replace the `<a>` link code in lines 26 and 27.

   https://twitter.com/settings/widgets

6. Open the hour1604.js file and add the following `.ready()` and `addTwitter()` functions that will load the Twitter library code into a `<script>` element and add it to the `<head>`:

```
01 function addTwitter(){
02   if ( $("#twitter-wjs").length == 0 ) {
03     var twitter = $("<script></script");
04     twitter.attr("id", "twitter-wjs");
05     twitter.attr("src", "https://platform.twitter.com/widgets.js");
06     $("head").append(twitter);
07   }
08 }
...
17 $(document).ready(function() {
18   addTwitter();
19   addTweet();
20 });
```

7. Add the following `addTweet()` function that dynamically builds the Tweet button and adds it to the `#tweet` page element. You should replace the `data-url`, `data-via`, and `data-related` values with values from your own Twitter account.

```
09 function addTweet(){
10    var tweet = $('<a href="https://twitter.com/share" class="twitter-share-
      ➥button">Tweet</a>');
11    tweet.attr("data-url", "http://dayleycreations.com");
12    tweet.attr("data-via", "bwdayley");
13    tweet.attr("data-related", "bwdayley:Dayley Creations");
14    tweet.attr("data-lang", "en");
15    $("#tweet").append(tweet);
16 }
```

8. Save all three files and then open the HTML document in a web browser, as shown in Figure 16.8. You should be able to tweet, follow, and see the tweet and timeline in the window.

FIGURE 16.8
Adding Twitter elements to a web page.

LISTING 16.4-html   HTML Document That Adds the Web Page and Implements Many of the Twitter Elements

```
01 <!DOCTYPE html>
02 <html>
```

```
03   <head>
04    <title>Hour 16-4</title>
05    <meta charset="utf-8" />
06    <script type="text/javascript" src="../js/jquery.min.js"></script>
07    <script type="text/javascript" src="js/hour1604.js"></script>
08    <link rel="stylesheet" type="text/css" href="css/hour1604.css">
09   </head>
10   <body>
11    <div id="tweet" class="header"><p>Tweet Button</p></div>
12    <div class="header"><p>Follow Button</p>
13      <a href="https://twitter.com/bwdayley" class="twitter-follow-button"
14         data-show-count="true" data-lang="en">Follow @bwdayley</a>
15    </div>
16    <div class="header"><p>Display Existing Tweet</p>
17      <blockquote class="twitter-tweet"><p>Hour 13-2
18        <a href="http://t.co/n9Pfzfsc" title="http://dayleycreations.com">
19           dayleycreations.com</a>via @<a href="https://twitter.com/bwdayley">
20              bwdayley</a></p>&mdash;Brad Dayley (@bwdayley)
21        <a href="https://twitter.com/bwdayley/status/291612551190564865"
22           data-datetime="2013-01-16T18:27:04+00:00">January 16, 2013</a>
23      </blockquote>
24    </div>
25    <div class="header"><p>Display TimeLine</p>
26      <a class="twitter-timeline"  href="https://twitter.com/bwdayley"
27         data-widget-id="291617670590251008">Tweets by @bwdayley</a>
28    </div>
29   </body>
30  </html>
```

LISTING 16.4-js   jQuery and JavaScript Loads the Twitter Library and Dynamically Adds a Tweet Button

```
01  function addTwitter(){
02    if ( $("#twitter-wjs").length == 0 ) {
03      var twitter = $("<script></script>");
04      twitter.attr("id", "twitter-wjs");
05      twitter.attr("src", "https://platform.twitter.com/widgets.js");
06      $("head").append(twitter);
07    }
08  }
09  function addTweet(){
10    var tweet = $('<a href="https://twitter.com/share" class="twitter-share-
    ➥button">Tweet</a>');
11    tweet.attr("data-url", "http://dayleycreations.com");
12    tweet.attr("data-via", "bwdayley");
```

```
13    tweet.attr("data-related", "bwdayley:Dayley Creations");
14    tweet.attr("data-lang", "en");
15    $("#tweet").append(tweet);
16  }
17  $(document).ready(function() {
18    addTwitter();
19    addTweet();
20  });
```

LISTING 16.4-css   CSS Code That Styles the Page

```
1  .header {display:inline-block; border:1px solid black; border-radius:5px;
➥margin:5px; }
2  .header p{ background-image: -moz-linear-gradient(center top , #B1B1B1, #FFFFFF);
3    margin:0px; padding:3px; text-align:center; width:500px; font-size:20px;
4    border-bottom:1px solid; }
```

Adding Flickr Images to Your Website

One common external service that is integrated into web pages are Flickr photo streams. Flickr provides a nice interface that provides the photo stream information in an easily consumable JSON object via a JSONP request.

It is easy to implement a Flickr stream using the jQuery AJAX request $.getJSON() to make the JSONP request. All you need to do is make the AJAX request to Flickr and specify the feed id. The following shows a couple of examples of using the Flickr API: one to get a photos_public feed and the other to get a groups_pool feed.

```
$.getJSON(url, "http://api.flickr.com/services/feeds/photos_public.gne?
            341168865@N08&lang=en-us&format=json&jsoncallback=?");
$.getJSON(url, "http://api.flickr.com/services/feeds/groups_pool.gne?
            650323@N24&lang=en-us&format=json&jsoncallback=?");
```

To get the id attribute for the Flickr API request, go to the following location and enter the URL of the stream, as shown in Figure 16.9:

http://idgettr.com/

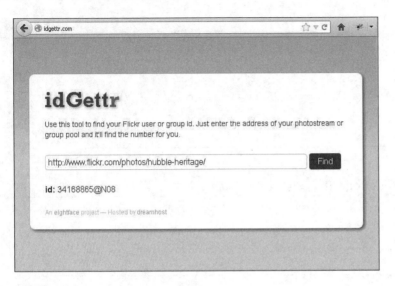

FIGURE 16.9
The idGettr tool allows you to get the stream ID of Flickr photo streams.

The following shows an example of the JSON object returned by the Flickr request:

```
{
  "title": "Uploads from Hubble Heritage",
  "link": "http://www.flickr.com/photos/hubble-heritage/",
  "description": "",
  "modified": "2012-12-19T14:26:47Z",
  "generator": "http://www.flickr.com/",
  "items": [
      {
        "title": "Planetary Nebula NGC 5189",
        "link": "http://www.flickr.com/photos/hubble-heritage/8286901075/",
        "media": {"m":"http://farm9.staticflickr.com/8199/8286901075_d9f154b8dd_
        ➡m.jpg"},
        "date_taken": "2012-12-19T09:11:05-08:00",
        "description": " <p>...<\/p>",
        "published": "2012-12-19T14:26:47Z",
        "author": "nobody@flickr.com (Hubble Heritage)",
        "author_id": "34168865@N08",
        "tags": "heritage v nebula mus hubble "
      },
          {
```

Adding a Flickr Stream

In this example, you get a chance to implement a couple of Flickr streams into a web page. You do two streams—one that is a public photos stream and the other that is a groups stream—to get a sense of how easy it is to add them and manipulate them dynamically with jQuery and JavaScript.

The code for the example is in Listing 16.5. Use the followings steps to create the dynamic web page:

1. In Aptana, create the hour16, hour16/js, and hour16/css folders, and then add the hour16/hour1605.html, hour16/js/hour1605.js, and hour16/css/hour1605.css files.

2. Add the code shown in Listing 16.5-html and Listing 16.5-css to the HTML and CSS files— some basic HTML and CSS. Notice on lines 14 and 15 that an `onclick` handler is added that passes the type and ID of the Flickr streams:

```
14          <p onclick="setImages('photos_public', '34168865@N08')">Hubble</p>
15          <p onclick="setImages('groups_pool', '650323@N24')">National
    ➥Geographic</p>
```

3. Open the hour1605.js file and add the `.ready()` function shown in lines 18–20.

4. Add the following `setImages()` function that will be called when the user clicks the left nav items. This function makes a JSONP request to Flickr to download the stream and calls the `updateImages()` handler function on completion.

```
13 function setImages(feedType, id){
14   var url = "http://api.flickr.com/services/feeds/" + feedType + ".gne?id="
    ➥+ id +
15              "&lang=en-us&format=json&jsoncallback=?";
16   $.getJSON(url, updateImages);
17 }
```

5. Add the following `updateImages()` AJAX completion handler that reads the response from Flickr, updates the page header `#feedName`, and then iterates through the `items` array to create the image elements on the page.

```
01 function updateImages(data){
02   $("#images").children("div").remove();
03   $("#feedName").html(data.title)
04   for (i=0; i<data.items.length; i++){
05     var imageInfo =data.items[i];
06     var img = $('<img />').attr("src", (imageInfo.media.m).replace
    ➥("_m.jpg", "_s.jpg"));
07     var title = $("<p></p>").html(imageInfo.title+" ");
08     var link = $("<a></a>").attr("href", imageInfo.link).append(img);
09     var div = $("<div class=\"item\"></div>").append(link,title);
```

```
10    $("#images").append(div);
11  }
12 }
```

6. Save all three files and then open the HTML document in a web browser, as shown in Figure 16.10. You should be able to click the left navigation items and load both the Hubble Heritage and National Geographic Group streams.

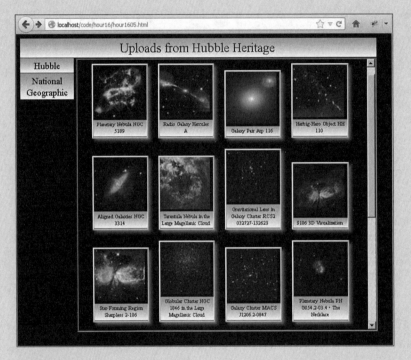

FIGURE 16.10
Flickr feed viewer that dynamically downloads a Flickr photo stream and updates the page with the images.

LISTING 16.5-html   HTML Document That Adds the Web Page

```
01 <!DOCTYPE html>
02 <html>
03   <head>
04     <title>Hour 16-5</title>
05     <meta charset="utf-8" />
06     <script type="text/javascript" src="../js/jquery.min.js"></script>
07     <script type="text/javascript" src="js/hour1605.js"></script>
08     <link rel="stylesheet" type="text/css" href="css/hour1605.css">
```

```
09    </head>
10    <body>
11     <div id="feedName">Select Feed</div>
12     <div>
13       <div id="leftNav">
14         <p onclick="setImages('photos_public', '34168865@N08')">Hubble</p>
15         <p onclick="setImages('groups_pool', '650323@N24')">National
           ➥Geographic</p>
16       </div>
17       <div id="images">
18       </div>
19     </div>
20    </body>
21   </html>
```

LISTING 16.5-js   jQuery and JavaScript That Interacts with Flickr

```
01 function updateImages(data){
02   $("#images").children("div").remove();
03   $("#feedName").html(data.title)
04   for (i=0; i<data.items.length; i++){
05     var imageInfo =data.items[i];
06     var img=$('<img />').attr("src", (imageInfo.media.m).replace("_m.jpg",
       ➥"_s.jpg"));
07     var title = $("<p></p>").html(imageInfo.title+" ");
08     var link = $("<a></a>").attr("href", imageInfo.link).append(img);
09     var div = $("<div class=\"item\"></div>").append(link,title);
10     $("#images").append(div);
11   }
12 }
13 function setImages(feedType, id){
14   var url = "http://api.flickr.com/services/feeds/" + feedType + ".gne?id="
       ➥+ id +
15              "&lang=en-us&format=json&jsoncallback=?";
16   $.getJSON(url, updateImages);
17 }
18 $(document).ready(function(){
19   $("#leftNav").children("p:first").click();
20 });
```

LISTING 16.5-css   CSS Code That Styles the Page

```
01 body { background-color: black;}
02 div { display:inline-block; }
03 .item {border:3px ridge white; box-shadow: 5px 5px 5px #888888; margin:10px; }
```

```
04 p, #feedName { background-image: -moz-linear-gradient(center top , #B1B1B1,
   ➥#FFFFFF);
05    margin:0px; padding:3px; text-align:center; width:100px; font-size:10px;
06    border-bottom:1px solid; }
07 img { width:100px; }
08 #images { background-color:black; padding:20px; width:550px; height:480px;
09    overflow-y:scroll; border:3px groove;}
10 #leftNav { width:106px; height:440px; vertical-align:top; }
11 #leftNav p { font-size:18px; cursor:pointer; }
12 #feedName { width:700px; font-size:25px; }
```

Summary

In this hour, you learned how to incorporate external services into your web pages. You got a chance to add Facebook Likes and Comments. You also got to play around with adding Google Maps and dynamically controlling them. Next, you implemented some of the Twitter elements to give your web pages a better social appeal. Finally, you implemented some code to apply Flickr feeds directly into your web page.

Q&A

Q. **What other external services should I look at?**

A. If you are planning to implement any kind of e-commerce on your web pages, look into Checkout by Amazon. There are a lot of good tools there with a name that customers trust.

Q. **You showed an example of converting the generated HTML tags from Google, Facebook, and Twitter into JavaScript and jQuery functions. Is it better to use the original scripts or convert them?**

A. That is totally up to you. They make the scripts so that web developers with absolutely no JavaScript or jQuery experience can still implement them. They are a bit awkward that way, so you can revise them so you can include the code in your general site JavaScript files.

Workshop

The workshop consists of a set of questions and answers designed to solidify your understanding of the material covered in this hour. Try to answer the questions before looking at the answers.

Quiz

1. How do you define a `<div>` element as a Facebook Like button?

2. How do you detect that the center position of a Google Map has changed?

3. How do you specify related Twitter accounts in a Tweet element?

4. What AJAX method should you use to get the Flickr photo feeds, and why?

5. How do you get the current center position of a Google Map object?

Quiz Answers

1. Set `class="fb-like"`.

2. Add a `center_changed` listener using `google.maps.event.addListener()`.

3. Set the `data-related` attribute of the element to the related account.

4. `.getJSON()` because the Flickr feed is a JSONP request.

5. Use `.getCenter()`.

Exercises

1. Open up the code in Listing 16.2 and modify the Google Maps example. Add a `<select>` element, and when the Mark button is clicked, use jQuery to add a new `<option>` element to the `<select>`. Use the `.data()` method to attach the coordinates of the position of the mark to the `<options>` jQuery object. Then, add a change event handler for the select that will set the center of the Google Maps to the position attached to the selected `<option>`.

2. Go to Flickr and find a new photo stream. Then go to idgettr.com and find the ID of the photo stream. Add a new left `nav` item to the example in Listing 16.5 that links to that photo stream. You will need to determine whether to use the `photos_public` or `groups_pool.gne` location type.

3. Go to the following URL and read through the page. Then use the web form to generate code to recommend some of the other examples in this chapter.

https://developers.facebook.com/docs/reference/plugins/recommendations/

Introducing jQuery UI

What You'll Learn in This Hour:

▶ How to download and add the jQuery UI libraries
▶ How to create custom jQuery UI themes
▶ New functionality jQuery UI provides over jQuery alone
▶ Using jQuery UI selectors
▶ How to dynamically position UI elements using jQuery UI

jQuery UI is an additional library built on top of jQuery. The purpose of jQuery UI is to provide a set of extensible interactions, effects, widgets, and themes that make it easier to incorporate professional UI elements in your web pages. In this hour, you get a chance to download and implement jQuery UI in some web pages. The purpose of this hour is to introduce you to how jQuery interacts with HTML, CSS, and JavaScript.

Getting Started with jQuery UI

jQuery UI is made up of two parts, JavaScript and CSS. The JavaScript portion of jQuery UI extends jQuery to add additional functionality specific to adding UI elements or applying effects to those elements. The CSS portion of jQuery UI styles the page elements so that developers don't need to style the elements every time.

jQuery UI saves developers time by providing prebuilt UI elements, such as calendars and menus, with interactions, such as dragging and resizing, right out of the box. The following sections introduce you to the library; you learn how to download it and apply it to your projects.

Getting the jQuery UI Library

To get started with jQuery UI, you need to download the library and add it to your web pages. The jQuery library can be downloaded from the following location by selecting the options that you would like to include, shown in Figure 17.1, and clicking the Download button at the bottom. This downloads the jQuery UI files: http://jqueryui.com/download.

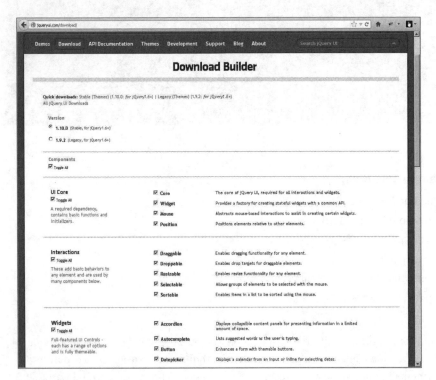

FIGURE 17.1
Using jQuery UI download builder to build and download a custom version of jQuery UI.

Using ThemeRoller

In addition to the basic jQuery UI theme, you can also use the jQuery UI ThemeRoller, shown in Figure 17.2, to select some different custom themes or even customize your own theme. A theme defines the colors, border radius, and multiple other styles applied to jQuery UI widgets and elements.

To access the jQuery UI ThemeRoller:

1. Open the following URL in your browser:

   http://jqueryui.com/download/

2. Scroll down to the bottom of the download page shown in Figure 17.1 and click the Design a Custom Theme link. This brings up the ThemeRoller shown in Figure 17.2.

3. Select the Gallery tab and view the gallery of prebuilt themes shown in Figure 17.2.

4. Select the gallery that most fits your needs.

Roll Your
Own settings

Gallery selection

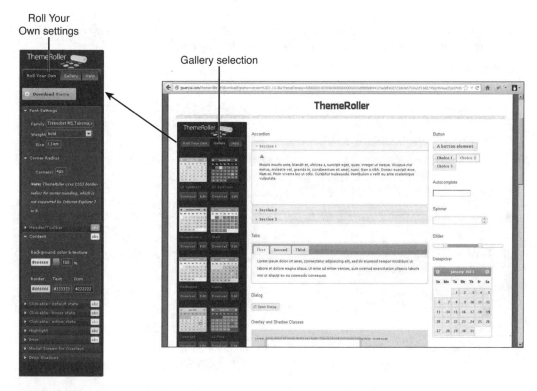

FIGURE 17.2
Using jQuery UI ThemeRoller to define a custom theme.

5. Select the Roll Your Own tab, also shown in Figure 17.2, and specify as many of the specific settings as you want to define.

6. Click the Download Theme button. This takes you back to the main download page.

7. Click the Download button to download the jQuery UI files.

TRY IT YOURSELF ▼

Adding jQuery UI to Your Project

When you download the jQuery UI library, you will get a zip file. Inside the zip file are three main folders that you need to understand:

▶ **js**—This is the folder that will contain the jQuery UI and jQuery libraries files. These files need to be deployed so they can be loaded in your web pages.

▶ **css**—This contains the theme named folders that will house the .css files and images used by the jQuery UI library. You need to place this folder in a location where you will be able to load the .css file from your web pages.

▶ **development-bundle**—This folder contains the full source for jQuery UI. If you are not planning to modify the jQuery UI code, you can ignore this folder.

Use the following steps to download the jQuery UI library and add it to the project you are using
for this book:

1. In Aptana, create the hour17, hour17/js, and hour17/css folders, and then add the
hour17/hour1701.html file. You also need to copy the images folder from the book's website at code/hour17 to the hour17 folder in Aptana.

2. Copy the code code/js/css folder and code/js/jquery-ui.min.js file to the js/ folder in your
Aptana project. jQuery UI 1.10.0 is already downloaded for you and included on the book's
website. This is the version that the examples are based on.

3. Add the code shown in Listing 17.1. This is straightforward code to validate that the jQuery
UI library is installed properly.

4. Make sure that the locations specified in lines 7 and 8 for the jQuery UI library and the
CSS file are correct:

```
07      <script type="text/javascript" src="../js/jquery-ui.min.js"></script>
08      <link rel="stylesheet" type="text/css" href="../js/css/
        ➥ jquery-ui.min.css">
```

5. Save all the files, and then open the HTML document in a web browser, as shown in
Figure 17.3. You should see the date picker displayed correctly if the libraries are installed
properly.

FIGURE 17.3
Simple jQuery UI date picker.

LISTING 17.1-html HTML Document That Adds the jQuery UI Libraries and
Renders a Date Picker

```
01 <!DOCTYPE html>
02 <html>
03   <head>
04     <title>Hour 17-1</title>
05     <meta charset="utf-8" />
06     <script type="text/javascript" src="../js/jquery.min.js"></script>
07     <script type="text/javascript" src="../js/jquery-ui.min.js"></script>
08     <link rel="stylesheet" type="text/css" href="../js/css/jquery-ui.min.css">
09     <script>
10       $(document).ready(function(){
11         $( "#datepicker" ).datepicker();
12       });
13     </script>
14   </head>
15   <body>
16     <div id="datepicker"></div>
17   </body>
18 </html>
```

Applying jQuery UI in Your Scripts

Now that you've got the jQuery UI library loaded and ready to go, you can learn about some of
the enhancements that jQuery UI adds over jQuery. This section covers some new functionality
as well as some enhancements to the jQuery library. The meat of jQuery UI—namely, the effects,
interactions, and widgets—are covered in upcoming hours.

Understanding Enhanced jQuery UI Functionality

jQuery UI is in many ways an extension of the jQuery library. To get you up to speed so that
you can begin implementing jQuery UI components, the following sections discuss some of the
important upgrades from jQuery.

Adding and Removing Unique IDs

jQuery UI provides a couple of additional methods to jQuery objects that allow you to easily add
and remove unique IDs to a set of elements. This is especially useful when you dynamically create a bunch of new elements that you must be able to access by ID later.

To add unique IDs, use the .uniqueId() method. This method checks each element in the set and adds an id attribute if one is not present. The new ID will have a prefix of "ui-id-". If the element already has an id attribute, it is not altered.

You can later delete the unique IDs using the .removeUniqueId() method on the set. Only elements that had IDs created by .uniqueId() are affected.

For example, the following code adds id values to all <div> elements and then later removes them:

```
var divs = $("div").uniqueId();
...
do something
...
$("div"). removeUniqueId ();
```

Getting Scroll Parent

Another helpful addition in jQuery UI is the .scrollParent() method. This method searches the ancestors of the element and returns the first parent element that is scrollable. This method works only on jQuery objects that have a single element in the set.

Getting the zIndex

Another helpful addition in jQuery UI is the .zIndex() method. This method returns a numeric z-index value of the element, if it has one, or the first ancestor that does. This enables you to quickly determine the stacking placement of any item on the page.

Async Focus

jQuery UI extends the .focus(delay [. callback]) method of jQuery objects to allow for a delay before setting the focus and including a callback function that will be executed when the element does get the focus. The delay is specified in milliseconds.

This functionality has a wide range of uses, from using a timer to automatically select a form element to forcing refocus of an element. For example, the following code adds a half-second delay before setting the focus to an element #timedInput:

```
$("#timedInput").focus(500, function(){
  $(this).val("Enter Text Now");
});
```

Using New Selectors in jQuery UI

One great feature of jQuery UI is the capability to extend the jQuery selectors that are already pretty extensive. These new selectors make it easier to narrow down selections specific to UI element needs. The following sections discuss each of the new selectors.

Using the `:data()` Selector

One of my favorite selectors in jQuery UI is the `:data()` selector. This selector enables you to filter elements based on a specific key that was added to elements using the `.data()` jQuery method. For example, the following code adds a `color` value to all `<span>`, `<div>`, and `<p>` elements, and then uses the `:data()` selector to set those colors on the elements:

```
$(p).data("color", "red");
$(span).data("color", "blue");
$(div).data("color", "green");
$(":data(color)").each(function(){
  $(this).css({color:$(this).data("color")});
});
```

`:focusable`

The `:focusable` selector allows you to limit elements to only those that can receive focus. For example, the following statement limits the changes to only those form elements that can receive focus:

```
$("form:focusable").each(function(){
  $(this).css({color:red});
});
```

`:tabbable`

The `:tabbable` selector is similar to the `:focusable` selector. It allows you to limit elements to only those that can be tabbed to. For example, the following statement limits the changes to only those form elements that can be tabbed to:

```
$("form:tabbable").each(function(){
  $(this).css({color:red});
});
```

This filter is very useful, especially when you're trying to exclude elements that are disabled.

TIP

Elements that have a negative tab index are `:focusable` but not `:tabbable`.

▼ TRY IT YOURSELF

Applying jQuery UI Selectors Based on Data Values

In this example, you add several `<div>` elements to the web page. Then in jQuery, you add an image data value to some of them. Using the `:data()` selector, you then apply different changes to the elements with image data than those without image data.

The code for the example is in Listing 17.2. Use the followings steps to create the dynamic web page:

1. In Aptana, create the hour17/hour1702.html, hour17/js/hour1702.js, and hour17/css/hour1702.css files.

2. Add the code shown in Listing 17.2-html and Listing 17.2-css to the HTML and CSS files. The following lines are used to load the jQuery UI library and CSS files:

```
07      <script type="text/javascript" src="../js/jquery-ui.min.js"></script>
...
09      <link rel="stylesheet" type="text/css" href="../js/css/
        ➥ jquery-ui.min.css">
```

3. Open the hour1702.js file and add a basic `.ready()` function.

4. Add the following three lines. These lines add the `image` data value to some of the `<div>` elements in the document.

```
02    $("#arch").data("image", "images/arch.jpg");
03    $("#volcano").data("image", "images/volcano.jpg");
04    $("#pyramid").data("image", "images/pyramid2.jpg");
```

5. Add the following `click` handler function that will first get all the `<div>` elements that have an `image` value and use the `image` value to set the `src` of an `<img>` element that gets prepended. Then the function will get all `<div>` elements that do not have an `image` value and append the generic insert.png image.

```
05    $("#add").click(function(){
06      $("div:data(image)").each(function(){
07        $(this).prepend($('<img></img>').attr("src", $(this).data("image")));
08      });
09      $("div:not(:data(image))").each(function(){
10        $(this).prepend($('<img></img>').attr("src", "images/insert.png"));
11      });
```

6. Save all three files and then open the HTML document in a web browser, as shown in Figure 17.4. When you click the Add Images button, you should see the images pop up for the `<div>` elements that had an `image` value and the generic image for those that do not.

FIGURE 17.4
Using the jQuery UI selector to update the elements that have an image data value.

LISTING 17.2-html   HTML Document That Adds the Web Page

```
01  <!DOCTYPE html>
02  <html>
03    <head>
04      <title>Hour 17-2</title>
05      <meta charset="utf-8" />
06      <script type="text/javascript" src="../js/jquery.min.js"></script>
07      <script type="text/javascript" src="../js/jquery-ui.min.js"></script>
08      <script type="text/javascript" src="js/hour1702.js"></script>
09      <link rel="stylesheet" type="text/css" href="../js/css/jquery-ui.min.css">
10      <link rel="stylesheet" type="text/css" href="css/hour1702.css">
11    </head>
12    <body>
13      <span id="add">Add Images</span>
14      <div id="arch">Arch</div>
15      <div id="river">River</div>
16      <div id="volcano">Volcano</div>
17      <div id="mountain">Mountain</div>
18      <div id="pyramid">Pyramid</div>
19    </body>
20  </html>
```

LISTING 17.2-js jQuery and jQuery UI Code That Uses the `:data()` Selector to Select Elements

```
01 $(document).ready(function(){
02    $("#arch").data("image", "images/arch.jpg");
03    $("#volcano").data("image", "images/volcano.jpg");
04    $("#pyramid").data("image", "images/pyramid2.jpg");
05    $("#add").click(function(){
06       $("div:data(image)").each(function(){
07          $(this).prepend($('<img></img>').attr("src", $(this).data("image")));
08       });
09       $("div:not(:data(image))").each(function(){
10          $(this).prepend($('<img></img>').attr("src", "images/insert.png"));
11       });
12    });
13 });
```

LISTING 17.2-css CSS Code That Styles the Page Elements

```
1 img {width:60px; margin-right:20px; vertical-align:middle; }
2 div { margin-top:15px; border:1px dotted; width:400px; font-size:35px;}
3 span { background-image: -moz-linear-gradient(center top , #B1B1B1, #FFFFFF);
4 border:3px ridge white; box-shadow: 5px 5px 5px #888888; padding:3px;
  ↪cursor:pointer; }
```

Positioning UI Elements with jQuery UI

A great advantage that jQuery UI provides is the capability to position elements relative to other elements and handle collisions. This is done by extending the `.position()` method to allow for an options object that defines the relative positions between the jQuery element and other elements or event locations.

For example, to position an element `#div1` to the right of `#div2`, you could use the following:

`$("#div1").position("my:"left", at:"right", of:"#div2");`

Pretty simple. Table 17.1 describes the options that jQuery UI provides to the `.position()` method.

TABLE 17.1 Option Settings Used When Positioning Elements with jQuery UI
`.postion()`

Option	Description

`my`	Specifies the relative position of the current jQuery object to use for alignment. Acceptable values are
	
	`"right"`, `"left"`, `"top"`, `"bottom"`, `"center"`
	
	You can also combine these; for example:
	
	`"left top"`, `"right bottom"`, `"left center"`, `"center center"`
	
	These positions can also be adjusted using numerical or percentage values. For example, the following places the item `-10` pixels to the left and `20%` of the height down:
	
	`"left-10 top+20%"`

`at`	Specifies the relative position in the target element to use for alignment. This option can be set to the same values as the `my` option.
`of`	Specifies a selector, a DOM element object, a jQuery object, or a JavaScript `Event` object. In the case of a jQuery object, the first element in the set is used. In the case of a JavaScript `Event` object, the `pageX` and `pageY` properties are used.
`collision`	Specifies how to handle instances where the element overflows the window in some direction. When this option is specified and the object overflows the current window, it is moved based on the collision value. Accepted values are as follows: ▶ `"flip"`—Flips the element to the opposite side of the specified target, then runs the collision detection again. Whichever side allows more of the element to be visible is then used. ▶ `"fit"`—Repositions the element away from the edge of the window. ▶ `"flipfit"`—Tries to apply the flip logic by placing the element on whichever side allows more of the element to be visible. Then it tries the fit logic to ensure as much of the element is as visible as possible. ▶ `"none"`—Does not apply any collision detection.
`using`	Allows you to specify a callback function that handles the actual positioning. The first argument passed to the function is the position value that can be used to set the CSS properties using `.css()`/`.animate()`. The second parameter is an object that contains the dimensions and relative positions of both the source and target elements.
`within`	Allows you to specify the container object to use when determining if there is a collision. This defaults to the JavaScript `window` object, but can be set to a selector, a DOM element object, or a jQuery object.

▼ TRY IT YOURSELF

Using jQuery UI to Position Images on a Web Page

The best way to help you understand jQuery UI positioning is to give you some hands-on experience. In this example, you use jQuery UI position to position static image elements as well as a dynamic one that moves with the mouse. You add some collision protections to keep the image from leaving a `<div>` element.

The code for the example is in Listing 17.3. Use the followings steps to create the dynamic web page:

1. In Aptana, create the hour17/hour1703.html, hour17/js/hour1703.js, and hour17/css/hour1703.css files.

2. Add the code shown in Listing 17.3-html and Listing 17.3-css to the HTML and CSS files.

3. Open the hour1703.js file and a `.ready()` function.

4. Inside the `.ready()` function, add the following lines to position #img2 at the right bottom corner of #img1, and #img3 at the right bottom corner of #img2:

```
2    $("#img2").position({my:"left top", at:"right bottom", of:"#img1"});
3    $("#img3").position({my:"left top", at:"right bottom", of:"#img2"});
```

5. Add the following `mousemove` event handler to reposition #img3 with the mouse movement. Notice that `collision` is set to `"flip"` within the `<div>` element so that the image will not be repositioned outside.

```
4    $("div").mousemove(function(e) {
5        $("#img4").position({ my:"left top", at:"center", of:e,
6                              collision:"flip", within:"div" });
```

6. Save all three files and then open the HTML document in a web browser, as shown in Figure 17.5. You should see three images placed on the page, and the fourth image will track with the mouse cursor as it is moved.

LISTING 17.3-html   **HTML Document That Adds the Images to the Web Page**

```
01 <!DOCTYPE html>
02 <html>
03   <head>
04     <title>Hour 17-3</title>
05     <meta charset="utf-8" />
06     <script type="text/javascript" src="../js/jquery.min.js"></script>
07     <script type="text/javascript" src="../js/jquery-ui.min.js"></script>
08     <script type="text/javascript" src="js/hour1703.js"></script>
09     <link rel="stylesheet" type="text/css" href="../js/css/jquery-ui.min.css">
10     <link rel="stylesheet" type="text/css" href="css/hour1703.css">
```

```
11   </head>
12   <body>
13     <div>
14       <img id="img1" src="images/arch.jpg">
15       <img id="img2" src="images/pyramid2.jpg">
16       <img id="img3" src="images/volcano.jpg">
17       <img id="img4" src="images/jump.jpg">
18     </div>
19   </body>
20 </html>
```

FIGURE 17.5
Positioning images using the .position() method in jQuery UI.

LISTING 17.3-js   jQuery and jQuery UI That Dynamically Positions the Images

```
1 $(document).ready(function(){
2   $("#img2").position({my:"left top", at:"right bottom", of:"#img1"});
3   $("#img3").position({my:"left top", at:"right bottom", of:"#img2"});
4   $("div").mousemove(function(e) {
5     $("#img4").position({ my:"left top", at:"center", of:e,
6                           collision:"flip", within:"div" });
7   })
8 });
```

▼ **LISTING 17.3-css   CSS Code That Styles the Page**

```
1 img { position: absolute; height: 130px; width:auto; }
2 div { height:500px; width:500px; border:3px ridge; }
```

Summary

In this hour, you downloaded and implemented jQuery UI in a few examples. You learned that jQuery UI extends jQuery with some additional functionality, such as new selectors, as well as enhances existing jQuery functionality, such as element positioning.

You implemented some examples to illustrate how to use jQuery in your web pages.

Q&A

Q. Is there anything that can be done in jQuery UI that I can't do myself in jQuery and JavaScript?

A. No. But that's not the point. The real point is that jQuery and jQuery UI will save you a ton of time.

Q. Can I use more than one theme at a time?

A. No, the themes will conflict with each other. You can, however, have multiple themes in different locations on your website and then dynamically adjust which .css files get loaded. This allows some users to have one theme and other users to have another.

Workshop

The workshop consists of a set of questions and answers designed to solidify your understanding of the material covered in this hour. Try to answer the questions before looking at the answers.

Quiz

1. What jQuery UI selector would you use to isolate elements that happen to have a specific data value assigned to them?

2. True or False: There is no way to get the scroll parent for an element.

3. How would you delay setting the focus on an element?

4. How can you easily reposition an element directly to the right of another element using jQuery UI?

Quiz Answers

1. `:data()`

2. False. You can use the `.scrollParent()` method to get the nearest scrolling container.

3. Use the `.focus()` method in jQuery UI with a delay value.

4. Use the `.position()` method with one element at `"right"` and the other `"left"`.

Exercises

1. Open the code in Listing 17.2, and modify it to add an additional data value that specifies the color; for example, `.data("color","red")`. Then, when the user clicks the Add Images button, change the color of the text using `.css()`.

2. Open the code in Listing 17.3 and modify it so that the images overlap each other as they cascade. The simplest way to do this is to add negative values to the `.position()` settings.

Using jQuery UI Effects

What You'll Learn in This Hour:

▸ Methods to apply effects using the jQuery UI library
▸ How easing effects make animation changes variable
▸ Ways to add cool effects when hiding/showing elements
▸ How to apply effects to class changes
▸ Applying animation effects when repositioning elements

jQuery UI provides a rich set of animation-type effects that can be applied to elements on your web pages. There are a couple of reasons why animating elements is a good thing. One is to leave the user with an impression that the website is interactive and fun to use. The second is to help users understand the visual changes that are taking place in your dynamic scripts.

In this hour, you see the improvements that jQuery UI provides in animation effects. You will be able to apply effects directly to elements, or you can apply effects when making class, visibility, or position changes.

Applying jQuery UI Effects

The purpose of this section is to introduce you to the effects that jQuery UI provides. This section discusses each of the effects and how to apply them using the .each() method. You are also introduced to the multitude of easing functions that provide a variable aspect to how values are applied during the effect animation.

Understanding jQuery UI Effects

jQuery UI effects are just animations to CSS position, size, and visibility properties. The animated changes are implemented in such a way as to create visual effects that give users a better experience.

For example, suppose a user tries to log in with an invalid password. In addition to the form validation message, you can also use jQuery UI effects to make the login button shake, which will catch the user's attention better letting the user know the login failed. These are subtle changes to the web page, but they can have a large impact on the user experience.

Table 18.1 lists the effects with values that can be applied to manipulate them. This should give you an idea of the effects possible with jQuery UI. You implement some of these effects later in this hour.

TABLE 18.1   jQuery UI Effects

Method	Options	Description
blind	direction	Provides the effect of "pulling the blinds" up by rolling the element up from the bottom.
		direction option can be set to up, down, left, right, vertical, or horizontal.
bounce	distance	Provides a bouncing effect by repositioning the element up and down vertically. distance is specified in pixels.
	times	times is the number of times the element bounces.
clip	direction	The element slides down as the bottom is erased, simulating the bottom being clipped off. direction option can be set to vertical or horizontal.
drop	direction	Slides the element as it fades in or out. direction option can be set to up, down, left, right.
explode	pieces	Slices the element into equal pieces that fade away in different directions. pieces should be a perfect square number (4, 9, ...).
fade		Slowly fades the element in or out.
fold	size	Folds the element in one direction and then a second. size is the number of pixels to fold down to.
	horizFirst	horizFirst specifies true or false on which direction to fold first.
highlight	color	Adds a color highlight to the image. color specifies the hex color value; for example, #FF0000.
puff	percent	Scales an element up at the same time it hides it. percent value specifies the percentage to scale the element to; for example, 50=smaller, 150=bigger.
pulsate	times	Fades the element in and out quickly, simulating a pulsing effect. times value is the number of times to fade.

Method	Options	Description
scale	direction origin percent scale	Shrinks or enlarges the element to a vanishing point. `direction` can be both `vertical` or `horizontal`. `origin` is an array specifying the vanishing point, which defaults to, for example: `["middle", "center"]` `percent` specifies the percentage to scale to. `scale` specifies what part of the element to resize: `box`, `content`, `both`.
shake	direction distance times	Animates rapid position changes vertically or horizontally. `direction` can be `left`, `right`, `up` or `down`. `distance` is the number of pixels to shake. `times` is the number of times to shake.

size	to
	origin
	scale
		Animates resizing the element.
		`to` specifies the new `height` and `width`:
		`{height:#, width:#}`
		
		`origin` specifies the vanishing point array; for example:
		`["middle", "right"]`
		
		`scale` specifies what part of the element to resize: `box`, `content`, `both`.

slide	direction distance	Animates the element to simulate a sliding effect. `direction` can be `left`, `right`, `up` or `down`. `distance` to slide up to the height or width of the element.
transfer	className to	Animates a wire frame transitioning from one element to another. `className` specifies class the transfer element will receive. `to` specifies the element to transfer to.

Setting the Effect Animation Easing

The easing function sets a value path that the effect uses when animating the effect. You have already seen the linear and swing easing in jQuery animations. jQuery UI adds a large number of new easing functions that can provide some fun animation effects.

The simplest way to illustrate how easing works is to show you the graphs published at the following location and shown in Figure 18.1. Think of the horizontal axis of the graphs as duration time, where left is 0 and the right is complete. Think of the vertical axis of the graph as how complete the transition of the effect is. For example, in a fade-out transition, the bottom would be fully opaque and the top would be fully transparent:

http://api.jqueryui.com/easings/

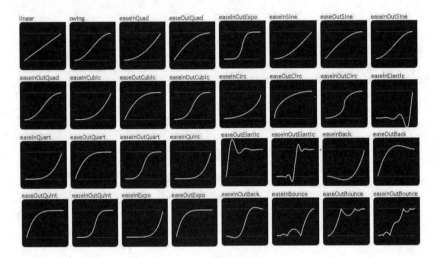

FIGURE 18.1
jQuery UI easing functions.

Adding Effects to jQuery Objects

There are multiple ways to apply effects to jQuery objects. Effects can be added as a part of another transition, such as a class change or visibility change. You can also apply effects to an element using the `.effect()` method. The `.effect()` method has the following syntax:

```
.effect( effect [, options ] [, duration ] [, complete ] )
```

In the `.effect()` method, effect is the name of the effect and `options` is an object containing the option values. Table 18.1 lists the effect names and options that you can apply to each effect. The `duration` is specified in milliseconds, and you can add an optional `complete` handler function that will be executed when the effect has been applied.

The following example illustrates the full syntax of applying a `size` effect to an element:

```
("img").effect("size",
              {to:{height:100, width:100}, origin:["right","top"], scale:"box"},
              3000,
              function(){alert("effect complete");});
```

Adding jQuery UI Effects

In this example, you apply several effects to `<img>` elements. You add four images to the web pages and apply a different effect on each when the user clicks the image. The purpose of the example is to familiarize you with how to implement different effects, set the effect `options`, and apply a `complete` function.

The code for the example is in Listing 18.1. Use the followings steps to create the dynamic web page:

1. In Aptana, create the hour18, hour18/js, and hour18/css folders, and then add the hour18/hour1801.html, hour18/js/hour1801.js, and hour18/css/hour1801.css files. You will also need to copy the images folder from the book's website at code/hour18 to the hour18 folder in Aptana.

2. Add the code shown in Listing 18.1-html and Listing 18.1-css to the HTML and CSS files.

3. Open the hour1801.js file and add a `.ready()` function.

4. Add the following `click` handler to #img1. The `click` handler applies a basic shake effect; 20 pixels in the down direction first and shake 5 times. 3000 milliseconds means the effect will take 3 seconds.

```
02    $("#img1").click(function(e) {
03       $(this).effect("shake", {direction:"down", distance:20, times:5},
         ➡3000);
04    });
```

5. Add the following `click` handler to #img2. The `click` handler applies a scale effect in both directions to the middle, right vanishing point. The effect scales the image down to 40 percent. Also notice that the `easeInBounce` easing is added to adjust the flow of the animation.

```
05    $("#img2").click(function(e) {
06       $(this).effect("scale",
07          {direction:"both", origin:["middle", "right"], percent:40,
         ➡scale:"box",
08           easing:"easeInBounce"}, 3000);
09    });
```

6. Add the following `click` handler to #img3. The `click` handler applies a double effect. The first effect is a slide in the downward direction for 200 pixels and the second, which slides right, is placed in the callback handler for the first effect, so it will not occur until the first effect is finished.

```
10    $("#img3").click(function(e) {
11       $(this).effect("slide", {direction:"down", distance:200}, 3000,
         ➡function(){
```

```
12        $(this).effect("slide", {direction:"right", distance:200}, 3000);
13    });
14  });
```

7. Add the following `click` handler to `#img4`. The `click` handler applies an explode effect, breaking the image into 16 pieces and having them fade as they move apart.

```
15  $("#img4").click(function(e) {
16      $(this).effect("explode", {pieces:16}, 3000);
17  });
```

8. Save all three files and then open the HTML document in a web browser, as shown in Figure 18.2. You should see the effects as you click the images.

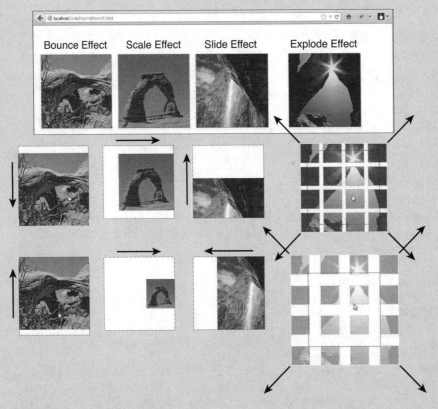

FIGURE 18.2
Applying jQuery UI effects to images.

LISTING 18.1-html   HTML Document That Adds the Web Page

```
01 <!DOCTYPE html>
02 <html>
03   <head>
04     <title>Hour 18-1</title>
05     <meta charset="utf-8" />
06     <script type="text/javascript" src="../js/jquery.min.js"></script>
07     <script type="text/javascript" src="../js/jquery-ui.min.js"></script>
08     <script type="text/javascript" src="js/hour1801.js"></script>
09     <link rel="stylesheet" type="text/css" href="../js/css/jquery-ui.min.css">
10     <link rel="stylesheet" type="text/css" href="css/hour1801.css">
11   </head>
12   <body>
13     <div id="frame1"><img id="img1" src="images/double.jpg"></div>
14     <div id="frame2"><img id="img2" src="images/arch.jpg"></div>
15     <div id="frame3"><img id="img3" src="images/cliff.jpg"></div>
16     <div id="frame4"><img id="img4" src="images/sunstar.jpg"></div>
17   </body>
18 </html>
```

LISTING 18.1-js   jQuery and jQuery UI That Apply Several Effects on Images

```
01 $(document).ready(function(){
02   $("#img1").click(function(e) {
03     $(this).effect("shake", {direction:"down", distance:20, times:5}, 3000);
04   });
05   $("#img2").click(function(e) {
06     $(this).effect("scale",
07       {direction:"both", origin:["middle", "right"], percent:40, scale:"box",
08        easing:"easeInBounce"}, 3000);
09   });
10   $("#img3").click(function(e) {
11     $(this).effect("slide", {direction:"down", distance:200}, 3000, function(){
12       $(this).effect("slide", {direction:"right", distance:200}, 3000);
13     });
14   });
15   $("#img4").click(function(e) {
16     $(this).effect("explode", {pieces:16}, 3000);
17   });
18 });
```

▼ **LISTING 18.1-css**   CSS Code That Styles the Page

```
1 img { height:200px; }
2 div { height:200px; width:200px; border:1px dotted;
3        display:inline-block; position:fixed; }
4 #frame1 { top:80px; left:20px; }
5 #frame2 { top:80px; left:240px; }
6 #frame3 { top:80px; left:460px; }
7 #frame4 { top:80px; left:720px; }
```

Adding Effects to Class Transitions

A very important part of jQuery UI effects is the capability to animate transitions when applying classes to elements. This is done by adding a duration to the class transition function and specifying the easing function to control the animation effect. Any numerical class values that are changing will be animated each step of the class transition.

NOTE
_____

Colors can be tricky; jQuery UI is not able to animate the transition from red to blue, but it can animate the transition from #FF0000 to #0000FF. If you want to animate color transitions, use the hex numerical value for them.
_____

The following is a list of the different class transition methods that you can use to apply effects on jQuery objects by setting `duration` and `easing` values:

▶ `.addClass( className [, duration ] [, easing ] [, complete ] )`—Adds the class and animates the changes to numerical class properties.

▶ `.removeClass( className [, duration ] [, easing ] [, complete ] ) )`—Removes the class and animates the changes to numerical class properties.

▶ `.switchClass( removeClassName, addClassName [, duration ] [, easing ] [, complete ] ) )`—First removes the `removeClassName` and animates the changes to numerical class properties, then adds the `addClassName` animating the numerical class property changes.

▶ `.toggleClass( className [, switch ] [, duration ] [, easing ] [, complete ] )`—Adds the class if the object(s) do not already have it or removes it if they do. Any changes to numerical class properties will be animated based on the `easing` function.

Applying Easing to Class Transitions

It's time to jump in and add some effects to class changes. In this example, you apply animation effects by applying different easing functions to `<span>` elements dressed up as buttons. The purpose of this example is to show each of the class transitions applying easing functions.

The code for the example is in Listing 18.2. Use the followings steps to create the dynamic web page:

1. In Aptana, add the hour18/hour1802.html, hour18/js/hour1802.js, and hour18/css/hour1802.css files.

2. Add the code shown in Listing 18.2-html and Listing 18.2-css to the HTML and CSS files. Notice the different class styles defined in the CSS file. These will be used to animate the class changes.

3. Now open the hour1802.js file and add the following `.ready()` function that implements a `click` handler for each of the `<span>` elements in the HTML document. The `click` handlers call the `.addClass()`, `.removeClass()`, `.switchClass()`, and `.toggleClass()` methods for the different button elements.

```
1 $(document).ready(function(){
2   $("#btn1").click(function(e) { $(this).addClass( "round", 2000,
    ➥"easeInElastic"); });
3   $("#btn2").click(function(e) { $(this).switchClass( "active", "inactive",
    ➥2000,
4                                           "easeInOutElastic");
                                          ➥});
5   $("#btn3").click(function(e) { $(this).toggleClass( "round", 2000,
    ➥"easeOutQuart"); });
6   $("#btn4").click(function(e) { $(this).removeClass( "round", 2000,
    ➥"easeInCirc"); });
7 });
```

4. Save all three files and then open the HTML document in a web browser, as shown in Figure 18.3. You should see the animated class transitions as you click each of the buttons.

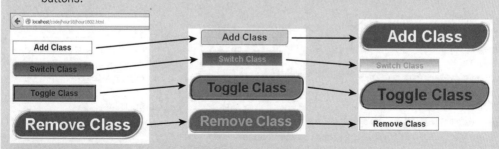

FIGURE 18.3
Adding animated effects to class transitions.

LISTING 18.2-html   **HTML Document That Adds the Web Page**

```
01 <!DOCTYPE html>
02 <html>
03   <head>
04     <title>Hour 18-2</title>
05     <meta charset="utf-8" />
06     <script type="text/javascript" src="../js/jquery.min.js"></script>
07     <script type="text/javascript" src="../js/jquery-ui.min.js"></script>
08     <script type="text/javascript" src="js/hour1802.js"></script>
09     <link rel="stylesheet" type="text/css" href="../js/css/jquery-ui.min.css">
10     <link rel="stylesheet" type="text/css" href="css/hour1802.css">
11   </head>
12   <body>
13     <span id="btn1">Add Class</span><br>
14     <span id="btn2" class="active">Switch Class</span><br>
15     <span id="btn3" class="square">Toggle Class</span><br>
16     <span id="btn4" class="round">Remove Class</span><br>
17   </body>
18 </html>
```

LISTING 18.2-js   **jQuery and jQuery UI Code That Implements the Class Transitions with Animation Effects**

```
1 $(document).ready(function(){
2   $("#btn1").click(function(e) { $(this).addClass( "round", 2000,
    ➥"easeInElastic"); });
3   $("#btn2").click(function(e) { $(this).switchClass( "active", "inactive", 2000,
4                                                       "easeInOutElastic"); });
5   $("#btn3").click(function(e) { $(this).toggleClass( "round", 2000,
    ➥"easeOutQuart"); });
6   $("#btn4").click(function(e) { $(this).removeClass( "round", 2000,
    ➥"easeInCirc"); });
7 });
```

LISTING 18.2-css   **CSS Code That Styles the Page**

```
1 span { display:inline-block; height:30px; width:200px; margin-top:20px;
2   border:1px ridge; text-align:center; font:bold 20px/30px arial; }
3 .round {border-width:6px; border-radius:120px 60px; height:60px; width:320px;
4   background-color:#0000FF; color:#FFFFFF; font-size:40px; line-height:60px; }
5 .square {border-width:6px; background-color:#FF0000; color:#000000; }
6 .active {background-image: -moz-linear-gradient(center top , #B10000, #FF0000);
7   border-radius:10px 10px; border:3px outset #FF0000; }
8 .inactive {background-image: -moz-linear-gradient(center top , #B1B1B1, #FFFFFF);
9   border-radius:0px; color:#A1A1A1; }
```

Adding Effects to Element Visibility Transitions

Another very cool effect that you can add to your web pages with jQuery UI is visibility changes. This can be one of the most useful in allowing users to visualize what is happening, and it provides them with a chance to follow the page flow better.

Visibility effects are applied in the same manner as the `.effect()` function you learned earlier in this hour. You specify an effect from Table 18.1 and then set the desired options, including an `easing` function if you want to control the animation.

The following is a list of the different element visibility transition methods that you can add effects to using jQuery UI:

- ▶ `.hide( effect [, options ] [, duration ] [, complete ] )`—Applies the effect with options while hiding the element.

- ▶ `.show( effect [, options ] [, duration ] [, complete ] )`—Applies the effect with options while showing the element.

- ▶ `.toggle( effect [, options ] [, duration ] [, complete ] )`—Either shows or hides the object based on its current visibility and applies the specified effect while doing so.

TRY IT YOURSELF ▼

Applying Effects to jQuery Visibility Transitions

In this example, you get a chance to apply effects to the visibility of menu items. The purpose of the example is to familiarize you with how to implement jQuery UI effects in jQuery's visibility methods.

The code for the example is in Listing 18.3. Use the followings steps to create the dynamic web page:

1. In Aptana, add the hour18/hour1803.html, hour18/js/hour1803.js, and hour18/css/hour1803.css files.

2. Add the code shown in Listing 18.3-html and Listing 18.3-css to the HTML and CSS files.

3. Open the hour1803.js file and add the following `.ready()` function that will hide the secondary menus initially:

```
01 $(document).ready(function(){
02    $("#showMenu, #showMenu2, #toggleMenu").hide();
...
11 })
```

4. Add the following click handlers for the different menu items. Notice that you use several, including `fold`, `scale`, `explode`, and `blind`. The reason is so that you can see how the effects work. On the `blind` effect, you set `easing` to `easeOutBounce`; this provides a simple `bounce` effect, as if the menu bounces at the bottom.

```
03  $("#show").click(function(e) { $("#showMenu").show("fold", {size:22},
    ➥2000); });
04  $("#show2").click(function(e) { $("#showMenu2").show(
05      "scale", {origin:["top","left"]}, 2000); });
06  $("#showMenu").click(function(e) { $("#showMenu").hide("fold", {size:22},
    ➥2000); });
07  $("#showMenu2").click(function(e) { $("#showMenu2").hide(
08      "explode", {pieces:9}, 2000); });
09  $("#toggle, #toggleMenu").click(function(e) { $("#toggleMenu").
    ➥toggle("blind",
10      {direction:"up", easing:"easeOutBounce"}, 2000); });
```

5. Save all three files and then open the HTML document in a web browser, as shown in Figure 18.4. You should be able to select the menus and see the `.show()`, `.hide()`, and `.toggle()` effects working.

Menus Collapsed

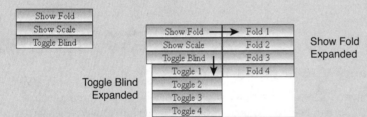

FIGURE 18.4
Using jQuery UI effects to improve showing and hiding menu options.

LISTING 18.3-html   HTML Document That Adds the Web Page

```
01  <!DOCTYPE html>
02  <html>
03    <head>
04      <title>Hour 18-3</title>
05      <meta charset="utf-8" />
06      <script type="text/javascript" src="../js/jquery.min.js"></script>
07      <script type="text/javascript" src="../js/jquery-ui.min.js"></script>
08      <script type="text/javascript" src="js/hour1803.js"></script>
09      <link rel="stylesheet" type="text/css" href="../js/css/jquery-ui.min.css">
```

```
10        <link rel="stylesheet" type="text/css" href="css/hour1803.css">
11      </head>
12      <body>
13      <span id="show">Show Fold</span><br>
14      <span id="show2">Show Scale</span><br>
15      <span id="toggle">Toggle Blind</span><br>
16      <div id="showMenu">
17        <span>Fold 1</span><br><span>Fold 2</span><br>
18        <span>Fold 3</span><br><span>Fold 4</span><br>
19      </div>
20      <div id="showMenu2">
21        <span>Explode 1</span><br><span>Explode 2</span><br>
22        <span>Explode 3</span><br><span>Explode 4</span><br>
23      </div>
24      <div id="toggleMenu">
25        <span>Toggle 1</span><br><span>Toggle 2</span><br>
26        <span>Toggle 3</span><br><span>Toggle 4</span><br>
27      </div>
28      </body>
29 </html>
```

LISTING 18.3-js   jQuery and jQuery UI That Implements the Visibility and Effects

```
01 $(document).ready(function(){
02    $("#showMenu, #showMenu2, #toggleMenu").hide();
03    $("#show").click(function(e) { $("#showMenu").show("fold", {size:22}, 2000);
   ➥});
04    $("#show2").click(function(e) { $("#showMenu2").show(
05      "scale", {origin:["top","left"]}, 2000); });
06    $("#showMenu").click(function(e) { $("#showMenu").hide("fold", {size:22},
   ➥2000); });
07    $("#showMenu2").click(function(e) { $("#showMenu2").hide(
08      "explode", {pieces:9}, 2000); });
09    $("#toggle, #toggleMenu").click(function(e) { $("#toggleMenu").toggle("blind",
10      {direction:"up", easing:"easeOutBounce"}, 2000); });
11 });
```

LISTING 18.3-css   CSS Code That Styles the Page

```
1 span { display:inline-block; width:130px; border:1px ridge; text-align:center;
2         background-image: -moz-linear-gradient(center top , #B1B1B1, #FFFFFF);
3         cursor:pointer; }
4 div span{ width:120px; margin-left:10px; }
5 #showMenu { position:fixed; left:130px; top:8px;}
6 #showMenu2 { position:fixed; left:130px; top:30px;}
```

▼ TRY IT YOURSELF

Adding Effects to Animations

The new easing functionality in jQuery UI can also be applied to the jQuery `.animation()` method. Using the different `easing` options, you can alter the effect of the animation through varying the rate that the transition occurs. One of the best examples of this is to apply a bounce transition to an animation that alters the position of an element.

The best way to illustrate this is through an example. In this example, you apply several animation effects to the movement of an image. The image is a simple ball that moves around the screen when clicked. At the final position, the ball hits a needle and "pops" using an `explode` effect. The purpose of the example is for you to see how the effects apply to the animation process.

The code for the example is in Listing 18.4. Use the followings steps to create the dynamic web page:

1. In Aptana, add the hour18/hour1804.html, hour18/js/hour1804.js, and hour18/css/hour1804.css files.

2. Add the code shown in Listing 18.4-html and Listing 18.4-css to the HTML and CSS files. The `<img>` elements are set to `fixed` positioning so their movement can be animated by changing the CSS position.

3. Open the hour1804.js file and add the `coords` array shown in lines 1–6 of Listing 18.4-js. This array provides positioning coordinates and easing function names that will be used by the `click` handler.

4. The following `.ready()` function adds the `click` handler to the ball.

```
14 $(document).ready(function(){
15   $("#ball").click(reposition);
16 });
```

5. Add the following `click` handler `reposition()` code. This function will pop off a coordinate and use the values in an `.animate()` call that will animate moving the ball. The easing value is set using the `easing` attribute of the `coord` object. Notice that the `callback` handler loops back to the `reposition()` function. When there are no more coordinates left, an explode effect is applied to the ball.

```
07 function reposition(){
08   if (coords.length){
09     coord = coords.pop();
10     $(this).animate(coord, 1000, coord.easing, reposition);
11   } else{
12     $("#ball").effect("explode", {pieces:25}, 2000); }
13 }
```

6. Save all three files and then open the HTML document in a web browser, as shown in Figure 18.5. When you click the ball, it should move around the web page with varying speed, illustrating the easing functions. At the end, it should hit the needle and disappear.

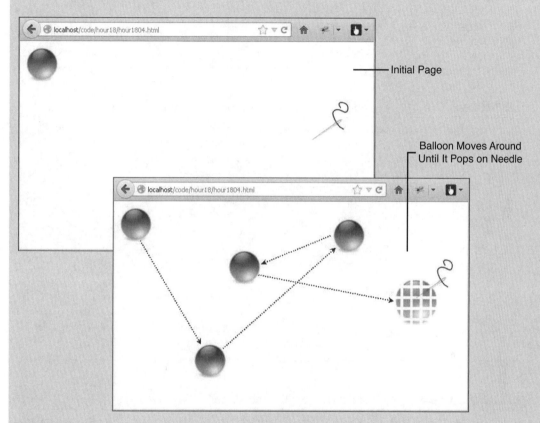

Initial Page

Balloon Moves Around Until It Pops on Needle

FIGURE 18.5
Using jQuery UI effects to adjust the timing of position animation.

LISTING 18.4-html   HTML Document That Adds the Web Page

```
01  <!DOCTYPE html>
02  <html>
03    <head>
04      <title>Hour 18-4</title>
05      <meta charset="utf-8" />
06      <script type="text/javascript" src="../js/jquery.min.js"></script>
07      <script type="text/javascript" src="../js/jquery-ui.min.js"></script>
08      <script type="text/javascript" src="js/hour1804.js"></script>
```

```
09        <link rel="stylesheet" type="text/css" href="../js/css/jquery-ui.min.css">
10        <link rel="stylesheet" type="text/css" href="css/hour1804.css">
11    </head>
12    <body>
13        <img id="ball" src="images/ball.png" />
14        <img id="needle" src="images/needle.png" />
15    </body>
16 </html>
```

LISTING 18.4-js   jQuery and jQuery UI That Implements the Reposition Effects

```
01 var coords = [{top:140, left:470, easing:"easeInBounce"},
02                {top:100, left:200, easing:"easeOutElastic"},
03                {top:300, left:200, easing:"easeInOutCirc"},
04                {top:20, left:300, easing:"easeInBounce"},
05                {top:10, left:10, easing:"easeOutExpo"},
06                {top:200, left:100, easing:"easeInSine"}]
07 function reposition(){
08    if (coords.length){
09      coord = coords.pop();
10      $(this).animate(coord, 1000, coord.easing, reposition);
11    } else{
12      $("#ball").effect("explode", {pieces:25}, 2000); }
13 }
14 $(document).ready(function(){
15    $("#ball").click(reposition);
16 });
```

LISTING 18.4-css   CSS Code That Styles the Page

```
1 img { position:fixed; }
2 #needle { left:500px; top:100px; }
```

Summary

jQuery UI effects are basically animations to the CSS properties of page elements. The benefit that they provide is that rather than having the effect happen instantaneously, you can have it happen gradually. Using easing functions, you can adjust the rate that the changes occur in the animation to give elements more of an interactive feel.

Q&A

Q. Is there a way to animate changing an `<img>` element from one source to another so that part of both elements are visible at the same time?

A. Not directly, but there is a trick you can employ. Use two `<img>` elements and animate the `opacity` property changes at the same time. As one disappears, the other one will become visible at the same time.

Q. Is there a way to create custom easing functions?

A. Yes, you can create a custom easing function and attach it to `$.easing`. The function needs to accept the following parameters and return a new value based on those parameters:

- `tPercent`—Percentage of time passed in the animation from 0.0 to 1.0.

- `tMS`—Milliseconds since animation started.

- `startValue`—Starting value of the property.

- `endValue`—Ending value of the property.

- `tTotal`—Duration of the animation.

```
$.easing.myCustom = function(tPercent, tMS, startValue, endValue, tTotal) {
    var newValue= <your code here>>...
  return newValue;
}
```

Workshop

The workshop consists of a set of questions and answers designed to solidify your understanding of the material covered in this hour. Try to answer the questions before looking at the answers.

Quiz

1. How do you control the amount of time the effect will take?

2. How do you define the number of pieces the explode effect will generate to 25?

3. True or False: You cannot animate changes to the `border-style`.

4. What effect would you use to simulate an element shrinking?

Quiz Answers

1. Setting the `duration` value.

2. Set the options value to `{pieces:25}`.

3. True. You can only animate numerical changes.

4. Scale or Size.

Exercises

1. Open the code in Listing 18.1 and change which effects are applied to the images. Try applying the `pulsate`, `drop`, and `puff` effects.

2. Modify the code in Listing 18.4. Add a `duration` attribute to each of the coordinates so that you can also adjust the `duration` time for each point in the ball's animation. Add a few new points, as well. The coordinate values should look something like this:

```
{top:20, left:300, easing:"easeInBounce", duration:1500},
```

Advanced Interactions Using jQuery UI Interaction Widgets

What You'll Learn in This Hour:

- ▶ Implementing drag-and-drop functionality
- ▶ Making elements and children resizable
- ▶ How to select multiple page elements using a bounding box
- ▶ Creating sortable tables, lists, and containers

A special set of jQuery UI widgets are intended to provide generalized interactions for various elements. These widgets allow you to make elements draggable and droppable and provide sorting, box selection, and resize functionality to elements.

The jQuery UI interaction widgets can be attached to elements to provide a rich set of predefined interactions. The following sections cover the different interaction widgets and how to implement them in your web pages.

Introducing jQuery UI Interactions

All jQuery UI interactions are based on two main components—the `jQuery.widget` factory and the mouse widget. The `jQuery.widget` factory provides the base functionality for all widgets including creation, disabling, enabling, and option settings. The mouse widget provides the base mouse interactions with the widget that captures mouse events and allows the widgets to interact with them.

Reviewing the `jQuery.widget` Factory

The `jQuery.widget` factory defines an interface that is used by all jQuery UI widgets. The options, methods, and events of the factory are available to all widgets. Table 19.1 lists the methods and events defined in the factory and available in all widgets.

TABLE 19.1 Methods and Events Available on All jQuery UI Widgets

Method	Description
`create`	Event triggered each time the widget is created.
`destroy()`	Removes the widget functionality completely.
`disable()`	Keeps the widget functionality, but disables it.
`enable()`	Enables the widget functionality.
`option([optionName] [,value])`	`option()` returns an object with all option keys/values. `option(optionName)` returns the specific option value. `option(optionName, value)` sets an option value.
`widget(name, [,base], prototype)`	Used to create custom widgets. Provides 3 parameters: `name` is the string used to access the widget, `base` is the existing widget to inherit functionality from, and `prototype` is an object defining the widget.

You can get more information about the `jQuery.widget` factory at http://api.jqueryui.com/jQuery.widget/.

Understanding the Mouse Interaction Widget

The mouse interaction widget is automatically applied to all widgets. Typically, you will not need to interact with it much. However, it does expose a few options that are very useful at times. Those options are the following:

▶ `cancel`—Cancels interaction for specific elements. For example, to cancel mouse interactions for elements with `class="label"` in the #item1, you would use

```
$( "#item1" ).mouse( "option", "cancel", ".label" );
```

▶ `delay`—Delays the time after the `mousedown` event occurs before the interaction takes place. For example, to add a 1-second delay for mouse interactions on #item2, you would use

```
$( "#item2" ).mouse( "option", "delay", 1000 );
```

▶ `distance`—Specifies the distance in pixels the mouse must travel after the mousedown event occurs before the interaction should start. For example, to set the distance to 10 pixels for mouse interactions on #item3, you would use

```
$( "#item3" ).mouse( "option", "distance", 10 );
```

Using the Drag-and-Drop Widgets

Now that you have reviewed the widget interface and the mouse interaction widget, you are ready to look at some of the most common jQuery UI widgets—the draggable and droppable widgets. These widgets are designed to work in tandem.

You can define one element to be draggable and then another to be droppable. When draggable elements are dropped on droppable widgets, you can apply JavaScript and jQuery code to provide whatever interaction for the user you would like.

Dragging Elements with the Draggable Widget

The draggable widget defines an element as draggable by holding down the mouse and moving it. This allows you to move the element to whatever position on the screen you would like.

The draggable widget will handle scrolling elements and provides several options to control the look and feel while dragging. Table 19.2 describes the more common draggable options. The following shows an example of attaching the draggable widget to an element with the `cursor` and `opacity` options:

```
$("#img1").draggable({cursor:"move", opacity:.5});
```

TABLE 19.2   Common Draggable Widget Options

Option	Description
axis	Can be set to x or y, or false. x drags horizontally only, y drags vertically only, and false drags freely.
containment	Specifies a container to limit dragging within. Possible values are "parent", "document", or "window".
cursor	Specifies the cursor to display while dragging.
helper	Defines what element is displayed when dragging. Values can be "original", "clone", or a function that returns a DOM object.
opacity	Sets the opacity while dragging.
revert	Boolean. Specifies if the "original" object should return to its original position when dragging stops.
	String. If set to "valid", revert occurs only if the object has been dropped successfully. "invalid" reverts only if the object hasn't been dropped successfully.
stack	Is set to false or a selector. If a selector is specified, the item is brought to the top z-index of the element specified by the selector.
zIndex	z-index value to use while dragging.

The draggable widget also provides the additional events so handlers can be attached to the element when dragging starts, is in progress, and stops. Table 19.3 lists the events that you can access on draggable items. The following shows an example of adding a `dragstop` event to apply a `bounce` effect when the item is dropped:

```
$("#drag1").draggable({cursor:"move", opacity:.5});
$("#drag1").on("dragstop", function(){$(this).effect("bounce", 1000); });
```

TABLE 19.3 Draggable Widget Events

Event	Description
drag(event, ui)	Triggered while dragging.
	event is the JavaScript event object.
	ui is an object with the following values:
	▶ helper—jQuery object representing the helper for the draggable item.
	▶ position—{top, left} object for the current CSS position.
	▶ offset—{top, left} object for the current CSS offset.
dragstart(event, ui)	Triggered when dragging starts.
dragstop(event, ui)	Triggered when dragging stops.

▼ TRY IT YOURSELF

Adding Draggable Images to a Web Page

In this example, you implement draggable multiple image elements. Each image behaves a bit differently, as described in the following steps. The purpose of the example is to help you see how easy it is to make web elements draggable.

The code for the example is in Listing 19.1. Use the following steps to create the dynamic web page:

1. In Aptana, create the hour19, hour19/js, and hour18/css folders, and then add the hour19/hour1901.html, hour19/js/hour1901.js, and hour19/css/hour1901.css files. You also need to copy the images folder from the book's website at code/hour19 to the hour19 folder in Aptana.

2. Add the code shown in Listing 19.1-html and Listing 19.1-css to the HTML and CSS files.

3. Open the hour1901.js file and add a `.ready()` function.

4. Add the following lines. Line 2 adds the draggable widget to #drag1 and sets the cursor to move while dragging; also, the `opacity` is at 50% while dragging. Line 3 adds a `dragstop` handler function that applies the `bounce` effect to the image when it is dropped.

```
02    $("#drag1").draggable({cursor:"move", opacity:.5});
03    $("#drag1").on("dragstop", function(){$(this).effect("bounce", 1000); });
```

5. Add the following lines that implement `draggable` on the #drag2 element. The `helper` option is set to `"clone"` so that the object stays in place while dragging; then in line 5, a `dragstop` event handler is added to animate changing the position from the original to the location of the helper clone. Notice that the `offset` is collected using the `ui` parameter.

```
04    $("#drag2").draggable({helper:"clone"});
05    $("#drag2").on("dragstop", function(e, ui){$("#drag2").animate(ui.
➥offset); });
```

6. Add the following lines that implement `draggable` on the #drag3 element. This time, you implement a drag handler in line 7 that updates a paragraph element with the current mouse coordinates while dragging. The `dragstop` handler will clear out the position text.

```
06    $("#drag3").draggable();
07    $("#drag3").on("drag", function(e){
08      $(this).children("p").html(e.pageX+", "+e.pageY); });
09    $("#drag3").on("dragstop", function(e){ $(this).children("p").html("");
➥});
```

7. Save all three files and then open the HTML document in a web browser, as shown in Figure 19.1. You should be able to drag the images around and test the interactions.

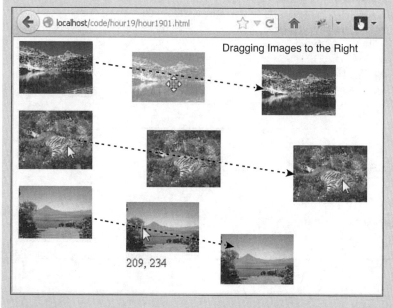

FIGURE 19.1
Applying jQuery UI dragging widgets to move images on the screen.

LISTING 19.1-html   HTML Document That Adds the Web Page.

```
01 <!DOCTYPE html>
02 <html>
03   <head>
04     <title>Hour 19-1</title>
05     <meta charset="utf-8" />
06     <script type="text/javascript" src="../js/jquery.min.js"></script>
07     <script type="text/javascript" src="../js/jquery-ui.min.js"></script>
08     <script type="text/javascript" src="js/hour1901.js"></script>
09     <link rel="stylesheet" type="text/css" href="../js/css/jquery-ui.min.css">
10     <link rel="stylesheet" type="text/css" href="css/hour1901.css">
11   </head>
12   <body>
13     <div id="drag1"><img id="img1" src="images/lake.jpg"></div>
14     <div id="drag2"><img id="img1" src="images/tiger.jpg"></div>
15     <div id="drag3"><img id="img1" src="images/volcano.jpg"><p></p></div>
16   </body>
17 </html>
```

LISTING 19.1-js   jQuery and jQuery UI Implements Draggable Images

```
01 $(document).ready(function(){
02   $("#drag1").draggable({cursor:"move", opacity:.5});
03   $("#drag1").on("dragstop", function(){$(this).effect("bounce", 1000); });
04   $("#drag2").draggable({helper:"clone"});
05   $("#drag2").on("dragstop", function(e, ui){$("#drag2").animate(ui.offset); });
06   $("#drag3").draggable();
07   $("#drag3").on("drag", function(e){
08     $(this).children("p").html(e.pageX+", "+e.pageY); });
09   $("#drag3").on("dragstop", function(e){ $(this).children("p").html(""); });
10 });
```

LISTING 19.1-css   CSS Code That Styles the Page

```
1 p {margin:0px; }
2 div {height:80px; width:100px; position:fixed; }
3 #drag2 { top:100px; }
4 #drag3 { top:200px; }
5 img { width:100px; }
```

Creating Drop Targets with the Droppable Widget

The droppable widget defines an element as a valid drop container usable by draggable items. This enables you to provide interactions between elements using simple mouse controls.

The droppable widget allows you to specify an accept function that can process the information about the event, such as mouse coordinates as well as the draggable item involved. Table 19.4 describes the more common droppable options. The following shows an example of attaching the droppable widget to an element and specifying the `tolerance` level:

```
$("#div1"). droppable ({tolerance:"touch"});
```

TABLE 19.4 Common Droppable Widget Options

Option	Description
accept	Specifies a selector used to filter the elements that will be accepted by the droppable item.
activeClass	Specifies a class that will be applied to the droppable item while a valid draggable item is being dragged.
greedy	Boolean. The default is `false`, meaning that all valid parent droppable items will receive the draggable item as well. When `true`, only the first droppable item will receive the draggable item.
hoverClass	Specifies a class that will be applied to the droppable item while a valid draggable item is hovering over it.
tolerance	Specifies the method used to determine if a draggable item is valid. Acceptable values are ▶ `fit`—Draggable overlaps droppable entirely. ▶ `intersect`—Draggable overlaps droppable at least 50% in both directions. ▶ `pointer`—Mouse hovers over droppable. ▶ `touch`—Draggable overlaps droppable in any location.

The droppable widget also provides the additional events so handlers can be attached to the element when dragging and dropping. Table 19.5 lists the events that you can access on droppable items. The following shows an example of adding a `dropactivate` event to apply a `shake` effect when a droppable item is activated by a drag start:

```
$("#drop1").droppable({tolerance:"pointer"});
$("#drop1").on("dropactivate", function(){$(this).effect("shake", 1000); });
```

TABLE 19.5 Droppable Widget Events

Event	Description
`dropactivate(event, ui)`	Triggered when a valid draggable item begins dragging. `event` is the JavaScript event object. `ui` is an object with the following values: ▶ `draggable`—jQuery object representing the actual draggable item. ▶ `helper`—jQuery object representing the helper for the draggable item. ▶ `position`—{`top`, `left`} object for the current draggable CSS position. ▶ `offset`—{`top`, `left`} object for the current draggable CSS offset.
`drop(event, ui)`	Triggered when a draggable item is dropped on droppable.
`dropout(event, ui)`	Triggered when draggable leaves droppable based on tolerance.
`dropover(event, ui)`	Triggered when draggable enters droppable based on tolerance.

▼ TRY IT YOURSELF

Applying Drag and Drop to a Web Page

In this example, you implement draggable and droppable on page elements. The first droppable element displays an image, and the second adds the image and `src` text to a list. The purpose of the example is to help you see how easy it is to make web elements droppable.

The code for the example is in Listing 19.2. Use the followings steps to create the dynamic web page:

1. In Aptana, add the hour19/hour1902.html, hour19/js/hour1902.js, and hour19/css/hour1902.css files.

2. Add the code shown in Listing 19.2-html and Listing 19.2-css to the HTML and CSS files.

3. Open the hour1902.js file and add a `.ready()` function.

4. Add the following lines that add the draggable widget to #drag1, #drag2, and #drag3. Use `clone` for the `helper` setting to keep the images in place, set the `cursor` and the `opacity`. Also, you set `zIndex` up so that the images will show on top of other page elements, even while dragging over them.

```
02    $("#drag1, #drag2, #drag3").draggable(
03        {helper:"clone", cursor:"move", opacity:.7, zIndex:99});
```

5. Add the following lines that implement droppable on #drop1. accept is set to "img" so that only <img> elements will be accepted. In line 5, a dropover event handler is added that applies a pulsate effect to the droppable box when the draggable item is hovering over it. Also, a drop event handler is added in lines 6 and 7 that will add an <img> element to #drop1 with the same src attribute as the draggable element. A bounce effect is also added to show the user the content changed.

```
04    $("#drop1").droppable({accept:"img", tolerance:"fit"});
05    $("#drop1").on("dropover", function(e,ui){ $(this).effect("pulsate"); });
06    $("#drop1").on("drop", function(e,ui){
07        $(this).html($("<img></img>").attr("src", ui.draggable.attr("src")));
08        $(this).effect("bounce");
09    });
```

6. Add the following lines that implement droppable on #drop2. Notice that in line 10 a hoverClass is added. The class will cause the background to turn light blue when the box is hovered over by a droppable item. Also in lines 11–16, the drop handler function is implemented that adds a <div> element with the <img> and src text to #drop2.

```
10 $("#drop2").droppable({accept:"img", tolerance:"intersect",
   ➥hoverClass:"drop-hover"});
11 $("#drop2").on("drop", function(e,ui){
12     var item = $("<div></div>");
13     item.append($("<img></img>").attr("src", ui.draggable.attr("src")));
14     item.append($("<span></span>").html(ui.draggable.attr("src")));
15     $(this).append(item);
16 });
```

7. Save all three files and then open the HTML document in a web browser, as shown in Figure 19.2. You should be able to drag and drop the images around and test the interactions.

LISTING 19.2-html   HTML Document That Adds the Web Page

```
01 <!DOCTYPE html>
02 <html>
03   <head>
04     <title>Hour 19-2</title>
05     <meta charset="utf-8" />
06     <script type="text/javascript" src="../js/jquery.min.js"></script>
07     <script type="text/javascript" src="../js/jquery-ui.min.js"></script>
08     <script type="text/javascript" src="js/hour1902.js"></script>
09     <link rel="stylesheet" type="text/css" href="../js/css/jquery-ui.min.css">
10     <link rel="stylesheet" type="text/css" href="css/hour1902.css">
11   </head>
12   <body>
13     <div id="images">
```

```
14        <img id="drag1" src="images/lake.jpg" />
15        <img id="drag2" src="images/tiger.jpg" />
16        <img id="drag3" src="images/volcano.jpg" />
17    </div>
18    <div id="drop1"></div>
19    <div id="drop2"></div>
20  </body>
21 </html>
```

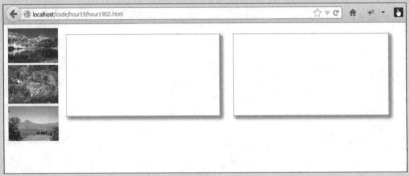

Dragging and Dropping Images

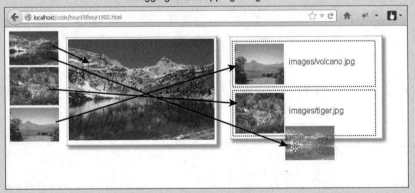

FIGURE 19.2
Applying jQuery UI drag and drop.

LISTING 19.2-js   jQuery and jQuery UI Implements Draggable and Droppable Elements

```
01 $(document).ready(function(){
02   $("#drag1, #drag2, #drag3").draggable(
03     {helper:"clone", cursor:"move", opacity:.7, zIndex:99});
04   $("#drop1").droppable({accept:"img", tolerance:"fit", hoverClass:"opaque"});
```

```
05   $("#drop1").on("dropover", function(e,ui){ $(this).effect("pulsate"); });
06   $("#drop1").on("drop", function(e,ui){
07     $(this).html($("<img></img>").attr("src", ui.draggable.attr("src")));
08     $(this).effect("bounce");
09   });
10   $("#drop2").droppable({accept:"img", tolerance:"intersect",hoverClass:
     ➥"drop-hover"});
11   $("#drop2").on("drop", function(e,ui){
12     var item = $("<div></div>");
13     item.append($("<img></img>").attr("src", ui.draggable.attr("src")));
14     item.append($("<span></span>").html(ui.draggable.attr("src")));
15     $(this).append(item);
16   });
17 });
```

LISTING 19.2-css   CSS Code That Styles the Page

```
01 div { display:inline-block; vertical-align:top; }
02 img {width:100px; margin:0px; }
03 #images { width:100px; height:300px; }
04 #drop1, #drop2 { width:300px; min-height:150px; padding:3px;
05   border:3px ridge white; box-shadow: 5px 5px 5px #888888; margin:10px;}
06 #drop1 img { width:300px; }
07 #drop2 div{ height:80px; width:280px; padding:4px; border:2px dotted;
   ➥margin-top:5px;}
08 #drop2 div img {height:80px; margin-right:10px; }
09 #drop2 div span { display:inline-block; vertical-align:top; font:16px/70px
   ➥arial; }
10 .drop-hover { background-color:#BBDDFF; }
```

Resizing Elements Using the Resizable Widget

A frequent request for users is the capability to define the size and shape of images, lists, tables, and so on. The resizable widget provides the capability to easily resize an image with mouse controls. This allows users to resize page elements as they desire.

The resizable widget attaches several handle controls to the page elements that interact with the mouse to resize the elements. You can also resize other elements at the same time.

Table 19.6 describes the more common resizable options. The following shows an example of attaching the resizable widget to an element and specifying the aspectRatio as true:

```
$("#div1"). resizable ({aspectRatio:true});
```

TABLE 19.6 Common Resizable Widget Options

Option	Description
alsoResize	Specifies a selector, jQuery object, or DOM object to resize synchronously with the currently sizable element.
aspectRatio	Can be set to true to maintain the current aspect ratio or a number to force a specific aspect ratio.
autoHide	Boolean. When set to true, the handles will disappear when not hovered over.
containment	Limits the resizing bounds to an object. Values can be a selector, DOM object, or a string containing "parent" or "document".
ghost	Boolean. When true, a semitransparent element is shown during resizing.
handles	Specifies a comma-separated list of compass style locations to place the image. Values can be the following, for example: {handles:"n,e,s,w,ne,se,sw,nw"}
helper	Same as for draggable.

The resizable widget also provides the additional events so handlers can be attached to the element when resizing. Table 19.7 lists the events that you can access on resizable items. The following shows an example of adding a `resizestop` event to apply a `pulsate` effect when a resizable item has finished being resized:

```
$("#resize1"). resizable ({aspectRatio:true });
$("#resize1").on("dropactivate", function(){$(this).effect("pulsate"); });
```

TABLE 19.7 Resizable Widget Events

Event	Description
resize(event, ui)	Triggered while resizing.
	event is the JavaScript event object.
	ui is an object with the following values:
	▶ element—jQuery object representing the element to be resized.
	▶ originalElement—jQuery object representing the original element before being wrapped.
	▶ helper—jQuery object representing the helper for the draggable item.
	▶ originalPosition—{top, left} object for the original position.
	▶ originalSize—{width, height} object for original size.
	▶ position—{top, left} object for the current position.
	▶ size—{width, height} object for the current offset.

Event	Description
`resizestart(event, ui)`	Triggered when a resizing starts.
`resizestop(event, ui)`	Triggered when a resizing stops (mouse up).

TRY IT YOURSELF ▼

Creating Resizable Elements

In this example, you implement draggable and resizable elements to allow users to customize the position and size of items on the web page. The purpose of the example is to illustrate the interaction between draggable and resizable.

The code for the example is in Listing 19.3. Use the followings steps to create the dynamic web page:

1. In Aptana, add the hour19/hour1903.html, hour19/js/hour1903.js, and hour19/css/hour1903.css files.

2. Add the code shown in Listing 19.3-html and Listing 19.3-css to the HTML and CSS files.

3. Open the hour1903.js file and add a `.ready()` function.

4. Add the following line that will add `draggable` to the main `<div>` elements:

   ```
   2    $("#resize1, #resize2, #resize3").draggable();
   ```

5. Add the following line that implements the resizable widget on `#resize1`. Notice that the `aspectRatio` is true, so it will force the aspect ratio to be constant when resizing. The `alsoResize` option is set to the image contained in #resize1 so that the `<img>` element will be resized.

   ```
   3    $("#resize1").resizable({aspectRatio:true, alsoResize:"#resize1 img" });
   ```

6. Add the following line that implements `resizable` on #resize2. This time, `aspectRatio` is not set, so you can adjust the box freely, which distorts the image.

   ```
   4    $("#resize2").resizable({alsoResize:"#resize2 img"});
   ```

7. Add the following lines that append a series of `<p>` elements to #resize3 and then add the resizable widget. You also resize the #list `<div>` when resizing the widget to shrink the scrollable list with the box. Also you changed the `handles` option to `"n,s,e,w"`, which will allow you to resize the elements from the top, bottom, or sides, but not the corners.

```
5    for(var i=0; i<100; i++){ $("#list").append($("<p></p>").html("Item "+i));
     ➥}
6    $("#resize3").resizable({alsoResize:"#resize3 #list", handles:"n,s,e,w"});
```

8. Save all three files and then open the HTML document in a web browser, as shown in Figure 19.3. You should be able to drag and resize the elements and test the interactions.

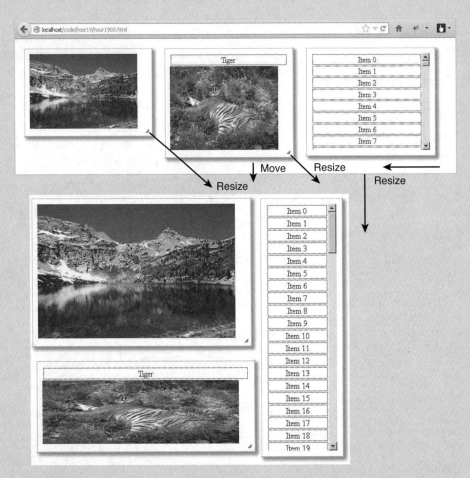

FIGURE 19.3
Applying jQuery UI resizing.

LISTING 19.3-html HTML Document That Adds the Web Page

```
01 <!DOCTYPE html>
02 <html>
03   <head>
04     <title>Hour 19-3</title>
05     <meta charset="utf-8" />
06     <script type="text/javascript" src="../js/jquery.min.js"></script>
07     <script type="text/javascript" src="../js/jquery-ui.min.js"></script>
08     <script type="text/javascript" src="js/hour1903.js"></script>
09     <link rel="stylesheet" type="text/css" href="../js/css/jquery-ui.min.css">
10     <link rel="stylesheet" type="text/css" href="css/hour1903.css">
11   </head>
12   <body>
13     <div id="resize1"><img src="images/lake.jpg" /></div>
14     <div id="resize2">
15       <p>Tiger</p>
16       <img src="images/tiger.jpg" />
17     </div>
18     <div id="resize3"><div id="list"></div></div>
19   </body>
20 </html>
```

LISTING 19.3-js jQuery and jQuery UI Implements Resizing and Moving the Page Elements

```
1 $(document).ready(function(){
2   $("#resize1, #resize2, #resize3").draggable();
3   $("#resize1").resizable({aspectRatio:true, alsoResize:"#resize1 img" });
4   $("#resize2").resizable({alsoResize:"#resize2 img"});
5   for(var i=0; i<100; i++){ $("#list").append($("<p></p>").html("Item "+i)); }
6   $("#resize3").resizable({alsoResize:"#resize3 #list", handles:"n,s,e,w"});
7 });
```

LISTING 19.3-css CSS Code That Styles the Page

```
1 img { width:230px; }
2 #resize1, #resize2, #resize3 {
3   width:250px; padding:10px; display:inline-block; margin:10px;
4   border:3px ridge white; box-shadow: 5px 5px 5px #888888;  vertical-align:top; }
5 p { margin:2px; border:1px dotted; text-align:center; }
6 #list { height:200px; overflow-y:auto; }
```

Applying the Selectable Widget

Another frequent request for users is the capability to easily select multiple items on a page using a bounding box. The selectable widget provides that functionality by allowing the user to draw a box, or "lasso," around selectable children inside the selectable element using the mouse. Items inside the box are selected in the list.

Table 19.8 describes the more common selectable options. The following shows an example of attaching the selectable widget to an element and specifying the tolerance as fit:

```
$("#ul1"). selectable ({tolerance:"fit"});
```

TABLE 19.8 Common Selectable Widget Options

Option	Description
appendTo	Specifies a selector that defines what element to attach the lasso to when dragging. This defaults to "body".
filter	Specifies a selector to use to define which child element can be selected in the bounding box.
tolerance	Can be set to "fit", meaning that the lasso overlaps the child element entirely, or "touch", meaning that any part of the lasso overlaps the child element.

The selectable widget also provides the additional events so handlers can be attached to the selectable element or its children when changing the selection. Table 19.9 lists the events that you can access on selectable items.

Each of the selectable events will pass the event object along with a ui object that will have a value for each of the events representing the selectable element. For example, the following code adds a selectableselected event to an element and then accesses the selected attribute:

```
$("#list1").selectable();
$("#list1").on("selectableselected ", function(e, ui){ ui.selected.effect("shake");
➥});
```

TABLE 19.9 Selectable Widget Events

Event	Description
selectableselected	Triggered at the end on the new elements selected.
selectableselecting	Triggered during select on each element selected.
selectablestart	Triggered on selectable when selecting starts.

Event	Description
`selectablestop`	Triggered on selectable when selecting stops.
`selectableunselect`	Triggered at the end on the elements unselected.
`selectableunselected`	Triggered during select on each element unselected.

NOTE

The `.ui-selecting` class is appended to child elements that are currently being selected. After a child element is selected, the `.ui-selected` class will be appended. This allows you to define some basic styles in CSS without having to add/remove classes in the selectable event handlers.

TRY IT YOURSELF ▼

Creating Selectable Sets

In this example, you implement `selectable` on a `<list>` and a group of images. The purpose of the example is to give you a look at a couple of ways to implement the selectable widget. You will get a chance to apply some of the options and use different event handlers to interact with the selection process.

The code for the example is in Listing 19.4. Use the followings steps to create the dynamic web page:

1. In Aptana, add the hour19/hour1904.html, hour19/js/hour1904.js, and hour19/css/hour1904.css files.

2. Add the code shown in Listing 19.4-html and Listing 19.4-css to the HTML and CSS files. Notice in Listing 19.4-css that `.ui-selected` and `.ui-selecting` classes are added for both `#set1` and `#set2`.

3. Open the hour1904.js file and add a `.ready()` function.

4. Add the following line that will populate the `#set1` list:

```
02    for(var i=0; i<100; i++){ $("#set1").append($("<p></p>").html("Item
    ➡"+i)); }
```

5. Add the following lines to implement `selectable` on `#set1` along with `selectablestart`, `selectableselecting`, and `selectablestop` event handlers. Notice in the `selectableselecting` event handler that the `ui.selecting.innerHTML` value is used to update the list of items being selected.

```
03    $("#set1").selectable({filter:"p"});
04    $("#set1").on("selectablestart", function(e, ui){ $("span").
    ➡html("Selecting "); });
```

```
05    $("#set1").on("selectableselecting", function(e, ui){
06       $("span").append(ui.selecting.innerHTML+", "); });
07    $("#set1").on("selectablestop", function(e, ui){
08       $("span").html("Selection Complete"); });
```

6. Add the following lines to implement selectable on #set2, which is a `<div>` full of images. Inside the `selectablestop` event handler, you use the `.ui-selected` class attribute to find the selected images. In line 12, a `pulsate` effect is applied to the selected images, and the `<span>` element is updated with the count of selected images.

```
09    $("#set2").selectable();
10    $("#set2").on("selectablestop", function(e, ui){
11       var selection = $("#set2 .ui-selected");
12       selection.effect("pulsate");
13       $("span").html("Selected "+ selection.length + " Photos"); });
```

7. Save all three files and then open the HTML document in a web browser, as shown in Figure 19.4. You should be able to drag to select items in the list as well as images.

LISTING 19.4-html   **HTML Document That Adds the Web Page**

```
01  <!DOCTYPE html>
02  <html>
03    <head>
04      <title>Hour 19-4</title>
05      <meta charset="utf-8" />
06      <script type="text/javascript" src="../js/jquery.min.js"></script>
07      <script type="text/javascript" src="../js/jquery-ui.min.js"></script>
08      <script type="text/javascript" src="js/hour1904.js"></script>
09      <link rel="stylesheet" type="text/css" href="../js/css/jquery-ui.min.css">
10      <link rel="stylesheet" type="text/css" href="css/hour1904.css">
11    </head>
12    <body>
13        <span>Nothing Selected</span><br>
14      <div id="set1"></div>
15      <div id="set2">
16        <img src="images/cliff.jpg" /><img src="images/flower2.jpg" />
17        <img src="images/lake.jpg" /><img src="images/tiger.jpg" />
18        <img src="images/flower.jpg" /><img src="images/volcano.jpg" />
19      </div>
20    </body>
21  </html>
```

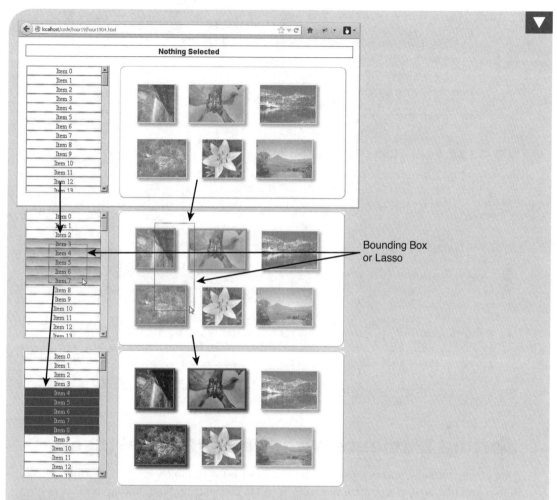

FIGURE 19.4
Applying jQuery UI selecting items in a list using a bounding box.

LISTING 19.4-js   jQuery and jQuery UI Implements Item Selection

```
01  $(document).ready(function(){
02    for(var i=0; i<100; i++){ $("#set1").append($("<p></p>").html("Item "+i)); }
03    $("#set1").selectable({filter:"p"});
04    $("#set1").on("selectablestart", function(e, ui){  $("span").html("Selecting
    ➥"); });
05    $("#set1").on("selectableselecting", function(e, ui){
06      $("span").append(ui.selecting.innerHTML+", "); });
07    $("#set1").on("selectablestop", function(e, ui){
08      $("span").html("Selection Complete"); });
```

```
09   $("#set2").selectable();
10   $("#set2").on("selectablestop", function(e, ui){
11     var selection = $("#set2 .ui-selected");
12     selection.effect("pulsate");
13     $("span").html("Selected "+ selection.length + " Photos"); });
14 });
```

LISTING 19.4-css   CSS Code That Styles the Page

```
01   span { display:inline-block; border:1px solid; font:bold 18px/26px arial;
02     width:800px; text-align:center; margin:10px;}
03   div { display:inline-block; border:3px ridge white; vertical-align:top;
     ➥margin:10px;}
04   p {border:1px dotted; margin:0px; }
05   #set1 {height:300px; width:200px; overflow-y:auto; text-align:center; }
06   #set1 .ui-selecting {
07     background-image: -moz-linear-gradient(center top , #88BBFF, #DDEEFF); }
08   #set1 .ui-selected { background-color:blue; color:white; }
09   img { height:90px; border:3px ridge white; box-shadow: 5px 5px 5px #888888;
10     margin:15px; opacity:.6; }
11   #set2 { width:500px; padding:25px; border-radius:15px; }
12   #set2 .ui-selecting{ border:5px ridge green; box-shadow: 5px 5px 5px #558822;}
13   #set2 .ui-selected{ border:5px ridge blue; box-shadow: 5px 5px 5px #225588;
14     opacity:1; }
```

Sorting Elements with the Sortable Widget

One of the coolest interactions provided by jQuery UI is the sortable widget. The sortable widget allows you to drag and reposition the order of HTML elements that are flowing together in a list, table, or just inside a container.

The sortable widget repositions the other elements as you drag an item. You can also link sortable containers together so that you can drag an item from one sortable container to another.

Table 19.10 describes the more common sortable options. The following shows an example of attaching a sortable widget to an element and specifying the tolerance as fit:

```
$("#ul1").sortable({tolerance:"fit"});
```

TABLE 19.10   Common Sortable Widget Options

Option	Description
axis	Specifies the direction that items can be dragged. Values are x for horizontal, y for vertical, or false for both.

Option	Description
`connectTo`	Specifies the selector of another selectable container that you want to be able to drag items from this container to.
`cursor`	Specifies cursor shown while sorting.
`helper`	Defines what element is displayed when sorting. Values can be `"original"`, `"clone"`, or a function that returns a DOM object.
`items`	Specifies a selector used to define what child elements are sortable inside the list.
`opacity`	Specifies the opacity of the helper while sorting.
`placeholder`	Specifies a class name that is applied to the placeholder while dragging.
`scroll`	Boolean. When true, the page will scroll when the sorting element comes to the edge.
`tolerance`	Specifies the method used to determine if a sorting item is in a new position. Acceptable values are ▶ `intersect`—Draggable overlaps droppable at least 50% in both directions. ▶ `pointer`—Mouse is over droppable.
`zIndex`	Specifies the `z-index` used when sorting.

NOTE

To sort table rows using `sortable`, you need to make `<tbody>` sortable, not `<table>`.

The sortable widget also provides the additional events so handlers can be attached to the sortable element or its children when sorting. Table 19.11 lists the events that you can access on selectable items.

TIP

jQuery UI will add the `.ui-sortable-helper` class to the helper element being sorted. You can define your own settings in the CSS for the helper class to control the look while moving the element in the `sortable`.

Each of the `sortable` events will pass the `event` object along with a `ui` object that will have the following values attached to it:

▶ `helper`—jQuery object representing the helper object being dragged.

- ▶ item—jQuery object representing the actual object being sorted.

- ▶ offset—{top, left} object for the current offset.

- ▶ originalPosition—{top, left} object for the original position.

- ▶ position—{top, left} object for the current position.

- ▶ sender—Sortable object that the item is being dragged from when dragging from one sortable to another.

For example, the following code connects #list1 to #list2 and then adds a sortreceived event that will add a pulsate effect on both the sender and recipient:

```
$("#list1").sortable({connectWith:"#list2"});
$("#list1").on("sortreceived", function(e, ui){
  ui.sender.effect("pulsate");
  $(this).effect("pulsate "); });
```

TABLE 19.11 Sortable Widget Events

Event	Description
sortactivate	Triggered when a connected list starts sorting.
sortbeforeStop	Triggered when sorting stops, but the placeholder is still available.
sortchange	Triggered when the DOM position changes during sort.
sortout	Triggered when a sorting item leaves the sortable list.
sortover	Triggered when a sorting item enters a sortable list.
sortreceive	Triggered on receiving container when a sortable item is moved from one sortable to another.
sortremove	Triggered on sending container when a sortable item is moved from one sortable to another.
sort	Triggered during sorting.
sortstart	Triggered when sorting starts.
sortstop	Triggered when sorting stops.
sortupdate	Triggered when a DOM position changes at the end of sorting.

Implementing Sortable Elements

In this example, you implement `sortable` on a list and a table. There are two lists that are connected together so you can sort from one list to the other. The purpose of the example is to provide some practical examples of using sortable elements along with handling sort events.

The code for the example is in Listing 19.5. Use the followings steps to create the dynamic web page:

1. In Aptana, add the hour19/hour1905.html, hour19/js/hour1905.js, and hour19/css/hour1905.css files.

2. Add the code shown in Listing 19.5-html and Listing 19.5-css to the HTML and CSS files. Notice on line 13 of Listing 19.5-css that `.ui-sortable-helper` classes are added to style elements while sorting.

3. Open the hour1905.js file and add a `.ready()` function.

4. Add the `images` array with image `name` and `src` locations and the `buildLists()` function shown in lines 1–15 of Listing 19.5-js. The `buildLists()` function uses the array to populate the elements in `#sorter1` and `#sortTable`.

5. Add the following line that makes `#sorter1` sortable and connects it to `#sorter2`:

```
19   $("#sorter1").sortable({cursor:"move", connectWith:"#sorter2"});
```

6. Add the following lines that implement sortable on `#sorter2` and adds the `sortreceive` event handler. The event handler adds a `pulsate` effect on both the sender and receiver when an item is added to `#sorter2` from the other list.

```
20   $("#sorter2").sortable({cursor:"move", connectWith:"#sorter1"});
21   $("#sorter2").on("sortreceive", function(e, ui){
22     ui.sender.effect("pulsate");
23     $(this).effect("pulsate"); });
```

7. Add the following code to implement `sortable` on the `#sortTable` `<tbody>` element. Notice that the sort `axis` is restricted to the `y` direction. Also the `sortupdate` event handler is added that makes the sorting item `pulsate` when it has been moved to a new position.

```
24   $("#sortTable").sortable({axis:"y", cursor:"n-resize" });
25   $("#sortTable").on("sortupdate", function(e, ui){
26     ui.item.effect("pulsate"); });
```

8. Save all three files and then open the HTML document in a web browser, as shown in Figure 19.5. You should be able to drag elements from the `div` on the left to the one in the middle and back. You should also be able to reorder elements in the table.

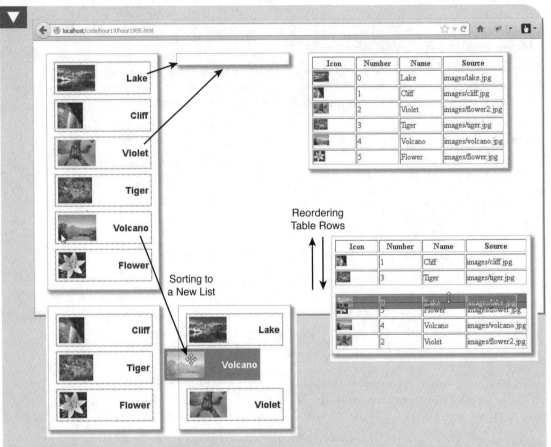

FIGURE 19.5
Applying jQuery UI selecting items in a list using a bounding box.

LISTING 19.5-html   HTML Document That Adds the Web Page

```
01 <!DOCTYPE html>
02 <html>
03   <head>
04     <title>Hour 19-5</title>
05     <meta charset="utf-8" />
06     <script type="text/javascript" src="../js/jquery.min.js"></script>
07     <script type="text/javascript" src="../js/jquery-ui.min.js"></script>
08     <script type="text/javascript" src="js/hour1905.js"></script>
09     <link rel="stylesheet" type="text/css" href="../js/css/jquery-ui.min.css">
10     <link rel="stylesheet" type="text/css" href="css/hour1905.css">
11   </head>
```

```
12    <body>
13      <div id="sorter1"></div>
14      <div id="sorter2"></div>
15      <table border=1>
16        <tbody><tr><th>Icon</th><th>Number</th><th>Name</th><th>Source</th></tr>
        ➥</tbody>
17        <tbody id="sortTable"></tbody>
18      </table>
19    </body>
20  </html>
```

LISTING 19.5-js   jQuery and jQuery UI Implements Sorting

```
01 var images=[{src:"images/lake.jpg",name:"Lake"},{src:"images/cliff.
   ➥jpg",name:"Cliff"},
02   {src:"images/flower2.jpg",name:"Violet"}, {src:"images/tiger.
   ➥jpg",name:"Tiger"},
03   {src:"images/volcano.jpg",name:"Volcano"}, {src:"images/flower.
   ➥jpg",name:"Flower"}];
04 function buildLists(){
05   $.each(images, function(i,item){
06     var img = $("<img></img>").attr("src", item.src);
07     var name = $("<p></p>").html(item.name);
08     $("#sorter1").append($("<div></div>").append(img, name));
09     var tr = $("<tr></tr>");
10     tr.append($("<td></td>").append($("<img></img>").attr("src", item.src)));
11     tr.append($("<td></td>").html(i));
12     tr.append($("<td></td>").html(item.name));
13     tr.append($("<td></td>").html(item.src));
14     $("#sortTable").append(tr);
15   });
16 }
17 $(document).ready(function(){
18   buildLists();
19   $("#sorter1").sortable({cursor:"move", connectWith:"#sorter2"});
20   $("#sorter2").sortable({cursor:"move", connectWith:"#sorter1"});
21   $("#sorter2").on("sortreceive", function(e, ui){
22     ui.sender.effect("pulsate");
23     $(this).effect("pulsate"); });
24   $("#sortTable").sortable({axis:"y", cursor:"n-resize", });
25   $("#sortTable").on("sortupdate", function(e, ui){
26     ui.item.effect("pulsate"); });
27 });
```

LISTING 19.5-css   CSS Code That Styles the Page

```
01 #sorter1, #sorter2, table { display:inline-block;
02   width:200px; padding:10px; vertical-align:top; margin:15px; height:auto;
03   box-shadow: 5px 5px 5px #888888; border:3px ridge white;  }
04 #sorter1 div, #sorter2 div { width:180px; display:inline-block; height:50px;
05   padding:5px; margin:5px; border:1px dotted;vertical-align:middle; }
06 p { float:right; margin:0px; display:inline-block; height:50px;
07   font:bold 18px/50px arial; vertical-align:top; text-align:center; }
08 img { height:50px; }
09 table { width:auto; padding:5px; }
10 tr { background-color:white; }
11 td {min-width:80px; }
12 #sortTable img { height:20px; }
13 .ui-sortable-helper { background-color:blue; color:white; opacity:.5; }
```

Summary

Using interaction widgets, you can easily provide some advanced features to your web pages. In this hour, you created some drag-and-drop elements by making some elements draggable and others droppable using jQuery UI draggable and droppable widgets.

Adding the selectable widget allowed you to draw a bounding box or lasso around multiple items. You used the resizable widget to make a container such as a `<div>` resizable. You also resized the content inside.

Finally, you learned how to implement the sortable widget to sort items in a `<div>` and `<tbody>`. Elements from sortable containers can also be dragged from one container to another.

Q&A

Q. Is it possible to create a custom interaction widget?

A. Yes. Using the jQuery UI `jquery.widget` factory, you can create a custom widget and provide whatever functionality in the prototype that you need.

Q. Is there a way to prevent mouse events from occurring on elements inside an item extended with a jQuery UI widget?

A. Yes. The following code cancels mouse events for items in an element `#myList` that have `class="notSelectable"`:

```
$("#myList").mouse({ cancel:".notSelectable"});
```

Workshop

The workshop consists of a set of questions and answers designed to solidify your understanding of the material covered in this hour. Try to answer the questions before looking at the answers.

Quiz

1. When making an item draggable, what option should you use to keep the original in place while dragging?

2. What droppable event will be triggered when a draggable item is ready to be dropped in it?

3. True or False: It is not possible to keep a fixed ratio when using the resizable widget on an image.

4. Is there a way to limit what items are selected by the selectable widget?

Quiz Answers

1. Set `helper` to `"clone"` or another DOM object.

2. `dropover`

3. False. You can set the `aspectRatio` option to set a fixed ratio.

4. Yes. Use the `filter` option.

Exercises

1. Open the code in Listing 19.3 and add a `resize` handler for the `#resize2` handler. Change the `font-size` attribute based on the width and height the element is resized to.

2. Open the code in Listing 19.5 and modify the `#sortTable` element so that it connects with `#sorter2`. You will need to remove the `axis` restriction and change the `width` of `#sort2` to handle the additional width.

Using jQuery UI Widgets to Add Rich Interactions to Web Pages

---

What You'll Learn in This Hour:

▶ Adding autocomplete, slider, and spinner elements

▶ How to add a `datepicker` calendar to your forms

▶ Ways to stylize dialogs and buttons

▶ Implementing tooltips

▶ Organizing your web pages with custom menus and tabbed panels

▶ How to apply status bars to your work flow

jQuery UI provides a wide array of prebuilt widgets that provide extended functionality to HTML elements. These widgets provide functionality that make forms and other input controls much more intuitive and easy to use, such as a calendar view for choosing dates and expandable menus.

This hour introduces you to each of those built-in widgets to get you started with them. The purpose of this hour is just an introduction so that you understand what widgets are available and how to implement them into your web pages. The examples are pretty basic, so you should also look at the docs at the jQuery UI site for more information about specific widgets that you might like to use: http://api.jqueryui.com/category/widgets/.

No "Try It Yourself" sections are included this hour because the examples are basic and easy to follow. The code for each of the listings and the supporting images can be found at the book's website at code/hour20.

Reviewing Widgets

Before you get started, this section reviews how options and attribute values are accessed on widget elements, because it is a little bit different than on normal jQuery objects.

When you are creating the widget, options are specified in the object passed to the constructor. For example, the following code sets the `min` and `max` options for a slider widget:

```
$("#mySlider").slider({min:2, max:10});
```

To access those options later, you need to specify `"options"` as a parameter to the `.slider()` call. For example, the following sets and then gets the `max` option:

```
var slider = $("#mySlider").slider({min:2, max:10});
slider.slider("option", "max", 100);
var currentMax = slider.slider("option", "max");
```

Attribute values for the widgets are accessed in a similar way. For example, the following code gets and then sets the value of the `value` attribute on a slider:

```
var value = $("#mySlider").slider("value");
$("#mySlider").slider("value", value+5 );
```

In fact, `value` and `options` are methods on the slider widget that get called when passed in as the first argument.

Adding an Expandable Accordion Element

The accordion widget combines pairs of headers and content into an expandable accordion view. The accordion widget is applied to a container element, and all the headers are identified. The `header` will become a tab and the content in between the headers will be attached to a separate `<div>` element that is expandable/collapsible.

The code in Listing 20.1 creates an accordion view with an image as the content in each tab. The visual can be seen in Figure 20.1. The following options are part of the example:

▶ `header`—Specifies a selector to use when determining the header elements.

▶ `collapsible`—Boolean. If `true`, all content in the accordion can be collapsed.

LISTING 20.1   jQuery, CSS, and HTML to Implement the Accordion

```
...jQuery...
11      $(document).ready(function(){
12        $( "#accordion" ).accordion({header:"p", collapsible:true});
...CSS...
16      div { width:200px; }
17      img { width:200px; }
...HTML...
20      <div id="accordion">
21        <p>Jungle</p><div><img src="images/jungle.jpg" /></div>
22        <p>Peak</p><div><img src="images/peak.jpg" /></div>
23        <p>Sunset</p><div><img src="images/sunset3.jpg" /></div>
24        <p>Lake</p><div><img src="images/beachhouse.jpg" /></div>
25      </div>
```

FIGURE 20.1
Simple accordion view.

Implementing Autocomplete in Form Elements

The autocomplete widget gets attached to text input elements. As the user types into the text input, suggestions from a list are displayed. This is especially helpful in circumstances where you have a finite set of possibilities that can be typed in and you want to make sure the correct spelling is used.

The code in Listing 20.2 creates a basic autocomplete input to specify the day of the week. The visual can be seen in Figure 20.2. The set of days to autocomplete are added by setting the `source` attribute to an array of day names in line 14.

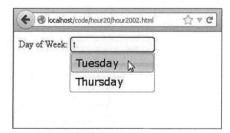

FIGURE 20.2
Autocompleting typing in a day of the week.

LISTING 20.2   jQuery, CSS, and HTML to Implement the Autocomplete Field

```
...jQuery...
13        $( "#autocomplete" ).autocomplete({
14          source: ["Monday", "Tuesday", "Wednesday", "Thursday", "Friday"]
15        });
...CSS...
19      input { border:2px ridge blue; border-radius:5px; padding:3px; }
...HTML...
22      <label for="autocomplete">Day of Week: </label>
23      <input id="autocomplete">
```

Applying jQuery UI Buttons to Form Controls

A great feature of jQuery UI is the work that has been done to stylize buttons. Let's face it, the HTML button styles are outdated and ugly. Using jQueryUI, you can quickly stylize buttons, check boxes, and radio elements.

To stylize a single item, all you need to do is call .button(options) on the jQuery object that represents it. To stylize a set of radios or check boxes, you call .buttonset().

The code in Listing 20.3 illustrates styling HTML elements as jQuery UI buttons. Notice in line 12, the icons option is set to "ui-icon-gear", which is one of the icons included with jQuery UI download. Also, the text option is set to true. If this option is false, only the icon would be displayed. The visual can be seen in Figure 20.3.

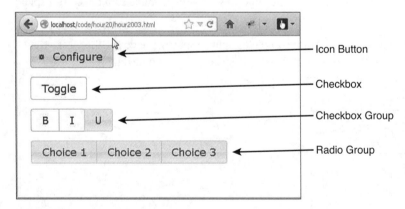

FIGURE 20.3
Styling form elements as jQuery UI buttons.

LISTING 20.3 jQuery, CSS, and HTML to Implement the Autocomplete Field

```
...jQuery...
12        $( "#button1" ).button({icons: {primary: "ui-icon-gear"}, text: true});
13        $( "#check" ).button();
14        $( "#format" ).buttonset();
15        $( "#radio" ).buttonset();
...CSS...
19     div {margin:15px; }
...HTML...
22 <div><button id="button1">Configure</button><br></div>
23 <div><input type="checkbox" id="check" /><label for="check">Toggle</label></div>
24 <div id="format">
25   <input type="checkbox" id="check1" /><label for="check1">B</label>
26   <input type="checkbox" id="check2" /><label for="check2">I</label>
27   <input type="checkbox" id="check3" /><label for="check3">U</label>
28 </div>
29 <div id="radio">
30   <input type="radio" id="radio1" name="radio" /><label for="radio1">Choice 1
     ➥</label>
31   <input type="radio" id="radio2" name="radio" /><label for="radio2">Choice 2
     ➥</label>
32   <input type="radio" id="radio3" name="radio" /><label for="radio3">Choice 3
     ➥</label>
33 </div>
```

Creating a Calendar Input

The datepicker widget provided with jQuery enables you to implement a calendar interface that allows users to select a specific day using a simple click of the mouse. This can save a lot of problems when users input dates incorrectly because they are typing them by hand.

The datepicker widget is attached to a text, date, or datetime <input> element. When the user clicks the <input>, the calendar is displayed. You also add an icon image to launch the datepicker.

The code in Listing 20.4 creates a date with an image icon. The visual can be seen in Figure 20.4. Settings for the following illustrate some of the available options:

▶ onSelect—Specifies a function that will be called each time a new date is selected.

▶ showOn—This is set to "button" so that the datepicker will be launched when the button icon is clicked.

▶ buttonImage—Specifies the location of the image file to use.

▶ buttonImageOnly—When true, the datepicker is launched only when the button icon is clicked and not the <input>.

▶ numberOfMonths—Specifies the number of months to display.

▶ showButtonPanel—When true, the Today and Done buttons are displayed on the bottom of the datepicker.

▶ dateFormat—String that describes the format that will be placed in the <input> field.

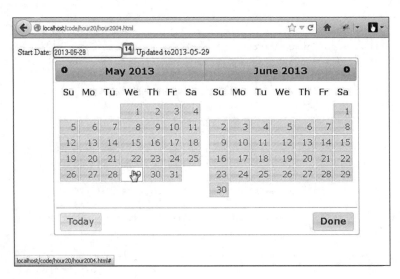

FIGURE 20.4
Adding a datepicker to a date input.

LISTING 20.4 jQuery, CSS, and HTML to Implement the Datepicker Widget

```
...jQuery...
13        $( "#month" ).datepicker({
14            onSelect:dateChanged,
15            showOn: "button", buttonImage: "images/calendar.png", buttonImageOnly:
              ↪true,
16            numberOfMonths:2,
17            showButtonPanel:true,
18            dateFormat: "yy-mm-dd"
19        });
...CSS...
23    input { border:2px ridge blue; border-radius:5px; }
...HTML...
26    <label>Start Date: </label><input type="text" id="month"></input>
27    <span></span>
```

Generating Stylized Dialogs with jQuery UI

The dialog widget is a very useful inclusion to jQuery UI. You can easily get rid of the plain dialogs provided in JavaScript and replace them with dialogs that have styled attributes and even forms.

The code in Listing 20.5 creates a jQuery UI dialog that includes an image, icon, button, and some stylized text. The visual can be seen in Figure 20.5. The following options are part of the example:

▶ modal—Boolean. When `true`, other items on the page are disabled until the dialog returns.

▶ buttons—This is an object where the key is the button name, and the text displayed in the button and the value is the function that will be called when that button is clicked. Notice that in line 13, a button named Sweet closes the dialog.

FIGURE 20.5
Stylized jQuery UI dialog.

LISTING 20.5   jQuery, CSS, and HTML to Implement the Dialog

```
...jQuery...
11    $(document).ready(function(){
12        $( "#dialog" ).dialog({ modal: true,
13            buttons: { Sweet: function() { $( this ).dialog( "close" ); }}});
...CSS...
17    img { height:60px; float:left; }
...HTML...
20    <div id="dialog" title="Upload Successful"><p>
```

```
21          <img src="images/peak.jpg" />
22          <span class="ui-icon ui-icon-circle-check"></span>
23          Image Uploaded Successfully.
24        </p><p>Currently using <b>76% of your storage space</b>.</p>
25      </div>
```

Implementing Stylized Menus

One of the most-often used jQuery UI widgets is the menu widget. The menu widget enables you to turn an element tree into an expanding menu. Typically, menus are created by using cascading sets of `<ul>`/`<li>` elements with an `<a>` element that defines the link behavior and menu text.

TIP

You can customize the element tags that are used to build the element using the `menus` option; for example, `menus:"div.menuItem"`.

The code in Listing 20.6 creates a jQuery UI menu from a set of list items. Notice in the HTML that some of the `<li>` fields include a `<span>` that has `class="ui-icon ui-icon-{type}"`. These items include the jQuery UI icon specified along with the menu text.

The selected item is displayed in the `<p>` element to show how the selection handler works using the `menuselect` event handler defined in line 14. Also, the width of the menu is defined in the CSS code on line 19 by setting the `width` value in the `.ui-menu` class. The visual can be seen in Figure 20.6.

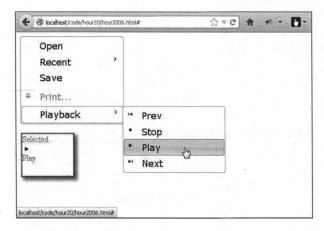

FIGURE 20.6
Stylized jQuery menu.

LISTING 20.6   jQuery, CSS, and HTML to Implement the Menus

```
...jQuery...
12        $( "#menu" ).menu();
13        $( "#menu" ).on("menuselect", function(e, ui){
14          $("p").html("Selected " + ui.item.children("a:first").html());
15        });
...CSS...
19     .ui-menu { width: 200px; }
20     p { box-shadow: 5px 5px 5px #888888; border:3px ridge red; color:red;
21          display:inline-block; height:80px; width:100px; }
...HTML...
24     <ul id="menu">
25       <li><a href="#">Open</a></li>
26       <li><a href="#">Recent</a><ul>
27         <li><a href="#">Some File</a></li>
28         <li><a href="#">Another File</a></li>
29         </ul></li>
30       <li><a href="#">Save</a></li>
31       <li class="ui-state-disabled"><a href="#"><span class="ui-icon
      ➥ui-icon-print">
32         </span>Print...</a></li>
33       <li><a href="#">Playback</a><ul>
34         <li><a href="#"><span class="ui-icon ui-icon-seek-start"></span>Prev
      ➥</a></li>
35         <li><a href="#"><span class="ui-icon ui-icon-stop"></span>Stop</a></li>
36         <li><a href="#"><span class="ui-icon ui-icon-play"></span>Play</a></li>
37         <li><a href="#"><span class="ui-icon ui-icon-seek-end"></span>Next</a>
      ➥</li>
38         </ul></li>
39     </ul>
40     <p></p>
```

Creating Progress Bars

The progress bar widget allows you to create some very simple-to-implement progress bars. The progress bar is controlled by changing the value property that ranges from 0 to 100. The progress is represented by an element with a class .ui-progressbar-value.

The code in Listing 20.7 provides an example of implementing a progress bar. The bar is updated in the inc() function, which illustrates getting and setting the value of the progress bar. setTimeout() is used for time delay. The visual can be seen in Figure 20.7.

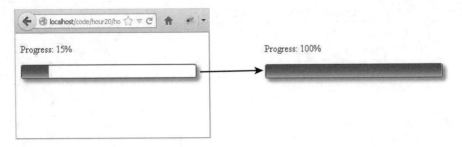

FIGURE 20.7
Progress bar being updated by `setTimeout()`.

LISTING 20.7   jQuery, CSS, and HTML to Implement the Progress Bar

```
...jQuery...
11    function inc(){
12       var value = $("#progressbar").progressbar("value") + 5;
13       if (value <= 100){
14          $("p").html("Progress: " + value + "%");
15          $("#progressbar").progressbar("value", value);
16          setTimeout(inc, 100);
17       }
18    }
19    $(document).ready(function(){
20       $("#progressbar").progressbar({ value: 0});
21       inc();
22    });
...CSS...
25    #progressbar { box-shadow: 5px 5px 5px #888888; border:2px ridge;
26         display:inline-block; height:20px; width:300px; }
27    #progressbar .ui-progressbar-value{
28       background-image: -moz-linear-gradient(center top , #0000FF, #88BBFF); }
...HTML...
31    <p></p>
32    <div id="progressbar"></div>
```

Implementing Slider Bars

The slider widget allows you to create slider controls that adjust a value by dragging the mouse. The slider has two components: the slide and the handle. The slide is styled by the `.ui-slider-range` class, and the handle is styled by the `.ui-slider-handle` class.

TIP

You can define both a min and max handle that allows you to use a single slider control to define a range instead of a single value.

The code in Listing 20.8 provides an example of implementing a set of sliders that are used to adjust the background color of another element. The slider is applied to the `<div>` elements in lines 22–29 and sets the following options:

- `orientation`—Can be set to `"horizontal"` or `"vertical"`.

- `range`—Can be set to `true`, `"min"`, or `"max"`. Used to define the range. `"min"` goes from the slider min to a handler, and `"max"` goes from the slider max to a handle.

- `max`—Specifies the maximum value.

- `value`—Specifies the current value.

- `slide`—Event handler to call when the slide moves.

- `change`—Event handler to call when the slide value changes.

Also pay attention to the class settings in lines 38–43 of the CSS. Those alter the appearance of the slider and handler. The visual can be seen in Figure 20.8.

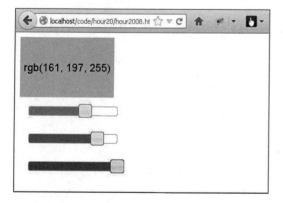

FIGURE 20.8
Sliders used to choose a color based on the RGB value.

LISTING 20.8 jQuery, CSS, and HTML to Implement the Sliders

```
...jQuery...
11      function cValue(selector){
12          var v = $(selector).slider("value").toString( 16 );
```

```
13        if (v.length ===1) { v = "0" + v;}
14       return v;
15     }
16    function refreshSwatch() {
17      $("#mix").css("background-color", "#" + cValue("#red") +
18        cValue("#green") +  cValue("#blue"));
19      $("#mix").html($("#mix").css("background-color"));
20    }
21   $(document).ready(function(){
22      $( "#red, #green, #blue" ).slider({
23        orientation: "horizontal",
24        range: "min",
25        max: 255,
26        value: 127,
27        slide: refreshSwatch,
28        change: refreshSwatch
29      });
30      $("#red").slider("value", 128);
31      $("#green").slider("value", 128);
32      $("#blue").slider("value", 128);
33   });
...CSS...
36   #mix { width:160px; height:100px; text-align:center; font:18px/100px arial;
}
37   #red, #green, #blue { float: left; clear: left; width: 150px; margin: 15px;
     ➥}
38   #red .ui-slider-range { background:red; }
39   #red .ui-slider-handle { border-color:red; }
40   #green .ui-slider-range { background:green; }
41   #green .ui-slider-handle { border-color:green; }
42   #blue .ui-slider-range { background:blue; }
43   #blue .ui-slider-handle { border-color:blue; }
...HTML...
46   <div id="mix"></div>
47   <div id="red"></div>
48   <div id="green"></div>
49   <div id="blue"></div>
```

Adding a Value Spinner Element

The spinner widget allows you to create a value input that has up and down arrows that enable you to increment/decrement the value with the mouse instead of typing in numbers.

The code in Listing 20.9 provides an example of implementing a basic spinner input and two currency spinner inputs. The spinners are defined with the following options. The visual can be seen in Figure 20.9.

- ▶ step—Specifies the step value to apply when incrementing or decrementing the spinner.

- ▶ culture—Specifies Globalize culture to use for the value; for example, en-US, eu-ES.

- ▶ numberFormat—Specifies the Globalize format for the number; for example, "n" is for decimal #.##, "C" for currency.

This example uses the Globalize jQuery plug-in to add additional cultures. For more information about the Globalize jQuery plug-in, go to https://github.com/jquery/globalize

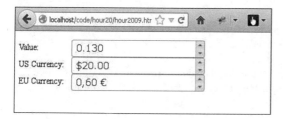

FIGURE 20.9
Simple decimal spinner input.

LISTING 20.9   jQuery, CSS, and HTML to Implement the Spinner

```
...jQuery...
14      $( "#spin1" ).spinner({step: 0.005, numberFormat: "n3"});
15      $( "#spin2" ).spinner({step: 5, numberFormat: "C", culture:"en"});
16      $( "#spin3" ).spinner({step: .1, numberFormat: "C", culture:"eu-ES"});
...CSS...
20      label { display:inline-block; width:100px; }
...HTML...
23      <label for="spin1">Value:</label><input id="spin1" name="value" /><br>
24      <label for="spin2">US Currency:</label><input id="spin2" name="value" /><br>
25      <label for="spin3">EU Currency:</label><input id="spin3" name="value" /><br>
```

Creating Tabbed Panels

The tabs widget allows you to create a series of tabbed panels. This provides the capability to easily break chunks of content up and yet have it easily accessible. Each tab represents a panel that contains content that can be revealed by activating the tab.

Tabs are a list of elements containing an <a>. The tabs widget links the tab with content using the href value of an <a> element. Tabs can be activated by clicking them, or you can set options to have the tabs enabled on mouseover or some other event.

The code in Listing 20.10 provides an example of three tabs: one with image content, one with text, and another with a list. The tabs are defined with the following options. The visual can be seen in Figure 20.10.

► `event`—Specifies what event on the tab element will cause the tab to become active; for example, `click` or `mouseover`.

► `collapsible`—Boolean. Specifies whether the active tab can be collapsed by clicking on it or by setting `active` to `false`.

► `active`—When set to `false`, the active tab is collapsed. Requires `collapsible` to be true.

NOTE

In the example, the tabs link to locations on the page using ID values. You can also specify links external to the web page or even retrieve data from the server via AJAX to populate the panel content.

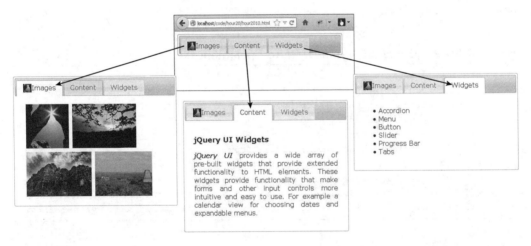

FIGURE 20.10
Three tabs with different content.

LISTING 20.10   jQuery, CSS, and HTML to Implement the Tabbed Panel

```
...jQuery...
12      $( "#tabs" ).tabs({event: "mouseover", collapsible: true, active:"false"});
...CSS...
16      * { vertical-align:top; }
```

```
17      img { height:120px; margin:5px; }
18      .mini {height:23px; margin:0px; }
19      #tabs { width:450px; }
20      p { text-align:justify; }
...HTML...
23   <div id="tabs">
24    <ul><li><a href="#tabs1"><img class="mini" src="images/sunstar.jpg"/>Images</
a></li>
25        <li><a href="#tabs2">Content</a></li><li><a href="#tabs3">Widgets</a>
         ➥</li></ul>
26    <div id="tabs1">
27        <img src="images/sunstar.jpg" /><img src="images/sunset3.jpg" />
28        <img src="images/peak.jpg" /><img src="images/jungle.jpg" />
29    </div>
30    <div id="tabs2">
31        <h3>jQuery UI Widgets</h3>
32        <p><b><i>jQuery UI</i></b> provides a wide array of prebuilt widgets that
33            provide extended functionality to HTML elements. These widgets provide
34            functionality that make forms and other input controls more intuitive
35            and easy to use. For example a calendar view for choosing dates and
36            expandable menus.</p>
37    </div>
38    <div id="tabs3">
39        <ul><li>Accordion</li><li>Menu</li><li>Button</li><li>Slider</li>
40          <li>Progress Bar</li><li>Tabs</li></ul>
41    </div>
42  </div>
```

Adding Tooltips to Page Elements

The tooltips widget allows you to easily add tooltips to form input, images, and just about any other page element. To implement tooltips, apply .tooltip(options) to the document or other container. Inside the options, specify the items that should include tooltips and then the tooltip content handler.

As the mouse hovers over an item supported by the tooltip, the tooltip message is displayed. The code in Listing 20.11 provides an example of implementing tooltips on <input> and <img> elements. The visual can be seen in Figure 20.11.

▶ items—Specifies the selector used to determine whether the page element supports tooltips.

▶ content—Tooltip handler function called when a supported element is hovered over. The function should return the content to be displayed. Notice that for the image, a mini version is displayed in the tooltip.

▶ position—Specifies the position to place the tooltip; for example:

```
position: {my: "left top+15", at: "left bottom", collision: "flipfit" }
```

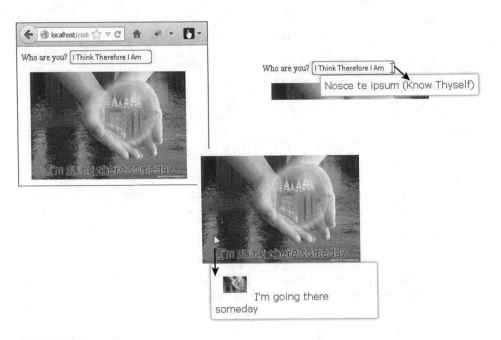

FIGURE 20.11
Tooltips are displayed when page elements are hovered over.

LISTING 20.11   **jQuery, CSS, and HTML to Implement the Tabbed Panel**

```
...jQuery...
11    $(document).ready(function(){
12      $(document).tooltip({
13        items: "img, input",
14        position: {my: "left+15 top", at: "left bottom", collision: "flipfit" },
15        content: function() {
16          var obj = $(this);
17          if (obj.is("input")) { return obj.attr( "title" ); }
18          if (obj.is("img")) {
19            var img = $("<img></img>").addClass("mini").attr("src",
                  ➥obj.attr("src"));
20            var span = $("<span></span>").html(obj.attr( "alt" ));
21            return $("<div></div>").append(img, span); }
22        }});
23    });
```

```
...CSS...
26     input { border:2px ridge blue; border-radius:5px; padding:3px; }
27     img { height:200px; margin:15px; }
28     .mini {height:30px;}
...HTML...
31     <label for="size">Who are you? </label>
32     <input id="size" title="Nosce te ipsum (Know Thyself)" /><br>
33     <img src="../images/someday.jpg" alt="I'm going there someday"/>
```

Creating Custom Widgets

Creating custom widgets is a fairly simple process. The $.widget() factory needs a name and then the prototype object shown next. The widget factory will handle setting everything up so that the widget can be applied to page elements.

The code in Listing 20.12 shows a basic outline for a custom widget. To create the widget, follow these steps:

1. Replace "custom.mywidget" with your own name.

2. Add the options with default values.

3. Add any additional code in _create(), _refresh(), _destroy(), _setOptions(), and _setOption().

4. Add additional attributes or methods to the prototype object to implement the widget.

LISTING 20.12 jQuery Code Outline to Implement a Custom Widget

```
01 $.widget("custom.mywidget", {
02   options : {
03     // custom options
04   },
05   _create: function() {
06     //creation code
07   },
08   _refresh: function() {
09     //refress code called when element refreshed
10   },
11   _destroy: function() {
12     //cleanup code called when widget is destroyed
13   },
14   _setOptions: function() {
15     // _super and _superApply handle keeping the right this-context
16     this._superApply( arguments );
17     this._refresh();
```

```
18    },
19    _setOption: function( key, value ) {
20      // set individual option value override code
21      this._super( key, value );
22    }
23 });
```

Summary

jQuery UI includes a large set of built-in widgets that provide some much-desired functionality and styling left out of conventional HTML elements. In this hour, you saw the widgets and how to implement them on pages, including autocomplete elements, buttons, datepicker, dialog, menu, progress bar, sliders, spinners, tabs, and tooltips.

Q&A

Q. What is the Globalize plug-in and why would I want to use it?

A. The Globalize plug-in is a project that simplifies the process of internationalizing your web pages to match currency, time, and other value formatting that varies from locale to locale. If you plan to have a website with elements that need localization, it is a good idea to at least check it out.

Workshop

The workshop consists of a set of questions and answers designed to solidify your understanding of the material covered in this hour. Try to answer the questions before looking at the answers.

Quiz

1. How do you get the value of a slider from the element #mySlider?

2. True or False: Datepicker widgets must be attached to an `<input>` element.

3. How do you attach an event handler to a button, a check box, or a radio stylized by jQuery UI?

4. How do you populate the possible values for an autocomplete element?

Quiz Answers

1. `$("#mySlider").slider("value");`

2. False.

3. The normal way you would with jQuery or JavaScript.

4. Set the value of the source option to a JavaScript array of values.

Exercises

1. Open the code in Listing 20.5 and add an Input element to the dialog box. Then add a second button that gets that value and displays it on the web page somewhere.

2. Open the code in Listing 20.10 and add a new tab called Sliders. Then have it link to the hour2009.html file that contains the sliders example.

HOUR 21
Introducing Mobile Website Development

What You'll Learn in This Hour:

▶ Why mobile web development is so important

▶ How jQuery Mobile can help build mobile-friendly web pages

▶ Using jQuery Mobile ThemeRoller to create a custom look and feel

▶ Implementing jQuery Mobile in your web pages

Mobile devices are the fastest growing development platform. Much of that development is geared toward making websites mobile friendly. It is much easier to implement and maintain a mobile website than it is to maintain a mobile application.

In this hour, you jump in to learn how jQuery—and especially the jQuery Mobile library—can help you create some clean, cool mobile web pages.

Jumping into the Mobile World

Before you get started creating mobile web pages with jQuery Mobile, the next section points out a few things about the mobile world we live in. It has changed rapidly, and the changes appear to be accelerating.

Is Mobile Still Mobile?

There used to be a very distinguishable line between mobile devices and computers/laptops. That is no longer the case, and here are the reasons why:

▶ Mobile device network speeds are very close to traditional PCs.

▶ Many mobile screen sizes are much larger than they used to be, especially in tablets.

▶ Mobile processors, disk IO, and available memory is no longer such a limiting factor.

▶ There are more smart mobile devices in use than PCs.

Those factors have gotten rid of a lot of the old problems and requirements for mobile solutions. However, they have created a few new ones:

▶ Mobile screen sizes vary wildly. You can't just define a small mobile version of your website.

▶ People are using mobile devices for many tasks, and they now expect the same level of features and performance as traditional apps and web pages. At the same time, they want the interfaces to their mobile tools to be clean and uncluttered.

▶ With the wild popularity of social tools such as Twitter and Facebook, users expect their social world to follow along with them into as many places as possible.

▶ People would often rather have mobile sites than mobile apps so that their links, profile information, and user experience remains consistent.

Based on those new problems, jQuery Mobile could become your new best friend in the upcoming shifts.

Size Matters

In today's mobile world, the fact that a user is on a mobile device is no longer the critical question. The new critical questions are first, how much screen space do users have to work with? And second, how much network bandwidth does their device connection support?

You can use the following JavaScript and `regex` statement to parse the `navigator.userAgent` value to determine whether a user is coming into your website on a mobile device:

```
if( /Android|webOS|iPhone|iPad|iPod|BlackBerry/i.test(navigator.userAgent) ) { }
```

That information is useful, but you also need to check the screen size of the device. Does it have a 3-inch, 4-inch, or 11-inch screen? There is a big difference. If you design your website for a 3- or 4-inch screen, but the user comes in on an 11-inch screen, it is awkward and frustrating. The same is true in reverse. A good idea is to get the screen size using `screen.height` and `screen.width` in JavaScript and then adjust your pages dynamically to support that size. For example:

```
$("#contentBody").width(screen.width).height(screen.height);
```

The network bandwidth is important because it may limit the amount of data you want to send. This is another situation where you can't err on the side of caution. If you send low-resolution images to a device where the user expects high resolution, your website looks lousy. If you send high-res images to slow devices, your website is too slow. If you are working with large data sizes, it is a good idea to time some of the AJAX requests to the server and back to determine how fast the user's device is.

Why jQuery Mobile?

Why would you want to learn jQuery Mobile? jQuery Mobile provides several advantages with developing mobile solutions, including the following:

▶ Hiding some of the complexities of resizing page elements to a wide array of mobile devices.

▶ Providing simple UI components with mobile event interactions already built in to them.

▶ JavaScript and jQuery are common and well-developed languages that are based on proven concepts.

▶ Developing a mobile web app, especially with jQuery Mobile, is so simple to do and does not require any installation on the user's part. That is why they are becoming more and more popular.

Getting Started with jQuery Mobile

How do you get started with jQuery Mobile? You download the library, put in your website path, and start using it. The following sections take you through the process of getting and implementing the jQuery Mobile library.

Adding the jQuery Mobile Library

To get started with jQuery Mobile, you will need to download the library and add it to your web pages. The jQuery library can be downloaded from the following location by selecting the version and options that you would like to include, and clicking the Download button at the bottom. This downloads zip files containing the jQuery Mobile library.
http://jquerymobile.com/download/

CAUTION

The .css files and the images folder that are included with the jQuery Mobile library come as a set. You need to make sure that they are installed in the same location and that you don't mix and match them from different custom downloads.

When you download the jQuery Mobile library, you will get a zip. Inside the zip file are three main components that you need to put where they can be loaded by your mobile web pages. They are as follows:

- **js files**—There will be a jquery.moble.###.js as well as a minified version. This is the main library file, and one of these needs to be placed in a location where you can add it to your project files in a `<script>` tag.

- **css files**—There will be jquery.mobile.###.css, jquery.mobile.###.structure.css, and jquery.mobile.###.theme.css files, as well as their minified forms. This is all the styling code and should be placed in the same location as the jquery.moble.###.js file.

- **images folder**—This folder contains the images and icons used by jQuery Mobile to style the elements. This should also be placed in the same location as the jquery.moble.###.js file.

After the library is downloaded, you can add it to your web pages in the header file by adding the `<script>` tag to load the JS file and a `<link>` tag to load the CSS file. For example, the following code loads the jQuery library first because it is required by jQuery Mobile and then loads the jQuery Mobile JS and CSS files:

```
<script type="text/javascript" src="../js/jquery.min.js"></script>
<script type="text/javascript" src="../js/jquery.mobile-custom.min.js"></script>
<link rel="stylesheet" href="../js/css/jquery.mobile-custom.min.css" />
```

Using ThemeRoller

In addition to the basic jQuery Mobile theme, you can also use the jQuery Mobile ThemeRoller shown in Figure 21.1 to create custom themes. You can specify the font family, colors, corner radius, and so on. When you set the `data-theme` attribute, the custom theme will be applied to the jQuery Mobile elements.

To access the jQuery Mobile ThemeRoller, follow these steps:

1. Open the following URL in your browser:

   http://jquerymobile.com/themeroller/

2. From the Global tab, shown in Figure 21.1, you can set the global values.

3. Select the theme letters to customize the alternative theme swatches.

4. When you are finished, click the Download Theme Zip File button. This takes you back to the main download page.

5. Click the Download button to download the customized jQuery Mobile files.

FIGURE 21.1
jQuery Mobile ThemeRoller page.

Understanding jQuery Mobile

Now that you are able to get the library downloaded and in place, you need to know a few things about the jQuery Mobile syntax and structure. Two of the main additions that you will see in jQuery Mobile are the `data` attributes and new mobile events.

Introducing jQuery Mobile Data Attributes

Much of the jQuery Mobile framework is built on extending the current HTML elements with additional functionality. The advantage of this aspect is that you keep the HTML conceptual knowledge that you already have and build on it.

The way the jQuery Mobile builds on the HTML framework is by adding `data` attributes to the HTML elements. The `data` attributes all begin with `data-` and end with some slightly descriptive word of what the attribute means. As those attributes are processed by the jQuery Mobile library, additional methods, events, styles, and values that fit the mobile needs are attached to the element. You will see this extensively in the examples to come.

Table 21.1 lists many of the attributes along with some of the values that they support. The table is a good way to visualize how the `data` attribute method works and can act as a reference.

TABLE 21.1 A Few of the Data Attributes Added in jQuery Mobile

Event	Description
data-role	This is used to define the role the HTML plays in the mobile page—for example, a dialog box, button, panel, and the like.
data-mini	Each UI element has a compact version that is used if this is set to true.
data-theme	Specifies the letter (a–z) that is used when rendering the UI component.
data-transition	Specifies a transition effect to use when transitioning from one page/state to another—for example, slide or pop.
data-direction	Specifies the direction of the animation so that it can match the transition—for example, reverse for page back.
data-rel	Defines the relationship that the element has to a link. Values include back, dialog, external, and popup.
data-title	Text displayed when page is shown.
data-icon	Specifies an icon to attach to an HTML element; possible values are home, delete, plus, arrow-u, arrow-d, check, gear, grid, star, custom, arrow-r, arrow-l, minus, refresh, forward, back, alert, info, search.
data-iconpos	Specifies the icon position when attached to an element: left, right, top, bottom, notext.
data-add-back-btn	For items with data-role="dialog", if true, a Back button will be added.
data-collapsed	For items with role="collapsible", specifies if the state is collapsed.
data-collapsed-icon	Defines the collapsed icon for role="collapsible" elements.
data-expanded-icon	Defines the expanded icon for role="collapsible" elements.
data-close-btn	For items with role="dialog", if true, a Close button will be added.

Understanding Swatches

The CSS files that come with jQuery Mobile include several versions of styling called *swatches*. A swatch is just a letter assignment that specifies what color scheme to use when rendering the mobile elements. Swatches are typically specified using the data-theme attribute. For example:

```
<div data-role="header" data-theme="b"><h1>Teach</h1></div>
```

Looking at New Mobile Events

One of my favorite features of jQuery Mobile is how easy it is to implement mobile events. The library automatically creates the events and adds them to elements based on the data attributes. If you want to add or remove a specific mobile event, you can do so using the `.on()` method from jQuery that you are already familiar with.

For example, to add a tap handler to an element `#myImage`, you would use the following:

```
$("#myImage").on("tap", function() { });
```

Table 21.2 lists some of the mobile events and describes their purpose.

TABLE 21.2   **New Events Added by jQuery Mobile**

Event	Description
tap	Triggered on a quick touch.
taphold	Triggered after the touch is held for more than a threshold. Default is 750ms.
swipe	Triggered by a quick horizontal drag.
swipeleft	Triggered by a quick horizontal drag to the left.
swiperight	Triggered by a quick horizontal drag to the right.
orientationchange	Triggered when the device orientation changes from portrait to landscape, or vice versa.
scrollstart	Triggered when scrolling starts.
scrollstop	Triggered when scrolling stops.
pagebeforeload	Triggered right before a mobile page is loaded into the DOM.
pageload	Triggered after a mobile a page is loaded into the DOM.
pagebeforechange	Triggered right before a mobile page is changed to a different page. The two pages may be in the same HTML document.
pagechange	Triggered after a mobile page is changed to a different page.
pagebeforeshow	Triggered right before a page transition occurs. The event is triggered on the new page.
pageshow	Triggered after a page transition has occurred.

NOTE

jQuery Mobile also includes several virtual mouse events that mask the mouse and touch events to allow developers to register just the basic mouse events. These work well for the most part, but there are still a few quirks with them. The virtual events are `vmouseover`, `vmouseout`, `vmousedown`, `vmousemove`, `vmouseup`, `vmouseclick`, and `vmousecancel`.

Defining the Viewport Meta Tag

A critical component of using jQuery Mobile is adding the viewport settings in a `<meta>` tag inside the page `<head>` tag. The viewport defines how the browser displays the page zoom level as well as the dimensions used.

Specifically, you need to set the `content="width=device-width, initial-scale=1"` as shown next. These settings force the device's browser to render the web page width at exactly the number of pixels available on the device.

```
<meta name="viewport" content="width=device-width, initial-scale=1">
```

Without specifying the viewport setting, the mobile page is at a much higher size than the screen width, making the page look very small. The user will still be able to zoom in on the web page.

Configuring jQuery Mobile Default Settings

jQuery Mobile is initialized when the library is loaded. Any page elements with jQuery Mobile tags will be initialized as well and use the default settings to create mobile versions of the elements.

Occasionally, you might want to override the default settings. To do this, you will need to add a `mobileinit` event handler to the document object before loading the jQuery mobile library, and then add your default override code in that handler function.

Use the `mobileinit` handler to change the default theme swatches because that can't be done on-the-fly after the library has been loaded. The following code shows an example of setting the default header and footer themes:

```
<script type="text/javascript" src="../js/jquery.min.js"></script>
<script>
  $(document).bind( "mobileinit", function () {
    $.mobile.page.prototype.options.headerTheme = "b";
    $.mobile.page.prototype.options.footerTheme = "b";
  });
</script>
<script type="text/javascript" src="../js/jquery.mobile-custom.min.js"></script>
```

Notice that the init `<script>` is placed after jQuery is loaded, but before jQuery Mobile is loaded.

▼ TRY IT YOURSELF

Building Your First jQuery Mobile Web Page

In this section, you follow the steps to get set up using jQuery Mobile in the Aptana environment set up for this book. You create a basic mobile web page and display on a mobile device, if you have one.

Use the following steps to download the jQuery Mobile library and add it to the project you are using for this book:

1. Find out the IP address of your PC. To connect with a mobile device, you need an external address.

2. Open the Apache configuration file in XAMPP and uncomment the following two lines and comment the third. This opens up Apache to support external connections on the IP address from step 1. You will also need to restart Apache.

```
Listen 0.0.0.0:80
Listen [::]:80
#Listen 80
```

3. In Aptana, create the hour21 folder and then add the hour21/hour2101.html file.

4. Copy the code/js folder from the book's website to the js/ folder in your Aptana project if you have not already done so. You can also download the latest version of the jQuery Mobile library and install it as described earlier in this hour. However, if you install your own, you need to make sure that the `<script>` and `<link>` tags that load the jQuery Mobile files are updated for the examples in the book.

5. Add the code shown in Listing 21.1. This is straightforward code to validate that the jQuery Mobile library is installed properly. The `<div>` elements build a mobile web page with a header, content, and a footer.

6. Notice that the function `checkForMobile()` will apply additional classes around the `#border` and `#frame` `<div>` elements. These elements are extras added to display a phone background image when the page is not viewed from mobile device. That helps you visualize what the page will look like on a mobile device when testing from a development browser.

```
11      function checkForMobile (){
12          if(!/Android|webOS|iPhone|iPad|iPod|BlackBerry/i.test
          ➡(navigator.userAgent)){
13            $("#border").addClass("border");}
14      }
```

7. Make sure that the locations specified in lines 8 and 9 for the jQuery Mobile library and the CSS file are correct for what you have installed:

```
08      <script type="text/javascript" src="../js/jquery.mobile-custom.min.js">
        ➡</script>
09      <link rel="stylesheet" href="../js/css/jquery.mobile-custom.min.css" />
```

8. Save all the files, and then open the HTML document in a web browser, as shown in Figure 21.2. You should see a basic web page inside the phone image with header and footer. Then try to open the page using your mobile device's web browser and the address from step 1. You should see the header, content, and footer, but not the phone image.

FIGURE 21.2
Simple jQuery Mobile web page.

LISTING 21.1   **HTML Document That Adds the jQuery Mobile Libraries and a Basic Mobile Web**

```
01  <!DOCTYPE html>
02  <html>
03    <head>
04      <title>Hour 21-1</title>
05      <meta charset="utf-8" />
06      <meta name="viewport" content="width=device-width, initial-scale=1">
07      <script type="text/javascript" src="../js/jquery.min.js"></script>
08      <script type="text/javascript" src="../js/jquery.mobile-custom.min.js">
        ➥</script>
09      <link rel="stylesheet" href="../js/css/jquery.mobile-custom.min.css" />
10      <script>
11        function checkForMobile (){
```

```
12          if(!/Android|webOS|iPhone|iPad|iPod|BlackBerry/i.test
        ➥(navigator.userAgent)){
13            $("#border").addClass("border");
14            $("#frame").addClass("frame");}
15          }
16        $(document).ready(function() {
17          checkForMobile();
18        });
19      </script>
20      <style>
21        .border { background-image:url("images/phone.png"); height:700px;
        ➥width:350px;}
22        .frame { height:475px; width:267px; margin-top:112px; margin-left:40px;
23          position:absolute; overflow:hidden; }
24        p { text-align:center; font:italic 45px Helvetica; color:blue; margin:5px;
        ➥}
25      </style>
26    </head>
27    <body>
28      <div id="border"><div id="frame">
29        <div data-role="page">
30          <div data-role="header"><h1>Teach</h1></div>
31          <div data-role="content">
32            <p>jQuery</p><p>and</p><p>JavaScript</p><p>In</p><p>24</p><p>Hours</p>
33          </div>
34          <div data-role="footer"><h4>Yourself</h4></div>
35        </div>
36      </div></div>
37    </body>
38 </html>
```

Summary

In this hour, you were introduced to the world of mobile web development. You learned how jQuery Mobile can help in building web pages that are mobile friendly and yet very powerful. You also downloaded, installed, and used the jQuery Mobile library in a basic mobile web page.

Q&A

Q. Is there a way to build native mobile apps using jQuery?

A. Yes, using PhoneGap. The PhoneGap platform allows you to build native phone apps using HTML5, CSS jQuery, and JavaScript. PhoneGap packages the web pages to run as a native application within the UIwebView or WebView on mobile devices.

Workshop

The workshop consists of a set of questions and answers designed to solidify your understanding of the material covered in this hour. Try to answer the questions before looking at the answers.

Quiz

1. How does jQuery Mobile extend HTML to provide mobile versions of the HTML elements?

2. What is the purpose of the viewport `<meta>` tag?

3. What mobile event is triggered when the user slides a finger horizontally across the touch screen on a mobile device?

Quiz Answers

1. Using additional `data` attributes.

2. To set the initial size and zoom of the mobile web page to match the screen size of the device.

3. `swipe`, `swipeleft`, or `swiperight`.

Exercise

1. Try using the jQuery Mobile ThemeRoller to create a custom theme and install it in your project.

Implementing Mobile Web Pages

What You'll Learn in This Hour:

- ▶ Basic structure of mobile pages
- ▶ How to link multiple mobile pages together
- ▶ How to load additional mobile pages
- ▶ Using navbars to navigate mobile sites
- ▶ Implementing dialogs in mobile pages

A good mobile website will act more like a mobile application than a traditional website. To implement a website as a mobile app style, you need to think about things a bit differently. You don't want a lot of controls, tables, or content all on the same page because mobile devices, even tablets, don't have the screen area.

To build a good mobile website, you need to break up the content of the major pages into sections that compose "mobile" pages with mobile formatted content. Then you can apply simple transitions from one section to another using swipes, buttons, toolbars, and menus.

The following sections discuss creating web pages, linking them together, and then using jQuery navigational controls and events to transition between them.

Building Mobile Pages

Creating mobile pages is very simple. Pages consist of `<div>` elements that are enhanced in jQuery Mobile using the data tags discussed in the previous hour. This section focuses on using the data tags to define mobile web pages.

Understanding Page Anatomy

Mobile pages are composed of three main parts: the header, the footer, and content in between. All three are not necessarily required; however, it is a good idea to at least have a header with the content, especially when working with multiple pages.

All these elements are defined by adding `data-role` attributes to `<div>` elements. The content inside the `<div>` elements can be just about anything—text, images, forms, lists, and so on. The following shows the basic code for defining a mobile page with all three elements:

```
<div data-role="page">
  <div data-role="header"><h1>Header</h1></div>
  <div data-role="content" id="content">
    <p>Images</p>
    <img src="../images/flower.jpg" />
  </div>
  <div data-role="footer"><h4>Footer</h4></div>
</div>
```

Notice that each of the components has a distinct value for `data-role`. Figure 22.1 shows the resulting mobile web page.

FIGURE 22.1
Basic mobile web page with a header, a footer, and a comment with text and images.

Everything else in mobile applications is based on these basic components. As you will see going forward, you can add buttons and toolbars to the header and footer and a wide array of elements to the content, but all mobile web pages start with these three components.

Creating Fixed Headers and Footers

Notice that in Figure 22.1, the footer is not at the bottom of the screen on the device. That is because it is flowing with the content. Both the header and the footer flow with the content, meaning if you scroll the content up or down, the header scrolls with the content, as shown in Figure 22.2.

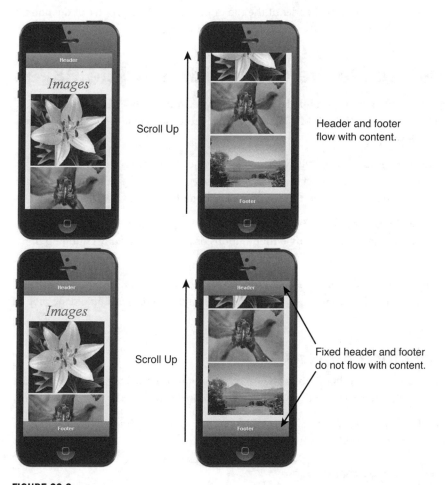

FIGURE 22.2
Setting the `data-position="fixed"` will make the header and footer stick to the device screen instead of scrolling with the content.

Flowing headers and footers are often a desired result; however, there are also many times that you want one or both to stay in a fixed position on the device screen so that it is always displayed. jQuery Mobile makes that adjustment very simple to make.

To make the header or footer—or a toolbar, for that matter—fixed, you add the `data-position="fixed"` attribute to the `<div>`. For example:

```
<div data-role="header" data-position="fixed"><h1>Header</h1></div>
...
<div data-role="footer" data-position="fixed"><h4>Footer</h4></div>
```

This will make them stay in place: the header at the top of the page and the footer at the bottom, regardless of how the content scrolls. This is illustrated in Figure 22.2.

Implementing Mobile Sites with Multiple Pages

Mobile sites are composed of either a single HTML document with multiple `<div data-role="page">` elements or multiple HTML documents with those elements. Each `<div>` element represents a single mobile page.

When using multiple pages in your mobile website, you need to implement code and UI controls to provide ways for the user to transition from one mobile page to another. The transitions should be smooth and intuitive based on the controls and content interaction.

Changing mobile pages is accomplished by linking to the second page from the first. This can be done using one of two methods: adding navigation buttons or programmatically changing the page in your jQuery code.

The pages can come from `<div>` elements in the same web page or external URLs downloaded to the device. The following sections describe the methods of implementing multiple page mobile sites.

Adding Navigation Buttons

Navigation buttons are links to other mobile pages. Typically, this is done in the header or footer element for easy visibility. However, you can also place them inside the mobile content.

The sole purpose of the navigation buttons is to allow the user to move from one mobile page to the next, so it is important to implement them with that in mind.

Creating Navigation Buttons

Navigation buttons are created by adding the `data-role="button"` attribute to an `<a>` link. The `href` attribute should point to the hash tag or URL of the mobile page you want to switch to. An example of the navigation buttons is shown in Figures 22.3 and 22.4. The following code shows the syntax for defining an `<a>` tag as a navigation link:

```
<a href="#page2" data-role="button">Next</a>
<a href="hour2201-page3.html" data-role="button">Next</a>
```

Positioning Navigation Buttons

You can position the button on the left or right side of the header or footer, adding the `.ui-btn-right` or `.ui-btn-left` class to the `<a>`.

The following code shows some examples of the navigation button links:

```
<a href="#page2" data-role="button" class="ui-btn-right">Next</a>
<a href="hour2201-page3.html" data-role="button" class="ui-btn-left">Next</a>
```

Creating a Back Button

Another useful feature included in jQuery Mobile is the capability to define a navigation button as a back button. A back button uses the browser history to navigate to the previous button mobile page. To define a link as a back button, you need to add the `data-rel="back"` attribute. For example:

```
<a data-rel="back data-role="button" class="ui-btn-right">Back</a></div>
```

Notice that there is not an `href` attribute. That is because the `href` attribute will be ignored; instead, the most recent URL will be popped off the browser's navigation history list.

Changing Pages with jQuery Code

The second method is to use the `$.mobile.changePage(URL, options)` function call where the URL is the link location. Table 22.1 shows the available options for the `.changePage()` call. The following is an example of adding a `swipeleft` event handler to load a remote web page when the user left-swipes the page on the device. Notice that a transition of "slide" is used, and reverse option is set to `true`:

```
$("#pageTwo").on("swipeleft", function(){
  $.mobile.changePage("newPage.html", {transition:"slide", reverse:true}); });
```

TABLE 22.1 Options for the `.changePage()` and `.loadPage()` Calls

Method	Description
changeHash	Specifies whether the hash in the location bar should be updated.
data	Object or string data to send with an AJAX request.
dataUrl	The URL used when updating the browser location. If not specified, the value of the `data-url` attribute is used.
pageContainer	Specifies the element that should contain the page.
reloadPage	Boolean. Reloads the page from the server if it is already in the DOM.
reverse	Boolean. Specifies the direction the page change transition runs.

Method	Description
role	The `data-role` value to be used when displaying the page.
showLoadMsg	Boolean. Specifies if the loading message should be shown.
transition	The transition to use when showing the page.
type	Specifies the method of the AJAX request: `"get"` (default) or `"post"`.

Loading Mobile Pages Without Displaying Them

Another helpful function is the `.loadPage(URL, options)` function. Load page downloads the mobile page from the web server using an AJAX call, but does not change the mobile page to the downloaded one. Actually, `.changePage()` calls `.loadPage()` underneath to retrieve the page. Most of the options listed in Table 22.1 are also available via `.loadPage()`, except `changeHash`, `dataUrl`, `reverse`, and `transition`.

The `.loadPage()` function is useful to preload pages in the initialization functions that you want available later but do not want to display yet. The following code shows an example of loading a page using POST data from a form:

```
$.mobile.loadPage("newPage.php", {data=$("form").serialize(), type="post"});
```

Events Triggered by Changing Pages

An important feature included with jQuery Mobile is the capability to trigger and handle events linked to changing and loading pages.

When you change pages, the following events are triggered:

▶ pagebeforechange, pagechange, pagebeforeload, pageload, pageshow, pagehide

When you load pages, the following events are triggered:

▶ pagebeforeload, pageload

These events allow you to implement code to handle new pages being transitioned and prevent pages from being downloaded from the server. The events are implemented as standard jQuery events, and the object passed back to the handler includes things like `url`, `absUrl`, `dataUrl`, and `xhr` objects, as well as the options used for changing pages.

The following shows an example of adding a `pageload` event handler:

```
$(document).on("pageload", function(e, obj){
  if($("#pageThree .ui-content").length) {
    $("#pageThree .ui-content").append("Page loaded from ."+ obj.url); }
});
```

Linking to Other Mobile Pages

Linked mobile pages displayed on the device can be prepared and displayed in one of three ways, which are listed next and are described in more detail in the sections that follow:

▶ Included in the original HTML document and linked by a local hash.

▶ Downloaded via AJAX request and inserted into the original DOM.

▶ Downloaded via non-AJAX request (traditional) and displayed as a new page.

The first two options provide the advantage that you are working with a single DOM. The benefits are that the libraries and CSS code are loaded only once, and it is easier to share data between pages because everything stays in memory. The downside is that for complex pages, the single DOM method may take a lot of browser memory because all pages remain in memory.

Local Hash

The simplest method in linking to another page is using a local hash. To do this, the page must already be loaded in the DOM. You can then link to the page by adding an `<a>` tag with the `data-role="button"` attribute set and an `href` value pointing to the `id` of the desired page.

For example, the following code adds a link button to the header of `#pageOne` that links to a second mobile page `#pageTwo` as shown in Figure 22.3:

```
<div data-role="page" id="pageOne">
  <div data-role="header"><h1>Page 1</h1>
    <a href="#pageTwo" data-role="button" class="ui-btn-right">Next</a></div>
...
</div>
<div data-role="page"  id="pageTwo">
...
```

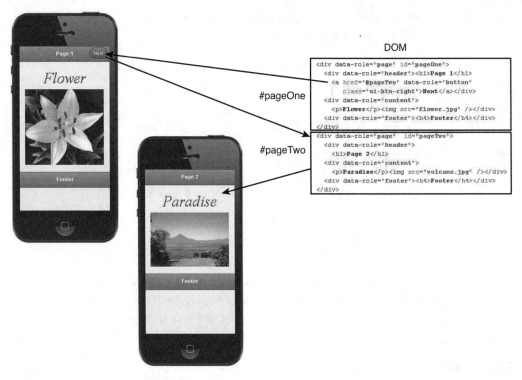

FIGURE 22.3
Linking to another page already loaded in the DOM.

AJAX DOM Insertion

This is the default functionality for `<a>` tags and `.changePage()` handling external URLs. The AJAX insertion occurs when you pass an external URL in the `<a>` tag or the `.changePage()` call. jQuery Mobile will first load the document from the web server, enhance it for jQuery Mobile, and then insert it into the DOM. Then the current page will be changed over to the new page.

CAUTION

In jQuery Mobile, AJAX is used to load the contents of external pages into the DOM as you navigate, but the DOM ready handler executes for only the first page. Therefore, to execute code whenever a new page is loaded and created, you need to put the initialization code in `$(document).on('pageinit')` instead of `$(document).ready()`.

For example, the following code adds a link button to the header of #pageOne that links to a second mobile page #pageThree that is in a separate HTML document, as illustrated by Figure 22.4:

```
<div data-role="page" id="pageOne">
  <div data-role="header"><h1>Page 1</h1>
    <a href="hour2201-page3.html" data-role="button"
       class="ui-btn-right">Next</a></div>
...
```

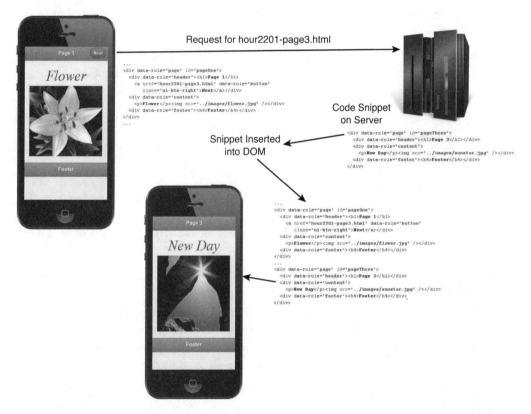

FIGURE 22.4
Linking to another mobile page on the web server.

HTML snippet file on web server:

```
<div data-role="page" id="pageThree">
  <div data-role="header"><h1>Page 3</h1></div>
  <div data-role="content">
    <p>New Day</p><img src="../images/sunstar.jpg" /></div>
  <div data-role="footer"><h4>Footer</h4></div>
</div>
```

NOTE

In reality, the best solution is to mix these two methods. Use a single DOM as much as possible and then load a fresh DOM when working with the larger amount of content.

Bypassing AJAX

At times, you do not want to have the mobile page inserted into the DOM. For example, when you have a large amount of data being transferred with pages, you might not want to have all of them loaded at once.

To prevent the AJAX DOM insertion when linking to a web page, you can use a `target` attribute in the `<a>` tag or specify a `rel="external"` or `data-ajax="false"`. For example:

```
<a href="hour2201-page3.html" data-role="button" target="_blank">New</a>
```

or

```
<a href="hour2201-page3.html" data-role="button" data-ajax="false">New</a>
```

or

```
<a href="hour2201-page3.html" data-role="button" rel="external">New</a>
```

In these instances, a normal HTTP request will be made to load the HTML link as a normal web page.

Adding Page Transitions

A great feature of linking pages is the animated transitions between them. This can be extremely useful in giving users a better experience. A good example of this is when you swipe to change pages and can swipe either left or right. It is nice to have the new page slide in the direction of the swipe, as if the user actually pulled the page in from off the device screen.

Transitions are added to the page links either by adding the `data-transition` attribute to the `<a>` tag or setting the transition option in the `.changePage()` call. You can also use the `data-direction="reverse"` attribute or `reverse:true` option to specify that a transition should happen in reverse, such as a slide backward. An example of using setting the page transition is shown next:

```
$.mobile.changePage("#pageTwo", {transition:"slide" });
<a href="#pageTwo" data-role="button" data-transition="slide">Next</a>
$.mobile.changePage("#pageOne", { reverse:true});
<a href="#pageOne" data-role="button" data-direction="reverse">Back</a>
```

Implementing a Mobile Web Page with Multiple Links

In this example, you will put the past few pages together and build a multipage mobile site. Two of the pages will be included in the initial HTML doc, and the third will be downloaded and injected on demand. You will also get a change to implement swipe events and a `pageload` event. The purpose of this example is for you to learn how to add multiple pages with linking and transitions.

The code for the example is shown in Listing 22.1. Use the following steps to create the mobile pages:

1. In Aptana, create the hour22, hour22/js, and hour22/css folders, and then add the hour22/hour2201.html, hour22/hour2201-page3.html, hour22/js/hour2201.js, hour22/js/initmobile.js, and hour22/css/hour2201.css files.

2. Add the code shown in Listing 22.1-initjs to the initmobile.js file. The code binds to the `mobileinit` handler and sets the default header and footer themes to `"b"`. Also, the code includes a `checkForMobile()` function that will adjust the CSS for nonmobile browsers. This function will put the phone image around the mobile content to visualize it better when developing.

3. Add the code shown in Listing 22.1-html, Listing 22.1-html-page3, and Listing 22.1-css to the HTML and CSS files.

4. Notice the following lines of code in Listing 22.1-html. This code defines the first mobile page using `data-role` attributes in the `<div>` elements. Also notice that there is a navigation button added to the header. This navigation button links to the next page #pageTwo.

```
16        <div data-role="page" id="pageOne">
17          <div data-role="header"><h1>Page 1</h1>
18           <a href="#pageTwo" data-role="button" class="ui-btn-right"
19              data-transition="slide">Next</a></div>
20          <div data-role="content">
21            <p>Flower</p><img src="../images/flower.jpg" /></div>
22          <div data-role="footer"><h4>Footer</h4></div>
23        </div>
```

5. Notice the code lines 24–34 of Listing 22.1-html. This code defines the second mobile page. In lines 26 and 27, a back button is defined to go back to the first page, and in lines 29 and 30, a navigation button is defined that goes to the external link hour2201-page3. html. This loads the external page and inserts it into the DOM.

```
26            <a href="#pageOne" data-role="button"
27              data-rel="back" data-direction="reverse">Back</a>
...
```

```
29              <a href="hour2201-page3.html" data-role="button"
30                 data-transition="slide" class="ui-btn-right">Next</a></div>
```

6. Check out the code in Listing 22.1-html-page3. This is just an HTML snippet, but it is enough to load the third page into the DOM.

7. Open hour2201.js and add a `.ready()` function with a call to `checkForMobile()`, as shown in line 2. Then add the following `swipeleft` and `swiperight` event handlers. These handlers will catch the user's horizontal finger swipes and use them to implement page changes. Notice that when the user swipes to the left, the reverse transition is used so that the page swipes with the direction of the user's finger.

```
03    $("#pageOne").on("swipeleft", function(){
04      $.mobile.changePage("#pageTwo", {transition:"slide"}); });
05    $("#pageTwo").on("swiperight", function(){
06      $.mobile.changePage("#pageOne", {transition:"slide", reverse:true});
      ➥});
07    $("#pageTwo").on("swipeleft", function(){
08      $.mobile.changePage("hour2201-page3.html", {transition:"slide", }); });
```

8. Add the following `pageload` event handler that will add the URL text to the third web page after it has successfully downloaded and is inserted into the DOM. The `url` is retrieved from the `obj` argument to the event handler.

```
09    $(document).on("pageload", function(e, obj){
10    if($("#pageThree .ui-content").length) {
11      $("#pageThree .ui-content").append("Page loaded from: "+ obj.url); }
12    });
```

9. Save all the files and then open the HTML document in your mobile device, as shown in Figure 22.5. You should be able to use the navigation buttons and finger swipes to navigate among the three pages.

LISTING 22.1-html   HTML Builds the Mobile Pages

```
01  <!DOCTYPE html>
02  <html>
03    <head>
04      <title>Hour 22-1</title>
05      <meta charset="utf-8" />
06      <meta name="viewport" content="width=device-width, initial-scale=1">
07      <script type="text/javascript" src="../js/jquery.min.js"></script>
08      <script type="text/javascript" src="js/initmobile.js"></script>
09      <script type="text/javascript" src="../js/jquery.mobile-custom.min.js">
      ➥</script>
10      <script type="text/javascript" src="js/hour2201.js"></script>
11      <link rel="stylesheet" href="../js/css/jquery.mobile-custom.min.css" />
```

```
12      <link rel="stylesheet" href="css/hour2201.css" />
13    </head>
14    <body>
15      <div id="border"><div id="frame">
16        <div data-role="page" id="pageOne">
17          <div data-role="header"><h1>Page 1</h1>
18            <a href="#pageTwo" data-role="button" class="ui-btn-right"
19              data-transition="slide">Next</a></div>
20          <div data-role="content">
21            <p>Flower</p><img src="../images/flower.jpg" /></div>
22          <div data-role="footer"><h4>Footer</h4></div>
23        </div>
24        <div data-role="page" id="pageTwo">
25          <div data-role="header">
26            <a href="#pageOne" data-role="button"
27              data-rel="back" data-direction="reverse">Back</a>
28            <h1>Page 2</h1>
29            <a href="hour2201-page3.html" data-role="button"
30              data-transition="slide" class="ui-btn-right">Next</a></div>
31          <div data-role="content">
32            <p>Paradise</p><img src="../images/volcano.jpg" /></div>
33          <div data-role="footer"><h4>Footer</h4></div>
34        </div>
35      </div></div>
36    </body>
37 </html>
```

LISTING 22.1-html-page3   HTML Snippet Used to Define the Third Mobile Page

```
1 <div data-role="page" id="pageThree">
2   <div data-role="header"><h1>Page 3</h1>
3     <a data-role="button" data-rel="back" data-direction="reverse">Back</a></div>
4   <div data-role="content">
5     <p>New Day</p><img src="../images/sunstar.jpg" /></div>
6   <div data-role="footer"><h4>Footer</h4></div>
7 </div>
```

LISTING 22.1-initjs   jQuery Mobile and JavaScript Code That Initializes Some
Default Settings and Adds a Phone Image Frame for Nonmobile Browsers

```
01 $(document).bind( "mobileinit", function () {
02   $.mobile.page.prototype.options.headerTheme = "b";
03   $.mobile.page.prototype.options.footerTheme = "b";
04 });
```

```
05 function checkForMobile (){
06   if(!/Android|webOS|iPhone|iPad|iPod|BlackBerry/i.test(navigator.userAgent)){
07     $("#border").css({ "background-image":'url(../images/phone.png)',
08       height:700, width:350});
09     $("#frame").css({height:475, width:267, "margin-top":112, "margin-left":40,
10       position:"absolute", overflow:"hidden" });
11   }
12 }
```

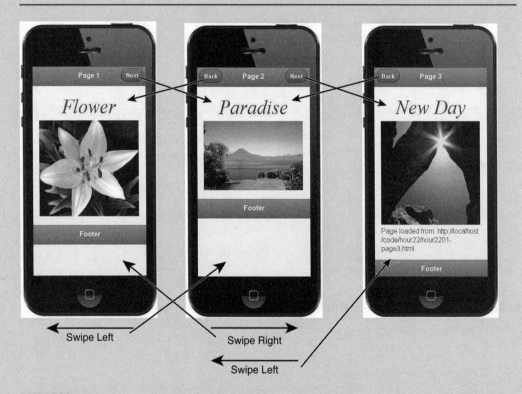

FIGURE 22.5
jQuery Mobile site with multiple pages.

LISTING 22.1-js   jQuery Mobile Code That Implements the Swipe Event Handlers and Changes the Page

```
01 $(document).ready(function() {
02   checkForMobile();
03   $("#pageOne").on("swipeleft", function(){
04     $.mobile.changePage("#pageTwo", {transition:"slide"}); });
```

```
05   $("#pageTwo").on("swiperight", function(){
06     $.mobile.changePage("#pageOne", {transition:"slide", reverse:true}); });
07   $("#pageTwo").on("swipeleft", function(){
08     $.mobile.changePage("hour2201-page3.html", {transition:"slide", }); });
09   $(document).on("pageload", function(e, obj){
10   if($("#pageThree .ui-content").length) {
11     $("#pageThree .ui-content").append("Page loaded from: "+ obj.url); }
12   });
13 });
```

LISTING 22.1-css CSS Code That Styles the Mobile Pages

```
1 p { text-align:center; font:italic 45px Helvitica; color:blue; margin:5px; }
2 img { width:235px; }
```

Creating a Navbar

Another method of navigating pages is using a navbar. A navbar is a set of buttons grouped together in a single bar element. Each button links to a different mobile page.

Navbars are defined by adding the role="navbar" to a div and then adding a list of pages to link to using <ul>, <li>, and <a> elements. For example, the following code will render a navbar similar to the one in Figure 22.6:

```
<div data-role="navbar" >
  <ul>
    <li><a href="#pageTwo">page 2</a></li>
    <li><a href="#pageThree">page 3</a></li>
    <li><a href="#pageFour">page 4</a></li>
  </ul>
</div>
```

The navbar <div> can be placed anywhere. You can put it in the header, footer, content, or it can stand alone between the other sections of the mobile page. A common place to put the navbar is in a fixed footer. This allows the navbar to remain present even as the content scrolls.

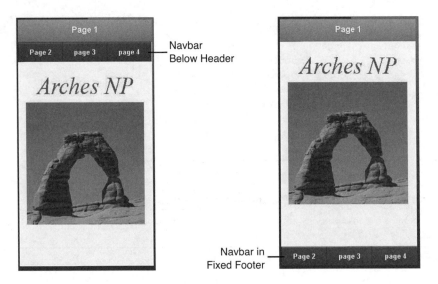

Navbar Below Header

Navbar in Fixed Footer

FIGURE 22.6
Mobile web page with navbar below the header and as a fixed footer.

▼ TRY IT YOURSELF

Adding Navbars to Mobile Web Pages

In this example, you add a navbar to a set of mobile web pages. Rather than using navigation buttons, the navbar will allow you to click to the other pages. The purpose of this example is to show you how navbars work.

The code for the example is shown in Listing 22.2. Use the following steps to create the mobile pages:

1. In Aptana, add the hour22/hour2202.html, hour22/hour2202.css, and hour22/hour2202.js files.

2. Add the code shown in Listing 22.2-css and Listing 22.2-js to the JS and CSS files. The jQuery code just calls the `checkForMobile()` function to initialize the phone image for nonmobile browsers.

3. Open the hour2202.html file and add the code shown in Listing 22.2. The code should be familiar to you because it is very similar to the previous example.

4. The big change is that there are now `<div data-role="navbar">` elements at lines 18–20, 26–26, and 34–36, as shown next. The content contains three mobile pages. Each of the pages contains a navbar with links to the other two. The link buttons are styled with `data-theme="a"` to make the menu more visible.

```
18        <div data-role="navbar" ><ul>
19          <li><a href="#pageTwo" data-theme="a">page 2</a></li>
20          <li><a href="#pageThree" data-theme="a">page 3</a></li></ul>
          ➥</div>
...
26        <div data-role="navbar" ><ul>
27          <li><a href="#pageOne" data-theme="a">page 1</a></li>
28          <li><a href="#pageThree" data-theme="a">page 3</a></li></ul>
          ➥</div>
...
34        <div data-role="navbar" ><ul>
35          <li><a href="#pageOne" data-theme="a">page 1</a></li>
36          <li><a href="#pageTwo" data-theme="a">page 2</a></li></ul></div>
```

5. Save all the files and then open the HTML page in a browser on your mobile device. The web pages should look similar to Figure 22.7. You should be able use the navbars to link between web pages.

Navbar Links

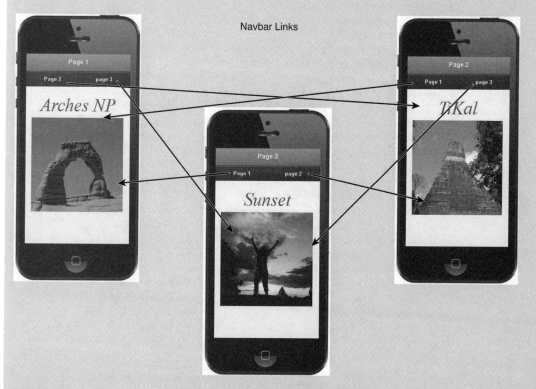

FIGURE 22.7
jQuery Mobile site with multiple pages.

▼ **LISTING 22.2-html**   **HTML Builds the Mobile Pages**

```
01 <!DOCTYPE html>
02 <html>
03   <head>
04     <title>Hour 22-2</title>
05     <meta charset="utf-8" />
06     <meta name="viewport" content="width=device-width, initial-scale=1">
07     <script type="text/javascript" src="../js/jquery.min.js"></script>
08     <script type="text/javascript" src="js/initmobile.js"></script>
09     <script type="text/javascript" src="../js/jquery.mobile-custom.min.js">
       ➥</script>
10     <link rel="stylesheet" href="../js/css/jquery.mobile-custom.min.css" />
11     <script type="text/javascript" src="js/hour2202.js"></script>
12     <link rel="stylesheet" href="css/hour2202.css" />
13   </head>
14   <body>
15     <div id="border"><div id="frame">
16       <div data-role="page" id="pageOne">
17         <div data-role="header"><h1>Page 1</h1></div>
18         <div data-role="navbar" ><ul>
19           <li><a href="#pageTwo" data-theme="a">Page 2</a></li>
20           <li><a href="#pageThree" data-theme="a">page 3</a></li></ul></div>
21         <div data-role="content">
22           <p>Arches NP</p><img src="../images/arch.jpg" /></div>
23       </div>
24       <div data-role="page" id="pageTwo">
25         <div data-role="header"><h1>Page 2</h1></div>
26         <div data-role="navbar" ><ul>
27           <li><a href="#pageOne" data-theme="a">Page 1</a></li>
28           <li><a href="#pageThree" data-theme="a">page 3</a></li></ul></div>
29         <div data-role="content">
30           <p>TiKal</p><img src="../images/pyramid2.jpg" /></div>
31       </div>
32       <div data-role="page" id="pageThree">
33         <div data-role="header"><h1>Page 3</h1></div>
34         <div data-role="navbar" ><ul>
35           <li><a href="#pageOne" data-theme="a">Page 1</a></li>
36           <li><a href="#pageTwo" data-theme="a">page 2</a></li></ul></div>
37         <div data-role="content">
38           <p>Sunset</p><img src="../images/jump.jpg" /></div>
39       </div>
40     </div></div>
41   </body>
42 </html>
```

LISTING 22.2-js   jQuery Mobile Code That Calls the Check for Mobile Devices ▼

```
01 $(document).ready(function() {
02   checkForMobile();
3 });
```

LISTING 22.2-css   CSS Code That Styles the Mobile Pages

```
1 p { text-align:center; font:italic 45px Helvitica; color:blue; margin:5px; }
2 img { width:235px; }
```

Implementing Dialogs

Another type of page in jQuery Mobile is the dialog. A dialog is just a mobile page that is presented as a dialog using the `data-rel="dialog"` attribute in the `<a>` link. Instead of displaying the page as a normal full page, it will be displayed as a dialog with a close button in the header.

The following code shows an example of a dialog link in the header of a mobile page with the `data-rel="dialog"`:

```
<a href="#imageDialog" data-role="button" class="ui-btn-right"
   data-rel="dialog" data-icon="gear">Options</a>
```

When the link above calls is clicked, the following mobile page is loaded as a dialog, as shown in Figure 22.8:

```
div data-role="page" id="imageDialog">
  <div data-role="header"><h1>Select Image</h1></div>
  <div data-role="content">
    <a href="#pageOne" data-role="button"><img src="../images/lake.jpg" />Lake</a>
    <a href="#pageTwo" data-role="button"><img src="../images/peak.jpg" />Peak</a>
    <a href="#pageThree" data-role="button"><img src="../images/river.jpg"
/>River</a>
  </div>
</div>
```

A dialog is not treated as a page link as far as the browser history is concerned; it is just an overlay on top of the page with the `<a>` link that launched it, so pressing the back button will navigate to the previous page, not back to the calling page.

You can chain multiple dialog pages together, one linking to the other. Closing subsequent dialogs will automatically link back to the previous dialog.

FIGURE 22.8
Page loaded as a dialog box.

NOTE
_____

The dialog UI container is styled by the `.ui-dialog-contain` class. It has a width of 92.5 to render the dialog smaller than the original page.
_____

▼ TRY IT YOURSELF

Adding Dialogs to Mobile Web Pages

In this example, you add an options dialog page that links to two additional dialog pages. You also add a `pageshow` event handler that will allow you to capture the dialog show event and make adjustments during the event using jQuery. The purpose is to illustrate how to implement dialogs in mobile pages.

The code for the example is shown in Listing 22.3. Use the following steps to create the mobile pages:

1. In Aptana, add the hour22/hour2203.html, hour22/hour2203.css, and hour22/hour2203.js files.

2. Add the code shown in Listing 22.3-css to the CSS file.

3. Add the code shown in Listing 22.3-js to the JS file. The following lines of that code implement the `pageshow` event handler that will be called when the `#random` dialog page is shown. The code selects a random image and displays it in the dialog.

```
3    $("#random").on("pageshow", function(){
4      var images=["lake","peak","sunset2","falls"];
5      $("#randomImg").attr("src", "../images/" +
6        images[Math.floor(Math.random()*4)] + ".jpg");
```

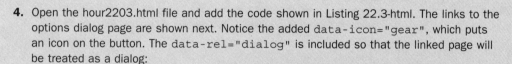

```
7    return false;
8  });
```

4. Open the hour2203.html file and add the code shown in Listing 22.3-html. The links to the
   options dialog page are shown next. Notice the added data-icon="gear", which puts
   an icon on the button. The data-rel="dialog" is included so that the linked page will
   be treated as a dialog:

```
18          <a href="#options" data-role="button" class="ui-btn-right"
19             data-rel="dialog" data-icon="gear">Options</a>
...
27          <a href="#options" data-role="button" class="ui-btn-right"
28             data-rel="dialog" data-icon="gear">Options</a>
```

5. The following code shows the options page. It is just a normal page, but because the links
   to it specify data-rel="dialog", it will be rendered as dialog. It also contains links to
   two additional pages, which will be treated as dialogs.

```
34          <div data-role="page" id="options">
35            <div data-role="header"><h1>Options</h1></div>
36            <div data-role="content">
37              <a href="#imageDialog" data-role="button"
              ➥data-rel="dialog">Switch Page</a>
38              <a href="#random" data-role="button" data-rel="dialog">Random
              ➥Image</a>
39            </div>
40          </div>
```

6. The #imageDialog page shown in lines 41–47 of Listing 22.3-html adds links to other
   mobile pages in the content.

7. The #random page in lines 48–53 of Listing 22.3-html contains a single image element
   that is updated by the pageshow event handler in the jQuery code.

8. Save all the files and then open the HTML code in a browser on your mobile device. The
   web pages should look similar to Figure 22.9. The dialogs should show up as dialogs when
   you click the links to them.

LISTING 22.3-html   HTML Builds the Mobile Pages with Dialogs

```
01 <!DOCTYPE html>
02 <html>
03   <head>
04     <title>Hour 22-3</title>
05     <meta charset="utf-8" />
06     <meta name="viewport" content="width=device-width, initial-scale=1">
07     <script type="text/javascript" src="../js/jquery.min.js"></script>
08     <script type="text/javascript" src="js/initmobile.js"></script>
```

```
09    <script type="text/javascript" src="../js/jquery.mobile-custom.min.js">
   ➥</script>
10    <script type="text/javascript" src="js/hour2203.js"></script>
11    <link rel="stylesheet" href="../js/css/jquery.mobile-custom.min.css" />
12    <link rel="stylesheet" href="css/hour2203.css" />
13  </head>
14  <body>
15    <div id="border"><div id="frame">
16      <div data-role="page" id="pageOne">
17        <div data-role="header"><h1>Page 1</h1>
18          <a href="#options" data-role="button" class="ui-btn-right"
19            data-rel="dialog" data-icon="gear">Options</a>
20        </div>
21        <div data-role="content">
22          <p>Silver Lake</p><img src="../images/lake.jpg" class="full" />
23        </div>
24      </div>
25      <div data-role="page" id="pageTwo">
26        <div data-role="header"><h1>Page 2</h1>
27          <a href="#options" data-role="button" class="ui-btn-right"
28            data-rel="dialog" data-icon="gear">Options</a>
29        </div>
30        <div data-role="content">
31          <p>Zion NP</p><img src="../images/peak.jpg" class="full" />
32        </div>
33      </div>
34      <div data-role="page" id="options">
35        <div data-role="header"><h1>Options</h1></div>
36        <div data-role="content">
37          <a href="#imageDialog" data-role="button" data-rel="dialog">Switch
   ➥Page</a>
38          <a href="#random" data-role="button" data-rel="dialog">Random Image</
a>
39        </div>
40      </div>
41      <div data-role="page" id="imageDialog">
42        <div data-role="header"><h1>Select Page</h1></div>
43        <div data-role="content">
44          <a href="#pageOne" data-role="button"><img src="../images/lake.jpg" />
   ➥Lake</a>
45          <a href="#pageTwo" data-role="button"><img src="../images/peak.jpg" />
   ➥Peak</a>
46        </div>
47      </div>
48      <div data-role="page" id="random">
49        <div data-role="header"><h1>Random</h1></div>
50        <div data-role="content">
```

```
51              <img id="randomImg" class="medium"></img>
52          </div>
53        </div>
54      </div></div>
55    </body>
56  </html>
```

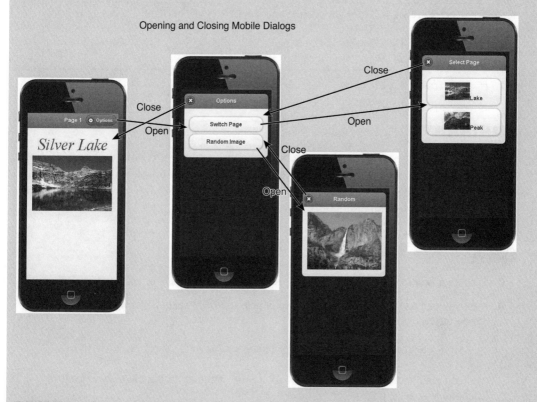

FIGURE 22.9
jQuery Mobile dialogs.

LISTING 22.3-js jQuery Mobile Code That Handles the `pageshow` Event for the `#random` **Page**

```
1 $(document).ready(function() {
2   checkForMobile();
3   $("#random").on("pageshow", function(){
4     var images=["lake","peak","sunset2","falls"];
5     $("#randomImg").attr("src", "../images/" +
6       images[Math.floor(Math.random()*4)] + ".jpg");
```

```
7      return false;
8    });
9  });
```

LISTING 22.3-css   **CSS Code That Styles the Mobile Pages**

```
1  p { text-align:center; font:italic 45px Helvitica; color:blue; margin:5px; }
2  img {height:50px; width:auto; }
3  img.full { width:235px; height:auto; }
4  img.medium { width:220px; height:auto; }
```

Summary

In this hour, you learned about mobile web pages. You learned how the parts of the mobile page are header, footer, content, and occasionally a navbar. You learned how to link multiple mobile pages together by adding navigation links to the headers and footers, or by using a navbar with a list of pages to link to. You also implemented dialog boxes.

Q&A

Q. Is there a way to cache mobile pages in the DOM so I don't have to keep reloading them?

A. Yes, you can use the following setting to enable the DOM cache. This will enable caching for all pages.

```
$.mobile.page.prototype.options.domCache = true;
```

You can also add the `data-dom-cache="true"` attribute to the page if you want to cache only specific pages. For example:

```
<div data-role="page" id="cacheMe" data-dom-cache="true">
```

Additionally you can do it programmatically using the following:

```
pageContainerElement.page({ domCache: true });
```

Workshop

The workshop consists of a set of questions and answers designed to solidify your understanding of the material covered in this hour. Try to answer the questions before looking at the answers.

Quiz

1. How do you define a `<div>` as a page header?

2. How do you add transitions to page changes?

3. True or False: A jQuery Mobile link to an external HTML document will not load the scripts in that file.

4. How do you define a page as a dialog box?

5. Name three events that are triggered by a page change.

Quiz Answers

1. Add the `data-role="header"` attribute.

2. Add the `data-transition` attribute in the `<a>` link that points to the page.

3. True. The jQuery Mobile page load defaults as an AJAX request.

4. Use the `data-rel="dialog"` attribute in the `<a>` link that points to the page.

5. `beforepageload`, `pageload`, `beforepagechange`, `pagechange`, `pagehide`, and `pageshow`.

Exercises

1. Open the code in Listing 22.1. Add an `id` attribute to the `<img>` tag. Then in the jQuery `.ready()` function, add a click event that resizes the image. For example:

```
$("#img1").on("click", function(){
  $(this).css({width:400})
});
```

2. Open the code in Listing 22.3 and add an additional mobile page to the HTML. Then add a link from the `#options` dialog to that page. The link should include the `data-rel="dialog"` so that your page opens as a dialog.

Formatting Content in Mobile Pages

What You'll Learn in This Hour:

▶ Organizing data into listviews
▶ Adding dialogs and pop-up menus
▶ Creating panels for auxiliary information
▶ Implementing mobile friendly tables
▶ Applying collapsible content to mobile pages

One of the most important parts of mobile pages is content formatting. Many mobile devices have very limited screen space, so it is critical to get things formatted correctly. jQuery Mobile provides several good tools that allow you to format the mobile content to fit the goals you are trying to achieve.

In this hour, you learn the basic framework provided to lay out mobile content. You see how to implement grids, lists, collapsible elements, pop-ups, dialogs, panels, and tables to present data in a variety of ways.

Adding Basic HTML

The jQuery Mobile content `<div>` supports the basic HTML elements styled for the most part exactly as they appear on web pages. You can add the content in the standard way that you are very familiar with. You can use lists, tables, headings, paragraphs, `<div>`, `<span>`, and other elements just as you normally would.

The data in the content `<div>` is styled using the `data-content-theme="c"` attribute, which defaults to theme swatch `"c"`; however, you can set the theme by adding the `data-content-theme` attribute to the `<div data-role="page">` element.

In addition to the standard HTML elements, you can add the same CSS styling that you would normally apply to your HTML pages. To illustrate this, look at the following code:

HTML:

```
<div data-role="page" id="pageOne" data-content-theme="c">
  <div data-role="header"><h1>Page 1</h1></div>
```

```
<div data-role="content">
  <h1>Heading 1</h1>
  <img src="../images/flower.jpg" />
  <h2>Heading 2</h2>
  <ul><li>jQuery</li><li>jQuery UI</li><li>jQuery Mobile</li></ul>
  <p>This is some simple text.</p>
  <p><b>Bold</b> and <em>ephasized</em> and <a>Linked</a>.</p>
  <table border="1">
    <tr><th>Heading 1</th><th>Heading 2</th></tr>
    <tr><td>Data 1</td><td>Data 2</td></tr>
  </table>
</div>
</div>
```

CSS:

```
h1, h2 { background-color:blue; color:white; border-radius:5px; padding:2px;
margin:3px;}
img { width:50px; }
ul {border: 3px ridge blue; margin:5px; list-style-type: none;padding:3px; }
li {border:1px dotted; margin-left:0px; text-align:center; }
p {font:italic 16px arial; }
td { border:5px inset red; }
```

Figure 23.1 shows the basic HTML elements stylized with theme "a", then "c", and then with the CSS styling applied. The elements appear pretty much as they would appear in a browser.

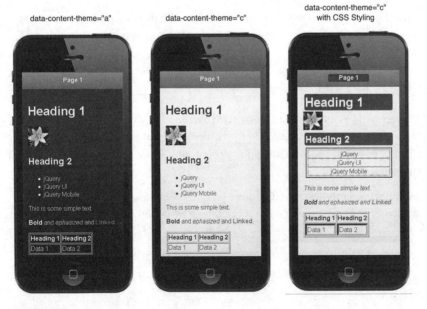

FIGURE 23.1
Mobile web page with the standard HTML formatting applied.

Creating a Grid Layout

One of the basic layouts provided by jQuery Mobile is the grid layout. The idea behind the grid layout is to split the page into equal-sized blocks, similar to an HTML table. Content can then be placed in those blocks and will automatically be laid out correctly.

To add a grid layout, you need to add a `<div class="ui-grid-#">` where # specifies the number of columns to include. The values are a (2 columns), b (3 columns), c (4 columns), and so on. For example, the following defines a three-column grid:

```
<div class="ui-grid-b"> </div>
```

Items are added to the grid by using a `<div ui-block-#>` where # is the column letter, a (first), b (second), and so on. The first time a column letter is specified, the item will be placed in row 1 of the grid in that column position. The second time it will be placed in row 2. For example, to create a 2 by 2 grid you would use the following code:

```
<div class="ui-grid-a">
  <div class="ui-block-a">Row 1 Column 1</div>
  <div class="ui-block-b">Row 1 Column 2</div>
  <div class="ui-block-a">Row 2 Column 1</div>
  <div class="ui-block-b">Row 2 Column 2</div>
</div>
```

You can also create a single column grid using `<div class="ui-grid-solo">`. For example:

```
<div class="ui-grid-solo">
  <div class="ui-block-a"><p id="number"></p></div>
</div>
```

TRY IT YOURSELF ▼

Adding a Grid Layout to a Mobile Page

The best way to help you see how grid layouts work is to walk you through an example. In this example, you implement three grid layouts in a single page. The first is a basic single-item grid with a number display, then a three by four grid with calculator digit elements, and the last grid is a five by one grid with calculator buttons.

The purpose is to see how the grid column and row blocks are implemented. The code for the example is shown in Listing 23.1. Use the following steps to create the mobile page:

1. In Aptana, create the hour23, hour23/css, and hour23/js folders, and add the hour23/hour2301.html, hour23/hour2301.css, and hour23/hour2301.js files. Then copy the hour23/js/initmobile.js file into the hour23/js folder.

2. Add the code shown in Listing 23.1-css to the CSS file.

3. Add the code shown in Listing 23.1-js to the JS file. There are two `click` event handlers: one attached to the `<p>` elements appends the number or operator to the #number element, and the second is for `<span>` elements that will either clear #number or evaluate the contents.

```
3    $("p").on("click", function(){ $("#number").append($(this).html()); });
4    $("span").on("click", function(){
5        if ($(this).html() === "="){
6            $("#number").html(eval($("#number").html()));
7        } else {$("#number").html(""); };
8    });
```

4. Open the hour2301.html file and add the code shown in Listing 23.1-html. The code defines a basic page and adds three grid layouts in the following lines. The first grid is a single column defined by `"ui-grid-solo"`, the second is a three-column grid defined by `"ui-grid-b"`, and the third is a five-column grid defined by `"ui-grid-d"`:

```
19          <div class="ui-grid-solo">
...
22          <div class="ui-grid-b">
...
36          <div class="ui-grid-d" id="logic">
```

5. The code inside the grid layout `<div>` elements are all `<div "ui-block-#">` elements. Notice that the letters a, b, and c are used to define each row of the three-column grid cycle `a,b,c,a,b,c,a,b...` Each cycle begins a new row.

```
23          <div class="ui-block-a"><p>1</p></div>
24          <div class="ui-block-b"><p>2</p></div>
25          <div class="ui-block-c"><p>3</p></div>
26          <div class="ui-block-a"><p>4</p></div>
27          <div class="ui-block-b"><p>5</p></div>>
```

6. Save all the files and then open the HTML code in a browser on your mobile device. The web pages should look similar to Figure 23.2. The calculator should accept click input and evaluate when the = button is pressed.

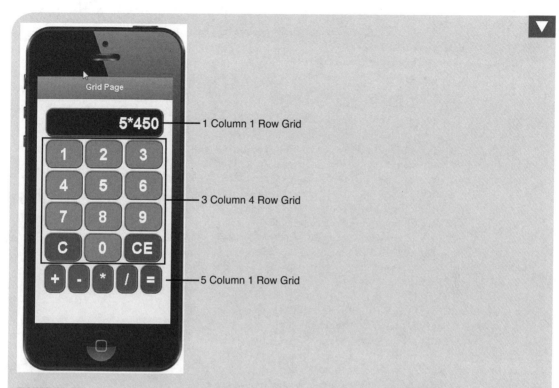

FIGURE 23.2
Using a series of grid layouts to lay out a basic calculator.

LISTING 23.1-html   HTML Code That Builds the Grids for the Calculator Controls

```
01  <!DOCTYPE html>
02  <html>
03    <head>
04      <title>Hour 23-1</title>
05      <meta charset="utf-8" />
06      <meta name="viewport" content="width=device-width, initial-scale=1">
07      <script type="text/javascript" src="../js/jquery.min.js"></script>
08      <script type="text/javascript" src="js/initmobile.js"></script>
09      <script type="text/javascript" src="../js/jquery.mobile-custom.min.js">
        ➥</script>
10      <script type="text/javascript" src="js/hour2301.js"></script>
11      <link rel="stylesheet" href="../js/css/jquery.mobile-custom.min.css" />
12      <link rel="stylesheet" href="css/hour2301.css" />
13    </head>
14    <body>
15      <div id="border"><div id="frame">
16        <div data-role="page" id="pageOne">
```

```
17          <div data-role="header"><h1>Grid Page</h1></div>
18          <div data-role="content">
19            <div class="ui-grid-solo">
20              <div class="ui-block-a"><p id="number"></p></div>
21            </div>
22            <div class="ui-grid-b">
23              <div class="ui-block-a"><p>1</p></div>
24              <div class="ui-block-b"><p>2</p></div>
25              <div class="ui-block-c"><p>3</p></div>
26              <div class="ui-block-a"><p>4</p></div>
27              <div class="ui-block-b"><p>5</p></div>
28              <div class="ui-block-c"><p>6</p></div>
29              <div class="ui-block-a"><p>7</p></div>
30              <div class="ui-block-b"><p>8</p></div>
31              <div class="ui-block-c"><p>9</p></div>
32              <div class="ui-block-a"><span>C</span></div>
33              <div class="ui-block-b"><p>0</p></div>
34              <div class="ui-block-c"><span>CE</span></div>
35            </div>
36            <div class="ui-grid-d" id="logic">
37              <div class="ui-block-a"><p>+</p></div>
38              <div class="ui-block-b"><p>-</p></div>
39              <div class="ui-block-c"><p>*</p></div>
40              <div class="ui-block-d"><p>/</p></div>
41              <div class="ui-block-e"><span>=</span></div>
42            </div>
43          </div>
44        </div></div>
45      </body>
46  </html>
```

LISTING 23.1-js   jQuery Mobile Code That Handles Clicks

```
1 $(document).ready(function() {
2   checkForMobile();
3   $("p").on("click", function(){ $("#number").append($(this).html()); });
4   $("span").on("click", function(){
5     if ($(this).html() === "="){
6       $("#number").html(eval($("#number").html()));
7     } else {$("#number").html(""); };
8   });
9 });
```

LISTING 23.1-css   **CSS Code That Styles the Mobile Page**   ▼

```
1 p, span {  margin:2px; border-radius:15px; background-color:#888888;
  ➥color:white;}
2 p, span { font:bold 30px/50px arial; text-align:center; border:3px ridge blue;}
3 #number {background-color:black; min-height:50px; text-align:right;
  ➥padding-right:5px;}
4 span { background-color:#555555; display:block; }
5 #logic span { background-color:#B10000; }
6 #logic p { background-color:#0066AA;  }
```

Implementing Listviews

One of the most common ways to organize mobile content is with listviews. Listviews organize the content into scrollable, linkable lists that are easy to view and navigate. jQuery UI does a great job providing a framework to easily implement listviews in your code.

The application of listviews varies a lot depending on the amount and type of data that is being placed in them. To handle this, jQuery provides an array of different types of lists. The following sections cover the most commonly used.

CAUTION

If you dynamically add items to lists, tables, and the like in jQuery code, you will need to call the `refresh()` action on that element to refresh the contents with jQuery Mobile.

Understanding Basic Lists

Lists are created by adding the `data-role="listview"` to a `<ul>` or `<ol>` element. jQuery automatically handles formatting the `<li>` elements into a list form. For `<ol>` elements, the formatted listview contains the numbering for each line item.

For example:

```
<ul data-role="listview">
  <li><a href="#nested">Nested</a></li>
  <li><a href="#split">Split List</a></li>
  <li><a href="#divided">Divided List</a></li>
  <li><a href="#search">Searchable List</a></li>
  <li>Non Linkable Item</li>
</ul>
```

Nested Lists

Nested lists are created by nesting additional `<ul>` elements inside the list view. jQuery Mobile automatically detects this and builds up linkable pages to the sublists. The following shows an example of implementing nested lists, as shown in Figure 23.3:

```
<ul data-role="listview" >
  <li>Hobbits<ul><li>Frodo</li><li>Sam</li><li>Bilbo</li></ul></li>
  <li>Elves<ul><li>Legolas</li><li>Elrond</li><li>Galadriel</li></ul></li>
  <li>Men<ul><li>Aragorn</li><li>Boromir</li><li>Theoden</li></ul></li>
</ul>
```

Split-Button Lists

Split-button lists are lists that include multiple options on each line. This can be useful in a variety of ways. A common use might be when listing products for sale, the main part might link to more details and the secondary link adds the item to the cart. The following code shows an example of implementing a split-button list, as shown in Figure 23.3:

```
<ul data-role="listview">
  <li><a href="#">Jeep</a><a href="#" data-icon="star">Like</a></li>
  <li><a href="#">Ford</a><a href="#" data-icon="star">Like</a></li>
  <li><a href="#">Chevy</a><a href="#" data-icon="star">Like</a></li>
</ul>
```

Adding Dividers to Lists

A divided list is one where elements of the list are divided from each other by a simple bar. The idea is to make it easier for the user to see the list items by splitting up the view.

Divided lists can be created manually by injecting your own dividers by adding a `data-role="list-divider"` to one of the `<li>` elements. For example:

```
<ul data-role="listview" >
  <li data-role="list-divider">Numbers</li>
    <li>1</li><li>2</li><li>3</li>
  <li data-role="list-divider">Letters</li>
    <li>A</li><li>B</li><li>C</li>
</ul>
```

You can also automatically add dividers by adding `data-autodividers="true"` to the `<ul>` element. This splits the elements every time the first character changes and then creates a divider for that letter. For example, the following code adds an `autodivider`, as shown in Figure 23.3:

```
<ul data-role="listview" data-autodividers="true">
  <li>Alex</li><li>Alice</li><li>Brad</li><li>DaNae</li><li>David</li>
  <li>Isaac</li><li>Jordan</li><li>Nancy</li>
</ul>
```

Implementing Searchable List

Another very useful feature is the searchable list. jQuery Mobile has a nice search feature built in that allows you to search the current list. The search feature adds a text input at the top of the list and will filter the items as you type text into the list. Only the items that match the filter text will be displayed.

Searchable lists are created by adding `data-filter="true"` to the `<ul>` element containing the list. For example, the following code adds a searchable list, as shown in Figure 23.3:

```
<ul data-role="listview" data-filter="true">
  <li>Rome</li><li>Milan</li><li>Florence</li><li>Genoa</li><li>Venice</li>
  <li>Naple</li><li>Balonga</li><li>Bari</li><li>Turin</li><li>Palermo</li>
</ul>
```

TRY IT YOURSELF ▼

Adding Listviews to a Mobile Page

In this example, you implement several types of listviews. You have already seen the code for most of the lists in the previous sections, which will help you follow the example more easily. The purpose is to allow you to implement the web page and see the interactions.

The code for the example is shown in Listing 23.2. Use the following steps to create the mobile page:

1. In Aptana, add the hour23/hour2302.html file.

2. Add the code shown in Listing 23.2-html to the file.

3. Review the code in lines 25–32. This is the main list that links to the other list pages.

4. Review the code in the Thumbnails List section. This illustrates adding the thumbnails images to the list items using `<img>` elements.

5. The code in the other sections are from the snippets you have already seen in this section.

6. Save all the files and then open the HTML code in a browser on your mobile device. You should be able to display and link the lists shown in Figure 23.3.

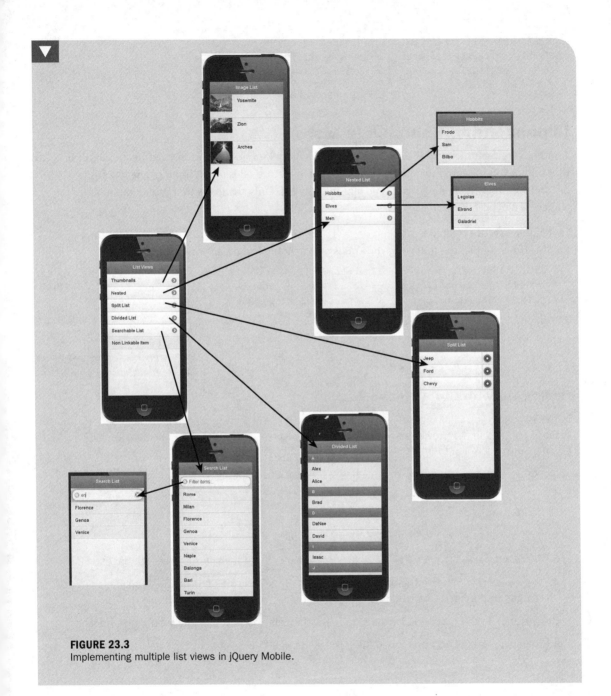

FIGURE 23.3
Implementing multiple list views in jQuery Mobile.

LISTING 23.2-html   HTML Code That Builds the Listviews   ▼

```
01  <!DOCTYPE html>
02  <html>
03    <head>
04      <title>Hour 23-2</title>
05      <meta charset="utf-8" />
06      <meta name="viewport" content="width=device-width, initial-scale=1">
07      <script type="text/javascript" src="../js/jquery.min.js"></script>
08      <script type="text/javascript" src="js/initmobile.js"></script>
09      <script type="text/javascript" src="../js/jquery.mobile-custom.min.js">
        ➥</script>
10      <link rel="stylesheet" href="../js/css/jquery.mobile-custom.min.css" />
11      <link rel="stylesheet" href="css/hour2302.css" />
12      <script>
13        $(document).ready(function() {
14          checkForMobile();
15        });
16      </script>
17      <style>
18      </style>
19    </head>
20    <body>
21      <div id="border"><div id="frame">
22        <div data-role="page" id="pageOne">
23          <div data-role="header"><h1>List Views</h1></div>
24          <div data-role="content">
25          <ul data-role="listview">
26            <li><a href="#thumbs">Thumbnails</a></li>
27            <li><a href="#nested">Nested</a></li>
28            <li><a href="#split">Split List</a></li>
29            <li><a href="#divided">Divided List</a></li>
30            <li><a href="#search">Searchable List</a></li>
31            <li>Non Linkable Item</li>
32        </ul></div></div>
33  <!--                  Nested List                        -->
34        <div data-role="page" id="thumbs">
35          <div data-role="header"><h1>Image List</h1></div>
36          <div data-role="content">
37          <ul data-role="listview">
38            <li><img src="../images/falls.jpg" />Yosemite</li>
39            <li><img src="../images/peak.jpg" />Zion</li>
40            <li><img src="../images/sunstar.jpg" />Arches</li>
41        </ul></div></div>
42  <!--                  Nested List                        -->
43        <div data-role="page" id="nested">
44          <div data-role="header"><h1>Nested List</h1></div>
```

```
45          <div data-role="content">
46          <ul data-role="listview">
47             <li>Hobbits<ul><li>Frodo</li><li>Sam</li><li>Bilbo</li></ul></li>
48             <li>Elves<ul><li>Legolas</li><li>Elrond</li><li>Galadriel</li></ul>
               ➥</li>
49             <li>Men<ul><li>Aragorn</li><li>Boromir</li><li>Theoden</li></ul></li>
50          </ul></div></div>
51 <!--                        Split List                           -->
52        <div data-role="page" id="split">
53          <div data-role="header"><h1>Split List</h1></div>
54          <div data-role="content">
55          <ul data-role="listview">
56             <li><a href="#">Jeep</a><a href="#" data-icon="star">Like</a></li>
57             <li><a href="#">Ford</a><a href="#" data-icon="star">Like</a></li>
58             <li><a href="#">Chevy</a><a href="#" data-icon="star">Like</a></li>
59          </ul></div></div>
60 <!--                        Divided List                         -->
61        <div data-role="page" id="divided">
62          <div data-role="header"><h1>Divided List</h1></div>
63          <div data-role="content">
64            <ul data-role="listview" data-autodividers="true">
65               <li>Alex</li><li>Alice</li><li>Brad</li><li>DaNae</li><li>David</li>
66               <li>Isaac</li><li>Jordan</li><li>Nancy</li>
67          </ul></div></div>
68 <!--                        Searchable List                      -->
69        <div data-role="page" id="search">
70          <div data-role="header"><h1>Search List</h1></div>
71          <div data-role="content">
72          <ul data-role="listview" data-filter="true">
73             <li>Rome</li><li>Milan</li><li>Florence</li><li>Genoa</li><li>Venice
               ➥</li>
74             <li>Naple</li><li>Balonga</li><li>Bari</li><li>Turin</li><li>Palermo
               ➥</li>
75          </ul></div></div>
76        </div></div>
77     </body>
78 </html>
```

Using Collapsible Blocks and Sets

Another useful way to represent content is by dividing it into collapsible elements. A header is presented that the user can see, but the content the header represents is hidden until the header is clicked.

This enables you to show and hide the content inline, rather than linking to another page. Collapsible elements can be represented as a standalone block or as a set of connected blocks.

To create a collapsible item, you add the `data-role="collapsible"` to a `div` element. The `<div>` element needs to have a header as well to display in a bar when collapsed. To group items together, you add multiple `<div data-role="collapsible">` elements inside a `<div data-role="collapsible-set">` element.

The code in Listing 23.3 shows an example of a single collapsible element followed by a set of collapsible elements, illustrated in Figure 23.4.

LISTING 23.3   **HTML Code That Builds the Listviews**

```
19      <div data-role="collapsible" data-collapsed="false"
20          data-theme="b" data-content-theme="c">
21        <h3>Photo Information</h3>
22        <p>These photos were taken by Brad Dayley in Arches National Park,
          ➥Utah.</p>
23      </div>
24      <div data-role="collapsible-set" data-theme="b" data-content-theme="a">
25        <div data-role="collapsible">
26          <h3>Delicate Arch</h3><img src="../images/arch.jpg" /></div>
27        <div data-role="collapsible" >
28          <h3>Double Arch</h3><img src="../images/double.jpg" /></div>
29        <div data-role="collapsible">
30          <h3>Morning View</h3><img src="../images/sunstar.jpg" /></div>
31      </div>
```

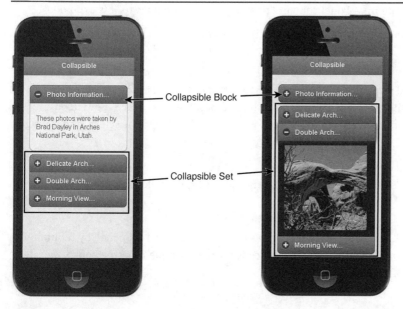

FIGURE 23.4
Collapsible content allows you to provide more information to users inline by allowing them to expand only what they want to see.

To force an item to be expanded, you add the `data-collapsed="false"`. This sets the initial state to expanded, although you can still collapse and expand it by clicking the header.

You also can control the themes used to render the collapsible sets, using `data-theme` to define the header and `data-content-theme` to define the collapsed content.

The full code for this example can be found on the book's website in code/hour23/hour2303.html.

Adding Auxiliary Content to Panels

A useful way to present data that is not necessarily part of the page but relevant is by using panels. A panel is similar to the page, but sits off to the left or right side. When opened, the panel transitions into revealing the additional information.

Panels are defined using `data-role="page"` and must be siblings to the header, content, and footer elements inside a mobile page. Panels are opened by linking to the `id` value, similar to opening a new page. When the link is clicked, the panel is displayed using one of the following three display modes:

- `data-display="overlay"`—Panel elements overlay the existing page with a transparent background.

- `data-display="push"`—Panel content "pushes" the existing page as it is exposed.

- `data-display="reveal"`—Panel is under the current page and is revealed as the current page slides away.

The panel is positioned using `data-position="right"` or `data-position="left"`. When opened, it will scroll with the page. You can force a fixed position using `data-position-fixed="true"`, in which case the panel contents will appear relative to the screen and not scroll position.

To close the panel, add a link button with the `<a data-rel="closed">` attribute set to the panel page. You can also close a panel from jQuery code using the following:

```
$( "#panelId" ).panel( "close" );
```

The code in Listing 23.4 shows an example of a basic panel. The panel is opened by a button on the main page, as shown in Figure 23.5. The full code for the example is on the book's website at code/hour23/hour2304.html.

LISTING 23.4   jQuery Mobile Panel Page with Configuration Options

```
17    <div data-role="header"><h1>Page</h1></div>
18    <div data-role="content">
19      <a data-role="button" href="#config" data-icon="bars">Configuration</a>
20    </div>
21      <div data-role="panel" id="config" data-position="right"
      ➥data-display="reveal">
22        <div data-role="header" data-theme="a"><h3>Panel</h3></div>
23        <h3>Settings</h3>
24        <label for="Option1">Option 1</label>
25        <input type="checkbox" id="Option1"></input>
26        <label for="Option2">Option 2</label>
27        <input type="checkbox" id="Option2"></input>
28        <a  data-role="button" data-icon="delete" data-rel="close" data>
      ➥Close Config</a>
29      </div>
30    </div>
```

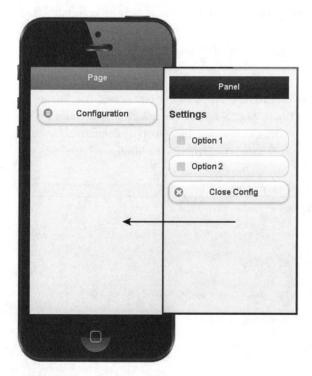

FIGURE 23.5
Using a button to slide in a configuration panel.

Working with Pop-ups

One of your best friends when implementing mobile page content is the pop-up. A pop-up is different from a panel in that it can be displayed anywhere on the page currently being viewed. This allows you to add additional bits of information that the user can easily click and see.

Pop-ups are defined using `data-role="popup"` and can be placed anywhere inside the content of a mobile page. Pop-ups are also opened by linking to the `id` value of the `<div data-role="popup">` tag. However, you must add a `data-rel="popup"` to the `<a>` tag that links to the pop-up. You can also manually open a pop-up using the following from jQuery code:

```
$("#popupId").popup();
```

The pop-up is positioned using a `data-position-to` attribute that can be set to `window`, `origin`, or the `#id` of an element. jQuery Mobile will try to center the pop-up over that element.

To close the pop-up, click the page somewhere other than the pop-up. You also can add a close button to the pop-up `<div>` by adding an `data-role="button"` attribute with a `data-rel="back"` attribute. For example, following is a close button with the `delete` icon and `notext` specified:

```
<a href="#" data-rel="back" data-role="button" data-theme="a"
   data-icon="delete" data-iconpos="notext" class="ui-btn-right">Close</a>
```

The code in Listing 23.5 shows an example of three pop-ups: a simple text pop-up, an image pop-up, and a menu pop-up, illustrated in Figure 23.6. Note that the image pop-up has a `class="photopopup"`; this provides class settings to style the image pop-up container. The full code for the example is on the book's website at code/hour23/hour2305.html.

LISTING 23.5   HTML Implementing jQuery Mobile Pop-ups

```
25    <a data-role="button" href="#simple" data-rel="popup" id="simpleLink">
      ➥Simple Popup</a>
26    <div data-role="popup" id="simple" data-position-to="#simpleLink">
27      <p>Simple text popup.<p>
28      <p>Put whatever text you want here.</p>
29    </div>
30    <a data-role="button" href="#photo" data-rel="popup" id="imageLink">
      ➥Image Popup</a>
31    <div data-role="popup" id="photo" data-position-to="#imageLink"
      ➥class="photopopup">
32      <a href="#" data-rel="back" data-role="button" data-theme="a"
        ➥data-icon="delete" data-iconpos="notext" class="ui-btn-right">Close</a>
33      <img src="../images/falls.jpg" />
34    </div>
35    <a data-role="button" href="#menu" data-rel="popup" id="menuLink">
      ➥Popup Menu</a>
36    <div data-role="popup" id="menu" data-position-to="#menuLink">
```

```
37      <ul data-role="listview">
38        <li><a>Setting A</a></li><li><a>Setting B</a></li>
39        <li><a>Setting C</a></li><li><a>Setting D</a></li>
40      </ul>
41    </div>
```

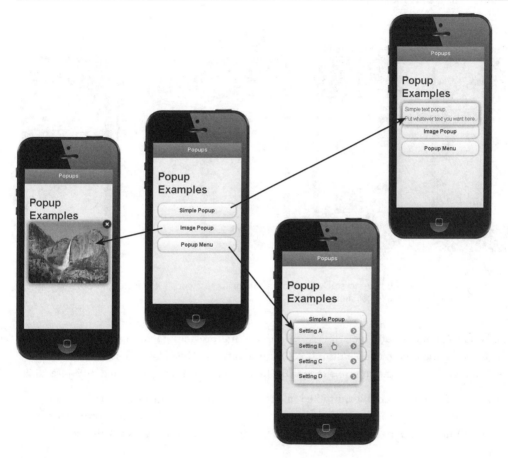

FIGURE 23.6
Simple, image, and menu pop-ups in jQuery.

Building Mobile-Friendly Tables

jQuery Mobile adds a few very useful features for implementing tables in mobile pages. Tables
are a tough sell for mobile pages because they typically take up too much room. That is why
jQuery Mobile has come up with a couple of nice solutions by adding a data-mode attribute to
the <table> tag.

The first solution is to add a `reflow` mode that allows the cells in the table to be repositioned so that they flow with the rest of the page. In reflow mode, when the table is too wide, the columns get broken up into individual cells stacked on top of each other. Then the headers in the column get added as labels to the cells so that each cell contains the column header to the left to identify the value. This is illustrated in Figure 23.7.

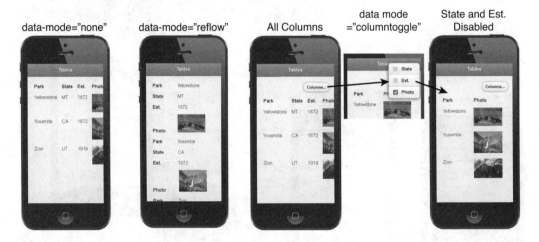

FIGURE 23.7
The `reflow` mode allows the table to stack each row's columns into groups with labels; the `columntoggle` mode allows the user to disable columns.

The second solution is to add a `columntoggle` mode that provides a button with a pop-up menu allowing the user to enable/disable columns to display. This allows users to keep the table formatting, but see only the columns they want to look at. This is also illustrated in Figure 23.7.

The columns that can be enabled/disabled in `columntoggle` mode are designated by adding a `data-priority=#` attribute to the `<th>` items in the first line of `<thead>`. Columns without the data-priority cannot be disabled. The # value of data-priority ranges from 1 (highest) to 6 (lowest).

Listing 23.6 shows a table that is set up for jQuery Mobile's table modes. The `<table>` tag includes the `data-role="table"` attribute and the required `data-mode` and `id` attributes. Figure 23.7 shows how setting the different values to data-mode changes the look on the mobile device. The full code for this example can be found on the book's website at code/hour2306. html.

LISTING 23.6   HTML Implementing jQuery Mobile Table Modes

```
21    <table data-role="table" data-mode="columntoggle" id="parkTable">
22      <thead><tr><th>Park</th><th data-priority="1">State</th>
23        <th data-priority="2">Est.</th><th data-priority="3">Photo</th></tr>
24      </thead>
25      <tbody>
26        <tr><td>Yellowstone</th><td>MT</td><td>1872</td>
27          <td><img src="../images/bison.jpg" width="100" /></tr>
28        <tr><td>Yosemite</th><td>CA</td><td>1872</td><td>
29          <img src="../images/falls.jpg" width="100" /></tr>
30        <tr><td>Zion</th><td>UT</td><td>1919</td><td>
31          <img src="../images/peak.jpg" width="100" /></tr>
32      </tbody>
33    </table>
```

Summary

This hour covered all the basics in implementing content in mobile web pages. There are several types of containers for content, and each of them has a different look and feel and can be used for different purposes. For example, listviews are great for displaying lists of items, menu choices, and even cascading data, whereas pop-ups and panels are good for providing users access to auxiliary data on demand, without having it encumber the page.

You saw how to make tables mobile friendly using the `reflow` and `columntoggle` modes. You also implemented some dialogs that can be used for a variety of purposes.

Q&A

Q. Does jQuery Mobile support responsive media queries and responsive web design?

A. Yes. Mobile elements such as tables and grids are meant to support responsive web design to support and adapt the layout for different screen sizes.

Q. How do you turn the corners on and off on buttons, collapsible sets, and the like?

A. Corners can be turned off on many elements by adding the `data-corners="false"` attribute.

Workshop

The workshop consists of a set of questions and answers designed to solidify your understanding of the material covered in this hour. Try to answer the questions before looking at the answers.

Quiz

1. How many columns are there in `<div class="ui-grid-a">`?

2. True or False: It is not possible to nest a listview inside another listview.

3. How do you make a collapsible item default to an expanded state?

4. What data attribute does a link need to open a pop-up?

5. How do you make a column available to be toggled on or off?

Quiz Answers

1. Three.

2. False.

3. `data-collapsed="false"`

4. `data-rel="popup"`

5. Add a `data-priority` attribute to the `<th>` element in the `<thead>`.

Exercises

1. Extend the code in Listing 23.5. Add another pop-up that has an expandable set of items. This is another common type of pop-up.

2. Extend the code in Listing 23.4 to include a second panel, the new one on the left.

Implementing Mobile Form Elements and Controls

What You'll Learn in This Hour:

▶ Adding mobile versions of HTML form elements to mobile pages

▶ Stylizing buttons, check boxes, selects, and other form elements

▶ Implementing a flip switch and slider elements to make users happy

▶ How the mobile form framework treats form elements

▶ Using selects to create custom menus

▶ Adding icons to buttons

jQuery Mobile provides an excellent framework that stylizes the HTML form elements to fit better with mobile pages. Using these stylized elements, you can add much better interaction and control to your web pages and a better experience for your users.

In this hour, you get a glimpse into how the mobile framework treats the form elements and how to utilize the framework in applying the form elements as controls on the mobile page—for example, combining check boxes, radios, buttons, and the like into groups that look and act as a single control.

Understanding Mobile Forms

Before you get started implementing mobile forms, you should understand a few differences from normal HTML forms controls. The following sections discuss those difference so that you understand how to implement the mobile form elements.

Form Data Attributes

jQuery Mobile introduces several attributes for elements that help extend and define the behavior to support mobile devices. Table 24.1 lists some of those attributes that you will need to be familiar with as you begin implementing mobile forms. The list is not comprehensive.

TABLE 24.1 jQuery Mobile Data Attributes for Form Elements

Attribute	Description
data-role="fieldcontain"	This allows for multiple form elements to be styled together as a single group.
data-role="controlgroup"	Allows you to group buttons into a single block similar to a navigation bar.
data-type	Specifies whether the items in the controlgroup should be organized "vertical" or "horizontal".
data-corners="true"	Adds corner radius to elements.
data-icon	Specifies an icon that will be added to an element: home, delete, plus, arrow-u, arrow-d, check, gear, grid, star, custom, arrow-r, arrow-l, minus, refresh, forward, back, alert, info, search
data-iconpos	Specifies the location the icon is placed: left, right, top, bottom
data-mini	Boolean. If true, a mini version of the element is rendered with limited padding and margins.
data-theme	Applies a theme swatch to the element (a-z).

Adding/Hiding Labels

Labels are required on form inputs in jQuery Mobile. This allows the library to format the form elements appropriately for mobile devices. Therefore, you need to add a label and use the for attribute to link it to the form input. The good news is that jQuery Mobile provides a class that you can easily hide the label with. For example:

```
<div data-role="fieldcontain" class="ui-hide-label">
  <label for="username">Username:</label>
  <input type="text" name="username" id="username" value="" placeholder="Username"/>
</div>
```

Disabling Form Elements

Form elements can be disabled by adding the ui-disabled class to them in the HTML definition or programmatically in your jQuery code. Disabling the elements prevents the control from accepting input from the user. jQuery Mobile also has special styling that is applied to disabled controls to make it apparent to the user that the form element cannot be used.

Refreshing Form Elements

When programmatically changing items in a form, such as adding options to a select, you need to call the `refresh` function on the item. The following shows some examples of adjusting form elements using jQuery and then refreshing them:

```
var mySelect = $("#mySelect");
mySelect[0].selectedIndex = 1;
mySelect.selectmenu("refresh");
$("#myCheckbox").prop("checked",true).checkboxradio("refresh");
$("#myRadio").prop("checked",true).checkboxradio("refresh");
$("#mySlider").val(100).slider("refresh");
```

Submitting Forms

jQuery automatically submits forms using AJAX. The submission will default to `get` and the action will default to the current page's path, found using `$.mobile.path.get()`, unless you specify an `action` and `method` attribute in the form.

Forms also support the `data-transition` and `data-direction="reverse"` attributes that allow you to transition back to the original page.

CAUTION

Using a multipart form with a file input is not supported by AJAX. Therefore, you need to add the `data-ajax="false"` to the parent form element to ensure that the form is submitted properly to the server.

Using Text Elements

jQuery Mobile text inputs are, for the most part, standard. It supports the HTML 5 input types, such as `search`, `password`, `email`, `tel`, `number`, and so on. This allows for standard HTML format checking and on some devices quick entry, such as a phone number.

You can enclose the text input field in a `<div data-role="fieldcontain" class="ui-hide-label">` container to hide the labels. You can also set the text input theme by using `data-theme`.

Listing 24.1 shows an example of some basic HTML elements being added to a web page. The results are shown in Figure 24.1. The full code can be found on the book's website in code/hour24/hour2401.html.

LISTING 24.1   HTML Code That Implements Textual Elements

```
20      <div data-role="fieldcontain" class="ui-hide-label">
21          <label for="search">Search</label>
22          <input type="search" name="search" id="search" value="" />
23      </div>
24      <div data-role="fieldcontain" class="ui-hide-label">
25        <label for="username">Name</label>
26        <input type="text" name="username" id="username" placeholder="your name
          ➥here"/>
27        <label for="title">Title</label>
28        <input type="text" name="title" id="title" value="" placeholder="some
          ➥title"/>
29        <label for="email">Email</label>
30        <input type="email" name="email" id="email" value="" placeholder="email"/>
31      </div>
32      <label for="area">Textarea:</label>
33      <textarea name="textarea" id="area" data-theme="a">
34      Simple text area input
35      </textarea>
```

FIGURE 24.1
jQuery Mobile text inputs.

Defining Buttons

jQuery Mobile provides a good set of options to create and style buttons for mobile use. You have already seen that adding the `data-role="button"` to an `<a>` tag will render the link as a button. You can also create buttons using the standard HTML methods in `<button>` and `<input>` elements.

jQuery Mobile styles the buttons automatically and enables you to add icons, adjust the theme, and render mini versions by adding the appropriate data attributes to the HTML tag.

A nice benefit of jQuery Mobile is that you can add icons to a button just by using the data-icon attributes. You can position it using `data-iconpos`. You can even render only the icon by using `data-iconpos="notext"`.

Another feature jQuery Mobile provides is the capability to group buttons together so they appear as a single set. To create a button set, add the buttons inside a

```
<div data-role="controlgroup" data-type="vertical">
```

or

```
<div data-role="controlgroup" data-type="horizontal">
```

element.

To illustrate the use of buttons, Listing 24.2 renders several types of buttons—some with icons, some in mini form. It also includes both vertical and horizontal button groups. The rendered results are shown in Figure 24.2. The full code can be found on the book's website in code/hour24/hour2402.html.

LISTING 24.2 HTML Code Mobile Button Elements

```
22      <a href="" data-role="button">Link Button</a>
23      <button data-inline="true" data-theme="b">Accept</button>
24      <button data-inline="true" data-theme="e">Decline</button>
25      <div data-role="controlgroup" data-mini="true" id="vGroup">
26        <button data-icon="arrow-u">Increment</button>
27        <button data-icon="arrow-d">Decrement</button>
28      </div>
29      <div data-role="controlgroup" data-type="horizontal" data-mini="true">
30        <button>b</button><button>i</button><button>u</button>
31      </div>
32      <div data-role="controlgroup" data-type="horizontal" data-mini="true">
33        <button data-icon="grid" data-iconpos="notext">b</button>
34        <button data-icon="gear" data-iconpos="notext">b</button>
35        <button data-icon="star" data-iconpos="notext">b</button>
36      </div>
37      <input type="submit" value="Submit" data-icon="check" data-iconpos="right"/>
```

FIGURE 24.2
Different buttons and button groups in a mobile web page.

Adding Sliders and Toggle Switches

An extremely useful control that you can add to your mobile pages is the slider. The slider makes it much easier for users to input data because they can use finger swipes to adjust values rather than clicking a text box for input.

To add a slider to the mobile page, use an `<input type="range">` element and then set the `value`, `min`, `max`, and `step` attributes. You also need to add a `<label>` element with the `for` attribute linking to the slider.

After you have created the slider, you can style it. The `data-theme` attribute allows you to select a swatch. You can also have the data side of the slider highlighted using the `data-highlight="true"` attribute. The code in Listing 24.3 shows two sliders to control the zoom and opacity of an image. I put the sliders in a `fieldcontain` so that the labels would track next to them and they would be closer together.

Another useful visual control similar to the slider is the toggle switch. The toggle switch has two states, on and off. This is another feature that makes it easier for users to interact with because it is not as easy to accidentally trigger as a check box or radio button because it takes a bit of a slide to toggle it on or off.

A toggle is created by implementing a `<select data-role="slider">` element with two options. The first option is styled as the on state, and the second option is styled as the off state. Listing 24.3 also contains an example of a slider element with options to show or hide the image.

Using Toggles and Switches Allows Users to Manipulate Elements

In this example, you implement the sliders and toggle switches discussed in this section. The purpose of the example is to show you the interaction that the slider and toggle switches can have with the mobile page.

The code for the example is shown in Listing 24.3. Use the following steps to create the mobile page:

1. In Aptana, create the hour24, hour24/css, and hour24/js folders, and add the hour24/hour2403.html, hour24/hour2403.css, and hour24/hour2403.js files. Then copy the hour22/js/initmobile.js file into the hour24/js folder.

2. Add the code shown in Listing 24.3-css to the CSS file.

3. Add the code shown in Listing 24.3-html to the HTML file.

4. Look at the following code in Listing 24.3. This code defines two sliders. The first has a range from 50 to 200 to control the zoom percentage. The second has a range from 0 to 1 in .05 `step` increments to control the opacity. The `data-highlight` option is set to `true` in both so that the slider will indicate the data side. The `fieldcontain` element around the sliders allows the labels to track to the side. Notice the code uses the `data-mini` display option.

```
20          <div data-role="fieldcontain">
21            <label for="sizeSlide">Zoom</label>
22            <input type="range" name="sizeSlide" id="sizeSlide"
23              value="100" min="50" max="200" data-mini="true"  />
24            <label for="fadeSlide">Fader</label>
25            <input type="range" name="fadeSlide" id="fadeSlide"
              ➥data-highlight="true"
26              value="1" min="0" max="1" step=".05" data-mini="true" />
27          </div>
```

5. Look at the following lines that define a toggle switch. The `data-role="slider"` is set on the select to define it as a mobile toggle switch. The toggle switch is put into a `fieldcontain` element to make the label track to the side:

```
28              <div data-role="fieldcontain">
29                <label for="flip">Image</label>
30                <select name="flip" id="flip" data-role="slider">
31                  <option value="off">Hide</option>
32                  <option value="on">Show</option>
33                </select>
34              </div>
```

6. Open hour2403.js and add the following `.ready()` function. The code adds three event handlers. The first two event handlers are for the `change` event on the slider switches. The `width` of the image is adjusted by the first and the `opacity` by the second using the `.val()` value from the slider element. The third handles the `change` event handler for the toggle switch `<select>` element. If the switch is on, the `<img>` element is displayed. If it is off, the `<img>` element is hidden.

```
1 $(document).ready( function() {
2    checkForMobile();
3    $("#sizeSlide").on("change", function(){ $("img").width(210*$(this).
val()/100); });
4    $("#fadeSlide").on("change", function(){ $("img").css({opacity:$(this).
val()}); });
5    $("#flip").on("change", function(){
6       if($(this).val() == "on") { $("img").show(); }
7       else { $("img").hide(); } });
8 });
```

7. Save all the files and then open the HTML code in a browser on your mobile device. The web page should look similar to Figure 24.3. You should be able to adjust the zoom and fade in the image with the sliders and turn the image on and off with the toggle switch.

FIGURE 24.3
The sliders and toggle switch allow a user to adjust the image using finger swipes.

LISTING 24.3 HTML Code Implementing Mobile Slider Elements to Control an Image

```
01 <!DOCTYPE html>
02 <html>
03   <head>
04     <title>Hour 24-3</title>
05     <meta charset="utf-8" />
06     <meta name="viewport" content="width=device-width, initial-scale=1">
07     <script type="text/javascript" src="../js/jquery-1.9.0.min.js"></script>
08     <script type="text/javascript" src="js/initmobile.js"></script>
09     <script type="text/javascript" src="../js/jquery.mobile-custom.min.js">
        ➥</script>
10     <script type="text/javascript" src="js/hour2403.js"></script>
11     <link rel="stylesheet" href="../js/css/jquery.mobile-custom.min.css" />
12     <link rel="stylesheet" href="css/hour2403.css" />
13   </head>
14   <body>
15     <div id="border"><div id="frame">
16       <div data-role="page" id="pageOne">
17       <div data-role="header"><h1>Buttons</h1></div>
18       <div data-role="content">
19         <div id="imgFrame"><img src="../images/peak.jpg" /></div>
20         <div data-role="fieldcontain">
21           <label for="sizeSlide">Zoom</label>
22           <input type="range" name="sizeSlide" id="sizeSlide"
23             value="100" min="50" max="200" data-mini="true"  />
24           <label for="fadeSlide">Fader</label>
25           <input type="range" name="fadeSlide" id="fadeSlide" data-
              ➥highlight="true"
26             value="1" min="0" max="1" step=".05" data-mini="true" />
27         </div>
28         <div data-role="fieldcontain">
29           <label for="flip">Image</label>
30           <select name="flip" id="flip" data-role="slider">
31             <option value="off">Hide</option>
32             <option value="on">Show</option>
33           </select>
34         </div>
35       </div>
36     </div></div>
37   </body>
38 </html>
```

LISTING 24.3-js   jQuery Mobile Code That Handles Changes in the Sliders and Toggle Switches

```
1 $(document).ready( function() {
2   checkForMobile();
3   $("#sizeSlide").on("change", function(){ $("img").width(210*$(this).val()/100);
➡});
4   $("#fadeSlide").on("change", function(){ $("img").css({opacity:$(this).val()});
});
5   $("#flip").on("change", function(){
6     if($(this).val() == "on") { $("img").show(); }
7     else { $("img").hide(); } });
8 });
```

LISTING 24.3-css   CSS Code That Styles the Image and Frame

```
1 img {width:210px;}
2 #imgFrame {width:210px; height:137px; border:1px solid; overflow:hidden;
3   border:4px ridge white; box-shadow: 5px 5px 5px #888888;}
```

Defining Radios and Check Boxes

jQuery Mobile also has a mobile-friendly version of radio and check box inputs. Most notable is the capability to group them together into control groups that can be displayed vertically or horizontally. When added to the `controlgroup`, the elements share a common outer border so it becomes obvious that they are connected.

Listing 24.4 shows examples of radio groups and check box groups, and both a horizontal and a vertical version of each. Notice that the `<fieldset>` element sets the data attributes for the radio groups rather than creating a separate `<div>`.

The full code can be found on the book's website in code/hour24/hour2404.html. You can download that code and play around with it. The rendered results are shown in Figure 24.4. It contains the standard change event handlers to adjust the image size.

LISTING 24.4   HTML Code Implementing Radio and Check Box Groups

```
24    <fieldset data-role="controlgroup" data-mini="true">
25      <input type="radio" name="rc" id="rc1" value="rc1" />
➡<label for="rc1">Family</label>
26      <input type="radio" name="rc" id="rc2" value="rc2" />
➡<label for="rc2">Friend</label>
27      <input type="radio" name="rc" id="rc3" value="rc3" />
➡<label for="rc3">Acqaintance</label>
```

```
28      </fieldset>
29      <fieldset data-role="controlgroup" data-type="horizontal" data-mini="true">
30        <input type="radio" name="hrc" id="hrc1" value="hrc1" />
          ➥<label for="hrc1">Accept</label>
31        <input type="radio" name="hrc" id="hrc2" value="hrc2" />
          ➥<label for="hrc2">Decline</label>
32        <input type="radio" name="hrc" id="hrc3" value="hrc3" />
          ➥<label for="hrc3">Maybe</label>
33      </fieldset>
34      <div data-role="controlgroup">
35        <input type="checkbox" name="cb" id="cb1" /><label for="cb1">Newsletter
          ➥</label>
36        <input type="checkbox" name="cb" id="cb2" /><label for="cb2">Special
          ➥Offers</label>
37        <input type="checkbox" name="cb" id="cb3" /><label for="cb3">Partner
          ➥Offers</label>
38      </div>
39      <div data-role="controlgroup" data-type="horizontal" data-mini="true"
        ➥data=theme="a">
40        <input type="checkbox" name="hcb" id="hcb1" /><label for="hcb1">Road
          ➥</label>
41        <input type="checkbox" name="hcb" id="hcb2" /><label for="hcb2">Topo
          ➥</label>
42        <input type="checkbox" name="hcb" id="hcb3" /><label for="hcb3">Sat
          ➥</label>
43      </div>
```

FIGURE 24.4
Custom mobile check box and radio groups.

Implementing Select Menus

Mobile menus are often accomplished with listviews and collapsible elements. However, at times, a traditional select is easier to implement under the covers because of the support for multiple selections and value accessibility.

jQuery Mobile provides basic support for `<select>` elements out of the box with no additional formatting. However, the actual select elements are not styled like the rest of the mobile elements, as shown in Figure 24.5.

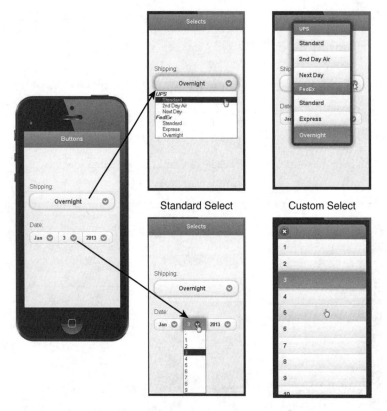

FIGURE 24.5
Mobile select and select group.

You can have jQuery Mobile generate custom select menus that have the mobile formatting. These custom menus do a good job of implementing the full `<select>` functionality across browsers and mobile OSes. The reason that custom select enhancements are not enabled by default is that it can be a bit of a performance hit, especially when dealing with large select menus.

To enable the custom select menus, you need to set the following option in the `mobileinit` handler. You should already be familiar with that handler because it was covered in the previous hour.

```
$(document).on('mobileinit',function(){
   $.mobile.selectmenu.prototype.options.nativeMenu = false;
});
```

When this option is set, jQuery Mobile converts the `<select>` element into a mobile version. This option provides the benefit that if the menu is too large, the framework will create a new page for it and switch to that page as a standard listview of options. That is shown in Figure 24.5 when day is selected.

You can also use a `<fieldset data-role="controlgroup">` element to wrap multiple selects into a single element. Listing 24.5 and Figure 24.5 show a `controlgroup` as a date selector.

The full code for Listing 24.5 can be found on the book's website in code/hour24/hour2405.html. You can download that code and play around with it. The rendered results are shown in Figure 24.5. It contains the standard change event handlers to adjust the image size.

LISTING 24.5 HTML Code Implementing Custom Selects

```
25          <label for="select-choice-0" class="select">Shipping:</label>
26          <select name="ship" id="ship">
27            <optgroup label="UPS">
28             <option value="us">Standard</option>
29             <option value="uex">2nd Day Air</option>
30             <option value="und">Next Day</option>
31            </optgroup>
32            <optgroup label="FedEx">
33             <option value="fs">Standard</option>
34             <option value="fex">Express</option>
35             <option value="fnd">Overnight</option>
36            </optgroup>
37          </select>
38          <br>
39          <fieldset data-role="controlgroup" data-type="horizontal"
            ➥data-mini="true">
40            <legend>Date:</legend>
41            <select name="mon" id="mon">
42               <option>Jan</option><option>Feb</option><option>Mar</option>
43               <option>Apr</option><option>May</option><option>Jun</option>
                 ➥</select>
44            <select name="day" id="day">
45               <option>-</option><option>1</option><option>2</option><option>3
                 ➥</option>
46               <option>4</option><option>5</option><option>6</option><option>7
                 ➥</option>
```

```
47              <option>8</option><option>9</option><option>10</option><option>11
            ➥</option>
48              <option>12</option><option>9</option><option>13</option><option>14
            ➥</option>
49              <option>15</option></select>
50          <select name="year" id="year">
51              <option value="13">2013</option>
52              <option value="14">2014</option>
53              <option value="15">2015</option></select>
54      </fieldset>
```

Summary

In this hour, you learned how to apply the different form elements to implement forms and page controls. You learned that you can combine buttons, check boxes, and even selects to create `controlgroups` that appear as a single control on the mobile page.

You were introduced to the jQuery Mobile toggle switches and learned how to use them and sliders to allow users to provide input with finger swipes instead of mobile keyboard input.

Q&A

Q. Is there a way to only use native form elements?

A. Yes, you can add `data-enhance="false"` to a form element and it will not be enhanced for mobile users. You need to activate this functionality by setting `$.mobile.ignoreContentEnabled=true;`.

Q. Is it possible to apply my own custom icons to buttons?

A. Yes. You need to add the `data-icon` attribute to the button and use a unique name for the button name—for example, `data-icon="cool-button"`. jQuery Mobile automatically creates a style for the custom button named `ui-icon-cool-button`. Then all you need to do is add a CSS rule that applies the image as the `background-image` to that class. The button must be an 18×18 pixel PNG-8 file with transparent background. See the code that follows:

HTML:

```
<button data-icon="cool-button">Coolness</button>
```

CSS:

```
.ui-icon-cool-button {
  background-image: url("cool-button.png");
}
```

Workshop

The workshop consists of a set of questions and answers designed to solidify your understanding of the material covered in this hour. Try to answer the questions before looking at the answers.

Quiz

1. How do you set the mobile theme for one text input in a set but not another?

2. How do you hide labels in a `fieldcontain` element?

3. How do you add an icon to a button?

4. How do you create a toggle switch?

5. How do you enable custom selects?

Quiz Answers

1. Add `data-theme=` {swatch letter} text input.

2. Use `class="ui-hide-label"`.

3. Use `data-icon` to add the button and `data-iconpos` to position it.

4. Create a `<select data-role="slider">` with two options. The first is on, the second is off.

5. Add the following statement to the `mobileinit` handler function:

```
$.mobile.selectmenu.prototype.options.nativeMenu = false;
```

Exercises

1. Open the code in Listing 24.3 and add two additional sliders with `change` events that adjust the position of the image. You will need to change the `position` property of the image and the image frame to `absolute` and then move the page elements down. In the change handler, you need to figure out how to adjust the position of the image element inside the frame.

2. Create your own mobile web app from the ground up. Start by copying code from one of the examples and then implement some list data, form elements, and other mobile content. Enjoy—it's been a pleasure!

Index

concat() method, 164-166, 169-170

conditional logic, 148-149

configuring

  Aptana Studio, 19-20

  browser development tools, 21-22

    Firebug on Firefox, 21-22

    Internet Explorer developer tools, 22-23

    JavaScript console in Chrome, 22

  jQuery Mobile default settings, 548

confirm() method, 287, 295

confirmation pop-ups, 295

connectTo option (sortable widget), 513

container elements, 75-78

containment option

  draggable widget, 495

  resizable widget, 503

content jQuery selectors, 193-196

content option (tooltips widget), 535

content size, setting with CSS, 123

CONTENT-LENGTH header, 11

CONTENT-TYPE header, 11

.contents() method, 208

continue keyword, 152

continueNotify() function, 298

controls attribute (Map), 434

converting

  arrays to strings, 171

  objects, 188-189

COOKIE header, 11

cookies, 291-294

cos() method, 176

create event, 494

createElement() method, 267

createEvent() method, 241

createPopup() method, 287

createTextNode() method, 267

creditcard rule (form validation), 354

cross-domain requests, 397-398

CSS (Cascading Style Sheets), 9

  adding, 27-30

    to headers, 99

    to HTML body, 99

  animating CSS settings, 301-303

  applying, 97-98

  debugging, 46

    with Firebug CSS inspector, 46

    with Firebug Layout inspector, 47-52

    with Firebug Style inspector, 47

  defining in HTML elements, 99-100

  design properties

    applying, 111-116

    backgrounds, 111

    borders, 117-121

    color, 103-105

    cursor, 121

    getting and setting, 257-258

    opacity, 121-122

    text styles, 106-110

    visibility, 122

graphical equalizer display, 385-389

layout properties, 122

  box model, 122-123

  content size, 123

  element flow, 124-125

  getting and setting, 257-258

  laying out web page components with, 127-130

  margins, 124

  overflow, 126

  padding, 123

  positioning, 125-126

  z-index, 126, 277-282

loading from file, 98

overview, 97

preparing for dynamic design, 130

selectors, 102-104

sparkline graphics, 389-392

syntax, 100-102

css files, 544

CSS inspector (Firebug), 46

.css() method, 188, 258, 277

ctrlKey property (events), 225

culture option (spinner widget), 533

currentTarget property (events), 225

cursor option

  CSS (Cascading Style Sheets), 121

  draggable widget, 495

  sortable widget, 513

<li>, 79

<link>, 72

<meta>, 69-70

<noscript>, 71-72

<ol>, 79

<option>, 83

<script>, 70-71, 136

<select>, 83

<style>, 70

<table>, 80

<tbody>, 80-83

<td>, 80-83

<textarea>, 83

<tfoot>, 80-83

<th>, 80-83

<thead>, 80-83

<title>, 68-69

<tr>, 80-83

<ul>, 79

event handers, assigning, 231-232

overview, 8, 65-66

structure, 66-68

XML/HTML response data, handling, 412-414

.html() method, **188, 267, 269**

HTML5, 8

<canvas>, 91-93

<ellipse>, 87

<path>, 88-91

<polygon>, 87

<svg>, 87

<video>, 94

HTTP (Hypertext Transfer Protocol)

GET requests, 11

headers, 10-11

overview, 10

POST requests, 11

Hypertext Markup Language.
See HTML (Hypertext Markup Language)

Hypertext Transfer Protocol.
See HTTP (Hypertext Transfer Protocol)

I

id attribute, 73, 187

IDEs, installing, 18-20

IDs

finding DOM objects by, 189

unique IDs, 463-464

if operator, 146

image elements, 78-79

image gallery, 365-370

images. *See* graphics

images folder, 544

<img> element, **78-79**

inc() function, 529

indexOf() method, 165-166, 170-171

initialization

jQuery initialization code, 230

page load events, 229-230

inline elements, 73-75

innerHeight() method, 259

innerHeight property (window object), 286

innerHTML attribute (DOM objects), 187

innerWidth() method, 259

innerWidth property (window object), 286

<input> element, **83**

installing

Aptana Studio, 18-19

development web server, 24-25

Firebug, 21-22

IDEs, 18-20

XAAMP stack, 24-25

instances of objects, creating, 161

interactive tables with sorting and filters, 371-377

interation widgets. *See* widgets

Internet Explorer developer tools, 22-23

interrupting loops, 152-153

.is() method, 212, 328

isDefaultPrevented() method, 227

isImmediatePropagationStopped() method, 227

isNaN() function, 163

isPropagationStopped() method, 227

items option

sortable widget, 513

tooltips widget, 535

iterating through arrays, 169

J

JavaScript

accessing DOM with, 137-141

adding to web pages, 136-138

browser values, accessing, 260-266

positioning, 125-126

z-index, 126, 277-282

layouts, grid, 581-585

<legend> element, 83

letter-spacing property (CSS), 106

<li> element, 79

Like button, adding, 427

line-height property (CSS), 107

lineTo() function, 92

<link> element, 72

linking mobile web pages, 559-562

links

adding with <a> element, 78

external links, controlling, 290

link elements, 78

lists, 585-590

adding to mobile web pages, 588-590

adding to web pages, 79

basic lists, 585

dividers, 586-587

list elements, 79

nested lists, 586

searchable lists, 587

split-button lists, 586

LN10() method, 176

load event, 228

.load() method, 230, 401

loading

CSS styles, 98

jQuery library, 135-136

.loadPage() method, 557

local hash, 559-556

location object, 285

login requests, handling with AJAX, 405-408

loops, 149-150

do/while loops, 150

for loops, 151, 169

for/in loops, 151-152, 169

interrupting, 152-153

while loops, 150

low-level AJAX requests, handling, 420-422

M

manually validating forms, 351-352

Map() function, 433-434

.map() method, 212-217

Map object, 434

mapOptions object, 433-434

Maps (Google), adding, 432-439

mapTypeId attribute (mapOptions), 433

maptypeid_changed event, 434

margins, adding with CSS, 124

match() method, 165

Math object, 175-176

max() method, 176

max option (slider widget), 531

max rule (form validation), 355

maxlength rule (form validation), 355

media elements, 94

memory flag (callbacks), 251

menu widget, 528-529

menus

dynamic menus, 314-316

menu widget, 528-529

in mobile forms, 610-612

messages, validation, 356-358

<meta> element, 69-70

metaKey property (events), 225

methods. See also individual methods

accessing, 162

adding to JavaScript objects, 177-178

assigning to objects, 162

min() method, 176

min rule (form validation), 354

minlength rule (form validation), 355

mobile forms, 599. See also mobile web pages

buttons, 603

data attributes, 599

disabling, 600

labels, 600

radio and check box groups, 608

refreshing, 601

select menus, 610-612

sliders, 604-608

submitting, 601

text elements, 601

toggle switches, 604-608

mobile web pages. See also jQuery Mobile; mobile forms

basic HTML, adding, 579-580

building, 549-551, 564-567

bypassing AJAX, 562

challenges of, 541-542

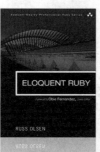
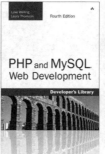

FREE
Online Edition

Your purchase of *Sams Teach Yourself jQuery and JavaScript in 24 Hours* includes access to a free online edition for 45 days through the **Safari Books Online** subscription service. Nearly every Sams book is available online through **Safari Books Online**, along with thousands of books and videos from publishers such as Addison-Wesley Professional, Cisco Press, Exam Cram, IBM Press, O'Reilly Media, Prentice Hall, Que, and VMware Press.

Safari Books Online is a digital library providing searchable, on-demand access to thousands of technology, digital media, and professional development books and videos from leading publishers. With one monthly or yearly subscription price, you get unlimited access to learning tools and information on topics including mobile app and software development, tips and tricks on using your favorite gadgets, networking, project management, graphic design, and much more.

Activate your FREE Online Edition at
informit.com/safarifree

STEP 1: Enter the coupon code: IHKYNGA.

STEP 2: New Safari users, complete the brief registration form.
Safari subscribers, just log in.

If you have difficulty registering on Safari or accessing the online edition,
please e-mail customer-service@safaribooksonline.com